2-12, 17-36, 41-62, 94-129
163-196, 223-258
C0-DAN-716

MANAGEMENT SCIENCE/OPERATIONS RESEARCH:

A Strategic Perspective

MANAGEMENT SCIENCE/OPERATIONS RESEARCH:

A Strategic Perspective

MANAGEMENT SCIENCE/OPERATIONS RESEARCH:

A Strategic Perspective

Peter C. Bell

SOUTH-WESTERN College Publishing

An International Thomson Publishing Company

Publishing Team Director:	Dave Shaut
Acquisitions Editor:	Charles McCormick
Developmental/Production Editor:	Mardell Toomey
Media Production Editor:	Robin Browning
Production House:	Maryland Composition Company, Inc.
Internal Design:	Craig Ramsdell
Cover Design:	Karla Stover Design Cincinnati, Ohio
Marketing Manager:	Joe Sabatino
Manufacturing Coordinator:	Sue Kirven

Copyright © 1999
by South-Western College Publishing
Cincinnati, Ohio

ALL RIGHTS RESERVED

The text of this publication, or any part thereof, may not be reproduced or transmitted in any form or by any means, electronic or mechanical, including photocopying, recording, storage in an information retrieval system, or otherwise, without the prior written permission of the publisher.

Library of Congress Cataloging-in-Publication Data

Bell, Peter C.
Management science/operations research : a strategic perspective / Peter C. Bell.
p. cm.
Includes index.
ISBN 0-324-00158-4
1. Management science. 2. Operations research. 3. Strategic planning. I. Title.
T56.B385 1999
658.4--DC21 98–8106
CIP

2 3 4 5 6 7 8 9 BB 6 5 4 3 2 1 0 9

Printed in the United States of America

I(T)P®

International Thomson Publishing
South-Western College Publishing is an ITP Company. The ITP trademark is used under license.

BRIEF CONTENTS

CONTENTS

Chapter 5
Simulating the Future 163

Chapter 6
Management Science/Operations Research in Support of Management Decision Makers 223

PREFACE

This text presents management science/operations research (MS/OR) from the perspective of the general manager. I believe that this approach to teaching MS/OR is appropriate for business students at all levels (undergraduate, M.B.A., or Executive programs) who seek a career in management rather than in MS/OR.

In this text, I attempt to demonstrate that the use of MS/OR is now widespread in competitive industries, and that the future manager who understands some basic MS/OR will have a career advantage over one who does not. Achieving understanding, however, is as much about understanding how MS/OR models are being used effectively in practice, as it is about understanding the theory behind the models. The text, therefore, pays as much (perhaps more) attention to the practice of MS/OR as it does to the theory.

The "strategic perspective" on MS/OR presented here has been developed from my own teaching experience, which has been almost exclusively in business programs that take a management viewpoint. This new "strategic" general management perspective on MS/OR is a response to the need for the teaching of MS/OR in business schools to continuously evolve to respond to the changing needs of our students and our business programs, competitive pressures from other fields, and the changing nature of MS/OR itself. We MS/OR instructors are involved in a process of continuous improvement of our courses, our classroom sessions, and our programs that will enable our teaching to keep up with the practice of MS/OR and will allow MS/OR to grow and prosper.

In my view, the greatest satisfaction in teaching comes from seeing students display mastery by applying MS/OR to real problems. Consequently, this text contains more than 40 cases, almost all based on real problems set in real companies. Teaching MS/OR with cases provides many pedagogical benefits including engaging the students actively in the classroom case sessions. The cases, however, also expose students to the useful practice of MS/OR in a variety of settings and situations: a student who has worked even a dozen cases will emerge with a dozen new ideas about how and where ideas from MS/OR can be successfully applied.

This book represents many years of learning about teaching, teaching with cases, and teaching MS/OR. A great many individuals have contributed to this experience, and it is simply not possible to list them all. I would, however, like to mention my colleague Peter Newson at the Ivey School, and former colleague Christoph Haehling von Lanzenauer who have taught me a great deal. Many students over the years have contributed to this book, some knowingly, some unknowingly. I would especially mention the contributions of Chris Anderson, Matt Brudzynski, Patrick Chau, Sulaiman Al-Hudhaif, Drew Parker, Arshad Taseen, Iris Tiemessen, and Betty Vandenbosch.

My special thanks to the thousands of Ivey H.B.A. and M.B.A. students who have participated in the development of these ideas, read drafts of these chapters, and offered countless suggestions that have greatly improved this text. Any errors or omissions that remain are, of course, my own.

Finally, my special thanks to Jennifer, who has supported my career in more ways than I can recount, to Caroline and David, and to my parents Mary and Stanley Bell for their sacrifices that allowed my education in MS/OR to begin early and to last a lifetime.

Peter C. Bell
1998

ABOUT THE AUTHOR

Professor Peter C. Bell has been at the University of Western Ontario since 1977, and Professor since 1989. He has also held short-term appointments as Visiting Professor, London Business School, C-I-L Distinguished Lecturer at Wilfred Laurier University, and Chevron Distinguished Visiting Professor at Simon Fraser University. He holds degrees from Oxford University (B.A. [Honors], M.A.) and the Graduate School of Business, University of Chicago (M.B.A., Ph.D.). He is a consultant to corporations, hospitals, small businesses, charities, and government agencies in the areas of manufacturing, operations, and/or computer systems.

The author of numerous texts, including *Statistics for Business with MINITAB; Text and Cases* and *Statistics for Business with Spreadsheets: Text and Cases*, and articles that have been published in academic and business journals, Peter Bell is also Editor-in-Chief of *International Transactions in Operational Research* and Associate Editor of *Omega* and *INFOR*.

He was an elected Member of the Council and the OR/MS Board of the Institute of Management Science. In addition, he has served as the President of the International Federation of Operational Research Societies and was North American Vice President from 1989 to 1991. He has also served as President of the Canadian Operational Research Society.

INTRODUCTION

The objective of this book is to introduce management science and operations research from the perspective of the general manager of a corporation. The text will emphasize the strategic role that management science and operations research are playing in globally competitive corporations today, rather than examine the details or attempt an encyclopedic review of the field of management science.

Management science and operations research (or "management science" for simplicity) are two terms that are used to describe a scientific approach to management. Management science is multifaceted:

- Ability in management science is *an essential management skill:* knowledge of management science helps the manager to analyze decision situations, prevent problem situations from arising, identify new opportunities, and often enables many millions of dollars to be added to the bottom line for the organization.
- Management science is *a vital functional area* in many organizations, although the function is not always known as "management science." "Decision Technologies," "Decision Sciences," or "Operational Research" are some other names used for the management science function. Some firms have very large "Management Science" functions: "Decision Technologies" at American Airlines is a separate division employing several hundred management scientists providing management science services to American Airlines and other organizations. These organizations seek to distribute management science services throughout the corporation by offering courses, training sessions, and support services in management science.
- Management science is *a source of competitive advantage* that, under the right conditions, can be sustainable over a long period of time. Organizations that are good at management science can create a cost advantage over their competitors. Many documented cases exist where this cost advantage is hundreds of millions of dollars.
- Management science is an *industry* made up of hundreds of firms and individuals who provide management science services to business, government, and individuals.
- Management science is also *an academic discipline* where most leading-edge ideas in management first appear. This discipline insists that ideas be theoretically sound or proven effective (unlike many other areas where new concepts, often expressed as buzz words, appear and disappear according to the rumblings of the "guru-of-the-month").

Throughout this book, we will examine a number of firms that have been very successful using management science. One example of such a firm is San Miguel Corporation of the Philippines that sees its very successful Operations Research Group as a functional area, providing vital help to the general management of the corporation:

> Operations Research plays a big role in the five-year . . . approximately one billion dollar expansion and modernization program that we launched in 1987. Under the program we have built 22 manufacturing plants—we would not have dared to undertake the expansion at all without Operations Research. In our strategic planning meetings every year, whenever a division or business unit manager presents a project, we always make sure that Operations Research has gone through the proposal.

> San Miguel's Senior Management appreciates the vital role of Operations Research in attaining our corporate goals, and in implementing the strategies that enable us to achieve adequate growth and satisfactory returns for our various stakeholders.
>
> Francisco Eizmendi Jr., President
> San Miguel Corporation, The Philippines

In contrast, Daniel Elwing, Chief Executive Officer of ABB Electric, emphasizes management science as an essential management skill:

> Management science is not a project or a set of techniques; it is a process, a way of thinking and managing.

Both ABB Electric and San Miguel Corporation have effectively used management science to create and sustain a strategic advantage. Understanding more about the use of management science strategically involves learning some essential skills that all general managers need to have in their tool bag, coupled with achieving an understanding of how these skills can be mobilized to bring an advantage to the competitive firm (to the disadvantage of the competition).

THE ORGANIZATION OF THE BOOK

The chapters of this book are organized in four parts. The first part introduces a problem area and presents some basic management science concepts that have been successfully used to address the problem area. The objective of this material is to provide you, the manager of the future, with a general understanding of the tools and techniques used by the management science analyst.

Felix Rohatyn of the New York investment banking firm, Lazard Freres & Co., quoted in the *New Yorker* magazine, provides a rationale for achieving a basic level of understanding:

> Too many high-level executives are prisoners of their staffs. They have never really done the nitty-gritty stuff, which is not terribly mysterious once you tackle it. And if you haven't done these things the technicians can absolutely wrap you up in the details, and you never find your way out.

The second part of each chapter is a series of short descriptions of organizations that have effectively used the tools described in the first part of the chapter. These readings are designed to demonstrate that the tools introduced in the chapter are not some obscure theory, but rather have been used, are being used, and will continue to be used by corporations and other organizations seeking to enhance profits or improve effectiveness or productivity.

To help you achieve an understanding of the basic concepts of management science, two sets of problems are included in each chapter. The first set of problems are small "exercises" that allow the concepts presented in the chapters to be practiced in simple but artificial situations. By working these exercises you can familiarize yourself with the basic ideas and models presented in the chapter.

The second set of problems are "cases" that describe real-world situations where the use of the concepts is more challenging and, usually, less definitive: many of these cases have no "correct" answer, although some answers are always better than others. Working these cases can provide an experience similar to that found "on-the-job": you may have to cope with ambiguity and extraneous or missing data. You may feel that you do not have enough information to proceed, but the situation demands action. The emphasis in these cases is to derive a recommendation for sensible action: what should the decision maker do? How should the action be implemented?

Working the exercises and the cases will provide an opportunity to learn about the concepts presented in the chapters and, importantly, how to achieve useful results by applying these concepts in the real world.

THE CHALLENGE

The recurring theme of this text is that managers who understand management science are better trained and better equipped to manage the modern corporation than those who do not. Of course, there is much more to management training than management science. However, management scientists have been instrumental in pushing forward the leading edge of management practice in many industries as we move into the twenty-first century. The challenge is to understand how and where this is happening, so that management science can provide our firm, not our competition, with a competitive advantage.

I

AN INTRODUCTION TO STRATEGIC MANAGEMENT SCIENCE

The 1990s have seen the emergence of a new type of corporation. These firms have prospered as a direct consequence of developing and exploiting special skills in management science, allowing them to gain and hold a competitive advantage in their marketplaces. In certain industries, a high level of management science sophistication has emerged; the very existence of firms in these industries depends not only on their marketing, financial, and human resource skills, but also on their ability to use the concepts and tools of management science on a day-to-day basis.

A VIEW OF THE CORPORATION

In thinking about strategic management science, it is helpful to have a common view or "model" of the corporation. The model used in this book is one of global competition. Competition is a concept that is familiar to us through the world of sports but, at its extreme, competition can be a matter of life or death. A metaphor from the animal world illustrates this point.

> Every morning, when the sun comes up a gazelle wakes. It knows that it must outrun the fastest lion or it will be eaten.
>
> When the sun comes up, the lion also wakes. The lion knows that it must outrun the slowest gazelle, or it will starve.
>
> **In the end, it doesn't really matter whether you are a lion or a gazelle; when the sun comes up, you had better be prepared to run for your life.**

Major global corporations often exist in an environment of intense competition where comparisons with warfare are common. Some corporations "win" and others "lose." Some win local skirmishes or achieve temporal advantage, while others move more slowly, conquer new territories gradually, and consolidate and hold positions for long periods of time.

Comparisons between global competition and warfare may not be too farfetched. Here is the view from the head of Matsushita Electric Corporation of Japan, one of the world's leading manufacturers of electronic equipment with brand names that include Panasonic and Quasar:

> We are going to win and the industrial West is going to lose; there's nothing much you can do about it . . . business, we know, is now so complex and difficult, the survival of firms so hazardous in an environment increasingly competitive and fraught with danger, that their continued existence depends on the day-to-day mobilization of every ounce of intelligence.
>
> Konosuke Matsushita of Matsushita Electric Industrial Company

Robert Cross, who has spent his career at the leading edge of developments in the practice of management, is also comfortable with the warfare metaphor:

> War—that's really what it's all about in today's business world. The generals, captains, and lieutenants may wear gray flannel suits and carry black leather briefcases, but they're still fighting a war. Every day, they march off to a new battle over some piece of turf, and the headlines of the *Wall Street Journal* scream about bombs being dropped, predators swooping down on their prey, winners and losers, bloody battles in the boardroom, and wounded companies. . . For some, this new kind of cold war is exciting as hell. For others, it is hell. But make no mistake about it—it's war all right.
>
> Robert G. Cross, Revenue Management (New York: Broadway Books, 1997, p. 100.)

All corporations engaged in global competition possess certain advantages and disadvantages. For example, corporations located in Japan have the advantages of a cooperative and well-trained work force and a supportive government structure, but also have the disadvantages of being a long distance from their major markets and their supplies of raw materials. North American firms are closer to resources and markets, but have more expensive labor, more costly regulations, and less support (in some cases, even hostility) from governments.

The outcome of the economic war is important. Countries where corporations prosper will enhance their economic well-being, allowing them to implement extensive (and often expensive) social programs. Countries where corporations struggle or die will suffer economic decline or stagnation, and will not be in a position to afford modern health care or social services.

An innovative new product, a particularly appealing advertising campaign, or a cost-savings resulting from an innovation in production methods may create a temporary victory for a corporation in the battle against the competition. However, a temporary victory is just one battle won: the war goes on and new combatants will appear. To survive in the long term, the corporation must create and maintain a **sustainable competitive advantage.**

Often a sustainable competitive advantage results from structural considerations that prevent or discourage the competition. For example, locating a plant in a major market may create a niche that competitors choose to allow to continue. Another example is a patent awarded by the government that may prevent direct competition. But for firms in most markets, the only way to sustain a competitive advantage is to keep one step ahead of the competition: a process of **continuous improvement.** A successful advertising campaign must be followed by an even more successful campaign; the firm must continuously improve its marketing. Production innovation must be ongoing as the firm continuously improves its production systems.

Management science can help this process of continuous improvement through constantly striving to improve the corporation's **decision making.** Can the corporation choose to ignore the potential benefits of management science? Almost certainly not, because others are already gaining advantages from using management science as a competitive weapon.

In the final analysis, to survive in the intensely competitive marketplaces of today, the firm must be good at everything. Certainly marketing is important, certainly human resources management is important, certainly finance is important, but if the firm is to survive, it must be as good as, or better than, its competitors at decision making. If two firms face the same problem and one makes a more profitable decision, then it has won a local skirmish. In the long term, battles are won by stringing together victories in local skirmishes.

DECISION MAKING

The emphasis of this book is on **decision making** in the context of the corporation. Making decisions is just one of many things that corporations do, but it is a critical activity. The moments at which decisions are taken differentiate successful organizations from unsuccessful ones. The successful organization has a history of making decisions that are timely, opportunistic, and that generally "work out."

Decision making in a corporation is a carefully controlled activity, where responsibility for decisions is formally assigned to particular individuals or groups (or committees). The human resources or personnel group generally has responsibility for hiring decisions, the marketing group for decisions about sales force planning and advertising spending, the financial manager has the responsibility to make decisions relating to investing surplus funds. These individuals, however, do not set their own decision-making rules, but make decisions within a framework that originates from the highest levels of management and ownership (the board of directors or the shareholders). This framework is articulated through statements about the corporation's *vision, mission,* and *strategy.*

While these statements can be criticized on the grounds that they don't vary much from corporation to corporation and appear to be largely aimed at an outside audience, they do generally define the objectives of the corporation and set guidelines for decision making within the corporation. As an example, here is a statement of "Mission, Values, and Guiding Principles" from the Ford Motor Company:

Note the recurring themes of profitability, competitiveness, and continuous improve-

Box 1-1

STATEMENT OF MISSION, VALUES, AND GUIDING PRINCIPLES BY FORD MOTOR COMPANY

MISSION

Ford Motor Company is a worldwide leader in automotive and automotive-related products and services as well as in newer industries such as aerospace, communications, and technical services. Our mission is to improve continually our products and services to meet our customers' needs, allowing us to prosper as a business and to provide a reasonable return for our stockholders, the owners of our business.

VALUES

How we accomplish our mission is as important as the mission itself. Fundamental to success for the Company are these basic values:

- **People.** Our people are the source of our strength. They provide our corporate intelligence and determine our reputation and vitality. Involvement and teamwork are our core human values.
- **Products.** Our products are the end result of our efforts, and they should be the best in serving customer needs worldwide. As our products are viewed, so are we viewed.
- **Profits.** Profits are the ultimate measure of how efficiently we provide customers with the best products for their needs. Profits are required to survive and grow.

GUIDING PRINCIPLES

- **Quality Comes First.** To achieve customer satisfaction, the quality of our products and services must be our number one priority.
- **Customers Are the Focus of Everything We Do.** Our work must be done with our customers in mind, providing better products and services than our competition.
- **Continuous Improvement Is Essential to Our Success.** We must strive for excellence in everything we do: in our products, in their safety and value, and in our services, our human relations, our competitiveness, and our profitability.
- **Employee Involvement Is Our Way of Life.** We are a team. We must treat each other with trust and respect.
- **Dealers and Suppliers Are Our Partners.** The company must maintain mutually beneficial relationships with dealers, suppliers, and other business associates.
- **Integrity Is Never Compromised.** The conduct of our company worldwide must be pursued in a manner that is socially responsible and commands respect for its integrity and for its positive contributions to society. Our doors are open to men and women alike without discrimination and without regard to ethnic origin or personal beliefs.

Source: Ford Motor Company, *Annual Report,* 1995.

ment. Ford Motor Company sees itself in a highly competitive industry in which it must continuously improve "everything we do" to generate the profits required to "survive and grow." Decision making at Ford is expected to take place within this framework.

A large corporation, such as Ford, makes hundreds of decisions every day. In many cases decisions are made deliberately but, perhaps more often, decisions are a consequence of inaction resulting in opportunities being missed because the corporation failed to recognize them. Decisions not made explicitly often are made anyway. There is little difference in result between a firm that carefully considers a new business opportunity but decides not to proceed, and a firm that did not identify the opportunity in the first place. To use an example closer to home, this business class will not include a number of students who carefully thought about taking a business degree, but decided not to, nor will it include students who didn't even think of taking a business degree, but who would have benefited from (and enjoyed!) the program.

Consistently, good decision making results when the corporation has processes in place to identify and evaluate decision situations. This is what management science is all about: management science provides the vehicle for the systematic improvement of decision-making processes in organizations. Through management science, organizations can improve the way they make decisions.

Management science should not, however, be seen as an isolated activity; the greatest benefits accrue when management science is highly integrated with the other business functions. For example:

> After the financial specialists have arrived at the desired financial characteristics for a portfolio, the management science specialist can help choose the best stocks to include. Having an 'optimal' portfolio provides an immediate advantage over the competition.
>
> or:
>
> After the marketing group has decided which markets to enter, the management science specialist can provide advice on how many warehouses to build, which cities to build them in, and how to ship products around the distribution system. A low cost or high response distribution system provides a competitive advantage.

One objective of this book is to make you, the manager of tomorrow, a better decision maker. Developing individual decision-making skills is one path to improved organizational performance. Much of what you will learn is taken from real life and contains lessons immediately transferable to your future work. However, improving individual decision-making skills is not enough: there are organizational issues that also must be addressed. A second objective is to understand the organizational issues: What can we learn by examining some of the many examples of corporations that have flourished by excelling at management science? Which corporations appear to have very good decision-making processes? How does an organization organize to do management science well? How do successful organizations transfer management science technology into improved decision making?

Can a corporation use management science to achieve a sustainable competitive advantage? The answer to this critical question is a definite "Yes." We can document more and more examples of firms that are very good at management science and very successful in their competitive marketplaces. While it is difficult to conclude that their competitive success is the result of their skill at management science, there are many people inside and outside the firms who are making this claim, including CEOs and members of boards. In some cases, spectacular growth in the number of people employed in the management science area has occurred: American Airlines had eight people employed in management science in 1982, but by 1993 this had risen to almost 400. The actions of other air carriers in hiring large numbers of management scientists (Figure 1-1) also support a view that American Airlines has gained a competitive advantage through the activities of its management science group.

THE FUTURE FOR MANAGEMENT SCIENCE

Personal computers, spreadsheets, and other information technologies are now ubiquitous in management. The great majority of management decision making now involves some form of computer input: the issue is no longer whether a computer should be used, but rather how the computer can be used to assist the human decision maker(s). Since human–computer decision-making systems are the domain of management science, the future for management science specialists looks bright. The United States Bureau of Labor Statistics forecast in 1992 that management science would be the third fastest growing occupation in the United States during the period 1990–2005. Only home health care aides and systems analysts were forecast to have a faster rate of growth. (See Table 1-1.)

This promising future is not limited to western economies. Chinese Vice-president Rong

Figure 1-1 | MS/OR IS A GROWTH AREA

USAir

OPERATIONS RESEARCH CONSULTANTS, PROJECT LEADERS & MANAGEMENT

Based upon its past contribution, USAir's OR Department is growing by 40 professionals.

As the world's "Most Frequent Flyer", USAir offers more daily departures than any of our competitors - creating some of the most challenging OR problems in an extremely demanding industry. Our existing Operations Research Department of 37 professionals provides management consulting and decision technology to all divisions of the Airline. This interdisciplinary department is comprised of Operations Research Consultants and Software Engineers who develop cost/benefit based improvements to the business process and create user-friendly systems which better utilize all of USAir's resources. We create models using innovative OR techniques (such as Neural Networks and Simulated Annealing) as well as the latest object-oriented design technology on UNIX and PC platforms.

Grow with us as we find solutions to some of the most complex real-world problems in:

Business Process Re-engineering

Transportation Scheduling & Routing

Forecasting & Marketing

Revenue Management

Operations & Maintenance Planning

We seek exceptional, business-oriented, energetic professionals to join our talented staff. Your reward will be seeing your problem-solving skills and effort make a direct impact on the bottom line.

You should have an M.S. or Ph.D. in Operations Research (or Statistics or Industrial Engineering), strong programming skills and excellent communication skills with professional experience preferred. USAir offers competitive starting salaries, excellent benefits, liberal travel privileges, and most importantly, a stimulating environment which fosters excellence and pride of achievement.

For immediate consideration, please mail or fax a cover letter, resume and salary information to: **USAir Operations Research, Attention: M. Cumming, Crystal Park Four-DCA/H700, 2345 Crystal Drive, Arlington, VA 22227, FAX: (703)418-5903.** We are an Equal Opportunity Employer M/F/D/V.

Source: Reprinted with permission from *OR/MS Today* INFORMS. (October 1995).

Yiren has said that "administrative systems based on scientific theory are important for economic development and social progress in both developed and developing countries." (Cao Min, *China Daily,* October 9, 1996, p. 1.)

Part of the reason for the forecast growth in management science is the increasing competitiveness and increasingly global nature of business. To survive, firms and countries must continually seek sources of competitive advantage that they can sustain over periods of time.

In seeking a sustainable advantage, it is important to concentrate on the **process** of decision making rather than individual decisions. An organization with effective decision-making processes will make some decisions that turn out badly; the organization was simply unlucky. It is important to distinguish between **decisions** and **outcomes**; a good decision can produce a bad result. Consider the following example:

> You are offered a chance to play the following game: a coin (selected at random from those in your pocket) will be flipped by a disinterested third party. If the coin shows "heads" you will receive $1,000, but if it comes down "tails" you will have to pay $1.

Choosing to play this game is a correct decision for most of us. If we could play it over and over again, we would become very rich, but if we were only able to play the game once, we could end up losing a dollar. A spectator seeing us lose a dollar might conclude that our decision to play was a poor one: they would be incorrect, we made a good decision—we

Table 1-1 **United States Bureau of Labor Statistics Forecast—1992**

Occupation	Number of Jobs in 1990	Number of Jobs in 2005	Percentage Increase
Home health aide	287,000	550,000	92
Systems analysts	463,000	829,000	79
Operations research analysts	57,000	100,000	73
Computer equipment repairers	83,000	134,000	60
Computer programmers	565,000	882,000	56
Management analysts	151,000	230,000	52
Marketing and public relations managers	427,000	630,000	47
Accountants	985,000	1,325,000	34
Veterinarians	47,000	62,000	31
Emergency medical technicians	89,000	116,000	30
Financial managers	701,000	894,000	28
Police and detectives	655,000	815,000	24
Education administrators	348,000	434,000	24
Budget analysts	64,000	78,000	22
Economists	37,000	45,000	21
Aeronautical engineers	73,000	88,000	20
Architects	108,000	134,000	20

Source: United States Department of Labor. "Outlook, 1990–2005," *Bureau of Labor Statistics Bulletin 2402* (May 1992).

were simply unlucky as to the outcome. Of course, the reverse is also true: firms that make bad decisions sometimes 'get lucky' and experience a good outcome.

An organization cannot avoid bad outcomes, but it can control the risks that it takes and act in a way that enhances its chances of survival. To do this, the organization must continuously work to improve the **processes** by which its decisions are made.

An interesting example of the partnership between management science and the other business functions leading to improved decision making was given by Richard Caldwell, Executive Vice President of Harris Trust and Savings Bank. Caldwell said:

> We became familiar with some of the academic work on decision making only after we discovered that a simple computer program could in some cases outperform our experts.

The process of continuous improvement is emphasized as Caldwell continued:

> Puzzled by this phenomenon, we turned to the literature and were able to fine tune our decision process and use the knowledge of our experts more effectively.

Presumably, with more effective experts, even more effective "simple computer programs" can be developed, leading to even more effective experts, and the cycle continues.

The first step toward implementing sound decision making is to examine the decision-making process itself.

THE DECISION-MAKING PROCESS

Decision making requires that three basic tasks be performed: **pathfinding, analysis,** and **managerial review and action** (Figure 1-2).

Pathfinding is the step at which possible acts that can be taken are identified. Pathfinding involves answering questions such as:

What alternatives (or options) do we have?

If we have a problem, what can we do about it? What are the possible solutions?

The organization is not doing as well as we feel it should. What can we change?

The competition is killing us. What can we do?

How do we get to where we want to be from where we are?

Figure 1-2 THE MANAGEMENT DECISION-MAKING PROCESS

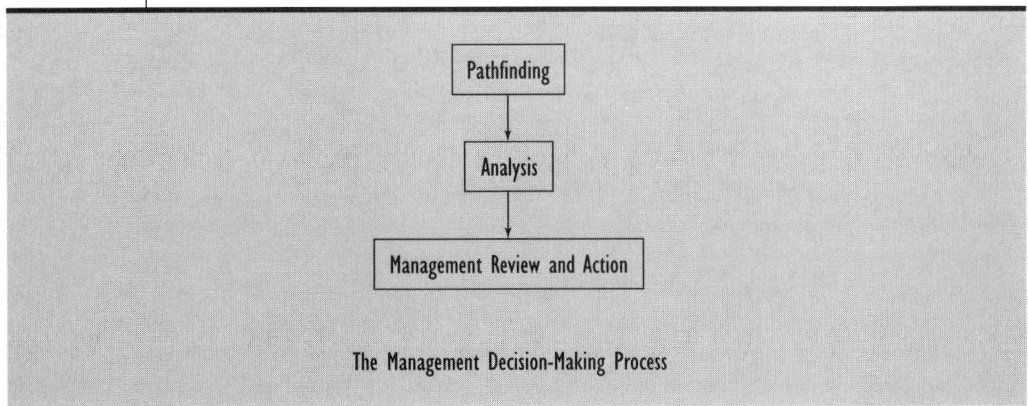

The Management Decision-Making Process

Pathfinding requires managerial expertise coupled, sometimes, with creativity and intuition. A "creative" option may emerge, but in other cases, the options may be straightforward. There may be a large number of options, or a few options. There may be some that, while strictly possible, are easily discarded. As an example, one option is almost always to close down the business, but in most instances this is not worth spending much time analyzing.

Analysis involves "laying out" the possible acts in some way and comparing and contrasting them. Typical questions include:

Box 1-2

FOUR DECISIONS THAT DID NOT WORK OUT WELL

In August 1981 IBM launched the IBM Personal Computer (PC) and in this one bold move, seized control of the PC market. For a few short months IBM dominated this market, but in a series of decisions made over about a 10-year period, IBM handed the PC market to Microsoft. Based on the capitalized value of Microsoft in 1991, the cumulative result of these decisions was a "gift" of about a billion dollars from IBM to Microsoft—IBM may well be the only company that has given $1 billion to a competitor and survived!

On December 6, 1994, Orange County, California filed under Chapter 9 of the Bankruptcy Code being unable to repay $1,200,000,000 owed to investment bankers. This was the culmination of a series of decisions whereby Orange County officials, lead by 69-year-old County Treasurer Robert Citron, had decided to invest their $20 billion investment pool in derivatives of Federal National Mortgage Association and Federal Home Loan Mortgage debt in an effort to increase investment returns.

Federal Express Corp (FedEx) launched its ZapMail service in July 1984. ZapMail was a 2-hour door-to-door electronic mail service. A FedEx courier would pick up a document and deliver it to a FedEx office from where the document was transmitted by a high-quality facsimile machine, specially developed for FedEx by NEC Corporation (Japan). The cost for this service was $25 for the first page and $1 for each additional page. In the first 5 months of operations, ZapMail lost $83 million but FedEx was undeterred and began offering machines for installation directly at customers' premises. At the end of September 1986 FedEx announced that it was ending its ZapMail service and taking a pretax writeoff of $340 million. A FedEx spokesperson is rumored to have "deadpanned": "We like to think that we were ahead of our time."

In 1988, Canadian real estate "baron" Robert Campeau purchased Federated Department Stores Inc. for $6.7 billion following a bidding "war" with Macy's, which saw Campeau's initial offer of $47/share increased to $73.50/share. Federated included Bloomingdale's, a 17-unit department store chain (sales of $1.2 billion in 1988), which many thought was the best retail franchise in the United States (and perhaps the world). Even after selling off eight store chains and laying off more than 3,500 employees, retail cash flow still failed to cover the interest on the staggering debt. In September 1989, under tight financial pressure, Campeau very reluctantly put Bloomingdale's up for sale. In early January 1990 Campeau terminated its plans to sell Bloomingdale's because of inadequate bids and filed for protection under Chapter 11 of the US bankruptcy code. In August 1990 after 9 months of effort at restructuring Campeau Corporation in order to stave off creditors, Robert Campeau was ousted as Chairman and Chief Executive.

...AND ONE THAT WORKED OUT REALLY WELL FOR MICROSOFT

Microsoft purchased all rights to a fledgling personal computer operating system called 86-DOS in July 1981 for two payments which totalled $75,000. 86-DOS had been developed by the Seattle Computer Products company in response to the need they perceived for a general purpose PC operating system. Development began in April 1980 and the first version (called QDOS 0.10 for "Quick and Dirty Operating System") was released in August having been thrown together in 2 people-months (although it worked surprisingly well). Version 0.3, now known as 86-DOS, was released in the last few days of 1980. Seattle passed this new version on to Microsoft, which initially purchased nonexclusive marketing rights: it had just one customer at the time. In April 1981, Seattle released version 1.0, which was essentially MS-DOS as used on the first IBM PCs. In July 1981, Microsoft purchased all rights to the DOS outright. Shortly afterward, IBM announced the IBM PC using essentially this operating system, now bearing the Microsoft name.

What are the consequences of each act?

How can we choose one act over some other act?

What relevant data are available?

Is there some additional data that we can collect?

Can expert opinion help us decide?

Is there some number crunching that we should do?

Can some type of model help us decide?

Analysis usually concentrates on the "harder" facts and the quantitative aspects of the decision, because these are easier to analyze, and draws conclusions based on data, calculations, and perhaps some theory (particularly economic theory).

A management science specialist or trained analyst can often provide assistance at the analysis stage, but the manager cannot stand completely aside. Many "management issues" emerge at the analysis stage: What are our goals? What are appropriate criteria?

Managerial review and action follow the analysis step. Analysts do not make decisions; this is the manager's responsibility. The manager must review the pathfinding step (Were the 'right' actions considered? Were there others that were missed?) and the analysis step (Was the analysis valid? What conclusions were reached? What was learned from the analysis?).

At this stage, other managerial issues might emerge: the analysis may suggest one route forward, but management may feel that some other action may be more consistent with the organization's long-term strategy. The review stage brings in the "softer" issues that could not be adequately addressed during the analysis.

Finally, after management becomes comfortable with a decision, steps must be taken to implement the required action. This may include testing the decision in some way (one form of testing is to try out the new system in parallel with the old system), and also may include monitoring and reviewing the results of the action. Implementing decisions is one of the basic tasks of line management. It requires skill and perseverance, coupled with attention to the process by which the decision is implemented.

TWO USEFUL FRAMEWORKS

Two useful frameworks for understanding decision making within organizations are the **strategic/tactical/operational framework,** which identifies different types of decision making at different levels in the organization, and the **data/models/knowledge (DMK) framework,** which examines the input into making a decision.

In the strategic/tactical/operational framework the organization is thought of as having a pyramid structure (Figure 1-3). At the bottom of the pyramid is the **operational** layer, while the top of the pyramid represents the **strategic** layer. Between these two are the middle management or **tactical** layers.

Operational decision making takes place at the lower levels of the firm. These decisions are required for the day-to-day running of the corporation and have mainly short-term consequences—they can be changed fairly easily, often at low cost. Examples include how much of a product to order when the stock has (or is about to) run out, how much fuel to load into an airplane, and how many equipment operators to hire.

Tactical decision making takes place in the middle managerial levels of the organization. These decisions have longer lasting effects than operational decisions and are more

Figure 1-3 **DECISION-MAKING LEVELS**

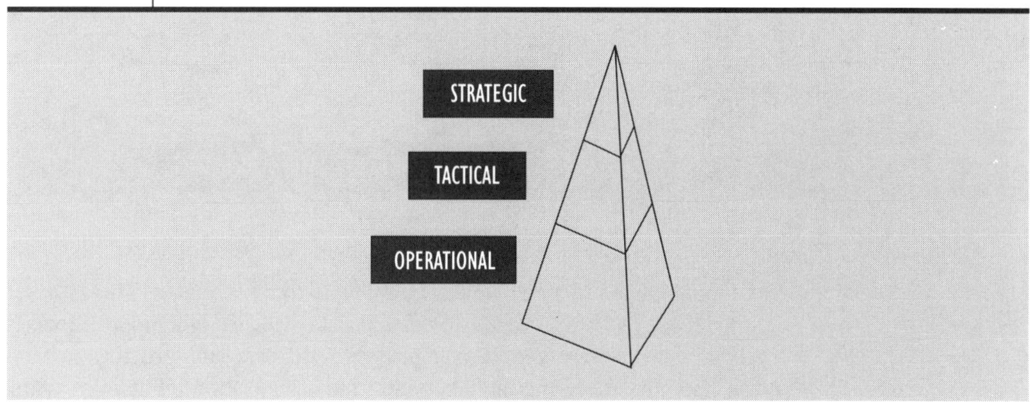

costly to change. Examples include deriving the manufacturer's master production schedule, deciding on the organization's operating budget, and hiring management staff.

Strategic decision making is the task of top management, often including the board of directors. Strategic decisions affect the long-term direction and vitality of the organization. Generally, strategic decisions, once taken, are very costly and difficult to change. Examples include leasing or buying a new building, launching a major new product, acquiring another company, and selecting the chief executive officer for the organization.

Knowing whether a decision is strategic, tactical, or operational says much about the process of making the decision. Clearly, each individual strategic decision is worth spending time and effort on since the cost of a mistake here generally is very high. Operational decisions, however, may not justify as high an expenditure of effort on each decision individually because these are easier and less expensive to change if a poor choice is made. Operational decisions, however, often recur: each time an airplane lands, the airline has to decide how much fuel to load on board. While each operational decision may not have great consequences, the total of all the operational decisions may lead to a source of significant competitive advantage. The airline that can implement a set of refueling decisions that takes best advantage of fuel price differences at different airports, avoids the cost of flying excess fuel around the skies, arranges refueling so as not to interfere with its flight timetable, and importantly, ensures that no plane runs out of fuel while flying, will have lower fuel costs than the competition. Implementing a good solution to the refueling problem is therefore of strategic importance. (Fuel costs are the single largest cost item for the major airlines amounting to approximately $2 billion per year for a major carrier.)

The strategic/tactical/operational framework looks at where decisions are made, while a second framework looks at what goes into making a decision.

The **DMK framework** breaks down the inputs to a decision into **data, models,** and **knowledge** (Figure 1-4). **Data** is an important input to decision making: there are few decision situations that can be resolved in an informed way without reference to data. Organizations contain vast amounts of data. Some is specific to the organization (e.g., payroll numbers), while other data is public (e.g., today's stock prices). Some data is captured in the organization's data bases (in libraries and in computer storage devices), while other data exists in the minds of employees or is available externally (e.g., through public, electronic data bases). Managing the organization's data is often a multimillion dollar activity in which providing access to the data is as important as managing the entry of new data.

Looking at data, however, rarely is sufficient. The data must be compiled, abstracted,

Figure 1-4 THE "DMK" FRAMEWORK

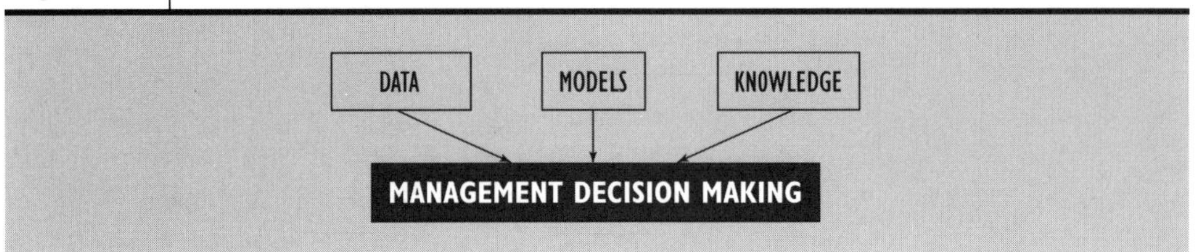

and manipulated in some way to be relevant to the decision. This is the role of the model: a model is a construct that *adds value* to data. The use of a model allows an informed analysis of a decision situation, bringing relevant data and structure to the decision-making task. Taking care of the models within the organization includes providing access, model maintenance and updating, and developing new models. These tasks provide many managerial challenges.

Few decisions are made without **knowledge.** Organizations contain vast amounts of knowledge, most of it in the minds of employees. Increasingly, knowledge can be extracted from humans, represented in some structured way, and stored in a *knowledge base.* For the most part, however, knowledge relevant to today's decisions comes from the people involved in the decision-making process. This includes knowledge about the data, knowledge about models and model building, and managerial knowledge about this decision and similar situations that have occurred in the past.

The DMK framework raises many probing questions about how a decision was made. For example:

What data was used to make this decision? Where did it come from? Was it reliable?

Was current data used? If forecasts were used, how were these obtained?

What model was used? Was this a valid model?

What knowledge went into the decision making? Whose knowledge was it? Does this individual have this knowledge? How do we know?

Successful decision making requires that appropriate data, useful models, and relevant knowledge be mobilized in the decision-making process.

SUMMARY

To survive in the long term, the corporation must create and maintain a **sustainable competitive advantage.** For most firms, in most markets, the only way to sustain a competitive advantage is by keeping one step ahead of the competition: a process of **continuous improvement.** Management science can help this process of continuous improvement through continually improving the corporation's **decision making.**

Two frameworks were presented that are useful in analyzing decision-making processes. The strategic, tactical, operational framework identifies decisions according to their importance in the organization, while the DMK framework looks at the inputs to each decision. The manager who understands these two simple frameworks is well equipped to ask many probing questions about the firm's decision making.

EUROTUNNEL: THE FOLKESTONE TERMINAL

December 1990; British and French workers have just met some 300 feet below the surface of the English channel linking England to the Continent for the first time in recorded history; an important milestone in the construction of the channel tunnel. About 35 kilometers of the tunnel is under the English channel, making this the longest undersea tunnel ever built. At a current cost estimate of $14.5 billion, the tunnel is also the largest privately financed engineering project in history.

By the end of 1991, 3 million tons of concrete will have been used to construct two running tunnels plus a smaller service tunnel. Construction is in the hands of Trans-Manche Link, a consortium of five French and five United Kingdom construction companies responsible for building the tunnel and the terminals at either end.

Dave Mustard, a management scientist who joined Eurotunnel in 1989, had been given the assignment of assisting in the design of the Folkestone terminal of the tunnel. The milestone meeting under the sea brought with it a sense of urgency; time was advancing, and much still needed to be done before the tunnel opened for business in 1993. Dave decided to review the progress in the design of the Folkestone terminal. He was particularly interested in identifying the decisions that had to be made, the people who would make those decisions, and what help he could provide with their decision-making process.

Eurotunnel

Eurotunnel is the company within the Channel Tunnel Group responsible for operating the tunnel on its completion in 1993. The tunnel will be a rail tunnel linking terminals at Folkestone in southeast England and Coquelles, near Calais, France. The distance between the terminals is about 50 kilometers that will be traversed by two types of rail traffic:

1. British, French, and Belgian railways (all major shareholders in the Channel Tunnel Group) will operate high-speed passenger and rail freight services from London and other points in the United Kingdom to Paris and other major European cities.
2. Eurotunnel will run shuttle trains on which owners of cars, heavy goods vehicles (HGVs), campers, buses, and other vehicles will be transported through the tunnel.

Shuttle trains will traverse the tunnel at about 140 kilometres per hour, making the passage time about 33 minutes. British, French, and Belgian railway trains will run slightly slower.

Initial daily capacity of the tunnel is expected to be 200 passenger or freight trains and 200 shuttle trains. It is estimated that 16 million passengers and 8 million tons of freight will travel through the tunnel annually.

The Folkestone Terminal

The Folkestone terminal is to occupy a restricted site bounded on the north and west by Shakespeare cliff (which has been excavated to the maximum possible extent). To the south are the main railway lines, the main London-Ashford-Dover road (A20/M20), and the town of Folkestone, while at the eastern extremity of the site is the tunnel portal. (In contrast, the terminal at Coquelles is situated on a large flat tract of open land some distance from Calais.)

Some decisions about operation of the terminal already have been made:

> Vehicles will not be able to reserve spaces on the shuttles, but will be processed as they arrive. Traffic intensity, particularly for tourist vehicles, is expected to be highly seasonal, with the major peak at the beginning of the school summer holidays (July). At very busy times, it is likely that long queues of vehicles will form.
>
> Drivers entering either terminal (in their vehicles) must pass through British and French customs and immigration, Eurotunnel security checks, and must buy their tickets for the crossing prior to departure. On arrival at the other end of the tunnel, they will be able to drive into France with no further formalities.
>
> The site of Folkestone is very confined, and it is not clear whether the shuttle trains will be able to turn (or loop) at Folkestone. If the shuttle trains are not able

to turn at Folkestone, they will have locomotives on both ends to facilitate the change of direction required at Folkestone.

Vehicles will be driven on and off the shuttle by their owners, who will be responsible for all movements of their vehicles on the terminal site.

HGVs require more complex processing than tourist vehicles and will be segregated from them. About one in five HGVs will be subject to an extensive customs and security check including vehicle-scale X-ray and MRI scans. HGVs will drive onto flatbed shuttle wagons and be taken through the tunnel on shuttles that carry HGVs only. Drivers will not ride in their vehicle but in a passenger wagon attached to the end of the shuttle.

Private cars and other tourist vehicles taller than 1.85 meters will drive onto single-deck shuttle wagons for their trip through the tunnel. In general, occupants will travel in their vehicles, although a passenger wagon will be provided for the use of occupants of campers or cars pulling housetrailers because the bottled gas in these vehicles is seen as a safety hazard to vehicle occupants while in the tunnel.

Private cars less than 1.85 meters tall will travel through the tunnel on double-deck flat shuttle wagons with the drivers and passengers traveling in their cars. These vehicles may also be carried on single-deck shuttle wagons if space is available.

The site will contain an amenities building offering meals and snacks, rest room facilities, and a display of the tunnel with exhibits covering construction and operation. Some drivers will want to stop to visit this building.

Assignment:

1. What decisions have to be made concerning the Folkestone Terminal?
2. Who makes these decisions?
3. How might these decisions be resolved?

DECOMMISSIONING NUCLEAR POWER STATIONS

Nuclear-powered electricity generating stations have a finite lifetime of about 40 years. As we approach the year 2000, we are starting to see power stations reaching the end of their useful life. When this occurs, the nuclear plant must be "decommissioned," that is, shut down and "retired." Decommissioning involves making some difficult decisions.

THE DECOMMISSIONING PROCESS

A closed, shutdown nuclear plant remains very dangerous. The materials inside the reactor vessels (there may be several reactors in a single plant) remain highly radioactive for thousands of years. In addition, large quantities of surrounding materials, particularly concrete stacks and containment structures, retain low levels of radioactivity for centuries. A retired plant cannot, therefore, be abandoned in the usual sense: the owner must do something to decommission the plant.

The plant can be "mothballed"—the reactors are shut down, the fuel is removed, and the buildings are abandoned except for ensuring continuing safety and security. This requires that the premises be guarded around the clock to prevent unauthorized entry and essential maintenance be performed to ensure that the closed plant remains safe. In general, periodic engineering inspections must be conducted that identify the need for maintenance. This may include the patching and repair of cracked or crumbling concrete and reinforcement of corroding steel structures.

The maintenance requirements are typically modest initially, but they can be expected to increase over time as the concrete ages and crumbles and the metals and materials continue to corrode. Every 5 years or so, a requirement for major maintenance can be expected. This could involve significant new concrete work, building new containment structures, replacing drainage, or replacing failing roofing. In addition, every now and then, very large costs might have to be incurred, for example, at some point in time, the tops might need to be taken off the stacks since the deteriorating condition of the construction materials will eventually make it too dangerous to ascend the stacks to perform other kinds of needed maintenance.

Alternatively, the plant could be dismantled and the site left vacant. Dismantling the plant will produce large quantities of three kinds of waste: nonradioactive material, low-level radioactive waste, and high-level radioactive waste. Nonradioactive waste is safe and can be buried on site or trucked to a landfill. Low-level radioactive waste, which can be safely handled by humans wearing suitable protective clothing, can be transported to low-level nuclear waste disposal sites for burial. Such sites charge a fee per cubic meter for disposing of this hazardous material (typically, this fee is increasing dramatically over time, because the numbers and capacities of these sites are finite and new sites are difficult to open).

High-level radioactive waste, however, is difficult and dangerous to handle, and robots and mechanical devices must be used exclusively. These materials must be loaded into concrete, lead-lined, sarcophaguses and shipped to nuclear processing plants where the radioactive materials are extracted and stabilized leaving a bulk of low-level radioactive waste that can be buried. The extracted high-level waste, often intensely radioactive and dangerous, must be handled with extreme care for the foreseeable future. In some cases, the processing plants can dispose of these radioactive materials for a large fee (in fact, they must be stored in permanent high-radiation waste storage facilities since the radioactivity cannot be destroyed). In other cases, the intensely radioactive materials are returned to the plant owners for them to arrange permanent storage.

EVALUATING THE DECOMMISSIONING OPTIONS

When a nuclear power station is to be closed down, management must consider what to do with the closed facility. The basic options are to mothball the plant or to dismantle it. Many other hybrid strategies are possible that involve dismantling those parts of the plant that will require the most maintenance or those that are the most (or least) dangerous, while mothballing the balance of the facility. Dismantling may take place immediately or may be postponed 30 or more years into the future.

Evaluating the possible choices is complicated by the uncertainties surrounding many of the important parameters. What will be the cost of low-level radioactive waste disposal 50 years from now? What about processing and storing high-level waste? What maintenance can be expected to be required, and at what cost? How fast will the abandoned plant "age"? How are expenditures 20 or 50 years from now to be compared with expenditures today (i.e., how can the "time value of money" be incorporated into an analysis)?

These are very difficult issues, but these decisions must be made.

Assignment:

1. What process should be used to decide how to decommission a closed nuclear facility?
2. What data is required to reach a decision, and how might the various required data items be estimated?
3. How might the "time value of money" issue be addressed?

2

MODELS AND MODEL BUILDING

The distinguishing feature of the management science approach to decision making is the use of "models." We are all familiar with models of various kinds. Architects use small-scale models to help them design new buildings; automobile designers build models of new cars to test out design features; and crash-test dummies are used to model the effects of automobile accidents on car occupants. These are all examples of physical models that can be seen and touched. Management science models, however, are **mathematical** or **computer models** in which relationships from the real world are approximated by the use of mathematical equations or logical statements: management science models exist on paper or in the computer.

Managers from many organizations can attest to the fact that the systematic use of models has improved their management decision making. The basic steps in the use of a model to address a decision problem are illustrated in Figure 2-1.

Figure **2-1** | **BASIC STEPS IN THE USE OF A MODEL IN DECISION MAKING**

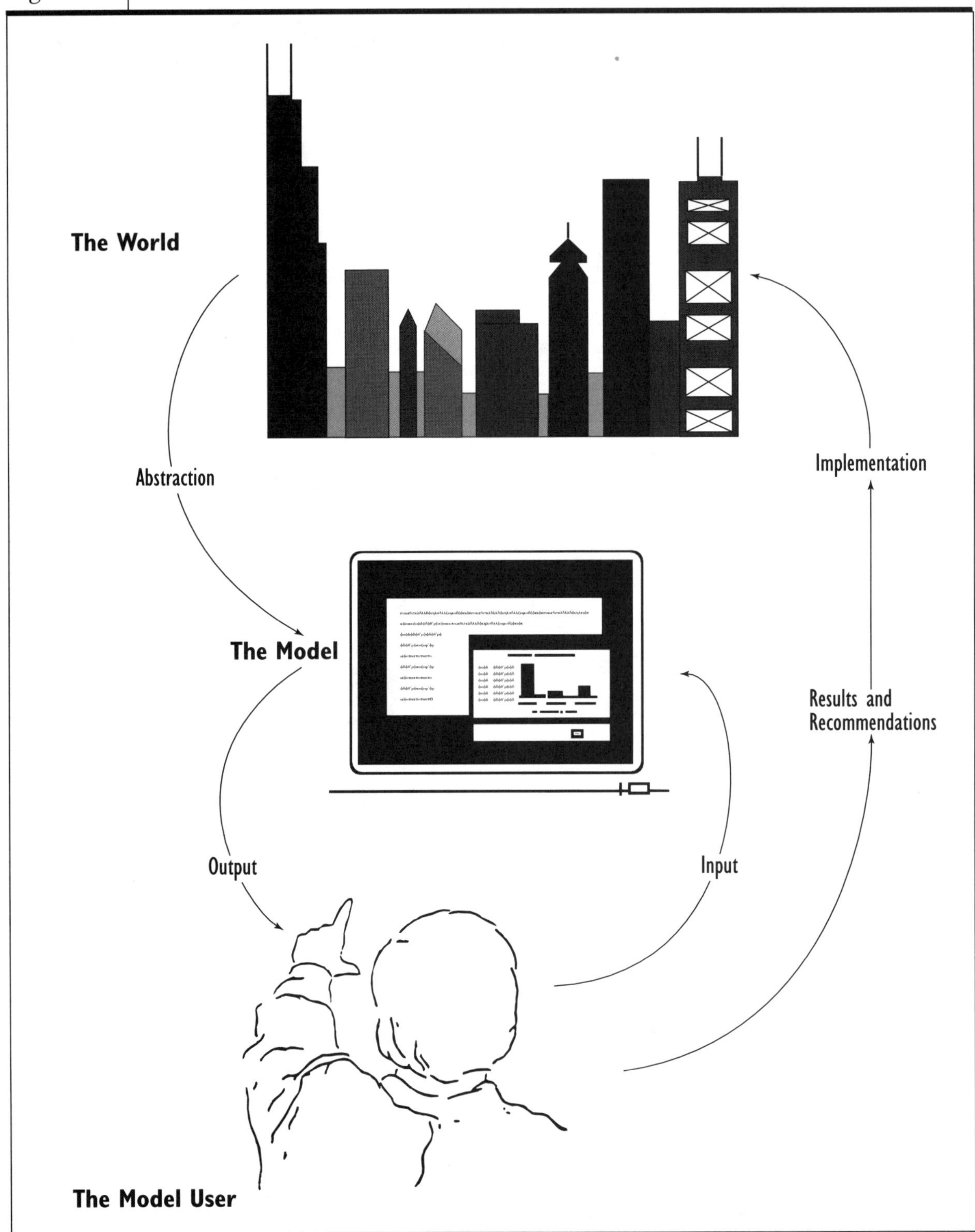

Model Building. The model builder studies the real world in which the decision issue exists and **abstracts** from the real world to construct a model. The model is designed to allow the model user to vary the decision variables (the **inputs** to the model) and to see how the decision criteria (the **outputs** from the model) vary in response. The **logic** of the model, although much simpler than that of the real world, is designed to accurately reflect the real world relationships between the decision variables and the decision criteria.

Using the Model. The model user (who may be an individual or a group or may be the decision maker or the model builder) works with the model and gains an understanding of the decision issue. After a period of time, the model user is able to identify values for the input variables (the decision variables) that produce "good" or perhaps even "the best" values for the decision criteria. These modeling results then are translated into recommendations for change.

Implementation. Translating the results of the modeling effort into effective change in the real world is the final step. Considerable management skill may be required to do this in some instances because implementation may affect the way people work. Often, implementation may also require software to be designed or modified, equipment to be purchased, or factories to be built.

In general, these steps are iterative rather than sequential. Model building and model use often follow an iterative design, or "prototyping," methodology in which a simple prototype model is built quickly and made available to the model user. The user experiments with the model and determines the direction for future model development jointly with the model builder. This leads to a second prototype, and the process is repeated until a final model, if there is one, emerges as an advanced prototype.

The effective use of management science within the organization requires that models be constructed that are appropriate, users be able to use these models to investigate the need for change and the direction that the change should take, and managers have the skills, and perhaps the courage, to translate the results from the modeling into action.

MODELS IN MANAGEMENT DECISION MAKING

The development and use of models to aid management decision making began during World War II when a group of scientists were assembled at Royal Air Force Fighter Command in England. This group was asked to provide a scientific point of view on various operational problems relating to fighter aircraft. The first problem concerned how to translate data on approaching aircraft from the air defense warning system into an organized fighter response. In May 1940, however, this group was involved in some very critical strategic decision making. As Harold Larnder recounts:

> When the Germans opened their offensive against France and the Low Countries, Fighter Command was quickly involved to the extent of ten of its Home Defence squadrons... maintained and operated from airfields on the Continent. [By May 1940,] British losses were running at a rate of some three squadrons every two days.... On 14 May, [Air Chief Marshal Sir Hugh] Dowding learned that the French Premier was asking for an additional ten squadrons and that Churchill, because of his strong sense of loyalty to Britain's ally, was determined to accede to the request. On the morning of May 15, [Dowding] invited Larnder to see him and... finished by saying, "... is there anything you scientists can sug-

> gest bearing on this matter?" Anything that could be done had to be done before he would leave for the Cabinet meeting two hours later.
>
> "So, at the suggestion of E.C. Williams, a rapid study was carried out based on current daily losses and replacement rates, to show how much more rapid this would become if additional squadrons were sent. For ease of presentation, Larnder converted Williams' findings from numerical to graph form. [At the Cabinet meeting,] Dowding, feeling that he was making little headway in dissuading the Prime Minister from his determination to reinforce France, got up, walked round the table and said to Churchill, "If the present rate of wastage continues for another fortnight, we shall not have a single Hurricane left in France *or* in this country"...he laid his graphs in front of the Prime Minister. In Dowding's considered view, "That did the trick." Not only were the requested ten additional squadrons not sent to France, but of those already there all but three were returned to the United Kingdom within a matter of days.
>
> H. Larnder, The Origin of Operational Research in K.B. Haley (Ed.) Operational Research, 78, North-Holland, Amsterdam, 1979.

This was clearly a pivotal decision. The Battle of Britain, which began about 2 months later, was fought with an average strength of 650 to 700 fighter aircraft; with 20 squadrons of fighters in France for a single week, the loss of 250 to 260 aircraft was expected.

This incident from the early history of management science exemplifies three characteristics of the strategic use of management science. First, the decision maker (prime minister) was in the upper ranks of the organization; second, the model was produced in timely fashion and was appropriate to the problem; and third, some effort was made to present the results in a way that the decision maker could understand.

In this example, the model was a **mathematical** model; the loss of aircraft was approximated by a mathematical function (in fact, an exponential decay curve). The mathematical model, solved by hand, was the mainstay of management science before the arrival of the computer. Usually, solving the model was a time-consuming and laborious task that involved rooms full of people with calculators who worked long hours, often overnight. The new electronic computers were first seen as particularly good calculators with which to solve this computational problem (their accuracy was an important benefit), but it was soon recognized that the computer could drive other kinds of models, particularly **simulations** that emulate the function of the real world in the computer.

The early computers were batch processing devices; the modeler produced a program that was submitted to the computer, and the output was returned some time after the job was submitted. The appearance of **interactivity** has had a profound impact, with managers now routinely using the kind of programming-free modeling environments offered by spreadsheet programs (such as Lotus 1-2-3 or Excel). For the model builder, there are now sophisticated environments that permit the interactive construction of highly graphic and interactive models with the extensive use of color and graphics to aid communication between user and model.

TYPES OF MODEL

Different types of models are appropriate for particular decision issues.

Decision analysis models (see Chapter 3) provide a useful vehicle for exploring sequential decision situations involving uncertainty. These models have been widely used for the analysis and management of risk and uncertainty.

Optimizing models (e.g., mathematical programming models; see Chapter 4), which provide the solution with the maximum profit, minimum cost, or maximum rate of return, have been widely applied to structured operational problems (e.g., day-to-day operation of an oil refinery, planning maintenance, transportation, production scheduling). Often, such models are embedded in an interactive system that permits the data to be easily entered or modified and allows the results to be viewed from several different perspectives. Optimizing models are also referred to as **normative** models because they seek to find the best possible solution; they determine what should be done in a normal situation.

Another broad class of models is the **analytical** models (e.g., queuing theory, Markov processes), which do not provide an optimum solution but allow the calculation of performance statistics for a given set of input parameters (e.g., queuing models provide mean customer waiting times for a wide variety of different types of queuing systems). Results for these kinds of models were once published in tabular form, but now these models are routinely used in interactive environments that allow the user to vary the inputs and observe the resulting changes in the performance statistics.

Simulation modeling (see Chapter 5) has become a very big business. Computer simulation is routinely used to review the operation of manufacturing plants before construction begins, to design warehousing and materials handling systems, in military operations and gaming, and in a broad range of service sector applications (including airports, banks, and so on). Simulation models are **descriptive** models in that they describe the way things are (versus normative models, which describe the way things should be). Descriptive models are used to evaluate different alternatives; however, because a descriptive analysis examines only a given set of alternatives (and not all possible alternatives), the result of this kind of modeling may not be optimal.

Knowledged-based models, or "expert systems" (see Chapter 6), attempt to solve problems by following the same kinds of logic that human experts use. The development of knowledge-based models is revealing that human expertise often is not very mysterious (or very "expert") and that fairly simple computer problems often can add value to the work of the human expert.

MANAGEMENT ISSUES SURROUNDING THE MODELING PROCESS

A manager equipped with a spreadsheet can perform much useful modeling, but in many situations in which substantial returns are available, management science models are highly complex and are developed and operated by specialists. For example, the linear programming models, which are the heart of the operation of an oil refinery, are built and maintained by groups of technicians who report to the plant management. Although actual model construction or model use can be delegated to the management science specialist, there are many issues where management must be involved in the modeling effort.

Problem formulation is the process of studying the real world and deciding which decision issue (or problem) should be addressed. Sometimes, problem formulation is straightforward: "We are going to build a new factory and must come up with a design." On other occasions, problem formulation may be very difficult: "Our production process does not seem to be operating as well as that of our competitor." Deciding what problem to address, and hence what model to construct, is an important management issue within the management science approach.

Model validation is the process of ensuring that the mathematical model adequately captures the relationships between the model inputs and outputs. Modeling the past often is a useful aid to model validation, even though the purpose of the model is to predict future behavior. Managers should play a key role in model validation because they have the best understanding of how the real process works. A useful model is one that supports the manager's understanding of the decision, not one that contradicts this understanding.

Sensitivity analysis addresses the sensitivity of the results of the modeling to the values used for the inputs or to the assumptions made in the modeling. If sales increase by 12% instead of the 10% that we assumed, what effect does that have? If the rate of inflation were 4% instead of the 6% that was used in our model, would we make a different decision? Management should be sure that any decision is sufficiently **robust**; that is, it is a good (perhaps the best) decision for the assumptions that have been made, but it is not a disastrous decision if reality differs a bit from what was assumed.

The design of the model *interface* may also be an important management issue. Modelers are paying increasing attention to the displays produced by the model and how the user interacts with the model. Color and graphics are widely used to communicate model results to the user. With the announcement of computers that include facilities for high-quality stereophonic sound, in addition to color and graphics, modelers will soon be incorporating a sound track into their models. Managers should ensure that the model interface is useful and sufficiently "user friendly," particularly if the model is designed to be used by the manager. A good interface can do much to help the user understand both the model and the real decision issue that it addresses.

To conclude this introductory section on the managerial issues around modeling, it is useful to reinforce the reasons why models are proving to be useful to senior managers. Frederick W. Smith, Chairman, CEO, and founder of Federal Express Corporation (FedEx), which is one of the world's largest air-package transportation companies, is convinced of the benefits management science models have provided FedEx. Smith has said:

> By modeling various alternatives for future system design, FedEx has, in effect, made its mistakes on paper. Computer modeling works; it allows us to examine many different alternatives and it forces the examination of the entire problem.
>
> P. Horner (1991) Eyes on the Prize, *OR/MS Today*.

AN EXAMPLE OF DECISION MAKING WITH A SPREADSHEET MODEL

The development of an understanding of models and modeling must begin with a simple example. The following is an example of a decision consumers often have to make.

"New Convenient Monthly Pay Plan!"

My automobile insurance renewal came today. The insurance company is offering the usual payment options:

Option 1. Pay the annual premium ($1,500) in full by the beginning of the month.

Option 2. Pay in three equal installments, with the first due by the beginning of the month and the remaining installments paid at 2-month intervals. A $3.50 service charge is added to each payment.

This year, for the first time, a third "convenient monthly pay plan" is offered.

Option 3. Under this plan, I pay for 2 months of insurance by the beginning of the month and then pay monthly, in advance, for the balance of the year. The last 10 payments are made directly through my bank (at no additional cost to me). A 3% service charge is added to each payment.

How Should I Pay?

At first it appears that option 1 represents the best deal because option 2 costs $10.50 extra (three service charges of $3.50) and option 3 costs $45.00 extra (3% of $1,500). The problem is that under options 2 and 3, payments can be postponed until later, and this postponement has value in that the money can be invested until it is needed. If the interest earned on the invested money is included, the decision might be different. How can I decide?

To simplify the problem, let us assume that $1,500 is in a savings account at the bank and this account pays interest at a rate of 0.5% monthly (approximately 6% annually).

We can now use a spreadsheet program to model the three options. Under each option, we compute the amount in the bank at the beginning of each month.

For option 1, this is zero for every month because the payment of $1,500 is made immediately.

For option 2, the initial balance is $1,500 less the first payment of $503.50, or $996.50. This amount earns interest for the first month, and the account is credited with interest of 0.5% of $996.50, or $4.98, leaving a balance at the beginning of month 2 of $1,001.48. This now earns interest for month 2 (0.5% of $1,001.48 is $5.01), but then the second installment of $503.50 must be paid, leaving a balance at the start of month 3 of $502.99. Interest is earned in months 3 and 4 with the third installment due at the end of month 4. Finally, the remaining balance earns interest to the end of the year.

For option 3, the monthly payment is $1,500 divided by 12 plus 3%, or $128.75. The initial balance is $1,500 less two monthly payments (or $257.50). For the next 10 months, interest is earned on the balance, and a payment of $128.75 is made each month.

The formulas for a spreadsheet model are as follows:

	A	B	C	D
1	Month	Option 1	Option 2	Option 3
2				
3	1	0	=1,500-503.5	=1,500-2*128.75
4	2	0	=C3*1.005	=D3*1.005-128.75
5	3	0	=C4*1.005-503.5	=D4*1.005-128.75
6	4	0	=C5*1.005	=D5*1.005-128.75
7	5	0	=C6*1.005-503.5	=D6*1.005-128.75
8	6	0	=C7*1.005	=D7*1.005-128.75
9	7	0	=C8*1.005	=D8*1.005-128.75
10	8	0	=C9*1.005	=D9*1.005-128.75
11	9	0	=C10*1.005	=D10*1.005-128.75
12	10	0	=C11*1.005	=D11*1.005-128.75
13	11	0	=C12*1.005	=D12*1.005-128.75
14	12	0	=C13*1.005	=D13*1.005

which give the following values:

	A	B	C	D
1	Month	Option 1	Option 2	Option 3
2				
3	1	0	996.50	1,242.50
4	2	0	1,001.48	1,119.96
5	3	0	502.99	996.81
6	4	0	505.50	873.05
7	5	0	4.53	748.66
8	6	0	4.56	623.65
9	7	0	4.58	498.02
10	8	0	4.60	371.76
11	9	0	4.62	244.87
12	10	0	4.65	117.35
13	11	0	4.67	-10.82
14	12	0	4.69	-10.87

The lowest-cost option is the three-payment plan (option 2), which saves $4.69 over the one-payment plan. The monthly payment plan (option 3) costs $10.87 more than the one-payment plan and $15.56 more than the three-payment plan. Under option 2, the interest earned by delaying the second payment for 2 months and the third payment for 4 months more than covers the $3.50 service charge added to each payment.

The model constructed above is a type of **simulation** model because in the model, we simulated making payments under each of the payment options and then compared the results. In building this simulation model, we have made several assumptions. For example, we assumed that the interest rate on our savings account will not change during the year, that the interest rate on the negative balance in month 11 under option 3 is the same as that on the positive balance, and that there is no postage or other cost of making the payments. We also assumed that we receive interest for the full month for payments that are due at the insurance company by the first of the following month.

One of the great benefits of modeling decision problems such as this is the precision imposed by the modeling task. Construction of a model raises many issues that must be addressed and requires assumptions to be made and challenged. Construction of a useful model requires a precise and detailed understanding of the problem, which can rarely be achieved by any other means.

BUILDING USEFUL MODELS

The model constructed above provides an answer but is unsatisfactory in several respects. For example, suppose that we checked with the bank and found that the interest rate was 0.6% per month (approximately 7.2% annually) rather than the 0.5% per month that we assumed. To modify the model, we have to change the 1.005 (which appears in 22 different cells) to 1.006. This requires editing 22 formulas one at a time. To avoid this, it is useful to **parameterize the model**.

Parameterizing the model means that we take the parameters that appear in several places in the model and place them in labeled locations. When the parameters are needed in formulas, they are referred to by absolute address rather than by value. For example, to make the interest rate a parameter for the model, we set up a cell (C16) containing the interest rate parameter (1.006) and change the formulas replacing 1.005 with the absolute address of the interest rate parameter ($C$16). The model formulas now look as follows:

	A	B	C	D
1	Month	Option 1	Option 2	Option 3
2				
3	1	0	=1,500-503.5	=1,500-2*128.75
4	2	0	=C3*$C$16	=D3*$C$16-128.75
5	3	0	=C4*$C$16-503.5	=D4*$C$16-128.75
6	4	0	=C5*$C$16	=D5*$C$16-128.75
7	5	0	=C6*$C$16-503.5	=D6*$C$16-128.75
8	6	0	=C7*$C$16	=D7*$C$16-128.75
9	7	0	=C8*$C$16	=D8*$C$16-128.75
10	8	0	=C9*$C$16	=D9*$C$16-128.75
11	9	0	=C10*$C$16	=D10*$C$16-128.75
12	10	0	=C11*$C$16	=D11*$C$16-128.75
13	11	0	=C12*$C$16	=D12*$C$16-128.75
14	12	0	=C13*$C$16	=D13*$C$16
15				
16	Interest rate:		1.006	

We now can change the value of the interest rate by changing only one cell. One immediate benefit of this paramaterization is the ability to quickly and easily perform a **validation** check; if the monthly interest rate were zero, the only difference between the payment plans should be the service charges. If the logic of the model is correct, it should reflect this result.

Month	Option 1	Option 2	Option 3
1	0	996.50	1,242.50
2	0	996.50	1,113.75
3	0	493.00	985.00
4	0	493.00	856.25
5	0	-10.50	727.50
6	0	-10.50	598.75
7	0	-10.50	470.00
8	0	-10.50	341.25
9	0	-10.50	212.50
10	0	-10.50	83.75
11	0	-10.50	-45.00
12	0	-10.50	-45.00
Interest rate:		1	

By varying the interest rate in the modified model, we can begin to understand the **sensitivity** of the decision to the value of the interest rate. At low interest rates, option 1 is preferred because the interest earned does not cover the service charges. Through trial and error, we can quickly determine the interest rate at which we are indifferent between options 1 and 2. This rate is 0.003503 monthly, and we call this an **indifference point** because at this parameter value, we are indifferent between options 1 and 2 (they have the same cost).

Month	Option 1	Option 2	Option 3
1	0	996.50	1,242.50
2	0	999.99	1,118.10
3	0	499.99	993.27
4	0	501.75	868.00
5	0	0.00	742.29
6	0	0.00	616.14
7	0	0.00	489.55
8	0	0.00	362.51
9	0	0.00	235.03
10	0	0.00	107.11
11	0	0.00	-21.27
12	0	0.00	-21.34
Interest rate:		1.003503	

Box 2-1

NOTE ON TRIAL-AND-ERROR SEARCHING

When conducting a trial-and-error search on a single parameter, a simple systematic procedure will quickly converge to an indifference point. Choose a value for the parameter that leads to one decision; then, choose a second value (perhaps quite different from the first) that leads to the other decision. Now try a parameter value midway between the first two and determine which decision it indicates. From the three parameter values that have been tried, choose the pair that are closest but lead to different decisions; then, repeat the process. Because half the values of the parameter being searched are eliminated in each step, this process quickly leads to a narrow interval in which both decisions have essentially the same objective value. (Some care is necessary because there may be more than one indifference point: if this is the case, it may be necessary to search for several local "optima" and then select the overall "global" optimum from the set of local optima.)

For high interest rates, we might expect option 3 to be the best deal (under option 3, we postpone payment for the longest period of time). We can quickly determine whether this is the case by searching for the indifference point between options 2 and 3:

Month	Option 1	Option 2	Option 3
1	0	996.50	1,242.50
2	0	1,005.38	1,124.82
3	0	510.84	1,006.09
4	0	515.39	886.31
5	0	16.48	765.45
6	0	16.63	643.52
7	0	16.78	520.51
8	0	16.92	396.40
9	0	17.08	271.18
10	0	17.23	144.84
11	0	17.38	17.38
12	0	17.54	17.54
interest rate:		1.00891	

We can now "solve" our decision problem without knowing the exact interest rate:

Option 1 is preferred for monthly interest rates of less than 0.3503%.

Option 2 is preferred for monthly rates between 0.3503% and 0.891%.

Option 3 is preferred for monthly rates of more than 0.891%.

This is called a **contingency solution**: the decision has been stated as being **contingent** on the value of an important parameter. To determine our best decision, it may be sufficient to know a reasonable range for our interest rate rather than its exact value. Of course, if we think the interest rate is close to one of the indifference points, we may need to know its exact value to make the right decision. However, because the total cost is approximately the same at the indifference points, for interest rates close to the indifference points, the extra cost incurred as a result of making the wrong choice will be quite small. For example, if the interest rate is around 0.35% monthly, it does not really matter whether option 1 or option 2 is chosen; the total cost is about the same.

Generalizing the Model. The model developed so far specifically applies to an annual premium payment of $1,500. To make our model useful to more people, who presumably pay different annual premiums, it would be useful to parameterize the premium amount. Because the payments are related to the annual premium, these also can be located in separate cells, although they are computed from the premium amount. We now have a model in which we can easily vary the annual premium and the interest rate. The formulas are:

	A	B	C	D
1	Month	Option 1	Option 2	Option 3
2				
3	1	0	=$C$17-$C$18	=$C$17-2*$C$19
4	2	0	=C3*$C$16	=D3*$C$16-$C$19
5	3	0	=C4*$C$16-$C$18	=D4*$C$16-$C$19
6	4	0	=C5*$C$16	=D5*$C$16-$C$19
7	5	0	=C6*$C$16-$C$18	=D6*$C$16-$C$19
8	6	0	=C7*$C$16	=D7*$C$16-$C$19
9	7	0	=C8*$C$16	=D8*$C$16-$C$19
10	8	0	=C9*$C$16	=D9*$C$16-$C$19
11	9	0	=C10*$C$16	=D10*$C$16-$C$19
12	10	0	=C11*$C$16	=D11*$C$16-$C$19
13	11	0	=C12*$C$16	=D12*$C$16-$C$19
14	12	0	=C13*$C$16	=D13*$C$16
15				
16	Interest rate:		1.005	
17	Annual premium:		1500	
18	Payment option 2:		=C17/3+3.5	
19	Payment option 3:		=C17/12*1.03	

Using this model, we could conduct a **two-way sensitivity analysis**, varying both the interest rate and the annual premium together. Such an analysis can be complex, and considerable searching and plotting may be required to arrive at a good solution.

Considering the User. The model above is fine for us to use because we developed it and we understand the terminology (e.g., 1.005 is the interest rate). Some minor changes would make the model much more user friendly for a user who was familiar with the problem but not the details of the model. First, we "hide" all the details of the model by moving them to an area of the spreadsheet away from the home screen. Second, we add a title and some friendly labels, and we display the parameter values and the results (both linked to the model through the cell formulas) in the terms that the user understands:

```
          A         B         C         D         E         F         G
 1
 2
 3                       Automobile Insurance Decision Model
 4
 5
 6
 7             Annual premium ($)    2,000
 8             Interest rate:          0.5% monthly
 9
10
11
12
13             Cost of option 1 (annual payment):               2,000.00
14             Cost of option 2 (3 payments):                   1,990.08
15             Cost of option 3 (monthly payment plan):         2,014.49
16
17
18
19
21
```

We now have a screen display that clearly presents the annual premium and the interest rate (**inputs** to the model) in a way that the decision maker understands. It also provides for easy changes to these inputs and presents the cost of the various options (**outputs** from the model) in terms familiar to the user. Nontechnical users could work with this screen to explore their personal decision situations and make informed decisions.

A second approach for communicating the results of the modeling effort is to develop some form of **decision aid**. A decision aid is a device that presents a summary of the dependence between the decision criteria and the decision variable or variables in a user-friendly form. Decision aids come in many forms, including formal reports (which may include recommendations from the modeler to the decision maker) and various kinds of charts and graphs.

For the automobile insurance example, the modeling results can be summarized in a series of graphs. For each premium amount, we can vary the interest rate per month over a reasonable range (from 0% to 2% per month) and plot the cost of the three payment options. (This is a bit tedious to do by hand, but the spreadsheet includes a macro command language that can be used to do this simply and quickly.) This graph is a very useful decision aid for this problem; for any interest rate, the lowest-cost payment plan can be quickly determined (Figure 2-2).

Figure 2-2 | COST OF AUTOMOBILE INSURANCE

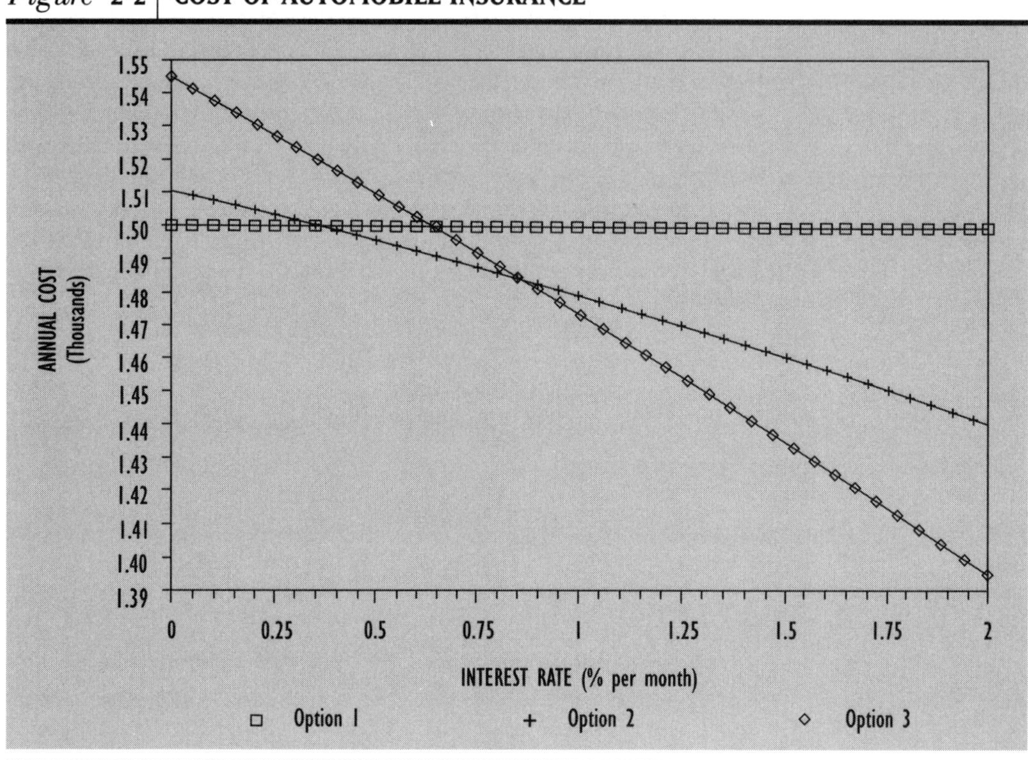

SUMMARY

In this chapter, the concept of the management model and some of the issues surrounding the development and use of models in management decision making were introduced. In the following chapters, several different types of management models will be examined in more detail, as will examples of organizations that have used these models to their competitive advantage.

MANAGEMENT SCIENCE MODEL BUILDERS AT WORK

Models for Project Management

Models have proved to be very useful over the years in assisting with the management of projects.

A **project** is an activity that has a beginning and an end. Building a building, executing an advertising campaign, and reengineering a production process are three examples of projects. A project can be considered to be made up of many related **tasks**. For example, building a building requires that many tasks be done, including architectural design, development of engineering plans, pouring concrete floors, building walls, putting on the roof, and finishing the interior.

Tasks generally have a **precedence structure**; that is, some tasks must be done before others. When building a building, for example, the roof supports must be in place before the roof is added.

Project management can be a complex activity that includes planning the project, arranging the hiring of workers and the acquisition of any necessary equipment at the appropriate times, setting due dates and performance requirements for contracts, and monitoring the project to ensure work is completed on time and unnecessary expenses are not incurred. People or equipment may also need to be moved among tasks in response to changing conditions, such as the weather. Project management models have been developed to help managers responsible for decisions such as these.

Two modeling approaches that have been widely used are the Project Evaluation and Review Technique (known as PERT) and the Critical Path Method (CPM). These approaches usually are implemented today through the use of project management software. A review in 1986 (R.D. Filley, *Industrial Engineering*, January) that listed 68 available project management software packages attests to the early market interest in implementation of these methods. Today, there are hundreds of packages available covering all price ranges. The market leaders implement hybrid PERT/CPM modeling approaches that pick up the most popular features from PERT and CPM and make extensive use of graphics to communicate with the model user.

An Example of Project Management. As an example of a project, we will consider a highly simplified version of an advertising campaign by an advertising agency. Execution of this particular campaign involves only seven tasks. First, the campaign team must be assembled from the people available at the agency or by using freelancers; second, a media plan must be developed that allocates the available media budget among the various different media (e.g., television, radio, newspapers, and billboards). Once the media plan is determined, the creative work can be done, and the required advertisements can be designed. Once designed, the advertisements can be produced. While the creative design work is being done and the advertisements produced, media purchasing can be undertaken; once the media purchases are completed, media contracts can be signed and exchanged. When all these tasks are completed, the entire program must be presented to the client for final approval.

Once we understand what is involved in the project, we can identify the individual tasks and their precedence and estimate the time each task will take. Table 2–1 presents a summary of this information.

There are several ways of depicting a planned schedule for this project graphically. First, we can use a "planning board" representation in which each row of the table represents a particular task, with the shading indicating when the task is scheduled to be done (Figure 2-3).

The planning board shows that task A is scheduled for week 1, but task B cannot start until week 2 because task A must be completed before task B can begin. Similarly, tasks C and E cannot be scheduled until week 6 because both require that task B be completed. Task D is scheduled to follow task C, and task F to follow task E. Finally, task G can be scheduled to begin only when tasks D and F (and all other tasks) are finished.

Table 2-1 | **TASK SUMMARY FOR EXAMPLE PROJECTS**

Task I.D.	Task	Time Estimate (weeks)	Required Preceding Tasks
A	Assemble campaign team	1	None
B	Develop media plan	4	A
C	Design advertisements	3	B
D	Produce advertisements	6	C
E	Buy media	4	B
F	Exchange media contracts	2	E
G	Final client approval	2	D and F

Figure **2-3** | **PLANNING BOARD REPRESENTATION OF PROJECT SCHEDULE**

Task																
A	■															
B		■	■	■	■											
C						■	■	■								
D									■	■	■	■	■	■		
E						■	■	■	■							
F										■	■					
G															■	■
Week	1	2	3	4	5	6	7	8	9	10	11	12	13	14	15	16

A common variant of this graphic format is a PERT chart, which can take several different forms. Figure 2-4 is a version for our example:

In the PERT chart display, the horizontal axis represent the flow of work, with tasks linked according to precedence. Horizontal dashed lines are used to illustrate required precedence in situations in which there are no tasks to perform. The PERT chart illustrates two key properties of the project: **slack time** associated with tasks and the key idea of a **critical path**.

Slack time is depicted on the chart as a horizontal dashed line. In the example, 3 weeks of slack time is associated with the subpath that includes tasks E and F. The managerial implication of this is that tasks E and F can be scheduled within this 3-week time window without otherwise affecting the project. For example, task E could be delayed from starting in week 5 to starting in week 8 without delaying completion of the project.

A **critical path** is a set of tasks that span the project from start to finish and contain no slack time; in the example, path A/B/C/D/G is a critical path. The managerial implications of scheduling a project that contains a critical path are that the project is scheduled for completion in minimum elapsed time and that any delays to tasks that form part of the critical path will delay completion of the project. A conservative approach to scheduling the project would leave some slack time in all paths.

Sometimes, after a preliminary scheduled is derived, the scheduled completion time for the project is found to be too long. To reduce the completion time, slack time must be eliminated until one, or more, critical paths emerge. At this point, the only mechanisms to bring

Figure **2-4** | **PERT CHART VISUALIZATION OF PROJECT**

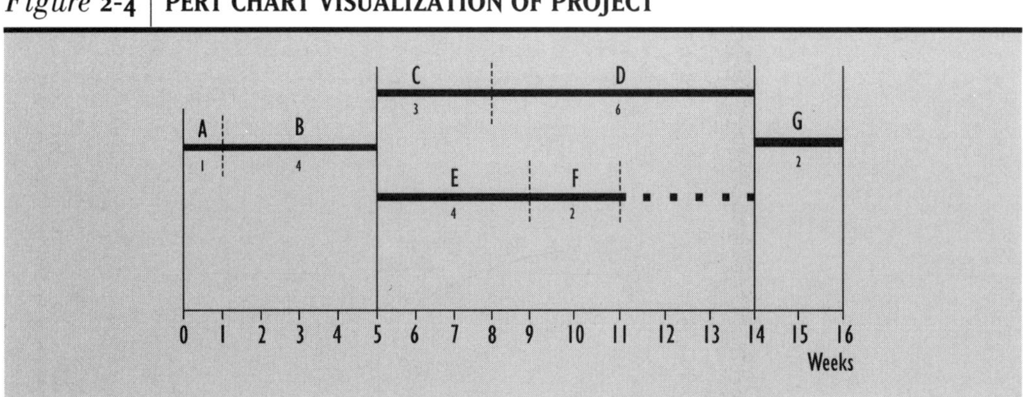

Table 2-2 **TASK SUMMARY FOR THREE-PERSON CAMPAIGN**

Task I.D.	Task	Time Estimate (weeks)	Required Preceding Tasks	Person
A	Assemble campaign team	1	None	Jane
B	Develop media plan	4	A	Jane
C	Design advertisements	3	B	Steve
D	Produce advertisements	6	C	Fred
E	Buy media	4	B	Steve
F	Exchange media contracts	2	E	Fred
G	Final client approval	2	D and F	Jane

the completion date forward are to start the project earlier or to shorten one or more tasks that make up the critical path.

An important extension of PERT/CPM involves scheduling tasks when these tasks require shared resources. As an example, suppose our advertising agency is quite small, and only three employees, Jane, Fred, and Steve, are assigned to work on the campaign. The task assignments are shown in Table 2-2.

We assume that all tasks require full-time attention from the designated employee for the duration of the task (in reality, resource assignments would be much more complex than this). A useful model for scheduling this resource-constrained problem is a planning board visual display (which may be some type of actual physical board) in which the horizontal lines represent the resources. Tasks are assigned to the resources according to capacity. In our example, this means that only one task can be assigned to each employee in each week. The completed board is shown in Figure 2-5.

Note that the resource constraints have lengthened the completion time of the project by 2 weeks and that the critical path is now longer; the only task for which there is slack time now is task E (which can be completed any time between weeks 9 and 16). If we wish to reduce the project completion time, we can shorten tasks on the critical path or consider the resource allocations. If we reassign task D to Jane or task F to Jane or Steve, we can reduce the completion time by 2 weeks. Another option is to add more resources; if we can hire a freelancer to do task F, then we can bring the completion time 2 weeks forward. Whether adding this extra resource is a good decision will depend on economic factors: the cost of the additional resource and the economic benefit of completing the project 2 weeks earlier.

Project scheduling with resource constraints therefore becomes a resource allocation problem in which tasks must be allocated among competing resources to produce the most

Figure 2-5 **PLANNING BOARD: EMPLOYEE UTILIZATION VIEW**

Resource																		
Jane	A	B	B	B	B												G	G
Steve						C	C	C	E	E	E	E						
Fred									D	D	D	D	D	D	F	F		
Week	1	2	3	4	5	6	7	8	9	10	11	12	13	14	15	16	17	18

beneficial balance between the cost of the resources and the time taken to complete the project. In many projects, such as construction, in which resources are purchased on a temporary basis, project management models have enabled managers to address the problem of integrating resource requirements with considerations of completion dates (and possible due date penalties) to arrive at a feasible, cost-effective work schedule. A second important benefit is the ability to monitor work on the project against the planned schedule. If a critical task is delayed, the models provide managers with the ability to reallocate resources and reschedule the project to minimize the impact of the delay on the completion date.

An Issue: Uncertain Task Times. The PERT/CPM model assumes that the times specified for the tasks are known. How must the model be modified if task times are uncertain? What happens to the important concept of the "critical path?"

Modeling Inventory Decision Making

A firm will hold an inventory (or stock) of parts or product for a number of reasons. One reason is purely economic: processing an order to acquire additional stock may impose additional cost on the firm. This "ordering" cost may include the cost of preparing the order, transmitting the order to the vendor, paying for the order, and shipping the order. When this is the case, we can use a simple model to determine *when* to order and *what quantity* to order.

Suppose that the sum of all the costs associated with placing an order is \$K, which does not depend on the quantity ordered.

Carrying a unit of a product in inventory incurs costs. The unit must be purchased and paid for, so there is capital tied up in the inventory that must be borrowed from the capital markets; even if we do not have to arrange a loan to finance the inventory explicitly, there is an "opportunity cost" of not having the funds invested in inventory available for other purposes. There also may be storage costs, such as rent for the space occupied by the inventory, the cost of heating or cooling this space, insurance, and the cost of theft (or "shrinkage"), spoilage, and so on. Assume that the total of all these costs is \$h per year for each unit in storage.

A common model to determine how many units to order and when to place each order is as follows:

> If demand for the product is D units/year and we order Q units at a time, then we make D/Q orders/year at a cost \$KD/Q.
>
> If we order Q units at a time and we assume that demand is constant over time so we can plan our orders such that the new order arrives when our inventory reaches exactly zero, then our average on-hand inventory is Q/2 units and the holding cost is \$hQ/2 per year.
>
> Now, the annual order cost (\$KD/Q) is a *decreasing* function of Q, and the annual holding cost (\$hQ/2) is an *increasing* function of Q, so we can find the value for Q at which these two costs are "balanced" (call this value Q^*).
>
> $$KD/Q^* = hQ^*/2$$
>
> implies
>
> $$Q^{*2} = 2KD/h \quad \text{or} \quad Q^* = \sqrt{(2KD/h)}$$

This well-known result is called the **economic lot size formula** and lies at the heart of many inventory control systems (although usually in a modified form). Many firms use a formula similar to this as a basis for decision making about the size of their orders (Q^*) and how often to place an order (every Q^*/D years).

In deriving this formula, many assumptions were made. Some were made explicitly (the order cost is a fixed cost $K, and the holding cost is a variable cost $h), but many other assumptions were made implicitly. To illustrate some of these assumptions, consider the following cases (all were taken from real companies).

Case A. For this company, demand is fairly predictable but not absolutely so; demand varies from day to day, and efforts to forecast these fluctuations have failed. How could the model be sensibly adapted for this situation?

Case B. A hospital pharmacy was using this formula as the basis for its ordering. A flyer arrived in the mail announcing that the price of albuterol, a drug dispersed by inhaler, was being increased from $1.52 to $15.00. The pharmacy was offered a one-time chance to order at the old price. Does the model help to determine the quantity to be ordered?

Case C. The same pharmacist received two flyers on the same day. One of the manufacturers of a well-known drug announced 10% "free goods" on orders received in the next month. The second flyer, from the manufacturer of several "generic" (i.e., non-brand name) drugs, announced that a generic form of this same drug would be available in 3 months (when the original manufacturer's patent expired) at 30% below the current prices for the brand-name product. Does the model help the pharmacist decide what to order?

Case D. We live in a world of inflation in which product prices increase by 5% to 10% annually, usually in one or two increments. Does this fact affect the usefulness of the economic lot size formula?

Bombardier versus Transmanche Link

Bombardier, Inc. was a Canadian-owned company that specialized in manufacturing railroad rolling stock, airplanes, and snowmobiles. Transmanche Link (TML) was the consortium that was behind construction of the Channel Tunnel linking England and France.

TML contracted with Bombardier's Euro Shuttle Consortium Wagon division (ESCW) to supply 254 double- and single-deck wagons for *Le Shuttle*, the railway system that was to carry automobiles, buses, and heavy goods vehicles through the Channel Tunnel. The single-deck wagons were built at BN in Bruges, Belgium, and the double-deck wagons were built at ANF-Industrie at Valanciennes, France. ESCW subcontracted the manufacture of 19 single-deck loader wagons to Fiat Ferroviaria in Turin, Italy.

The contract between Bombardier and TML was signed in 1989 for C$820 million. Unfortunately, after the contract had been signed and manufacturing had begun, a large number of changes, some major and some minor, were made to the design of the wagons by British and French government safety inspectors. As a result of these changes, Bombardier's projected final cost of completing the wagons was about double the original contracted price. Bombardier wanted reimbursement for the cost overrun, but TML balked at the amount requested. Bombardier held up delivery of the wagons, leading to the prospect of a delay in the opening of *Le Shuttle* service through the tunnel. Both parties were anxious to settle, but how could an agreement on the amount be reached?

Enter the international commercial lawyers who began to document a large detailed claim based on ESCW's cost of responding to TML's requests for design changes. A team of Dutch engineers went through every document that had passed between the parties and obtained evidence that TML had been slow to respond to design documentation and that this had imposed delay and disruption on ESCW. The problem remained of how to quantify the effect of design-documentation delays and the other elements of the claim.

ESCW called in Colin Eden, professor and head of the Management Science Department at the University of Strathclyde, Glasgow, Scotland, and three of his management science colleagues. The team began by interviewing a large number of senior members of ESCW's project team to determine what management perceived the problems to have been. From these interviews, the management scientists began to build a model of the project. This model was validated with the input of groups of senior managers and lawyers.

As work progressed, the model was refined and expanded and became the repository of all knowledge about the project. The final, very large model used the Bombardier/TML interactions as exogenous variables; when these were switched off (corresponding to completion of the contract as originally specified), the model provided a cost of completion of the contract without disruption, but when switched on, the model provided an estimate of Bombardier's actual completion cost. The model was designed to be used within a court situation; if the judge upheld some parts of the claim and not others, the model could be rerun to provide new cost estimates.

The completed model acted as a structure for discussions, became the communications mechanism by which the management scientists and ESCW exchanged ideas, and provided a rich history of the progress of the project. The management scientists became convinced of the validity of the cost estimates produced by the model and believe ESCW management was also convinced. The model and results of the modeling were shown to TML managers.

The claim was settled out of court at a value that (presumably) was satisfactory to both parties. ESCW received FFr700 million in phased payments, and Bombardier received up to 25 million Eurotunnel shares.

From Scuttler's COPE with delay and disruption, T. Williams, *OR Newsletter*, May 1994, and The Channel Tunnel, *Financial Times Survey*, May 6, 1994.

Information Systems Strategy Development at Sainsbury's

Sainsbury's was a leading supermarket chain in the United Kingdom with a turnover of approximately $10 billion in 1989. Sainsbury's operated approximately 300 supermarkets and in 1989 was expanding at a rate of about 30 new markets each year. Innovation was seen as a key component of Sainsbury's pursuit of its objectives of offering customers quality products, value for money, and service, to high trading and hygiene standards.

There was widespread recognition that information technology had contributed significantly to Sainsbury's record of profitable growth. Reduced warehouse stocks, enhanced service, and the ability to reliably handle large volumes of a wide variety of products in a dynamic market environment underpinned Sainsbury's growth, and management readily acknowledged that this growth would not have been possible without information technology.

The foundations for Sainsbury's information technology systems had been developed in an information technology strategy formulated in the late 1970s. Early in 1988, the company concluded that the implementation of this strategy, which they believed had provided them with a competitive advantage in the marketplace, was now largely complete and that there was an opportunity to develop a new information technology strategy that would sustain this competitive advantage. The Corporate Systems Strategy Project (CSSP) was initiated to develop a new information technology strategy for the company.

CSSP began in February 1989 with the objective of "involving a new generation of managers, fostering creativity and mind broadening, [and] producing an information technology strategy." The project involved four phases: in phase 1, the business and its environment were examined; in phase 2, candidate systems for investment were identified; in phase 3, the candidate systems were compared from the perspective of costs and benefits, and each system was given a priority score; and in phase 4, the prioritized portfolio of candidate systems was used to produce a strategy that took into account the current systems development program and the operational constraints of the business. By the end of 1989, after 9 months of investigation, a $73 million investment strategy had been developed.

This strategy involved pursuing six initiatives designed to electronically support all operations of the supply chain. The six initiatives chosen were:

CARES: A customer complaints analysis and response system

EPICS: A system to integrate existing employee-related systems, such as payroll, time and attendance, and staff scheduling, with additional new systems (absenteeism and training); the scope and complexity of personnel management in this large retail chain made development of this system a major challenge

SABRE: A sales-based reordering system designed to establish branch stock levels from scanner data and use these as a basis for the automatic generation of orders

MARC: A market analysis and range control system designed to use analysis of market research data and scanner data to tailor the range of products carried by each local store

SCION: A supply chain ordering network that would allow more frequent and efficient ordering from suppliers, leading to just-in-time deliveries

EMIS: An executive management information system designed to provide information and modeling systems to enhance decision making and control

By March 1995, five of these six initiatives had been implemented, and it was possible to evaluate the results (summarized in Table 2-3).

Although a number of assumptions were necessary to make the comparison between the planned systems and those implemented, because the scope of several of the systems changed, it seems clear that development costs were higher than planned ($90 million compared with $73 million) but the benefits realized were correspondingly greater.

Management science models were used throughout this successful strategy development process, both as aids to development of the strategy and to involve all levels of Sainsbury's management in the strategy development process.

From Putting soft OR methods to work: Information systems strategy development at Sainsbury's, R. Ormerod, *Journal of the Operational Research Society*, March 1995, and Information Systems Strategy Development at Sainsbury's Supermarkets, R. Ormerod, *Interfaces*, 26: January-February, 1996.

Table 2-3 **RESULTS OF SIX INITIATIVES BY SAINSBURY'S**

	1989 (estimated)		March 1995			
System	Cost ($ million)	5-Year Benefits ($ million)	Delivered (%)	Development Cost so far ($ million)	Total Projected Cost ($ million)	Benefits Projected ($ million)
CARES	4	17	100	1	1	22
EPICS	21	99–115	85	25	30	68
SABRE	23	114	88	32	38	135
MARC	11	37–72	100	4	4	24
SCION	9	20	75	9	12	108
EMIS	5	7	60	3	5	33
Total	**73**	**294–345**		**74**	**90**	**390**

EXERCISES

1. We acquired new furniture for the office. The invoice for $6,000 offers two ways to pay: We can pay the entire amount by September 1, or we can pay $3,060 by September 1 and $3,000 by January 1. How does our decision depend on the interest rate at which we can invest our funds?
2. An underground depository for the disposal of medium level nuclear waste can be built in 1994 for a cost of £2500 million, but construction of the facility can be deferred for 50 years, when the construction cost will be £5000 million. Additional interim "storage" costing £135 million per year will be required if construction is deferred (all costs in 1994 £). Assume a 6% real interest rate. Which option is preferred? Does your answer change if a 2% real interest rate is assumed?

   (This is a simplified version of the Nirex Ltd. decision discussed in Review of Radioactive Waste Management Policy Preliminary Conclusions: A Consultative Document, Department of the Environment, August 1994, as presented by Chapman and Howden, July 1995.)
3. Your corporate office is in New York. You must visit the distribution centers in Boston, Chicago, Cleveland, Detroit, and Toronto. The available airfares between these cities are given in Table 2-4.

   Use a spreadsheet to determine the minimum cost "tour" that begins and ends in New York and includes one visit to each city.

Table 2-4 | **AIRFARES BETWEEN DISTRIBUTION CENTERS**

From:	To: New York	Boston	Chicago	Cleveland	Detroit	Toronto
New York	—	$79	$179	$115	$165	$195
Boston	$99	—	199	129	105	199
Chicago	195	155	—	55	59	175
Cleveland	137	149	79	—	45	65
Detroit	165	135	55	55	—	65
Toronto	285	255	295	79	125	—

VIDEO MART OUTLET, INC

THIS CASE IS MODIFIED FROM AN EXAMPLE DEVELOPED BY MARY JACKSON.

"Work for Yourself and Earn $100,000 a Year!"

The advertisement was appealing. Joe was interested; this might be what he had always wanted, so he wrote to the company, Video Mart, Inc., for more details.

The literature that arrived described a videotape rental store service arrangement. For a one-time fee of $4,000, Video Mart would provide details on how to set up an outlet store for Video Mart's retail video rental business, including the type and relative number of videos to stock, where to obtain them, and how often to replace them. Video Mart would provide advice on the store design, location, and layout, and the literature suggested that you could expect to make $100,000 in the first year.

The facts were quite simple. To set up a video rental business, Joe had to buy an initial stock of 1,000 videos from Video Mart plus an additional 50 tapes a month to keep up with new releases. Video Mart advertised the lowest tape prices ("wholesale") but stressed that its particular skill was in selecting the most profitable titles: Video Mart's data base of tape rentals from its several stores enabled them to identify the fastest moving titles. Each video tape would cost Joe $60, and the tapes were guaranteed to be both "legal" and of the best quality. Video Mart, however, pointed out that customers are notoriously rough on tapes and that the industry average was about 30 rentals before the tape had to be replaced.

Video Mart left the price at which tapes are rented out up to the individual operator but suggested charging $3.99 per day. At that price, they expected the stock, on average, to be rented out once a week. However, Video Mart suggested that a lower price coupled with a faster turnover made sense in some situations but would be unlikely to have much impact on the total rental revenues received.

Joe was impressed by the literature and did some legwork. He found what he thought was a promising site that rented for $1,000 per month. He checked with his bank loan officer and found that with $10,000 of his own money invested in the business, he could borrow the balance at 12% per annum.

Joe knew that there was more work to be done; he still had not looked into insurance, marketing, and advertising, hiring store personnel, and so on. Joe thought, however, that he should now have enough data to be able to push some numbers around. Was $100,000 per year possible, or was he just another dreamer in the movies?

HINTS ON BUILDING A CASH-FLOW MODEL FOR JOE

A number of assumptions must be made to complete the model. Start with simple modeling assumptions that later can be made more realistic (and hence more elaborate). Of course, any analysis based on the model should include an investigation of the sensitivity of the results to the key assumptions.

Time period for analysis. Because many figures are given per month, a monthly cash-flow model seems appropriate.

Plays per month. A rental of once per week is equal to 4.33 (52 divided by 12) plays per month. An assumption of steady use for each tape at a rate of 4.33 plays per month from startup considerably simplifies the analysis.

Replacements. A tape lasts an average of about 7 months (30 divided by 4.33). Assuming a mixed stock of tapes (some used, some semiused, and some new), approximately one seventh of the existing stock of tapes would need to be replaced every month.

Purchases. In addition to replacing worn-out tapes, 50 new tapes are to be purchased each month.

Interest. A convenient assumption is that both the loan from the banks and deposits at the bank are at the same interest rate.

Shop Rental. The shop rental will be paid over time; assume that it is paid quarterly in January, April, July, and October.

Opening Cash Balance. Assume this is $6,000 (Joe's original $10,000 less the $4,000 paid to Video Mart).

Assignment

1. Build a spreadsheet model to assess the feasibility of the Video Mart.
2. What assumptions have you incorporated into your model?
3. What are the decision variables and decision criteria?
4. Would you go ahead with a Video Mart store?

PROFESSIONAL MEDIA, INC.

Professional Media, Inc. was an organization that specialized in providing media-planning and media-buying services for firms and advertising agencies.

In the 1970s, it was typical for a firm to hire a "full-service" advertising agency to handle its advertising. These firms had creative departments, planning departments, and media buyers, so they could design and develop the promotional materials, plan their placement in the various forms of media (television, radio, print media [magazines and newspapers], and outdoor signs and billboards), and purchase the required media positions to execute the media plan.

During the 1980s and into the 1990s, the benefits of scale became important in media buying; one very large buyer could negotiate more effectively with the various media sellers and could capture better rates for television and radio time and print and outdoor space. As a result, large specialized media-buying firms emerged; firms wanting to run an advertising campaign could now independently hire creative talent and media-planning and media-buying services. By 1995, almost half the media time and space purchased were bought through specialized media-buying firms.

Professional Media, Inc. was one of the largest of the media-planning and -buying specialists. Professional Media worked with the advertiser to lay out a direction for an upcoming campaign, then planned the media purchases, contacted the media outlets, and arranged purchase of the space.

Exhibit 2 | **VALUES OF SALES FROM 1% PRODUCT AWARENESS**

Week	Sales from 1% Product Awareness
1	$8,000
2	7,500
3	8,000
4	8,200
5	8,500
6	8,000
7	8,800
8	12,500
9	17,500
10	20,200
11	20,000
12	19,800
13	18,000
14	14,000
15	12,000
16	16,000
17	16,000
18	11,000
19	8,000
20	22,000*

* The sales value for week 20 reflects the fact that there is a residual value to the campaign after the advertising has ceased.

THE FABLITE CAMPAIGN

Julie Cronshaw of Professional Media, Inc. was in the process of planning the Spring 1996 television campaign for FabLite. The campaign budget was $7 million, which was to be spent on 7 weeks of advertising during the first 20 weeks of the year. Each week of advertising involved a carefully selected series of advertisements on network and local television, and each week of advertising cost $1 million.

Exhibit 1 | **EFFECT OF ADVERTISING ON PRODUCT AWARENESS**

Week	Beginning Awareness	Media Spend	Ending Awareness
1	20%	$1 million	28%
2	28%	$1 million	35%
3	35%	$1 million	40.25%
4	40.25%	$1 million	44.275%
5	44.275%	$1 million	48.7025%
6	48.7025%	$1 million	53.57275%
7	53.57275%	$1 million	58.930025%

The objective of the campaign was to build awareness of the FabLite product and to convert this awareness into product sales. In a recent survey conducted during December 1995, 20% of potential customers surveyed had recalled the FabLite brand name.

The effect of advertising on product awareness was quite dramatic. The first week of advertising had been shown to increase awareness by 40%, the second consecutive week by 25%, the third consecutive week by 15%, and each consecutive week from then on by 10%. Consequently, if Julie scheduled all 7 weeks of advertising at the start of the year, awareness would build as shown in Exhibit 1.

Julie knew that this level of awareness was quite transient and would fall rapidly if advertising was discontinued. Recent data from carefully controlled experiments suggested that awareness would fall by 20% after just 1 week without advertising, by an additional 10% after a second week without advertising, and at a rate of 5% per week after that, for as long as the advertising was off the air.

Julie's objective was, therefore, to schedule the 7 weeks of advertising to build awareness and to try to maintain awareness at a high level during the 20 weeks of the campaign. However, awareness was only part of the problem; the major objective was to capture sales.

AWARENESS AND SALES

The demand for FabLite was quite seasonal; in particular, there was a considerable peak in demand in early spring. The size of the market was expressed in dollars per awareness point; that is, a 1% increase in awareness translated into a higher volume of sales when demand was greater. The values of sales for each 1% of product awareness for the 20 weeks of the campaign were as shown in Exhibit 2.

The problem facing Julie is clear; she must schedule the 7 weeks of advertising during the 20-week period in a way that will maximize sales.

Assignment

1. Use the worksheet in Exhibit 3 to "simulate" 20 weeks of advertising by hand and to compute the value of sales generated during the period.
2. Build a spreadsheet simulation model that computes the sales associated with any feasible advertising schedule.
3. Use your model to search for the advertising schedule that leads to the maximum value for sales over the 20-week period.

Exhibit 3 | WORKSHEET FOR PROFESSIONAL MEDIA PROBLEM

Week	Beginning Awareness	Advertising Spent	Ending Awareness	Sales from 1% Product Awareness ($)	Total Sales ($100,000)
1	20%			8,000	
2				7,500	
3				8,000	
4				8,200	
5				8,500	
6				8,000	
7				8,800	
8				12,500	
9				17,500	
10				20,200	
11				20,000	
12				19,800	
13				18,000	
14				14,000	
15				12,000	
16				16,000	
17				16,000	
18				11,000	
19				8,000	
20				22,000	
Total		**$7 million**			

3

ANALYZING SEQUENTIAL DECISIONS

How many units should be produced? What price should be charged? How many workers should be hired? Should the offer be accepted? Which advertisement should be run? Managers make a host of decisions like these every day of their working lives.

Management is about making decisions. To be an effective manager, you must be able to make **good** decisions. You also must be able to explain to others why your recommendations constitute good decisions.

From the perspective of the organization, it is essential that decision making be handled throughout all levels of management in a way that encourages good decisions. In extreme cases, just one bad decision can put a firm out of business. The successful organization has good control of its decision making and has processes in place to ensure that important decisions are made in a timely way after appropriate analysis and discussion.

BASIC ELEMENTS OF A DECISION

Every decision involves a choice among a number of **alternatives** or **options**. There may be hundreds of alternatives (What list price do we set for our new product?) or just two (Should we accept their offer, or not?).

To make an intelligent choice, there must be some **criterion** (or several **criteria**) associated with each alternative that provides a basis for making a choice. In the world of business, the decision criterion often is money (e.g., the government usually awards contracts to the lowest bidder, the one that will fulfill the contract for the least money), but multiple criteria also are common (Should we hire contractor A, who is cheaper than contractor B but will take longer to complete the job?).

Most often, decision situations involve **uncertainty**. The future, after we have chosen a particular alternative, may not be entirely known (If we set our product price at $6.95, how many will we sell?). The elimination of uncertainty is rarely possible, although effective **forecasting** can reduce or control uncertainty.

Finally, there is an important **timeliness to decision making**. If a decision is made too late, the chosen option may no longer be available, whereas a decision made too early may result in vital, but late-arriving, information being missed.

A USEFUL MODEL FOR HELPING TO UNDERSTAND DECISION SITUATIONS

Important decision situations are rarely simple: the first step in intelligent decision making is to attempt to understand the decision situation. A useful vehicle to assist in grappling with the complexities of a decision is the **decision tree**. A decision tree presents a **model**

Figure 3-1 | THIS DECISION TREE INDICATES THAT A CHOICE MUST BE MADE BETWEEN ALTERNATIVE A AND ALTERNATIVE B

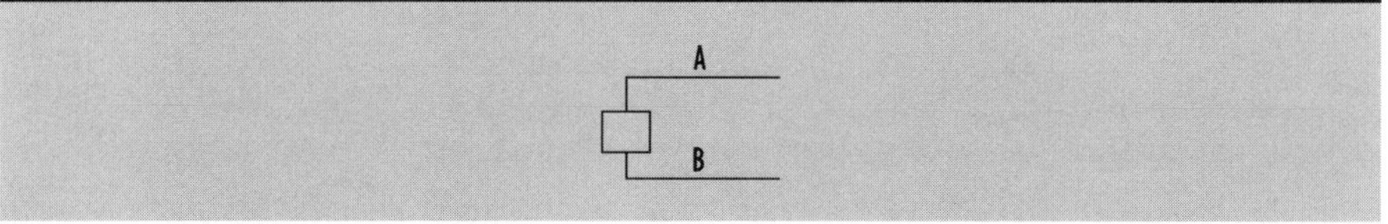

Figure 3-2 | A DECISION TREE INDICATING A CHOICE MUST BE MADE AMONG FIVE ALTERNATIVES (A–E)

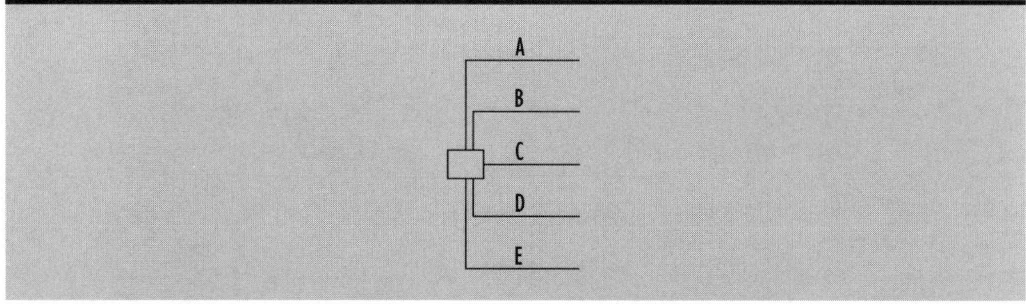

Figure 3-3 **A DECISION TREE REPRESENTATION OF THE OUTCOME OF A COIN FLIP**

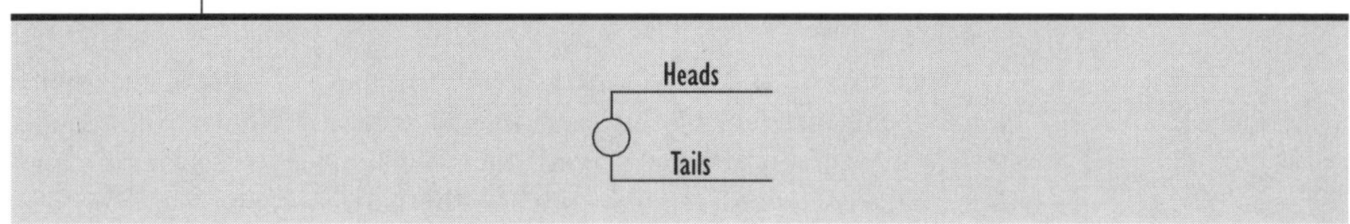

(or abstraction) of a decision situation. The tree does not "make" the decision or "solve" the problem but rather lays out the situation in a way that makes the choices and their ramifications more easily understood. Decision trees have also proved to be useful time and time again in providing a basis for a group of managers to talk about a decision (leading to a more effective group choice).

A decision tree is constructed from a few simple icons. A square is used to denote a decision point (Figure 3-1).

A decision to be made from five alternatives (A, B, C, D, and E) would be as shown in Figure 3-2.

A circle is used to denote a point of uncertainty, or **event**. At these points, there is no choice to be made; rather, one of a number of **outcomes**, over which we have no control, occurs. For example, a flip of a coin is an event with the outcomes "heads" and "tails"; this is indicated on a decision tree as shown in Figure 3-3.

In assembling a decision tree, the horizontal axis represents time; e.g.: Figure 3-4 denotes that decision B is made **after** decision A.

The sequence in Figure 3-5 indicates that if we choose the decision "market" and if the outcome of the next event turns out to be "low sales," then we are faced with decision B, between "price cut" or "no price cut."

The basic building blocks of the decision tree allow very complex decision situations to be laid out on paper. The process of doing this significantly improves understanding of the decision and often is a useful and worthwhile way to improve managerial decision making.

The exercise of constructing the tree raises questions and issues that would not emerge in a less rigorous analysis.

Figure 3-4 **A DECISION TREE INDICATING TIME SEQUENCE OF TWO CHOICES**

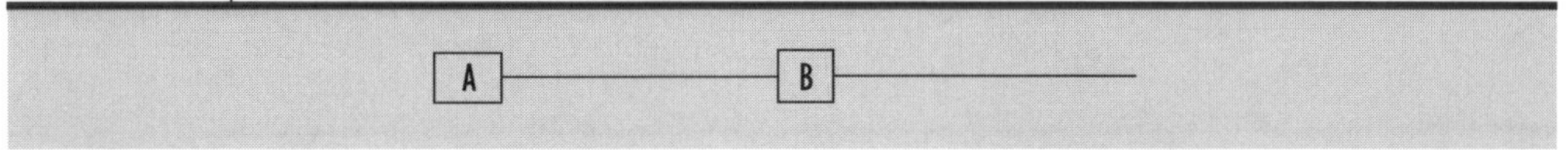

Figure 3-5 **A DECISION TREE FOR A SEQUENCE OF EVENTS AND DECISIONS**

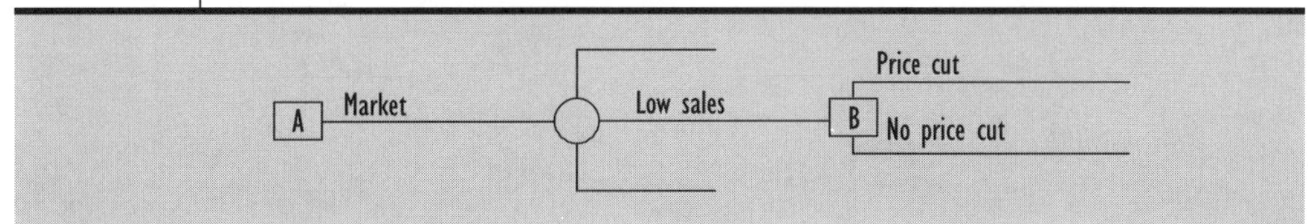

AN EXAMPLE: TESTING AN ATHLETE FOR DRUG USE

Whether athletes should be tested for the illegal use of performance-enhancing drugs is an issue of concern to many involved in athletics and sports. Why are the issues surrounding testing so complex? Perhaps laying out a decision tree will provide some insight.

The first decision is straightforward: should we test an athlete for illegal drug use? The decision tree, therefore, begins as shown in Figure 3-6.

Next, consider what happens if we decide to test the athlete. The **event** of conducting the test produces two possible **outcomes** (we cannot control which occurs): a "positive" test result or a "negative" test result. This event is added to the tree (Figure 3-7).

After we find out the result of the test, we must decide what to do with the athlete. If the test result is "negative," this decision presumably is straightforward: the athlete is pronounced to be "clean" and is allowed to compete. If the test is "positive," the decision is more difficult: what are the **alternatives**? To keep the tree manageable, only two of the sanctions often mentioned will be examined: a 2-year suspension or a lifetime suspension for the offender. The type of sanction to be imposed is a decision that must be made. The addition of this decision to the tree leads to Figure 3-8.

We next consider the "do not test" option. If we decide not to test, what happens? We have athletes competing who are drug users and others who are not (if no athletes used illegal drugs, there would be no reason to test). We therefore add this **event** to the tree (Figure 3-9).

We now raise a critical issue: How good is the test? Most medical tests are not perfect; sometimes the test indicates a condition that is not present (a **false-positive**), and at other times, the test fails to identify a condition that is present (a **false-negative**). The inclusion of these events produces the tree shown in Figure 3-10.

We can label the end points of the tree according to the final result (Figure 3-11).

The final outcomes are not all ideal. Outcomes 6 and 7 (nonuser allowed to compete) are ideal, whereas outcomes 2 and 4 (suspension of an offender) achieve the objective of rooting out illegal drug users. Outcomes 1 and 3 are of concern because they raise the possibility (perhaps probability) that nonusers will be labeled as users and suspended, perhaps for life. Outcome 5 raises the issue that some users will probably "escape" the drug testing and still end up competing, which could undermine the credibility of any testing program. The final outcome on the tree (outcome 8 [offender allowed to compete]) points out the reality that if no testing is done, there will be illegal drug users competing.

The analysis raises important issues that should be addressed before decisions are taken:

How many drug users are there competing? (Or, what is the extent of the problem?)

How accurate is the proposed test? Critically important is the number of false-positive results that occur, but the number of false-negative results also is important.

Figure 3-6 | **FIRST STEP IN DECISION TREE REGARDING TESTING FOR DRUG USE**

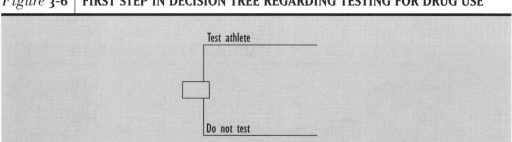

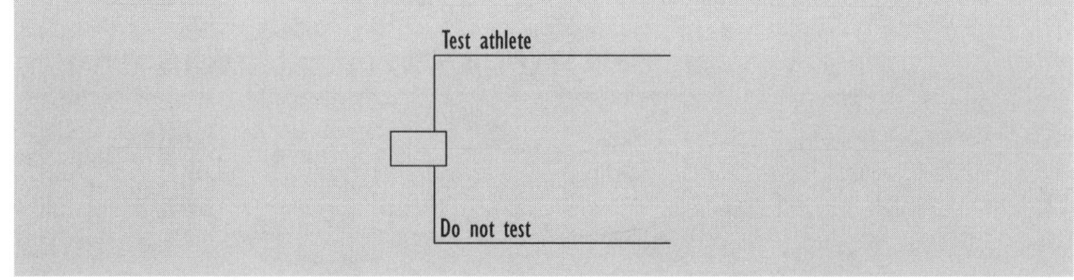

Figure 3-7 **ADDITION OF TEST OUTCOME TO DRUG TESTING DECISION TREE**

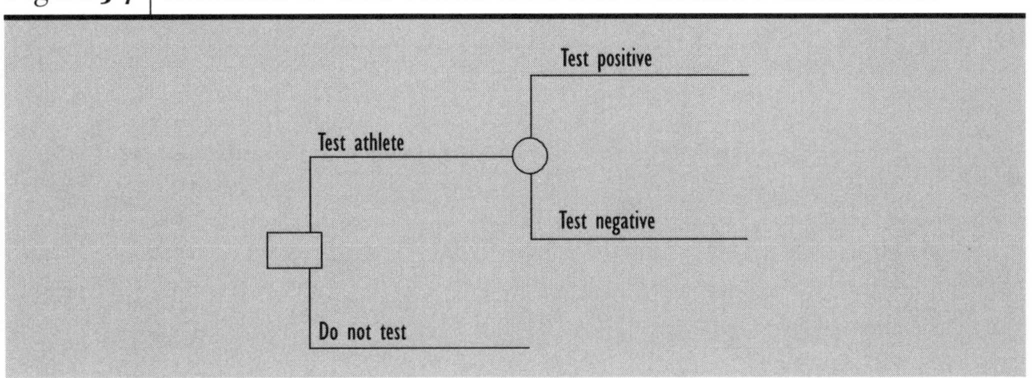

Figure 3-8 **ADDITION OF SANCTION DECISION TO DRUG TESTING DECISION TREE**

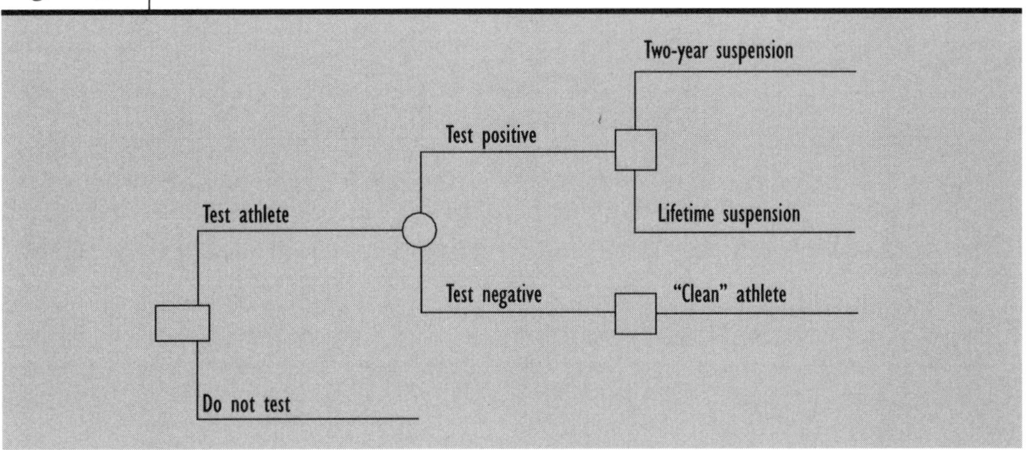

Figure 3-9 **DECISION TREE WITH `` DO NOT TEST'' OUTCOMES**

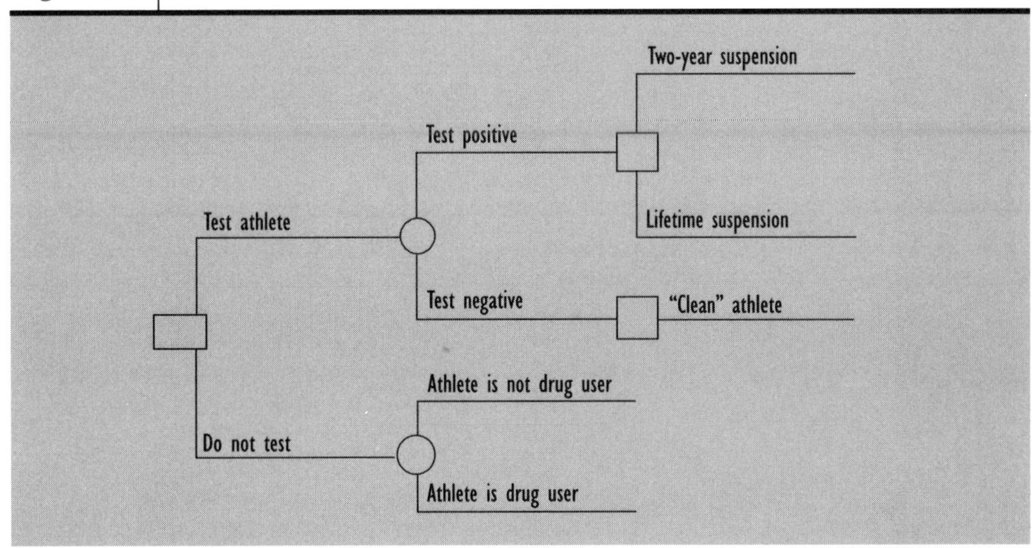

Figure 3-10 | **DECISION TREE TAKING INTO ACCOUNT THE IMPERFECTION OF DRUG TESTS**

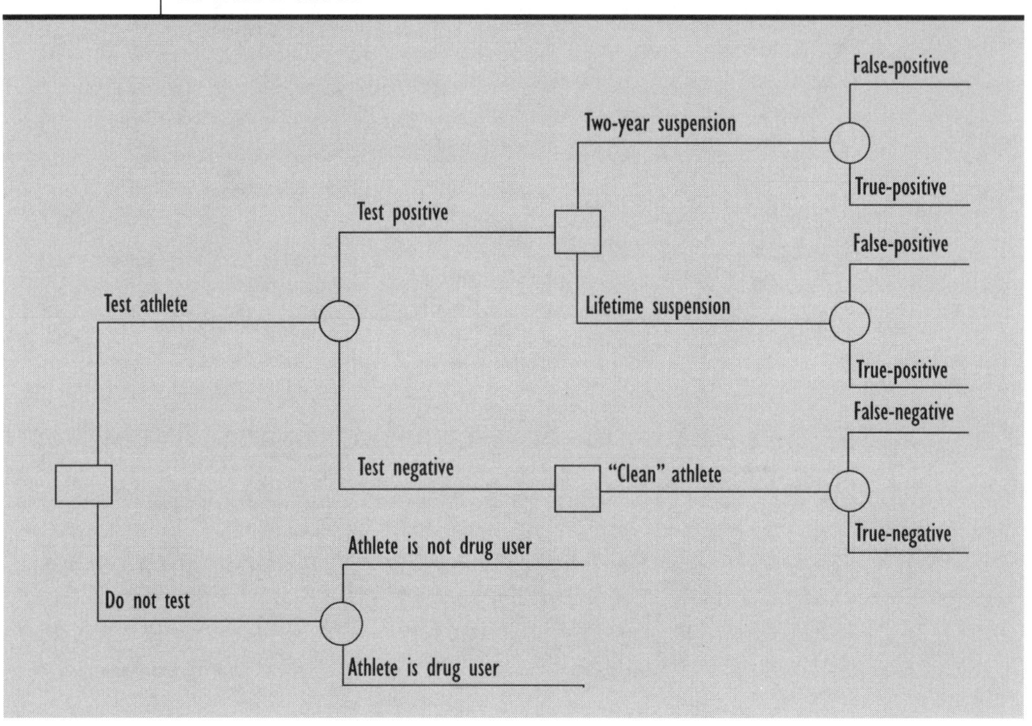

Figure 3-11 | **FINAL LABELED DECISION TREE**

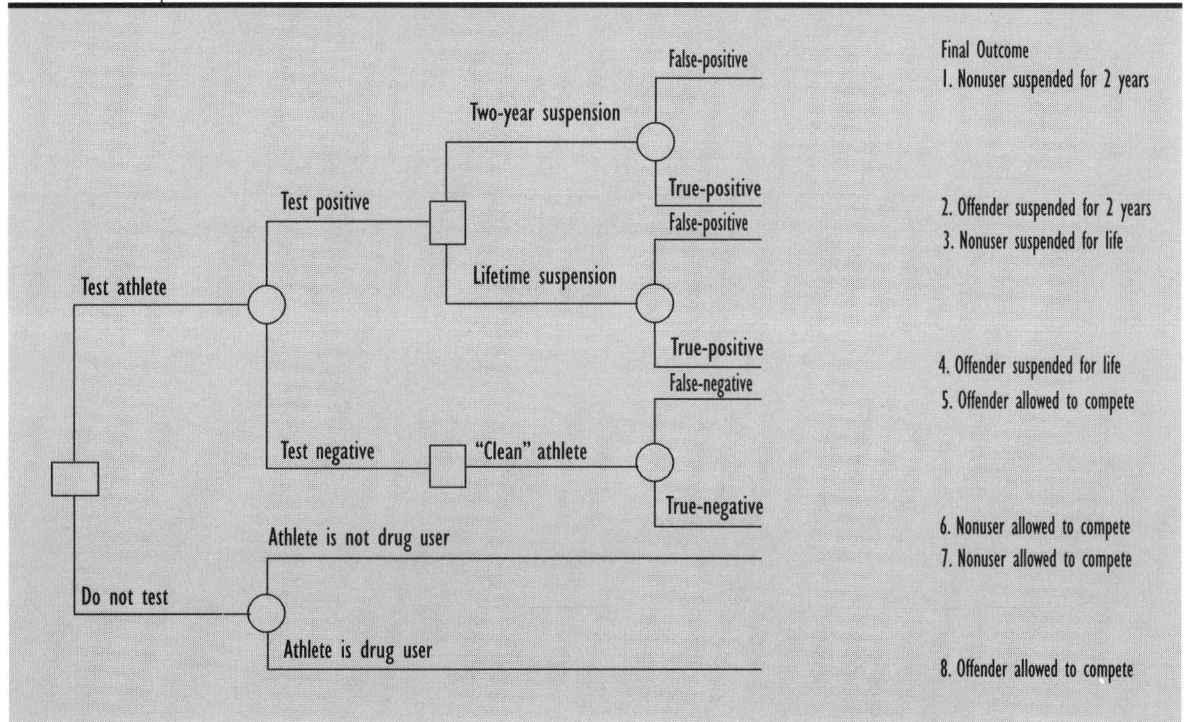

How do we handle the very undesirable outcome in which an innocent athlete is identified as a drug user and suspended?

The decision analysis also identifies the **risks** of the testing policies. The risk of not testing is that an offender may be allowed to compete. The major risk of a testing policy is that a nonuser may be suspended, perhaps for life.

An informed group could discuss these issues, weigh the alternatives, and reach a set of decisions. Note that the group would have to decide what to do with an athlete who had a positive test result before considering the decision of whether athletes should be tested. In general, when addressing sequential decisions, it is necessary to first evaluate the decisions that come later in time; that is, to work through the decision tree from right to left. This process is called a **roll-back** through the decision tree.

In considering the alternatives, the group would likely talk about **probabilities**.

COPING WITH UNCERTAINTY USING PROBABILITIES

Uncertainties exist in most business decision situations. This is inevitable because most decisions are concerned with the future. Uncertainty can rarely be assumed away but rather has to somehow be handled. One way of doing this is through the use of **probabilities**.

The use of **probabilities** enables us to cope with uncertain events in the decision tree. Recall that an event denotes a situation that we cannot control and that generates several outcomes. The example of flipping a coin has some probability of producing a "head" and some probability of producing a "tail" (Figure 3-3). If the coin is "fair," these outcomes are equally likely. There are several equivalent ways of making a probability statement about this event. We could say that if we flipped the coin 100 times, we would expect to see 50 "heads" and 50 "tails." We could say that on average, half of the flips will produce a "head" (or a "tail"), or we could say that if we flip the coin, the probability of the outcome being a "head" is 50% (or 0.5).

In business situations, probabilities can rarely be measured in any reasonable way but rather are usually assigned by someone with a good understanding of the uncertainties. Your stockbroker might tell you, "There is a 70% probability that the market will go up today." Assigned probabilities like these are called **subjective probabilities**. A subjective probability is an informed opinion of the likelihood of the occurrence of some outcome given by a knowledgeable individual or group.

The assignment of useful subjective probabilities requires a close familiarity with the uncertain events and with whatever data are available that have a bearing on the uncertainties. A familiar example is the weather forecast, which includes the "probabilities of precipitation." These are subjective probabilities usually assigned by a trained weather forecaster with a great deal of experience with weather systems who is armed with the most recent data on current weather conditions.

AXIOMS OF PROBABILITIES

In assigning probabilities, there are certain rules, or **axioms**, that must be followed if the values are to have meaning to others. Two basic axioms are:

> An outcome is **certain** if the probability of occurrence is 1 (or 100%); therefore, probabilities cannot be greater than 1 (or 100%).

An outcome is **impossible** if the probability of occurrence is 0, therefore, probabilities cannot be less than 0.

A third axiom states that if we define a set of outcomes for an event in such a way that no two outcomes can occur simultaneously and if the set of defined outcomes covers every possible result, then the sum of the probabilities assigned to this set of outcomes must equal 1.

Outcomes that cannot occur simultaneously are called **mutually exclusive** outcomes. A set of outcomes is **exhaustive** if every possible consequence of an event is included in at least one of the outcomes. The third axiom can be restated as follows.

The probabilities of a set of **mutually exclusive** and **exhaustive** outcomes must equal 1.

We often can choose how to define the outcomes from an event. For example, consider a single roll of a die. Some of the possible outcomes are "1," "2," "3," "4," "5," or "6," "odd," "even," "not 1," "not 5," "less than 3"; and so on.

There are many outcomes that are not **mutually exclusive** (e.g., "even" and "2"). We also can define many sets of outcomes that are not **exhaustive** (e.g., the set {"odd," "2," "4"}, which does not include "6").

Defining a set of **mutually exclusive** and **exhaustive** outcomes is important if we are to compute an **expected value** for an event.

EXPECTED VALUE

The expected value of an event can be interpreted as a long-run average; if we were to observe an event a very large number of times and average the outcomes, we would arrive at an average outcome very close to the expected value. However, in many management decision situations, particularly many of the important ones, events occur only once. When the outcomes of an event have a numerical value, the **expected value** of the event can be computed. Consider an event (Figure 3-12) in which the three outcomes constitute a set of mutually exclusive and exhaustive outcomes (with probability sum equal to 1). The **expected value** of event A is computed as:

$$(0.1 * 1{,}000{,}000) + (0.3 * 1{,}000) + (0.6 * 0)^{AQ1} = 100{,}300$$

In general, the expected value of an event is the value of each outcome multiplied by the probability of that outcome, summed over all outcomes. Or:

$$E(A) = \sum_i p_i * x_i$$

where
E(A) is the expected value of event A,
Σ_i denotes summation over all outcomes i from a set of mutually exclusive and exhaustive outcomes of event A.
p_i is the probability that outcome i occurs, and
x_i is the value of outcome i

The expected value is important in analyzing decisions because it provides a guide as to the "average" value of the event. Other characteristics of events are also important, notably their **riskiness**. Managerial decision making involves balancing expected values and risks. The decision depicted in Figure 3-13 would not be easy for most of us.

Choice A has an expected value of $[0.9 * 1000 + 0.1 * (-1000)]$, or \$800, which suggests that it is a better choice than \$600 for certain, but A is also riskier because we could

Figure 3-12 | **DECISION TREE FOR EXAMPLE EVENT**

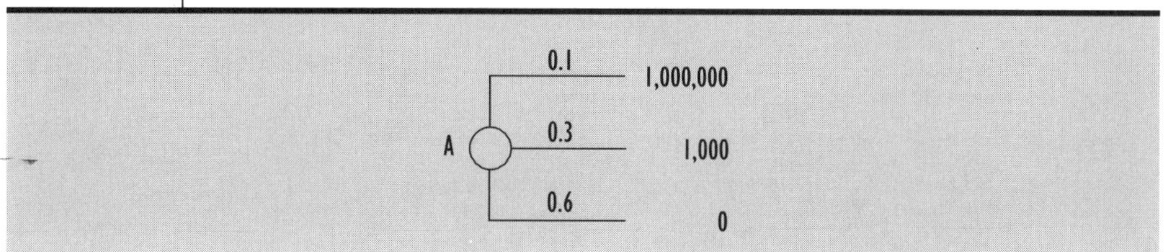

Figure 3-13 | **DECISION TREE ILLUSTRATING A DIFFICULT PERSONAL CHOICE**

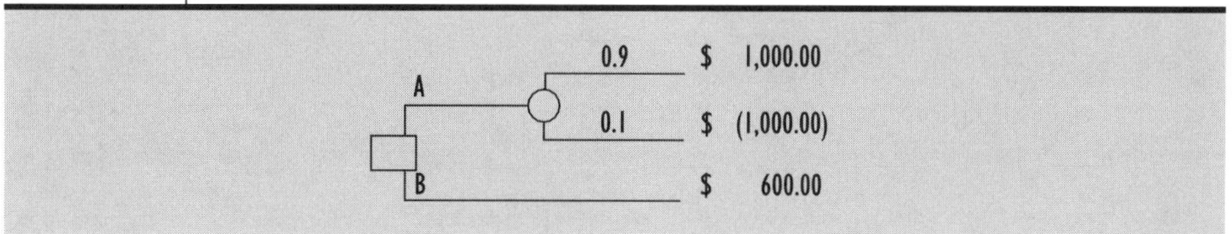

end up losing $1000 (but with 90% probability, we could end up with $1000). The final decision depends on whether the individual will give up $200 in expected value to avoid the risk of losing $1000 or to accept the risk of winning an extra $400. There is no correct answer here; different individuals will make this decision differently.

Expected value is, therefore, only a guideline for individual decision making. A large firm makes a great number of decisions, and the firm that acts to maximize expected value will, on average, come out the best. While acting to maximize expected value, however, it is important that management control the risks accepted and consider very carefully any decision that may catastrophically affect the firm. As an example of this kind of behavior, airline operators carry insurance to cover the civil liabilities that would result from the crash of one of their airplanes. In doing so, they give up expected value (the insurance companies profit from these policies, on average) but avoid the catastrophic impact on the firm should this unlikely event occur.

INCORPORATING EXPECTED VALUES INTO THE DECISION TREE: ROLL-BACK

Expected values can be used to assist in the analysis of the decision tree. Consider the following decision situation.

We have $10,000,000 in "spare cash" in our corporate account. We do not need these funds for 48 hours. We know that we can invest these funds through our bankers in overnight commercial paper and receive an annual interest rate of 7% (the interest rate for 48 hours will be $0.07 * 2/365$, which yields interest of $3,835.62). Our second choice is to offer these funds to a broker, who, for a fee of $100, will try to place them in the premium overnight market for 48 hours, where we will receive an 8% annual interest rate (or $4,383.56 less the $100 commission). The broker tells us that these placements can be successfully negotiated 90% of the time. If placement in the premium market is not successful, we will be too late to go to the overnight market and the funds will be idle for 24 hours, but tomorrow, we will have the same options: that is, we can go to the 7% overnight market for 24 hours (interest of $1,917.81) or pay the broker an additional $100 commission to try for a 24-hour premium placement at 8% (interest of $2,191.78).

Figure 3-14 | DECISION TREE FOR INVESTMENT PROBLEM

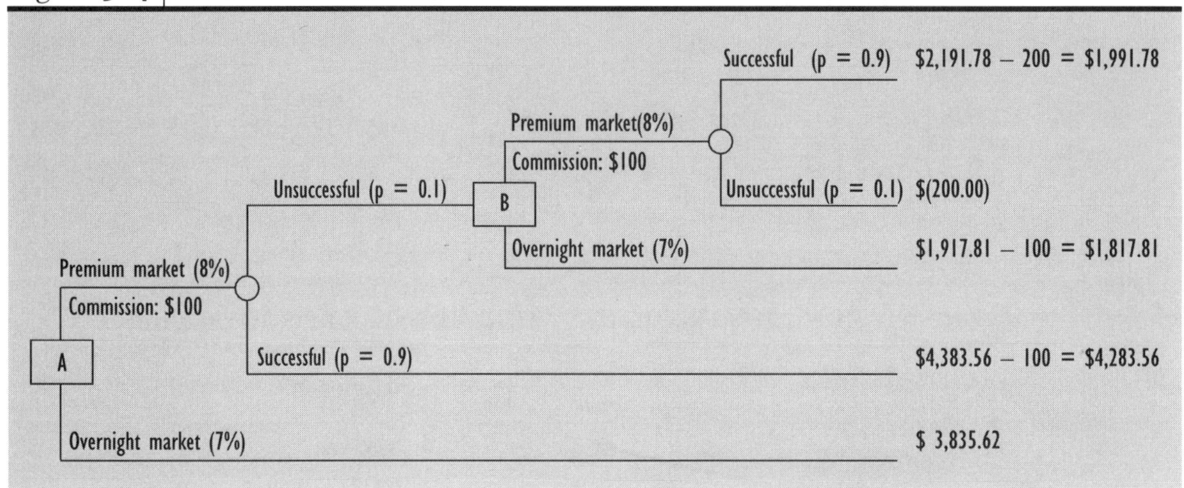

The decision tree for this decision situation is illustrated in Figure 3-14.

Note that at the end of the branches, we have computed the actual conditional payoffs (in dollars) if the decisions and events lead us to that result. Although other approaches are possible, this approach minimizes the possibility of confusing real dollars and opportunity dollars.

The decision of immediate concern is today's decision: **whether to try for a 48-hour premium placement or stay with the certain overnight investment at 7%**. This decision has been labeled "A" in the tree (see Figure 3-14). We cannot, however, make this decision until we understand the conditional decision (labeled "B" in Figure 3-14) concerning what we should do if our broker fails to find us a 48-hour premium placement. Therefore, to analyze the decision tree, we have to examine the decisions moving backward in time (from right to left in the tree). This process is called **roll-back**.

In rolling-back through the tree, we first address the conditional decision at "B" (Figure 3-15): if decisions are made and events unfold such that we arrive at point "B," what is our best plan of action?

Figure 3-15 | DECISION TREE FOR ANALYSIS OF DECISION B

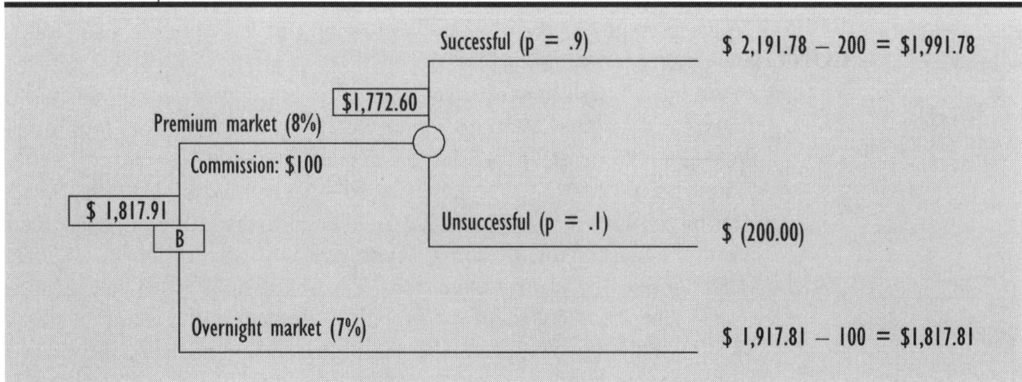

Figure 3-16 **INVESTMENT PROBLEM WITH DECISION B REMOVED**

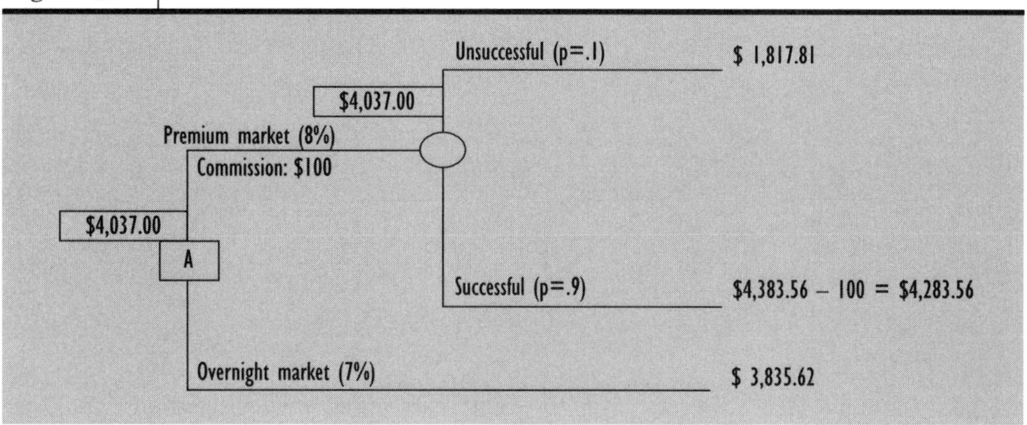

The choice we have is between \$1,817.81 for certain in the 24-hour overnight market or an event with a 90% chance at \$1.991.78 in the premium market coupled with a 10% chance at negative \$200 (we pay two commissions but receive no interest) (Figure 3-15). The expected value of this event is 0.9 * \$1,991.78 + 0.1 * (−200), or \$1,772.60. On an expected value basis, we prefer the overnight market (\$1,817.81 versus \$1,772.60). Because the option with the higher expected value is also less risky, we can be confident that the 24-hour overnight market is the best decision at "B."

The branch of the tree beyond "B" can therefore be eliminated and replaced by the expected payoff from the best decision at point "B" (\$1,817.81) (Figure 3-16).

We can now resolve the immediate decision "A."

We must choose between \$3,835.62 for certain in the 48-hour overnight market or an event having a 90% chance of a payoff of \$4,283.56 and a 10% chance of an expected payoff of \$1,817.81.

The expected value of this event is 0.9 * \$4,283.56 + 0.1 * \$1,817.81, or \$4,037. If our decision criterion is to maximize expected value, then the optimum decision is to try the 48-hour market (\$4,037 versus \$3,835.62).

We have now resolved our decision situation. Our best decision strategy is to first try the 48-hour premium market; if this is unsuccessful, and if nothing changes during the next 24 hours, then tomorrow we place the funds in the 24-hour overnight market.

CONTINGENCY ANALYSIS

A decision often depends critically on the value assigned as a subjective probability. In these situations, it is often helpful to conduct a contingency analysis.The contingency analysis seeks to determine the critical value or values of the probability, that is, the value or values that **change the decision**.

As an example, consider the following decision: a supplier made a mistake, and as a result, we incurred extra costs of \$1,000,000. Should we sue to recover these costs? The lawsuit will cost us \$50,000. This decision depends critically on our perceived probability of winning the suit.

The decision tree is shown in Figure 3-17.

Figure 3-17 **DECISION TREE FOR CONTINGENCY ANALYSIS**

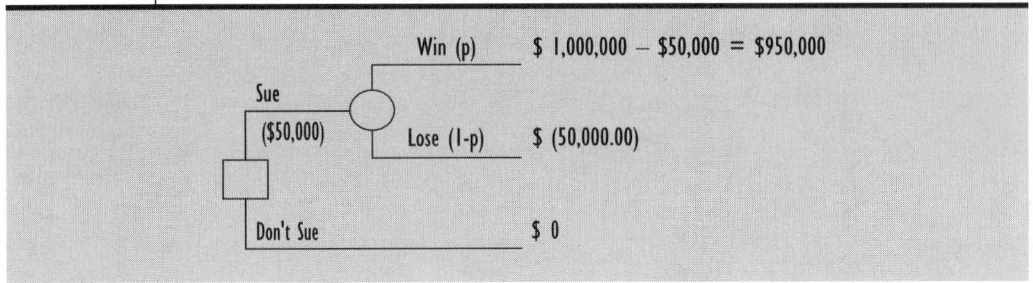

We have entered the probability of winning the suit as the unknown p and the probability of losing the suit as $(1 - p)$. To roll-back the tree, we compute the expected value of the "sue" option:

$$\text{Expected value} = \$950{,}000\,p + (-\$50{,}000)(1 - p) = \$1{,}000{,}000\,p - \$50{,}000$$

The expected value of "don't sue" is $0, so based on expected values, we prefer "sue" if:

$$\$1{,}000{,}000\,p - \$50{,}000 > \$0$$

or

$$p > \$50{,}000/\$1{,}000{,}000$$

or

$$p > 0.05$$

The expected value maximizing decision is, therefore, **contingent on the value assigned to the subjective probability *p***. We do not need to know an exact value for p; we only need a range. If we think p is greater than 0.05, we sue: if we think p is less than 0.05, we do not.

Risk Analysis and Risk Management

Risk analysis involves identifying the various types of risk to which the firm is exposed, whereas risk management is the process of managing to reduce these risks or to limit the firm's exposure if any of the various risks materialize.

Before risks can be managed, the specific risks facing the firm must be identified, and the management actions that can modify each specific risk must be spelled out. For example, if the risk item is identified as exposure to claims arising from injuries to workers on the job, then the kinds of management tools available to modify this risk include training programs, on-the-job supervision, and investment in safety equipment. Purchasing insurance is a risk management tool that limits the cost to the firm in the event that an injury to a worker does occur.

In terms of probabilities, risk analysis and risk management can be described as follows:

Let $P[x]$ be the probability that an undesirable outcome x occurs and $C[x]$ be the cost to the firm if x occurs.

Then the expected value of the risk is $P[x]C[x]$.

Table 3-1 | **RISK FACTORS CONTRIBUTING TO A RESIDENTIAL GAS SHORTAGE**

Sources of Risk	**Possible Controlling Actions**
Weather—a long, very cold spell	Build more storage facilities to begin the season with larger inventories; develop a priority allocation scheme; install larger pipes from gas suppliers to utility.
Transmission pipe failures	Build redundancy into transmission system; maintain strategic inventories close to residential centers.
Supply shortages—suppliers cannot meet contracts	Diversify purchases—use many suppliers; include penalty clauses in contracts.
Labor disputes	Build and maintain adequate inventories; train management to operate key facilities.

In general, x will occur when any one or more of a number of different "elementary" events occurs. Thus, $P[x]$ is a complex probability made up from accumulating the probabilities of several independent and dependent "elementary" events.

The **risk analysis** task is to identify the elementary events and probabilities that make up $P[x]$.

The **risk management** task is to take actions to reduce the expected value of the risk (i.e., $P[x]C[x]$) either by reducing the probabilities of the elementary events occurring, and hence reducing $P[x]$, or by reducing the cost, $C[x]$, to the firm if x occurs.

As an example, consider the case of a natural gas distribution utility. An outcome that is particularly unsatisfactory for such a utility is being unable to supply gas to residents in the distribution area. There is some probability "$P[x]$" that such a shortage will occur. A shortage, however, is a consequence of one or more "elementary" events occurring, each of which can produce a residential gas shortage. For each of these specific events (or risks), there are possible actions that the utility could take to modify that risk and thereby reduce the probability of a residential gas shortage occurring; Table 3-1 provides examples of some of these.

Finally, there exists the possibility of purchasing an insurance policy to reduce the cost of claims against the utility (i.e., $C[x]$) in the event that a residential gas shortage does occur. The risk management task facing the utility is to choose which specific risks to address and which actions to implement as part of a balanced, cost-effective strategy aimed at controlling the probability and cost of residential gas shortages.

DECISION ANALYSIS IN ACTION

THE *S.S. KUNIANG*

The *S.S. Kuniang* ran aground on April 9, 1981, off the coast of Florida. The ship was declared a total loss by its owners, who offered to sell the salvage rights to the vessel by way of a sealed bid auction. Anyone wishing to acquire the salvage rights could submit a sealed offer to the auctioneer, who would sell the rights to the vessel to the highest bidder.

The New England Electric System (NEES) served more than 1 million customers in Massachusetts, Rhode Island, and New Hampshire and required colliers to transport coal from Virginia to its power stations in New England. A NEES subsidiary, New England Energy Incorporated (NEEI), had already purchased a 36,250-ton self-loading ship at a cost of $70 million for this purpose. If the *S.S. Kuniang* could be repaired, its coal-carrying capacity would be 51,000 tons, although the shallowness of Brayton Point harbor would limit its capacity to 45,750 tons.This was sufficient to accommodate NEES's remaining collier needs. NEEI used a decision tree to help decide whether to bid and how much to bid for the *S.S. Kuniang*.

IMPORTANCE OF THE JONES ACT

The Jones Act, which was passed by the U.S. Congress in 1920, gave significant priority in U.S. ports to U.S.-manufactured and -crewed ships ("Jones Act" ships). These priorities were important: the wait for coal loading at ports like Newport News and Norfolk sometimes reached 45 days, whereas a round trip for NEEI took only 8 days if there was no wait for loading. The *S.S. Kuniang* was not American built, but there was a possibility under a 1852 statute for it to be declared a Jones Act ship. For this to happen, the cost of repairs to the ship had to be more than three times its "salvage value" as estimated by the U.S. Coast Guard.

NEEI had an estimate that the cost of salvaging the ship was around $15 million. Would the U.S. Coast Guard estimate the salvage value of the ship at its value as scrap (clearly less than $5 million), or would they consider the winning bid as an indication of the ship's true salvage value? Qualifying the *S.S. Kuniang* as a Jones Act vessel was so important that if NEEI bid more than $5 million, they would have to find some way of increasing the cost of repairs to meet the act's requirements.One way to do this was to install self-loading equipment on the vessel at an extra cost of $21 million. This equipment would reduce the round-trip time from 8 days to 5, but the extra weight of the equipment would reduce the coal-carrying capacity of the *S.S. Kuniang* from 51,000 to 40,000 tons.

THE DECISION

Three million tons of coal per year were required for existing NEES coal-burning plants. An additional 750,000 tons would be required at Salem Harbor if the environmental hearings on an additional plant conversion were successful. Some years down the road, an additional 250,000 tons of coal might be required for the Providence plant, making a coal requirement of 4,000,000 tons of coal per year, although this level might not be reached for several years, if ever. The General Dynamics vessel already purchased could move 2,250,000 tons per year. A sister to this vessel could be purchased, or chartered barges could be hired. The four options for the additional vessel are summarized in Table 3-2.

Table 3-2 | **DATA FOR THE FOUR OPTIONS**

	General Dynamics	Tug/Barge	*Kuniang* (Gearless)	*Kuniang* (Self-loader)
Capital cost	$70 million	$32 million	Bid + $15 million	Bid + $36 million
Capacity	36,250 tons	30,000 tons	45,750 tons	40,000 tons
Round trip (coal)	5.15 days	7.15 days	8.18 days (as Jones Act vessel)	5.39 days
Round trip (Egypt)	79 days	134 days	90 days	84 days
Operating cost/day	$18,670	$12,000	$23,000	$24,300
Fixed cost/day	$2,400	$2,400	$2,400	$2,700
Revenue/trip coal	$304,500	$222,000	$329,400	$336,000
Revenue/trip Egypt	$2,540,000	$2,100,000	$3,570,000	$2,800,000

Any excess shipping capacity acquired by NEEI would have to find open market business, likely grain transportation, which was substantial and almost always available.

Decision Analysis

NEEI used a decision tree to evaluate this decision. There were a number of additional complications. The *S.S. Kuniang* was 15 years old, and it was not clear how long it would last; the dates of conversion of the Salem and Providence plants to coal burning were unknown. Appropriate discount rates were not easy to estimate. NEES was sufficiently large that the dollar amounts involved in the *S.S. Kuniang* decisions, although significant, did not create any unacceptable financial risk; therefore, maximization of the expected value provided an appropriate guideline for bidding. Part of a decision tree representation of the problem (from Bell, *Interfaces,* 14:2, 1984 *op. cit.*) is shown in Figure 3-18.

Some of the probabilities assessed were as follows:

> The U.S. Coast Guard was thought likely to assess the salvage value at the bid price with a probability of 0.7 and at scrap value with a probability of 0.3.
>
> NEES was sure that a bid of $10 million would win the auction and that a bid of $3 million would definitely not win. A bid of $5 million was assessed a one-sixth chance of winning; $6 million, two sixths; $7 million, three sixths; $8 million, four sixths; $9 million, five sixths; and $10 million, six sixths.

The analysis showed that using the *S.S. Kuniang* initially as a gearless ship and converting it to a self-loader only if the demand for coal materialized was worth about $500,000 in expected value terms.

Results. NEES bid $6.7 million for the *S.S. Kuniang* but lost the auction to a bid of $10 million. The Coast Guard valued the vessel at its scrap value. The winning bidder had the option of operating the vessel as a full-time grain ship, which NEES could not do for regulatory reasons.

The decision analysis proved a remarkably effective tool for structuring this complex problem, lending insight into the most relevant information to collect and developing a rationale for the eventual solution. Ed Brown, Chairman and CEO of the New England Power Service Company, stated, "The analysis was a useful contribution to our deliberations and

Figure **3-18** **A DECISION TREE REPRESENTATION OF HOW MUCH TO BID FOR THE KUNIANG**

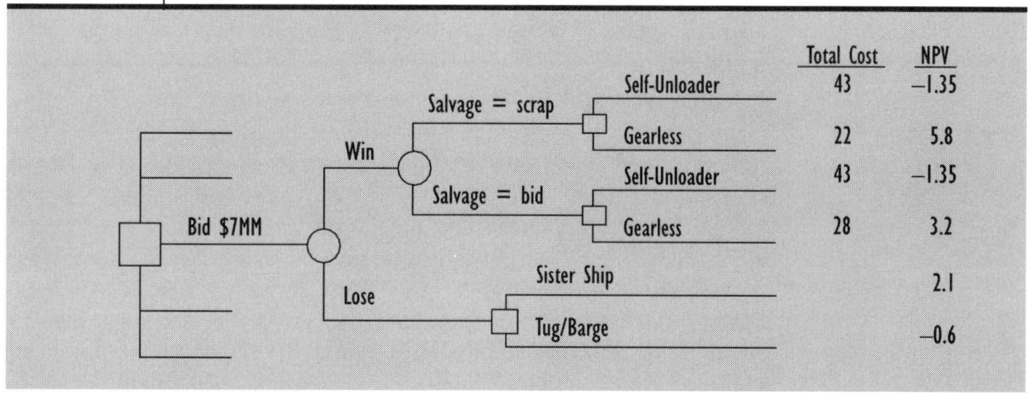

to our decision regarding an appropriate bid for the ship. The process was both interesting and valuable as well as being an excellent learning experience."

From D.E. Bell, Bidding for the *S.S. Kuniang*, *Interfaces*, 14:2, 1984.

DU PONT BELIEVES THAT DECISION AND RISK ANALYSIS CONTRIBUTES TO ACHIEVING OUTSTANDING FINANCIAL RESULTS

> Decision and risk analysis enables Du Pont's business teams to develop creative strategic alternatives, evaluate them rigorously, and select those with the greatest expected shareholder value.
>
> From F.U. Krumm and C.F. Rolle, Management and Application of Decision and Risk Analysis in Dupont, *Interfaces*, 22:6, 1992.

In the mid-1980s, Du Pont began acquiring major medical, agricultural, chemical, and automotive finishing businesses. At the same time, the company was reducing its staff. Consequently, many difficult decisions had to be made by a smaller management group. Further complications included the facts that these decisions involved vastly different markets from all over the globe, and in many cases, time was short and the environment was uncertain. Du Pont chose to move responsibility for these decisions to the business units by empowering local management to make important decisions.

Du Pont developed decision and risk analysis (D&RA) tools to help managers with these decisions. A core group of decision and risk consultants (DRC) was established. DRC organized training programs, consulted with Du Pont businesses, and produced a D&RA newsletter and annual forum. DRC became the focal point of a network of D&RA champions deployed throughout the organization who promoted the value of D&RA through education and networking, consulted with businesses having more complex problems, and integrated D&RA with strategic thinking and planning activities throughout Du Pont.

Business Z

One example of D&RA at work occurred in mid-1990. Business Z, an actual Du Pont business based in the United States with sales and facilities worldwide, found its financial performance declining as a result of eroding prices and market share. Business Z's products had fallen behind some competitors, and its production facilities were unable to produce the customized products now in demand. Moreover, the industry's rate of growth was slowing, although still outpacing the general economy.

The Du Pont director responsible for Business Z formed a decision board consisting of himself and senior management. The board's purpose was to select from the strategic options developed by the D&RA project team, which consisted of 10 Business Z managers as well as a full-time DRC consultant. The D&RA plan was conducted in several segments, as follows.

Framing the Problem. The team developed and shared with the decision board a wide-ranging set of alternative strategies.

Assessing and Analyzing the Options (Analysis). At this stage, uncertainties (such as competitors' market shares and prices) were assessed separately by region using small groups of experts. A spreadsheet model was used to construct net present values (NPV) of each strategy, and *Supertree* (software that evaluated decision trees) was used to construct the probability distributions of these NPVs. This analysis stage took 4 months.

Making Decisions. The decision board arrived at a new strategy that was expected to increase business Z's value by $175 million.

Planning Implementation (connection with the real world). Steps were identified to connect the recommendations to an implementation plan. Major activities, actions to minimize risk, contingency plans, measures of progress, and required changes to the organizational culture were identified.

Other Results

By the end of 1992, more than 10 Du Pont businesses had used D&RA to develop, select, and implement business strategies. Each of these businesses was competing globally, had annual sales in excess of $150 million, and possessed multiple production facilities.

Management has stressed the intangible results of D&RA even more than the tangible ones. For example, because so many employees take part and contribute to the decision making, a sense of personal commitment is fostered. The process enhances team building and increases effective communication among participants through the common purpose outlined within D&RA. Moreover, as greater attention is paid to strategy development, innovative new hybrid strategies often emerge.

D&RA has been particularly useful in allowing decision makers to focus on shareholder value as the primary decision criterion, and it has been an extremely useful framework for involving critical uncertainties such as customer behavior, competitive response, and the impact of society on the business operation.

Michael T. Sharples, Vice President Finance, Du Pont, writes, "We consider D&RA a best practice at Du Pont. The value of D&RA became even more vivid to me... as I sat on the decision board of another major Du Pont business. D&RA was used to structure and evaluate an opportunity that we believe will improve its NPV by a minimum of $200 million. The D&RA process improved communication within the business team as well as between the team and... management, resulting in rapid approval and execution. As a decision maker, I highly value such a clear and logical approach to making choices under uncertainty... ."

From F.V. Krumm and C.F. Rolle, Management and Application of Decision and Risk Analysis in Du Pont, *Interfaces*, 22:6, 1992.

OPERATIONS RISK MANAGEMENT AT A MAJOR BANK

When the operations of a business are disrupted, losses usually result. When that business is a financial institution, the losses can be considerable. Some sources of potential disruption include fire or earthquake, employee accidents or illness, and criminal activities. Historically, banks protected their financial assets from major theft using vaults and security guards, but the advent of electronic funds transfer has produced new security problems for financial institutions. Today, the fact that the value of electronic "paperless" transactions far exceeds the value of the banks' physical assets justifies devoting considerable resources to risk management.

What Is Risk Management?

Risk management is the management of the uncertainties surrounding unlikely events that have the potential to have an adverse impact on the operation of a business. The objective of risk management is to limit the impact of major disruptions to an acceptable level.

There are generally three options available to manage an identified risk:

Management may take action to reduce the probability that the event occurs.

Management may prepare and implement a contingency plan to minimize the effect of the event if it occurs.

Management may choose to do nothing.

In the case of electronic funds transfer, management would like to take steps to minimize the probability that theft occurs and to put controls in place so if theft does occur, it is speedily identified, and the amount lost by the bank is minimized. This set of controls might include purchasing insurance so if large losses occur, the bank is repaid for some or all of these losses.

Decision makers must determine whether to act and how to proceed. To do this, they must assess the severity of the risk and estimate the cost of controlling the risk. Good decisions must balance the probability of a risk occurring with the extent of the possible losses and must be effective in limiting the losses to manageable levels.

Risk Management Methodology at the Bank

The first step taken by the bank was to develop a risk management methodology. This methodology was a step-by-step process, based on decision analysis, to determine the appropriate response to an identified risk. Terms that were defined during planning are as follows:

A **threat** was a potential disaster that would lead to a loss of resources.

An **event** was an actual loss of resources that disrupted service delivery and affected earnings.

Losses were economic reductions in the company's wealth.

Next, the bank identified services where contingency plans were necessary and reviewed the resources needed to deliver those services. Management at the bank also had to predict what threats the bank's operations faced, and came up with a list that included power outages, fire, acts of nature, sabotage, and strikes. Once these threats were identified, management determined what resources and services would be affected if any of the various threats materialized.

The losses that would result from the various events were then estimated. Losses could be direct, indirect, or simply a loss of assets. For example, a fire would result in a loss of assets if a building were destroyed, but direct losses would also occur as a result of not being able to carry out contracted services, and indirect losses would result from a loss of future customers. In making these predictions and estimates, management reviewed historical data and discussed event likelihoods with experts. Computer simulation was used to blend historical data and subjective opinions to arrive at occurrence rates.

The next step was to develop alternatives to deal with the possible events, either by reducing the probability of an event or by reducing losses. Checklists were developed to assess similar risks and alternatives in different areas of operation. Management calculated the annualized cost of each alternative and compared it with the expected annual risk exposure and considered existing insurance coverage and the positive effect on premiums that a comprehensive risk management plan could have. At this point, a decision tree was constructed to evaluate each alternative. One branch of the tree denoted that the alternative was adopted, and a second denoted that it was not. Probabilities of various events were attached along with the estimated conditional losses that would result. In some situations, the values made decision making very easy, whereas in others, the outcomes were so close that a more detailed analysis was necessary.

To understand the level at which decisions would be considered material, the project team interviewed senior management to assess their attitude to risk. Risks were found to be significant only at very large monetary values, with the result that only risks with a large possible loss would be an issue; smaller losses would be "self-insured" (i.e., the bank would take the risk and fund any losses that occurred). This final framework was not intended to replace a manager's judgment but rather to support it; consequently, the results were compared with the operations manager's intuitive judgment, and any disagreements were closely examined and resolved.

Some Specific Projects

Several specific areas were examined using this methodology.

Power Generator. Intuitively, management believed that a backup generator was necessary. Because other banks had acquired backup generators, there was not likely to be a holiday in the event of a regional blackout. The decision analysis indicated that a small backup generator was needed only for the funds transfer division because this division was the most deadline dependent.

Multilocation Contingency Strategy. Dual data processing operations at geographically separate sites were proposed, with production computers at one site and development computers at the other.There was a strategic influence on the decision to go ahead because the bank managers wanted to see whether this decision could be used to further strategic initiatives.

Transaction Processing. The bank considered various threats to a basement data center that handled a small portion of the bank's business. The decision was taken to move the center to the third floor.

Pricing Risk into Coin and Currency. Operational risks were identified for each coin or currency product (e.g., theft by employees or outsiders); the controls inherent in the production process also were determined. The analysis methodology was used to ensure that the price charged for each product included the appropriate risk premium.

Authentication of Funds Transfers. The risk that someone might intercept, modify, and retransmit electronic funds transfers was quantified and used by management to assess the need for internal authentication.

Success of the Project

Management completely accepted the institutionalization of a decision analysis methodology to ensure uniform compliance with corporate policy with respect to risk:

> Management proved to be surprisingly receptive to such concepts as events, probability, expected value, and utility, as long as they were presented in an intuitive rather than a mathematical framework.

The project had the support of the president of the bank, and the bank was able to report yearly to its board of directors on a corporation-wide contingency planning program.

As a result of this work, the OR group became a department with worldwide responsibility for contingency planning and information security.

From K.J. Engemann and H.F. Miller, Operations Risk Management at a Major Bank, *Interfaces*, 22:6, 1992.

RESEARCH AND DEVELOPMENT PROJECT SELECTION AT THE GAS RESEARCH INSTITUTE

In the 1970s, the natural gas industry was struggling with the perception that natural gas was "a fuel with no future." Without new products and services that made use of natural gas, it appeared as though oil and electric technologies would win out.

To change this perception, and in competitive retaliation to the formation of the Electric Power Research Institute (EPRI), the industry formed a research and development (R&D) group called the Gas Research Institute (GRI) in 1978. The GRI has been credited with the development of 132 successful commercial products and processes that have transformed natural gas into "the fuel of the future." The success of the GRI R&D program was partly attributed to the use of a decision analysis technique known as the project appraisal methodology, or PAM.

PAM was used to evaluate the commercial feasibility of R&D projects by quantifying subjective decisions that, in turn, helped GRI management decide on the allocation of funds among competing projects.

R&D Branch of the GRI

The GRI was composed of representatives of producers, pipeline operators, and local distribution companies; was made up of 270 staff members; and had an annual budget of $200 million. The budget was determined each year when the GRI submitted a 5-year plan to the Federal Energy Regulatory Commission, which decided the level of funding to be raised through a surcharge on interstate gas pipeline shipments. The institute had no laboratories but essentially was a planning and funding organization that contracted out all R&D work. GRI's role was to decide which projects to fund and the level of funding so as to provide the industry with new products. By the early 1990s, 800 projects had been undertaken, of which 450 were complete.

PAM Process

PAM is the integrated decision-making tool central to the planning process. Through PAM, management science methods are combined with judgmental inputs to determine which products are worth pursuing. The first PAM step is to answer a sequence of questions about each project:

What Will the Project Accomplish? Each proposed project has performance goals that might include efficiency, reliability, emission levels, as well as initial cost, operating cost and payback period. These goals are quantified within PAM and compared to competing and existing technologies.

What Impact Will the Project Have in the Potential Markets? The GRI conducts an analysis of supply, demand, and prices each year, that serves as a major input to PAM. PAM estimates the impact of each proposal for funding on 65 end-use markets for energy, broken down by type of fuel and region. Expert judgment is included as PAM calculates a maximum market share and rate of market entry. From this process, a score is computed for each project on five criteria: consumer savings, new gas demand, energy saved, environmental and safety, and maintenance and reliability.

What Benefits and Costs Result from the Projected Market Impacts? The PAM software does this calculation based on the expected performance, cost data, and market projections.

What Is the Probability that the Calculated Benefits Will Be Achieved? Critical inputs are the probability of technical success and the probability of commercial success that must be determined judgmentally.

What Benefits (if any) Will Result if GRI Does Not Fund the Project? This process is repeated for four different GRI funding assumptions (zero funding, current, minimum or accelerated).

What Is the Expected Impact of GRI Funding? The impact of GRI funding at a given level is found by subtracting the impact at zero funding from the impact on any level of GRI funding.

The PAM software provides a ranking of all projects according to the highest expected cost/benefit. This list determines the GRI's preliminary budget, that is then submitted to four board-level advisory bodies for evaluation and final approval. These boards include representatives of scientific, consumer, industrial, regulatory commissioners and other interest groups, groups of technical and industry experts, and representatives of publicly owned gas utilities.

Success of PAM

PAM has successfully balanced subjective judgment and formal decision analysis methodology. The GRI has had 132 commercial successes out of 450 completed projects; more than twice the U.S. industry-wide average success rate for R&D projects. The benefit to cost ratio of GRI projects to date has been 6.8 to 1, representing $11 billion in consumer savings at a development cost of $1.6 billion. There is also greater gas availability at lower prices due to breakthrough technologies such as coal-bed gas and tight sands gas recovery. In addition, natural gas has increased its market share notably through the success of high efficiency gas furnaces to heat homes. The steel industry has also been a major beneficiary with new ladle preheaters, high-temperature heat exchangers and furnaces. Some 30 new technologies have saved $2 billion of the costs of transmission and distribution of natural gas.

Skeptics argue that it was easy to pick winners in an industry with so little previous R&D funding. However, there is a consensus that PAM was crucial to choosing the proper R&D mix for success, and can be credited with about half of the total benefits achieved. These benefits have been scrutinized by the U.S. General Accounting Office and the National Research Council, and have been estimated to be at least $11 billion and perhaps as high as $132 billion.

From W.M. Burnett, D.J. Monetta, and B.G. Silverman, How the Gas Research Institute (GRI) Helped Transform the U.S. Natural Gas Industry, *Interfaces* 23:1, 1993.

EXERCISES

1. Chad operated an automobile sales business. A major dealer in town offered Chad a one-time opportunity to help them sell some “trade-ins.” Under this deal, Chad could take one used car at a time from the dealer and try to sell it. If he sold it, he could take another. There were three cars they wanted Chad to try to sell (Table 3-3).

   The dealer concluded the offer as follows: “Chad, we have not dealt with you before, so we plan to proceed cautiously. I’m sure you understand. If you accept this deal, you must take the compact first. If you sell the compact, then you can choose either of the other two, or you can end the deal. If you sell the second car, then you can take the third if you wish.”

Table 3-3 | **DECISION ANALYSIS FOR CHAD'S AUTOMOBILE SALES BUSINESS**

Automobile	Chad's Commission (on Sale)	Chad's Selling Costs	Chad's Estimate of Probability of Sale
Compact	$900	$600	3/4
Standard	$1,500	$200	2/3
Luxury	$3,000	$600	50/50

   If he took a car, Chad would incur the selling costs in trying to sell the car but might not make the sale. What should he do?

2. Carlie needed a personal computer (PC) for school, but her budget was tight, so she decided on a used machine. After some searching, she was down to two possibilities. One she had found in a national franchised computer store, where she could purchase the PC for $800 with a 1-year guarantee. She was intrigued by a second possibility: a local charity store was offering a used machine for $500 that had been donated (exactly the same model as in the store).

Carlie talked to a computer repair specialist, who said the principal problem with this model of PC was the hard drive, which was prone to failure: he estimated that half of the PCs of this model and age would require a new drive. He offered to test the computer and check the condition of the drive for \$60. If the drive was no good, a new drive could be fitted for \$300 and would be guaranteed for 1 year. He added a qualification that his testing was not perfect; about 25% of drives that passed his testing failed soon afterward requiring a new drive (\$300) plus a service charge of \$100 for diagnosing the problem.

What should Carlie do?

from the wine room, the increased lot size, and the additional off-floor storage space.

The wine room was difficult to evaluate because Mike had never sold wine, and his existing customers were not wine buyers. The plans called for building a very attractive, "high-end" wine display and sales area, with the hope of attracting a new type of customer. If this was successful, these new customers would also buy beer and spirits. Mike reasoned that "there is no way sales can decline as a result of the addition of the wine room. Sales will probably increase, and if the wine room is accepted, it could be a great success." After some detailed discussions with a consultant, Mike translated this into a 10% chance of no change in net, a 50% chance of a 10% increase in net, a 30% chance of a 25% increase in net, and a 10% chance that the wine room would be a great success and would double the store's net.

The increased off-street parking space could only improve his drive-up business, although the improvement would be evident only at busy times. During these busy periods, Mike planned to assign additional staff to the drive-up window to serve two vehicles at a time, while additional vehicles waited off the street. Mike was convinced that his drive-up window would do more business but worried that some of this business would come from customers who would otherwise have walked into the store. Unsure about how many walk-in customers he would lose to drive-up or how often he would need additional staff at the drive-up window, he was unable to attach a single value to the increased lot size but thought a number of outcomes were possible. An increase in net of about 5% appeared most likely, although the increase could easily be more than this, whereas his "worst case" outcome, that he considered a fairly remote possibility, was no change in net. After discussion with a consultant, Mike settled on the following: a 50% chance of a 5% improvement in net, a 40% chance of a 10% increase, and only a 10% chance of no change in net as a result of the larger lot. Mike further reasoned that because drive-up customers also bought wine, the effect of the larger lot would multiply any increase in net that resulted from the wine room. That is, if the larger lot contributed an extra 10% to his "net" and the wine room contributed 50%, then the resulting increase in "net" would be 110 * 150%, or 165%.

With the additional off-floor storage space, Mike would be able to order larger quantities less often, and the wholesalers would pass on their transportation cost savings in the form of price discounts. With a larger warehouse area and more storage space, inventory would increase and, with it, inventory carrying costs. Mike noted, however, that product prices had increased steadily for many years and felt that these price increases, and the resulting inventory appreciation, would partially offset, and perhaps even totally offset, the increased inventory carrying costs. Taking into account the availability of discounts and the inventory appreciation, Mike believed that the additional off-floor storage space would add at least 5% to his eventual "net." Because these discounts were available on whatever volume of business he ended up with, this 5% increase would apply to "net" after adjustment for the new wine room and the added lot size.

Mike visited his banker and explained his general plans. He was delighted to find his banker supportive and that his credit was good. The bank would finance whatever he wanted to do with a 100% loan at 10% interest repayable monthly over 5 years. The monthly principal and interest payments were approximately as follows:

Loan Amount	Payment
$144,000	$3,060 per month
$320,000	$6,800 per month
$440,000	$9,348 per month
$1,000,000	$21,248 per month

Assignment

1. What should Mike do?

GILBERT & GILBERT

THIS CASE IS BASED ON A REAL SITUATION BUT HAS BEEN DISGUISED.

Barb Gilbert listened intently to her lawyer, Jen Miles: "I recommend you offer Thaddia Gladstone a settlement of $5,000 on condition that she sign a statement that her termination from Gilbert & Gilbert was not motivated by racial discrimination, that there has been no human rights law violation, and that the claimant drops this and all other claims against you."

Should Barb follow this recommendation?

GILBERT AND GILBERT

Barb and John Gilbert established Gilbert & Gilbert in 1988 just after they were married. Dr. John Gilbert was a obstetrics/gynecology specialist at the major hospital in town, where he spent long hours working in a successful practice. Barb came up with the concept of an up-market women's clothing store, and the two of them established the business as Gilbert & Gilbert, operating out of a rented space in the most prestigious shopping mall in town.

For the first 5 years, the business had flourished, but their success encouraged several new entrants. In 1993, one particular "high-end" fashion emporium opened nearby that particularly hurt Gilbert & Gilbert's business by "creaming off" the top of the market, leaving Gilbert & Gilbert in a midmarket niche. As competition grew, Gilbert & Gilbert began to struggle, and since 1994 the business had done no better than break even.

The Gilberts were divorced in 1992. The business (at that time highly profitable) was transferred to Barb as a major part of the property settlement. As the business stagnated after 1994, Barb had invested her own money to keep operating. She had also tried to find ways to cut costs.

THADDIA GLADSTONE

Barb Gilbert had initially hired three full-time sales people. As the store prospered, she had hired one additional full-time employee and then hired Thaddia Gladstone as a full-time salesperson in June 1990. Two of the full-time salespersons had left voluntarily (in 1994 and 1995) and had been replaced by part-time people (mostly students from the local university). Replacing a full-time person with part-timers saved approximately $5,000 annually in salary and benefits costs.

In January 1997, seeking to further cut costs, Barb had "restructured" the operation. In this restructuring, she proposed to operate with one full-time manager (herself) and two full-time assistant managers, with the remainder of the sales staff as part-timers. This meant that she had to let go one full-time employee. Thaddia was the most recently hired of the three remaining full-time employees, so she offered Thaddia a part-time position with the associated reduction in salary and loss of benefits. When Thaddia refused this offer, she was paid $2,250, representing 6 weeks' severance pay (according to the statutory guideline of 1 week's pay for each complete year of employment), and terminated.

THE LAWSUIT

On March 12, 1997, Thaddia Gladstone filed suit against Barb Gilbert operating as Gilbert & Gilbert. In this suit, Thaddia claimed that her dismissal was racially motivated (she was the only nonwhite full-time employee that Gilbert & Gilbert had ever had) and that she had been unable to find work since her termination. In the suit, she asked for restitution to her full-time position, back pay and benefits in the amount of $1,500 per month from date of dismissal, $15,000 in punitive damages for violation of the human rights law (which provided for damages for acts of discrimination based on race), and payment of her legal costs.

Barb hired Jen Miles, a junior associate with the most prestigious law firm in town, to advise her on a response to the suit. Miles quickly assessed the situation, and Barb was gratified to learn that she had, in Miles' opinion, behaved quite correctly. Corporate "restructuring" as a result of financial pressure was a well-established reason for employee terminations, and "last-in, first-out" was a well-established method for deciding which employees were to be let go. Miles suggested that Barb had a very good chance of successfully defending the suit, but it would take at least 1 year for the case to be heard. Miles estimated Barb would have to pay an additional $3,000 in legal fees to defend this action, and there was little chance that these costs could be recovered from the plaintiff.

A second option was to offer Thaddia her job back immediately, with back pay. Miles suggested that if this offer were made, there was almost no chance that the case would continue, and the claim for punitive damages would, therefore, be dropped.

The third option was to offer Thaddia an "enhanced" redundancy payment in return for her dropping the suit and waiving any claim resulting from a human rights law violation. Miles suggested an amount of $5,000, but any offer could be made: presumably, the higher the offer, the more likely it was to be accepted.

Finally, Miles noted that she was fairly comfortable with the legal aspects of the case but that she could call in a senior partner to review the situation and provide a second opinion. She estimated this review would cost $700.

Miles concluded by recommending the third option but asking Barb to let her have a decision as soon as possible so that, if necessary, a response to the suit could be filed or a second legal opinion could be sought promptly.

Assignment

1. What are Barb's options?
2. Should Barb seek a second opinion?
3. What should she do?

RESEARCH AND DEVELOPMENT AT ICI: ANTHRAQUINONE

WITH ACKNOWLEDGMENT TO SIDNEY W. HESS.

Anthraquinone (AQ) was an agent used to reduce pollution in the effluent of a pulp mill. The addition of AQ to the waste stream precipitated out certain paper and pulp waste products, allowing them to be filtered out of the mill effluent.

AQ was produced by distilling coal tar, a by-product of coke production at a steel works, with the result that the amount of AQ produced was highly dependent on the demand for steel. AQ had uses in dyestuffs as well as pulp mill waste control, but developing new uses for AQ was contingent on development of a new process to manufacture AQ synthetically. BASF, one of ICI's competitors, was known to have developed such a process.

ICI's research division had discovered a new, but unpatentable, use for AQ. Without its own process to synthesize AQ, this discovery was unexploitable and would only benefit BASF, which would have an uncatchable head start. ICI had to decide whether to accelerate research on a process to synthesize AQ and develop the commercial application or to terminate the on-going modest R&D effort. A decision to go forward would have to be approved by the board.

COSTS AND BENEFITS OF R&D

The costs and benefits of R&D were subject to considerable uncertainty. If successful, the benefit of the new venture into AQ was estimated to have a net present value of $25 million, plus or minus 50%. If the venture was unsuccessful, even after successful process development and best efforts at commercial development, a break-even outcome was expected.

The research expenses to find a new process were estimated at $0.8 million plus or minus 25%; if successful, this research would be followed by process development expenses of $3.0 million plus or minus 25%. Research on the new production process would need to be accompanied by some preliminary market development at a cost of $200,000 plus or minus 25%. If this initial market development suggested significant market potential, preliminary commercial development would have to be undertaken at an estimated cost of $0.5 million plus or minus 25%. Additional commercial development expenses of $1.0 million plus or minus 25% would be necessary after the board approved full-scale commercialization of the product.

QUANTIFYING THE UNCERTAINTIES

Any R&D project is subject to a high degree of uncertainty. The project team assessed the conditional probabilities for the AQ R&D project as follows:

Probability that research will find a new AQ synthesis process: 0.6 ± 0.15

Probability that initial market development will indicate a significant market: 0.6 ± 0.15

Probability that the board will approve final commercial development (if market and initial commercial development are successful): 0.8 ± 0.2

Probability of final commercial success: 0.8 ± 0.2

Assignment

1. Develop a model to assess the desirability of investment in research on anthraquinone.

LAYING OIL AND GAS PIPELINES IN THE NORTH SEA

WITH ACKNOWLEDGMENT TO CHRIS CHAPMAN.

The oil fields of the North Sea are connected to the mainland by a series of pipelines that carry crude oil and natural gas from the production wells to the on shore refining and distribution facilities. Firms laying these undersea pipelines have many decisions to make under conditions of significant risk.

Five major activities are involved in laying an underwater pipeline: design of the pipeline, procurement of the pipe, delivery of the pipe, coating the pipe, and laying the pipe. Pipeline design and pipe procurement are relatively straightforward, and delivery of the pipe has not historically posed many problems for most suppliers, although the promised delivery dates for some suppliers are subject to greater uncertainty than those of others.

The 32-inch diameter steel pipe is coated with 6 inches of concrete and anticorrosive materials to protect the pipe from corrosion before sinking to the sea floor. Coating the pipe involves three main sources of uncertainty: when a coating yard will be available, how productive the yard will be on a normal shift basis, and whether overtime or second-shift work will be required (with obvious cost implications). Coating can generally be arranged in advance, and rarely does a shortage of coated pipe interfere with the pipe laying. Laying the pipe, however, provides many opportunities for management decision making under conditions of significant risk.

PIPE-LAYING PROCESS

A pipeline is placed using a large floating vessel known as a **lay barge**. Coated pipe sections are transported from shore to the lay barge, welded together on the barge, and then dropped slowly to the sea floor. The lay barge inches forward as the pipe sections are added to the working end of the pipeline by winching itself forward on a series of cables connected to anchors. These anchors are placed in front of the barge by tug boats: as the barge closes in on one of the anchors, the tug picks up the anchor and moves it farther in front of the barge. This repositioning of anchors is an ongoing process and a sufficient number of anchors are used (typically three to four on each corner of the barge) to ensure that the barge can maintain its position while one or two anchors are being repositioned by the tugs.

The pipeline is strung over the back of the barge under sufficient tension (sustained via the leading anchors) to maintain the pipeline in a smooth "S" curve, even in water as deep as several hundred meters. High seas pose several problems. If the waves are too high, the tugs may not be able to pick up the anchors, or the lay barge may be moving up and down so much that the strain on the pipeline becomes too great and a pipe **buckle** becomes likely. When a buckle occurs, the pipe kinks and drops to the ocean floor, filling with water, mud, and other debris resulting from the suction of the breached pipe. In the past, a pipe buckle led to abandonment of the pipe and starting over, but repairing a pipe buckle is now possible although a major delay in pipe laying. To try to reduce the likelihood of buckles, several different types of lay barges are available that are designed to operate at different wave heights, allowing the choice of barges to be tailored to the sea conditions in the lay area.

A standard lay barge can operate in waves up to 1.6 meters in height, whereas some larger barges can operate in waves up to 5 meters high as long as they have anchor-handling tugs that can also work in seas that rough. However, the larger barges are significantly more expensive than the standard lay barges. A 1.6-meter barge and associated equipment costs about $250,000 per day to operate, and the costs for a 5-meter barge are about $500,000 per day.

Lay barges must be contracted well in advance and cannot be switched once pipe laying begins, but they sometimes are available during the season as jobs finish early or barges have some idle time between contracts.

A pipeline can be laid using one lay barge or two. If

one barge is used, it starts at one end and lays until it reaches the destination of the pipe. If a second barge is to be used, the barges start at opposite ends of the pipeline route; when they meet in the middle, the pipeline is joined. If an additional lay barge can be found, it may be possible to accelerate a single-barge pipe laying project that is running late by adding a second barge starting from the destination.

RISK FACTORS IN LAYING THE PIPE

Laying Rate

A prime risk factor is the weather, specifically, the wave heights from day to day. In March, a standard barge may be unable to lay any pipe, or it may achieve 31 lay days, depending on the sea conditions in the lay area. Sea conditions generally improve toward midsummer, with a maximum expectation of about 25 operating days per month in July, and then decline to November conditions that are comparable to those in March. The winter months are so rough in the North Sea that a standard barge cannot function.

Historical weather records provide an assessment of operating days available in each month. Approximate probabilities of the number of operating or lay days in each month for a standard barge are shown in Exhibit 1. For example, the probability of having 20 lay days in July is 0.2; the probability of having at least 20 days in July is 0.9.

A standard lay barge can lay an average of 3 kilometers of pipe per operating day, thus, Exhibit 1 provides estimates of the probability of laying a given number of kilometers in any of the given months. The larger, newer barges, although generally able to operate in higher sea states, involve uncertain lay rates in the range of 1 to 5 kilometers per day.

Pipe Buckles

One or more pipe buckles during the laying season are possible. The probability of a pipe buckle in each month is indicated in Exhibit 2. When laying is in progress, buckles are most likely in high seas, but laying is less likely to be attempted when seas are high. Consequently, the chance of a buckle in April is greater than the chance of a buckle in March because more laying is likely to be attempted in April. However, the chance of a buckle drops off again in May because of the improved weather conditions despite the fact that laying activity likely increases. This trend continues through June and July. The pattern reverses itself during the fall months as bad winter weather approaches.

Repairing a pipe buckle usually takes 20 to 30 working days. Therefore, buckle repair can be equated to an equivalent loss of kilometers of pipe laid (see Exhibit 3). For example, once a buckle occurs, a standard barge has a 0.7 chance that it will lose 75 km or more of pipe laying capacity.

A secondary risk is created if a buckle occurs and repair is attempted. Part of the repair process involves sending a "pig" through the pipeline to clear it before raising the end. If the pig sticks in the pipeline, the hydrostatic pressure in the pipeline is raised to pop the pig through, but this creates a risk of bursting the pipeline. If this happens, the repair process is lengthened considerably.

OTHER RISKS

Because the pipe laying equipment is contracted from other companies, there is always a risk that it may not be available when needed. For example, if a lay barge gets behind on a previous contract, it may not be available for the planned start date of the next project. Also, using

Exhibit 1 | LAY DAYS AVAILABLE EACH MONTH FOR A STANDARD LAY BARGE

Days	March	April	May	June	July	August	September	October	November
0	0.3	0.2	0.1				0.1	0.3	0.2
5	0.4	0.3	0.2	0.1		0.1	0.2	0.4	0.3
10	0.2	0.3	0.3	0.1		0.1	0.3	0.2	0.3
15	0.1	0.2	0.2	0.2	0.1	0.2	0.2	0.1	0.2
20			0.1	0.3	0.2	0.3	0.1		
25			0.1	0.2	0.4	0.2	0.1		
30				0.1	0.3	0.1			

Exhibit 2 **PROBABILITY OF A PIPE BUCKLE IN EACH MONTH**

	March	April	May	June	July	August	September	October	November
Buckle	0.05	0.07	0.05	0.03	0.01	0.05	0.07	0.05	0.03
No buckle	0.95	0.93	0.95	0.97	0.99	0.95	0.93	0.95	0.97

a second lay barge in a second season to overcome first-season delays could become necessary if project delays occur in the first season; however, unless substantial retainers are paid, a barge may not be available for unplanned additional seasons and replacements may not be easy to find. If a pipeline is completed earlier than necessary, there will be a high opportunity cost associated with the idle capital, but if a pipeline is finished late, the opportunity cost of the nonproductive platforms and wells may be very much greater.

Start dates have other risks associated with them. For example, the ability to start construction could depend upon obtaining government approval. Delaying the start date by a few weeks could push the project into the next season with severe cost implications.

Laying an offshore pipeline may involve crossing other existing pipelines. In this situation there is a considerable risk that the lay barge's anchors will damage the other pipelines. If that happened, the equipment onsite would have to be diverted from the project to repair the damage to the existing pipeline, resulting in delays for the project and possibly payments to compensate the owners of the damaged pipeline.

Although the risks associated with offshore pipe laying are complex, an analysis of the risk is an essential part of a good project plan. Assumptions will likely have to be made to make the analysis manageable. Useful models will facilitate checking the sensitivity of the analysis to the assumptions (by allowing the analysis to be quickly repeated under different assumptions).

Assignment

You have been given responsibility for the task of laying 350 kilometers of oil pipeline in the North Sea during the summer of 1995. This pipeline will carry crude oil from a new production platform in the North Sea to the Scottish mainland: the oil platform is expected to begin production in November 1995, and there will be substantial penalties if the pipeline is not completed by this date.

Lay barge and tug availabilities for the 1995 season are currently very good but are expected to be taken up very quickly. For the next 2 weeks, at least two standard (1.6 meter) barges are available for 1995, as well as one large (5 meter) barge (in 1993, this large barge achieved a 2.7 kilometers/day average lay rate on days when it was able to operate).

1. What decisions will you have to make?
2. Outline one or more models that you will use to help you to make these decisions. What additional information will you need to build your models?
3. What criteria will you use to make your decisions?
4. How will you assess the "riskiness" of your plan of action? (Be sure to explain "riskiness.")

Exhibit 3 **DISTANCE LOST FOR A BUCKLE REPAIR BY A STANDARD LAY BARGE**

Lost Kilometer for Repair (R)	P(R)
65	0.1
70	0.2
75	0.3
80	0.3
85	0.1

LISTERINE LOZENGES

THIS CASE WAS PREPARED BY MR. T. MOSS UNDER THE DIRECTION OF PROFESSOR ANDREW GRINDLAY, THE UNIVERSITY OF WESTERN ONTARIO. REVISION BY PETER C. BELL, 1997.

Warner-Lambert Canada Limited was considering introducing throat lozenges to the Canadian pharmaceutical market. Lozenges distributed under the company brand name had sold well in the United States and become a profitable venture. The lozenges were designed to provide temporary relief from sore throats caused by coughs and colds.

One of the products sold throughout the world by the parent company and its subsidiaries was Listerine Antiseptic, a well known mouthwash. It has been on the market for many years and was highly regarded by both dealers and consumers. Distributed through both food and drug stores, Listerine mouthwash held nearly 40% of the mouthwash market.

The U.S. parent had successfully test marketed a throat lozenge under the Listerine brand name, and national distribution was undertaken the following year, leading to an early 9.5% market share.After the addition of orange and lemon-mint flavors, Listerine rose to second in throat lozenge sales, with 16.5% of the total U.S. market.

Mr. R.T. Demarco, Product Manager in the Consumer Products Division of Warner-Lambert Canada Limited, decided to investigate the possibilities of manufacturing and distributing Listerine Throat Lozenges in Canada. Chris Seymour, Assistant Brand Manager in the Consumer Products Division, was assigned the task of recommending to the company an action plan for the proposed product.

THE MARKET

Seymour's first step was to investigate the throat lozenge market, where he found about 40 brands of **proprietary throat lozenges** were being sold. These nonsubscription products did not contain any active drug ingredient; rather, they contained ingredients that relieved throat irritation temporarily without specifically acting on the cause of the irritation. Consequently, there were no unique product claims because all brands offered the same benefit (i.e., temporary relief from sore throat pain). About 85% of the throat lozenges available were sold through drug stores, whereas the remainder were distributed through food stores or other mass merchandisers. Sales of these types of lozenges had increased 55% in the past 3 years.

PACKAGING AND PRICING

There were several different types of packages in the marketplace (Exhibit 2, p. 72), with the number of throat lozenges per package ranging from 9 to 50. The price range for the main competitors was $2.95 to $4.45.

Listerine Throat Lozenges manufactured and sold in the United States were packaged 18 to a pocket-sized box. The lozenge itself was a candy disk about ¾ inch in diameter and about ¼ inch thick. A "bunch wrapper" was used to "bunch" foil around the lozenge. The wrapped lozenges were placed in holes in a rectangular piece of cardboard, a backing was applied, and finally a plastic bubble was placed over each lozenge. This process was referred to as "blister packaging." Each card held six lozenges, and there were three cards per box. The user, after withdrawing the card from the box, simply pressed the plastic bubble, and the lozenge dropped from the back of the card.

Warner-Lambert management believed the product introduced into Canada should be the same product as was being sold in the United States. This would eliminate any product development cost and allow the Canadian market to be supplied initially by the U.S. parent if desired. The necessary proprietary number was obtained to allow distribution of the lozenges in food stores. Warner-Lambert expected to obtain quick, wide penetration by capitalizing on the existing distribution channels between the company salespeople and the food stores that handled Listerine mouthwash.

Demarco was in general agreement with the proposals but urged Seymour to find out if the U.S. parent could indeed supply the Canadian market. The U.S. production planner informed Seymour that they could supply a limited quantity of the lozenges, bunch wrapped and inserted into cards. To print the Canadian proprietary number and have bilingual printing, however, it would be necessary to box the lozenges in Canada.

Seymour also learned that the Canadian plant could manufacture the lozenges, but the plant did not have the specialized equipment necessary to bunch wrap and insert the lozenges into the holes in the cards. They did have, however, the equipment required to print the boxes and insert the cards in the boxes. Ten months would be required for delivery and installation of the specialized equipment for bunching and blister packaging.

THE TEST MARKET

Warner-Lambert often conducted a test market study before introducing a new product. Seymour realized that a national campaign could not be undertaken until next fall, but time and facilities existed to conduct a test market in one area this winter if management thought it was desirable. Management chose to price the product in direct competition with the market leader and accordingly set the price of Listerine lozenges at $4.45 per package of 18. Retailers would purchase the lozenges from Warner-Lambert for $2.75 a box. Seymour originally estimated that test market sales would be $302,500 (net factory value), which would represent 12.8% of the test market for lozenges. Because they could not have the necessary equipment for the test period, the blister packaged lozenges would have to be imported from the United States and would be boxed in Canada in boxes with bilingual labeling. The cost of the test was estimated to be as shown in Exhibit 1.

The lozenge cost was fixed because none of the imported product could be salvaged if it was not sold. Seymour used three volume estimates to represent the possible sales outcomes. He defined a successful test market sales of 110,000 boxes ($302,500) of lozenges, and he assessed the chance of achieving this level at 70%. He realized that even if they did not sell 110,000 boxes during the test year, they might sell a sufficient amount to label the test as inconclusive. He believed there was a 20% chance that an inconclusive test having sales of 90,000 boxes ($247,500) would occur. He would label the test a failure if sales were as low as 60,000 boxes ($165,000).

To give the product an adequate test and to be operating efficiently during the cold season, it would be necessary to have the product on the store shelves by the end of October. This would require shipments from the factory to start by September 16. J. O'Keefe, Sales Manager, informed Seymour that the very latest that they could begin to take orders for September delivery was August 12; this meant that July 15 would have to be the deadline for a decision to test market the product. As long as the order for the bunch wrapped and carded lozenges was sent to the United States before that date, there would be sufficient time to have them packaged in bilingual boxes in Canada and delivered to the stores for the fall cough/cold season.

EQUIPMENT DECISION

The machinery necessary for Canadian production would cost $440,000, with an additional $40,000 for installation expenses. If the order was placed in October, the equipment would be ready to produce the lozenges for the introduction of the national campaign the next fall. Equipment ordered in October would require a deposit of $125,000, which would be forfeited if the order was cancelled before the end of February. After February, the order could not be cancelled. Seymour believed that by the end of February, the company would know whether the test market was going to be successful, inconclusive, or a failure.

An alternative to ordering in October was to wait until the end of February, when the test market outcome could be determined. Under this alternative, the equipment would not be ready for the start of the fall campaign, and if Warner-Lambert decided to go national, 85% of the first-year sales would have to be imported. The total variable cost to the Canadian division for lozenges imported from the United States was $1.40 per box, but this could be reduced to $0.70 if the product were made entirely in Canada. Because Warner-Lambert Canada based their decisions on the profit contribution to the Canadian division only and because the U.S. division would guarantee to supply only 85% of the first year demand, and none after that, it was decided that the equipment should be ordered no later than February 28 if a national campaign was to be launched. In addition, the machine manufacturer would not guarantee current price and delivery terms beyond February.

Exhibit 1 | **COST OF TEST MARKET**

Advertising	$220,500
Promotion	100,000
Research	50,000
Direct Selling	25,000
Direct Operating	23,000
Lozenge Cost (Including Packaging)	154,000
Total	**$572,500**

PROFIT POTENTIAL

Seymour estimated before the test market that there was a 50% chance of achieving high sales of 800,000 boxes from the national campaign. He believed medium sales of 650,000 boxes and low sales of 400,000 boxes had a 30% and 20% chance of occurrence, respectively. National introduction would increase fixed costs due to advertising, research, and direct operating and selling expenses. Initial forecasts suggested these costs would be approximately $1,275,000 per year; this did not include equipment or test marketing costs. The product would be dropped after 1 year if national sales were medium or low. If the product reached the high sales forecast in the first year, Seymour thought it was conservative to assume that the level would be maintained for the expected 10-year life of the equipment.

The test market results would allow Seymour to make more accurate estimates for the sales outcome of the national campaign. He did not think there was any chance of achieving medium or high sales nationally if the test market sales volume was considered a failure. On the other hand, a successful test would suggest a 90% chance for high sales nationally and a 10% chance for medium sales; an inconclusive test result would suggest a 65% chance of low national sales and a 35% chance for high sales.

Seymour learned that the new equipment had no other use and would have negligible value if the new product was dropped. He decided to make an initial projection on a before-tax basis because all the revenues and expenses, with the exception of the equipment purchase, were period flows and were subject to the same tax rate. If the analysis did not make the optimum course of action obvious, he planned to recalculate considering the tax effects.

At the same time, Seymour realized that $1 received in the future was of less value than $1 received immediately. Because the company looked for new projects that returned 10% to 15% after taxes, he decided to discount the before-tax income figures for the national campaign at 22% (Exhibit 3). With these assumptions, he thought he could determine the best strategy for the new product.

Assignment

1. Develop an action plan for Mr. Demarco.

Exhibit 2 | **SAMPLE OF THROAT LOZENGE MARKET PACKAGING AND PRICE**

Product	Package Type	No. of Lozenges	Retail Price ($)	Retail Price per Lozenge ($)
Aspergum	Carton	16	5.27	0.33
Bentasil	Plastic bag	20	2.99	0.15
Bradosol	Plastic case	20	2.67	0.13
Cepacol	Carton	24	3.53	0.15
Cepastat	Carton	16	3.55	0.22
Chloraseptic	Carton	18	3.43	0.19
Dequadin	Tube carton	20	3.43	0.17
Fisherman's Friend	Bag	22	1.33	0.06
Ricola	Bag	19	1.96	0.10
Ricola	Tube	9	0.96	0.11
Strepsils	Carton	24	3.67	0.15
Sucrets Extra Strength	Plastic case	18	3.27	0.18
Sucrets Regular Strength	Plastic case	18	2.77	0.15
Valda	Tin can	50	4.76	0.10

Exhibit 3 **LISTERINE LOZENGES PROFIT CONTRIBUTION FROM NATIONAL SALES**

Equipment Ordered October	Sales High	 Medium	 Low
Sales (boxes)	800,000	650,000	400,000
Contribution margin per box ($2.75–0.70)	$2.05	$2.05	$2.05
Contribution margin	1,640,000	1,332,500	820,000
Fixed costs	1,275,000	1,275,000	1,275,000
Profit	365,000	575,000	(455,000)
Years	10	1	1
Present value discount factor at 22%	3.923	0.82	0.82
Present value of expected profit	1,431,895	47,195	(373,100)

Equipment Ordered February	Sales High	 Medium	 Low
Year 1			
Sales (boxes)	800,000	650,000	400,000
Contribution margin per box year 1 ($2.75 – ([0.85 * 1.40] + [0.15 * 0.70])	$1.455	$1.455	$1.455
Contribution margin year 1	1,164,000	945,750	582,000
Fixed costs	1,275,000	1,275,000	1,275,000
Profit year 1	(111,000)	(329,250)	(693,000)
Present value of expected year 1 profit	(91,020)	(269,985)	(568,260)
Years 2 to 10			
Contribution margin per box	$2.05		
Contribution margin per year	1,640,000		
Fixed costs	1,275,000		
Profit	365,000		
Present value discount factor at 22%	3.104		
Present value of expected profit (years 2–10)	1,132,960		
Present value of expected profit	1,041,940	(269,985)	(568,260)

ST. SWITHIN'S HOSPITAL

BY PROFESSORS PETER C. BELL AND CHRISTOPH HEAHLING VON LANZENAUER, WHO WISH TO THANK DR. ANN KIRBY, MD, FRCP(C), FOR HER HELP WITH THE MEDICAL FACTS IN THE CASE. STUDENTS ARE CAUTIONED NOT TO USE THE FACTS PRESENTED IN THIS CASE AS A BASIS FOR PERSONAL MEDICAL DECISION MAKING.

Dr. Susan Smith, Director of the Internal Medicine Department at St. Swithin's Hospital, had just read an article in the *New England Journal of Medicine* on the use of impedance plethysmography (IPG) for the diagnosis of deep vein thrombosis (DVT) (314[13]:823-828). St. Swithin's did not have the equipment or the trained staff to perform this diagnostic test; Dr. Smith wondered whether she should recommend that St. Swithin's acquire this capability.

Dr. Smith decided to review the options available at St. Swithin's Hospital for the diagnosis or treatment, or both, of DVT and to use this review as the basis for a recommendation on the acquisition of IPG capability.

DEEP VEIN THROMBOSIS

DVT is a blood clot in the major veins deep within the leg, resulting in clinical symptoms that include a red, swollen, and painful leg. DVT was difficult to diagnose, and finding the precise location of the clot was even more difficult. If the clot was in the upper leg or lower abdomen, the DVT was more serious than if the clot was located below the knee.

The difficulty of clinical diagnosis of DVT resulted from the fact that many other conditions caused similar symptoms (including sprains and tears, cellulitis, phlebitis, and even gout); in fact, only 40% of patients with the clinical symptoms of DVT actually had DVT.

Dr. Smith was well aware that an untreated DVT could lead to serious complications; in about half the patients with untreated DVT, the clot dislodged and traveled to the lungs (pulmonary embolus [PE]). For about one in four patients who had an untreated PE, the consequences were fatal. If the patient survived the PE, only minor lung damage remained, which rarely resulted in further problems for the patient. Because of the risk of fatality from PE, it was imperative that a patient with DVT be treated promptly.

TREATMENT OF DEEP VEIN THROMBOSIS

The treatment for DVT was anticoagulant therapy with the drug heparin. Heparin treatment reduced both the likelihood that a blood clot would break loose and cause a PE and the severity of any PE that did occur, resulting in a much lower mortality rate from treated PE.

Heparin treatment, however, was itself risky because anticoagulant therapy could cause internal bleeding. In about 1% of patients on heparin therapy, bleeding occurred in the brain (a cerebrovascular accident [CVA]), resulting in a brain haemorrhage that could be fatal or lead to varying degrees of disability. Dr. Smith recalled that a heparin-induced CVA would occur within 72 hours of first treatment with heparin. About 90% of patients with CVAs survived, but about 60% of those surviving would have serious long-term disability. For the remainder, any resulting disability would be minor or temporary.

The risk of CVA made Dr. Smith reluctant to prescribe heparin treatment unless she was reasonably sure the patient had DVT. Further diagnostic testing was required to improve the diagnosis of DVT.

DIAGNOSTIC TESTING FOR DEEP VEIN THROMBOSIS

Doppler Test

St. Swithin's Hospital had the capability to conduct a Doppler test, which Dr. Smith could use to try to diagnose the patient's actual condition. If this test produced a positive indication of DVT, then treatment would be given, because treatment of an identified DVT was the only acceptable standard of medical practice. The Doppler study was a safe, noninvasive test that did not involve puncturing the patient's skin or administering any drugs to the patient.

Doppler studies had been used in the diagnosis of DVT for many years, and the average accuracy of the test was well known, as was the fact that skilled testing physicians were able to achieve above-average accuracy. St. Swithin's, an affiliate of a major medical school, expected to be able to achieve better-than-average results with Doppler testing. The reported average sensitivity of the Doppler test, which is the probability of testing positive if the patient had DVT, was 0.83, and the average specificity, which is the probability of testing negative if the patient did not have DVT, was 0.86.

Venography

Venography also was available at St. Swithin's Hospital and was routinely used to investigate circulatory problems. When used as a test for DVT, venography was accurate but risky.

When venography was used to detect DVT, a contrasting dye was injected into a vein in the leg (i.e., the test was "invasive") and observed using x-rays. However, because DVT often was the result of a blood clot forming at a point at which a deep vein had been damaged, the puncture of the vein during venography could actually induce DVT in a patient who did not have DVT. Although this happened to only about 3% of cases, it was serious because the patient who exhibited the symptoms of DVT but did not have DVT would test negative on venography. DVT induced by the venography, which would appear after the venography, would remain undetected and untreated, and thus the patient could subsequently develop a fatal PE.

Venography was a tricky test; about 9% of the time, the test was "nondiagnostic"; that is, the physician performing the test could not find a vein to inject the dye, or the dye would not run into the correct veins to enable the DVT to be seen on the x-rays. Whether the test was diagnostic did not affect the probability of venography-induced DVT.

When a clear venography test was obtained (i.e., the test was "diagnostic"), it was error free (i.e, both 100% sensitive and 100% specific). If the venography test produced a positive indication of DVT or was nondiagnostic, then treatment would be given, because treatment of an identified DVT or a suspected but unconfirmed DVT was the only acceptable standard of medical practice. Dr. Smith had shied away from venography because of the risks of induced DVT but wondered whether the greater accuracy of venography over Doppler made taking these risks worthwhile.

Impedance Plethysmography

IPG was a new diagnostic test for suspected DVT that also was noninvasive and therefore perfectly safe. The potential of IPG resulted from its ability to locate the more dangerous DVTs; that is, those in the veins above the knee.

In the study reported in the *New England Journal of Medicine*, 426 patients with the clinical symptoms of DVT were tested using IPG; 289 patients tested "negative" and were not treated (none of these patients had a PE in the following 6 months). The remaining 137 patients had a "positive" IPG test; these 137 patients were carefully retested using more complex tests that were only practical in research studies. These tests confirmed the presence of DVT in 126 of these patients. (In the other 11 cases, the cause of the abnormal IPG was identified and was determined not to be DVT.)

Patients who tested "negative" in the study apparently did not have DVT or had less serious DVT (in the veins below the knee); in neither situation were these patients liable to develop PE. All the patients who had a DVT that was likely to produce a PE (above the knee) tested "positive" with the IPG test.

This test appeared to be very good at identifying patients who were at risk of PE and should be started on anticoagulant therapy.

PLAN OF ACTION

Dr. Smith had several options when confronted by a patient with the clinical symptoms of DVT. Should she administer treatment immediately on the chance that DVT was present and accept the risk that the treatment itself might cause serious complications or death? Should she first order Doppler testing or venography? What about IPG, if it were available?

Should only a single test be used? Was there a case for multiple tests? Were Doppler and venography sufficient for St. Swithin's, or would IPG render these tests obsolete? Should the hospital invest in IPG equipment? Dr. Smith wondered whether she should or could make a case to the administrators of St. Swithin's to persuade them to invest in this new procedure.

To review diagnostic and treatment strategies, Dr. Smith thought about her own clinical experience with DVT and of her objectives in treating patients. She wondered whether her criteria were consistent with the patient's objectives. In addition, in this age of increasing malpractice litigation, the hospital was most concerned that patients subjected to risky treatments or tests be correctly handled. Was there a single diagnostic treatment plan that optimized everyone's criterion? How sensitive was the best diagnostic treatment plan to the choice of criterion?

Was there a general treatment plan that was best for all patients? Dr. Smith's clinical experience led her to believe that the 40% probability that a patient with the clinical symptoms of DVT actually had DVT was best interpreted as an average taken over a large number of cases. After examining an individual with DVT symptoms, Dr. Smith thought that she would be able to assign a more accurate probability that the patient actually had DVT. This probability might be higher or lower than 40%. If Dr. Smith's assigned probability differed from 40%, did this call for the use of a different diagnostic/treatment plan?

Cost was not normally a major factor in determining how a patient was tested or treated, although it could be a secondary factor if tests or treatments were equally effective.

Finally, Dr. Smith consulted her medical library for more precise estimates of the likelihood of PE and of the effects of heparin treatment on reducing both the probability of PE and the mortality rate of a PE if one occurred. She found a recent journal that contained a table of best-estimate data that had been collected by pooling an enormous amount of clinical evidence (reproduced in Exhibit 1). She wondered whether these data could help her in developing her strategy.

Assignment

1. What are the options?
2. What criterion should be used to decide?
3. Is the IPG test "better" than the Doppler test?

PROBABILITIES

Dr. Smith recognized that some probabilities needed to be developed. She needed to know:

1. The probability that the Doppler test would yield a "positive" result
2. The probability that a patient actually had DVT given a "positive" Doppler test
3. The probability that a patient did not have DVT given a "positive" Doppler test in addition to:
4. The probability that the Doppler test would yield a "negative" result
5. The probability that a patient actually had DVT given a "negative" Doppler test
6. The probability that a patient did not have DVT given a "negative" Doppler test

The testing of 1000 patients using the sensitivity and specificity probabilities presented in the case leads to the structure in Exhibit 2.

Exhibit 1 **OBSERVED PROBABILITIES AND MORTALITIES FOR DEEP VEIN THROMBOSIS**

Probability of:	
Pulmonary embolus (PE) without heparin treatment	0.50
PE while on heparin treatment	0.16
Heparin-induced cerebrovascular accident	0.01
Probability of:	
Death from untreated PE	0.25
Death from PE while on heparin treatment	0.01

Exhibit 2 **DOPPLER TEST SENSITIVITY AND SPECIFICITY PROBABILITIES**

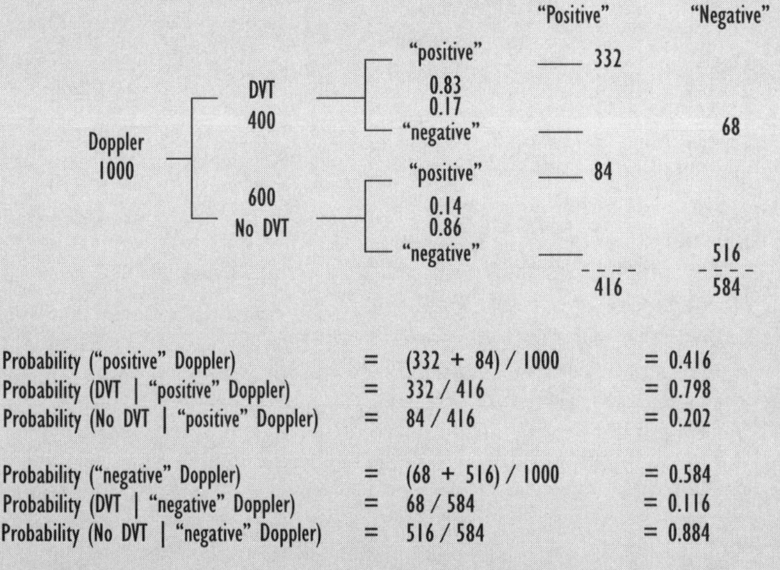

Probability ("positive" Doppler)	=	(332 + 84) / 1000	= 0.416
Probability (DVT | "positive" Doppler)	=	332 / 416	= 0.798
Probability (No DVT | "positive" Doppler)	=	84 / 416	= 0.202
Probability ("negative" Doppler)	=	(68 + 516) / 1000	= 0.584
Probability (DVT | "negative" Doppler)	=	68 / 584	= 0.116
Probability (No DVT | "negative" Doppler)	=	516 / 584	= 0.884

BRENT-HARBRIDGE DEVELOPMENTS, INC.

Sheila Harbridge, Chief Executive Officer of Brent-Harbridge Developments (B-H), had just received confirmation of several upcoming property auctions. B-H was currently "asset short" after some successful recent disposals, which made Sheila keenly interested in three of the properties being auctioned. She needed to acquire some more development properties; her task now was to prepare a bidding strategy.

BRENT-HARBRIDGE DEVELOPMENTS

B-H developments purchased real property that they developed or, in some instances, resold undeveloped. Over the past few years, they had prospered by being successful at acquiring properties "at the right price." A major source of acquisitions for B-H were the auctions conducted from time to time to unload various properties that had not sold through realtors. Properties that could be purchased at these auctions included commercial and residential buildings that had been declared "abandoned" by the mortgage holder or seized for back taxes and land that had been acquired for various government projects but that was now surplus.

B-H specialized in commercial and residential properties that they attempted to purchase at auction, develop or renovate, and then resell. At any one time, B-H held an inventory of 10 to 20 properties in various stages of development.

UPCOMING AUCTIONS

Three auctions during the next few weeks attracted Sheila's attention. The properties to be auctioned and their values as estimated by B-H's appraiser Tim Peters are listed in Exhibit 1.

The auctions were to be conducted by "sealed bids," in which buyers had to submit their bids in sealed envelopes by 9:00 a.m. on the day of the sale. At noon on the day of the sale, the auctioneer provided a report that listed the bid received by each bidder and confirmed that the property had been sold to the highest bidder. In the case of a tie (which was rare), a coin flip decided the winner. Because the bidding data were disclosed to the public, B-H maintained a file summarizing previous auctions. Exhibits 2 through 4 (pp. 79–82) summarize data from the last 51 property auctions, which involved 59 different bidders (B-H is bidder 25).

BIDDING STRATEGY

As she began to prepare her bids, Sheila recognized that B-H had been "shut-out" of these 51 auctions: that is, they had acquired no properties (they had bid on only 10 occasions). She attributed this to the increasingly competitive auction market that she thought was a consequence of two factors. The first was the aggressive bidding by Arthur MacNeil Properties, which had been high bidder (and, hence, the winner) in 15 of the previous 51 auctions, amassing properties that had cost Arthur MacNeil more than $31,500,000. The second factor was the increasing interest in these auctions as demonstrated by the increasing number of bidders: in the "good old days," there seemed to be only two or three serious bidders, but now there were often eight or more.With more bidders, it appeared likely that higher bids would be required to win the auctions.

In looking at the upcoming auctions, Sheila saw some hope. First, she knew that success had stretched MacNeil financially, and he was not interested in bidding on any new properties costing more than $1,000,000. Sheila also knew that MacNeil considered the property to be auctioned December 5 to have "great potential," and she inferred from this that he *would* bid on this property. Second, she saw the two major properties coming up for auction (November 29 and December 11) as "sleepers": she did not think that there would be much interest in either, probably fewer than four bids for each. MacNeil's views on the December 5 property,

Exhibit 1 | **UPCOMING AUCTIONS**

Auction Date	Type of Property	Estimated Value
November 29	Commercial	$1,226,000
December 5	Residential	$423,350
December 11	Commercial	$1,552,000

however, seemed typical: this could attract many bids, perhaps as high as 10.

Sheila's assessment of B-H's position was that they had done well by "playing the averages." By this, she meant that they bid in so many auctions, they could bid so as to maximize their average return and not take any undue risks in the process. She was, however, quite concerned that B-H had had a long run of "bad luck" at the auction and felt that they really needed $1,500,000 worth of new properties. When asked how badly they needed $1,500,000 of new properties, Sheila replied that she would give up $100,000 of expected value if this would help B-H acquire properties of at least $1,500,000 appraised value.

PREPARING THE BIDS

The first task was to prepare a bid for the November 29 auction. If B-H was successful, then Sheila thought she should bid very aggressively in the auction on December 5 because a second success on that date would put B-H over the $1,500,000 requirement. But what should she bid at the December 5 auction if she was unsuccessful on November 29? Finally, she reasoned that if she was unsuccessful on November 29 and December 5, she should bid very aggressively on December 11, again in an attempt to acquire the necessary $1,500,000 of property. But then, there would be other auctions after December 11, so how aggressive did she need to be?

Assignment

1. Report to Sheila Harbridge: Chief Executive Office of Brent-Harbridge Developments, recommending a bidding strategy for the auctions on November 29, December 5, and December 11.
2. Explain why you believe that the strategy you propose is an appropriate one for Brent-Harbridge Developments.

Exhibit 2 | DATA FROM 51 PREVIOUS PROPERTY AUCTIONS

Auction Item	Estimated Value	Winning Bid	Number Bidders	Type of Property
1	1,586,000	1,386,652	6	Commercial
2	575,700	502,042	4	Residential
3	1,469,300	1,266,892	7	Residential
4	748,900	637,815	5	Land
5	453,900	389,196	6	Residential
6	2,323,200	2,058,210	9	Land
7	3,295,600	2,919,754	7	Commercial
8	7,903,300	6,900,000	4	Land
9	970,000	871,520	5	Residential
10	1,143,000	1,012,702	4	Commercial
11	2,093,800	1,759,614	6	Residential
12	1,211,300	1,053,099	6	Land
13	750,300	625,501	4	Land
14	632,900	584,833	5	Residential
15	1,624,300	1,429,218	5	Land
16	936,200	842,319	2	Residential
17	375,100	284,947	9	Residential
18	520,100	447,021	5	Commercial
19	3,224,900	2,858,191	9	Land
20	8,425,000	7,646,123	8	Residential
21	4,143,100	3,705,840	7	Commercial
22	661,100	573,485	6	Land
23	1,731,700	1,558,574	5	Commercial
24	1,289,200	1,179,413	8	Residential
25	2,969,200	2,636,397	5	Commercial
26	581,300	469,663	7	Residential
27	2,017,300	1,526,553	4	Land
28	2,339,100	2,062,491	7	Commercial
29	654,600	499,888	5	Land
30	2,837,400	2,538,005	6	Commercial
31	787,500	599,429	5	Land
32	601,300	530,190	6	Commercial
33	917,800	792,966	5	Land
34	2,500,300	2,085,151	6	Land
35	937,300	821,617	6	Commercial
36	851,900	743,788	6	Land
37	7,825,800	6,631,664	9	Residential
38	636,500	508,985	5	Commercial
39	1,076,300	538,600	6	Commercial
40	2,370,700	2,087,946	7	Residential
41	1,695,100	1,503,739	6	Residential
42	4,012,000	3,624,453	8	Residential
43	799,300	629,164	5	Residential
44	2,421,700	2,187,217	5	Residential
45	1,392,100	1,202,916	3	Commercial
46	3,071,500	2,772,626	7	Residential
47	1,544,500	1,381,542	8	Commercial
48	848,500	698,161	7	Residential
49	284,800	248,733	4	Residential
50	416,000	351,803	5	Land
51	746,300	527,692	6	Land

'Estimated Value' is the value of the property as appraised by Tim Peters for B-H.
'Winning Bid' is the highest bid submitted.
'Number Bidders' is the number of bids submitted for each auction.

Exhibit 3 | BIDDING DATA ON AUCTIONS 1 THROUGH 8 (EXTRACT FROM DATA FILE)

Auction Number	**1**	**2**	**3**	**4**	**5**	**6**	**7**	**8**
Estimated value	$1,586,000	$575,700	$1,469,300	$748,900	$453,900	$2,323,200	$3,295,600	$7,903,300
No. of bids received	6	4	7	5	6	9	7	4
Winning bid	1,386,652	502,042	1,266,892	637,815	389,196	2,058,210	2,919,754	6,900,000
Winning bidder	MacNeil	43	41	8	14	MacNeil	MacNeil	2
Bidder MacNeil	1,386,652	498,793	1,262,638		389,178	2,058,210	2,919,754	6,764,661
1						1,950,809		
2								6,900,000
3	1,315,327							
4								
5	1,258,439				374,282		2,569,740	
6					365,168			
7			1,200,642					
8				637,815				
9			1,256,132					
10						1,946,454		
11								
12								
13			1,256,997					
14					389,196	1,963,076		
15								
16								
17	1,304,529					1,999,543	2,685,708	
18						1,820,312		
19								
20	1,318,789						2,719,819	
21								
22	1,325,437	474,340						
23		487,708			388,544			
24								
25							2,697,867	
26 and 27								
28							2,503,515	
29							2,589,581	
30								
31			1,202,628					
32						1,917,765		5,874,743
33				574,568				
34								6,425,350

(continued)

Exhibit 3 | **BIDDING DATA ON AUCTIONS 1 THROUGH 8 (EXTRACT FROM DATA FILE) *(continued)***

Auction Number	**1**	**2**	**3**	**4**	**5**	**6**	**7**	**8**
35, 36, 37, 38, and 39								
40				637,815				
41			1,266,892					
42								
43		502,042						
44				578,658				
45						1,928,429		
46						1,982,812		
47, 48, 49, 50, and 51								
52			668,239	577,804				
53					360,903			
Bidders 54–59								

Exhibit 4 | AUCTION RESULTS SUMMARIZED BY BIDDER

Bidder	No. of Bids Submitted	No. of Bids Won	Value of Bids Won
MacNeil	34	15	$31,571,615
1	3	1	842,319
2	2	1	6,900,000
3	8	1	469,663
4	1	1	248,733
5	20	1	447,021
6	6	0	0
7	2	0	0
8	4	1	637,815
9	4	0	0
10	2	0	0
11	1	1	499,888
12	3	0	0
13	3	0	0
14	4	1	389,196
15	2	1	871,520
16	2	1	508,985
17	12	0	0
18	5	1	2,636,397
19	3	0	0
20	6	1	6,631,664
21	9	1	2,085,151
22	12	2	3,847,560
23	5	1	629,164
24	2	1	1,202,916
25	10	0	0
26	4	0	0
27	3	0	0
28	3	0	0
29	5	1	3,624,453
30	7	1	1,526,553
31	6	0	0
32	10	1	792,966
33	3	0	0
34	4	1	1,503,739
35	3	1	743,788
36	3	0	0
37	5	0	0
38	7	2	1,447,118
39	3	0	0
40	8	2	5,630,817
41	3	1	1,266,892
42	2	0	0
43	7	1	502,042
44	2	1	573,485
45	3	0	0
46	4	1	698,161
47	3	1	1,429,218
48	8	0	0
49	3	0	0
50	1	1	527,692
51	2	1	538,600
52	2	0	0
53	3	0	0
54	2	2	1,184,262
55	2	1	284,947
56	4	0	0
57	4	0	0
58	3	0	0
59	4	0	0
TOTAL	**301**	**51**	**82,694,340**

MICHIGAN AUTO PRODUCTS, INC.

"As the final item of business for this meeting, I'd like to begin discussions on our upcoming contract negotiations with the union."Dave McGuire, President and Chief Executive Officer of Michigan Auto Products Inc., was addressing the weekly meeting of the Executive Committee.

"Let me remind you," Dave continued, "our union contract, which covers all our hourly paid workers, expires in 6 months. We expect the union negotiators to play hardball this year, but we must come up with a good contract to remain competitive in our industry. Six months may seem like a long lead time, but this contract is so important that I'd like to have our general negotiating strategy in place within the next 3 weeks. If we wait much longer than this, we may lose control over the timing of the negotiations, or not have sufficient time to prepare our position."

MICHIGAN AUTO PRODUCTS, INC.

Michigan Auto Products occupied a 46-acre site about 2 miles from the Ford plant in Dearborn, Michigan. The company was just less than 70% owned by a foreign, heavy-industrial conglomerate, with the balance of the stock publicly held and traded on the American Stock Exchange.

The company's major business was the manufacture of rubber and plastic automobile parts (mouldings, bushes, grommets, and boots), which it supplied to the major auto and truck manufacturers in Canada and the United States. Michigan's plant was mostly constructed in the late 1960s, although there had been several newer additions, particularly to the plastics division, where the rapid increase in the use of plastic in automobiles had resulted in a major expansion of the plastic moulding shop in the 1980s.

Michigan Auto Products had survived the recession of the early 1990s, but along with most firms connected with the auto industry, had shown an operating loss for fiscal years 1990/1991 ($6.1 million) and 1991/1992 ($2.9 million). In 1992/1993, Michigan had shown a net income (after tax) of $5.1 million on sales of $69.2 million, reflecting the recovery of the auto industry after the recession. Sales revenues for 1993/1994 were forecast at $76.8 million, with costs broken down as follows: direct labor, $14.1 million; materials and supplies, $27.4 million; and indirect labor plus depreciation, overhead, and other operating expenses, $23.5 million, leaving a forecast net income (before tax) of $11.8 million.

Michigan's workforce of some 550 hourly paid workers was represented by local 1481 of the Rubber and Plastics Workers Union (RPWU), and the existing contract expired at midnight on September 1, 1994. This contract had been negotiated in the midst of the recession, and although the RPWU had not made the kind of concessions that were common in the industry, the union thought that its members had "lost ground" over the life of the contract.

EXECUTIVE COMMITTEE MEETING, MARCH 1, 1994

Meetings of the Executive Committee were scheduled for Thursday mornings at 8:30 a.m. The members of this committee were Dave McGuire, President and CEO (Chairman); Harvey Smith, Comptroller; Gerhard Muench, Director of Finance; Terry Winegard, Director of Personnel; Henri Hanscom, Sales Manager; Burt Enison, Vice President Manufacturing; and Cecil Roussel, Chief Information Officer. Gerhard Muench was absent from the meeting of March 1.

The meeting of the Executive Committee had begun with a sense of optimism. The early agenda items had dealt with preliminary plans for an expansion of the tool-making department, a progress report on the new computer networks, and some staffing realignments. Dave McGuire's introduction of the upcoming contract negotiations introduced some unease to the group; everyone knew that this contract was key to Michigan's profitability and perhaps even its survival as an autonomous unit.

"Perhaps I can put you in the picture on our latest thinking about a new contract," Terry Winegard began. "We have had some preliminary discussions with the union representatives, and while they haven't given us any firm numbers, they are talking about a cut in working hours from a basic 38 hour week to a 35-hour week, plus a raise of 6% on base rates immediately followed by 9% a year from now, plus some nonmonetary items and changes in the fringe benefits package, mostly increases in medical and pension plan contributions. We've costed these nonmonetary items plus the extra fringe benefits they want at about $900,000 a year."

"Can I clarify something?" Harvey Smith interrupted. "Are they after a 6% immediate raise in the hourly rate or in the weekly rate?"

"The union is quite vague on this," responded Terry, "but their basic premise seems to be that they should get the same pay for the 35-hour week as for the 38-hour week and the 6% raise would come on top of that. We should be careful not to take this opening demand too seriously, but it's worth looking at the cost implications."

There was silence for a few minutes as Harvey did some calculations. He then began, "I costed the RPWU demand as follows: The 35-hour week amounts to a 21.4% increase in hourly rate, because we'll have to pay 3 extra hours at time-and-a-half for the same work that we previously got in the 38-hour week; that is, we now pay for 42.5 hours to get 35 hours, and 7.5 divided by 35 is 21.4%. Including in this the 6% increase they are asking for leads to a 28.68% increase in the hourly rate, to which we must add the $900,000 extra fringe benefits. Using this year's direct labor figure of $14.1 million means that we are looking at an increase in direct labor costs of $4.94 million in the first year of the contract!"

At this point, several committee members wanted to speak, but Dave McGuire took control. "These numbers look very grim, even as an opening demand," he began, "and it's important that we all understand our projections and plans for the next couple of years. Henri, why don't you review your marketing plans?"

Henri Hanscom, Sales Manager, took over. "As you all know, 90% of our sales are to the auto OEMs [original equipment manufacturers], with the remaining 10% to Caterpillar, John Deere, and some small Canadian equipment manufacturers. The size of our market is determined by the OEM sales, and we have been able to maintain our share of this market by keeping our prices down. We have a slight advantage in Detroit, because of our location, but we also compete successfully in much of the United States and Canada.We have about 20% of our sales in Canadian dollar accounts. Every product we make has an alternate supplier within 100 miles of us.

"Right now, we are producing at about $1.5 million in sales per week,[†] we could produce more but can't sell it unless auto sales pick up even higher, but we don't expect that to happen because General Motors, Ford, and Chrysler are all having record years already. Achieving this $1.5 million weekly sales takes tremendous sales effort; I don't think we can expect to improve on this very much. What really worries me is that a strike, or even rumors of a strike, will put a big dent in our sales projections."

[†]Michigan's working year was made up of 12 months. All months were 4 weeks except March. June, and September, which were 5 week months. The plant was closed the last week of December.

"I was talking to Jim Marbent at a trade show last June," continued Henri. "As you know, the RPWU called a strike against Jim's firm, but it was settled just before the strike date. Nevertheless, Jim said they lost 2 weeks' sales; apparently, the OEMs were convinced that a strike was imminent and had scrambled to put in place some alternate contracts with other suppliers, and Jim lost the business. My guess is that this same thing would happen to us: as soon as a strike appears likely, we are looking at $3.0 million in lost sales and, of course, every week of the strike will cost us a further $1.5 million in lost sales. While its important that we take a tough stand on a new contract, it's also important that we don't get struck."

"But suppose we had lots of inventory," interrupted Burt Enison, "wouldn't that cover some of these losses?"

"It certainly would," replied Henri. "What we would do is ship all goods to our customers on consignment; that is, the goods would be on the customers' premises, but they wouldn't pay for them until they were used. Because the goods would be on hand, the customers wouldn't bother about the strike until this extra inventory was used up. If we can get an extra week of inventory to our customers, then we could survive a 1-week strike without any costs."

"Just a minute," said Burt. "I don't understand. The strike is usually called 48 hours in advance. If the strike lasts 1 week, then toward the end of the week, the OEMs will be negotiating other arrangements, and we'll lose the 2 weeks' sales. How can we survive a 1-week strike with no loss of sales, even if we have a week's inventory on hand?"

"The logistics here are pretty clear," explained Terry. "Once the RPWU is on strike, they will insist on a member ballot before accepting any offer. This ballot will take 2 days. If the union executive is supporting the offer, then it's almost certain to pass, and we'll know of the end of the strike with 48 hours' notice. We can communicate this to our customers, and I'm quite sure we'll keep their business."

"I'd then like to propose that we start building inventory to help us survive a strike," said Burt. "We can accumulate a fair bit of extra inventory between now and the end of the contract simply by adding a bit of overtime and doing some rescheduling. We are looking at some extra costs for carrying the inventory but much less then that $3.0 million; if you give me a couple of minutes to do some figuring, I can estimate a cost for you."

"Go ahead," responded Dave McGuire. "While

Burt's doing that, I'd like to ask Terry what she thinks of this idea of building inventory."

"I suppose it's a useful precautionary move," began Terry, "but I'm worried about the union's reaction. If they find out that we are preparing for a strike, then it could sour the contract negotiations and might even make a strike more likely."

"Why don't I fill the others in about our discussions on the strategy for these negotiations?" said Dave. "Maybe this background is needed here. Basically, we think that the final settlement will be within one percentage point of 'market.' While the RPWU claims to have 'lost ground' over the life of the existing contract, they haven't fallen behind other autoworkers; times have been tough for everyone in this industry. We'll start with the usual games, and we expect the RPWU to reciprocate, but when we get down to serious negotiating, we expect to be working very close to a market increase. To help our thinking, we have simplified things by putting together three packages that we might offer.

"These packages are quite complex, but what they amount to is as follows:

"The first package (we'll call it P1) contains a wage increase averaging 4% per year for 2 years plus some fringe benefit changes that amount to $300,000 annually.

"The second package (P2) includes a wage increase of 5% per year for 2 years plus $300,000 annually in extra fringe benefits.

"The third package (P3) is for a 6% per year wage increase for 2 years plus $600,000 annually in extra fringe benefits.

"To compute the cost to us, recognize that the $14.1 million direct labor cost mentioned by Harvey is the cost of the last year of our existing contract with the RPWU. You'll notice that these are all 2-year contracts; the union is already on record against another 3-year contract but have indicated that they will accept a 2-year contract, so I think we should assume that we are discussing a two-year arrangement."

"Why did you pick these three packages?" asked Harvey Smith. "Clearly, there are many other possible offers."

"What we tried to do," replied Dave, "was to identify packages that we thought had 10%, 50%, and 90% chances of being accepted by the union. We think P3 has a 90% chance of acceptance as an early offer, even though it's well below what the union executive is talking about; it's better than all but one recent settlement. P2 reflects these other settlements fairly accurately, so we put its chances at 50/50, and P1 is pretty much our bottom offer, but it might be a useful negotiating tool. Of course, these chances of acceptance are 'first offer' chances. Clearly, a second offer will never be accepted if it's lower than the first offer (for example, if we offer P2 and it's rejected, we would never then offer P1), but sometimes a first offer can make the second offer look more attractive. In particular, if we put P1 on the table and explain how tough things have been for the last 3 to 4 years, then if we introduce P2 at the appropriate time, I'd raise its acceptance odds to 60/40. Similarly, if we discuss P2 long and hard and then introduce P3, I'd raise the chance of accepting P3 to 95%."

"There's a big difference between 4% and 6%," remarked Harvey Smith. "Can't we get the RPWU to put up the first offer?"

"We are not talking about the first offer here," replied Terry. "Rather, we are talking about what we expect to be offering during the hard and serious bargaining that will occur as a strike date approaches. Where we see ourselves ending up is almost independent of the initial offers."

At this point, Burt returned with his estimates. "Accumulation of inventory will cost us $60,000 in extra costs, mostly overtime, for each week of sales up to a maximum of 3 weeks' sales accumulation over the next 6 months. Any more than 3 weeks in additional inventory will really cost a bundle, but the first 3 weeks seems to me to be a small price to pay for the extra security it will provide."

"What happens to all this inventory if there is no strike?" asked Harvey.

"We'll use it up after the new contract comes into effect," replied Burt. "By doing this we can recover about half of these extra costs (by cutting back production and overtime), so with no strike, the net cost will be $30,000 for each extra week of sales we accumulate in inventory."

"I'm worried about Terry's point that the union may find out; what happens if the union hears of this?" asked Henri.

"This is a bit tricky," said Dave. "Clearly, we, as management, have the prerogative to set production rates and policies, and so the union wouldn't try to stop us, but they would probably see us as acting in bad faith and would toughen their negotiating stance."

"How would this affect the numbers you gave us?" asked Henri.

Dave McGuire and Terry Winegard held a short conference. As they broke up, Dave answered, "Our best guess is that to achieve the same acceptance chances as before, P1, P2 and P3 would have to be raised by half a percentage point; that is, to get a 90%

chance of acceptance, we would have to offer 6.5% annually for 2 years plus $600,000 in extra fringe benefits. This is a bit simple minded, but is the best we can do right now."

Burt returned to the discussion. "I don't think there's much chance that they will find out. We've come through a period of gradually increasing sales and production, so the shop floor is used to seeing higher production levels and working a few hours extra overtime. The inventory won't be kept in our plant but will be shipped to our customers, so there won't be any obvious accumulation. If we are discovered, it will happen immediately as we change production levels because quite a number of people will have to be involved in changing the master schedule. Several of these people will know that we don't have orders to support the extra production. I don't think there's more than a 1-in-5 chance that the right contacts would be made in casual conversation for the inventory buildup to be recognized by the union and the reasons for it identified."

"For this inventory buildup to be useful to us, we need to have a better idea of how you see the negotiations proceeding, Dave," began Henri. "What's your thinking on how you plan to negotiate?"

"We haven't yet firmed up our strategy," explained Dave, "but Terry will tell you how we are thinking." Terry shuffled through some papers, found the notes she needed, and began.

"Our original premise was that we will not take a strike—we just can't handle the lost sales that occur immediately, but Burt's idea to build up some inventory implies that we could now handle a 3-week strike with no loss of sales, so perhaps our original premise needs to be modified. Of course, we don't know the economics yet."

"But, Terry," interrupted Burt, "how can you resolve not to take a strike; doesn't this depend on the union, because even your best offer has only a 95% chance of acceptance?"

"We think that we can handle this at the conciliation stage," explained Terry. "As you know, our contract with the RPWU requires that a conciliation officer, who is an independent consultant, meet with both parties and attempt to effect a settlement. If this fails, the union has the right to strike after 3 days. At the conciliation stage, we'll have a very good idea, through the conciliation officer, of the union's bottom demand. After conciliation, there's still the possibility of arbitration. After the last negotiation, a clause was written into our contract with the RPWU to provide for binding arbitration as a means of settling contract terms. This clause is very vague, and we've no experience with arbitration, but this route is open if both we and the RPWU agree to go to arbitration and agree on the form of arbitration."

"I don't much like that idea of just paying up to the Union's bottom demand," added Henri. "What do we know about the attitude of the union? Suppose their bottom demand is outrageous?"

Terry explained, "First, I think we can agree with the union on the fringe benefits package. Our offer of $300,000 annually is almost certainly acceptable, on its own. It's much better than the commitments we have made, and this area is not as political or visible as the wage increase. We'll get the fringe benefits package out of the way before conciliation or arbitration so we can concentrate on the wage increase. If we go to arbitration, how this will come out is anybody's guess; I've been reading about other settlements through arbitration, and they seem to vary all over the place. My inclination is to assume that the arbitrator will take a position halfway between our final offer and the union's final offer. This means, of course, that if we go to arbitration, we would prefer to have P1 on the table, and we really don't want to have P3 on the table. We recognize that we need to understand the arbitration process better, and we've arranged to meet with an attorney specializing in this area next week."

"But you still haven't given us any idea of the union's positions; can you guesstimate how they will react to our offers?" asked Henri.

"This is really difficult," replied Dave. "We've had friendly discussions so far, but when we start serious negotiations, anything can happen. The problem is that we have to make some decisions now, but only when serious negotiations start in 4 or 5 months will we find out how they are thinking."

"So why don't we start negotiating right now?" asked Henri.

"The union can't really settle until midnight on the strike date," replied Dave, "because if they settle earlier, their members will think the executive has not been tough enough. We should probably plan on making our first serious offer 48 hours before the end of the contract."

"Suppose we offer P1?" said Henri, trying to pin Dave down.

"Then I guess that if they don't accept, there's a 50/50 chance that they will be publicly disgusted with our offer and stick to their informal preliminary offer or make a formal response that makes some minor concession, probably cutting the fringe benefits additions to $600,000 annually."

"Suppose we offer P2?" said Henri, continuing his attack.

"If they don't accept P2, then I think they will want to be specific; I would guess they will come back with a cut in weekly hours to 36 with a 6% wage increase (weekly). Their actual offer might be higher or lower than this, but I think this is a reasonable average position. They will probably go along with the $300,000 annually in extra fringe benefits."

"Suppose we offer P3?" said Henri concluding this inquisition.

"If they turn down P3, then they will simply try to stretch us up a little higher; my guess is that they will try for an extra 1% on the wage increase. I'm sure that they will give up on the shorter working week under these conditions. Let me add that these three scenarios are sort-of averages; the actual responses could be higher or lower."

"We all have a lot to think about here," concluded Dave. "We should talk about this again and clarify our strategy at next week's meeting. See you all same time next week."

MARCH 2, 1994

On the following day, Terry Winegard had a call from Dave McGuire's secretary to say that Dave had been working on the contract negotiations and wanted Terry to drop by. Terry was tied up temporarily, but a meeting was set up for immediately after lunch.

Dave began, "Terry, I know you have been busy with the Parker grievance and haven't had time to think further about the contract negotiations we discussed yesterday, but I woke up at 2 this morning worrying about it. The first thing I tried to resolve was Burt's idea of building inventory to help reduce the cost of a strike. This seems like a good idea, but this conflicts with our premise that we would always avoid a strike at the conciliation stage or through arbitration. Clearly, it doesn't make any sense to build inventory if we are not at risk of a strike."

"I was concerned about that yesterday," responded Terry.

"The idea of building inventory opened up some options that we had not seriously thought about before," continued Dave, "but there's another problem here: the RPWU executive may not come up with an offer we can accept at conciliation or may not agree to arbitration.

"Ted Caplan—you know Ted, he's Vice President Operations at Baker Hydraulic—was saying last night at the club that Baker had a devil of a time getting the RPWU to settle. Apparently, Baker thought that if they put up a low-ball offer and stuck with it, then the conciliator would take account of this and Baker might come away with a good settlement. Problem was the union accused them of bargaining in bad faith and struck for a month. By the end of the month, Baker had given the store away to get them back to work."

"I was thinking along similar lines," said Terry.

"The way we were talking yesterday suggested that we could offer our below market package (P1) and sit on that offer until the end of the contract, even after the union turned it down, but I'm pretty sure if we do that, we'll be struck."

"Yes, I agree," said Dave. "I'm just guessing here, but after talking with Caplan last night, I think I can construct a reasonable scenario. First, we'll know whether P1 is accepted or not very quickly because if they are not going to accept, the RPWU will give us a public blast to gain some political mileage. If we stick with P1 through conciliation and into arbitration, there's some chance that the RPWU will come back with an offer at 'market' that we can accept, but my guess is that there are 3 chances in 4 that the RPWU will call for a strike. If this happens, then I don't think there's any point in us sitting on P1, so we up our offer to P2. One thing that I'm not sure about is arbitration; it may be a good strategy to go to arbitration with P1 on the table, but we'll have to figure that out."

"Where does this leave us if they again turn us down?" asked Terry.

"A strike," replied Dave, "but remember that P2 is 'market.' I don't think they will refuse that offer for very long with their members on strike, but the timing here is quite complex. Once the strike is called, they are going to be out for a week; there will be just too much mental investment in the strike to come back sooner. But in weeks 2, 3, and 4, there will be increasing pressure on the union to settle; there's just too much unemployment around for the union members to be comfortable on strike. Remember also that many of the members are still paying off debts incurred during the layoffs of the last couple of years. I think the chance of our offer of P2 being accepted is evenly spread during this 3-week period."

"What's this 'evenly spread' stuff?" interjected Terry. "It sounds like something my son would put on bread."

"Yea, I know I didn't say that very well," laughed Dave. "My statistics are really rusty, but what I meant to say was that there are equal chances of the strike being settled by the start of the second week, the third week, or the fourth week."

"But we could also sweeten the pot; offer P2 plus, say, half a percent," added Terry.

"In that case, we'll have them back at work within 1 or 2 weeks, 50/50," answered Dave.

"Suppose we upped our offer to P3?" asked Terry.

"Any strike with P3 on the table has to be a union screw-up," responded Dave. "Once the members recognize that they are being offered one of the best settlements in the country, they will be back at work pronto. I wouldn't think such a strike could last 1 day more than the 1-week minimum."

"I'm still concerned about taking a strike," began Terry, after a short pause. "We work very hard between contracts to develop good relations with the blue-collar workers, we tell them over and over that 'we care,' and then at contract time, all this changes and we put them out on the street. After settlement, we have to start back at square one. You know, Burt said yesterday that if we built up some inventory, we could survive a strike without losing sales, but there are other costs to a strike in addition to lost sales."

"You are right, of course," responded Dave. "The kind of costs you are talking about are really soft and difficult to get a handle on, but there are also some hard costs. One that Burt didn't mention was mismatched orders: if we have to ship inventory on consignment, then we have to guess which items to ship—these shipments won't exactly match what the customer wants, and we'll lose some business because we shipped the wrong products. On the other hand, orders are fairly stable, and the OEMs' schedules are known, so we should be able to do a reasonable job of providing what the customer will want."

"To evaluate this decision to risk a strike, it seems to me we have to be prepared to put some numbers on the cost of a strike," began Terry, "How much are these lost orders going to cost us?"

"I'll tell you that if you put a number on your soft costs," replied Dave.

"Well, I'll take a guess," replied Terry. "As far as I'm concerned, a 1-day strike is as bad as a 4-week strike in terms of its impact on employee goodwill. On the other hand, strikes are fairly common in our industry and tend not to generate the kind of anger that they do in some industries." Terry paused at this point, tapping her pencil on Dave's desk. "A hundred thousand dollars—that sounds like a reasonable average value for these costs."

"I'd be disappointed if we lost any more than fifty thousand dollars a week during the strike because of mismatched orders," said Dave, fulfilling his side of the bargain.

"Whew!" said Terry after a pause. "I'm suffering from information overload; maybe we should continue this discussion after we've talked to the attorney next week." "I agree. See you on Monday," said Dave, ending the meeting.

MONDAY, MARCH 7

Bob Stockton had earned MBA and LLB degrees from prestigious universities and now practiced with a major Detroit law firm, where he specialized in labor law and arbitration. He met with Dave McGuire and Terry Winegard in his office. After introductions, the business began with Dave McGuire summarizing the situation at Michigan Auto. Terry listened to Dave's clear but succinct review with admiration, realizing why Dave had been appointed President and CEO. After 10 minutes or so, Dave's review turned to questions and answers, and Terry began to realize that Stockton had a good grasp of many of the essential trade-offs that Michigan faced—perhaps he had seen this all before.

At a short pause in the conversation, Terry brought this point up."I suppose our situation is fairly similar to that of many other firms," she offered.

"Yes, I would say so," replied Stockton. "My firm handled negotiations for about 25 corporations in the past year and consulted with dozens of others; although each case has some unique features, the general problems and options are quite similar. As I understand the purpose of today's meeting, you have some specific points where you would like my advice."

"First," began Dave, "we feel we must understand conciliation and arbitration better. We are having difficulties trying to evaluate the effect of conciliation."

"As you know," replied Stockton, "the conciliator has no power to impose a settlement, but his or her presence can be very useful to you because it may provide the first real evidence of the union's rock-bottom demand. First, let me say, that this is a pretty good time to be negotiating. The public sector is still operating under the threat of major layoffs and zero percent wage increases, and these are having a major effect on settlements in the private sector. Also, and perhaps more important to you, there is high unemployment, and further, many people are just back to work after layoffs or prolonged periods of being unable to find work. In several of my recent negotiations, the unions have given up 10 to 25 cents an hour, perhaps even more, to avoid a strike.

"Regarding arbitration," replied Stockton, "you probably know there are two basic types of arbitration for a collective agreement. These are known by a number of names, but we can call them 'final offer selection' and conventional 'arbitration.' In final offer selection, each side makes a final offer, and if no agreement is reached, the arbitrator chooses between these two offers—he is not allowed to select any kind of compromise. This scheme has worked well but has only been used in a few cases; it's used by major league baseball to resolve salary disputes.

"In conventional arbitration the final offers are submitted to the arbitrator who can then impose any settlement, although it's usually some compromise between the two final offers."

"You said that final offer selection is rare," replied Terry. "Does this mean we should rule it out?"

"Yes," replied Stockton. "Stick with conventional arbitration, in which, in my experience, settlements average about halfway between the final offers of the two sides. This is assuming, of course, that neither side goes into arbitration with an outrageous final offer. What is 'outrageous' depends on the market; all arbitrators pay a great deal of attention to recent settlements in similar industries."

"Our second offer (P2) is really 'market,' " interjected Terry. "We looked at all the settlements in the automobile industry over the past 6 months and then put together an offer that was right in line with these settlements."

"The difficulty is in making this case to the arbitrator," said Stockton. "You have to persuade him that at this point in time, in this industry, in this location, your offer is 'market.' This is not easy."

"I suppose it would be a mistake to offer P1 and stick with it?" queried Terry.

"Hold on a minute," said Stockton. "That one has to be thought through. If you offer P1 and sit on it, then the union may give you a public dressing down and will come back with a pretty outrageous demand. This demand will raise expectations within the union, and they may not be able to back out of it without losing face. They may therefore submit to arbitration so they can blame the arbitrator for the low settlement."

"This becomes a real game," said Dave. "It appears that we start to lose all control of the situation if we continue along these lines. Just suppose the arbitrator sides with the union's 'outrageous demand,' perhaps costing us 20%; then we would be bankrupt."

"If you could show that to the arbitrator, then you'd have a strong case!" said Stockton, flippantly. "Seriously," Stockton continued, "I'd try to avoid arbitration if I had P1 on the table. There's a chance that the arbitrator will think you are not negotiating seriously in which case this gets pretty risky. Also, don't forget you have to live with the union when this is all over. There is no point in stonewalling with an offer that could get you in real trouble at arbitration. As I mentioned earlier, I don't think you'll be far off if you assume a settlement at the midpoint of the two final offers."

"This is all well and good," began Dave, "but will the union agree to arbitration?"

"Actually, that may not be as difficult as you think," replied Stockton. "Arbitration promises sort-of average settlements without the loss of income of a strike; of course, you have to be careful and may have to play a few games along the way. The times are right, but you must decide whether you want to go to arbitration first and then negotiate the arbitration details before anything else. You would be foolish to try to negotiate details of an arbitration procedure after you have made an offer. The union members want a fair settlement without a strike. I think they see arbitration as one way to get that, so if you want arbitration, I'd say there was an 80% chance that the union would agree."

At this point, there was a considerable pause. "I assume that you are available to help us out if we need you," said Dave finally.

"Yes," replied Stockton. "If you like, I'll send you my fee schedule together with the results of the negotiations I've handled over the past year."

"Please do that," responded Dave. "Then we'll get back to you."

The drive back was mostly relaxed, but toward the end of the drive, Terry brought up the subject of hiring Stockton to handle the negotiations.

"No, I think we should try it on our own first," replied Dave. "The worst thing that could happen here is if the union finds out about our negotiating plans. I'd like to keep this strictly in house and limited to members of the Executive Committee. There should be no memos and no written reports—nothing that the union can get its hands on. I think that between us we can come up with a good strategy; it's just a question of laying out our options and choosing the best one."

"The thing that really scares me," concluded Terry, "is that we have made a lot of guesstimates and assumptions.

"Many of these are not going to affect us very much, but some of these numbers are going to critically affect how we proceed. We need to know where errors in our estimates will have a big impact on our decisions, and which assumptions that we've made, and which are critical to our strategy selection."

"I agree," said Dave, standing up to get his coat. "We should aim to have something to talk about at Thursday's meeting. Why don't you try to come up with a strategy?"

"OK," said Terry, "see you on Thursday."

Assignment

1. Develop a strategy for the negotiations.

PCB MANUFACTURING, INC.

THE AUTHOR THANKS PROFESSOR A.H. CHRISTER FOR PROVIDING THE SITUATION AND DATA USED IN THIS CASE.

Management at PCB Manufacturing, Inc. was concerned that a significant number of faulty printed circuit boards (PCBs) were reaching their customers.

PCB Manufacturing, Inc. produced PCBs for inclusion in television sets. The company sold quantities of boards produced to customer specification and made PCBs for use in its own television sets. Each board cost $5.00 to produce and sold (wholesale) for $8.00.

The production run of a typical board was one or two batches of 1,000 boards, although there were longer and shorter runs. Many different boards were produced during the year.

QUALITY CONTROL AT PCB MANUFACTURING, INC.

All PCBs produced at PCB Manufacturing, Inc. were subject to a series of tests to determine whether the board was acceptable for shipment. Shipping defective boards was costly: it was estimated that shipped defective boards cost PCB an average of $25.00 each. The quality control procedure that was followed was:

> Each PCB was sent to a testing station, where it was subject to a standard battery of electronic tests; boards that passed this initial check were shipped.
>
> Boards that failed this initial check were resubmitted to the testing station, and the tests were performed a second time; any board that passed at the second attempt was shipped.
>
> Boards that failed the second time were resubmitted to the testing station a third time; any board that passed at the third attempt was shipped.
>
> Boards that failed at the third submission were discarded.

The electronic testing process used was quite passive, and there was no reason to believe that testing affected the boards in any way. Each setup for the test of a batch of boards cost $15.00 but once set up, the variable cost of testing each board was essentially zero.

TESTING THE TESTING

PCB Manufacturing, Inc. was concerned that a significant number of faulty boards were being shipped. Professor A.H. Christer, Professor of Operational Research at the University of Salford, was called in to investigate the situation. Professor Christer began by considering a theoretical model:

Let

α be the proportion of boards that are actually good,

p be the probability that a board will pass the test if the board is actually good,

and

q be the probability that a board will fail the test if the board is actually bad.

From these assumptions, Professor Christer computed the theoretical proportion of shipped boards that were expected to be faulty.

To investigate the accuracy of this prediction, Professor Christer studied one lot of 1,136 boards. Of these boards, 1,087 passed quality inspection at the first attempt. The 49 boards that failed were resubmitted, and 21 passed. The remaining 28 boards were again resubmitted, and all failed at the third attempt.

Professor Christer set out to demonstrate that these data were consistent with his theoretical results.

THE FINAL TEST

After a good deal of persuasion, Professor Christer was able to arrange for a sample of the boards that passed quality inspection the first time to be retested. The firm agreed to reexamine 200 boards; in this process, 7 failed.

Professor Christer wondered whether this result affected his analysis.

IMPROVING THE QUALITY ASSURANCE PROGRAM

The real purpose of the project was to design a quality control program to reduce the costs associated with shipping faulty boards. Professor Christer turned to the possibility of rearranging the quality control program to improve the quality of the shipped PCBs. The same series of electronic checks would have to be used because nothing better was available.

Assignment

1. Can you propose a testing scheme to improve the quality of the shipped boards?

4

THINKING SIMULTANEOUSLY

Management decision problems are often complex. To cope with this complexity, the decision tree model presented in Chapter 3 can be used to structure a complex problem as a series of sequential decisions. Often, however, a number of **dependent** decisions must be made where an attempt to address each decision sequentially will produce a poor solution. Here are two examples in which decisions made on a one-at-a-time basis will likely produce high-cost results:

1. Suppose that we must decide how many units of several different products to produce this week. First, we might look at our most profitable product and decide a production level for that product; then, we move on to our second most profitable product and decide how many of that product to produce, continuing until we have moved through our entire product line.
2. The marketing manager might decide to tour the company's sales territories by traveling to the closest territory first, then the next closest, and so on.

In this chapter, we identify situations where this kind of thinking may be fundamentally flawed because the dependence between decisions may produce high-cost or inefficient solutions. Good solutions for many management problems can be derived only when the values of several (perhaps many) decision variables are determined simultaneously. We call this type of problem a **simultaneous decision problem**.

A simultaneous decision problem is a problem where there are benefits to simultaneously making multiple decisions, even though the decisions may be implemented over a period of time. Production scheduling is a common example where most firms achieve significant benefits by deriving a schedule for some time horizon (often weekly) *simultaneously* even though the production levels derived are implemented sequentially.

We can improve our decision making if we develop the skills to recognize simultaneous decision problems and the capability to solve these problems simultaneously. An example to present the concept of a simultaneous decision problem follows.

THE AB COMPANY

The AB Company will produce only two products this week: product A and product B. Management must decide how much of each product to produce (in tons). Product A yields a contribution margin of $25 per ton, and product B yields $10 per ton. All products produced will be sold.

Products A and B are made by mixing materials from inventory. For this week, there are three materials available in the following amounts:

Material 1:	12,000 tons
Material 2:	4,000 tons
Material 3:	6,000 tons

Product A is made up of 60% material 1 and 40% material 2.
Product B is made up of 50% material 1, 10% material 2, and 40% material 3.

In a **sequential approach** to try to decide how much of each product to produce, the product that has the highest contribution margin might be examined first. This is product A; if we try to produce the maximum possible amount of A, we are limited by the quantity of material 2, which makes up 40% of A. If we use all 4,000 tons of material 2 to produce product A, we can produce 10,000 (4,000/0.4) tons of A, for a contribution of $250,000. This consumes 6,000 tons (10,000*0.6) of material 1, leaving 6,000 tons of material 1 and 6,000 tons of material 3 unused. Because we need material 2 to produce product B, we can produce none of product B. The decision would be to produce 10,000 tons of product A and none of product B, for a contribution of $250,000.

But there is a better solution: if we produce 6,250 tons of product A and 15,000 tons of product B, we have a contribution of $306,250. The materials requirements are:

For product A,	
60% Material 1 (0.6*6,250)	3,750 tons
40% Material 2 (0.4*6,250)	2,500 tons
For product B,	
50% Material 1 (0.5*15,000)	7,500 tons
10% Material 2 (0.1*15,000)	1,500 tons
40% Material 3 (0.4*15,000)	6,000 tons
Total materials used:	
Material 1: 3,750 + 7,500	11,250 tons
Material 2: 2,500 + 1,500	4,000 tons
Material 3: 6,000	6,000 tons

Therefore, we use up all of materials 2 and 3 but have 750 tons of material 1 left over.

Those with some knowledge of algebra will recognize that this solution is found by solving equations **simultaneously**. This is a simple example of the value of **simultaneous thinking** over **sequential thinking**. By attempting to solve this problem sequentially, $56,250 was left "on the table." A competitive firm will not last long if it continues to make mistakes like this.

An essential skill for every manager is the ability to recognize situations where sequential decision making fails to deliver a competitive decision. It is also important to have some understanding of how to derive a better solution.

IDENTIFYING SIMULTANEOUS DECISION PROBLEMS

The kinds of decisions where a simultaneous solution approach has resulted in major profit or productivity improvements are widespread. Some examples are:

- American Airlines' decisions about which aircraft to use on which flights and which flight crews to assign to each aircraft
- The U.S. Defense Department's decisions on how to transport the necessary personnel and materiel for the Gulf War from existing locations to the Gulf
- The Chessie Rail System's decisions on the purchase and repair of more than $4 billion worth of freight cars
- Hydro Quebec's decisions on which reservoirs to use to meet the demand for electricity each day
- The Federal Land Banks of the Farm Credit System's decisions on how to refund maturing bonds and sell new bonds to generate new funds (amounting to some $6 billion annually) for growth
- American Edwards Laboratories' decisions concerning which artificial heart valves to produce to best meet the available demand
- EXXON refineries' decisions regarding adaptation of its refining capacity to adjust to the legislated changeover to no-lead automobile fuels
- North American Van Lines' decisions on how to dispatch thousands of trucks each week

These are just a few examples where organizations have saved millions of dollars through understanding the need for simultaneous thinking. These happen to be large firms where documented savings of several million dollars have been reported and are the kinds of applications that are important enough to be written up in the literature. Small firms can also use these techniques; the savings will not be as large but can still have an important impact on their "bottom line."

Although these examples occur in different industries and different sectors and involve different issues, they have several common features:

1. They involve many **decision variables** (often thousands, sometimes literally millions) that are interrelated.
2. There are some **scarce resources** that must be allocated among competing uses.
3. There are **constraints** on what can be achieved or what the manager wants to achieve.
4. There is a fairly clear and definite **objective**.
5. The decision problem is fairly well understood.

The approach used to solve such simultaneous decision problems goes by the general term of **mathematical programming** (MP) (MP has nothing to do with computer programming—the approach predates the computer). To understand MP, we need to take a look at a more rigorous statement of the problem.

FORM OF THE GENERAL MATHEMATICAL PROGRAMMING PROBLEM

A very general statement of the MP problem is:

- The MP problem seeks to find values for a set of decision variables that maximize (or minimize) a single objective and satisfy a set of constraints.

By restricting the algebraic form of the objective and the constraints, various more-limited MP problem types emerge. The most important of these is the **linear programming problem**.

Linear Programming Problem

The LP problem is one limited version of the general MP problem. If we define X_1, X_2, X_3, X_4 ... X_n (the $\boldsymbol{X_j}$**s**) as the set of decision variables (or activities), then the LP problem is stated in the form of **maximizing** a linear **objective function** subject to a set of linear **constraints** or:

$$\text{MAXIMIZE } Z = c_1X_1 + c_2X_2 + c_3X_3 + c_4X_4 + \ldots\ldots c_nX_n \ (\textit{the objective function})$$

SUBJECT TO: (*the constraints*)

$$\begin{aligned}
&a_{11}X_1 + a_{12}X_2 + a_{13}X_3 + a_{14}X_4 + \ldots\ldots a_{1n}X_n \le b_1\\
&a_{21}X_1 + a_{22}X_2 + a_{23}X_3 + a_{24}X_4 + \ldots\ldots a_{2n}X_n \le b_2\\
&a_{31}X_1 + a_{32}X_2 + a_{33}X_3 + a_{34}X_4 + \ldots\ldots a_{3n}X_n \le b_3\\
&\quad\cdot\\
&\quad\cdot\\
&a_{m1}X_1 + a_{m2}X_2 + a_{m3}X_3 + a_{m4}X_4 + \ldots\ldots a_{mn}X_n \le b_m
\end{aligned}$$

where

$c_1, c_2, \ldots c_n$ (the $\boldsymbol{c_j}$**s**) (which appear in the objective function only) are the values attached to a unit of each decision variable in the objective function,

$b_1, b_2, \ldots b_m$ (the $\boldsymbol{b_i}$**s**) are called the "right-hand sides" (or "rhs") and denote the total amounts of each of the constrained resources that can be taken up, and

$a_{11}, a_{12}, \ldots a_{mn}$ (the $\boldsymbol{a_{ij}}$**s**) are the **coefficients** and denote how much of each resource is taken up by a unit of each decision variable.

In this formulation, the decision variables (the X_js) can be positive or negative, but the procedures that solve this problem efficiently may not include solutions involving negative values of the X_js. We therefore customarily add a set of **non-negativity constraints** to the formulation. That is, we insist that:

$$X_1 \ge 0, \quad X_2 \ge 0, \quad X_3 \ge 0, \ldots\ldots X_n \ge 0$$

The LP problem can be written more succinctly as:

$$\text{MAX } Z = \sum_{j=1}^{n} c_jX_j$$

S.T.

$$\begin{aligned}
\sum_{j=1}^{n} a_{ij}X_j \le b_i &\qquad \text{for } i = 1,2, \ldots \text{m.}\\
X_j \ge 0 &\qquad \text{for } j = 1,2, \ldots \text{n.}
\end{aligned}$$

Note that the form of the LP problem is that of a **linear objective function** with **linear constraints**—hence, the name *linear* programming.

A number of other problems can be formulated into this form very easily. For example:

For a **minimization** problem, note that minimizing Z is equivalent to maximizing $(-Z)$. To formulate a minimization problem, we change the signs of the c_js. (We do not actually have to do this because most software for solving the LP problem can handle both maximization and minimization.)

The direction of the inequalities can be reversed by changing the signs of both sides of the equality. For example:

$$\sum_{j=1}^{n} a_{ij} X_j \geq b_i$$

is equivalent to:

$$\sum_{j=1}^{n} (-a_{ij}) X_j \leq -b_i$$

Again, we do not have to do this because LP software can handle $\leq$, $\geq$, or $=$ constraints.

There are many managerial decision variables that may take on negative values, such as the end-of-day balance in the firm's consolidated bank account, which would usually be secured through some type of line-of-credit arrangement with the bank. These variables can be included in an LP problem by using:

$$X_j = X_j^{+} - X_j^{-}$$

where X_j is the decision variable that may be negative, and X_j^{+} and X_j^{-} are two new nonnegative variables.

The general statement of the LP problem is formulated in terms of decision variables X_j (for $j = 1, 2, \ldots n$), but it is usually helpful to use meaningful variable names that clearly identify the decision variables in the real problem (Box 4-1).

Box 4-1

DOW CHEMICAL'S MANAGEMENT OF INTERNATIONAL PRODUCTION SCHEDULES

"Dow Chemical has devised one of the more sophisticated systems for juggling international production schedules. Using a computerized linear programming model that it began developing five years ago, the company weighs everything from currency and tax rates to transportation and local production costs to identify the cheapest maker of each product. For example, in making chlor-alkali and its derivatives, some of which require several intermediate chemicals, Dow's network chooses among factories on three continents to supply customers throughout the world."

Source: *Fortune* March 14, 1988.

Example of Linear Programming Formulation: The AB Company. As an example of an LP formulation, we consider the problem of the AB Company, which produces two products (A and B) from three materials (1, 2, and 3), as introduced earlier.

The problem is to decide how many tons of product A and how many tons of product B to produce. Therefore, we choose our decision variables as:

Let:

A be the number of tons of product A to be produced

and

B be the number of tons of product B to be produced.

Because the contribution from product A is \$25 per ton and that from product B is \$10 per ton, we can formulate our objective as the maximization of contribution, or:

$$\text{MAXIMIZE CONTRIBUTION} = \$25\text{A} + \$10\text{B}$$

We are prevented from making huge amounts of products A and B (and hence huge contributions) by limitations on the amounts of available materials. The quantities of materials available will therefore be the right-hand sides of the constraints. To complete the constraints, we must identify the coefficients, that is, how many tons of each material are used up producing 1 ton of each product.

Because 60% of product A is made up of material 1, then production of A tons of product A consumes $0.6A$ ton of material 1. The remaining 40% of product A ($0.4A$ ton) is material 2.

Similarly, production of B tons of product B consumes $0.5B$ ton of material 1, $0.1B$ ton of material 2, and $0.4B$ ton of material 3.

The total amount of material 1 consumed (producing A tons of product A and B tons of product B) is therefore:

$$0.6A + 0.5B$$

which cannot exceed the 12,000 tons of material 1 available. Our first constraint is therefore:

$$0.6A + 0.5B \leq 12{,}000 \quad \text{(material 1 supply constraint)}$$

Following similar logic, we derive material supply constraints for materials 2 and 3:

$$0.4A + 0.1B \leq 4{,}000 \quad \text{(material 2 supply constraint)}$$
$$0.0A + 0.4B \leq 6{,}000 \quad \text{(material 3 supply constraint).}$$

We now restate the complete formulation (leaving out the 0.0 coefficient):

$$\begin{aligned}
&\text{MAXIMIZE CONTRIBUTION} = 25A + 10B \\
&\text{S.T.} \\
&\quad 0.6A + 0.5B \leq 12{,}000 \\
&\quad 0.4A + 0.1B \leq 4{,}000 \\
&\quad 0.4B \leq 6{,}000 \\
&\quad \text{with } A \geq 0, \text{ and } B \geq 0.
\end{aligned}$$

This LP problem can be solved to find those values of A and B that maximize the objective while satisfying the constraints by using any of a large number of computer programs: examples include LINDO, What's Best, and IBM's OSL. Spreadsheet programs such as Lotus 1-2-3 and Microsoft Excel also contain "solvers" that can solve LP problems. Problems involving very large numbers of decision variables (several thousand or more) take some time to solve, and a great deal of development effort has gone into producing fast LP computer codes. An efficient, modern LP program running on a personal computer will solve most problems with 1,000 decision variables in just a few seconds. The solution obtained is both optimum and known to be optimum.

Solving the Linear Programming Problem

To understand the characteristic features of the LP problem, it is useful to work through a solution to an example problem. Consider the AB Company's problem:

$$\text{MAXIMIZE CONTRIBUTION} = 25A + 10B$$

S.T.

$$0.6A + 0.5B \leq 12{,}000$$
$$0.4A + 0.1B \leq 4{,}000$$
$$0.4B \leq 6{,}000$$
$$\text{with: } A \geq 0,\ B \geq 0$$

To find the maximum value of a function, we would normally plot the function and then be able to see the maximum point on the plot. For the AB Company, this would require three dimensions since CONTRIBUTION depends on both A and B. We can learn a lot about this problem, however, if we plot the **solution space**; that is, if we plot the constraints as equalities on a graph of A versus B (Figure 4-1).

The first constraint expressed as an equality is:

$$0.6A + 0.5B = 12{,}000$$

Thus, linear combinations A and B from ($A = 20{,}000$ at $B = 0$) to ($B = 24{,}000$ at $A = 0$) satisfy this equality. This line is plotted as "Material 1 Constraint" on Figure 4-1. Material 2 and 3 constraints can be plotted similarly.

Observation of the graph shows that there is no point at which the three constraints meet: that is, there is no (A, B) combination that satisfies all three constraints as equalities. This is a general result; problems with a large number of **equality** constraints may have no solution that satisfies all the constraints.

For the AB Company, however, the constraints are ≤ inequalities; a **feasible solution** (a solution that we can implement) may use less material than the maximum we have avail-

Figure 4-1 **FEASIBLE REGION FOR AB COMPANY PROBLEM**

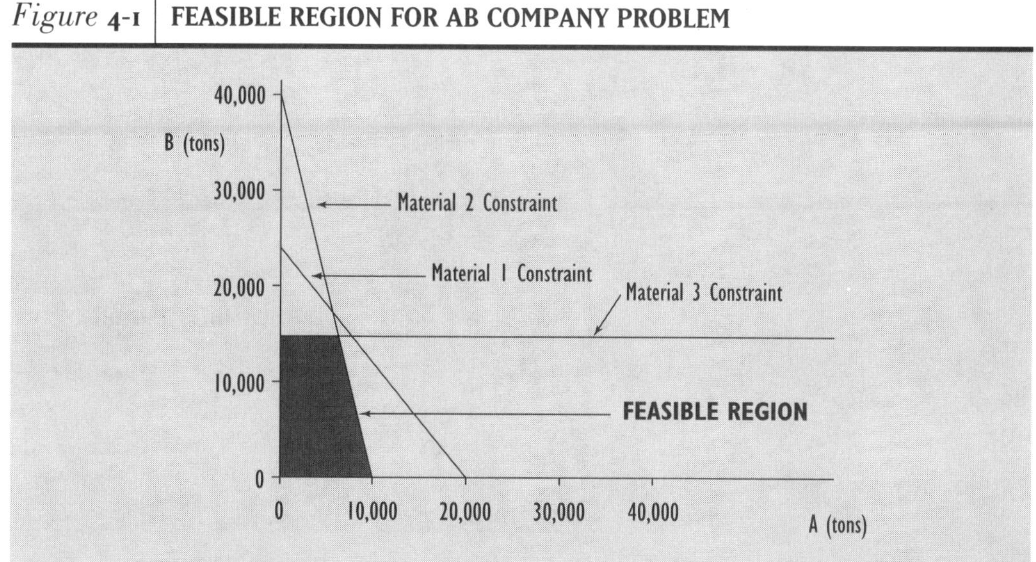

able. Feasible solutions for each constraint, therefore, lie on or *below* the constraint. The set of solutions that are feasible, because they use no more of each material than we have available, occur in the shaded area of Figure 4-1. This area is called the **feasible region**.

An important property of the feasible region is that it is **convex**; that is, all the corners point outward. (Technically, a line joining any two points in the feasible region is contained entirely within the feasible region.) No matter how many linear constraints we add to Figure 4-1, we cannot change the convexity of the feasible region. Furthermore, as we add more variables to the problem, this convexity property remains.

The problem now is to choose the solution that has the largest value of the objective from all the solutions contained in the feasible region. Because there are an infinite number of feasible solutions, this appears to involve an extensive search, but further understanding dramatically reduces the extent of the search required.

This understanding comes from a look at the objective function:

$$\text{MAXIMIZE CONTRIBUTION} = 25A + 10B$$

We cannot plot this function as it is, but we can use it to find solutions (that is, values for A and B) that yield a specific contribution. For example, let us try to find solutions that will yield $200,000 in contribution. To do this, we substitute CONTRIBUTION = 200,000 into the objective function, leading to:

$$200{,}000 = 25A + 10B$$

Then we solve for A and B. Clearly, there are a very large number of possible (A, B) combinations that will yield a contribution of $200,000: any point on this line. However, some of these combinations may not be feasible. How can we check? We superimpose a plot of this equation onto the plot of the feasible region (Figure 4-2). From the plot, we see that

Figure **4-2** **DETERMINATION OF OPTIMAL SOLUTION FOR AB COMPANY PROBLEM**

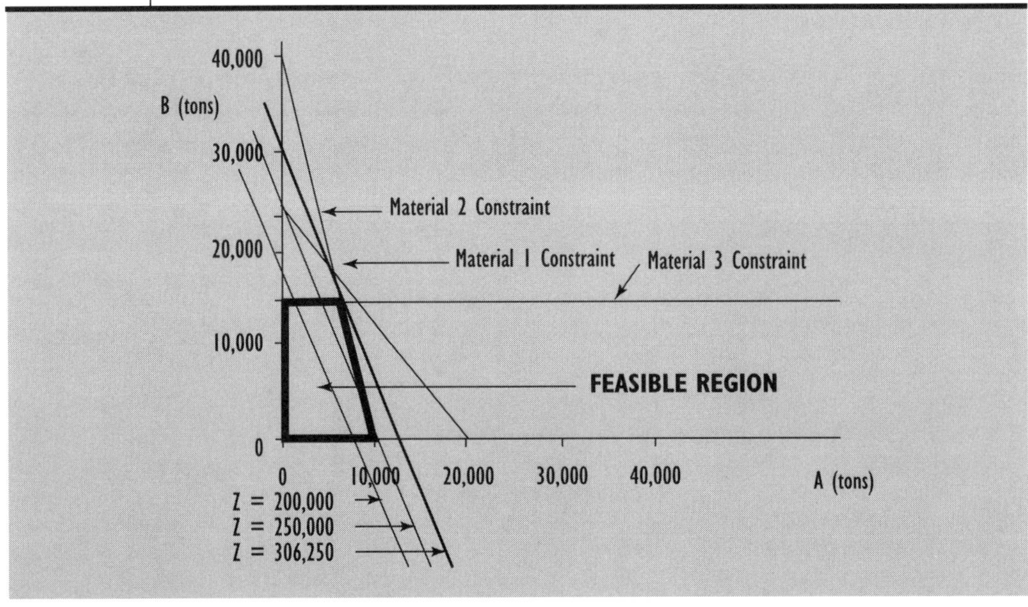

some of the solutions that produce a contribution of $200,000 lie outside the feasible region (that is, we do not have the materials to produce these (A, B) combinations; the solutions are **infeasible**): they require more of material 3 than we have available. However, there are still a very large number of solutions that lie within the feasible region and produce a contribution of $200,000 represented by all possible (A, B) pairs that are on that portion of the line contained in the feasible region.

Can we produce a contribution of $250,000? The line:

$$250{,}000 = 25A + 10B$$

is superimposed on Figure 4-2. Note that as we increase the contribution, the objective function line moves up (or to the right) but remains parallel to the $200,000 line. We now see how to find the optimum solution: we move the objective function line up (or to the right) as far as we can without losing contact with the feasible region. When we try to do this, a most important result emerges: **the optimum solution is always at a corner of the feasible region**.

The LP problem is now reduced to finite proportions: to find the optimum solution, we need only find that corner of the feasible region that produces the maximum value for the objective function. In our example problem, we need examine only four solutions corresponding to the four corners of the feasible region and choose the corner that yields the highest contribution. From our knowledge of the slope of the objective function obtained above (Figure 4-2), we can surmise that the corner at $A = 6{,}250$ and $B = 15{,}000$ with contribution $= 306{,}250$ represents the optimum solution (and it does!).

We now have a sense of how the LP problem can be solved. The solution procedure must examine the corners of the feasible region and find the one that optimizes the value of the objective function. This is not necessarily a trivial undertaking, as in large problems there may be millions of corners. Fortunately, procedures have been developed to find the optimum solution without having to examine each and every corner. These procedures follow one of two basic approaches:

Variations of the Simplex Method. This method was initially developed by George Dantzig during the 1940s. The solution procedure starts at a corner of the feasible region. Adjacent corners are inspected to determine whether the objective function can be improved by moving to an adjacent corner. If this is found to be the case, a procedure called a "pivot" is undertaken, which moves the solution to the adjacent corner that lies in the direction of the most rapid increase in the objective function value. The procedure terminates when no adjacent corner has a higher objective function value than the present solution.

Variations of Interior Point Methods. This method was initially developed by Narendra Karmarkar in the 1980s. These methods differ from the simplex methods in that intermediate solutions are developed that lie in the interior of the feasible region. Starting at a feasible solution, the interior point procedure generates new solutions across the feasible region in the direction of the optimum solution.

Both procedures have their proponents, and neither has been proved to be clearly superior. Most commercially available software use a variation of the simplex method. Some software, such as IBM's OSL, includes solvers that use both procedures, leaving the user free to choose which one to use.

The development of efficient solution procedures remains an important issue. Many large companies are solving problems that occupy large computers for many hours. In other cases, firms are limiting their application of optimization because of a lack of computer time, even though they know that improved solutions are available if they could run their solvers for a few more hours.

LEARNING FROM THE SOLUTION: POSTOPTIMALITY ANALYSIS

The graphic technique used to solve the example problem reveals some important properties of the optimum solution.

Property 1. The optimum solution (as denoted by the quantities of the decision variables) may not be very sensitive to changes in the objective function coefficients (that is, changes to the c_js).

Recall that the optimum solution is always at a corner of the feasible region. The slope of the objective function determines which corner of the feasible region is optimum, and this slope is determined by the relative values of the c_js in the objective function. These coefficients often have to be changed considerably before the slope of the objective function changes sufficiently to switch the optimum solution to an adjacent corner. When this does occur, the values of the decision variables may change considerably.

For example, for the AB Company, if we increase the contribution from product A, the slope of the objective function becomes **increasingly negative** (the objective function becomes more vertical). The geometry of the feasible region (Figure 4-3) suggests that the objective function will have to reach a slope parallel to constraint 2 for the optimum solution to switch from the current corner (A = 6,250, B = 15,000) to the corner at (A = 10,000, B = 0).

[We can compute the contribution of A at which this occurs as $40. Using some algebra:

Find the contribution of A (call it P_A) for the solution (A = 6,250, B = 15,000) to have the same contribution as the solution (A = 10,000, B = 0) given the contribution of B at $10:

$$6250\ P_A + 15000*10 = 10000\ P_A$$
$$150{,}000 = (10{,}000 - 6{,}250)\ P_A$$
$$P_A = 150{,}000/3{,}750 = \$40 \qquad]$$

Figure 4-3 | **INSENSITIVITY OF OPTIMAL SOLUTION TO INCREASE IN CONTRIBUTION OF A**

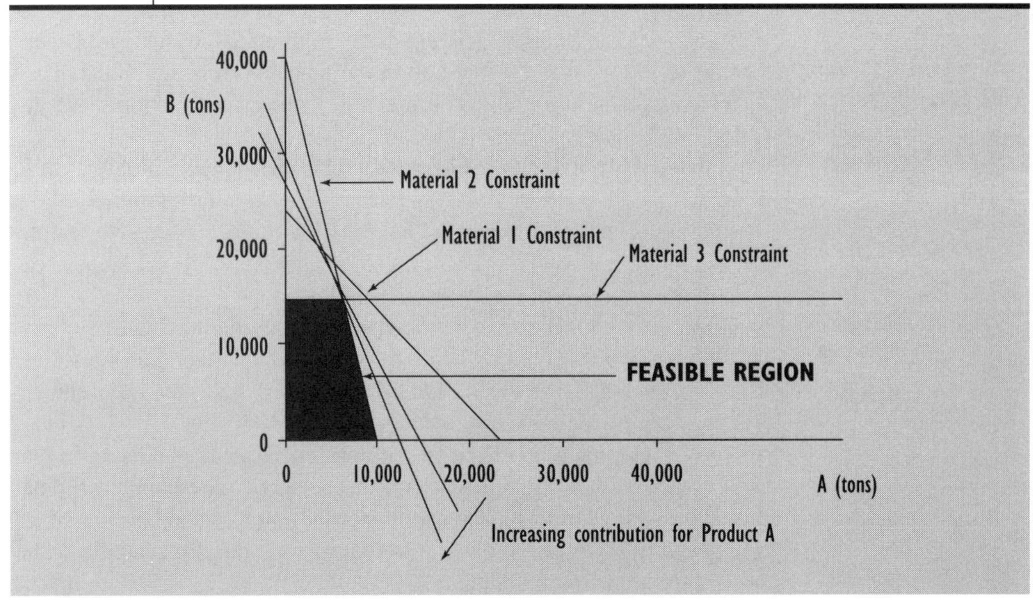

We conclude that for any contribution for *A* between \$25 and \$40 (with the contribution of *B* held at \$10), the contribution maximizing solution is to produce 6,250 tons of product A and 15,000 tons of product B. Note that if the contribution of A increases to exactly \$40, both corner solutions (A = 6,250, B = 15,000) and (A = 0,000, B = 0) are optimum, **as are all solutions that lie on the constraint joining these two corners**: we have an infinite number of optimum solutions. This leads to property 2.

Property 2. There may be a large number of optimum solutions to the LP problem, but one or more corners will always have the same objective function value as any optimum solution not at a corner.

Multiple optimum solutions arise when the slope of the objective is identical to the slope of a constraint bounding the feasible region. Knowing about multiple optimum solutions is important because there may be reasons for preferring one solution to another that were not part of the LP problem formulation (for example, one solution may be easier to implement than the others).

Property 3. The optimum solution to an LP problem has two types of constraints: **active** and **inactive**.

The **optimum solution** is at the intersection of the set of *active* constraints. The quantities of resources represented by the right-hand sides of the active constraints are fully used. In general, any change made to an active constraint will affect the optimum solution: the optimum solution will become infeasible if an active constraint is "tightened" (for example, the amount of a scarce material is reduced) or will generally become nonoptimum if an active constraint is "loosened" (for example, more of a scarce material is made available).

Inactive constraints represent resources where there is **slack** or **surplus**. Changing the value of the right-hand side of an inactive constraint by a small amount generally will not change the optimum solution.

We can define **slack** and **surplus variables** as follows:

The constraint

$$\sum_{j=1}^{n} a_{ij} X_j \leq b_i$$

can be written as:

$$\sum_{j=1}^{n} a_{ij} X_j + S_i = b_i$$

where S_i is the *slack variable* for resource i.

The constraint

$$\sum_{j=1}^{n} a_{kj} X_j \geq b_k$$

can be written as:

$$\sum_{j=1}^{n} a_{kj} X_j - S_k = b_k$$

where S_k is the *surplus variable* for resource $_k$.

It follows that in the optimum solution, the value of the slack or surplus variable in any active constraint is zero. Conversely, if the slack or surplus variable in a constraint does not have value zero, the constraint is inactive.

SOFTWARE FOR SOLVING MATHEMATICAL PROGRAMMING PROBLEMS

The graphic solution approach illustrates many important features of solutions to the LP problem, but it is not a practical method for solving realistic problems. A large number of computer programs have been developed to solve MP problems and to provide valuable decision-making information about the problem and the solution. MP problem "solvers" are included in the major spreadsheets (Microsoft Excel and Lotus 1-2-3), and many hundreds of special-purpose MP problem-solving programs are available. We will use the Microsoft Excel solver and LINDO, one of the special-purpose MP programs, to illustrate practical solution procedures.

Solving Linear Programming Problems with Microsoft Excel Solver

To solve MP programs using the Excel solver, we first load the Excel spreadsheet and enter the problem into the spreadsheet. The example problem of the AB Company introduced earlier will be used to demonstrate the approach. Recall the problem formulation:

$$\text{MAXIMIZE CONTRIBUTION} = 25A + 10B$$

$$\begin{aligned} &\text{S.T.} \\ &\quad 0.6A + 0.5B \leq 12{,}000 \\ &\quad 0.4A + 0.1B \leq 4{,}000 \\ &\quad 0.4B \leq 6{,}000 \\ &\quad \text{with: } A \geq 0,\ B \geq 0 \end{aligned}$$

The Excel solver can optimize problems presented in many different formats. For the AB Company problem, one possible format is shown in Table 4-1.

Cell **C5** corresponds to variable A and cell **C6** to variable B (the quantities to be determined to maximize contribution). The objective function coefficients appear in cells **B5** and **B6**, so the objective function value can be calculated in cell **C3** (using the formula =

Table 4-1 | **POSSIBLE EXCEL FORMAT FOR AB COMPANY**

	A	B	C	D	E	F	G
1		THE AB COMPANY					
2							
3	Contribution		35	*cell c3= b5*c5+ b6*c6*			
4							
5	A	25	1	*cell c5= quantity of product A produced*			
6	B	10	1	*cell c6= quantity of product B produced*			
7							
8	Availabilities						
9	Material 1	12000	1.1	*cell c9= .6*c5+ .5*c6*			
10	Material 2	4000	0.5	*cell c10= .4*c5+ .1*c6*			
11	Material 3	6000	0.4	*cell c11= .4*c6*			

Table 4-2 | **CONTRIBUTION-MAXIMIZING SOLUTION FOR AB COMPANY**

	A	B	C	D	E	F	G
1		THE AB COMPANY					
2							
3	Contribution		306250	*cell c3= b5*c5+ b6*c6*			
4							
5	A	25	6250	*cell c5= quantity of product A produced*			
6	B	10	15000	*cell c6= quantity of product B produced*			
7							
8	Availabilities						
9	Material 1	12000	11250	*cell c9= .6*c5+ .5*c6*			
10	Material 2	4000	4000	*cell c10= .4*c5+ .1*c6*			
11	Material 3	6000	6000	*cell c11= .4*c6*			

*b*5**c*5 + *b*6**c*6). Note that the values of the decision variables have been initialized to 1 so this calculation produces a result, but any initial variable values can be used.

The constraints are represented in rows 9 through 11. Column **B** contains the amounts of resources available, and column **C** contains the calculations for the respective amounts of each material used in the current solution. We could use this spreadsheet as a "deterministic simulator" by varying the values in cells **C5** and **C6** searching for a maximum value in cell **C3**, while being sure that the values in cells **C9**, **C10**, and **C11** did not exceed the respective values in cells **B9**, **B10**, and **B11**. If you are diligent and patient, you should be able to find the contribution maximizing solution shown in Table 4-2.

If you try this by hand, even for this very small problem, you will quickly come to appreciate the value of the "solver." To use the solver, we choose item **Solver** in the **Tools** menu and the *Solver Parameters* form appears (Figure 4-4). To operate the solver, we must:

1. Identify the *Target Cell* which contains a formula that computes the value of the objective function (in our example, **C3**).
2. Choose whether we want to maximize or minimize the value in the *Target Cell* (solver can also find variable values such that the target cell has a given *Value*).
3. Identify which cells contain the variables (*Changing Cells*).
4. Identify the constraints; when **Add**ing each set of constraints, we input the cell addresses that contain the left-hand sides and the right-hand sides and choose the sign ($\leq$, $=$, or $\geq$) from a menu item (hence, the signs do not appear in the spreadsheet).
5. Include non-negativity constraints explicitly if these are required. (Newer versions of Solver have an "Assume Non-negative" check box.) (The omission of required non-negativity constraints can result in one of two problems: negative values for the decision variables in the optimum solution, which is usually easy to see and correct, or a Solver error message stating that the solution procedure "does not converge." There are several causes of this message, one of which is the absence of non-negativity constraints.)

When the form is complete, we click the *Solve* button, and the solver will produce the contribution maximizing solution (Figure 4-5).

If the problem to be solved is linear but large or complex, choosing the option *Assume Linear Model* on the solver **Options** menu will result in the use of faster and more reliable solution algorithms (Figure 4-6).

Figure **4-4** | **SOLVER PARAMETERS FORM**

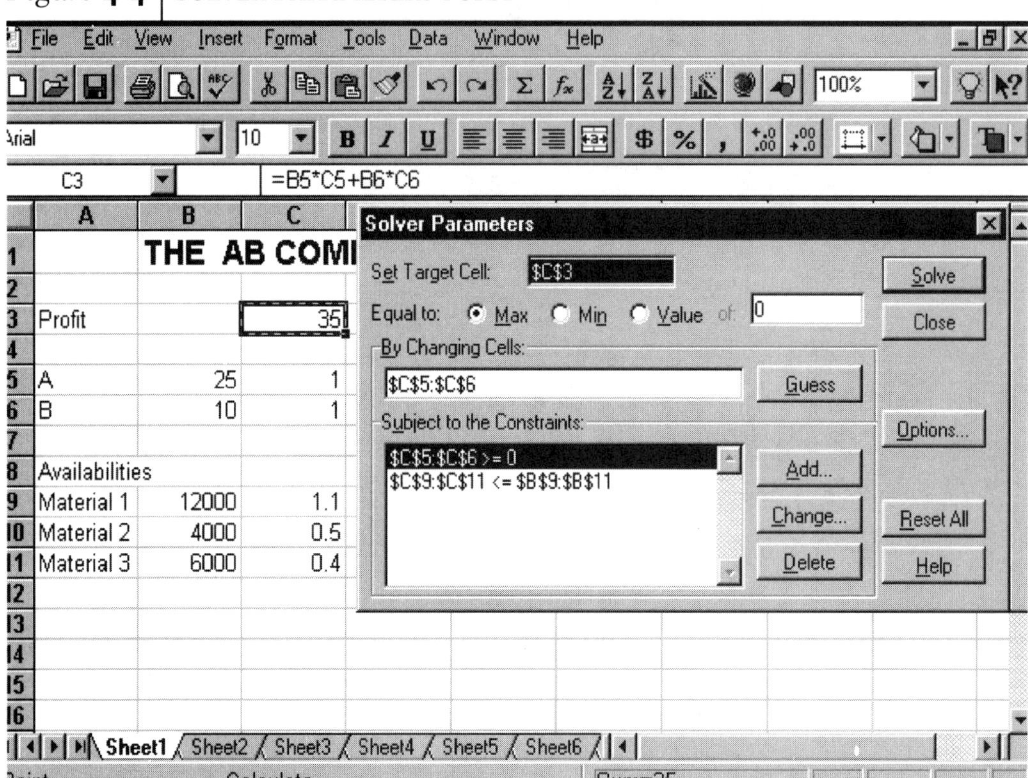

The **Solver Results** screen provides the option to generate two useful reports: the **Answer** and **Sensitivity** reports. The **Answer** report lists the starting and final values of the objective function (or *Target Cell*) and the variables (or *Adjustable Cells*), as well as the constraints indicating whether each constraint is active (or *Binding*) or inactive (or *Not Binding*). For the inactive constraints, the amount of slack is indicated (Figure 4-7).

The **Sensitivity** report provides two very useful columns of values: the **Reduced Costs** and the **Allowable Ranges** (Figure 4-8). This version of the **Sensitivity Report** is generated when *Assume Linear Model* is selected under **Solver Options** before clicking the **Solve** button.

The **Reduced Costs** for variables *A* and *B* are both zero, consistent with variables *A* and *B* both having nonzero values in the optimum solution. The range given for the reduced costs (from *Objective Coefficient* minus *Allowable Decrease* to *Objective Coefficient* plus *Allowable Increase*) gives the range for the objective function coefficients (the contributions) over which this same solution is optimum. We conclude that for any contribution of *A* between \$0 (25 − 25) and \$40 (25 + 15), the existing solution is optimum (although the value of the objective function will vary if the contribution of *A* is changed). The same is true for any increase in the contribution of *B* (the *Allowable Increase* is very large), but if the contribution of *B* falls below \$6.25 (\$10 − \$3.75), the optimum solution will change: we will produce less B.

Figure 4-5 | **SOLVER RESULTS**

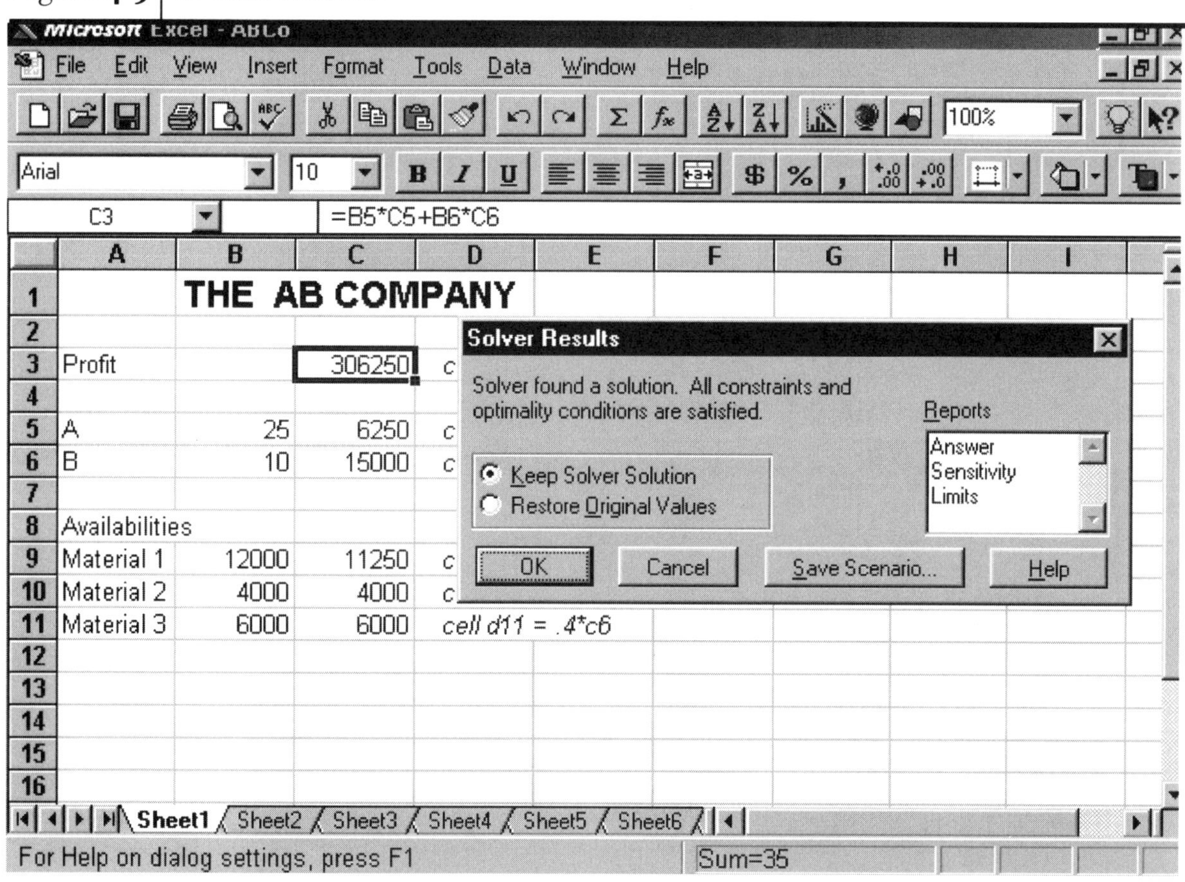

Figure 4-6 | **SOLVER OPTIONS FORM**

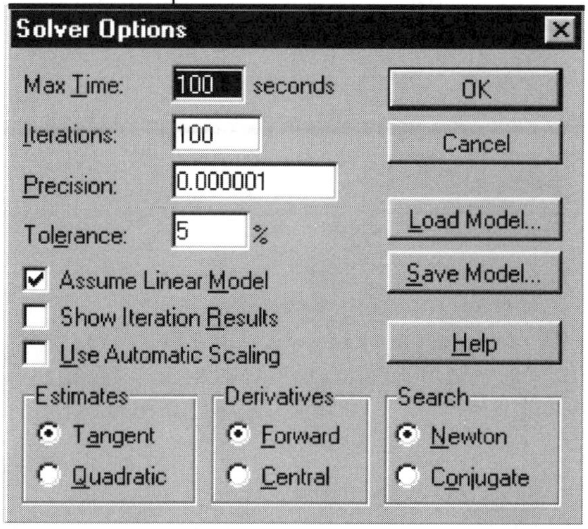

Solver Options

Max Time: 100 seconds

Iterations: 100

Precision: 0.000001

Tolerance: 5 %

☑ Assume Linear Model

☐ Show Iteration Results

☐ Use Automatic Scaling

Estimates: (•) Tangent ( ) Quadratic

Derivatives: (•) Forward ( ) Central

Search: (•) Newton ( ) Conjugate

OK | Cancel | Load Model... | Save Model... | Help

Figure 4-7 **EXCEL ANSWER REPORT**

Microsoft Excel 7.0 Answer Report
Worksheet: [ABCo.xls]Sheet1
Report Created: 12/12/96 12:40

Target Cell (Max)

Cell	Name	Original Value	Final Value
$C$3	Profit	35	306250

Adjustable Cells

Cell	Name	Original Value	Final Value
$C$5	A	1	6250
$C$6	B	1	15000

Constraints

Cell	Name	Cell Value	Formula	Status	Slack
$C$9	Material 1	11250	$C$9<=$B$9	Not Binding	750
$C$10	Material 2	4000	$C$10<=$B$10	Binding	0
$C$11	Material 3	6000	$C$11<=$B$11	Binding	0
$C$5	A	6250	$C$5>=0	Not Binding	6250
$C$6	B	15000	$C$6>=0	Not Binding	15000

A variable with value zero in the optimum solution will generally have a non-zero **Reduced Cost**. The value of the **Reduced Cost** gives the amount by which the objective function coefficient (the c_j) of this variable must change for this variable to appear at a nonzero value in the optimum solution.

For example, if we had a third product (product C) and the new line in the **Sensitivity Report** shown in Figure 4-9 appeared:

We conclude that the contribution of product C is too low for us to produce any. If, however, the contribution of C increased by $3.50, it would become profitable to produce C; however, we would have to reduce our production of A or B to accommodate this.

The last part of the **Sensitivity Report** lists the constraints (listed as Materials 1, 2, and 3), the *Final Value* of each constraint (or the amount of that material used in the optimum solution), and the **Shadow Price** for each constraint (Figure 4-8).

Figure **4-8** **EXCEL SENSITIVITY REPORT**

Microsoft Excel 7.0 Sensitivity Report
Worksheet: [ABCo.xls]Sheet1
Report Created: 12/12/96 12:40

Changing Cells

Cell	Name	Final Value	Reduced Cost	Objective Coefficient	Allowable Increase	Allowable Decrease
$C$5	A	6250	0	25	15	25
$C$6	B	15000	0	10	1E+30	3.75

Constraints

Cell	Name	Final Value	Shadow Price	Constraint R.H. Side	Allowable Increase	Allowable Decrease
$C$9	Material 1	11250	0	12000	1E+30	750
$C$10	Material 2	4000	62.5	4000	500	2500
$C$11	Material 3	6000	9.375	6000	857.1428572	6000

Recall that an *active constraint* has zero slack or surplus and that the constraints corresponding to materials 2 and 3 are *active* in the optimum solution, whereas the constraint corresponding to material 1 is *inactive*, with 750 tons of material 1 left over.

The **Shadow Price** is the marginal value of increasing the right-hand side of any constraint. The **Shadow Price** for material 1 is zero. Because, at the margin, the objective function value does not change if we change the right-hand side of an inactive constraint, the **Shadow Price** for an inactive constraint is always zero.

Material 2 is in short supply; if we relax the constraint by adding more material 2 (increasing the rhs from 4,000 tons), the value of the objective function will increase at a rate

Figure **4-9** **ADDITIONAL LINE IN SENSITIVITY REPORT**

Changing Cells

Cell	Name	Final Value	Reduced Cost
$C$7	C	0	3.5

of \$62.5 per ton of material 2. Similarly, the **Shadow Price** for material 3 shows that increasing the amount of material 3 available will add to the contribution at a rate of \$9.375 per ton of material 3. Note that the Shadow Prices are computed using the coefficients in the objective function (which are contribution margins in this example) and consequently assume the same materials costs for the additional materials as in the initial formulation.

The Shadow Prices provide **marginal rates of increase**: they do not tell us the range over which these rates apply. This information is provided by the *Constraint R.H. Side*, the *Allowable Increase*, and the *Allowable Decrease* (Figure 4-8).

The *Constraint R.H. Side* lists the value of the right-hand side of each constraint. The *Allowable Increase* and the *Allowable Decrease* provide the range over which the *Shadow Price* given for that constraint is valid. We conclude that the **Shadow Price** of zero for material 1 is valid over a range from 11,250 (12,000 − 750) to +infinity (12,000 + 1E+30) (1E+30 is 1 followed by 30 zeros, a very large number). Note that we have excess material 1 so adding additional material 1 will not change the optimum solution, but if we lose an amount of material 1 in excess of the amount of surplus (750 tons), then the present solution becomes infeasible. Thus, if the right-hand side of the material 1 constraint is less than 11,250, the **Shadow Price** for material 1 will change from zero to something positive.

Material 2 has a **Shadow Price** of \$62.5 per ton over a range from 1,500 tons (4,000 − 2,500) to 4,500 tons (4,000 + 500). We conclude that each additional ton, up to 500 tons, of material 2 that we can buy at the current price will add \$62.5 per ton to the total contribution. Conversely, if we can sell material 2 at a premium of more than \$62.5 per ton above current cost, selling up to 2,500 tons will also improve our contribution.

Similarly, the **Shadow Price** for material 3 of \$9.375 per ton is valid over the range from zero tons (6,000 − 1E+30 but non-negative) to 6,857.14 tons of material 3 and provides the value of Material 3 to the AB Company within this range.

Solving Problems with LINDO and Understanding LINDO Output

LINDO is a widely used software package for solving many classes of MP problems.

To solve our example problem using LINDO, we first load LINDO. To enter our problem into LINDO, we type EDIT and obtain the full-screen editor. We enter the problem by typing (LINDO is not fussy about the exact spacing in the formulation):

```
MAX 25A + 10B
ST
.6A + .5B < 12000
.4A + .1B <  4000
.4B < 6000
END
```

{ESCAPE} to return to the solver. Note that LINDO does not allow variables on the right-hand side of the constraint equations. We now type command GO to solve the problem.

LINDO command COM will list all the LINDO commands, and command HELP xxx will provide an explanation of command xxx.

LINDO responds with the output shown in Figure 4-10.

The first part of the output:

```
LP OPTIMUM FOUND AT STEP 2
```

informs us that the optimum solution was found in just two "pivots" of the simplex algorithm. The objective function (CONTRIBUTION) value and the decision variable values in the optimum solution follow:

```
OBJECTIVE FUNCTION VALUE
 1)            306250.00
VARIABLE        VALUE            REDUCED COST
   A         6250.000000           .000000
   B        15000.000000           .000000
```

We see that we obtain a profit of $306,250 by producing 6,250 (tons) of A and 15,000 (tons) of B. The REDUCED COSTS for *A* and *B* are both zero, consistent with variables *A* and *B* both being nonzero. A variable with value zero in the optimum solution will generally have a nonzero REDUCED COST.

> The value of the REDUCED COST gives the amount by which the contribution (the c_j) of this variable must change for this variable to appear at a nonzero value in the optimum solution.
>
> For example, if we had a third product (product C) and the following row appeared:

```
VARIABLE        VALUE            REDUCED COST
   C           .000000           3.500000
```

> We conclude that the contribution of product C is too low for us to produce any. If, however, the contribution of C increased by $3.50, it would become profitable to produce C; however, we would have to reduce our production of A or B to accommodate this.

The next part of the output lists the constraints (listed as rows 2, 3, and 4: the objective function is always row 1 in LINDO). For each constraint, the SLACK OR SURPLUS is listed alongside the DUAL PRICES.

```
ROW      SLACK OR SURPLUS     DUAL PRICES
 2)        750.000000           .000000
 3)           .000000         62.500000
 4)           .000000          9.375000
```

Figure 4-10 **LINDO OUTPUT**

LP OPTIMUM FOUND AT STEP 2

OBJECTIVE FUNCTION VALUE

1)	306250.00

VARIABLE	VALUE	REDUCED COST
A	6250.000000	.000000
B	15000.000000	.000000

ROW	SLACK OR SURPLUS	DUAL PRICES
2)	750.000000	.000000
3)	.000000	62.500000
4)	.000000	9.375000

NO. ITERATIONS = 2

RANGES IN WHICH THE BASIS IS UNCHANGED:

OBJ COEFFICIENT RANGES

VARIABLE	CURRENT COEF	ALLOWABLE INCREASE	ALLOWABLE DECREASE
A	25.000000	15.000000	25.000000
B	10.000000	INFINITY	3.750000

RIGHTHAND SIDE RANGES

ROW	CURRENT RHS	ALLOWABLE INCREASE	ALLOWABLE DECREASE
2	12000.000000	INFINITY	750.000000
3	4000.000000	500.000000	2500.000000
4	6000.000000	857.142900	6000.000000

Recall that an **active constraint** has zero slack or surplus; we therefore conclude that rows 3 and 4 (corresponding to the material 2 and 3 constraints) are **active** in the optimum solution (they have zero SLACK OR SURPLUS) and that row 2 (corresponding to material 1) is **inactive,** with 750 tons of material 1 left over.

The DUAL PRICES column contains important information; it provides the marginal value of increasing the right-hand side of any constraint. Because at the margin the objective function value does not change if we change the right-hand side of an inactive constraint, the dual price for an inactive constraint is always zero. Material 2 (row 3) is in short supply; if we relax the constraint by adding more material 2 (increasing the **rhs** from 4,000 tons), the value of the objective function will increase at a rate of $62.5 per ton of material 2.

Similarly, the dual price for row 4 (material 3) shows that increasing the amount of material 3 available will add to the contribution at a rate of $9.375 per ton of material 3.

Note that the DUAL PRICES provide **rates of increase**: they do not tell us the range over which these rates apply.

This information is contained in the final section of the output.

RANGES IN WHICH THE BASIS IS UNCHANGED:

		OBJ COEFFICIENT RANGES	
VARIABLE	CURRENT COEF	ALLOWABLE INCREASE	ALLOWABLE DECREASE
A	25.000000	15.000000	25.000000
B	10.000000	INFINITY	3.750000
		RIGHTHAND SIDE RANGES	
ROW	CURRENT RHS	ALLOWABLE INCREASE	ALLOWABLE DECREASE
2	12000.000000	INFINITY	750.000000
3	4000.000000	500.000000	2500.000000
4	6000.000000	857.142900	6000.000000

The first set of ranges given is the OBJ COEFFICIENT RANGES. Recall that the optimum solution is generally insensitive to the values of the contributions (the c_js): the OBJ COEFFICIENT RANGES list the range for each contribution for which the optimum solution remains at $A = 6{,}250$ tons, $B = 15{,}000$ tons (note that as a contribution changes, the objective function value also changes).

For VARIABLE A, we see that the current value is $25, the ALLOWABLE INCREASE is $15 (for a maximum contribution of $40), and the ALLOWABLE DECREASE is $25 (to $0). We conclude that the solution ($A = 6{,}250$, $B = 15{,}000$) is optimum for any contribution/unit for product A between $0 and $40 (with the contribution/unit from product B held at $10). Similarly, if the contribution/unit for product A is held at $25, the present solution is optimum for any contribution/unit for product B above $6.25 ($10.00 − 3.75). The allowable increase of INFINITY denotes that the current solution remains optimum for any contribution of B above the current contribution and that the current solution maximizes the quantity of B produced.

The RIGHTHAND SIDE RANGES provide the ranges for which the DUAL PRICES are valid. Row 2 is the inactive constraint associated with material 1. This constraint has a zero dual price because we have 750 tons of material 1 left over. The ranging output indicates that the dual price remains at zero for any increase in the 12,000 tons of material 1 available (we have too much of this material now; adding more does not improve our contribution). However, if the rhs decreases by 750 tons (to 12,000 − 750 = 11,250 tons), row 2 will become an **active constraint** because we need 11,250 tons of material 1 to produce the optimum solution. When row 2 becomes an active constraint, the dual price will switch from zero to a positive value.

Rows 3 and 4 are active constraints. The ranging output provides limits for applicability of the current dual prices. The dual price for row 3 (material 2) is $62.5, and this is valid over a range from 1,500 (4,000 − 2,500) tons to 4,500 (4,000 + 500) tons.

Similarly, row 4 indicates that material 3 has the dual price of $9.375 per ton in the range from 0 (6,000 − 6,000) tons to 6,857.1429 (6,000 + 857.1429) tons.

Interpreting the Shadow or Dual Prices and Right-Hand Side Ranging

The **shadow prices** (Excel) or **dual prices** (LINDO) and the right-hand side ranging output enable a number of important questions to be addressed without rerunning the solver. For example:

We have been offered 500 tons of material 1 for $1 per ton. Should we take it?

Answer: Not unless we can inventory material 1 for future use. We already have surplus material 1.

We have been offered 500 tons of material 2 at $50 per ton. Should we accept?

Answer: Yes. Additional material 2 contributes $62.5 per ton to contribution for up to an additional 500 tons. If we accept this offer, we make $12.5 per ton for the 500 tons, or $6,250. We would have to rerun our solver to find the new production quantities of A and B if we accept this offer.

The firm down the road has run short of material 3 and has offered us $15 per ton for all the material 3 that we are willing to sell. Should we sell them any?

Answer: Let them have all 6,000 tons if they will ship it. We give up $9.375 for each ton of material that we take out of the solution down to zero tons. If we sold all our 6,000 tons of material 3 at $15 per ton, our total contribution will be $33,750 greater (15 − 9.375) * 6,000.

The LP problem is one important form of MP problem. Three other important variants of MP problems arise when (unlike in the LP problem) all or some of the decision variables are restricted to integer values.

The General Integer Programming Problem

The integer programming (IP) problem is identical in form to that of the LP problem except that one or more variables are restricted to having **integer** values. Examples of such problems are those that involve indivisible resources such as vehicles, airplanes, or people, where an optimum solution that requires a fraction of the resource is not implementable.

Solving integer problems as LP problems and then rounding the values of the decision variables to integers sometimes gives good (near-optimum) integer solutions but sometimes it does not. This approach can easily produce integer solutions that violate one or more of the constraints: that is, the integer solution is not feasible.

IP problem formulation is identical to the LP formulation with the additional constraint that one or more decision variables are restricted to integer values. IP problems are more difficult to solve than LP problems, although most commercial codes (such as LINDO, IBM's OSL, and the spreadsheet solvers) have IP solvers included. These solvers use a variety of rules-of-thumb or "heuristics" and for most problems, the solutions are very close to optimum, but in general, there is no way of knowing whether a better solution can be found. IP problem solvers generally take longer to reach a solution than LP solvers.

The 0/1 Integer Programming Problem

An important group of problems are those in which all the decision variables are restricted to having the value 0 or 1. The general statement of the 0/1 IP problem is identical to that of the LP problem presented above except that all the decision variables (the X_js) are restricted to the value 0 or 1.

Some example problems:

- Assignment problems: An example is assigning aircraft hulls to flights: the decision variables take on value 1 if the hull is assigned to a particular flight and 0 otherwise.
- Truck loading problem: Should this load be placed on this truck or on another truck?
- Investment problems: Should we invest in this stock or not?
- Bidding problems: Should we bid on this issue or project or not?

The IP problem is generally more difficult to solve than the LP problem, and the "optimum" solution produced by the solver cannot usually be guaranteed to be the true optimum solution.

The Mixed-Integer Programming Problem

Mixed-integer programming (MIP) problems may include integer decision variables, 0/1 integer decision variables, and linear decision variables. The form of the problem is identical to that of the LP problem but concludes with a list of those decision variables restricted to integer and/or 0/1 values.

Good solutions to MIP problems can be found with most commercially available codes: the time taken to solve the problem increases with the number of integer variables, and the solution obtained will usually be very close to optimum but cannot generally be guaranteed to be optimum.

Nonlinear Programming Problems

The nonlinear programming (NLP) problems are the general class of MP problems where the structure of the objective function and/or the constraints are not linear and the variables are not all integers. In general, these problems are difficult to solve and require specialized techniques. When faced with such a problem, it may be worthwhile to try to approximate the problem with an LP or MIP form and arrive at a good solution by solving the approximation. The spreadsheet solvers can solve small nonlinear problems, but care is needed.

An important application of NLP optimization is **optimum dynamic pricing**.

Optimum Dynamic Pricing. Product pricing is an important component of any competitive strategy. Over the past 10 years, optimization has dramatically changed the way some firms set prices, and this method of price setting has transformed some industries (and looks like it may be spreading to many others). The leader in applying optimum dynamic pricing has been American Airlines, which has managed the introduction of new pricing techniques in the airline, hotel, cruise ship, and holiday businesses.

Traditionally, firms have set prices for their products and have waited for the market, often prompted by advertising, to determine how much product was sold. Discounting was commonly used to clear out excess inventory if prices were set too high to generate the required volume of sales. American Airlines, faced with fixed airplane capacities, recognized that their objective was to maximize the revenue from sale of a fixed number of tickets for each flight. American developed the concept of using prices deliberately and consciously to achieve this objective.

Some notation will be useful to introduce a highly simplified example that will present the concept:

Suppose a firm has a maximum of I units of product to sell and has just 2 days to sell this inventory. We will allow the firm to change the price of the product at the end of the first day.

Let p_1 be the price set for day 1,
q_1 be the quantity sold on day 1,
p_2 be the price set for day 2, and
$q2$ be the quantity sold on day 2.

The revenue received from sales is $p_1q_1 + p_2q_2$, and the quantity sold is $q_1 + q_2$. The firm then faces the following two-period optimization problem:

$$\text{MAXIMIZE REVENUE } Z = p_1q_1 + p_2q_2$$
$$\text{SUBJECT TO: } q_1 + q_2 \leq I$$

Now the quantity sold is linked to the price of the product through its **demand curve**:

the lower the price (all other things being equal), the greater is the quantity sold. Assume that the demand curves for the product over some price range can be approximated by linear functions:

Demand curve for day 1: $q_1 = A_1 - b_1p_1$ for $p_{1\min} \leq p_1 \leq p_{1\max}$; $A_1, b_1, p_{1\min}, p_{1\max} \geq 0$

Demand curve for day 2: $q_2 = A_2 - b_2p_2$ for $p_{2\min} \leq p_2 \leq p_{2\max}$; $A_2, b_2, p_{2\min}, p_{2\max} \geq 0$

The two-period revenue maximization can now be restated as a constrained price optimization problem by eliminating q_1 and q_2:

$$\text{MAXIMIZE REVENUE Z} = p_1(A_1 - b_1p_1) + p_2(A_2 - b_2p_2)$$

$$\text{SUBJECT TO:} \quad A_1 - b_1p_1 + A_2 - b_2p_2 \leq I$$

$$p_{1\min} \leq p_1 \leq p_{1\max}$$

$$p_{2\min} \leq p_2 \leq p_{2\max}$$

Solving this optimization problem at the start of day 1 provides planned (revenue maximizing) prices for day 1 and day 2 that will, in general, be different.

After posting the optimum day 1 price (p_1), the firm will observe a certain level of day 1 sales, but in general this will differ from the planned quantity q_1. The optimum price for day 2 is now recomputed by solving a new **one-period** optimization (for p_2) in which the initial inventory is depleted by the actual sales in period 1:

$$\text{MAXIMIZE REVENUE Z} = p_2(A_2 - b_2p_2)$$

$$\text{SUBJECT TO:} \quad A_2 - b_2p_2 \leq I - q'_1 \qquad \text{where } q'_1 = \text{actual sales on day 1.}$$

$$p_{2\min} \leq p_2 \leq p_{2\max}$$

This highly simplified example illustrates the essential features of optimum dynamic pricing:

The firm seeks to vary prices optimally to maximize revenues while selling a given quantity of product over a certain number of pricing periods.

The firm computes new optimum prices at the end of each pricing period. These new prices take into account actual sales (or actual inventory levels).

The number and length of the "pricing period" depends on the nature of the product. In existing applications, the pricing period is generally 1 day, with the largest problems having product life cycles of 3 to 6 months.

In general, prices will vary from pricing period to pricing period. In periods of high demand, prices will tend to be higher than in periods of low demand.

In general, prices will deviate from planned prices according to actual sales. If actual sales are below planned sales, prices will generally fall. If actual sales are above planned sales, prices will tend to increase.

Several variations of the basic problem can be added where appropriate:

Where increasing prices is unacceptable to the firm, constraints can be added to require

$$p_i \geq p_{i+1} \quad \text{for all } i$$

(although this will result in "lost" revenue).

Large price fluctuations can be eliminated by adding constraints to restrict the range of prices or the magnitude of period-to-period price changes (although these will result in lost revenues and may lead to positive ending inventories if price cannot be reduced fast enough to clear the inventory).

Implementation of Optimum Dynamic Pricing. Effective implementation of dynamic pricing requires both advanced information technology and state-of-the-art algorithms. Beginning with accurate real-time data on sales volumes or inventory levels for each product, the firm must develop the procedures to use periodic sales data to estimate product demand curves. These procedures may include collection and analysis of exogenous variables (such as competitor's prices, weather, economic activity levels, and so on). For given demand curves, the optimum pricing problem is a nonlinear MP problem (which may be large) that the firm must be able to solve for every product every pricing period. Finally, the firm must have the capability to "deliver" the new product prices back into the marketplace in time for the next pricing period.

Is implementation possible? American Airlines is able to revise the prices of up to 50,000 products each day. Yes, implementation is certainly possible.

Solving Integer, 0/1 Integer, and MIP Problems with Excel Solver

General integer variables are identified in Excel Solver formulations by formulating the problem in the normal way and then adding constraints that the variables be integers by choosing **int** as the sign in the integer constraints (Figure 4-11).

0/1 integer variables are identified by constraining them to be integer, and greater or equal to 0, and less than or equal to 1. (Newer versions of Excel Solver allow 0/1 variables to be input as binary variables in the constraint box.)

Solving Integer, 0/1 Integer, and Mixed-Integer Programming Problems with LINDO

General integer variables and 0/1 integer variables are identified to LINDO by commands GIN and INTEGER. After entering the problem formulation, command:

GIN X

restricts decision variable X to integer values. Command

INTEGER Y

restricts decision variable Y to value 0 or 1.

Figure 4-11 CONSTRAINING VARIABLES TO BE INTEGER IN EXCEL SOLVER

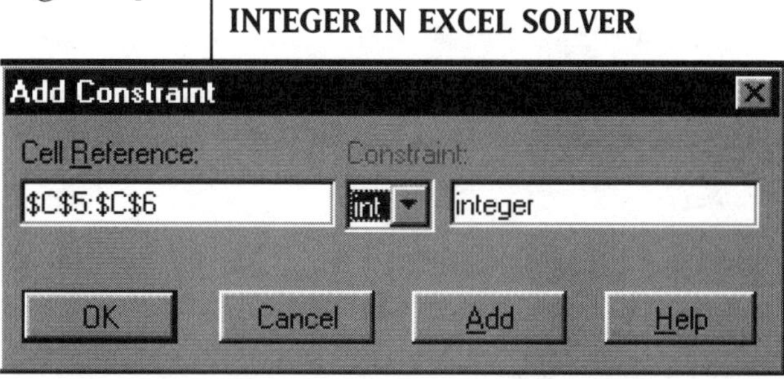

For problems that include integers, LINDO will list several intermediate solutions before listing the best solution found. The final output (for the best solution found) is displayed using commands SOLUtion and RANGe and contains the same information as the LP output. In interpreting this output, attention should be paid to the integer nature of some of the variables.

Table 4-3 **OPTIMIZATION SOFTWARE**

Package Name	Linear Optimization	0-1 (Only) Integer Optimization	General Integer Optimization	Price for Largest Version ($)
AXA	√	No	√	5,000
C-WHIZ	√	No	√	Variable
CPLEX	√	√	√	1,000
Fort LP	√	√	√	4,200
Fort MP	√	√	√	1,250–3,750
HS/LP	√	√	√	—
LAMPS	√	√	√	—
LINDO	√	√	√	4,995
LINGO	√	√	√	4,995
LOQO	√	No	No	15,000
LP/MIP Solver	√	No	√	1,495
LSSOL	√	—	—	2,000
MILP LP	√	—	—	895
MINOS	√	√	√	5,000
MINOS (IIS)	√	—	—	—
MPL System	√	√	√	4,600
MathPro	√	√	√	6,000
OMNI LP	√	√	√	—
OMP	√	√	√	—
ORSYS	√	√	√	299
OSL	√	√	√	19,200
PC-PROG	√	√	√	1,069
Premium Solver for Excel	√	No	√	1,495
ROI EXPRESS	√	No	√	25,000
SCICONIC MGG	√	No	√	—
SOPT	√	√	√	—
VMP/PC	√	No	No	950
What's Best	√	√	√	4,995
XLSol for AMPL	√	No	√	1,495
XPRESS-MP	√	No	√	—

Source: R. Sharda, *OR/MS Today,* October 1995.

Optimization Software

MS/OR professionals have produced and marketed a vast array of MS/OR applications software, including many optimization packages. In addition to the solvers available in the major spreadsheets, a large variety of stand-alone optimizing software is available (for examples, see Table 4-3).

What the Manager Needs to Know

Optimization using MP techniques (particularly LP, IP, or MIP) are valuable competitive tools. To apply these tools effectively, the manager needs to:

- Be able to recognize these problem types within the organization
- Be able to formulate these problems in a sensible way to attain the highest possible benefit from use of the available tools
- Understand how to obtain an optimum solution for these problems
- Be able to interpret the solutions and understand how the results obtained can be used to improve the firm's competitiveness

When the problems are large and solved repeatedly, the manager will likely not solve these problems personally, but rather the manager's role switches to that of supervision. In this role, it is important that the manager can explain how the problem is to be solved (what is the objective, the constraints, and so on) and can *validate* the solution derived. Validation requires that the manager be able to inspect the output from the solver and determine that the formulation was correct and that the solution is feasible and implementable. Validation also requires an assessment that the data used in the model were correct and up to date.

When the optimization is performed repeatedly over time, particularly if the model is large, the manager also must take responsibility for the introduction and control of some form of **data management system**. Such a system ensures that the data required for the model are available and are maintained to ensure that the model is always solved using current data. The manager also needs to know enough about the structure of the formulation to be able to recognize when the model requires reformulation.

MATHEMATICAL PROGRAMMING IN ACTION

FORMULATING ANIMAL FEED FOR FARMERS

The Shur-Gain division of Canada Packers manufactured and distributed more than 400 complete feeds and supplements for poultry, swine, cattle, horses, rabbits, dogs, and other animals at 14 plants and 10 company-owned feed mills throughout Canada and the United States. Marketing of Shur-Gain products in more than 400 local areas was undertaken by independent franchised feed mills that bought supplements from Shur-Gain, added required feed grains, and marketed locally the finished Shur-Gain products. A recent development for dairy or beef cattle was the Shur-Gain custom supplement: individual farmers who formulated their own feeds could request a custom supplement that, when mixed with the farmers' own farm-grown feed grains, produced a feedstock nutritionally balanced for each particular herd.

The feed and supplements were made up from about 600 basic materials, premixes, and additives, with the mixture of ingredients being combined to meet appropriate nutritional specifications which varied by feed type. LP models were developed and used to determine the formulas for manufacturing each basic feed that minimized the costs of all feeds, based on the availability and cost of ingredients, while ensuring that nutritional requirements were met.

Formulation of custom feeding programs for cattle required the development of more complex LP models. The nutritional and feed energy needs of cattle depend on the breed of cattle, their sex and age, and feedlot conditions (temperature, wind chill exposure, bedding, amount of mud, and so on), as well as the desired weight gain or milk production. The dairy cattle LP model developed by Shur-Gain provided a least-cost feed program for a specified milk production level, a range of milk production levels, or for non-milk-producing cows. For beef cattle, the LP model calculated the feeding program that provided a fixed growth rate at minimum cost or optimized the growth rate at minimum cost, in all cases meeting the nutritional requirements for given weight animals.

The custom feed models were run on request: about 200 runs per year for the beef model and 500 runs per year for the dairy model. To use the models, a producer submitted information on the herd and feedlot conditions, together with samples of locally available hay, grains, and other feedstuff. After an analysis of the samples and entry of the local conditions, the appropriate model was run, and the optimum feeding program was determined (both the feed formulation and the amount of feed per head per day). After adoption of the custom feed program, the weight gain forecast for beef cattle was usually within 2% of that predicted by the model. The dairy cattle model also was highly successful: a 20% increase in production in 1 year accompanied by reduced feed cost was common.

From Russ McGillivray, Formulating Animal Feeds for Canada's Farmers, in Peter C. Bell (ed), *Successful Operational Research in Canada*, Canadian Operational Research Society, Ottawa, 1984.

SCOTT PAPER USED LINEAR PROGRAMMING FOR FOREST RESOURCE ALLOCATION

Scott Paper operated a pulp mill and two sawmills and supplied roundwood and wood byproducts to about 40 privately owned sawmills, another pulp mill, and a hardboard plant. Scott Paper faced the problem of how to allocate the wood resources available to the company to its own plants and those of its customers to maximize profits.

Scott Paper obtained wood to supply these plants from three sources: logs cut on company-owned or leased land, roundwood purchased from landowners, and wood chips purchased from various sawmills. The availability of logs was dependent on the amount of forest available to harvest and the availability of skilled wood crew labor.

An LP model was used to determine what tonnage of each type of wood (hardwood, softwood, pulp or sawlog, chips, or bark) should be harvested from each of 162 forest compartments or purchased from Scott Paper's or privately owned sawmills or pulp mills over a 5-year time horizon. The objective was to maximize net profit for Scott Paper and all their customers, where net profit was calculated as selling price less cutting and transportation costs. Constraints in the model included the availabilities of wood in each area of forest and of labor to harvest the wood, as well as the demand for roundwood, chips, and bark at each plant. The model developed included 2,200 activities and about 800 constraints.

The model enabled Scott Paper's management to determine which operations were the most or least profitable to evaluate the impact of a shortage of skilled woods labor and some measures to cope with this shortage, to determine a value to place on wood chips, and to determine the overall impact of management decisions that imposed annual cut restrictions in certain forest areas. The model was used for more than 7 years, during which it also provided valuable insight into the long-term effect of a severe inventory shortage resulting from spruce budworm infestation and the economic feasibility of building a third Scott Paper sawmill.

From T.B. Nickerson (Nova Scotia Research Foundation), Forest Resource Allocation for Scott Paper, in Peter C. Bell (ed), *Successful Operational Research in Canada*, Canadian Operational Research Society, Ottawa, 1984.

OPTIMIZING VEHICLE ROUTING PROBLEMS

Optimization is routinely used by a great variety of organizations to solve various routing problems. There are a number of these problems that although they have some similarities, they are sufficiently different to require special solution techniques. Although most of these can be formulated as IP or MIP problems, they often become very large when realistic size problems are considered. For this reason, the solution techniques used often make use of a variety of heuristics to assist the optimizing software. Close to optimum solutions have been found and implemented for most of these problems using available software or with the aid of consulting services from vehicle routing specialists.

The Traveling Salesman Problem

A traveler (vehicle or person) must visit a number of locations and wants to minimize the cost of travel or the time spent traveling. In the single traveling salesman problem (TSP), there is only one traveler. In the multiple TSP, there are several travelers, each constrained as to the number of locations that can be visited.

The Package Delivery and/or Pickup Problem

A delivery organization must deliver (and/or pick up) objects to (and/or at) several different locations. Many complexities to this basic problem are common in practice: more than one vehicle may be required as a result of vehicle capacity or time worked constraints, mixed pickup and delivery may require consideration of vehicle loading patterns, a schedule of one-time pickups or deliveries may have to be merged into a schedule of fixed routes operated periodically, or vehicles may operate from a single depot or multiple depots.

The Package Delivery Problem with Time Windows

The package delivery problem becomes significantly more difficult if deliveries (or pickups) are constrained to occur only within certain times of the day which vary by location.

The Haulage Problem

Quantities of materials (which may be multiple loads) must be moved from existing locations to new locations using a fleet of trucks.

The School Bus Problem

Children living at known locations must be bused to school on vehicles that travel fixed routes at fixed times and have maximum capacities.

The Mass Transit Problem

People need to be carried on a daily basis around a geographic area (usually a city or town) by a fleet of vehicles running on fixed schedules along predetermined routes.

The Real-Time Dispatching Problem

Calls are received requiring pick up of a person or object from one location and delivery to another location. The vehicles being dispatched may be spread out over a city (such as taxicabs) or a country (such as long-range road haulage).

The "7-Up" Truck Problem

This is a delivery problem except that the driver sells off the truck. The size of each delivery is not known until the truck visits a location where a sale is made.

The Traveling Lunch Problem

A mobile canteen vehicle must plan a day's operations. The sales made at each location visited depend on the time of day when the visit occurs.

The Garbage Truck/Mail Delivery Problem

A route system must be derived in which every location in a given area is visited each time period. (The vehicle may or may not have to be on the same side of the street as the location being serviced.)

Transportation Planning Problems

A regional authority must plan new roads, rail tracks, canals, dock facilities, and so on to allow for an integrated transportation policy.

AT&T'S TELEMARKETING SITE SELECTION SYSTEM

Since deregulation of the telephone industry, AT&T has faced increasing competition. Specialist low-cost suppliers have entered AT&T's most lucrative market segments, providing keen competition. As a result, AT&T was having great difficulty competing as a supplier of telephone sets, switches, or long distance calls—all markets in which AT&T was perceived to be the highest priced vendor (although AT&T tried to retain an image as the highest *quality* vendor).

AT&T's strategic response to this competition was to aggressively market new products that were made up of packages of telecommunications hardware, software, and services. One example of this type of product was a corporate telephone system that consisted of handsets, exchanges, software, outside lines, toll call services, and "800" numbers, together with required training and decision support, all individually tailored for a given company. By offering such inclusive, customized products, AT&T hoped to entice companies to choose AT&T as the supplier of all their telecommunications needs. Another example of a new product being offered by AT&T was telemarketing systems.

The Growing Business of Telemarketing

Telemarketing is a business tool or concept that encompasses four major areas:

- Order processing (such as handling catalogue sales)
- Customer service (such as managing a product service fleet)
- Sales support (such as shipment tracking, billing problem resolutions)
- Account management (such as direct telephone sales)

In 1990, it was estimated that there were more than 180,000 telemarketing centers in the United States employing more than 2 million people. It was predicted that by the year 2000, there would be more than 700,000 companies in the United States employing approximately 8 million people in telemarketing, generating annual revenues of about $500 billion. AT&T has been a major supplier to the telemarketing industry, providing many services at no extra cost. Such services included telephone training, consultation on the integration of telemarketing into the firm's business strategy, and helping with the very difficult problem of selecting the best locations for telemarketing centers.

Telemarketing Site Selection

Companies developing a new telemarketing operation face the problem of deciding how many telemarketing centers they should have and where they should be located. The location of the site or sites affects the cost of operations because labor and real estate costs vary geographically and the cost of calls to the center or centers depends on the origin of the calls and the location of the center or centers. Finding a minimum cost solution to the site-selection problem is quite complex.

AT&T's National Technical Center recognized that providing "optimum" site selection as part of its telemarketing products would provide a competitive edge. Furthermore, prompted by a query from a large catalogue-based sales customer that revealed the inadequacy of existing site-selection procedures, AT&T set out to solve the site-selection problem systematically.

A procedure to determine the optimum solution to the site selection problem would have to have data on every possible site, but the work involved in collecting this data clearly makes this impractical. AT&T resolved this issue by recognizing that politics was an important factor in site selection. Consequently, there was no point in suggesting sites that were not politically acceptable. The problem could, therefore, be restated: identify those sites that were politically acceptable and then choose the set of optimum sites from this group.

The system developed to perform this task was designed to be highly user-friendly and run on a personal computer. LINDO was used to perform the optimization. The system included graphic displays of the possible sites, as well as access to a host of demographic information, economic forecasts, and other potentially significant information about each site. The output of the system provides suggestions as to the number of sites and their geographic locations, the areas of the country to be served from each site, and the amount of labor required at each site. After using the system, several customers who had preconceived ideas as to where their sites should be located changed their minds and agreed with the suggestions from the system.

Mixed-Integer Programming Model

The problem formulation is fairly straightforward:

For each site j (where $j = 1, 2, \ldots M$ denotes the M sites under consideration):

Let the fixed costs, such as real estate costs, of operating a center at the site be $F(j)$.
Let $X(i,j)$ be the fraction of calls originating from area code i to be routed to site j.
Let the upper limit on the size of the site j (indicating how much labor was needed) be $U(j)$, and the lower limit be $L(j)$.
Let $Y(j) = 1$ denote the site was selected, and $Y(j) = 0$ denote that the site was not selected.

Let the total hours of calls expected to originate from area code i be $T(i)$, for $i = 1, 2, 3, \ldots N$.

Let the per-unit communication costs from each possible telephone area code i to the telemarketing site j be $C(i, j)$.

Let MAXSITE be the maximum number of sites to be selected, and MINSITE be the minimum number of sites to be selected.

The objective is to find values for the 0-1 integer variables $Y(j)$ (M values in all) and for the fractional variables $X(i,j)$ ($i \times j$ values in all) so the sum of the fixed costs plus the communications costs is minimized.

Constraints that must be met include the following:

- The volume of calls handled at each center ($X(i, j)*T(i)$ summed over all area codes i) must be within the capacity of the center, that is, in the range from $L(j)Y(j)$ to $U(j)Y(j)$.
- All calls must be handled by some center (the sum of the $X(i, j)$ for all centers j must be equal to 1 for all area codes i).
- The number of sites selected (the sum of the $Y(j)$) must be in the range from MINSITE to MAXSITE.

An Example

A national manufacturer and distributor had 42 branch offices containing groups of six to 40 people who supported the field sales force by handling orders and problems when the salespeople were unavailable. Management decided to expand and consolidate this telemarketing operation to cut sales expenses. The AT&T sales team presented the AT&T site-selection process to senior management at the firm and worked with the firm to select a new set of sites.

Within 1 week, AT&T sent the customer a set of sites. These were modified by the customer, and new sites were suggested. Within 2 weeks, AT&T presented five configurations with cost comparisons for 1, 2, and 5 years. Four weeks after the original presentation, the customer selected a chosen configuration that saved $1,040,000 annually (or 12% off the cost of its own candidate locations).

The company awarded AT&T the 800 service (worth approximately $7.5 million annually) and decided to buy the telephone switching equipment needed from AT&T without competitive bids.

Results

The model has been successful in progressing AT&T's competitive strategy. It has provided a new value added service for AT&T's customers, enhanced AT&T's reputation as a provider of superior and comprehensive service, and increased the likelihood that the customer will use AT&T for future business.

In 1988, 46 customers of AT&T used the model to make decisions on sites swiftly and confidently while committing to $375 million in annual network services and $31 million in equipment sales. Of these 46 customers, 12 reported that they had saved an average of $1 million annually by using locations identified by the model as opposed to those sites that the companies developed independently.

From Thomas Spencer III, Anthony J. Brigandi, Dennis R. Dargon, and Michael J. Sheehan, "AT&T's Telemarketing Site Selection System Offers Customer Support," *Interfaces*, January-February 1990.

MATHEMATICAL PROGRAMMING AT MILITARY AIRLIFT COMMAND

Air transportation for the U.S. Department of Defense is provided by Military Airlift Command (MAC), whose corporate headquarters is at Scott Air Force Base near St. Louis, Missouri. MAC used 5,000 pilots to fly some 700,000 hours annually with 1,700 aircraft operating from 850 locations in 24 countries. On a typical day, MAC would fly 1,700 flights, move 5,000 passengers and 1,000 tons of cargo, fly nine rescue missions, and move 200 patients on medical evacuation flights.

The Commander in Chief of the MAC (a four-star general) had a group of 23 analysts who were actively employed in decision making involving mobilization of MAC's air fleet. This analysis group had to make the best possible decisions in the time available: their continued existence hinged on their performing credible, responsive, timely analyses.

This group has used LP extensively to arrive at efficient solutions to large and complex problems. Examples include:

Optimizing Scheduled Cargo Flights

MAC spends 35% of its flying hours for C-5, C-141, and C-130 aircraft, flying regularly scheduled cargo flights over a global network. However, the volume of cargo to be transported exceeds the capacity of MAC's fleet, consequently significant amounts of cargo capacity must be purchased from commercial air carriers. The problem facing the analysis group is to derive a network of scheduled cargo flights that minimizes the cost of purchased cargo capacity.

This problem is formulated as an LP problem with 18,000 variables and 13,000 constraints. The variables specify the number of times each month to fly a particular aircraft on a particular route. The problem takes about 1 hour to solve using a fast commercial interior-point LP code.

Solution of this problem has yielded impressive benefits. In 1988, $164 million was spent to buy commercial cargo capacity, and it is expected that this can be reduced by about 15%. In addition, improved routing has eliminated the need to purchase at least one additional airplane (valued at $3.5 million).

Cargo Distribution in the United States

In the continental United States, 650,000 cargo shipments originate at 10,000 locations, and they must be shipped (by air or truck) through MAC terminals and onto overseas destinations through the MAC scheduled global network. The problem is to find a low-cost set of MAC ports combined with the global network that takes into account where cargo originates and where it is going.

The problem is formulated as an LP problem with 60,000 variables and 6,000 constraints and takes about 20 minutes to solve. The variables specify the number of times each month to fly a particular aircraft or drive a truck on a particular route. The solution suggested a major change in operations of the port system: eight major ports were reduced to five, with one primary port for each overseas destination, leading to more timely cargo delivery and financial gains from closing ports.

Patient Evacuation

Wartime medical evacuation will, in the future, be carried out with Boeing 767 aircraft of the Civil Reserve Air Fleet. The problem is to find an optimum set of distribution hubs that are near hospital bed concentrations in the United States and to determine an optimum set of routes to these hubs from potential overseas locations.

The LP problem formulation has 250,000 variables specifying the number of casualties to be transported on a particular route, the number of beds required in U.S. hospitals, and the number of aircraft that should fly particular routes. The 90,000 constraints involve casualty and hospital bed availability by type (burn, orthopedic, and so on) and aircraft capacity and ranges. The problem takes about 4 hours to solve.

As a result of this modeling, an ideal set of nine hubs has been chosen from 52 possible hubs to minimize the average distance patients must travel to reach an appropriate hospital bed.

From Robert Roehrkasse, "Linear Programming in Operations Research," *IEEE Potentials*, December 1990.

OPTIMIZATION OF POULTRY OPERATIONS AT SADIA

The Sadia Group is Brazil's largest producer of poultry, processed meat, pork, and beef and the second largest processor of soybeans. The group has an annual income of more than $2.5 billion and exports its products to 40 countries around the world. Sadia's poultry business area represents 30% of the group's income. Sadia recently collaborated with UniSoma, a management sciences and operations research company, to develop PIPA, an integrated planning and support system for poultry operations.

Poultry Process

The process begins with the purchase of grandparent chicks from poultry genetics companies. These grandparents are used to produce a second generation of chicks called **breeders**. The breeders are housed in strict male/female proportions and used to hatch the final generation of chicks, called **broiler chicks**, which are distributed to growers in flocks of approximately 12,000.

The flocks, together with feed and necessary technical support, are delivered to farmers, who house and raise the chicks until the slaughter date, at which time the farmer is paid a negotiated price based on performance and efficiency—determined on the basis of the amount of feed used and the average chicken weight achieved.

Scheduling the processing plants requires determining which flocks will be slaughtered and processed, and this involves many variables such as flock availabilities, weight distribution of flocks, and plant capacity utilization. The plant process itself includes plucking, evisceration, inspection, chilling, weighing, sorting, optional deboning, cutting, packing, and shipping. Plant processing equipment is adjusted for each range of live weight.

PIPA

PIPA, which is an acronym for Integrated Planning for Poultry Production (in Portuguese), is a modular system organized into strategic, tactical, and operational level systems (Figure 4-12). The modules make extensive use of MP optimization supported by statistical methods and complemented by the feed formulation module.

On the strategic level, the **Integrated Global Planning** module plans the material flow of eggs to incubators, chicks to growers, broilers to farmers, and products to market. In addition, it permits what-if analysis of new plant, product, or market investments.

The tactical-level **Chick Planning** module synchronizes the production and replacement of grandparent chicks with the demand for broilers, minimizing the cost of broiler chick production. This module is closely integrated with the **Site Planning** system, which determines housing, slaughtering, and production schedules based on available processing

Figure 4-12 | **SADIA PIPA SYSTEM SCHEMATIC**

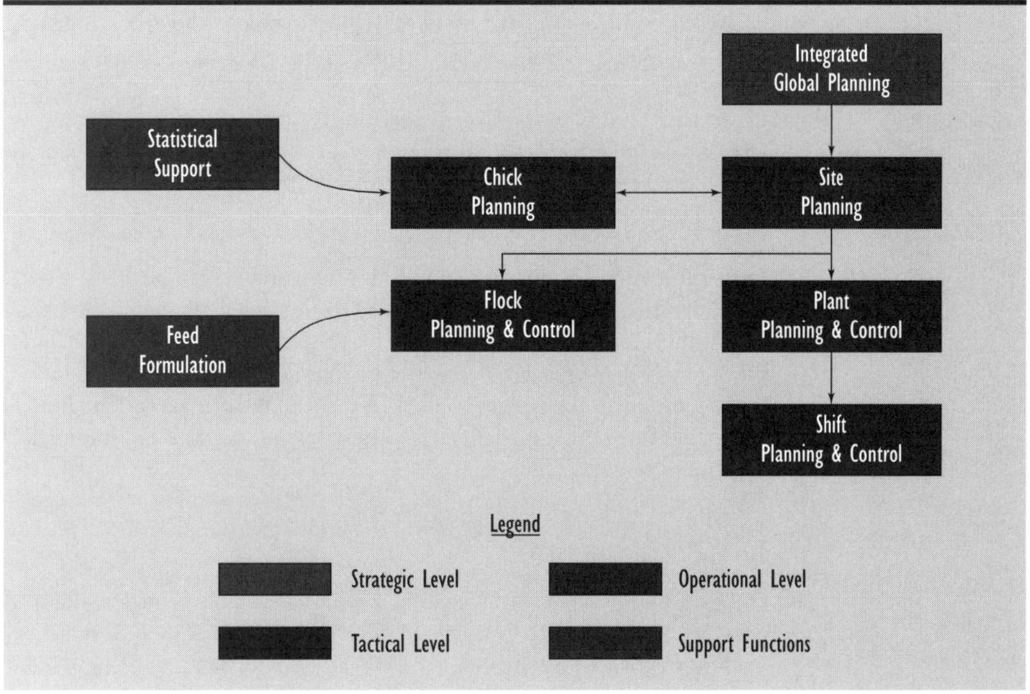

capacities; demand and prices for final products; and feed and chick costs to maximize each site's margin.

The housing schedules are used by the **Flock Planning and Control** module to determine a slaughter date for that flock based on previous performance with a particular grower with respect to expected weight distribution. The **Plant Planning and Control** module takes this slaughtering schedule and, based on the weight distribution, determines a production schedule for the following 1 to 2 weeks. Once a production schedule is developed, a deterministic simulation is used to attempt to predict exact weight distributions for production shifts. This information is merged with the capacity of the processing lines for use by the **Shift Planning and Control** system to assign labor.

The problems addressed by the PIPA system are large and complex; the Chick Planning module alone contains 130,000 decision variables and 35,000 constraints. In total, the PIPA system optimizes more than 180,000 variables involving some 51,000 constraints.

Benefits of the PIPA System

Three main areas have seen significant improvements as a result of the implementation of the PIPA system: feed to live weight conversion, higher value products, and market responsiveness.

Feed-to-Live Weight Conversion. A young chick gains roughly 1 kilogram of weight for each 2 kilograms of feed consumed, but as the chickens grow, their feed needs increase and the feed efficiency decreases. Once a flock reaches a certain age, delaying slaughtering by 1 day increases the marginal cost of achieving weight gain; therefore, there is a cost-minimizing slaughter date.

Comparisons of the feed-to-weight ratio before and after PIPA implementation showed a 3.2% to 3.9% improvement. Sadia uses 105,000 tons of chicken feed each month, with each ton costing about $165. This 3.9% improvement, therefore, translates into a saving of almost $25 million over a 3-year period, with an additional $5 million in savings for turkey production.

Greater Value Products. The ability to plan production at a strategic level has led to an 11% increase in the weight of higher margin products produced, or increased revenues of $18 million over a 3-year period.

Faster Response Times to Market Fluctuations/Opportunities. Chicken profiles differ quite significantly among growers. The PIPA system allows Sadia to select growers who will produce birds with qualities that best match current market demands. In addition with the help of PIPA, changes in chicken processing age and sales mix have shown the potential to increase gross margin by 14%. Nearly all the critical production plans developed by PIPA have been implemented successfully, resulting in timely shipments to both domestic and export markets.

BENEFITS

Over the past 3 years, PIPA benefits have totaled more than $50 million—a figure that is expected to rise as PIPA is refined. These benefits do not include nonfinancial benefits that PIPA has provided by increasing managerial understanding of individual roles and of the interdependencies in the decision chain.

From M. Taube-Netto, "Integrated Planning for Poultry Production at Sadia," *Interfaces*, January-February 1996.

EXERCISES

1. An automobile parts manufacturer has sufficient stamping capacity available to stamp out parts for 1,000 luxury car jacks or 2,000 economy car jacks (or any combination thereof). They also have the metal shop capacity to produce 1,000 luxury jack handles or 1,200 economy jack handles (or any combination thereof). Painting facilities can paint any number of economy jacks (they are unpainted) but no more than 900 luxury jacks. Contribution is $10 per economy jack and $15 per luxury jack. How many jacks (with handles) should be produced to maximize contribution?
2. A farmer grows soybeans and wheat. Soybeans yield a profit of $36 per ton, and wheat yields a profit of $0.25 per bushel. Production of 1 ton of soybeans requires 1 acre of land, 1 hour of labor, and no fertilizer. Growing 1 bushel of wheat requires 0.01 acre of land, 0.005 hour of labor, and 0.01 sack of fertilizer. The farmer plans to plant 50 acres of land and has 20 labor hours and 5 sacks of fertilizer available. What should he plant?
3. Janet paid exactly $60 for 60 old thimbles priced at $0.39, $0.97, or $1.19 each. How many of each did she buy?
4. Transworld Nickel Company operates a nickel mine. Nickel ore is mined in three pits, from where it is conveyed to the crusher and mill. Pit details are as given in Table 4-4.

Table **4-4** | **CHARACTERISTICS OF THE THREE PITS**

	Pit 1	Pit 2	Pit 3
Conveyer capacity (tons/week)	20,000	25,000	21,000
Variable mining cost ($/ton)	10	9	9.5
Nickel in ore (%)	2.5	1.8	2.4

The crusher can crush the ore to a fine grind for $1 per ton or to a coarse grind for $0.90 per ton. The type of grind affects the handling of the ore at the mill (Table 4-5).

The current market price of nickel is $2.40 per pound. How should the mine and crusher be operated to maximize contribution?

Table **4-5** | **GRINDING CHARACTERISTICS**

	Fine Ground	Coarse Ground
Mill capacity (tons/week)	16,800	21,000
Nickel recovery rate (%)	96	85
Milling cost ($/ton)	2.00	1.90

CASES

RED BRAND CANNERS

REPRINTED WITH PERMISSION OF STANFORD UNIVERSITY, GRADUATE SCHOOL OF BUSINESS.
COPYRIGHT© 1965 BY THE BOARD OF TRUSTEES OF THE LELAND STANFORD JUNIOR UNIVERSITY.

On Monday, September 13, 1965, Mr. Mitchell Gordon, Vice-President of Operations, asked the Controller, the Sales Manager, and the Production Manager to meet with him to discuss the amount of tomato products to pack that season. The tomato crop, which had been purchased at planting, was beginning to arrive at the cannery, and packing operations would have to be started by the following Monday. Red Brand Canners was a medium-size company that canned and distributed a variety of fruit and vegetable products under private brands in the western states.

Mr. William Cooper, the Controller, and Mr. Charles Myers, the Sales Manager, were the first to arrive in Mr. Gordon's office. Dan Tucker, the Production Manager, came in a few minutes later and said that he had picked up Produce Inspection's latest estimate of the quality of the incoming tomatoes. According to their report, about 20% of the crop was grade A quality and the remaining portion of the 3,000,000-pound crop was grade B.

Gordon asked Myers about the demand for tomato products for the coming year. Myers replied that they could sell all of the whole canned tomatoes they could produce. The expected demand for tomato juice and tomato paste, on the other hand, was limited. The Sales Manager then passed around the latest demand forecast, which is shown in Exhibit 1. He reminded the group that the selling prices had been set in light of the long-term marketing strategy of the company, and potential sales had been forecasted at these prices.

Bill Cooper, after looking at Myers' estimates of demand, said that it looked like the company "should do quite well [on the tomato crop] this year." With the new accounting system that had been set up, he had been able to compute the contribution for each product, and according to his analysis the incremental profit on the whole tomatoes was greater than for any other tomato product. In May, after Red Brand had signed contracts agreeing to purchase the grower's production at an average delivered price of $0.06 per pound, Cooper had computed the tomato products' contributions (Exhibit 2).

Dan Tucker brought to Cooper's attention that although there was ample production capacity, it was impossible to produce all whole tomatoes because too small a portion of the tomato crop was A quality. Red Brand used a numerical scale to record the quality of both raw produce and prepared products. This scale ran from 0 to 10, with the higher number representing better quality. Rating tomatoes according to this scale, grade A tomatoes averaged 9 points per pound, and grade B tomatoes averaged 5 points per pound. Tucker noted that the minimum average input quality for canned whole tomatoes was 8 points and for juice it was 6 points per pound. Paste could be made entirely from grade B tomatoes. This meant that whole tomato production was limited to 800,000 pounds.

Gordon stated that this was not a real limitation. He had been recently solicited to purchase 80,000 pounds of grade A tomatoes at $0.085 per pound and at that time had turned down the offer. He felt, however, that the tomatoes were still available.

Myers, who had been doing some calculations, said that although he agreed that the company "should do quite well this year," it would not be by canning whole tomatoes. It seemed to him that the tomato cost should be allocated on the basis of quality and quantity rather than by quantity only as Cooper had done. Therefore, he had recomputed the marginal profit on this basis (Exhibit 3), and from his results, Red Brand should use 2,000,000 pounds of the B tomatoes for paste and the remaining 400,000 pounds of B tomatoes and all of the A tomatoes for juice. If the demand expectations were realized, a contribution of $48,000 would be made on this year's tomato crop.

Assignment

Ignore for the present the opportunity to purchase additional grade A tomatoes.

1. Address the following questions:

What is management's objective?

What does management need to know?

What constraints are there?

What do you think Red Brand Canners should produce?

2. Formulate Red Brand Canners' production problem as a linear program. Use a solver to solve this problem and address the following questions:

How much whole tomatoes, juice, and paste should be made?

Are there any tomatoes left over? Of what grade?

What is the average point count (quality) of whole tomatoes, juice, and paste?

How much would Red Brand Canners pay for 1 additional pound of grade A tomatoes?

What is the contribution?

Should Red Brand Canners buy the extra 80,000 pounds of grade A tomatoes at the offered price?

How do solutions derived using Cooper's contribution figures and Myer's profit figures differ from your own? Why are there differences?

The purchasing manager of a supermarket chain offered \$3.60 per case for all the whole tomatoes that RBC could produce at a minimum quality level of 7 points. Should the offer be accepted?

Suppose an unlimited supply of grade A tomatoes were available at \$0.085 per pound. How much should Red Brand Canners buy? What would be the product mix?

Exhibit 1 | **RED BRAND CANNERS: DEMAND FORECASTS**

Product	Selling Price per Case	Demand Forecast (Cases)
24–2½ whole tomatoes	\$4.00	800,000
24–2½ choice peach halves	5.40	10,000
24–2½ peach nectar	4.60	5,000
24–2½ tomato juice	4.50	50,000
24–2½ cooking apples	4.90	15,000
24–2½ tomato paste	3.80	80,000

Exhibit 2 | RED BRAND CANNERS: PRODUCT ITEM PROFITABILITY

Product	24–2½ Whole Tomatoes	24–2½ Choice Peach Halves	24–2½ Peach Nectar	24–2½ Tomato Juice	24–2½ Cooking Apples	24–2½ Tomato Paste
Selling price	$4.00	$5.40	$4.60	$4.50	$4.90	$3.80
Variable costs						
Direct labor	1.18	1.40	1.27	1.32	0.70	0.54
Variable OHD	0.24	0.32	0.23	0.36	0.22	0.26
Variable selling	0.40	0.30	0.40	0.85	0.28	0.38
Packaging material	0.70	0.56	0.60	0.65	0.70	0.77
Fruit[1]	1.08	1.80	1.70	1.20	0.90	1.50
Total variable costs	3.60	4.38	4.20	4.38	2.80	3.45
Contribution	$0.40	$1.02	$0.40	$0.12	$1.10	$0.35
Less allocated OHD	0.28	0.7	0.52	0.21	0.75	0.23
Net profit	$0.12	$0.32	($0.12)	($0.09)	$0.35	$0.12

Product usage

Product	Pounds per case
Whole tomatoes	18
Peach halves	18
Peach nectar	17
Tomato juice	20
Cooking apples	27
Tomato paste	25

Exhibit 3 | RED BRAND CANNERS: MARGINAL ANALYSIS OF TOMATO PRODUCTS

$Z =$ Cost per pound of A tomatoes in cents

$Y =$ Cost per pound of B tomatoes in cents

(1) (600,000 lbs. $\times$ Z) + 2,400,000 lbs. $\times$ Y) = 3,000,000 lbs. $\times$ 6)

(2) $\frac{Z}{9} = \frac{Y}{5}$

$Z =$ 9.32 cents per pound

$Y =$ 5.18 cents per pound

Product	Canned Whole Tomatoes	Tomato Juice	Tomato Paste
Selling price	$4.00	$4.50	$3.80
Variable cost (excluding tomato costs)	2.52	3.18	1.95
	$1.48	$1.32	$1.85
Tomato cost	1.49	1.24	1.30
Marginal profit	($ .01)	$ .08	$ .55

NESBITT THOMSON: MONTHLY PAYMENT PLAN—SERIES 30

Mike Mackasey, Vice President, Corporate Finance at Nesbitt Thomson Deacon Inc. (Nesbitt), had just been handed the list of long-term bonds issued by senior Canadian corporations that were eligible for inclusion in Nesbitt's Series 30 Monthly Payment Portfolio (Exhibit 1). The Series 30 portfolio was to have a face value of $50 million, and Mike's task for the remainder of the day (and the night, if necessary) was to choose the portfolio of bonds to be included in the portfolio. Speedy action was essential so the portfolio could be purchased at the prices now being quoted (see Exhibit 1).

THE COMPANY

Nesbitt, a fully integrated, international investment dealer, has been engaged in the trading of securities and commodities and in the underwriting and distribution of securities since 1912. The company did business in Canada, the United States, and Europe and dealt in equity, money market, and debt securities issued by the government of Canada and provincial and municipal governments as well as in certain other specialized investment instruments. Nesbitt also provided its clients with research and advisory services and provided individuals and small institutions with portfolio management services, registered retirement savings plans, provincial stock savings plans, and related services.

The company generated significant revenue from many business sectors, including retail and institutional brokerage, equity trading, corporate and government finance, and syndication.

PORTFOLIO OFFERING

Nesbitt had introduced its Monthly Payment Plan (MPP) in 1986 with the offering of Series 1. The objective of the MPP was to provide an even, secure flow of investment income by providing regular monthly payments of income to unitholders and to ensure, to the greatest extent practicable, the eventual return of principal invested.

The product was a closed-end investment trust comprised of several "A" or better rated bonds. The investment objective was to provide investors with regular monthly payments of income through investment in a professionally selected portfolio of long-term, high-quality debt obligations issued primarily by senior Canadian corporations and government. The trust would not be a managed fund, and the underlying securities would not be traded in an attempt to achieve capital gains or higher returns; once the portfolio was chosen, it was held to maturity unless extraordinary circumstances arose. The Royal Trust Company, one of Canada's largest trust companies, acted as trustee, collecting and distributing the bond interest.

The public response to Nesbitt's MPP had been excellent. Most series had sold out quite quickly, and new series were now a regular feature of Nesbitt's business. The face value of the portfolios had increased from $15 million for the early series to $50 million for series 30.

MONTHLY PAYMENT PLAN—SERIES 30

On April 1, 1996, Mike Mackasey had been instructed to establish another MPP (Series 30) for offering to the public. He was provided with a list of 27 corporate bonds that could be included in the portfolio (see Exhibit 4-4).

In selecting the portfolio, it was important to meet certain rules:

The portfolio had to have a face value of $50 million.

No more than 15% of the portfolio could be in any one bond or in the bonds of any single issuer.

The average term to maturity must be close to 10 years.

Nesbitt was also concerned about the offering price of the portfolio to the public. The plan was offered to the public in units of $500 face value each. The offering price per unit (net of interest accrued from the date of purchase to the date of sale) was determined from the purchase price of the units plus a sales commission of 4.059%. It was desirable that this price be "close" to the face value of the units, but some latitude was allowed if slight deviation led to a higher yield. Previous series had been offered at costs per unit between $470 and $530 (before the addition of accrued interest).

Mike called in Sandra Schumacher and Rob Wonnacott. This "team" had assembled several MPP Series and had evolved a procedure to select the bonds to be included. The possible bonds were entered in a spreadsheet, and a process of trial and error was used to select the portfolio that produced the highest **running yield**—the running yield for each bond was calculated by expressing the coupon rate as a percentage of the asked price. This procedure was very time consuming, and also somewhat frustrating because it was not possible to guarantee that the best portfolio had been chosen.

Mike Mackasey did not look forward to another long day. He wondered if there was a better way to choose the Series 30 MPP portfolio.

Assignment

1. Is this a resource allocation problem?
2. Formulate this problem as an LP problem. What is a suitable objective? What are the constraints?
3. What help will the solution provide to Nesbitt management (in addition to the make up of the optimum portfolio)?

Exhibit 1 | **BONDS ELIGIBLE FOR INCLUSION IN SERIES 30**

Company	Bond Coupon	Bond Maturity	Bond Bid	Bond Ask	Bid YTM%	Ask YTM%
BNS	9.38%	03-Feb-04	102.250	102.500	9.47%	9.41%
TRANSALTA	10.75%	17-Nov-04	106.500	106.750	9.30%	9.25%
PROVIGO	10.80%	15-Sep-04	105.625	106.125	9.53%	9.43%
GAZ METRO	11.00%	01-Dec-04	106.250	106.750	9.60%	9.51%
NOVACORP	11.25%	31-Dec-04	106.375	106.875	9.83%	9.73%
EATON ACC	11.50%	30-Dec-04	108.375	108.875	9.71%	9.62%
HYDRO QUE	9.75%	16-Jul-04	101.750	102.000	9.20%	9.15%
IMASCO	10.50%	28-Apr-05	104.375	104.625	9.42%	9.37%
UNION GAS	10.50%	31-May-05	103.750	104.250	9.53%	9.44%
J LABATT	10.38%	21-Apr-05	104.500	104.875	9.27%	9.20%
ONT HYD	10.25%	12-Jul-05	104.750	105.125	9.08%	9.02%
BELL	10.50%	15-May-05	105.750	106.000	9.17%	9.12%
TRANSALTA	10.38%	06-Jul-05	104.500	104.750	9.26%	9.21%
PROV QUE	10.25%	07-Apr-05	104.125	104.375	9.21%	9.17%
TD CNTR	10.70%	12-May-05	106.250	106.750	9.28%	9.19%
ROYAL BK	10.80%	01-Jun-05	106.250	106.500	9.38%	9.34%
NAT BANK	10.88%	01-Jun-05	106.000	106.500	9.50%	9.41%
BC FOREST	11.00%	30-Jun-05	105.000	105.500	9.81%	9.72%
NOR FOR	11.00%	15-Jul-05	105.000	105.500	9.81%	9.72%
O & Y	11.00%	04-Nov-05	106.500	107.000	9.53%	9.44%
MARK PRP	10.75%	19-May-05	105.000	105.500	9.56%	9.47%
BMO	10.60%	20-Dec-05	106.175	106.375	9.18%	9.14%
RBC	10.90%	15-Jan-06	106.750	107.000	9.38%	9.34%
BELL	9.88%	01-Apr-06	101.625	102.125	9.21%	9.12%
WARDAIR	11.20%	31-Oct-06	107.750	108.000	9.50%	9.46%
NOVA	10.75%	14-Apr-06	104.000	104.250	9.70%	9.65%
WARDAIR	10.95%	29-Apr-07	106.125	106.375	9.51%	9.47%

DOFASCO—FUEL MANAGEMENT

The Works Manager at Dominion Foundries and Steel (DOFASCO) was faced with rapidly increasing market prices for fuel oil and natural gas. Anticipating that similar price increases were likely to continue for the foreseeable future, the Works Manager wanted to be certain that the steel works was making the best use of its energy dollars and, in particular, that the fuels produced as byproducts from plant operations were being efficiently used.

THE COMPANY

DOFASCO, founded in 1912, was an important steel producer that manufactured a variety of flat rolled steel products and castings. The company began as a foundry operation that supplied castings for the rail car manufacturing sector, but by the mid-1970s, it had grown into a fully integrated steel-making operation with over 10,000 employees. The company produced over 3 million ingot tons of steel and had annual sales of $621 million.

Major production facilities located at its 700-acre plant included six coke oven batteries, four blast furnaces, two steel-making shops, a hot strip mill, and cold rolling and associated finishing lines. DOFASCO's product line included:

Hot rolled sheet and strip—for automotive frames, wheels, and miscellaneous stampings, as well as construction and agricultural applications

Cold rolled sheet and strip—for automobile parts, appliances, metal containers, mechanical tubing, and agricultural equipment

Tin plate and chromium-coated steels—for food and beverage cans, crown, caps, and aerosol containers

Galvanized steel—for building and road construction, appliances, and automotive parts

Electrical steel—for transformers and motors

Prepainted steel products—for building cladding, automobile parts, and miscellaneous end uses

Steel castings—for railway components, gears, valves, and other industrial uses

ENERGY SOURCES

Fuel was produced within the plant from the blast furnaces and coke ovens. The blast furnaces produced 15,500 cubic feet (CF) of blast furnace gas (BFG) during production of each ton of iron. BFG had a low heat content (only 90 BTUs per CF), but because production was forecast at 3.3 million tons of iron, BFG represented a major energy source for DOFASCO. Furthermore, because BFG was an essential byproduct of blast furnace operation, the only cost associated with using BFG as a fuel gas was a cost of maintaining the BFG lines and necessary equipment. This cost was estimated at $5.00 per million CF used.

Coke oven gas (COG) produced during coking by the coke ovens had a much higher BTU content than BFG (540 BTUs per CF), and each ton of coke produced was accompanied by the production of 12,000 CF of COG. Coke production was forecast at 1.3 million tons. The maintenance cost of the COG lines was estimated at $45.00 per million CF used.

The fuel gas produced internally was augmented by natural gas and fuel oil purchased at market prices. Commercial fuel oil was currently available at $40 per 1,000 pounds and natural gas was available at $2,200 per 1,000,000 CF, although these prices were expected to increase dramatically in the future. One thousand pounds of fuel oil had a heat content of about 18.75 million BTUs, whereas natural gas produced 1,000 BTUs per CF. Maintenance costs for the natural gas lines were estimated at $0.10 per million CF, and those for the fuel oil lines at $8.00 per 1,000 pounds used.

ENERGY REQUIREMENTS

Production of steel was an energy-intensive process, consuming large quantities of electricity, coal, and fuel gas. There was considerable flexibility as to how the demands for fuel gas could be met from the available supplies.

The coke ovens, annealing and finishing operations, and the foundry were major users of fuel gases. Each of these plants required a gas of a certain heat content (measured by BTU value) that could be made by combining different fuels. There were, however, restrictions on the amounts of some fuels that could be used to make up the BTUs necessary to produce 1 ton of steel by each process, which resulted from the physical characteristics of the process. Exhibit 1 summarizes the fuel gas requirements and restrictions for the eight major user plants.

Coke ovens had somewhat different but strict requirements. There were three types of fuel used by the coke ovens:

1. Primary fuel (BFG), providing 1.6 million BTUs per ton
2. "Sweetened" gas, a mixture of BFG and COG averaging 100 BTUs per CF and providing 0.37 million BTUs per ton
3. "Enriched" gas, a mixture of BFG and COG averaging 250 BTUs per CF and providing 0.23 million BTUs per ton

The above three fuels, in combination, met the fuel requirement of 2.2 million BTUs per ton of coke produced.

DISTRIBUTION

Although the actual flow of gas at the plant was complex and conditions changed from hour to hour, the Works Manager decided to consider, for the purpose of long-run analysis, that the distribution of fuel gases in the steel works was limited only by the requirements of the producer and user plants. If the analysis demonstrated that fuel costs could be reduced by improved allocation, then the necessary changes in equipment and operating rules could be implemented to effect this.

The Works Manager requested that the Manufacturing Controls Department determine the most efficient pattern for fuel use within the plant.

Assignment

1. Formulate DOFASCO's problem as an LP problem.
2. Solve the problem. What information does the solution provide to management?

Exhibit I | **USES OF FUEL GAS**

User Plant	Fuel Gases Currently Used	Fuel Gases that Could Be Used	Requirements for Fuel (million BTU/ton)	Production Forecast (thousand tons/month)	Maximum Quantities (million CF/month)	
Soaking pits	NG, COG, OIL	NG, BFG, COG, OIL	1.16	275	2,147	(NG)
					510	(COG)
Batch anneal	COG	NG, BFG, COG	1.02	52	166	(COG)
Galvanizing lines	NG, COG	NG, BFG, COG	1.16	45	45	(COG)
					56.8	(NG)
Coreplate line	NG	NG, BFG, COG	.54	2.6	17.4	(NG)
Specialty steels	NG	NG	.57	7		
Foundry	COG	NG, BFG, COG	12.34	2.8	1,080	(COG)
Normalizing lines	NG	NG, BFG, COG	1.15	10.8	9	(NG)
Coke ovens	BFG, COG	BFG, COG	Primary fuel 1.6 "Sweetened" gas 0.37 "Enriched" gas 0.23	108.3		

NG, natural gas; BFG, blast furnace gas; COG, coke oven gas; OIL, fuel oil.

AGREVO INTERNATIONAL, INC.

BY PROFESSOR THOMAS A. GROSSMAN, JR., FACULTY OF MANAGEMENT, UNIVERSITY OF CALGARY.
REPRODUCED WITH PERMISSION. COPYRIGHT © 1997 THOMAS A. GROSSMAN JR.

Calvin Sonntag, Manager of Strategic Planning for AgrEvo International, Inc. (AgrEvo), is leaving Frankfurt-am-Main, Germany, and the headquarters of Hoechst Schering AgrEvo GmbH, the parent company of AgrEvo. As he settles in to his airplane seat, he reflects on the series of meetings he had attended. Global

Exhibit 1 | **PROJECT RESOURCE REQUIREMENTS ($thousand)**

Department	Year	Project Identification Code											
		A1	A3	A4	B2	B17	B18	B19	B21	D11	D12	E	F
Research	1997	266	239	11	96	15	14	32	12	41	50	6	24
	1998	68	132	2	0	0	0	32	4	50	75	0	0
Scientific Affairs	1997	81	239	5	5	15	17	5	7	23	10	17	1
	1998	68	56	5	0	0	0	5	9	32	11	0	0
Field Development	1997	145	125	42	16	34	7	10	28	15	18	5	1
	1998	60	82	23	0	0	0	6	4	12	18	0	0
Regulatory Affairs	1997	81	56	11	2	3	12	3	17	3	1	1	1
	1998	15	48	19	0	0	0	3	24	6	4	0	0

competitive pressures are increasing, and he wonders what he is going to recommend to senior management in AgrEvo's North American headquarters regarding AgrEvo's portfolio of R&D projects.

AgrEvo is a crop protection and biotechnology firm that manufactures and sells crop protection products (herbicides, insecticides, fungicides, and so on) and has a rapidly growing business in the development and sale of the products of plant biotechnology. Sales currently exceed $2 billion worldwide.

Their business is characterized by increasing competition and rapid technological change and requires substantial investment in research and development of new technologies and products. Over the past two decades, AgrEvo has introduced several innovative technologies that have allowed farmers to produce crops in a more sustainable manner. This commitment to developing and marketing environmentally responsible crop protection technologies has formed an important component of the company's competitive advantage.

Because increasing competition is causing sales margins to decline and increasing regulatory requirements are causing costs to rise, AgrEvo has recognized a need to more thoughtfully manage their R&D portfolio. In particular, they want to focus their R&D investment on a portfolio of projects that deliver the highest net present value.

As Calvin had explained in his presentation in Frankfurt, different R&D projects require different amounts of departmental resources over time. AgrEvo has instituted a **Strategic Project Management** (SPJM) system that has accurately determined the necessary resources and net present value (NPV) for each project. There are 12 projects that AgrEvo could include in their project portfolio (see Exhibits 1 and 2). Each department has its own director and its own budget, as summarized in Exhibit 3.

Calvin is wondering what he should recommend to the firm's senior management. Which projects should be funded, and which should be canceled? Some senior managers have expressed the opinion that R&D is underfunded at AgrEvo, and Calvin is wondering if this opinion is correct. If it is, he will have to carefully build a business case for additional funding before recommending to senior management that they go back to Frankfurt seeking additional resources from an increasingly tight-fisted parent company.

Shortly after takeoff on the connecting flight from London, Calvin opens his laptop computer and reflects that he is fortunate that the SPJM system has generated hard numbers that are highly credible within AgrEvo. As he opens the Excel file containing these data, he wonders what insights he can get into the R&D portfolio and the manner in which AgrEvo manages R&D resources and what he is going to recommend to his superiors when he gets home.

Exhibit 2 | **PROJECT NET PRESENT VALUE ($million)**

Project Identification Code											
A1	A3	A4	B2	B17	B18	B19	B21	D11	D12	E	F
25	33	2.3	5	10	6.1	3.5	0.5	8.4	9.4	3.4	11

Exhibit 3 | **DEPARTMENT BUDGETS ($thousand)**

Department	1997	1998
Research	600	240
Scientific Affairs	760	250
Field Development	340	250
Regulatory Affairs	292	220

Assignment

1. Create a spreadsheet model to analyze which projects should be funded and which should be cancelled. Try to determine a solution by trial and error.
2. Use Solver to optimize your model. How does the solution differ from your trial-and-error solution?
3. Is there a good case to be made for additional funding?

BISHOP'S UNIVERSITY: CLASS SCHEDULING

BY ARSHAD TASEEN AND PETER C. BELL WITH ASSISTANCE FROM CHRIS ANDERSON.

In October 1996, Bishop's University Registrar, Ann Montgomery, and her staff were notified that promised new course and examination scheduling software would not be purchased. This decision by Bishop's new principal, Janyne Hodder, had serious implications for the scheduling of Fall term examinations and the next semester's courses.

After the decision, Professor Arshad Taseen, a faculty member from the Business School was contemplating the scheduling of classes for the school's spring semester. The Business School was one of four divisions at Bishop's University; the others were Social Science, Natural Science, and Humanities. There also was a large-scale continuing education program and a graduate program in education. Professor Taseen thought that if he was able to schedule next semester's classes within the Business School, then his approach could perhaps be extended to the other divisions of the university.

BISHOP'S UNIVERSITY

Bishop's University, a small, mostly residential liberal arts university, decided during the early 1990s to prepare itself for future challenges through a series of renovations and computer system upgrades. However, the university was plagued by a series of budgetary cutbacks, and by the mid-1990s, it was faced with an administrative and financial crisis. The principal resigned and was replaced; faculty and staff were offered early retirement packages; and many ongoing projects were either frozen or severely curtailed. So severe were the budget cuts that every aspect of the university was affected.

UNIVERSITY COMPUTER SYSTEM

The university's old mainframe AZTEC computer became expensive to maintain and was replaced by a microcomputer-based system. The old mainframe system had handled many functions, including Registrar's Office activities such as student records, transcript production, registration, and timetabling, as well as being used by the Business Office for accounting. As part of the changeover, university personnel were required to convert all records and data to the new microcomputer system. Also part of the conversion was the implementation of new software to perform the many functions required within the university at a cost of about $100,000.

During Summer 1996, when the changeover was nearing completion, the decision was made not to purchase software specifically for the scheduling of course and examination timetables because the cost ($85,000 plus 12% annual maintenance fee) could not be justified. Fall semester classes had already been scheduled before the decommissioning of the old AZTEC system, and it was thought that more cost-effective solutions would become available in due time.

CRISIS

With AZTEC gone, the Registrar's Office had no software for scheduling course or examination timetables. As a result, Fall semester examinations had to be scheduled manually by staff from the Registrar's Office. The results were unsatisfactory to many students. The examination period was 3 days shorter than usual, and many students were faced with several back-to-back examinations. Frustrated with the structure of the examination schedule, many students vented to faculty. It was at this point that the scheduling problem became apparent to Professor Taseen, and he thought he might assist in the next semester's course schedule.

TIMETABLING PROCEDURE

Each division of the university prepared a minitimetable and submitted it to the Registrar's Office. This timetable contained the courses that would be offered by the division, including the name of the faculty member and a preferred time and desired classroom to teach each course. The minitimetables ensured that:

> The seating capacity of the classroom requested was greater than the possible course enrollment, and a faculty member was not teaching more than one course at the same time.

Continuing education courses were offered exclusively during the evening, and the Graduate School of Education had its own classrooms.

In the days of the AZTEC computer, the Registrar's Office would then feed the division timetables into the timetabling software and produce one universitywide timetable. This was then sent back to the divisions for their approval. If the results were not satisfactory to the division, they would resubmit their minitimetable with changes. The process would generally go through a couple of iterations before the timetable was satisfactory to all.

Sandra Gallup-Palme, Executive Secretary to the Registrar, suggested that the minitimetables produced by the divisions often contained many conflicts over rooms or timeslots, and she had to juggle courses and classrooms all the time. To make things worse, changes were frequent: Linda Fisk from the Records Office estimated that there had been more than 100 changes during the previous semester. It was estimated that seven person-months of work went into preparing timetables, not including the time spent by the divisions.

Professor Taseen collected the following information to prepare a timetable for the Business Division:

> Teaching time periods
> Classrooms available and their capacities
> Courses to be offered, with possible enrollment
> Faculty teaching a given course

A sample of this information is presented in Exhibits 1 through 3.

Professor Taseen thought that if he could develop a procedure to prepare a timetable for the Business School, then perhaps this procedure could be extended to the entire university.

Assignment

1. Formulate the problem as an IP problem and use a solver to solve the example problem.
2. Is this approach feasible for the department or universitywide problems?

Exhibit 1 | COURSE OFFERINGS AND FACULTY

Course Number	Course	Expected Enrollment	Faculty	Preferred Time Slot	Preferred Classroom
1	BUS 120	35	Schenk	Mon-Wed-Fri 9:00	H302
2	BUS 121	35	Schenk	Mon-Wed-Fri 10:30	H303
3	BUS 200	25	Lalibert	Mon-Wed-Fri 10:30	H303
4	BUS 210	23	Lalibert	Mon-Wed-Fri 9:00	H301
5	BUS 230	65	Kaltenba	Tue-Thur 10:00	H301
6	BUS 300	38	Schenk	Tue-Thur 8:00	H304
7	BUS 310	55	Cunningham	Tue-Thur 10:00	H303
8	BUS 405	10	Cunningham	Tue-Thur 8:00	H303
9	BUS 406	15	Bequet	Mon-Wed-Fri 10:30	H302
10	BUS 410	65	Bequet	Tue-Thur 8:00	H301
11	BUS 420	20	Taseen	Tue-Thur 10:00	H304
12	BUS 000	72	Kaltenba	Tue-Thur 8:00	H302

Exhibit 2 | CLASSROOM CAPACITIES

Capacity	Room Number
72	H301
38	H302
25	H303
38	H304

Exhibit 3 | TIME SLOTS

Time Slot	Days	Time
1	Mon-Wed-Fri	9:00
2	Mon-Wed-Fri	10:30
3	Tue-Thur	8:00
4	Tue-Thur	10:00

Each of the four time slots provides 3 hours of teaching time per week. The Monday-Wednesday-Friday classes (Mon-Wed-Fri) are 1 hour long each day. The Tuesday-Thursday (Tue-Thur) are 1½ hours long each day.

NORTHWEST NEWSPRINT, INC.

BY PETER C. BELL AND JOHN S. HULLAND.

The recent stabilization of the price of newsprint was welcome news for Northwest Newsprint, Inc., and John Smithers was now eager to exploit existing market conditions to the fullest. Northwest was a major producer of newsprint with pulpmills in the Pacific Northwest and Canada from which they supplied various North American markets.

Smithers, Assistant Controller in Northwest's Core Business-Papers Department, recognized that Northwest's shipping patterns had been derived when market conditions were very different from those today. Reviewing which mill supplied which market would likely reveal some opportunities for cost savings. He initially planned to develop and use a model to investigate the immediate newsprint allocation problem, but he hoped that the model could also be used to address some longer term "strategic" issues.

NORTHWEST NEWSPRINT'S OPERATIONS

In the late 1980s, the Northwest Forest Products Company of Tacoma, Washington, purchased a majority interest in Clark Newsprint Ltd. of British Columbia. By the mid-1980s, it had increased its holding in the latter company to almost 100%, and in 1988, the corporate name was changed to Northwest Clark, Inc.

After the acquisition, Northwest Clark Inc. became one of the world's largest producers of newsprint and ranked as one of the five largest forest products enterprises, with plants and mills located in both Canada and the United States. The company also maintained extensive woodlands operations. By 1994, Northwest had sales approaching $2 billion.

The company's sales could be broken into six product lines; newsprint, groundwood papers, fine papers, kraft products, building products, and lumber (Exhibit 3). Northwest Clark had always been primarily a pulp and paper products producer; however, beginning at the time of the merger, an increasing proportion of the company's total sales were attributable to the lumber and building product lines. Growth in these lines was largely dependent on U.S. housing starts, whereas newsprint had been, and continued to be the company's largest product line, using 75% of the firm's pulp and paper capacity. In recognition of the importance of newsprint, Northwest Clark established Northwest Newsprint Inc. as a separate subsidiary in 1986, with responsibility for all of Northwest Clark's pulp and paper operations.

Pulp and paper operations used about 85% of the company's effective capacity by 1990. Breaking out the production figures by product line, however (Exhibit 4, p. 145), indicated that some products made more efficient use of the available facilities than others. Highly efficient use of available capacity was essential if profitability was to be maintained in this capital-intensive and highly competitive industry. The 85% utilization rate achieved by Northwest was about the industry norm; rates lower than this would be viewed with concern.

Newsprint

Newsprint was a type of paper that had only one use; it was the paper on which newspapers were printed. The world demand for newsprint was, therefore, highly dependent on the demand for newspapers, which was in turn dependent on business conditions around the world that influenced the demand for newspapers and newspaper advertising.

Canada, the United States, and Japan were the world's largest producers of newsprint, and the United States was by far the largest consumer, consuming more than 40% of the total world supply. Japan, the United Kingdom, and West Germany were other major newsprint users. Because the United States and Japan consumed virtually all of their own production, Canada was left as the world's largest newsprint exporter. Because Northwest's newsprint mills were in Canada, prices received were considerably affected by fluctuating exchange rates, particularly that of the U.S. dollar.

The price of newsprint had fluctuated in the range from $410 per tonne to $500 per tonne since mid-1993, but a recent increase in demand beginning in 1994 had led to a surge in prices. The present price was U.S. $750 per tonne, representing a 47% increase over the past 12 months. It appeared that additional price increases were unlikely: this morning's newspaper suggested that one manufacturer was now considering reducing prices by $58 per tonne.

Allocation Problem

Northwest Newsprint operated a total of 10 newsprint mills in the United States and Canada, with the majority

Exhibit 1 | **1995 PRODUCTION (projected)**

Mill	Daily (tonnes)	Annual (tonnes)
Spruce Mills	462.0	166,320
Naomee Mills	756.5	272,340
Duchesne	737.0	265,077
Total capacity		**703,737**

The daily figures (the number of tonnes of newsprint that can be produced during a 24-hr operating day) are multiplied by 360 to calculate the annual projection. This allows for about five days of scheduled down time annually.

located in the Pacific Northwest. Three of the mills were located in Canada. Because more than 85% of the company's newsprint demand came from the United States, the Canadian mills shipped most of their output to the south. The company's seven U.S. mills were assigned specific customers that effectively required their entire newsprint output. These assignments seemed generally quite logical; a mill located close to a large-demand center would naturally supply that center, or in other cases, mills that were quite isolated from major demand centers exported the majority of their production to Japan or elsewhere on the Pacific Rim. Although these assignments were somewhat arbitrary, the company was satisfied that they yielded acceptable results.

As Smithers examined the 1995 production plan, he noted that reassignment of newsprint from the three Canadian mills to North American customers might provide some opportunities for cost savings. The projected 1995 production at the three remaining unassigned mills—Spruce Mills, Naomee Mills, and Duchesne—was 703,737 tonnes split among the three mills, as indicated in Exhibit 1.

Northwest Newsprint's 3,000 customers could all be supplied from one of nine major centers: Seattle, Washington; Chicago, Illinois; Denver, Colorado; Dallas, Texas; New Orleans, Louisiana; Los Angeles and San Francisco, California; Vancouver, British Columbia; and Calgary, Alberta. The projected 1995 annual demand for these centers is indicated in Exhibit 2.

On merging, Northwest and Clark had signed an agreement that production would be equitably shared among all the mills; that is, one mill could not be scheduled to operate at 100% capacity utilization while another mill was left idle. This was now interpreted as meaning that each mill must operate at least 6 of every 7 days.

Northwest Newsprint was expecting prices for newsprint to remain constant over the next year at a

Exhibit 2 | **1995 PROJECTED DEMAND**

Distribution Center	Annual Demand (tonnes)
Seattle	40,727
Chicago	55,608
Dallas	92,680
New Orleans	92,680
Denver	23,832
Los Angeles	211,841
San Francisco	52,960
Vancouver	32,581
Calgary	8,145
Total Demand	**611,054**

delivered price of $750 per tonne to customers located in the United States and $700 per tonne to Canadian customers. (All currency values have been converted to $U.S. at an exchange rate of $0.75 U.S. equal to $1.00 Canadian.)

Production of newsprint was a relatively capital-intensive process, but the production of 1 tonne of newsprint still involved significant variable costs. These costs included raw materials (wood, supplies, chemicals), direct labor, and energy but excluded fixed costs such as salaries, insurance, taxes, administration, depreciation, and similar service-department expenses. Using a direct costing approach, Northwest estimated newsprint production costs at $390 per tonne for Spruce Mills and $415 per tonne for both Naomee Mills and Duchesne.

Shipping finished newsprint from the mills to the distribution centers was an expensive process. Shipping costs, estimated for 1995, are summarized in Exhibit 5. (Not all rates are quoted. In some cases, no reliable shipping method had been found.)

In November 1994, the company had assigned newsprint production for 1995 (Exhibit 6) using this information. Spruce Mills' and Duchesne's production was assigned to the nearest respective markets, whereas Naomee Mills production was used to meet the remaining demand. The resulting allocation appeared acceptable, but Smithers wondered whether or not a better set of assignments could be determined: had he left money "on the table"?

Freight Rates and Delivery Swaps

An initial operating plan for 1995 was a key output from the model, but Smithers also planned to address two other important issues: freight rate discounts and "delivery swaps."

Freight rate discounts were common for large volumes, and in the past, Northwest had managed to negotiate such discounts with most carriers when volumes were sufficient. Smithers believed that he could negotiate a freight rate reduction of about 5% in 1995 for any mill-to-destination shipments greater than 100,000 tonnes. He wondered whether the availability of such discounts would affect the operating plan and the projected profit.

"Delivery swaps" were under negotiation between Northwest Newsprint and some of its major customers, including *The Los Angeles Times*, Knight-Ridder, and Hearst chains. Delivery swaps traded off customers to other newsprint suppliers to reduce freight costs. Under a swap arrangement, Northwest's contract to supply customer A would actually be delivered by another newsprint supplier, most likely one of Northwest's U.S. mills, which could meet the contract at lower cost. Usually, the alternate supplier was a mill that was closer to customer A then Northwest's Canadian mill and consequently had lower freight costs. Smithers hoped to use the model to identify the center or centers that would make the proposed delivery swaps cost attractive.

Longer-Term Issues

Northwest Newsprint's management recognized that the model could be useful for addressing some capacity planning issues. The operating plan projected 1995 capacity utilization for newsprint production of about 86%. Some major capital decisions under consideration could, however, dramatically alter the availability of newsprint capacity.

Alternative 1 involved the conversion of a newsprint machine at Naomee Mills to groundwood specialties' production. Groundwood specialties were types of paper used for printing advertising inserts, telephone directories, and computer forms, and this was a faster growing segment of the printed paper business than was newsprint. In 1994, the groundwood speciality business had operated at 96% of effective capacity, leading to concern that customers for these products might have to be turned away in the future if additional production capacity was not made available. Converting one newsprint machine at Naomee Mills would shift 58,000 tonnes per year of paper-making capacity from newsprint to groundwood specialties at a minimal cost.

Alternative 2 was to reduce newsprint capacity by selling off an older machine located at Naomee Mills, reducing capacity by 44,000 tonnes per year (it was unlikely that the company would make much money on the sale of this equipment). As an alternative to selling this second machine, it could be converted to groundwood specialties production, along with the first, at minimal cost.

Alternative 3 was to expand existing capacity. A new newsprint machine with a capacity of 150,000 tonnes of newsprint/year could be installed at any of the three mills for a total cost of $120 million. The new machines produced paper of a higher quality than that obtained from most of the older existing machines.

Higher-quality newsprint was emerging as a major competitive factor within the industry. In the early 1990s when there had been worldwide oversupply of newsprint, customers had been demanding a higher-quality product from suppliers. As the market had picked up, these demands had faded somewhat, but as new capacity came on line and production expanded, it seemed clear that this trend would reappear. To respond to this demand for higher quality, Northwest could install completely new equipment (as mentioned above) or upgrade existing machinery. Older equipment could be reengineered to deliver a higher-quality product (comparable to newsprint from the new machine) for an expenditure of about $8 million per machine. However, it was not clear to Smithers how the availability of higher-quality newsprint would affect sales.

Alternative 4 was to construct a new mill in Jasper, Georgia. This new operation would cost at least $250 million and would include woodlot operations, pulping facilities, a complete newsprint mill, controls, and administrative facilities. In addition, new newsprint machinery, similar to that mentioned in alternative 3, would have to be purchased at an additional cost. A significant advantage of such expansion would be a dramatic reduction in the cost of delivery to Northwest's southern U.S. customers.

Demand Forecasts

Smithers believed that the original 1995 demand forecasts were both reasonable and realistic, but he wanted to explore the options available to Northwest under more optimistic and under more pessimistic (Exhibit 7) demand projections. He was particularly concerned about which strategic alternatives should be considered under the differing demand conditions.

Northwest Newsprint was operating its newsprint operation using existing capacity and the assignment plan developed late in 1994. Smithers hoped to use the information he had collected to investigate alternate allocation plans, as well as to examine some of the strategic options facing Northwest.

Assignment

1. Formulate the problem as an LP problem and solve the LP model.
2. How does the solution differ from the original allocation? What are the benefits?
3. Can Northwest save money through freight rate discounts on volumes larger than 100,000 tons? If so, how much?
4. Should a 58,000-tonne-per-year machine at Naomee Mills be converted to groundwood specialities?
5. Can you recommend specific "delivery swap" arrangements to improve Northwest's bottom line?

Exhibit 3 | **NORTHWEST NEWSPRINT NET SALES BY PRODUCT**

	Net Sales by Product					
	1992		1993		1994	
Product	**$000**	**%**	**$000**	**%**	**$000**	**%**
1. Newsprint	$724,356	43.6	$808,591	49.5	$ 908,376	51.5
2. Groundwood papers	195,804	11.8	208,918	12.8	194,039	11.0
3. Fine papers	415,372	25.0	371,901	22.7	402,350	22.8
4. Kraft products	51,883	3.1	57,948	3.5	66,512	3.8
Total (pulp + paper)	**$1,387,415**	**83.6**	**$1,446,548**	**88.5**	**$1,571,277**	**89.1**
5. Building products	164,432	9.9	128,008	7.8	115,361	6.5
6. Lumber	108,333	6.5	59,706	3.7	76,747	4.4
Total (5 + 6)	**$272,765**	**16.4**	**$187,714**	**11.5**	**$192,108**	**10.9**
Total sales	**$1,660,180**	**100.0**	**$1,634,262**	**100.0**	**$1,763,385**	**100.0**

The Net Sales figures include adjustments for fluctuations in foreign exchange rates, but are calculated before other period and product costs.

Exhibit 4 | NORTHWEST NEWSPRINT PULP AND PAPER PRODUCTION

	Primary Production—Pulp and Paper Operations			
	Newsprint	**Groundwood Papers**	**Fine Paper**	**Kraft Products**
Effective capacity* 1994 000s tonnes	1,937	333	127	207
As percent of total 1994 effective capacity	74.4	12.8	4.9	7.9
Actual production (1994)	1,575	321	101	173
Capacity utilization (1994)	81.3%	96.4%	74.5%	83.6%

Effective capacity is calculated from the number of tonnes of newsprint produced per day per machine and the number of available days (allowing for scheduled downtime) for that machine. The effective capacities for each machine are then aggregated.

Exhibit 5 | NORTHWEST NEWSPRINT TRANSPORTATION COSTS

		Transportation Costs (US $/tonne delivered)	
Distribution Center	**Spruce Mills**	**Naomee Mills**	**Duchesne**
Seattle	—	$46.68	$52.80
Chicago	$89.77	128.82	97.17
Dallas	162.24	204.13	210.42
New Orleans	166.18	195.08	200.62
Denver	151.77	162.83	142.82
Los Angeles	—	147.46	150.14
San Francisco	151.11	115.49	124.83
Vancouver	—	72.42	42.17
Calgary	—	77.50	87.94

Exhibit 6 | NORTHWEST NEWSPRINT 1995 PLANNED DISTRIBUTION

		Original 1995 Allocation (tonnes delivered)	
Distribution Center	**Spruce Mills**	**Naomee Mills**	**Duchesne**
Seattle	—	40,727	—
Chicago	55,608	—	—
Dallas	64,976	27,704	—
New Orleans	—	92,680	—
Denver	23,832	—	—
Los Angeles	—	22,401	189,440
San Francisco	—	52,960	—
Vancouver	—	—	32,581
Calgary	—	—	8,145

Exhibit 7. | **NORTHWEST NEWSPRINT 1995 FORECASTS**

Distribution Center	1995 Forecast Annual Demand (tonnes) Optimistic	Pessimistic
Seattle	45,028	29,557
Chicago	61,481	45,518
Dallas	102,468	75,863
New Orleans	102,468	75,863
Denver	26,349	19,507
Los Angeles	234,213	173,401
San Francisco	58,553	43,350
Vancouver	36,022	23,646
Calgary	9,006	5,911
Total	675,588	492,616

BERBARIAN BALL BEARINGS, INC.

BY THOMAS H. BEECHY.

Ms. Katherine Berbarian, President of Berbarian Ball Bearings, called a meeting of the Executive Committee to discuss several issues that had recently arisen within the company and to plan the firm's operations for the remainder of the year.

BACKGROUND

Berbarian Ball Bearings was the largest integrated producer of ball bearings in the region and had attained a sales level of almost $15 million. The industry was composed of a large number of small firms, but Berbarian had succeeded in establishing a reputation for quality products and reliable deliveries that permitted market penetration throughout parts of the Midwestern United States and Canada. Nevertheless, the bulk of Berbarian's customers were concentrated in the highly industrialized "auto belt" running from Detroit up through Hamilton, Toronto, and Oshawa.

The firm was founded in 1923 by a machinist, Hector Berbarian, to manufacture screws. It was initially called Berbarian Fasteners. The screw business was (and is) very highly competitive because the capital necessary for entry into the industry is very small. Therefore, Hector soon began to move into products requiring specialized machinery, such as bearing collars, rings, and grommets. After only 2 years, Hector decided to emphasize the production of bearing components and changed the name of the company to its present form. Hector also began to develop specialized machinery that could produce bearings more quickly and reliably than could most existing techniques. The firm prospered for several years until the depression brought a decline in sales.

The Second World War brought prosperity back to Berbarian but coincided with the death of Hector Berbarian. In 1943, control of the firm passed to Hector's son, Archibald, who proved to not be much interested in bearings. The firm was not really managed by Archibald; it was actually run by a group of foremen who were skilled machinists. The foremen saw to it that good products were produced, but the sales prices were generally too low to return much profit to the firm.

In 1963, Archibald had a heart attack in a Detroit nightclub, and control of the firm in due course went to Archibald's daughter, Katherine. Katherine Berbarian was already familiar with the operations of the company and saw that the firm's production expertise could be a powerful selling point for penetrating the quality-conscious automobile and airframe manufacturing market. She therefore resolved to expand the plant, strengthen the sales force, and establish a reputation for quality that would permit a selling price higher than average for the industry.

To achieve her goals, she sought to acquire a steel ball manufacturer that had been supplying most of Berbarian's requirements for steel balls for its bearing assembler. The manufacturer was located nearby, and the owner had indicated a willingness to sell out. However, no bank seemed willing to finance such a purchase. Ms. Berbarian believed it was vital for Berbarian to control the production of its own balls to achieve maximum product reliability. The firm could, of course, enter into production of balls without buying out its supplier, but such a course of action would cost more and take longer.

Eventually, Ms. Berbarian was able to obtain a $1 million loan (in the form of a private placement of debentures of varying maturities) from a Detroit bank. In 1965, the ball supplier was purchased, and both the ball operations and Berbarian's bearings production were moved to a leased, larger, general-purpose, one-story building.

When the combination and the move were completed, Ms. Berbarian launched the company into the production of a new line of precision balls and bearings made from titanium. The new line had bearings in which the balls had outside diameters as small as 1/40 inch, and tolerances were held to 1 millionth of an inch (0.000001 inch). The line was well timed, and the firm achieved great success in selling the bearings to manufacturers of items such as gyroscopes, autopilots, synchros, fuel control systems, aircraft cameras, and high-speed dental handpieces.

OPERATIONS

The plant was divided into two divisions: the Ball Division and the Bearing Division. They occupied the same building but were physically separate operations with different personnel. Each division produced both precision and commercial (nonprecision) products, but there was no physical or operational separation by type of product within each division. The products were costed by a job-order system.

The basic manufacturing operation in the Bearing Division was the removal of metal from the heat-hardened rings by abrasive grinding. Grinding, although relatively slow, was semi-automatic and permitted close control of the rate at which metal was removed. After grinding and punching, the rings passed to the finishing department, where they were finished to extreme fineness. The finishing department also refined the finish on any externally purchased balls that were being used. The rings and balls were then assembled into a finished bearing. Although there were a total of 38 distinct steps in producing a finished bearing, Berbarian divided these steps into only two departments, grinding and finishing, for cost control and production planning purposes.

The Ball Division also was classified into two departments: machining and finishing. The Ball Division was highly automated, so relatively little labor input was required for production in that division. The bulk of the output of the Ball Division was transferred to the Bearing Division, but a small part of the output was sold externally to manufacturers requiring highly finished balls. Some was also sold to independent bearing manufacturers.

Last year, Berbarian's engineers conducted a detailed study of the input requirements of the products of both divisions. They found that there was a remarkable similarity in the production requirements of the products of each division and that changes in the product mix (that is, in the sizes of the balls or bearings) were quite gradual. Therefore, they summarized the results of their study in a table for each division that showed the input requirements for an "average"product (Exhibit 3, p. 150). This "average" product description was considered to be reliable enough for general production planning, although the detailed input specifications for each product were used in actual production scheduling and cost analysis.

COST AND PROFIT RESPONSIBILITY

Each of the two divisions had a division manager who was primarily responsible for controlling costs and generating profits in his division. Ms. Berbarian expected these two managers to tend to the day-to-day operations of the plant, as well as to give specific direction to the salesmen who were dealing with the customers.

There were six full-time sales representatives for the firm in the United States and Canada. The U.S. representative worked out of Chicago and covered the Chicago/Northern Indiana area with occasional forays into northern Ohio. In other parts of the United States, the company was represented by manufacturers' sales agents who also represented several noncompeting firms and who operated strictly on commission. Two Canada representatives shared the Ontario-Quebec region (plus Detroit).

The sales representatives were under the general direction of Ms. Berbarian, who set the marketing strategy and occasionally helped to win major new customers herself. The salesmen were directed to sell the bearing assemblies but also to keep their eyes open to possible sales of balls. Therefore, the divisional managers provided specific product direction for the salesmen but not much general strategy.

The Ball Division was considered by Ms. Berbarian to be primarily a component supplier to the Bearing Division. The Bearing Division was under specific orders to use only internally produced balls if at all possible because Ms. Berbarian believed that the firm could be ensured of maintaining quality only if all components were produced by Berbarian. Nevertheless, the Ball Division was not required to turn down external orders to provide the Bearings Division's requirements.

Ball Division production was transferred to the Bearing Division at cost. This procedure had caused dissatisfaction in both divisions. The Ball Division manager would have liked his precision balls to be transferred because much of the profitability of the firm was obtained from the precision line, yet the Bearing Division currently got full credit for all the profit on that line.

In the Bearing Division, dissatisfaction arose primarily from the transfer price of the commercial balls. The average sales price of Berbarian's steel balls was $15 per dozen bearings, but the transfer cost was higher than that. Furthermore, the Bearing Division could obtain steel balls from external sources at an average price of only $9 per dozen bearings. The manager of the Bearing Division felt that he should be charged no more than the market value of competitive balls. In the precision line, external balls could be obtained for $24 per dozen bearings, although Berbarian's precision balls were currently selling at an average of $30 per dozen bearings. Ms. Berbarian hoped to resolve this issue.

LAST YEAR'S OPERATIONS

The firm had had a good year last fiscal year. The production and sales were as given (in dozens of bearings) in Exhibit 1).

The Bearing Division had obtained all of its balls from the Ball Division in accordance with company policy. The managers of both divisions kept costs under very good control. Input consumption did not vary significantly from specifications.

The raw material prices were:

$0.048 per ounce for stainless steel and $0.435 per ounce for titanium.

Labor rates were:

$22.80 per hour for grade 4, $27.60 per hour for grade 5, and $30.00 per hour for grade 6.

Overhead assignable to the Ball Division amounted to a total of $1,592,640. Variable overhead was applied in the Machining Department at the rate of $0.60 per machine hour and in the Finishing Department at the rate of $3.00 per machine hour. The remainder was considered to be fixed overhead and was applied to production on the basis of machine hours, using the same rate in both departments.

In the Bearing Division, assignable overhead amounted to $2,635,800. The variable overhead application rates were $1.80 per machine hour in the Grinding Department and $3.60 per machine hour in the Finishing Department. As in the Ball Division, the remainder was allocated uniformly to production based on machine hours in the division as a whole.

In addition, the factory incurred generally fixed costs of $342,000, which were not meaningfully assignable to either division. These factory costs were considered to be period costs; no attempt was made to allocate them to production.

During the past year, the raw material inventory fluctuated somewhat, but overall, purchases were just sufficient to replace withdrawals for production. The Finished Goods Inventory on December 31 was as shown in Exhibit 2.

Finished Goods were accounted for on a FIFO basis.

Selling and administrative expenses amounted to $908,040 last year..These expenses were assumed to vary by 2% of total sales per period.

The firm's fixed assets were depreciated by the

Exhibit I | **PRODUCTION AND SALES**

	Production	Outside Sales	Average Price
Ball division			
Commercial	144,000	40,000	$15
Precision	84,000	11,000	$30
Bearing division			
Commercial	104,000	104,000	$66
Precision	73,000	73,000	$99

Exhibit 2 | **FINISHED GOOD INVENTORY**

	Units (dozen)	Unit Cost	Total Cost
Balls			
Commercial	6,000	$16.35	$98,100
Precision	2,000	23.40	46,800
Bearings			
Commercial	1,000	52.50	52,500
Precision	4,000	69.15	276,600
Total			**$474,000**

straight-line method on the books. The tax savings that arose from the difference between book depreciation and the tax-deductible capital cost allowance were credited to deferred income taxes. Last year, book depreciation amounted to $540,000, distributed as $180,000 for the Ball Division, $240,000 for the Bearing Division, and $120,000 for general factory depreciation.

These amounts were included in the overhead costs given earlier. The capital cost allowance for tax purposes amounted to $720,000. The firm's tax rate was 50%. The fixed assets had an average life of 20 years, so on a common-dollar basis, 5% were replaced each year. However, average annual inflation of 3% caused the replacement cost to exceed the original cost of the assets.

OUTLOOK

Ms. Berbarian and the sales representatives had been successful in generating new business, especially for the precision balls and bearings. The current projections for next year's sales were for balls, 48,000 dozen for commercial and 30,000 dozen for precision, and for bearings, 120,000 dozen for commercial and 84,000 dozen for precision.

However, Ms. Berbarian was concerned about the plant's capacity to produce the level of demand. The Ball Division currently had a maximum annual capacity of 540,000 machine hours in the Machining Department and 144,000 machine hours in the Finishing Department. The Bearing Division had a current annual capacity of 306,000 machine hours in the Grinding Department and 432,000 machine hours in the Finishing Department.

Therefore, Ms. Berbarian wanted the Executive Committee to consider what level of production should be assigned for each product to generate the highest profit. Although the sales projections might be attainable, there was some question as to whether they were desirable, and Ms. Berbarian wanted a consensus on which products were more important. It was important, however, to continue to supply the current customers to at least last year's levels.

It also seemed to be a logical time to review the company policy on the transfer price for the balls. The manager of the Ball Division had been speaking with a professor at a local university, Dr. P. Petersen, who had suggested that shadow prices might be used to set transfer prices. Ms. Berbarian wanted a system with which both division managers would be comfortable.

In addition to discussing the points above, Ms. Berbarian wanted the committee to review the financial and cost flows from last year, to plan the operating budget (assuming that the sales projections could be met), and to plan an operating budget that should be followed if projections did not achieve the maximum profit.

The company was about to enter labor negotiations, and Ms. Berbarian was concerned about how much the firm could afford in increased wages before the relative importance of the products was altered, thereby necessitating a shift in the company's product emphasis and marketing strategy.

Assignment

1. Formulate the problem as an LP problem and solve.
2. Interpret the solution. Why are balls being purchased externally while there is excess capacity in the ball-making division?
3. What does your solution say about the transfer pricing problem?

Exhibit 3 | BERBARIAN BALL BEARINGS, LTD.

Variable Inputs—Ball Division (per dozen bearings)		
	Commercial Grade	**Precision Grade**
Raw material (oz)		
Stainless steel	25	
Titanium		20
Labor hours (hr)		
Grade 4	0.2	
Grade 6	0.1	0.2
Machine hours (hr)		
Machinery dept.	2.4	1.5
Finishing dept.	0.2	0.8
Variable Inputs—Bearing Division		
Raw material (oz)		
Stainless steel	30	
Titanium		16
Labor hours: Using internally manufactured balls (hr)		
Grade 4	0.50	
Grade 5	0.10	0.4
Grade 6	0.19	0.5
Labor hours: Using purchased balls (hr)		
Grade 4	0.70	
Grade 5		0.55
Grade 6	0.25	0.6
Machine hours: Using internally manufactured balls (hr)		
Grinding dept.	1.5	1.0
Finishing dept.	2.5	2.0
Machine hours: Using purchased balls (hr)		
Grinding dept.	3.0	1.0
Finishing dept.	2.0	2.5

Exhibit 4 **BERBARIAN BALL BEARINGS, LTD. CONSOLIDATED BALANCE SHEET (dollars in thousands)**

Assets		
Current assets		
Cash	$ 414	
Accounts receivable (net)	918	
Raw material inventory	129	
Finished goods inventory	474	$1,935
Property, plant, and equipment	$10,719	
Less accumulated depreciation	5,145	5,574
Total assets		**$7,509**
Equities		
Current liabilities		
Notes payable	$ 279	
Accounts payable	225	
Accrued taxes	231	
Current portion of long-term debt	120	$ 855
Long-term debt (10%)		2,025
Deferred income taxes		504
Total liabilities		$3,384
Stockholders' equity		
Common stock	$ 100	
Capital in excess of par value	219	
Retained earnings	$3,806	$4,125
Total equities		**$7,509**

NEW ENGLAND FEED SUPPLY

BY DREW PARKER AND PETER C. BELL.

On April 14, 1996, Jeff Smith, Formulation Analyst for New England Feed Supply Inc. (NEFS), was evaluating next week's requirements for three animal feed mixes produced by the Burlington plant. A shortage of one ingredient, meat meal, meant that NEFS would find it difficult to meet the orders on hand. Smith needed to determine which, if any, of the mixture formulas should be altered, and in what way; alternately, he could elect to buy additional meat meal on the spot market, at a significantly higher price.

THE COMPANY

NEFS was an animal feed-blending company with 12 plants located in major centers throughout New England. The principal ingredients were purchased from farmers and brokers each month and mixed into a number of standard animal feed products that were sold to feedlots, individual farmers, and large corporate farms. NEFS mixed products to meet orders and kept no product inventory. Because ingredients were purchased at different times and prices, the cost of each ingredient in inventory was recorded as the total price paid for an ingredient divided by the number of tons in stock.

Each product mix sold had a standard nutritional content that met or exceeded the requirements set by the National Research Council (NRC). Ingredient costs were more than 80% of the total product cost, with the result that the determination of least-cost formulas was critical if the company was to remain competitive and profitable.

FORMULATION

Customer orders for various types of animal feed were taken directly by the producing plants. The Formulation Department, located at the head office, advised each plant on appropriate feed formulations. From the standard feed formulas supplied by the Formulation Department, each plant would determine the amounts of the ingredients required for the following week and forward these requirements to the head office by Wednesday morning. Because the delivery of ordered products was critical for the customer's livestock, it was company policy that an order, once taken, must be filled. Shortages (or back orders) were not acceptable.

NEFS faced a relatively steady and predictable demand for each of its products. This, and the fact that each plant offered between 150 and 200 different product mixes, necessitated that the plants follow standard mix formulas on a day-to-day basis, even though minor changes in market prices or ingredient costs could occur. Occasionally, however, shortages of raw ingredients required the Formulation Department to recalculate the feed formulas. The alternative to recalculating formulas was to buy additional units of the short ingredient on the spot market at a price significantly higher than that they normally paid.

BURLINGTON PLANT

The Burlington plant mixed and sold three products that potentially used meat meal as an ingredient: *15% Pig Grower*, *40% Pig Supplement*, and *17% Cage Layer* (the percentages identify the amount of protein in the product). In preparing these products, the company had to ensure that the minimum nutritional standards set by the NRC were met. The NRC standards for these products are given in Exhibit 1. For example, 1 ton of 15% Pig Grower required 0 units of ME: Poultry, 3,000 units of ME: Swine, 15 units of Protein, and so on. Exhibit 4-16 also indicates the demand, in tons, that the firm faced for the coming week.

The necessary nutrients could be formulated into each of the three end products by combining appropriate quantities of the raw ingredients. The ingredients used include corn, barley, soy meal, meat meal, lime, and dical. A ton of each ingredient contained a certain amount of each nutrient; for example, 1 ton of corn contained 3,500 units of the ME: Poultry nutrient. The nutrient contents, together with the current cost of each ingredient, are given in Exhibit 2.

The basic feed formulation problem faced by Smith, then, was to determine a combination of the raw ingredients that satisfied the nutrient requirements for each product, at minimum cost.

In deciding on a mixture for each end product, Smith needed to ensure that the combination of ingredients that were selected to make up 1 ton of a product did not, in fact, weigh more than 1 ton. If the combined ingredients weighed less than 1 ton, the weight difference could be made up by adding non-nutritive filler at essentially no cost.

JEFF SMITH'S PROBLEM

The company's head office had received an order for 168 tons of meat meal from the Burlington plant for the following week. This was the amount of meat meal the plant needed to fulfill its orders, using the standard mixing formulas then in effect. Because there were only 80 tons in stock, Smith had been advised of the shortage.

In evaluating the current formulas for the three mixes sold in the Burlington plant, Smith noted that each required meat meal. He was well aware that the availability of meat meal was determined by the month's purchase contracts and that the meat meal on hand had a weighted average cost of $339.00 per ton. Any additional requirements would have to be bid for on the spot market. The spot market was managed by independent commodity brokers who could supply a purchaser on short notice but at a significantly higher price.

The constraint of a maximum availability of 80 tons of meat meal could be taken into consideration and the formulas recalculated, or a spot market bid could be made. The immediate problem was to determine an appropriate bid, if one was to be made on the next day's market, or to determine new mix formulas with the meat meal limitation taken into account. The result of whatever action was taken would have to be sent back to the plant by Friday morning.

The other ingredients were not in short supply, even if the formulas changed somewhat, because inventories had been built up for the summer season.

Assignment

1. Formulate the mix problem for each product separately. What are the minimum cost solutions?
2. Would the formulation differ if all three products were included together?
3. Solve the combined problem. Then add the 80-ton meat meal constraint and solve again.
4. Determine a spot market bid (price and quantity) or bids for meat meal.
5. What would Smith's options be if he could purchase as much meat meal as needed at $365 per ton?

Exhibit 1 **NEW ENGLAND FEED SUPPLY: DEMAND AND REQUIRED NUTRIENTS FOR EACH PRODUCT—BURLINGTON PLANT**

Product	**15% Pig Grower**	**40% Pig Supplement**	**17% Cage Layer**
Demand for coming week (tons)	400	120	600
	Units of nutrients required per ton		
ME: Poultry	0	0	2,675
ME: Swine	3,000	2,500	0
Protein	15	40	17
Calcium	0.75	5.50	3.80
Phosphates	0.60	2.50	0.70
Lysine	0.61	2.00	0.68
Methionine	0.20	0.45	0.28
Meth and cystine	0.30	0.80	0.48
Tryptophane	0.10	0.25	0.15

Exhibit 2 **NEW ENGLAND FEED SUPPLY: NUTRIENT MAKEUP AND COST OF INGREDIENTS**

Ingredient	**Corn**	**Barley**	**Soy Meal**	**Meat Meal**	**Lime**	**Dical**
Cost per ton ($)	127	145	314	339	25	405
	Nutrient makeup (units of nutrient per ton of ingredient)					
ME: Poultry	3,500	2,865	2,530	1,984	—	—
ME: Swine	3,325	2,870	3,485	2,540	—	—
Protein	8.70	10.00	48.4	50.9	—	—
Calcium	0.02	0.06	0.30	9.70	39	16.5
Phosphates	0.28	0.33	0.69	4.02	—	21.0
Lysine	0.20	0.35	3.20	2.82	—	—
Methionine	0.20	0.15	0.70	0.62	—	—
Meth and cystine	0.33	0.32	1.44	1.24	—	—
Tryptophane	0.09	0.12	0.63	0.31	—	—

PETRO PIPE LINES CORPORATION

BY SULAIMAN AL-HUDHAIF UNDER THE SUPERVISION OF PROFESSOR PETER C. BELL.

David Anderson, a management scientist, was asked by Mr. Andrew Fry, the president of a gas production company, to develop a model for allocating the gas supplied to the Petro Pipe Lines Corporation (PPL) gas plant among the various suppliers according to the terms of the gas supply contracts. The intent of the model was to minimize the penalties imposed at the end of each month on the gas suppliers as a result of daily differences between production (supply) and nomination (demand) for each contract.

It was September 15, 1993, and in the next few days, David wanted to formulate his model. He knew that an appropriate model would realize substantial benefits to the gas suppliers without the need to make any changes in production, operations, or facilities.

INDUSTRY AND COMPANY BACKGROUND

Traditionally, the natural gas industry consisted of three primary activities: exploration for and production of natural gas, transportation of the gas from producers to market regions, and distribution of gas to end users. Some companies were involved in all three areas, whereas others focused their efforts on only one or two. PPL was a natural gas transportation and marketing company and was classified as a natural gas transmission subindustry. PPL owned a mid-diameter natural gas pipeline in southwestern Alberta linking Nova's regional systems and their connections with large pipeline companies (TransCanada PipeLines and Pacific Transmission of the U.S). PPL bought, transported, and resold natural gas from and to regional gas distribution companies within Alberta and southeastern British Columbia. The company also owned and operated 2,550 kilometers of natural gas transmission pipelines throughout Alberta.

Natural gas is formed from ancient sediments rich in organic matter that in the past have been subjected to very high temperatures and pressures. Natural gas is a mixture of hydrocarbons, principally methane, extracted from the earth's crust through wells for use as a fuel or as a feedstock for chemical production. With the exception of the Soviet Union and Canada, where the use of natural gas started around the turn of this century, the natural gas industry is essentially a post-World War II development. The industry has grown rapidly since then to the point where it now supplies more than 20% of the world's primary energy demand. In the residential market, for example, natural gas is used in single-family home construction (for cooking, water heating, and space heating), and a well-established industrial use is for the generation of electricity.

The major activities of natural gas producers are to discover and tap into underground pools of crude oil and natural gas and to exploit already discovered pools as fully as possible. Whether a pool exists and, if it does, what kind of products it holds are typically unknown until a well is drilled. Some analysis, such as seismic reading, can be done from the surface before drilling takes place, and such analysis, plus a thorough knowledge of geological structure combined with an educated guess, can help with the decision regarding where to drill a well. Natural gas is obtained in two ways: either the pool contains natural gas, or it contains oil in which natural gas is dissolved. The quality of the natural gas varies from field to field and often between pools in the same field.

The risky nature of the exploration and development business makes it common for several companies to form a partnership or joint venture. By sharing in the costs and risks of the exploration, the partners earn a right to a share of (or, in industry parlance, a working interest in) the profits (if any) that result.

The flow of natural gas from a gas pool to the final consumers can be traced in the following stages: (see Exhibit 1).

Wellhead → gathering system → gas processing plant → pipelines → refineries → final consumers

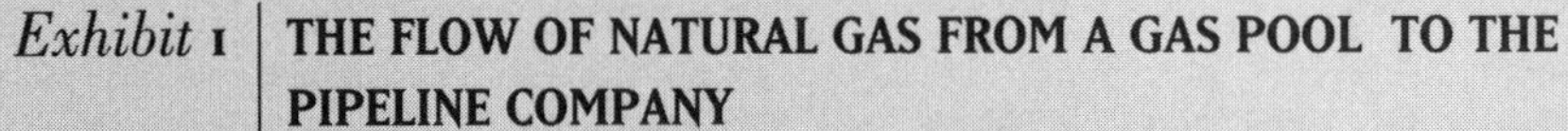
Exhibit 1 THE FLOW OF NATURAL GAS FROM A GAS POOL TO THE PIPELINE COMPANY

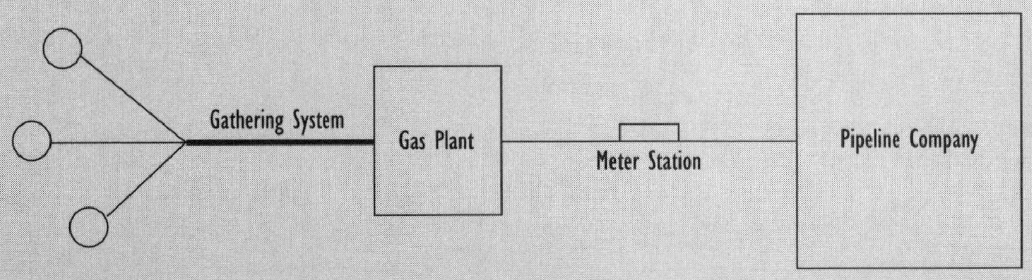

The main function of the gas processing plant is to extract the contaminants and compress the gas to feed into a pipeline. The plant may also extract other products, such as ethane, propane, and butane from the gas, which can be sold separately.

PRODUCERS' AND AGGREGATORS' RELATIONS

Typically, the pipeline companies state their specified demand (nominations), and then the natural gas is delivered by the producers. The pipeline companies buy the natural gas from producers to transport and resell. Because they buy from many producers and aggregate the product into the large volumes required by major customers, they are known as **aggregators**. The aggregators negotiate contracts with producers to supply natural gas for a certain term. These contracts specify the field or fields from which the gas is to be taken and how much may be taken each year.

In the natural gas business, the most successful contracts are those that have been freely negotiated and accepted by both sellers and buyers with minimal constraints imposed on them by third parties. Contractual terms that unduly favor the seller or the buyer have seldom stood the test of time. A contract usually does not specify in advance how much gas will be needed each day but rather allows the aggregator to specify or nominate the demand from day to day to avoid imbalances.

NATURAL GAS IMBALANCES

With more parties involved in natural gas transactions, the potential for differences regarding what is actually demanded and delivered has increased. These differences are called **imbalances**. Imbalances have always been present in the industry due to the physical properties of natural gas. Producers cannot guarantee with absolute certainty that a specific volume of gas will be produced from a given well in a particular time period. Significant variations in the system (such as pressure fluctuations and breakdowns) occur at wells, gathering systems, and plants. Pipeline disruptions also occur from time to time.

In the past, imbalances were generally short term in nature and were regarded as an internal pipeline problem. Because the pipeline companies were the primary purchasers of natural gas for the pipeline system, imbalances were often handled through informal handshake arrangements between the producers and pipeline companies. However, in a world of unbundled pipeline services, with tariff provisions for fees and penalties related to imbalances, serious economic consequences may result.

Exhibit 2 | **PENALTIES IN THEORY**

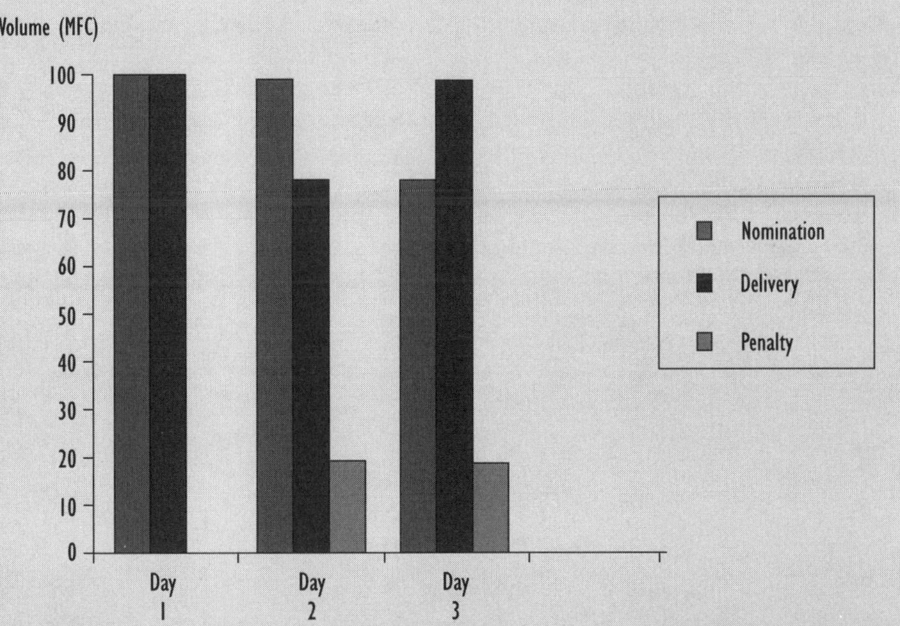

PENALTIES

The supply contracts usually give the aggregator the right to penalize the producer for underdelivery or overdelivery. The penalty for underdelivery is simply the sacrificing of the right to sell the undelivered gas to the aggregator, whereas the penalty for overdelivery can be even more extreme: in some cases, confiscation of the excess gas without compensation to the producer. Overdelivery penalties were not generally enforced until the early 1990s. Because of the certain penalty for underdelivery versus the possibility of a penalty for overdelivery, many producers chose to err on the side of overdelivery. The following simplified example illustrates the concept of penalties.

Let us assume that the aggregator nominates the following quantities (measured in 1 million cubic feet [MCF]) for 3 days: the first day 100 MCF, the second day 100 MCF, and the third day 80 MCF. On the other hand, the producer delivers the following quantities: the first day 100 MCF, the second day 80 MCF, and the third day 100 MCF. In this example, there is no penalty on the first day, but on the second day, there is a penalty of 20 MCF because the aggregator's obligation to take gas from the producer is reduced from what had been nominated to what had been delivered (from 100 MCF to 80 MCF). On the third day, the producer delivers 20 MCF extra to the aggregator (100 MCF minus 80 MCF); thus, the producer incurs an oversupply penalty for this 20 MCF. Exhibit 2 illustrates the penalties imposed in this example. In theory, the aggregator might not pay for the extra 20 MCF, but in practice, such a penalty was not generally enforced. This example illustrates that even though the total quantity nominated over the 3-day period is equal to the total quantity delivered, penalties still apply.

Because each aggregator may hold several contracts at a gas plant, each involving many wells and producers with different working interests, it is not possible, with the measurements available, to determine who supplied what and when and, therefore, who should be penalized.

CURRENT ALLOCATION PROCESS

One straightforward technique for solving the allocation problem would be **pro rata allocation**. Pro rata allocation is based on two rules: (1) calculate each contract's share of the monthly total, and (2) allocate the daily totals in the same proportions as the monthly total. The problem with this method is its assumption that nominations are constant over the course of the month. If the nominations were to stay constant, or if the nominations for different contracts were to rise and fall in parallel, then the pro rata allocation process would pose no problems. Unfortunately, in practice, those conditions do not exist. Nevertheless, PPL's default method of allocating production was pro rata, and this had led in the past to penalties being applied that Andrew Fry's company believed to be unfair. In response to this, he and David Anderson had persuaded PPL to accept their allocation of production, subject only to the following two rules:

1. The total of the volumes allocated to the contracts on each day must equal the actual daily total volume.
2. The total of the volumes allocated to any one contract for all days of the month must equal the actual monthly total for the contract. See Exhibits 3 and 4 for known and unknown information.

Considering the daily total of the production volume as supply and the monthly total for the contract as demand, allocation was solved as a transportation problem. Because oversupply penalties were not enforced, any excess was allocated by the **northwest corner rule** or by pro rata allocation. The northwest corner rule is a procedure used to determine an initial solution to the transportation problem (for more details, see the Appendix). Applying this technique substantially reduced, and in some cases eliminated, the penalties caused by the pro rata allocation of the daily total volume.

In 1993, PPL became unhappy with producers tending to overdeliver to avoid penalties. To reduce this abuse, PPL decided to enforce the penalties for oversupply as it was entitled to do under the contracts. At the

Exhibit 3 | **NOMINATIONS (MCF)**

	Contract 1	Contract 2
Day 1	Known	Known
Day 2	Known	Known
—		
—		
Monthly total	Known	Known

Exhibit 4 PRODUCTION VOLUMES (MCF)

	Contract 1	Contract 2	Daily Total
Day 1	?	?	Known
Day 2	?	?	Known
—			Known
—			Known
Monthly Total	Known	Known	Known

Exhibit 5

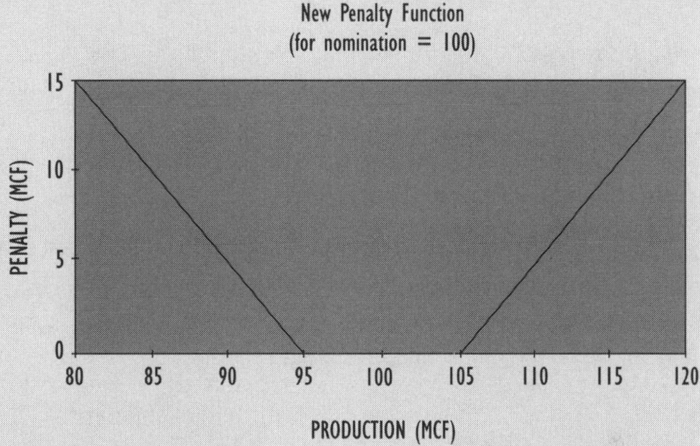

Exhibit 6 DAILY TOTAL SALES

Day	Sales
Day 1	211.8
Day 2	221.9
Day 3	225.7
Day 4	222.4
Day 5	219.5
Day 6	208.7
Day 7	224.2
Total	1534.2

Exhibit 7 CONTRACT TOTAL SALES

Contract	Sales
Contract 1	415.6
Contract 2	410.5
Contract 3	407.6
Contract 4	300.5
Total	1534

Exhibit **8** | **NOMINATIONS BY DAY BY CONTRACT**

	Contract 1	Contract 2	Contract 3	Contract 4
Day 1	40	20	50	40
Day 2	50	30	60	50
Day 3	60.5	52.5	50.5	55.5
Day 4	60.7	52.5	50.5	56
Day 5	60.6	52.5	50.5	55.5
Day 6	60	32	50	50
Day 7	41	33	41	30

negotiation meeting between PPL and the suppliers' representatives, which included both Andrew and David, the following rules were approved:

1. There was a penalty-free zone of 5% on either side of nomination. If the volume on a particular day was within this zone, there was no penalty.
2. If the volume delivered fell below the lower limit of the penalty-free zone, the aggregator was deemed to have taken a volume equal to the lower limit of the penalty-free zone (a penalty equal to the difference between volume delivered and the lower limit would be imposed).
3. If the volume delivered exceeded the upper limit of the penalty-free zone, a penalty equal to the difference between volume delivered and the upper limit would be imposed. Exhibit 5 illustrates the shape of the new penalty function.

David knew that the allocation process could no longer be treated as a transportation problem under these rules, but he still thought that once imbalances and their sources were identified, an opportunity would exist to do a better allocation if he developed a linear programming model. Implementation of this model would not just provide a solution to the problem but would also be adaptable to a continuously changing natural gas business environment.

To test his suggested optimization model, David collected 7 days of data for four contracts submitted by different suppliers. The contracts were served by a single meter station (see Exhibits 6, 7, and 8).

Given the daily total sales, the contract total sales for the week, and the daily nominations by contract, the objective of the optimization model was to find an allocation of the total sales to the contracts to minimize the penalties. A proper allocation had to satisfy the constraints that the daily totals and weekly contracts agreed with the known values.

APPENDIX

Transportation Problem

The transportation problem is a special type of allocation problem that involves the transportation or physical distribution of goods or services from several supply origins to several demand destinations. The transportation problem often involves minimizing the cost of shipping.

Northwest Corner Rule

The northwest corner method for finding an initial solution is an elemental logic process. Quite simply the process begins by starting in the northwest (the top left) corner of the table (where columns show destinations or demands and rows show sources or supplies). An allocation of as many units as are permitted by supply and demand restrictions is placed in that cell. The result is that either the supply or the demand in the first row or first column will be exhausted, respectively. If the demand is exhausted, the next allocation of units is placed in the first row, second column. If the supply is exhausted, the next allocation of units is placed in the second row, first column. This pattern is repeated until all units of supply have been distributed to meet the demand requirements. The result is an allocation of units that start in the northwest corner of the table and end up in the southeast corner of the table.

Assignment

1. Formulate the example problem in Solver.
2. Solve the problem. What savings result?

KUWAIT'S AL-MANAKH STOCK MARKET

BY SAM RIDESIC UNDER THE SUPERVISION OF PROFESSOR PETER BELL. REPRODUCED WITH PERMISSION OF INFORMS. COPYRIGHT © 1998, INFORMS

The Kuwait al-Manakh Stock Market crash in 1982 resulted in outstanding debts of some $94 billion and left the country in a state of economic panic. The Kuwaiti judicial system faced the near impossible task of assigning criminal and financial liability among the 6,000 investors caught in a web of 29,000 "bounced" postdated checks and IOUs with the associated bankruptcies and business failures.

Postdated checks and IOUs, written on behalf of speculative Kuwaiti investors and traders, funded the market's boom and led to its dramatic crash. Developing a method to disentangle the web of outstanding debt could save many years and nearly $10 billion in court and attorney fees. In addition, the disentanglement would "net out" offsetting debts and reduce the magnitude of the total outstanding debt resulting from the crash, thereby reducing the negative impact of the market crash on the economy.

The government of Kuwait recognized that this complex web had to be disentangled quickly, fairly, and in a way most beneficial to the economy. His Excellency Shaikh Ali Al-Khalifa Al-Sabah, Minister of Finance and Oil of Kuwait, turned to the Kuwait Institute for Scientific Research for help.

EVENTS LEADING UP TO THE CREATION OF THE AL-MANAKH STOCK EXCHANGE

The al-Manakh Stock Market was established in 1979 by Kuwaiti trading companies and speculative investors to take the place of a very tightly controlled official stock market of Kuwait (KSE). After the KSE had undergone a major crash in 1977, permanent government controls were put in place to control Kuwait's highly speculative investors, who were motivated by high liquidity coupled with poor returns on Kuwaiti investments abroad as a result of volatile exchange rates. Oil-rich Kuwaitis had few places to invest their money other than in the country's stock market, but as the KSE began to boom, speculative traders entered the market, and the rapid speculative growth eventually caused the KSE to crash. Speculators writing postdated checks for investments that they could not afford meant that the market's boom was supported by funds that did not exist. Once out of control, when one investor defaulted, a chain reaction of bankruptcies was inevitable because investors could not honor their checks and IOUs because their accounts receivable and expected market returns were needed to fund these debts.

After the crash, the complicated puzzle of unpayable debts led to the bottom falling out of the KSE, which produced widespread panic in the Kuwaiti economy. As a result, the government bailed out creditors at a cost of $525 million. After the crash, tight government controls, including new laws severely restricting the use of postdated checks on the KSE, were established to curb further speculative trading.

EVENTS LEADING UP TO THE AL-MANAKH CRASH

The Kuwaiti government owned nearly half of the country's share-holding companies, and with very few investment opportunities other than oil, wealthy Kuwaitis had few investment alternatives at home. After a third major oil hike in 1979, wealthy Kuwaitis enjoyed a time of prosperity, and public spending and the demand for places to invest money rose. This increase in liquidity combined with few investment alternatives led to another speculative bubble. Because returns on foreign investments were poor, investors looked at the al-Manakh Stock Exchange as a place where they could carry out the speculative trading that had occurred on the KSE before the 1977 crash.

The al-Manakh exchange was unregulated, and in the absence of government regulation or supervision, the heavy use of postdated checks soared along with stock prices. Traders created numerous Gulf companies in neighboring Arab states solely for speculative purposes to avoid domestic regulations governing new companies. Investors poured money anywhere they could. At the peak of the stock market's explosion, traded shares amounted to 3.5 billion, or more than four times the 837 million of the KSE. A 100% increase in stock value within a few weeks was not surprising to the 6,000 individuals and corporations feverishly trading in the al-Manakh market.

By 1982, the al-Manakh stock exchange was out of

control. Untrained and uncertified brokers were trading worthless securities at astronomical P/E ratios. With a complicated mesh of postdated checks being traded to fund the explosion, traders used crude and often illegal methods of settlement. The inevitable crash left traders in a complicated puzzle of postdated checks and IOUs, making it difficult to determine who was responsible for each trade. Traders faced the disastrous implications of having written postdated checks against funds that they expected to receive in the future from the sale of stocks for a profit before the postdated checks came due.

THE CRASH

In August 1982, the bubble burst when one of the largest of the 18 major trading companies defaulted on its debts. During the month, traded shares fell from 602 to 72 million, whereas securities traded in the market lost 60% to 98% of their value.

The crash was a huge shock to the Kuwaiti economy. Initially, neither the central bank nor the government knew the magnitude of the crash and the resulting outstanding debt. Traders were left with worthless stocks in defunct Gulf companies as well as a web of two-way IOU notes and postdated checks.

First calculations of the resulting outstanding debt after the crash produced a figure of $94 billion, or 4.3 times the Kuwaiti gross domestic product. The majority of this value was the sum of the face value of nearly 29,000 postdated checks. In addition, 95% of the total outstanding debt involved only 18 traders who were caught in a mesh of entangled debt responsibilities.

ATTEMPTS TO RECTIFY THE SITUATION

In late 1982, the government took some steps to attempt to contain the damage. It established a clearinghouse with the purpose of collecting, matching, verifying, and systematizing the financial accounts of individuals and brokers and set aside a $1.7 billion trust fund to compensate small investors (losses of less than $1.7 million). Finally, an arbitration panel was established to effect settlements and to sanction and finalize settlements reached voluntarily between traders.

Unfortunately, the government's initial strategy of forcing traders to pay their debts as part of the solution did not work. Many traders had become insolvent, and few were willing to meet their accounts payable before collecting their receivables, especially when their accounts receivable were needed to pay off their debts. This problem, and the fact that a resolution did not seem to be arising in the near future, led the Kuwait government to form the **Corporation for the Settlement of Company Forward Share Transactions**. This company established a special task force made up of A.A. Eliman (San Francisco State University), M. Girgis (LTC Techno-Economics Research Group, Inc.), and S. Kotob (Kuwait Institute for Scientific Research). Under the supervision of the Kuwaiti Minister of Oil and Finance, the task force began the high-priority task of untangling traders and settling debts.

APPRECIATING THE TRADERS' ENTANGLEMENT

Exhibit 1 illustrates the example of four entangled traders. Each trader had some assets, had (potentially)

Exhibit 1 **EXAMPLE OF TRADER ENTANGLEMENTS**

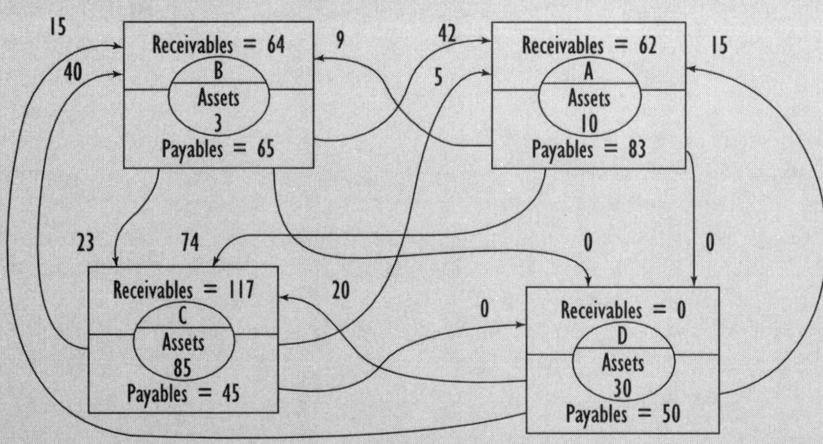

an uncollected receivable from each other trader, and had (potentially) an unpaid payable to each other trader.

Each trader's assets were further broken down into four asset classes. These were, in order of decreasing risk, cash and KSE shares, real estate, receivables from other entangled traders, and shares of Gulf companies. For the example, consider the four traders' assets to be as shown:

Exhibit 2 | **ASSETS OF FOUR TRADERS**

	Trader			
	A	B	C	D
Cash and KSE shares	1	0.6	15	5
Real estate	4	1.2	24	7
Receivables from solvents	3	0.2	27	3
Shares of gulf companies	2	1	19	15
Total assets	**10**	**3**	**85**	**30**

In this situation, three of the traders (A, B, and D) could not determine how much of their debt they could pay before knowing what portion of their receivables they would collect from the other entangled traders. Therefore, one can appreciate how the situation could not be resolved without outside intervention to decide who could and should pay what and to whom. In addition, there was the issue of how the different asset types were to be treated and in what proportion they were to be paid.

The task force first defined the debt settlement ratio (DSR):

$$\text{DSR} = \text{Minimum}\left[\frac{\text{Assets} + \text{Actual Receivables}}{\text{Actual Payables}}, 1\right]$$

To determine the portion of debt that could be honored by each trader, the task force set out a series of equations to determine each trader's DSR that was dependent on actual receivables: computing each trader's DSR would essentially require first determining the payments that each trader would make. A further problem with this method was the necessity to restrict the payments from solvent traders to the amount they actually owed. The task force, however, was able to use DSRs as a method of trader classification without knowing what portion of actual receivables would be collected (Exhibit 3).

METHOD FOR DISENTANGLING THE TRADERS

After considering the dilemma faced in determining the traders' DSRs, the task force realized that determining DSRs would actually disentangle the traders because each intertrader payment would have to be calculated to determine traders' actual receivables. However, the rationale behind these payments needed to be decided.

Exhibit 3 | **CLASSIFICATION OF TRADERS**

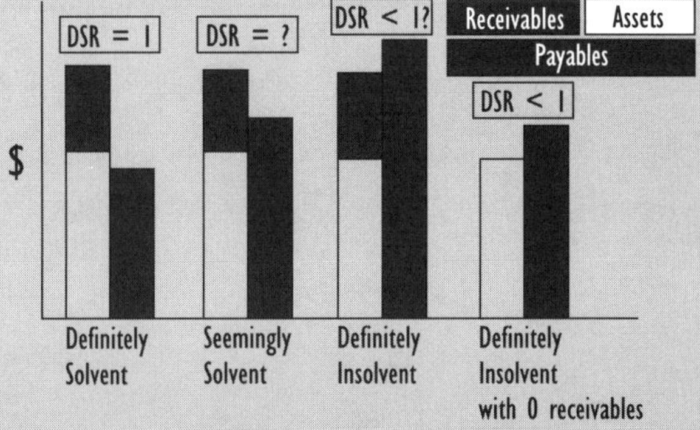

What should these payments accomplish? What possible settlement options were the fairest and/or the most beneficial to the economy?

Possible payment disentanglement rationales considered included attempting to:

Limit the number of bankruptcies

Pay off as many solvent creditors as possible

Achieve the largest possible total payments to all creditors

Maximize the sum of insolvent traders' DSRs

Minimize insolvent traders' deficits (assets plus receivables minus payables)

Determine DSRs that were least susceptible to further deterioration in asset value

Determine DSRs while keeping equal the DSRs of the largest 18 insolvent traders

The task force also needed to consider the following factors:

All traders had to be treated equally and in accordance with the strengths and weaknesses of their financial portfolios, al-Manakh stock trading, and their choice of trade cohorts.

Maximizing the ability for traders to pay their debts in full would minimize the negative effect of the crash on the economy.

A trader's DSR could not be higher than 1 because that would imply that the trader would be paying out more than the amount owed.

By Kuwaiti law, debts to multiple creditors had to be paid in equal proportion of the amount owed to each creditor.

All solvent traders should honor their payables in cash (even if this required them to liquidate other assets).

The disentanglement solution must prevent traders who actually owed money from making net gains.

The task force had many decisions to make to arrive at an equitable solution that would disentangle the web of debts and "net out" the actual loss to the economy. If a credible solution could not be found, each of the 29,000 postdated checks and IOUs would require three court cases to settle: a criminal case, a commercial case, and a bankruptcy case. The outcome of this legal process would send many Kuwaiti entrepreneurs to jail, including many with strong political and social ties; would cost the government some $380 million; and would require the judicial system to increase capacity 18-fold for 5 years. Most importantly, the Kuwaiti economy's state of panic and recession would not improve until the situation was resolved. Time was of the essence.

Assignment

1. Determine a method of allocating payments between traders using the example given in the case, while ignoring the asset breakdown.
2. How should the total payments be allocated among asset classes?

5

SIMULATING THE FUTURE

Computers were first seen as large, fast calculating devices, but a breakthrough occurred in the 1950s when it was realized that the arithmetic engine in the computer could be used to "mimic" the future by driving a *simulation model.* The use of computer simulation is now widespread in well-managed companies; major facilities or products constructed today are "run in the computer" to debug the design and to check out the host of decisions that must be made before construction can begin. Some examples include the following:

Simulation was used to evaluate the design of the terminals of the channel tunnel linking Britain and France.

Simulation is routinely used to assist in the design of new airplanes. A new airplane makes thousands of simulated "flights" in the computer before a single piece is constructed.

General Motors and British Leyland (and most other automobile manufacturers) make extensive use of simulation studies to identify design changes that would improve the efficiency of their existing manufacturing facilities and to design new facilities.

Hospitals use simulations to plan the layout and capacity of operating theaters, outpatient clinics, and guided vehicle systems.

And the list goes on.

Simulation is widely used as a tool to improve operations, but there are also many examples of simulations being used for tactical and strategic decisions. Simulation models can assist management at all decision-making levels: a firm that makes a strategic decision to be a low-cost producer may well use simulation models to study its entire operation with a view to identifying cost savings or opportunities for efficiencies (see the later discussion on Vilpac Truck Manufacturing Company of Mexicali).

An important strategic use of simulation is the **strategic corporate simulation exercise**. Here, a simulation model of the strategic level of a firm is constructed, and the managers of the firm gather at a retreat at which they "play through" various possible strategic decisions using the simulation model to assess their impact and desirability. The organizations marketing these exercises claim that management emerge from these experiences with a much improved understanding of their organization as well as valuable insight into the impact of the chosen future strategy. Simulation models are also extensively used for lower-level management training purposes (for example, flight simulators to train pilots and "war game" simulators to train military officers).

Simulation is its own industry. One estimate put the size of this industry in 1992 at $4 billion annually. The simulation industry includes hardware and software suppliers, consultants, trainers, and specialists. The manager facing a problem for which simulation might be useful can tap into this industry in many different ways, such as buying software that makes simulation easy to do or hiring a consulting firm specializing in simulation.To be able to make an informed choice in a situation such as this, the manager must know some of the basic concepts of simulation.

Two basic types of computer simulations are **deterministic simulations** and **stochastic** (or **Monte Carlo**) **simulations**.

DETERMINISTIC SIMULATION

Deterministic simulation uses the computer as a calculator to compute a value for some decision strategy. Once the simulator has been developed, different strategies can be evaluated to obtain one that provides an acceptable, perhaps "optimal," result.

Deterministic simulation is conceptually straightforward: the decision maker determines the values for a set of decision variables, the computer crunches the numbers and displays (perhaps graphically) the values for one or more criteria, the decision maker reviews the criteria values and comes up with a new set of decision variables, and the cycle repeats.

For example, an accountant is trying to decide how to allocate overhead expenses to several product lines to minimize tax that is paid. A spreadsheet model of the accounting statements and tax calculations is set up, so the model computes the tax to be paid under any overhead allocation scheme. The accountant can now try different overhead allocation "scenarios," and the computer will determine the taxes paid under each scenario. By systematically evaluating several different scenarios, the accountant can decide the best overhead allocation. This is an example of deterministic simulation, although the accountant may just think of it as decision making through "trial and error."

Deterministic simulation often involves searching for values of decision variables to find a good solution.

The **Goal-Seeking** tool provided in most spreadsheets can be a useful aid in some problems. Here is a simple example based on a break-even analysis.

Table 5-1 | **EXAMPLE OF MICROSOFT GOAL SEEKING**

	A	B	C	D
1		BREAK-EVEN ANALYSIS		
2				
3	Fixed Costs		$225,450	
4				
5	Variable Production Cost			$4.53
6				
7	Product Price			$7.23
8				
9	Gross Margin			$2.70
10				
11				
12	Sales Volume		0	
13				
14	Profit		$(225,450.00)	

We want to find the break-even volume for a product for which we have fixed costs of $225,450 and variable production costs of $4.53 per unit. The selling price is $7.23 per unit. A Microsoft Excel model might appear as shown in Table 5-1.

The *Gross Margin* is the *Product Price* minus the *Variable Production Cost* (=D7-D5 in cell D9). Our *Profit* is the *Sales Volume* multiplied by the *Gross Margin* less the *Fixed Costs* (=C12 * D9-C3). A break-even analysis determines the *Sales Volume* required to cover our *Fixed Costs* (or at which *Profit* is zero). We can find this break-even volume through a trial-and-error search, varying *Sales Volume* (cell C12) until *Profit* (cell C14) is zero, or by using **Goal Seeking**. Goal Seeking enables us to set a given cell (the **Set cell**) to a certain **value** by changing a **changing cell**. In our break-even example, we **Set cell** C14 **to value** 0 **by changing cell** C12. The break-even volume appears almost immediately (83,500 units in cell C12) (Table 5-2).

Table 5-2 | **BREAK-EVEN ANALYSIS WITH SOLUTION**

	A	B	C	D
1		BREAK-EVEN ANALYSIS		
2				
3	Fixed Costs		$225,450	
4				
5	Variable Production Cost			$4.53
6				
7	Product Price			$7.23
8				
9	Gross Margin			$2.70
10				
11				
12	Sales Volume		83,500	
13				
14	Profit		$0.00	

Table 5-3 | **BREAK-EVEN ANALYSIS WITH ECONOMIES OF SCALE**

	A	B	C	D
1		BREAK-EVEN ANALYSIS 2		
2				
3	Fixed Costs		$225,450	
4				
5	Variable production cost			4.447513
6				
7	Product Price			$7.23
8				
9	Gross Margin			2.782487
10				
11				
12	Sales Volume		81,024	
13				
14	Profit		$ (1.78)	

Of course, a calculation provides this break-even point directly:

$$
\begin{aligned}
\text{Break-even Point} &= \text{Fixed Costs/Gross Margin}\\
&= 225450/(7.23-4.53)\\
&= 83{,}500
\end{aligned}
$$

The value of the **Goal-Seeking** tool emerges in more complex situations in which simple calculations fail. For example, change the break-even example given above to include economies of scale in production by assuming that the variable production cost per unit declines with quantity produced according to:

$$\text{Variable Production Cost/unit} = 10\ e^{-(\text{quantity}/100{,}000)}$$

To do this in the spreadsheet, replace the constant 4.53 in cell D5 with the expression: =10 * EXP(-C12/100000).

The identical application of **Goal Seeking** produces the new break-even volume (the result has been rounded to the nearest integer) as shown in Table 5-3.

STOCHASTIC (OR MONTE CARLO) SIMULATION

Stochastic simulations differ from deterministic simulations in that they are driven by computer-generated **random numbers**. The outputs of a stochastic simulation are statements about probabilities of events or situations occurring.

Random numbers can be generated with almost any computer software. In Microsoft Excel, the function =RAND() in a cell assigns that cell a value between 0 and 1 with **all values in this range equally likely**. We call these **0-1 uniformly distributed random numbers**. Each time the Excel spreadsheet is recalculated, the values assigned to cells that include RAND() are recomputed using new values for RAND().

Figure 5-1 **FREQUENCIES OF 10,000 EXCEL RAND( ) NUMBERS**

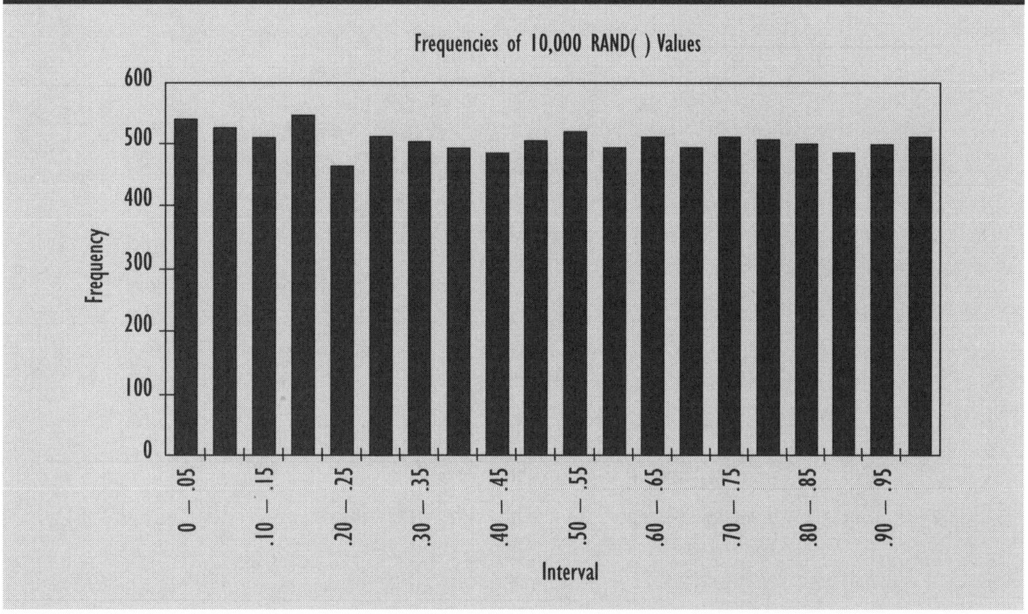

Try the following exercise: In any cell in the spreadsheet, enter =RAND(). Now recalculate the spreadsheet (function key 9), and observe the changes in the value generated by RAND(): each time the spreadsheet is recalculated, the values of all RAND() functions are recomputed.

Figure 5-1 shows a histogram of the frequencies of 10,000 random numbers generated by the Excel RAND() function. All class intervals are expected to occur with the same frequency, although in any sample that we collect, there will be observed variations from this expectation. Because frequencies accumulated in 20 class intervals are plotted, our expectation is to find 500 (10,000/20) values in each interval, and this is approximately the case. Theoretically, RAND() can produce the value 0.0 exactly but not the value 1.0 exactly; this is only a theoretical issue because the probability of generating 0.0 "exactly" is extremely low due to the high degree of precision of Excel (for example, Excel will not round the value 0.000,000,000,000,001 to 0).

A simple example will demonstrate how the RAND() function can be used to drive a simulation model. Suppose we want to determine how many "heads" we would get if we flipped a fair coin 10 times.We could, of course, conduct this experiment directly without great effort, but we can also **simulate** the experiment in Excel.

First, we need a random number for the first coin flip, so we enter =RAND() in cell A1. Because the probability of the result "head" is 0.5 (or 50%), we call any value generated by the function RAND() that is greater than 0.5 a "head." We now check whether the first flip was a "head" or "tail" by checking the random number in cell A1 using

=IF(A1>0.5,''Head,'' ''Tail'') in cell B1.

Because we want to simulate 10 flips, we copy A1:B1 for 10 rows:

	A	B
1	0.161192	Tail
2	0.044212	Tail
3	0.737801	Head
4	0.754327	Head
5	0.356878	Tail
6	0.586503	Head
7	0.497216	Tail
8	0.017443	Tail
9	0.040366	Tail
10	0.551318	Head

In 10 simulated coin flips, we observed four heads. Note that if you try this in your spreadsheet, you will generate different random numbers with, likely, different numbers of simulated "heads" and "tails."

Now recalculate the spreadsheet by hitting {function key 9}. You have just repeated the experiment and observed a new result:

	A	B
1	0.398746	Tail
2	0.730272	Head
3	0.696109	Head
4	0.505395	Head
5	0.173672	Tail
6	0.919423	Head
7	0.746155	Head
8	0.634045	Head
9	0.403714	Tail
10	0.234071	Tail

The Excel **Copy** command enables 100, 1,000, or 10,000 simulated coins to be flipped with very little extra effort (as long as we have enough memory in our computer!). It is easier to keep track of the number of "heads" if we assign a "head" a value of 1 and a "tail" a value of zero [using =IF(A1>0.5,1,0) in cell B1]. We can now use function SUM(B1:B10000) in cell C1 to count the number of "heads."

	A	B	C
1	0.696796	1	5022 = Number of "Heads"
2	0.794706	1	
3	0.647749	1	
4	0.474313	0	
5	0.191770	0	
6	0.574982	1	
7	0.344211	0	
•			
9994	0.769106	1	
9995	0.685820	1	
9996	0.752593	1	
9997	0.780581	1	
9998	0.729356	1	
9999	0.981430	1	
10000	0.878150	1	

When we try to recalculate the spreadsheet with 10,000 simulated coin flips, there will be a pause while recalculation occurs. This is a general occurrence: large-scale simulations can take quite a bit of computer time to work through. This example, however, clearly illustrates one advantage of using the computer to flip 10,000 simulated coins rather than conducting the same experiment "live." How long would it take to flip 10,000 coins and record the results?

The 0-1 uniformly distributed random numbers are an essential driver for two important classes of stochastic simulation: **process** simulation and **event** simulation.

Process Simulation

Process simulation has become an important tool for improving existing processes and designing more effective new processes. Process simulation attempts to model a real-world process "in the computer" so the process can be studied with the view to making process improvements.

Some of the many successes of process simulation include the following:

A process simulation model of a steel works plant has been used to streamline materials flow.

Process simulations are routinely used in business process reengineering projects.

A process simulation of a bank branch has been used to improve customer flow and service.

A process simulation of a hospital has been used to improve the floor plan of an outpatient clinic.

Event Simulation

Event simulations are used to construct distributions of outcomes. Some examples will help clarify this concept:

An event simulation was used to construct the distribution of the likely value of a star pitcher to a professional baseball team. The final distribution was dependent on the probabilities that the pitcher would start different numbers of games, the number of games that the pitcher might win, the distribution of the increase in attendance when the pitcher appeared, the probability of the team making the playoffs and World Series, and so on.

Event simulations are routinely used to construct payoff distributions for various group insurance plans. For example, an office workforce consists of a certain distribution of women and men of known ages, and the probabilities of various disabilities by age/sex classes are known to the insurance companies from experience with long-term disability plans. An insurance company quoting on a new long-term disability plan can simulate the claims distribution for any office workforce.

DEVELOPING A STOCHASTIC SIMULATION MODEL

Data Collection and Observation

Development of a stochastic simulation model generally begins with observation of an existing system and data collection (although if we are modeling a new plant, we may have to make some assumptions about the new plant based on our understanding of existing equipment).

Even when modeling the future, some things may not change. For example, changing the layout of a bank or outpatient department at a hospital may not have much of an effect on the stream of customers or patients arriving.

In general, it is important to understand both the frequency and timing of events. When "customers" are arriving for service, we would like to know when they arrive, not just how many arrive. In general, we will not be able (nor will it be economical) to collect sufficient data to run our simulation model on real data alone. For example, if a customer arrives about every 10 minutes, we could sit for half a day with a clipboard and a watch and record about 24 arrivals. This would generally be too few to run a simulation of a reasonable length; it would not be unreasonable to run 10,000 simulated "customers" through a process simulation (more about run lengths later).

Generating Streams of Events

How can we produce a long stream of simulated events that matches the characteristics of a much smaller sample? We use 0-1 uniformly distributed random numbers to **generate** a simulated stream of events. This can be done in two ways: either through the use of the empirical distribution or by fitting a theoretical distribution.

To illustrate the two approaches, we consider the example of generating a simulated stream of customers arriving at some facility. We assume that we sat for half a day and collected the following arrival times for 20 customers who arrived while we were observing. For simplicity, we have expressed all times in minutes from the time we started collecting observations. For each arriving customer, we have also computed the time (in minutes) since the last customer arrived.

Customer Number	Arrival Time	Minutes since last Arrival
1	17.4	17.4
2	20.2	2.8
3	27.1	6.9
4	37.9	10.8
5	52.8	14.9
6	67.4	14.6
7	103.7	36.3
8	106.5	2.8
9	108.4	1.9
10	120.6	12.2
11	120.8	0.2
12	156.7	35.9
13	157.4	0.7
14	162.2	4.8
15	167.2	5.0
16	184.6	17.4
17	188.7	4.1
18	202.3	13.6
19	208.0	5.7
20	226.9	18.9

Method 1: Using an Empirical Distribution. We can use this data and RAND() to generate an arrival stream of arbitrary length that will have the same distribution over time as the observed arrivals. The method is straightforward. We sort the times between arrivals into ascending order and place the values in a column (in our example, in column F). Because there are 20 values, the probability of any one value appearing is 1/20, or 0.05. We therefore load the values 0.00, 0.05, 0.1, . . . 0.95 in column E along the times between arrivals.

	E	F
1	**Probability**	**Interarrival**
2		**Time**
3	----	----
4	0.00	0.2
5	0.05	0.7
6	0.10	1.9
7	0.15	2.8
8	0.20	2.8
9	0.25	4.1
10	0.30	4.8
11	0.35	5.0
12	0.40	5.7
13	0.45	6.9
14	0.50	10.8
15	0.55	12.2
16	0.60	13.6
17	0.65	14.6
18	0.70	14.9
19	0.75	17.4
20	0.80	17.4
21	0.85	18.9
22	0.90	35.9
23	0.95	36.3

We are now in a position to transform a stream of 0-1 uniformly distributed random numbers into a set of interarrival times. We use the values in range E4:F23 with the vertical table look-up function =VLOOKUP(RAND(),$E$4:$F$23,2). This function will start at the top of the first column of the table in E4:F23 and move down if it finds the value to be less than the value given by RAND(), stopping when the next value is greater. The value of the cell in which the statement is entered is given as the value that appears in column 2 of the table. If this statement is copied into 100 (or 1,000 or 5,000) cells in a column, this column will contain 100 (or 1,000 or 5,000) simulated interarrival times. Summing from the top will generate a stream of simulated arrivals that have the same distribution over time as the observed sample.

Method 2: Fitting a Theoretical Curve. The 20 observed interarrival times are plotted as a cumulative frequency distribution in Figure 5-2. That is, the height of the curve at x gives the fraction of observations with an interarrival time of less than x. In addition, superimposed on Figure 5-2 is the mathematical function:

$$P = 1 - e^{(-t/11.3)}$$

Figure 5-2 **FITTING A THEORETICAL CURVE TO EMPIRICAL DATA**

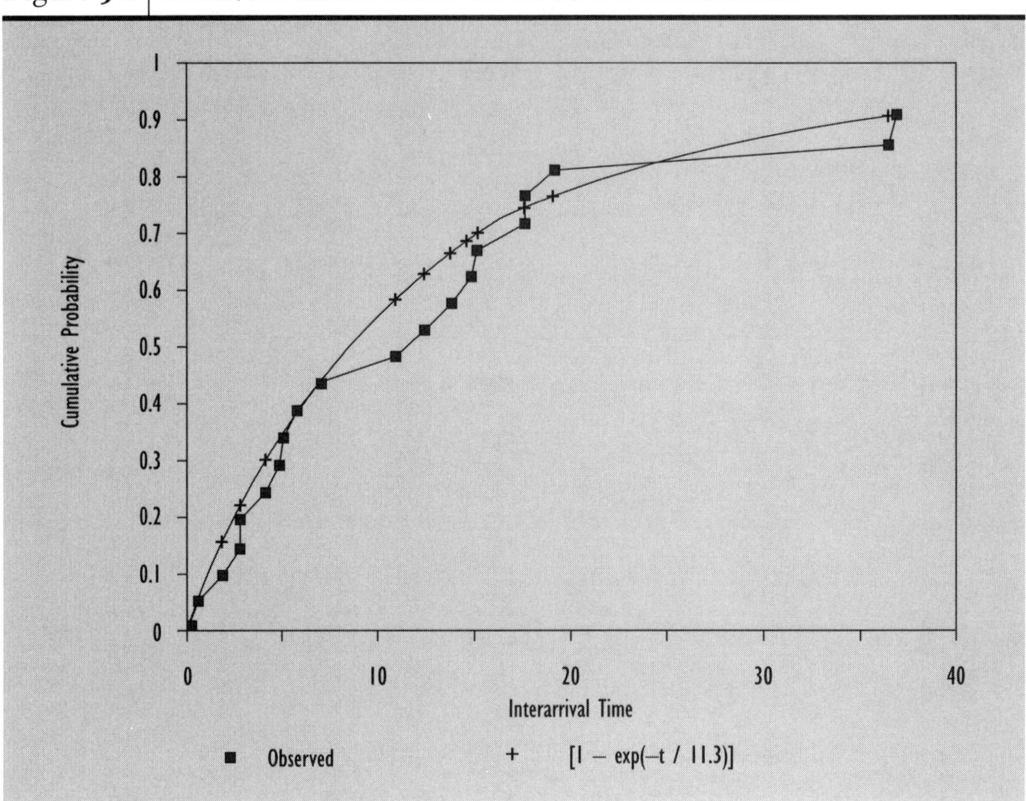

where P is the cumulative probability, t is the interarrival time, and 11.3 is the *mean interarrival time*.

This theoretical curve fits the observed points reasonably well. We can therefore use this theoretical curve to generate interarrival times. We note that P takes on a value between 0 and 1; by generating P values as 0-1 uniformly distributed random numbers and then inverting the theoretical function, we obtain the interarrival times. The inversion is accomplished as follows:

For

$$P = 1 - e^{(-t/11.3)}$$

then:

$$1 - P = e^{(-t/11.3)}$$

and

$$\ln(1 - P) = (-t/11.3)$$
$$t = -11.3 \ln(1 - P)$$

Because (1 − P) has the same distribution as P, we can generate an interarrival time that fits the empirical data using the statement:

$$= -11.3 * LN(RAND())$$

By varying the *mean interarrival time* (11.3 in the above example), this form of theoretical function can be used to generate interevent times that approximately match large numbers of "random" events. Some examples where this has proved useful include the arrival times of ships at a port and of customers at a bank and an ice cream shop, and the time between breakdowns of machinery and incidents of employee sickness.

Building the Logic of the Simulation

The logic of a simulation model attempts to replicate the real life system. The logic of an **event simulation** differs from that of a **process simulation**.

Event logic often follows a tree structure in which the tree is made up of uncertain events for which branching occurs. Event logic uses random numbers to simulate the uncertain events and generate paths through the tree (or "scenarios").

As an example, consider the problem of estimating the cost of claims for a group of employees covered by a long-term disability insurance plan. Typically, such plans pay the covered employees a percentage of their salaries in the event they suffer some kind of disability that keeps them from working for a period in excess of several months.

Actuaries, employed by the insurance companies, maintain records of past claims experience from which probabilities can be derived. Estimates of the probability of disability occurring and of the disability lasting any number of months are available for various customer classes (professionals, blue collar workers, various industry groups, and so on).

Using these probabilities, data on group members' salaries, characteristics, and a knowledge of the terms of the long-term disability policy, event simulation can be used to estimate the claims experience for the plan. The simulation would examine each individual in the group in turn and use random numbers to generate a claims scenario for that individual over the lifetime of the plan. This claims scenario would be derived by using a random number for each simulated time period to determine whether or not the individual became disabled. If disability occurred, a second random number (or set of random numbers) could be used to determine the duration of the disability (other random numbers could determine the type of disability or the benefit level if this was important to the claim).

By examining each individual in turn for each time period, a typical claims scenario for the group can be derived. Examining multiple claims scenarios (if the model were in a spreadsheet, generating a new scenario simply requires hitting the F9 recalculation key) enables the average value and variability of the groups' claims to be examined. Such a simulation would enable management at the insurance company to develop an understanding of the riskiness of the plan and to adopt a sensible pricing (and perhaps reinsurance) policy.

Process Logic. As an illustration of development of the logic of a process simulation, consider The Tennessee Tour Bus Company.

THE TENNESSEE TOUR BUS COMPANY

The Tennessee Tour Bus Company makes tour buses–the kind used for concert tours or other traveling shows. The basic bus is purchased from the manufacturer and is customized in a two-stage production process.

At the body work stage (the "bodyshop"), the interior of the bus is customized, including the fitting of sleeping rooms, lounge areas, and a kitchen and modifying the window arrangement. Each bus receives about the same body work, and this takes 10 working days. The bus is then moved to a painting area (the "paintshop"), where it is painted. The paint work on these tour buses is usually quite spectacular, including individual artwork, as well as a high-quality overall finish. In some cases, the name of the touring performer is painted on the outside of the bus, or the paint work may include images or motifs chosen by the performer. The time taken to paint a bus averages 10 days but is highly variable; sometimes the paint "wrinkles" and has to be redone. In a few cases, painting can be accomplished in 2 days, but there have been instances in which a bus took 18 days to paint satisfactorily.

"Raw" buses can be stored in a large lot outside, so there is always a bus for the bodyshop to work on; painted buses are weatherproof and can be stored outside, so the paintshop can always unload a finished bus. However, buses that are ready for painting must be kept inside, and the only place available is the bodyshop. If body work employees finish a bus, but painting employees are busy, then the bodyshop is "blocked"; work must stop until painting finishes and the bus can be moved into the paintshop. If painting employees finish a bus, they can begin work on the next bus only if the bodyshop has a finished bus ready: otherwise, they are "starved" and must wait for the bodyshop to finish a bus before they can start work again.

Managers have noticed that the bodyshop often is blocked and the paintshop often is idle, with no bus to paint. The suggestion has been made that a floor space large enough to park one complete fitted but unpainted bus be created between the two processes. Body work employees would then be able to "unload" a complete fitted bus into this space even though painting employees were still busy. Similarly, painting would sometimes be able to start a new bus if one was available in storage, even though the bodyshop employees were still working.

How much extra throughput will the additional storage space allow?

A Stochastic Simulation Model in a Spreadsheet

We begin the spreadsheet model in Table 5-4 by placing the key parameters in cells. Cell D5 contains the time taken at the "fitting" stage (10 days), and the minimum and maximum times to paint a bus are placed in cells B6 and C6.

We First Model the Existing System. To construct the logic of the model, we identify each bus passing through the shop as a row. Row 10 charts the flow of the first bus through the (empty) shop. This bus begins body work at time 0 and is finished at time 10 (=B10+$D$5). It then moves directly into painting (at time 10), and painting takes some time between 2 (=$B$6) and 18 (=$C$6) days. We generate the time to paint the bus as a random variable distributed uniformly between 2 and 18 days using =$B$6+($C$6-$B$6) * RAND(). This means that the completion time for the first bus is given by =D10+$B$6+($C$6-$B$6) * RAND() in cell E10.

Row 11 charts bus number 2 (=1+A10 in A11). This bus begins body work when the previous bus enters painting, freeing up the bodyshop (=D10 in B11), and completes body work at =B11+$D$5 (in cell C11). Bus 2 can enter the painting area only if it has finished body work **and** bus 1 has finished painting and the formula =MAX(C11,E10) in cell D11 captures this. In the example in Table 5-4, the delay between the end of body work (at time 20) and the entry into painting (at time 25.46) indicates that the bodyshop was blocked for 5.46 days and could not start the next bus. (Bus 3, therefore, begins body work at time 25.46 days.) Bus 2 completes painting at a time generated by =D11+$B$6+($C$6-$B$6) * RAND() in cell E11.

Rows 12 and the following rows chart as many buses as we wish to include (and we have memory space for) using the spreadsheet copy command from row 11. We copy A11:E11 to rows A12:E129 charting 120 buses through the simulated shop.

To obtain a performance measure for the shop, we note that because the shop always starts empty, the first few buses take less time to complete than later buses, which may be held up by congestion. A simple way to remove this "start-up" effect is to ignore the first few buses when computing the performance measures. One performance measure is therefore the total time taken to complete buses numbers 21 through 120, or =(E129-B30) (in cell E3) (Table 5-4).

We Now Model the Proposed System. The model with the one-bus inventory space is constructed in columns G through K of the same spreadsheet.

The logic is essentially the same, but we include an extra column to record the time at which the bus enters the inventory space. For bus 1, this is the same as the time of completion of body work, but for later buses, it is the maximum of the time when the bus completes body work (column H) and the time at which painting begins work on the previous bus (column J) (because the beginning of painting leads to removal of the bus from inventory into the paintshop, making the inventory space available, if needed). The appropriate formula is =MAX(J10,H11) in cell I11. The time at which the second bus enters painting

Table 5-4 **SIMULATION MODEL OF EXISTING SYSTEM OF TENNESSEE TOUR BUS COMPANY**

	A	B	C	D	E
1		**Tennessee Tour Bus Company**			
2		Existing System			
3		Time to complete 100 buses			1,209.35
4	**Parameters**				
5	Bodywork			10	
6	Painting	2	18		
7					
8	Bus	Start	End	Into	Finished
9	Number	Bodywork	Bodywork	Painting	Painting
10	1	0.00	10.00	10.00	25.46
11	2	10.00	20.00	25.46	40.11
12	3	25.46	35.46	40.11	42.43
13	4	40.11	50.11	50.11	60.26
14	5	50.11	60.11	60.26	70.14
15	6	60.26	70.26	70.26	80.74
16	7	70.26	80.26	80.74	91.92
17	8	80.74	90.74	91.92	99.40
18	9	91.92	101.92	101.92	117.29
19	10	101.92	111.92	117.29	132.81
20	11	117.29	127.29	132.81	147.90
21	12	132.81	142.81	147.90	159.50
:					
129	120	1,416.69	1,426.69	1,434.10	1,441.77

is the latest (maximum) of the time the first bus completed painting and the second bus entered inventory [=MAX(K10,I11) in cell J11]. The last change to make is to note that body work can start on the second bus as soon as the previous bus enters inventory (=I10 in cell G11).

Copying the formulas in G11 through K11 to the range G12:K129 simulates 120 buses passing through the proposed system. The time taken to complete the last 100 of these buses (=K129-G30 in cell K3) provides a performance measure for the proposed system. The spreadsheet containing both models appears in Table 5-5.

Table 5-5 | **SPREADSHEET CONTAINING TWO MODELS**

	A	B	C	D	E	F	G	H	I	J	K
1		**Tennessee Tour Bus Company**									
2		Existing System						Proposed System			
3		Time to complete 100 buses			1,209.35			Time to complete 100 buses			1,089.00
4	**Parameters**										
5	Bodywork			10							
6	Painting	2	18								
7											
8	Bus	Start	End	Into	Finished	—	Start	End	Into	Into	Finished
9	Number	Bodywork	Bodywork	Painting	Painting		Bodywork	Bodywork	Inventory	Painting	Painting
10	1	0.00	10.00	10.00	25.46		0.00	10.00	10.00	10.00	23.34
11	2	10.00	20.00	25.46	40.11		10.00	20.00	20.00	23.34	40.87
12	3	25.46	35.46	40.11	42.43		20.00	30.00	30.00	40.87	51.58
13	4	40.11	50.11	50.11	60.26		30.00	40.00	40.87	51.58	62.45
14	5	50.11	60.11	60.26	70.14		40.87	50.87	51.58	62.45	64.63
15	6	60.26	70.26	70.26	80.74		51.58	61.58	62.45	64.63	69.07
16	7	70.26	80.26	80.74	91.92		62.45	72.45	72.45	72.45	88.03
17	8	80.74	90.74	91.92	99.40		72.45	82.45	82.45	88.03	99.01
18	9	91.92	101.92	101.92	117.29		82.45	92.45	92.45	99.01	107.32
19	10	101.92	111.92	117.29	132.81		92.45	102.45	102.45	107.32	123.81
20	11	117.29	127.29	132.81	147.90		102.45	112.45	112.45	123.81	126.70
21	12	132.81	142.81	147.90	159.50		112.45	122.45	123.81	126.70	144.55
:											
129	120	1,416.69	1,426.69	1,434.10	1,441.77		1,263.96	1,273.96	1,276.57	1,286.00	1,295.32

Using the Model to Make Decisions

The RAND() function used in the model is recalculated each time the spreadsheet is recalculated (for example, by using the F9 recalculation key). Each use of F9, therefore, provides one snapshot of the operations of the two systems, each processing 100 buses. By repeatedly pressing F9, we can obtain a sense of the variability in our performance statistics. The results from 20 recalculations of these statistics are shown in Table 5-6.

Table 5-6 | **SIMULATION MODEL RESULTS OF 20 RECALCULATIONS**

	Existing System	Proposed System	Difference
	1,209.35	1,089.00	120.35
	1,214.36	1,069.96	144.40
	1,169.96	1,095.11	74.85
	1,220.62	1,101.32	119.30
	1,261.45	1,089.12	172.33
	1,249.74	1,034.96	214.78
	1,170.50	1,084.57	85.93
	1,212.27	1,056.99	155.28
	1,204.29	1,110.79	93.50
	1,202.89	1,047.34	155.55
	1,216.04	1,082.45	133.59
	1,232.45	1,085.77	146.68
	1,195.25	1,032.77	162.48
	1,222.16	1,099.14	123.02
	1,203.54	1,110.26	93.28
	1,184.61	1,017.11	167.50
	1,203.11	1,068.50	134.61
	1,198.58	1,092.95	105.63
	1,192.60	1,063.85	128.75
	1,174.76	1,120.98	53.78
Mean	**1,206.93**	**1,077.65**	**129.28**
Std. Dev.	**23.77**	**28.26**	**38.09**

We see that this sample of 20 observations provides an estimate that the addition of the inventory space will reduce the time to complete 100 buses by an average of 129.28 days, representing a time saving of 1.29 days per bus. In terms of an average productivity gain, if we operated the system with the inventory space for the same time as the original system (1206.93 days) we would average 100 * 1,206.93/1,077.65, or 112 buses, instead of 100, for a productivity gain of 12%.

This result is based on a sample of 20 runs of our model. If we ran the model a 21st time, what will be the time savings for the new sample of 100 buses? The **prediction interval** addresses this issue. The **prediction interval** is the interval from the mean minus two standard deviations to the mean plus two standard deviations. Approximately 95% of the time (or 19 times out of 20 times), the next model run will produce a result within this interval. We conclude that an approximate 95% prediction interval for the estimated savings in manufacturing time is the interval from 53.1 to 205.5 days. Computing this interval on a *per-bus* basis, we conclude that we expect the addition of the inventory space to save us between 0.53 day and 2.05 days per bus, 19 times out of 20.

The **prediction interval** provides an idea of the variability of the model result, and in this case, this wide interval suggests considerable variability. One method of narrowing this interval is to increase our sample size from 100 to 1,000 buses. To do this, we copy row 129 down to row 1,029 and recalculate the completion time for 1,000 buses by modifying the formulas in cells E3 and K3 to reflect the fact that row 1029 is now the final row of the model (that is, change E129-B20 in E3 to E1029-B30). Twenty replications of the 1,000-bus simulator produced the results shown in Table 5-7.

From these results, the **95% prediction interval** for the estimated time savings for a new sample of 1,000 buses is calculated as 1,278.67 ± 2 * 39.59 days, or (on a per-bus basis) 1.2787 ± 2 * 0.0396 days per bus. The prediction interval is between 1.199 days and 1.358 days per bus, 19 times out of 20; the increased sample size has narrowed this interval considerably.

Extending the sample size in this way imposes a cost: the model takes more memory and takes longer to run. Both of these are noticeable in the small simulator developed above and become even more of a factor in larger and more complex simulation programs. We therefore look for ways to achieve more precision in our estimates without increasing the sample size. Because these methods reduce the variance in our model results, they are called **variance reduction methods**.

Table 5-7 | **TWENTY REPLICATIONS OF THE 1,000-BUS SIMULATOR**

Existing System	Proposed System	Difference	Difference per Bus
12,139.66	10,900.52	1,239.15	1.239
11,984.13	10,665.72	1,318.41	1.318
12,201.25	10,862.62	1,338.63	1.339
11,908.07	10,634.58	1,273.50	1.274
11,997.66	10,666.02	1,331.64	1.332
12,048.57	10,806.04	1,242.52	1.243
11,925.03	10,656.97	1,268.07	1.268
12,017.70	10,753.29	1,264.41	1.264
12,081.35	10,854.13	1,227.22	1.227
11,930.21	10,693.05	1,237.16	1.237
11,944.47	10,598.82	1,345.65	1.346
11,833.91	10,587.75	1,246.16	1.246
12,090.19	10,879.47	1,210.72	1.211
12,096.82	10,791.06	1,305.77	1.306
11,770.65	10,492.56	1,278.09	1.278
12,091.28	10,829.69	1,261.59	1.262
11,987.41	10,678.94	1,308.47	1.308
12,027.18	10,704.44	1,322.74	1.323
12,126.91	10,840.52	1,286.40	1.286
12,123.65	10,856.55	1,267.10	1.267
	Mean	**1,278.67**	**1.2787**
	Std. Dev.	**39.59**	**0.0396**

One simple variance reduction technique enables the interval to be narrowed considerably. This technique is to simulate both the existing and the proposed system processing *the same buses*. Because the body work time for each bus is constant (at 10 days) in both systems, all buses are already the same in terms of body work. Painting times, however, are generated from separate random numbers in each system and are different in Table 5-5: bus 1 takes 25.46 − 10, or 15.46, days to paint in the existing system but 23.34 − 10, or 13.34, days to paint in the proposed system. Changing the formula in cell K10 to =J10+E10-D10 and copying to K11:K129 sets the painting time for each bus in the proposed system at the same duration as that generated using RAND() for the simulation of the existing system. We could accomplish the same effect by generating 120 simulated buses "off-line," each with its own processing times, and then feeding this data set of simulated buses through our simulators of the existing system and of the proposed system. Collecting real processing time for 120 buses and running this through both simulators would also have the same effect.

Twenty replications of the simulation now produced the results shown in Table 5-8.

Table 5-8 **RESULTS FROM 20 REPLICATIONS OF THE SIMULATION USING THE SAME SIMULATED BUSES FOR BOTH SYSTEMS**

Existing System	Proposed System	Difference
1,251.28	1,094.93	156.35
1,182.18	1,048.02	134.17
1,224.69	1,101.27	123.42
1,216.93	1,066.17	150.76
1,192.56	1,079.97	112.58
1,231.77	1,084.62	147.15
1,194.57	1,044.48	150.09
1,199.48	1,079.11	120.37
1,231.31	1,109.51	121.80
1,207.50	1,073.17	134.34
1,243.48	1,084.97	158.51
1,220.10	1,074.59	145.52
1,235.92	1,095.11	140.81
1,182.31	1,033.08	149.23
1,232.93	1,101.07	131.86
1,238.85	1,105.20	133.65
1,190.25	1,047.34	142.91
1,174.41	1,040.46	133.95
1,203.66	1,073.63	130.04
1,189.65	1,078.21	111.44
	Mean	**136.45**
	Std. Dev.	**13.80**

We note that the use of the same simulated buses has reduced the standard deviation of the mean processing time for 100 buses from 40.04 to 13.80 days, *with no additional computation requirements*. The prediction interval has slimmed from 0.53 to 2.05 days per bus to 1.08 to 1.64 days per bus.

A Second Look at Process Simulation Logic: The Flowchart

The flowchart provides another way of detailing the logic of a simulation. Flowcharts are particularly useful if a simulation model is to be coded into a computer language. We examine three types of process logic: **discrete time** logic, **discrete event** logic, and **entity life-cycle** logic.

A flowchart, illustrating **discrete time** logic for a simulation model of the Tennessee Tour Bus Company's existing operations, is shown in Figure 5-3. The following steps are involved:

Figure 5-3 **DISCRETE TIME FLOWCHART FOR TENNESSEE TOUR BUS COMPANY SIMULATION**

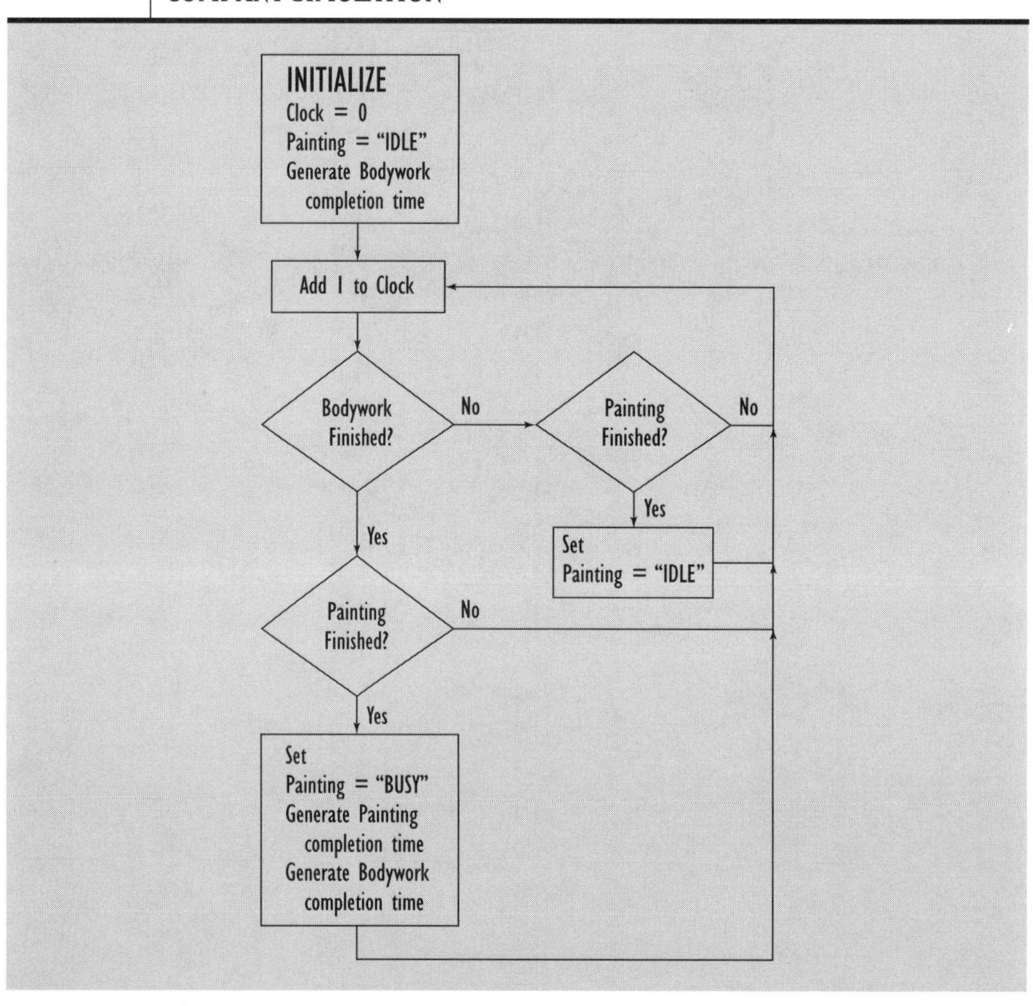

Initialization. We begin by setting the starting conditions for the model.We define a variable *CLOCK* that will keep track of the clock time and set its starting value to zero, set the state of the paintshop to *IDLE*, and generate the time at which the first bus will complete body work.

Main Loop. Now that the starting conditions are set, we enter the main loop of the model. Each time around this loop, we advance the clock by one "tick" and check to see whether an event has occurred that has changed the state of the system. We first check to see whether the bodyshop has finished working on its bus. If it has not, we check to see whether the paintshop has finished its work. If neither has finished, we move the clock forward one "tick" and loop again.

If the body work has finished, we check to see if the paintshop is *BUSY*. If it is busy, there is nothing we can do but go around the loop again: the bodyshop is "blocked." If painting is *IDLE*, we move the bus from the bodyshop to the paintshop; in the model, this involves setting the paintshop to *BUSY*, generating a new paintshop completion time, and generating a new bodyshop completion time (because moving the bus into the paintshop coincides with beginning body work on a new bus). We now go around the loop again.

There are a number of important items to be considered that are not included in the flowchart (Figure 5-3).

Stopping Rule. Note that the flowchart (Figure 5-3) contains no way of terminating the simulation. This could be done by exiting the main loop when the clock reaches a certain time or exiting when a certain number of buses have been processed through the plant. The appropriate stopping method will depend on the statistical design of the experiments and what data are being collected. To replicate the spreadsheet model (above), we would keep a count of the number of buses painted and terminate the simulation when this reached 120, printing out the value of *CLOCK* when this occurred.

Statistics Collection. The flowchart contains no statistics collection. We must determine what output we want to collect and then devise logic to collect the necessary statistics. For example, if we want to know the percentage of time that the paintshop is idle, we set up a counter that counts each "tick" of the clock when the paintshop is idle. At the end of the simulation, dividing the value of the counter by the ending value of the *CLOCK* variable provides the required rate.

Size of the "Tick." If we chose to "tick" the clock forward in very small time increments, than we spend a great deal of time spinning round the simulation loop with nothing happening. If we go to a larger time increment, we may not be able to recognize events when they actually occur; for example, if we compute processing time in minutes but tick the clock forward in hours, then a bus could be sitting completed in the bodyshop for up to 59 minutes before we move it into a vacant paintshop. This difficulty leads directly to **discrete event logic**.

Discrete Event Logic

In discrete event logic, we replace the even "ticking" of the clock by variable time increments. This recognizes that nothing happens in the simulation model unless some event triggers changes in the state of the system. To illustrate the concept, we return to the Tennessee Tour Bus Company. Figure 5-4 illustrates the flowchart for a discrete event simulation model.

For the discrete event simulation, we define three variables:

- *Clock* is the clock time.
- *Bodytime* is the completion time of the bus occupying the bodyshop.
- *Painttime* is the completion time of the bus occupying the paintshop.

Figure 5-4 **DISCRETE EVENT FLOWCHART FOR TENNESSEE TOUR BUS COMPANY SIMULATION**

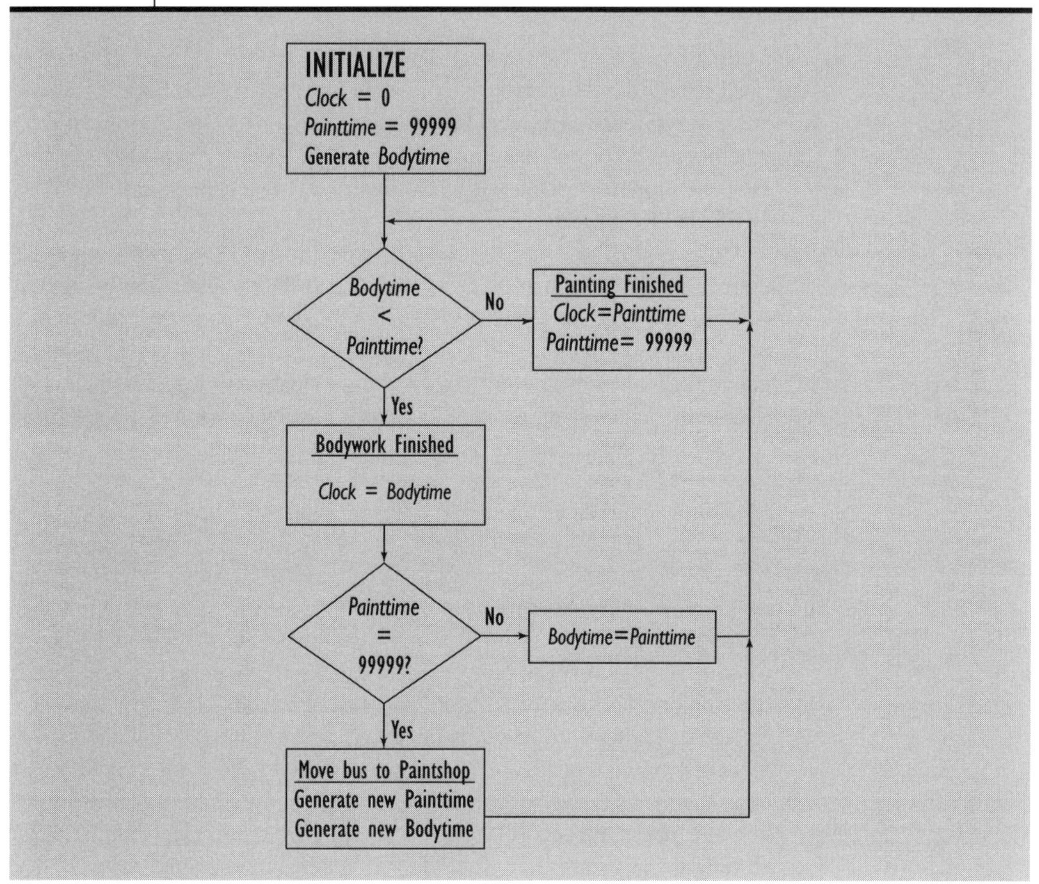

We will use *Painttime* = 99999 (a number larger than the maximum value of the clock variable) as a code to denote that the paintshop is empty.

Initialization requires that we set *Clock* to zero, set *Painttime* to 99999 (start with the paintshop empty), and generate the time of the first event, which is the completion of body work for the first bus.

The logic of the main loop (Figure 5-4) involves determining which event occurs first, body completion or painting completion; advancing the clock to the time of that event; and then processing that event.

If body work completes first, check to see whether the paintshop is empty (or *Painttime* = 99999); if so, move the bus from the bodyshop to the paintshop and generate completion times for both body work on the next bus and painting of this bus. If the paintshop is not empty, set *Bodytime* equal to *Painttime* so on the next loop, the end-of-painting event will be processed.

If painting completes first, set the clock to *Painttime*, empty the paintshop (*Painttime* = 99999), and loop again.

As a final example of the logic of simulation, we view the system from the perspective of the entities moving through the simulated process. This is known as **entity life-cycle logic**.

Entity Life-Cycle Logic

We can represent a bus moving through the Tennessee Tour Bus plant as an entity that goes through the following activities during its life-cycle: from the time of arrival at the plant to that of departure from the plant:

1. The bus seizes the bodyshop.
2. The bus occupies the bodyshop.
3. The bus releases the bodyshop.
4. The bus seizes the paintshop.
5. The bus occupies the paintshop.
6. The bus releases the paintshop.

The bodyshop and paintshop are also entities; these both go through the same simple life-cycle:

1. Open for business (at time 0)
2. Working
3. Closed for business (at end of simulation)

We could schedule working hours each day, but because we have assumed that the state of the system is unaffected by the close down and startup, this is unnecessary.

In the Tennessee Tour Bus example, there will be a stream of bus entities going through the same list of activities at different times. In more general simulation models, there may be many different types of entities, each with their own life-cycle description. These process may interact as entities compete for the same resources, resulting in the formation of queues, bottlenecks, and so forth.

Simulation software based on the special-purpose language GPSS, which was originally developed by IBM in the 1950s, uses entity life-cycle logic as the basis for input of the model. These packages include features that provide considerable help to the modeler in handling the advance of the clock, interactions between entities, processing queues and blockages, and statistics collection.

LARGE-SCALE SIMULATION MODELS

The modeler building a large-scale simulation model has many software options available. First, the model can be coded in a third-generation language, such as FORTRAN, Pascal, or BASIC. These languages are highly flexible but require that the model, including all input and output statements, be coded from scratch. To take advantage of the existing input and output formats provided by the spreadsheet, a simulation model can be coded in a spreadsheet macro language, such as the Visual BASIC macro language included in Microsoft Excel.

Special-purpose languages, such as GPSS, SIMSCRIPT, and SLAM, provide the modeler with a variety of skeletal simulation models: by filling in the "blanks," the modeler can access standard simulation model logic that may significantly shorten the programming task.

Finally, there are a large number of software packages that facilitate simulation model building, graphic animation, and model interaction capabilities (Table 5-9).

Table 5-9 | **SIMULATION SOFTWARE**

Package Name	Typical Applications	Animation Real-time	Animation Post-processed	Price for Standard Version ($)
ARENA (SIMAN/CINEMA)	General Purpose	√	√	—
@RISK	Risk Analysis	No	No	395
AutoMod	General Purpose 3-D Simulation	√	√	18,000–40,000
AutoSched	Manufacturing scheduling and capacity planning	√	√	41,000–61,000
BestFit	Statistical distribution fitting	No	No	299
Best Network	Analysis of communications networks	No	No	1,650
COMNET III	Voice and data network modeling	√	√	34,500–39,500
CSIM17	General purpose	No	No	450
Curve Fit I	Statistical distribution fitting	No	No	295
ExpertFit	Statistical distribution fitting	No	No	275–1,350
Extend	General purpose	√	No	695
Extend + BPR	Business process reengineering	√	No	990
Extend + Manufacturing	Simulating discrete industrial processes	√	No	990
FACTOR/AIM	Manufacturing	√	No	—
G2 Real-Time Expert System	On-line process control simulations	√	No	6,500–39,000
GPSS/H	General purpose	No	Yes	2,500–5,200
GPSS/PC	General purpose	√	√	1,995
GPSS World	General purpose	No	√	4,500
GSS	Communications networks	√	No	—
Hocus Simulation 8000	General purpose	√	No	9,000
ithink	Business process reengineering	√	No	949
Maintsim	Maintenance, repair shops	No	No	295
ManSim/X	Microelectronic fabrication plants	√	√	49,500
MAST	Cellular manufacturing	√	√	2,950
MEModel	Healthcare facility simulations	√	√	—
micro-GPSS	Teaching simulation	No	√	700
Micro Saint	General purpose	No	√	5,995
MODSIM II	General purpose	√	√	23,500–34,500
MOGUL	Computer systems and network simulations	√	√	4,995
NETWORK II.5	Computer systems and network simulations	√	√	23,500–29,500

Table 5-9 | **CONTINUED**

Package Name	Typical Applications	Animation Real-time	Animation Post-processed	Price for Standard Version ($)
OPNET Modeler	Simulating communications networks	√	√	16,000–25,000
PASION	Simulation of queueing systems	√	√	250
PC Model	General purpose	√	No	3,000
ProModel	General purpose	√	√	13,900
Proof Animation	Animation of simulation model output	No	√	3,000–5,200
PROVISA	Finite capacity scheduling	No	No	—
QueGAUSS	Simulation of queueing systems	No	No	275
QUEST	Simulation of queueing systems	√	No	—
ServiceModel	Business process reengineering	√	√	13,900
SIGMA	General purpose	√	√	4,995
SIMFACTORY II.5	Manufacturing systems simulations	√	√	11,500–15,000
SimGAUSS	Nonlinear dynamic simulations	No	No	375
SIMNET II	General purpose	No	No	—
SIMNON	Simulation of nonlinear systems	√	√	1,145
SIMPLE++	General purpose	√	No	<6,000
SIMPROCESS III	Business process analysis	√	√	11,500–15,000
SIMSCRIPT II.5	General purpose	√	√	23,500–34,500
SIMSTAT 2.0	Statistical analysis of input and output data	No	No	1,500
SIMUL8	General purpose	√	No	395
SLAMSYSTEM	General purpose	√	√	—
Taylor II	General purpose	√	No	—
TUTSIM	Simulation of non-linear systems	√	No	820
Witness	General purpose	√	No	—
Workflow Analyser	Business process improvement	√	No	10,000

From JJ Swain, Simulation Software Review, *OR/MS Today*, August 1995.

ANIMATION AND SIMULATION

Simulation modeling was once the world of the "black box" simulation model into which data were entered and from which numbers emerged. Simulation has now moved beyond this "batch simulation" toward **visual interactive simulation**, in which the model user or decision maker can watch a dynamic, color graphic display of model output and can interrupt the model, change data or decision rules, and continue.

The first visual interactive simulation models emerged from attempts to build interactive simulation models of automobile plants. Modelers ran into the problem of displaying the status of the model so the user could see when to interact (and the effect of the interaction). After experimenting with the display of intermediate numerical results and transferring these results to physical models of the system, the modelers began producing dynamic computer-generated graphic displays. As technology has developed, the quality of these displays has improved enormously, and we have simulation software that can produce multicolored, three-dimensional, dynamic graphics showing the operation of large systems, and all on a personal computer (see Figures 5-5 and 5-6 for two examples).

Animation can be used in two different ways: **postprocessed** animation and **visual interactive animation**. In **postprocessed animation**, the moving pictures are used to illustrate the results of running a nongraphic simulation model: software such as PROOF Animation can read an output file from a simulation model and replay the results through a visual display device. The user can watch the moving pictures but cannot interact with the model and cannot make changes. In **visual interactive animation**, the model is actually running while the pictures are being displayed: the user can stop the model, make changes, and continue, and can immediately see the results of the interaction visually. Simulation software that takes the visual interactive approach includes SEE-WHY (the first commercially available simulation software to include animation), GENETIK, SIMSCRIPT II.5, SIMAN/CINEMA, SLAMSYSTEM, AUTOMOD, and XCELL+.

Figure 5-5 **MAIN SCREEN DISPLAY OF VISUAL INTERACTIVE SIMULATION MODEL OF AN UNDERGROUND MINE FOR ANALYSIS OF ORE-FLOW OPERATIONS (Peter C. Bell and Insight Logistics Ltd.)**

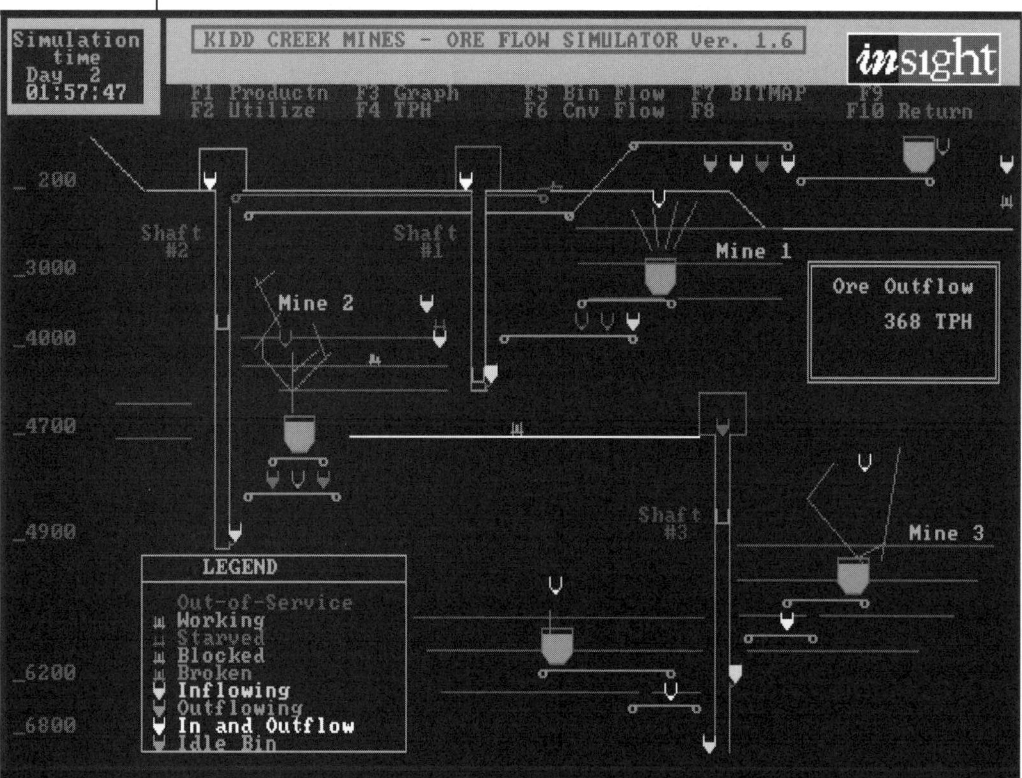

Figure 5-6 **PART OF VISUAL INTERACTIVE SIMULATION MODEL OF A PROPOSED ROCK CRUSHING OPERATION FOR CAPACITY PLANNING AND PROCESS FLOW ANALYSIS (Peter C. Bell and David Kolterman)**

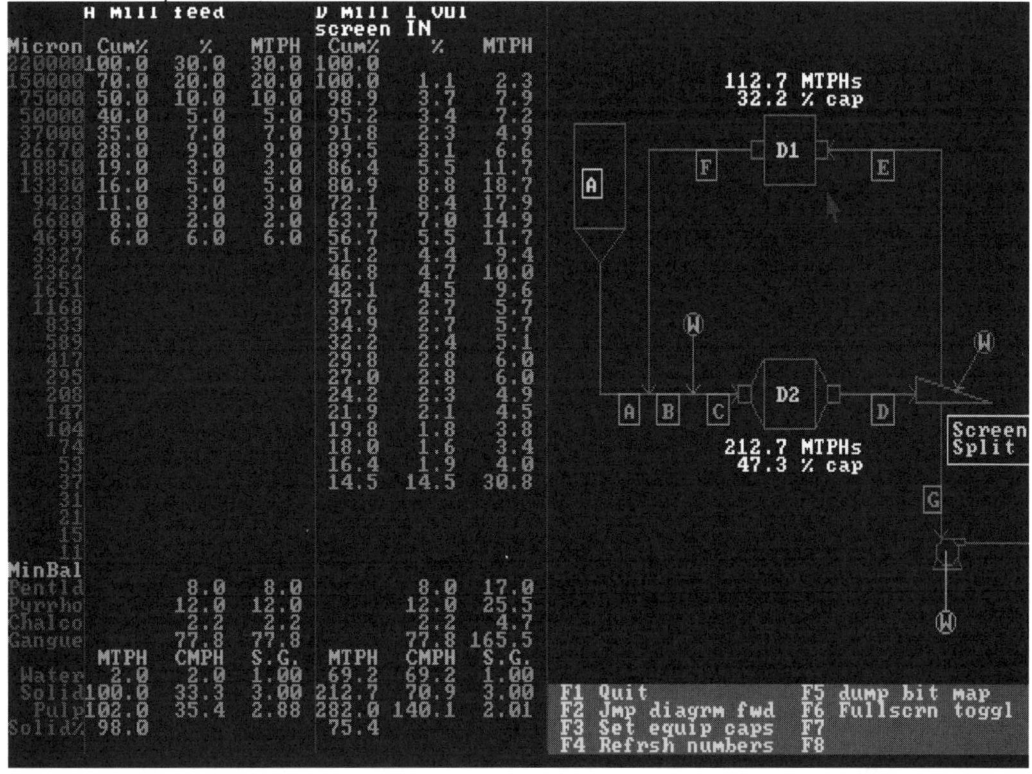

Benefits of Graphics and "Animation"

Simulation packages that include dynamic graphics or "animation" have been a huge market success; almost all commercial simulation software now includes this capability. This market success appears to be the result of several factors:

- Graphics output has wide appeal. Users enjoy seeing a visual display of their system in operation.
- Graphic displays and interaction help the user to understand the model and to take an active part in using and experimenting with the simulation.
- Interaction with the model increases confidence in it and increases the probability of results being implemented. Users feel that they are participants in the problem-solving process rather than spectators.
- The visualization helps to obtain managerial commitment to the simulation study by helping the decision maker and modeler to **validate** the simulation model. This increases the probability that useful change will occur.
- The picture enables the user to easily and quickly shift attention between different parts of the simulation.
- Graphic output may reveal situations that the modeler or decision maker never envisaged. A moving picture can capture unusual "transient" states (or "crises") that would not be visible in long run average results from a traditional simulation (Box 5-1):

Box 5-1

Robert Hurrion, a pioneer of visual simulation, discusses its value:

If the model progresses as the manager expects, then credibility in its use is increased. If, however, the model diverges from the expectations of the manager, then this leads to direct communications between the analyst and the manager. Either the model is correct, in which case the manager learns from the situation, or the model is logically incorrect. If the latter is true, then the manager can usually state the logical inconsistency in the model, since he is watching the dynamic visual representation. At the next interactive session with the inconsistencies rectified, the model soon ceases to become the analyst's model and becomes the manager's own management model. This observation has occurred on all management visual simulations developed to date.

Source: Robert D. Hurrion, *European Journal of Operational Research, Vol. 5, 1980.*

- Graphic displays provide a focal point that appears to be helpful for group decision making, particularly for investigating the causes of conflicting opinion within the group.
- Graphics appear to be useful when qualitative dimensions enter into the decision making and when the decisions depend on the state of the system.
- Animation appears to be useful for decision making in very complex systems (where there may be multiple decision criteria).

WHAT THE MANAGER NEEDS TO KNOW

Simulation can help the manager to be competitive in many important ways. To be make use of these valuable tools, the manager must be aware of the capabilities of simulation models and of the existence of the "simulation industry." The manager also needs to:

Be able to recognize the kinds of problems where simulation can yield useful solutions

Understand the basic types of simulation model and be able to give direction on how a simulation model is to be constructed

Understand the issue of simulation model validation and the steps necessary to determine whether a model is a valid representation of the real system

Understand and be able to interpret simulation model output and be able to participate intelligently in a discussion involving the results of a simulation study

A manager may well find opportunities to build and use small simulation models, likely in a spreadsheet or using user-friendly interactive software such as XCELL+. This will require that the manager be able to sketch out the logic of the model, enter the model into the software, and run the model and interpret the results.

SIMULATION IN ACTION

SIMULATION AT KENTUCKY FRIED CHICKEN

The Kentucky Fried Chicken (KFC) Operations Group used simulation models to assist in evaluating operations within its restaurant system in an effort to remain a key player in a highly competitive industry.

KFC was a member of the PepsiCo, Inc. conglomerate, whose restaurant system was the largest in the world. KFC, headquartered in Louisville, Kentucky, operated more than 8,100 restaurant sites with 5,000 in the United States, with the remaining 3,100 distributed among 58 other countries. KFC was a competitor in the **quick service restaurant** (QSR) industry and, as such, faced intense competition as new players and products were constantly entering the field. Customers demanded good food, good service, low prices, and, most of all, speedy delivery. Any resources wasted during production or delivery of the product, when multiplied by the number of sites in operation, represented a huge detriment to success.

To ensure continued financial returns and optimal productivity, KFC formed an Operations Research group to provide solutions for certain operational problems.Two examples of these operations were service systems for large-volume restaurants and drive-through operations.

Information from large-volume restaurants was developed into a representative customer order database. A simulation model was built that used this database to allow equipment configurations, queuing methods for producing menu items, order taking, and other service and packaging procedures to be analyzed. The model accepted alternative menu mixes and determined their impact on the restaurant. The results provided the optimal equipment configurations, minimum labor requirements, and alternate packing techniques required to increase restaurant volume substantially.

A similar simulation model was developed for KFC's drive-through operations. The analysis performed involved evaluating alternate drive-through layouts, varied numbers of pay/pick-up windows, and varied menu board locations. The results of the model provided the minimum capital expenditures required to increase drive-through capacity and profits.

Simulation models for other areas of operations are being developed in an effort to maintain KFC's competitive success.

From L. Cook, Simulation Applications at KFC, *Softletter,* 7:1, 1991; published by Pritsker Corporation, Indianapolis, Indiana.

KEEPING AHEAD OF THE $2 BILLION CANAL

The Welland Canal is a major link in the St. Lawrence Seaway. This seaway was built jointly by the United States and Canada to enable ocean-going freighters to travel up the Great Lakes to the ports of Duluth, Chicago, Thunder Bay, and so on. The Welland Canal enables these freighters to bypass Niagara Falls and was used in the 1960s and 1970s primarily for transporting grain from Duluth to the Atlantic (then overseas) and for transporting steel and iron ore from Europe and Eastern Canada to the heart of North America.

Efficiency was the primary reason the canal was so essential as a mode of transportation. Shipping was three times more efficient than rail and 12 times more efficient than road transportation because ships could carry large loads that exceeded the weight and capacity limitations of rail or road transport.

Capacity Problem of the 1960s and 1970s

In 1964, an average of 20 vessels were waiting at each end of the canal for passage through the lock system at an average cost of $12,000 per day. At the same time, there was heavy political pressure to transport grain overseas, demanding that the canal perform more efficiently. The whole situation turned into a simple problem; demand must meet supply, and that was how the success of the canal was measured.

By 1967, with $26 million in improvements to the canal recently completed, capacity of the canal was again exceeded by demand, although it was generally believed that this was temporary and that eventually a new canal would have to be built to satisfy the escalating demand from shipping. It was estimated that the cost of a new canal would exceed $2 billion. One official of The St. Lawrence Seaway Authority, the governing body in charge of the Welland Canal's day-to-day operations, stated:

> With increasing demand and growing ship sizes, how would The St. Lawrence Seaway Authority meet its mandate to maintaining an efficient level of service while delaying the inevitable $2 billion expenditure for building a new canal?

Solution Using Simulation

In 1974, the Operational Systems Analysis Section (OSAS) was created to try to understand the fundamental problems of the canal with the objective of keeping capacity ahead of demand. OSAS realized that the canal system was very complex. For example:

- There were eight locks in series, separated by bodies of water (known as "reaches") of varying lengths.
- There was one-way movement between some locks (some reaches were too narrow to allow passage of more than one ship at a time).
- Each lock had to provide service in two directions to raise or lower vessels.
- Several bridges between locks introduced delays because only one vessel could go under a bridge at a time.
- Arrivals of ships were random; there was no set schedule that ships followed.
- Vessel sizes and speeds varied considerably.

The OSAS team decided to build a simulation model to study activity in the canal. This would enable them to conduct "what-if" analyses with all the variables, including those listed above, that affected the performance of the canal. *Without such a model, it would be too expensive to test every proposed upgrading project because thousands of suggestions for improvements had been put forward.*

The OSAS team, with help from outside experts, built a very complex simulation model of the Welland canal in just 14 months at a cost of $116,400.

Use of the Simulation Model

The simulator could use historical data of ship arrivals or randomly generated data to make projections of the future. An early example of the use of the model to test ideas to improve canal throughput was the investigation of the "Lock 7 problem."

Lock 7 was thought to be the slowest area of the canal. Two options had been proposed. The first, a popular option of many experts, was to spend $10 million to reconstruct the approach wall above the lock to permit the exiting and entering vessels to pass much closer to the lock, reducing large vessel times above the lock by 10%. After analysis using the simulator, it was found that this option would not increase the capacity of the entire canal; in fact, there was no benefit to be gained by speeding up this one lock.

The second, albeit less popular, option was to widen the channel above Lock 7 to accommodate more ships and permit two-way traffic. After running this option through the simulator, it was quickly recognized as a very successful option, increasing the capacity of the canal by about 5% at a cost of $8 million.

Impact of the Work

Over a period of several years, the simulation model was used to investigate many innovative decision rules and canal alterations designed to increase the capacity of the canal. By

1980, management at The St. Lawrence Seaway Authority was confident that they would be able to modify existing canal operations to meet the expected demand on the canal until at least the year 2000. The $2 billion expenditure for the new canal was, therefore, delayed for at least 20 years.

This simulation model prevented many projects that were not cost-effective from being started, while enabling The St. Lawrence Seaway Authority to successfully keep ahead of demand, thus delaying construction of the new $2 billion canal. In recent years, demand at the Welland Canal has dropped off sharply as grain exports have dropped dramatically. The canal is not as busy as it was in the 1970s and early 1980s, but the lessons learned from the simulation project remain very valuable.

From W.A. Dawson, S.M. Lakshminarayan, A.A. Landry, and J.B. McLeod, Keeping Ahead of a $2 Billion Canal, *Interfaces*, 11:6 1981.

WAR GAMES WITH THE U.S. MILITARY

The U.S. military needed field training to improve the battlefield skills of military commanders and their staff, but federal budget cuts made real-life field exercises a rare and expensive luxury. As an alternative, the various branches of the U.S. military (Army, Navy, Air Force) developed computerized battlefield simulators.

Need for a New Kind of Military Training

Budget cuts and changes in military thinking brought about the age of **joint action**. Joint action was a coordinated military effort among air, land, and sea forces to bring the qualities and resources of each branch of the military to the battlefield. Joint action required close coordination and communication among forces with different equipment and procedures, in addition to different languages in the case of United Nations operations.

The various branches of the U.S. military used battlefield simulators for officer training but now needed to train its commanders for the new requirements of joint action. The existing simulators were very difficult to interconnect because of compatibility problems because they had not been designed with interconnection in mind. For example, one model allowed command of each individual tank or plane, whereas another model allowed control at the unit or battalion level only. The Army's simulator used a unique hardware/operating system and was designed to move from event to event, whereas the other simulators ran on a time scale (hours, days, and so on).

Preliminary work by the military was able to link together two of the simulators, but attempting to integrate additional simulators quickly became an impossible programming task.

New Approach

The Defense Advanced Research Projects Agency (APRA) approached the MITRE Corporation to develop a **distributed interactive simulation** (DIS). Using DIS, independent simulators would share an artificial battlefield, a concept known today as **virtual reality**. Each simulator was to operate independently, but they were to cooperate and interact by sending messages back and forth through a central communications system. Each simulator needed only one link with the communications system, so the programming task was made much easier.

The most difficult task was developing the computerized rules, called the Aggregate Level Simulation Protocol (ALSP), for sending messages back and forth between simulators and modifying the simulations to make them capable of sending, receiving, and reacting to messages.

The Result: A New Level of Training. ALSP was given its first major test in the Ulchi Focus Lens 1992 (ULF 92) training exercise. The military set up a global network with the Army's simulator run on hardware in Korea and the Air Force and Navy simulators run in Germany. Players from Europe, the United States, and Korea played together without leaving their bases.

The DIS was cheaper and faster to organize than a real exercise and had several other benefits:

- It allowed people in different functional areas to train together and practice coordinating their efforts.
- It made it possible to simulate environments that could not be used in real exercises.
- Military commanders could test what-if scenarios and assess their relative effectiveness.
- There was no damage to the environment from lead shells, depleted uranium shells, or heavy equipment.
- There was no risk of provoking adversaries, as might be the case when staging a real exercise.

From D.S. Hartley III, War Games, *OR/MS Today*, August 1993.

IDEAS TAKE FLIGHT

The U.S. Air Force's Theater Airlift provides cargo transport within a theater of operations. In the new world order, the U.S. Army expects to be involved in shorter engagements in various hot spots around the world. However, in many areas of the world, traditional forms of transportation will not be readily available, so the military will have to rely on air transport.

Designing an Effective Airlift Aircraft

The Air Force wanted a systematic way of finding the most effective aircraft design for the next generation of theater airlift aircraft to support Army operations in the new world order.

The Air Force's Aeronautical Systems Center (ASC) developed a simulation model that could be used to test the effectiveness of theater airlift systems under different battlefield conditions. The ASC used the Generalized Air Mobility Model (GAMM) to simulate the effectiveness of various theater airlift aircraft in carrying out a representative set of cargo movements.

FTAS developed three airlift scenarios: a central European war, a Soviet drive through Iran and into the Persian Gulf, and an invasion of Honduras and El Salvador by Nicaragua. The ASC recognized that the scenarios were no longer very realistic due to the new world order, but they were still used because they represented a wide variety of theater characteristics.

Objective: Aircraft Effectiveness

The critical aspects of theater airlift are timeliness, the ability to move cargo to specific locations in a short delivery window, the ability to move oversized or outsized items, and survivability in high-threat environments. The ASC decided on three measures of theater airlift effectiveness: ratio of cargo delivered, ratio of cargo delivered on time, and ratio of critical cargo delivered.

The ASC used a set of statistically determined experiments to test the effectiveness of design variables while simultaneously varying many other attributes and battlefield factors. Different design variables and battlefield conditions were entered into the model, and the effectiveness of the aircraft was measured. This process was repeated many times to produce a large data set of inputs and resulting outputs. A regression model was then developed in which effectiveness, the output, was the dependent variable and the design attributes were the independent variables. This resulting regression equation summarized how the various design variables affect aircraft effectiveness.

Result: An Effective Aircraft Design

In all scenarios, larger and more numerous aircraft were more effective. In-flight performance was significant in Southwest Asia because it was a large area with long flight times. Wheel loading was significant in many Southwest Asian scenarios and in all the Central American scenarios due to the lack of long, paved runways. Reliability and maintainability were not significant in terms of effectiveness, but they would be significant in terms of costs, which the model did not address.

An unexpected result was that aircraft with short take-off and landing abilities (STOL), capable of landing in forward areas on rudimentary airfields, had a negative impact on effectiveness because the aircraft were too easily damaged or destroyed.

By using simulation, the ASC was able to systematically study the effects of design concepts on theater airlift effectiveness. The design was able to benefit, in a sense, from combat testing even though no actual aircraft had been built. This approach allowed the Air Force to build an extremely effective airlifter without years of in-flight analysis and expensive redesign.

From P.F. Auclair, S.J. Wourms, and J.J. Koger, Ideas Take Flight, *OR/MS Today*, August 1993.

VILPAC TRUCK MANUFACTURING

The North American Free Trade Agreement (NAFTA) has provided a major new opportunity for North American manufacturers, including the Vilpac Truck Manufacturing Company of Mexicali, Mexico, which found itself positioned to take advantage of Mexico's increased competitiveness and prosperity.Vilpac was a joint venture between PACCAR Industries, a manufacturer of Kenworth trucks in Portland, Oregon, and the Vildosola family of Mexico, and was producing up to 22 units per day with a workforce of 1,200 and annual sales of $415 million.

The tremendous increase in cross-border hauling as NAFTA took effect, together with Mexico's expanding highway system, promised a solid future for Vilpac, but trade liberalization also posed the threat of increased competition from major truck manufacturers such as Volvo and General Motors. Vilpac, however, was not typical of many U.S./Mexico joint ventures under the Maquiladora program, where Mexico was used mainly for high labor content production. Vilpac recognized that it had to change to become a world class manufacturer, and the key to this transformation was investment in technology rather than labor.

World Class Manufacturing

For the world class manufacturer, manufacturing is seen as a competitive weapon and not simply just another functional area. To achieve a level of manufacturing that is "world class," the firm must attain a very high degree of understanding of its operations and processes. This understanding leads to control, in which the controlled operations can be manipulated with the effects being known before the consequences are incurred. The knowledge a company has about its operations can then be used for advanced planning, making the company proactive rather than reactive in the marketplace. At Vilpac, planning involved anticipating customers' needs in the future or implementing new manufacturing methods for increasing quality or reducing costs. The world class manufacturer uses a process of continuous improvement to sustain its competitive advantage, never being content to maintain the status quo.

Rengineering Vilpac

Before pursuing world class manufacturing standards, Vilpac underwent extensive process reengineering under the direction of CEO Don Gustava Vildosola. This reengineering process started with the development of a new understanding of the corporation and its strategic business objectives and a complete analysis of current operations and systems. The business processes were then reengineered to correct fundamental deficiencies in the existing system.

Process reengineering was not limited to manufacturing operations but also involved the mapping out of all existing processes with ideal processes being identified by viewing all operations from the customer's perspective. An essential part of this methodology was the development of a comprehensive detailed simulation model of the manufacturing system that was used to assess the performance of proposed manufacturing processes. Once identified, these ideal processes contained the correct amount of quality assurance, technology, and employee involvement and continually focused on the customer. By following these steps, redundancies were eliminated, and modifications were planned with a view to replicating the ideal process.

The existing plant and workforce had to be considered, so a migration plan was developed to implement the change from the status quo to the newly designed processes on a continuous improvement basis. Each step in the migration process was defined in terms of strategic objectives and activities that included training, defining metrics, establishing alliances, and further analysis and modeling.

Simulation Model

The simulation itself had to handle a great deal of randomness. Although the randomness made model construction more difficult, it enhanced its usefulness because no production engineer could account for all the possibilities when designing or assessing the impact of modifying plant procedures. More than 95 different machines with varying yields, 1,900 parts, 1,177 set-up times, 60 maintenance malfunctions, 30 critical tools, 26 material handling systems, 5 end products, and 11 production sequences were incorporated into the model. Clearly, the ability to balance and coordinate these processes through successive iterations with the aid of this model produced significant planning advantages.

The creation of the simulation program provided a great deal of impetus for managers to work together in both the strategy formulation sessions and the reengineering workshops. Managers realized that if their views were not expressed in the simulation, then future decisions would not address their concerns. Managers had to be (and were) convinced that this new technology would be used to determine future capital expenditures such as introducing a new product line, expanding capacity, or purchasing new equipment. The integration of strategy throughout the company was an unexpected but valuable benefit.

Another benefit of the model was the ability to test changes in the plant without spending any money unless the modifications proved successful. The managers were interested in altering capacity, product mix, inventory controls, set-up times, maintenance policies, and process flows. Only those improvements that could be seen to have a positive impact on the company were implemented. The simulation model enabled Vilpac to avoid common pitfalls such as shifting bottlenecks, accumulating inventories, and rejecting new products for fear of congestion, while concentrating attention on important constraints such as critical set-up times and equipment capacities.

The simulation provided several management criteria for each configuration tested, including throughput time, cycle time, cost, inventory level, utilization rates, and, most importantly, the value added in each process. Suggestions for change were evaluated and implemented based on their cost-effectiveness and overall priority.

Payoff

The computer simulation has dramatically increased the productivity and profitability of Vilpac Truck Manufacturing Company by focusing management attention on the aspects of the plant where improvements offered the largest rewards. The ability to assess the consequences of changing the plant before investing money has led to better decision making and a corresponding increase in company performance.

The results have been dramatic with an increase in net profits of 70% and a corresponding decrease in fixed costs of 26%, despite a 260% increase in production. Other intangibles include improved quality and market share, as well as the ability to offer the highest wages in the Baja region of Mexico.

From J.P. Nuño, D.L. Shunk, J.M. Padillo, and B. Beltrán, Mexico's Vilpac Truck Company Uses a CIM Implementation to Become a World Class Manufacturer, *Interfaces,* 23:1, 1993.

EXERCISES

1. Develop two simulation models of tossing two six-sided die (numbered 1 through 6 on the six faces).

   Model 1: Simulate rolling a single dice twice and add the total.
   Model 2: Simulate a combined roll giving a number from 2 through 12 with appropriate probabilities.

2. An advertisement in the newspaper offers a new automobile for sale or lease. The purchase price is $43,240, or the automobile can be leased for 24 months for a monthly payment of $458 with a $7,500 down payment. Under the lease option, there is a charge of 24 cents per mile for mileage above 30,000 miles for the 24 months, and a $550 security deposit, which is refundable at the end of the lease, must be deposited with the dealer. The automobile may be purchased at the end of the lease for $29,732. All other charges (taxes, maintenance, plates, and so on) are the same under both options.

   Develop a simulation model to compare the net present value of buying or leasing the automobile for 24 months. To compare the two options a number of assumptions must be made. Assume:

   The mileage driven over the 24 months can be approximated by an exponential distribution with a mean of 25,000 miles.
   The best estimate of the interest rate over the next 24 months is a normal distribution with mean of 8.5% and standard deviation of 1%.
   The value of the automobile at the end of 24 months is the same under both op-

tions (that is, if the car is purchased, the realizable value at the end of month 24 is $29,732 less 24 cents per mile for each mile over 30,000).

Use your simulation model to assess the probability that the lease option results in a lower net present value than the purchase option.

Notes: Excel statement =NORMINV(RAND( ),x,y) will generate normally distributed random numbers with mean *x* and standard deviation *y*. To generate exponentially distributed random numbers with mean *x*, use the functions: =x*LN(RAND()).

3. A narrow (single-lane) bridge over a railroad track slows traffic on a busy road. During the rush hour, vehicles traveling south were observed to arrive at the north end of the bridge at a mean rate of four vehicles per minute. Vehicles traveling north were observed to arrive at the south end of the bridge at a rate of 3.5 vehicles per minute. In both cases, vehicle interarrival times were well approximated by exponential distributions. Traversing the bridge took a single vehicle between 10 and 20 seconds, with any time in this interval equally likely. If a "batch" of vehicles traversed the bridge (in the same direction!), each vehicle in the batch added 3 seconds to the traverse time (that is, if a batch of five vehicles crossed the bridge in line together, the time taken was the time of the first vehicle plus 15 seconds).

One group of bridge users believed that the bridge should alternate vehicles; that is, the first vehicle to arrive at the bridge should cross first. If immediately after this vehicle had crossed, there was a vehicle waiting to cross *from the opposite direction*, then this vehicle had priority.If there was a queue of vehicles at either end of the bridge, then traffic on the bridge should switch direction after each vehicle.

A second group of users believed that traffic on the bridge should stay in the same direction until there were no more vehicles to cross. Once the bridge was free, vehicles traveling in the opposite direction could "capture" the bridge until the entire queue had crossed (by which time, there would likely be a new queue of vehicles coming from the other direction).

A third group of bridge users suggested that the only "fair" discipline was strict "first to arrive, first to cross": vehicles should cross the bridge in strict order of their arrival at the bridge, regardless of direction.

Develop a simulation model to show the impact of these three different "scheduling rules" for the bridge on the waiting times of vehicles at the bridge.

SUPERIOR GRAIN ELEVATOR, INC.

Mike Armstrong, manager of port facilities for Superior Grain Elevator, Inc. in Thunder Bay, Ontario, replaced the telephone and looked at his notes. He had just learned that the Canadian Government had negotiated a 5-year, 8-million ton grain deal with Poland and that a substantial volume of this grain was to be shipped through Superior's facility. Perhaps this was the opportunity that Superior had been waiting for to expand the Thunder Bay Wharf.

THE COMPANY

Thunder Bay, Ontario, was located on the shores of Lake Superior at the inland end of the Saint Lawrence Seaway. Although some 3,500 kilometers from the Atlantic Ocean, Thunder Bay was Canada's third busiest port and was particularly important for the shipment of grain because it was the closest port to large areas of the Manitoba and Saskatchewan wheat belt. Some 15 million tons of grain and oilseeds were loaded each shipping season, with the majority of this tonnage bound for Eastern Canada, although some was exported to the United States and overseas.

Superior Grain Elevator, Inc. had been established as a subsidiary of the Saskatchewan Grain Cooperative in 1949, and its 14 giant grain elevators gave Superior a prominent position on the Thunder Bay waterfront. The success of Superior had reflected the development of the seaway. A major expansion had accompanied the opening of the new St. Lawrence Seaway in 1959 after completion of new locks in the Welland Canal and the new "Soo" locks at Sault Ste. Marie that allowed ocean-going freighters with a draft of 7.9 meters to reach Thunder Bay. These larger freighters in the lakes, together with an increasing density of ship traffic, led to steady growth in tonnages through Superior's elevators.

In 1974, Superior was sold to local interests in Thunder Bay. A major landmark was reached in 1979 when, for the first time, Superior shipped 1 million tons during a single season. Since that year, however, volumes had hovered around the 1-million ton level; although there had been some good years since 1979, there had also been some not-so-good years.

SUPERIOR'S GRAIN FACILITY OPERATIONS

Superior's operations centered around the railroads and the Seaway. After the wheat harvest on the prairies, trains of specially built railcars hauled the grain from local silos in Manitoba, Saskatchewan, and parts of Ontario to Thunder Bay. The grain was stored in lakefront elevators for loading into the freighters that had made the long haul up the St. Lawrence. Apart from the 4 months of the winter when the seaway was closed because of ice, Superior loaded ships steadily, sending grain to all parts of Eastern Canada and the world.

The ships were contracted for by agents who lined up the required tonnage of shipping capacity to fulfill the various contracts held with Superior. During the last shipping season, Superior had handled 115 ships, averaging about 3.5 each week. Exhibit 2 shows the arrival times of ships during the months of May and June 1996 in days after 00:00 hours on May 1 (column 1) and the time between these arriving ships in days and fractions of a day (column 2). May and June were typical months—in fact, the arrival and loading of vessels went on at about the same rates all season.

Although the agents tried to arrange for ships to arrive at Thunder Bay in a steady stream, the vagaries of lockage transfer times in the seaway resulted in quite variable arrival times (as shown in Exhibit 2). If Superior's two wharfs were both busy, the arriving ships had to anchor in the lake while awaiting a berth. Because the ships were under contract from the moment they arrived at Thunder bay, if a ship had to drop anchor, Superior had to pay a standard demurrage charge at a rate of $2,000 per day (prorated for parts of a day) for any time that a ship was held up before loading.

Loading the ships was one of the easier parts of the operation. There was always sufficient grain in the elevators (except during rare strikes on the railway or the waterfront) to fill all available ships. Each of the two wharfs had its own loading equipment and could load one ship at a time, and because all freighters in the seaway were about the same size, loading times were fairly constant at "about" 2.5 days, although there was some variability. The loading times (including docking and casting off) for the ships in Exhibit 2 are shown in column 3.

THIRD WHARF AND THE POLISH CONTRACT

For some time, Superior had thought of adding a third wharf and had acquired the waterfront to the west of the present property for this purpose in 1990. This new wharf was estimated to cost $1,500,000 (in 1996), but the volume of shipments necessary to provide the 20% return on investment that the new owners thought prudent had not yet materialized, in part because the 8-month shipping season meant that the annual return had to be captured in only 8 months.

Mike Armstrong reviewed his notes of the telephone conversation. Apparently, Superior had been allocated 20 shipments to Poland for each year for the 5 years of the contract. Mike wondered whether this was the increase in volume that they had been waiting for. Could the Polish contract make a third wharf a profitable option ?

Assignment

1. How might you investigate this problem?
2. Where is the payoff from the third wharf going to come from?
3. How can you estimate a value for the savings?

Use the worksheet provided (Exhibit 1) to simulate the arrival and loading of 16 ships.

Exhibit 1 | **SUPERIOR GRAIN ELEVATOR HAND SIMULATION WORKSHEET**

				Wharf Clocks						
				Wharf 1		Wharf 2		Wharf 3		
Ship Number	Random Number	Inter Arrival Time	Arrival Time	Arrival	Departure	Arrival	Departure	Arrival	Departure	Idle Time
1	—	—	0.00							
2										
3										
4										
5										
6										
7										
8										
9										
10										
11										
12										
13										
14										
15										
16										

Exhibit 2 | SHIP ARRIVAL AND LOADING TIMES FOR MAY AND JUNE 1996

Time of Arrival (in days after 00:00 May 1)	Days Since Last Arrival	Loading Time (days)
1.54	1.57	2.18
2.59	1.05	2.53
4.52	1.93	2.24
5.26	0.74	2.10
11.77	6.51	2.24
19.33	7.56	2.62
21.52	2.19	2.36
25.70	4.18	2.81
29.49	3.79	2.10
30.84	1.35	2.06
31.77	0.93	2.57
33.83	2.06	2.86
34.50	0.67	2.49
34.71	0.21	2.56
34.80	0.09	2.14
37.43	2.63	2.52
37.71	0.28	2.75
37.77	0.06	2.45
38.09	0.32	2.71
39.05	0.96	2.76
40.72	1.67	2.87
40.74	0.02	2.18
41.91	1.17	2.91
47.73	5.82	2.77
48.46	0.73	2.60
50.99	2.53	2.16
55.63	4.64	2.91
56.56	0.93	2.27
57.59	1.03	2.57
59.80	2.21	2.50
62.60	2.80	2.68
MEAN	2.020	2.499

BIRMINGHAM MEGATRON, INC.

Caroline Miller, plant manager at Birmingham Megatron's manufacturing operation, listened intently as Mark Hill talked through design options for additions to the new automatic manufacturing system (AMS). The design of this facility, which represented the latest stage of Birmingham's advance into automatic manufacturing, was very important to Birmingham. A good design would (in addition to the obvious benefits in terms of profitability) maintain Birmingham's confidence in its ability to handle new manufacturing technologies effectively.

The plan was to modify the existing facility used to produce "TG96" cylinder blocks for a big-three automobile manufacturer to expand output for an additional contract. This new contract was still at the bidding stage, and cost accounting had proposed a bid of $64.00 per block for the required 1,400 blocks per week. (Appendix) Caroline saw this contract as critical to the future of advanced manufacturing technologies at Megatron and wondered if she could afford to offer a more competitive price.

THE COMPANY

Birmingham Megatron, Inc. started manufacturing automobile parts for original equipment manufacturers (OEMs) in the mid-1950s and expanded steadily; by 1995, their sales were $345 million.

Birmingham had been forward looking in the adoption of advanced manufacturing technologies, despite an early company tradition of a labor-intensive "craftsman" approach to manufacturing. As labor costs had risen faster than inflation, the pressure of the sealed bids competition that the OEMs used to award parts contracts had driven Birmingham to seek more efficient manufacturing technologies. Beginning in 1982, the company had invested in automatic manufacturing equipment whenever contract terms rendered such automation economical.

By Fall 1995, Birmingham's blue-collar workforce had declined to about half the 1981 maximum, although output had increased more than three times over the same time period.

TG96 CONTRACT

In December 1996, Birmingham had bid on and won a 5-year contract to supply 950 TG96 cylinder blocks for a popular full-size sedan each week (50-week year) at $56.00 each. To meet this contract, Birmingham purchased cast-iron cylinder blocks from Western Foundry and rough machined steel cylinder liners from United Steel. Birmingham fit the liners into the cast-iron cylinder blocks and then performed a precision grinding and boring operation to produce the finished TG96 block for shipment. Birmingham's management had decided to investigate a fully automatic line to perform this two-stage process and, after careful research, had invested in some advanced technology.

AUTOMATIC MANUFACTURING FACILITY

The heart of the automatic manufacturing facility was a Treller Black-MAX B7400 workstation. This complex machine was fed by three Imatzu C4 numerically controlled tools that were programmed to fit the cylinder liners into the blocks. The different speeds of the equipment were buffered using a work-in-process inventory held in an automatic storage/retrieval system (ASRS). The ASRS had a maximum capacity of just two blocks.

The Black-MAX B7400 had a nominal capacity of 10 cylinder blocks per hour, and there was little variability in the cycle time of this machine. Furthermore, human quality control inspection was unnecessary–the Black-MAX performed its own quality control (using LASER technology to scan finished work pieces). All work pieces completed by the Black-MAX had passed rigorous quality inspection. If the Black-MAX sensed a bad work piece that it could not finish to quality standards, it shut down, almost invariably the result of the grinding tools requiring replacement. Replacing the tools was usually a 15-minute job for the maintenance engineer, but sometimes other problems were found that took a lot longer to fix. Exhibit 1 summarizes data on failures and repair times for the Black-MAX, collected as part of a recent quality improvement project.

The Imatzu C4 environment had proved to be quite different. Both cycle time and quality were highly variable because the quality of the raw materials varied, and this determined how easily the fit between block and liner could be achieved. The cycle time had averaged 12 minutes per block, although any time between 8 and 16 minutes was equally likely, depending on the quality of the input materials. The C4 had proved to be highly reliable and almost never broke down during normal operation, but problems with the achieved fit between

Exhibit 1 | PERFORMANCE OF BLACK-MAX

Time Since Last Failure (min)	Repair Time (min)
274	64
198	30
70	10
97	7
230	7
138	0
54	20
237	50
15	3
8	8
128	18
600	3
10	83
107	4
130	27
465	28
355	51
647	49
22	20
306	7
352	10
215	38
7	30
110	37
116	6
52	16
169	22
74	7
Mean 185.3	**23.4**

block and liners rendered the work piece unsuitable for further work in 8% of the C4 output.

The ASRS was physically located between the C4s and the Black-MAX (Exhibit 2) and controlled all product flow from C4 to Black-MAX. Because the ASRS performed no work on the work piece, the cycle time was very short, and this machine did not interfere with operation of the other machines. ASRSs had a limited number of storage bins that were used to hold the inventory of work-in-process. Having too many storage bins in an ASRS was a waste of money in terms of both the cost of the bins and the increased work-in-process as bins were added. Access time to the ASRS storage was included in the Black-MAX processing time. Birmingham had opted for a single additional storage bin in the ASRS.

Exhibit 2 | **SCHEMATIC OF PRODUCTION LINE FOR TG96S**

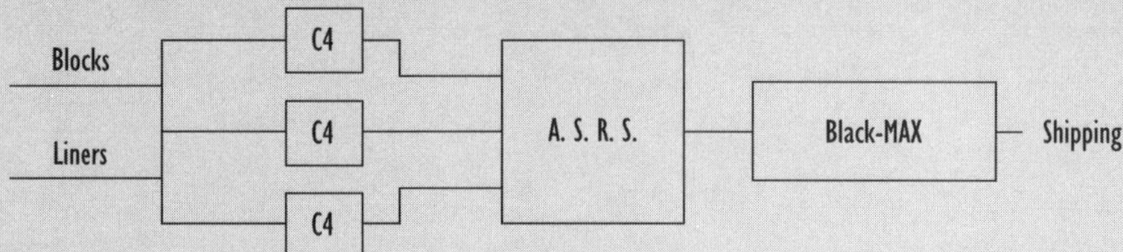

RESULTS FROM THE TG96 CONTRACT

The TG96 contract was viewed by Birmingham as being quite successful. There had been no shortages of raw materials (either blocks or liners) and no line delays as a result of accumulations of finished goods inventory, although the line had been shut down on some Saturdays when finished goods inventory had accumulated and the Saturday production was not needed. The 1-hour planned maintenance period between the second shift and the night shift, as well as the all-day Sunday preventative maintenance period, had been achieved most of the time. This time had also provided a useful buffer during the first few weeks when operation of the equipment was poorly understood.

There had been no major problems meeting delivery schedules, but there had been an issue of equipment utilization: the TG96 line appeared to have quite a bit of excess capacity. For this reason, Birmingham had been looking for other uses for this equipment.

TG101 CONTRACT

Birmingham now had an opportunity to bid on an additional contract to supply TG101 cylinder blocks to the same automobile manufacturer. The TG101 was a very similar block to the TG96; both had four cylinders and were the same dimensions, although the external shape of the 101 casting was slightly modified to allow for placement of the air conditioner. This contract appeared to be a particularly good fit for Birmingham because both blocks could be produced using exactly the same equipment with exactly the same processing times.

Mark Hill envisaged expanding the TG96 line by adding additional C4s and another Black-MAX. As Caroline listened to Mark Hill's presentation, she realized that important questions remained unanswered:

1. Should Birmingham go with one combined line or two separate lines? If they went with a combined line:
   How many C4s were needed to support two Black-MAX machines?
   Were two storage slots in the ASRS sufficient in the new line?
   What was expected to be the throughput of this line? Was there sufficient capacity for the combined contract without working on Sundays?
2. What should they bid on the contract?

Mark raised a further issue: Imatzu had recently announced the availability of a C5 machine. This machine cost 50% more than the C4 but was expected to be able to achieve a workable fit between block and liners 96% of the time (rather than the 92% for the C4) using the same materials. The C5 was also faster, with processing time varying from 5 to 9 minutes per piece. Perhaps the C5 offered Birmingham a cost-effective alternative to the C4?

FINANCIAL CONSIDERATIONS

Birmingham Megatron based financial projections on a 5-year payback of capital equipment purchases, especially those in high-technology equipment that was subject to rapid obsolescence. The hurdle rate of return for bids on new contracts was set at 20%, although it was common that once a bid was arrived at, it would be "shaved" to take into account the very highly competitive nature of their business.

APPENDIX

BIRMINGHAM MEGATRON INTERNAL MEMORANDUM

To: Fred Newper, Contracts Department
From: Harvey Smith, Cost Accounting
Re: TG101 contract

We have undertaken an analysis of the cost of supplying TG101 cylinder blocks at a rate of 1,400 per week (for a 50-week year). We recommend that the minimum bid price for this contract be $64.00 per block FOB Birmingham Megaton.

Our cost assumptions were based on us using an expanded AMS with the following equipment costs (which include installation) provided by the manufacturers:

Black-MAX B7400 . . . . $2,700,000
Imatzu C4 (each) $800,000
ASRS plus conveyors $750,000
For each storage bin add $10,000

Materials cost has been assumed at $31.00 for each block and four liners.

The additional operating cost imposed on Birmingham as a result of the expanded facility (including maintenance and tooling) was estimated at $3,000 per week. We have assumed a scrap value of $6 for spoiled blocks.

We have assumed that we will not have to run this line on Sundays. If Sunday operation is required, we would have additional costs of $4,500 per shift.

Assignment

1. Recommend to Caroline Miller a minimum bid price (per block) for the TG101 contract, together with recommended design changes to the AMS should the bid be successful.

DOFASCO, LIMITED: LANCE DESULFURIZING PLANT

The superintendent of blast furnaces at Dominion Foundries and Steel, Limited (DOFASCO) had to decide whether to recommend that engineering modifications costing $600,000 be made to the lance desulfurizing plant.

Lance desulfurizing was part of the process for converting liquid iron into steel. Molten pig iron from the blast furnaces was transported in special purpose railcars (torpedo cars) to the lance desulfurizing plant, where the sulfur content of the iron was reduced to a specified level. After desulfurization, a locomotive hauled the torpedo cars to the melt shop, where the molten iron was converted into steel.

COMPANY BACKGROUND

DOFASCO was a publicly owned steel producer that manufactured a variety of flat rolled steel products and castings. The company had been formed in 1912 as a foundry operation that supplied castings for the rail car manufacturing sector. The original workforce of about 150 people produced and shipped more than 3,600 tons of castings in 1912. Since then, DOFASCO had grown into a fully integrated steel making operation with over 10,000 nonunionized employees. In 1978, the company produced 3.56 million ingot tons of steel.

The company's iron ore mining interests included the Adams and Sherman Mines, the Wabush Mines in Labrador and Quebec, and the Eveleth Expansion Company in Minnesota. Lime and Limestone came from the wholly owned Beachville Lime Limited and its subsidiary, Guelph DoLime. DOFASCO also had an ownership interest in the Itmann Coal Company of West Virginia.

A subsidiary, National Steel Car Corporation Limited, manufactured railway rolling stock using hot rolled steels and castings produced at DOFASCO.The company owned Prudential Steel, which produced small-diameter pipe products for the oil and gas and construction industries, and was a 50% shareholder of Baycoat Limited, which produced prepainted steel.

LANCE DESULFURIZING PLANT

The lance desulfurizing plant consisted of two side-by-side ports, each of which could desulfurize a single torpedo car. At each port, a machine called a *lance car* was an essential part of the desulfurizing process. The problem arose when one of the two lance cars (one at each port) broke down because there was no back-up system, and repairs could take as long as 1 week. A back-up system was designed that would ensure that both desulfurizing ports were always operational. Installation of this system required engineering modifications that were estimated to cost $600,000.

The DOFASCO iron-making plant consisted of four blast furnaces. Each blast furnace discharge filled from one to four torpedo cars with molten iron. These were then picked up by the locomotives, moved to the weight station for weighing, and brought to the desulfurizing plant. Exhibit 1 summarizes the blast furnace discharges that determine the arrival of torpedo cars at the desulfurizing plant. After desulfurization was completed, the desulfurizing plant operator called by radio for a locomotive to remove the torpedo car from the desulfurizing port and haul it to the melt shop. Several locomotives were operating around the works, and one would usually arrive soon after being called. Occasionally, if all the locomotives were down at the blast furnaces or up at the melt shop, it might be half an hour before one arrived at the desulfurizing plant.

The plant had a limited number of torpedo cars (23) to serve the blast furnaces. When a blast furnace was ready to discharge, torpedo cars had to be available to take the iron. The superintendent was concerned that if the desulfurizing plant was operating at only 50% capacity as a result of a lance car failure, the queue of torpedo cars waiting for desulfurization would restrict the availability of cars to the blast furnaces and severely hinder their operation.

The superintendent asked the Manufacturing Controls Department to investigate whether he should recommend installation of the back-up system.

A few days were spent observing the desulfurizing plant in operation. During this time, the data summarized in Exhibits 2 and 3 were collected.

Assignment

1. Should the engineering modifications be made?

Exhibit 1 | **BLAST FURNACE DISCHARGES**

	Blast Furnace			
	1	2	3	4
Mean time between discharges (min)	205	205	205	180
Range	±45	±45	±45	±45
Relative frequency of 1 torpedo car	10%	10%	25%	
Relative frequency of 2 torpedo car	90%	90%	75%	10%
Relative frequency of 3 torpedo car				70%
Relative frequency of 4 torpedo car				20%

Exhibit 2 | OBSERVED PROCESSING TIME

Processing Time (min)	Frequency
6	1
8	1
10	1
11	2
12	5
13	7
14	9
15	10
16	8
17	5
18	6
19	2
20	2
21	2
22	3
23	2
24	1
26	1
27	2
30	1
31	2
32	1
36	1

The mean processing time was 17.2 minutes. (Processing time was the time interval, rounded to the nearest minute, between the arrival of a torpedo car to a vacant desulfurizing port and the completion of desulfurization of that torpedo car. The processing time included set-up, desulfurization, and sampling to test for sulfur content.)

Exhibit 3 | **OBSERVED WAIT TIME FOR LOCOMOTIVE**

Wait Time (min)	Frequency
0	4
1	8
2	6
3	8
4	6
5	5
6	2
7	4
8	3
9	5
10	3
11	2
13	3
14	2
15	1
16	1
17	2
18	1
19	2
21	1
23	1
25	1
26	1
28	1
≥30	2

The mean wait time was 8.3 minutes. (Wait time was the time interval, rounded to the nearest minute, between the operator's call for the locomotive anc the arrival of the locomotive at the desulfurizing plant.)

BABCOCK AND WILCOX: CONSOLIDATED FORECASTING

Mr. Jan D'Ailly, Manager, Marketing Services, at Babcock and Wilcox (B&W) was explaining his computer printouts.[16] Despite being quite sophisticated in our analysis, we are not quite getting the information we need for our shop-load planning and scheduling. Our sales projections also drive our accounting and business forecasts, so we need to improve the way we develop our basic forecasts."

THE COMPANY

For more than a century, B&W has been supplying boilers and related components and services for steam generation. Steam is the principal medium by which the heat of fossil fuel combustion or nuclear reaction is used to drive turbines that produce 75% of the world's electricity. In 1993, more than 800 B&W fossil fuel burners and more than 200 B&W nuclear steam generators produced in excess of 250,000 MW of power around the world.

B&W Power Generation Group supplied fossil-fueled steam generation systems and associated equipment, replacement nuclear steam generators, and environmental equipment and emission control systems. The group operated major manufacturing facilities in Barberton, Ohio, and Cambridge, Ontario, as well as offshore facilities in Beijing, China (B&W Beijing); Cairo, Egypt; Pune, India (Thermax B&W); Jakarta and Batam Island, Indonesia; Mexico City, Mexico (B&W Mexicana); and Ankara, Turkey (B&W Gama).

B&W is a wholly owned subsidiary of McDermott International that had 25,200 employees in 1996 and 1995 revenues of $3,043 million. McDermott, headquartered in New Orleans, was a marine construction company for the offshore oil and gas industry until the acquisition of B&W in March 1978. This acquisition, and a number of others since 1978, has resulted in McDermott emerging as a leading, global, broad-based energy services company.

B&W performed sales forecasting for 11 market segments. These were:

1. Fossil Utility North America
2. Fossil Utility Export
3. Environmental
4. Industrial Oil and Gas North America
5. Industrial Oil and Gas Export
6. Solid Fuel North America
7. Solid Fuel Export
8. Recovery North America
9. Recovery Export
10. Nuclear and Special Comp. Worldwide
11. Operations and Maintenance

AWARD OF CONTRACTS FOR NEW POWER PLANTS AND RETROFITS

B&W obtained their business by bidding and winning contracts for supplying or installing major power facilities or parts of facilities. B&W representatives and its salesforce around the world maintained contacts with organizations that constructed or operated power-generating facilities or other facilities related to B&W's business products and attempted to identify impending projects and the resulting contracts. An important component of the representatives' activities was the building of a close relationship between B&W and the potential client organizations. B&W also maintained contacts with a large number of contractors, engineers, and turbine suppliers in many different countries because many large projects ended up being joint projects with a contractor from the home country. Because many utility projects involved national or regional governments in some way, there often were political issues to be addressed with respect to the choice of domestic contractor and/or domestic suppliers.

When a representative heard of a potential project, details were communicated to B&W. B&W managers assessed whether the project was of interest to B&W and whether B&W would bid. Bidding was a costly process, especially in the Pacific Rim countries, which were the current high-growth area for construction of power generating facilities: a successful bid could cost up to 1 million dollars.

CONSOLIDATED FORECASTING PROCESS

If B&W was interested in bidding on the contract, B&W sales produced estimates of the dollar value of each potential contract in four areas: boiler manufacture, environmental controls manufacture, "EPC" (engineering and project management) and construction. The manufacturing dollars were used to estimate the number of shop hours that the project would require in each of B&W's eight fabricating shops. Exhibit 1 lists potential projects known in May 1996 for business units 2, 3, and 4 for 1997 through 1999 (dollar values are in thousands). (For competitive reasons, the data have been disguised.)

B&W management estimated the quarter when contracts for that project would be available for bid. These estimates were subject to considerable uncertainty. Often governments or bureaucracy would delay a contract for one to four quarters, but delay of a large job could throw off estimates, leading to incorrect financial projections. Serious unexpected delays could precipitate financing difficulties or lead to overcapacity or undercapacity at the various manufacturing facilities.

Two probabilities were estimated for each project: "P1," the probability that the contract would proceed in the specified year and quarter, and "P2," the probability that B&W would win the contract, if it were put out to bids. Finally, the manufacturing component of each potential project was tentatively assigned to a manufacturing facility.

The data on forthcoming contract tenders and the probabilities were communicated to Marketing Services and used to produce the consolidated forecast. This forecast was used as the driver to calculate work load (man-hours, engineering shop hours) and to produce the financial forecasts.

FINANCIAL FORECASTING AND SHOP CAPACITY PLANNING

For each of B&W's eight fabricating shops, and for each business unit, potential future contracts were aggregated by quarter and expected values for revenues (U.S. dollars) and shop hours calculated. The expected revenues computed in this way drove the consolidated financial forecasts, and the expected shop hours were used as input to capacity and workforce planning. International work was assigned between Cambridge and Barberton with the objective of producing a balanced shop loading because it was undesirable to have one shop working overtime while another was below capacity.

Assignment

1. What business can Babcock and Wilcox expect to win in the first quarter of 1998?
2. For the same quarter, for what range of business activity should they plan?

Exhibit 1 | INFORMATION ON FUTURE PROJECTS: BUSINESS UNITS 2,3,4

Year-Qtr	Customer	Country	Equipment	Mkt. Segt.	P1	P2	USA $ Value	Boiler $	Environ. $	EPC $	Const. $	Shop Hours	Shop Assign.	Financing
97-1	SCECO 3	SAUDI ARABIA	1 × 125 MW Oil EPC	2	95	100	89,345	11,115	0	78,230	0	8,000	C,ECA	EXIM
97-1	POWERGEN	INDONESIA	CHX	3	100	100	640	640	0	0	0	200	B	CUST
97-1	SHANGHAI	CHINA	1 × 480 MW Oil	2	80	10	120,000	120,000	0	0	0	33,000	C,EDC	OPEN
97-2	SCECO 1	SAUDI ARABIA	2 × 500 MW PC	2	90	20	101,000	101,000	0	0	0	12,000	ECA	OECF
97-2	TPC	TAIWAN	1800 MW FGD Upgrade	3	80	90	102,000	70,000	0	0	32,000	6,000	B	CUST
97-2	SHANDONG/ HIPDC	CHINA	2 × 660 MW PC	2	80	40	205,000	205,000	0	0	0	9,000	ECA	CUST
97-2	TPC	TAIWAN	2 × 230 MW DRY FGD	3	80	80	47,000	31,000	0	0	16,000	3,500	B	CUST
97-2	TEAS	TURKEY	2 × 700 MW FGD	4	10	50	9,000	9,000	0	0	0	1,000	B	EED
97-2	VASILIKOS POWER	CYPRUS	1 × 350 MW PC	2	90	90	134,000	134,000	0	0	0	2,000	C,ECA	EXIM
97-3	CONSOLIDATED EDISON	USA	2 × 550 MW FGD	4	50	50	700	700	0	0	0	500	B	CUST
97-3	IEC	ISRAEL	2 × 500 MW PC	2	50	10	418,000	418,000	0	0	0	7,000	ECA	EDC
97-3	FAUJI ELECTRIC POWER	PAKISTAN	2 × 800 MW FGD	4	80	60	68,000	68,000	0	0	0	5,400	B	EXIM
97-4	WAIGAO QIAO POWER	CHINA	1 × 400 MW FGD	4	60	20	21,000	21,000	0	0	0	1,900	B	ECA
97-4	BITOR	USA	2 ACID MIST PRECIP.	4	70	95	214,000	214,000	0	0	0	7,000	B	CUST
97-4	POWER GEN/ BUKIT SUNUR	INDONESIA	2 × 165 MW FGD	4	10	25	17,000	17,000	0	0	0	800	B	CUST
97-4	CNTIC	CHINA	2 × 550 MW FGD	4	25	10	58,000	58,000	0	0	0	2,300	B	ECA
97-4	COGEN TECH./ SABA POWER	PAKISTAN	2 × 350 MW PC	2	25	10	268,000	220,000	48,000	0	0	198	C,ECA	EDC
97-4	POWER CO. #1	VIETNAM	2 × 100 MW PC	2	60	30	25,000	25,000	0	0	0	0	B,ECA	CUST
97-4	TNB 1	MALAYSIA	2 × 500 MW PC	2	40	30	193,000	193,000	0	0	0	12,000	ECA	CUST
97-4	SCECO 4	SAUDI ARABIA	2 × 700 MW PC	2	60	35	138,000	123,000	15,000	0	0	3,200	C,ECA	EDC
97-4	IPP	ECUADOR	2 × 600 MW Oil/Gas	2	60	25	76,000	76,000	0	0	0	4,000		CUST
97-4	GUANGXI ELECTRIC	CHINA	2 × 600 MW PC	2	30	10	65,000	65,000	0	0	0	24,000	OPEN	ECA
98-1	KEPCO	KOREA	2 × 550 PC	2	25	20	76,000	63,000	0	0	13,000	5,000	B,ECA	EXIM
98-1	EGCO/UNION ENERGY	THAILAND	4 × 600 MW O/G or HRSG	2	40	10	113,000	113,000	0	0	0	6,800	B	ECA
98-1	WAPDA	PAKISTAN	8 × 300 MW Oil	2	80	15	182,000	182,000	0	0	0	3,200	C,ECA	WB
98-1	LPU	LAOS	2 × 550 MW FGD	4	50	50	41,000	41,000	0	0	0	2,100	B	EXIM
98-1	TPC	TAIWAN	4 × 250 MW Seawater FGD	4	50	10	72,000	72,000	0	0	0	3,500	B	CUST
98-1	SEI	INDONESIA	PRECIPS	4	75	30	6,000	6,000	0	0	0	400	B	CUST
98-1	SHAANXI ELECTRIC POWER	CHINA	1 × 700 MW SPIRAL SUP., C	2	20	20	76,000	64,000	12,000	0	0	3,100	B,OPEN	EXIM
98-1	TEAS	TURKEY	CHX/IFGT	4	20	10	10,000	10,000	0	0	0	1,000	B	EXIM
98-1	AES	HUNGARY	2 × 350 MW Anthracite	2	80	30	116,000	116,000	0	0	0	7,400	C,OPEN	OECF
98-1	POWER GEN	INDONESIA	2 × 900 MW SUPER.	2	50	10	67,000	67,000	0	0	0	3,000	B,OPEN	ECA

(continued)

Exhibit I | CONTINUED

Year-Qtr	Customer	Country	Equipment	Mkt. Segt.	P1	P2	USA $ Value	Boiler $	Environ. $	EPC $	Const. $	Shop Hours	Shop Assign.	Financing
98-1	GUANGDONG POWER CO.	CHINA	1 × 500 MW PC	2	80	30	115,000	115,000	0	0	0	45,000	C,EDC	ADB
98-1	PUB	SINGAPORE	2 × 350 MW Coal	2	25	10	139,000	139,000	0	0	0	70,000	C,EDC	ECA
98-2	TPC or a DEVELOPER	TAIWAN	2 × 600 MW PC	2	60	15	177,000	177,000	0	0	0	3,900	ECA	CUST
98-2	NIQUEL TOCANTINS/ CONFAB	BRAZIL	3 × 210 MW FGD	4	50	20	71,000	71,000	0	0	0	3,000	B	ECA
98-2	CEA	INDIA	2 × 660 FGD	4	60	10	70,000	70,000	0	0	0	4,200	B	ECA
98-2	NOVA SCOTIA POWER	CANADA	1 × 350 MW Oil	2	60	5	116,000	116,000	0	0	0	0	B	EXIM
98-3	INNER MONGOLIA	CHINA	2 × 660 MW PC	2	80	20	165,000	165,000	0	0	0	7,500	ECA	WB
98-3	PUB	COLORADO	4 × 550 MW SCR	4	80	20	32,000	32,000	0	0	0	1,250	B	CUST
98-3	JSW	JAPAN	2 × 550 MW Oil/Gas	2	60	15	157,000	157,000	0	0	0	6,200	B,OPEN	EXIM
98-3	ANHUI PROVINCIAL POWER	CHINA	6 × 120 MW O/G	2	40	20	55,000	55,000	0	0	0	3,550		CUST
98-3	SUNBURST ELECTRIC	CHINA	1 × 400 MW PC	2	10	20	120,000	120,000	0	0	0	11,500	C,ECA	ECA
98-3	CHINA PETROLEUM	TAIWAN	1 × 100 MW CC EPC	2	10	10	294,000	294,000	0	0	0	2,150	C,ECA	ECA
98-3	EGAT	THAILAND	2 × 350 MW PC	2	70	20	181,000	181,000	0	0	0	3,500	B,ECA	CUST
98-4	TPC	TAIWAN	4 × 200 MW FGD	4	50	20	79,000	79,000	0	0	0	1,870	B	CUST
98-4	CNTIC	CHINA	2 × 350 MW PC	2	30	25	134,000	22,000	0	112,000	0	8,000	EPC	EXIM
98-4	HIPDC	CHINA	1 × 400 MW FGD	4	20	20	67,000	67,000	0	0	0	3,400	B	OECF
98-4	HPI	CHINA	3 × 660 MW PC	2	50	25	370,000	370,000	0	0	0	35,000	C,OPEN	CUST
98-4	KEPCO	KOREA	2 × 660 MW PC	2	60	20	99,000	99,000	0	0	0	11,000	B,OPEN	CUST
98-4	ELECTRICITY LEBANON	LEBANON	2 × 300 MW Anthracite	2	20	20	230,000	167,000	63,000	0	0	5,500	C,OPEN	OECF
98-4	SHANXI ELECTRIC POWER BUR.	CHINA	2 × 660 MW PC	2	30	10	157,000	157,000	0	0	0	1,700	ECA	ECA
98-4	FORTALEZA DE MINAS	BRAZIL	2 × 350 MW PC	2	50	25	242,000	171,000	71,000	0	0	5,500	C,OPEN	EDC
98-4	EGAT	THAILAND	2 × 660 MW PC	2	50	20	18,000	18,000	0	0	0	500	C,OPEN	ECA
98-4	SEI	INDONESIA	4 × 375 MW Oil/Gas	2	10	90	111,000	111,000	0	0	0	0	B,OPEN	EDC
98-4	WAIGAO QIAO POWER	CHINA	2 × 360 MW Lignite	2	40	20	132,000	106,000	0	0	26,000	770	ECA	EDC
98-4	IPP	COLOMBIA	2 × 550 MW FGD & SCR	4	30	30	66,000	66,000	0	0	0	1,000	B	CUST
98-4	KEPCO	KOREA	2 × 500 MW PC	2	30	30	150,000	150,000	0	0	0	4,000	C,OPEN	ECA
98-4	RUPALI POWER CO.	PAKISTAN	6 × 350 MW Anthracite	2	50	20	139,000	139,000	0	0	0	22,000	C,ECA	CUST
98-4	MINISTRY OF ELECTRICITY	KUWAIT	2 × 660 MW FGD	4	50	25	65,000	65,000	0	0	0	1,000	B	ECA
98-4	UNION ENERGY/ TOMEN/IVO	THAILAND	3 × 500 MW FGD & Orimul	4	25	5	36,000	36,000	0	0	0	2,200	B	ARAB
99-1	ENTERGY/BAKRIE/ TOMEN	INDONESIA	2 × 600 MW FGD	4	50	20	70,000	70,000	0	0	0	1,200	B	WB
99-1	SHAANXI ELECTRIC POWER	CHINA	2 × 900 MW FGD	4	60	25	72,000	72,000	0	0	0	2,000	B	CUST

Exhibit 1 | CONTINUED

Year-Qtr	Customer	Country	Equipment	Mkt. Segt.	P1	P2	USA $ Value	Boiler $	Environ. $	EPC $	Const. $	Shop Hours	Shop Assign.	Financing
99-1	NATIONAL POWER	UK	CHX & UPGRADE	4	25	20	64,000	64,000	0	0	0	1,800	B	ECA
99-1		THAILAND	2 × 600 MW PC	2	25	20	146,000	146,000	0	0	0	21,000	C,ECA	ECA
99-1	CNTIC	CHINA	2 × 300 PC BOT	2	30	10	200,000	200,000	0	0	0	35,000	C,ECA	ECA
99-1	HPI	CHINA	FGD & Orimul Convers.	3	10	50	61,000	61,000	0	0	0	2,100	B	CUST
99-1	HENAN ELECTRIC P.B.	CHINA	1 × 180 MW OIL	2	50	20	111,000	111,000	0	0	0	1,900	C,OPEN	ECA
99-1	ENTERGY/BAKRIE/ TOMEN	INDONESIA	2 × 660 MW PC	2	30	20	266,000	266,000	0	0	0	40,000	C,ECA	EXIM
99-1	CEA 2	INDIA	2 × 800 MW Spiral Sup., C	2	40	10	58,000	58,000	0	0	0	6,600	B,OPEN	ECA
99-1	CNTIC	CHINA	4 × 250 MW O/G & Constr.	2	50	20	325,000	244,000	81,000	0	0	3,000	B,OPEN	WB
99-2	FUJIAN PROV.	CHINA	3 × 350 MW FGD & Orimul	3	30	30	90,000	47,000	0	0	43,000	1,250	B	CUST
99-2	TNB 2	MALAYSIA	2 × 250 MW PC	2	50	5	172,000	172,000	0	0	0	17,300	C,OPEN	ECA
99-2	SCECO 2	SAUDI ARABIA	2 × 600 MW PC	2	50	20	80,000	80,000	0	0	0	8,000	OPEN	ECA
99-2	THAI COPPER	THAILAND	2 × 350 MW Anthracite	2	25	20	177,000	177,000	0	0	0	11,000	C	ECA
99-2	EGAT	THAILAND	2 × 550 MW FGD	4	30	15	82,000	82,000	0	0	0	2,500	B	CUST
99-2	ANHUI EPB	CHINA	2 × 600 MW PC	2	30	15	260,000	141,000	84,000	0	35,000	12,500	B,OPEN	CUST
99-3	STEEL AUTHORITY INDIA	INDIA	1 × 400 MW FGD, ESP, SCR	3	30	30	82,000	59,000	0	0	23,000	4,000	B	CUST
99-3	IEC	ISRAEL	2 × 750 MW Oil/ Coal super.	2	10	20	220,000	220,000	0	0	0	21,000	B,OPEN	ECA
99-3	TPC	TAIWAN	1 × 300 MW Oil	2	20	20	167,000	167,000	0	0	0	16,000	OPEN	ECA
99-4	IPP	INDONESIA	1 × 550 MW PC EPC	2	20	60	202,000	202,000	0	0	0	20,000	B,OPEN	ECA
99-4	PUBLIC SERVICE NEW MEXICO	USA	2 × 600 MW PC	2	20	10	221,000	221,000	0	0	0	22,000	C,OPEN	ADB
99-4	UNION ENERGY/ TOMEN/IVO	THAILAND	1 × 300 MW PC	2	10	20	223,000	223,000	0	0	0	25,000	C,OPEN	EDC
99-4	IEC	ISRAEL	FGD	4	50	25	13,000	13,000	0	0	0	1,500	B	CUST
99-4	TPC	TAIWAN	2 × 100 MW Seawater FGD	4	50	25	63,000	63,000	0	0	0	6,000	B	CUST

COLUMBUS-AMERICA DISCOVERY GROUP AND THE *SS CENTRAL AMERICA*

BY BINU KOSHY UNDER THE SUPERVISION OF PROFESSOR PETER BELL. REPRODUCED WITH PERMISSION OF INFORMS. COPYRIGHT 1998, INFORMS.

In 1857, while carrying passengers and gold from California to New York, the *SS Central America* sank in a hurricane, taking gold bars and coins worth an estimated $400 million to the ocean floor. The Columbus-America Discovery Group was formed 128 years later with the objective of locating, exploring, and recovering the remains of the *SS Central America*. In the summer of 1985, Thomas G. Thompson, director and founder of Columbus-America, assigned Dr. Lawrence D. Stone the task of estimating the location of the wreck and participating in planning the search.

THE SINKING OF THE *SS CENTRAL AMERICA*

Between 1848 and the completion of the transcontinental railroad in 1869, the principal mode of transportation between California and the east coast of the United States was to travel by steamer from San Francisco to the west coast of Panama, cross the isthmus by train, and take a steamship to New York. In 1857, the *SS Central America*, one of the steamships operating on the Atlantic side of the Panama route, sank in a hurricane taking 425 people and an estimated $400 million worth of gold to the ocean bottom almost 8,000 feet below.

The ill-fated journey began on August 20, 1857 when the mail steamer *Sonora* left San Francisco harbor bound for New York carrying about 600 passengers and crew and 3 tons of gold. Arriving at the Pacific coast of Panama, the travelers were met by a train that took them to the Atlantic coast to board the mail steamer *Central America*. The *SS Central America* was a 280-foot wooden hulled steamship with two large iron side paddle wheels (Exhibit 1). In command was the captain of the ship, William Lewis Herndon, a commander in the United States Navy. On September 3rd, the *Central America* left Panama for New York. On the 9th a storm began to rise, and by the 10th it had developed into a hurricane. On Friday morning, September 11th, a leak was discovered, and the crew attempted to bail out the ship. By 2:00 p.m. the water covered the coal and

Exhibit 1 | **THE *SS CENTRAL AMERICA***

From a Lithograph in Frank Leslies' *Illustrated Newspaper*, October 3, 1857

smothered the fire in the main boilers, disabling the engines. Passengers and crew bailed heroically all night, and at daybreak the storm appeared to have abated, but by Saturday morning, Captain Herndon could feel the storm rising again and realized that the ship was certain to go down.

At noon, Herndon signaled the brig *Marine* to rescue passengers from the *Central America*. Fifty-nine women and children plus 41 male passengers and crew made it to the *Marine* before evening when darkness and distance prevented further rescue efforts. At 6:30 p.m. the schooner *El Dorado* approached the *Central America*. Captain Herndon relayed his last estimated position to the captain of the *El Dorado,* and then waved the schooner away from the sinking ship and asked it to stand by until morning. The *El Dorado* drifted away in the storm. That evening, a few minutes before 8:00 p.m., Captain Herndon climbed onto the port paddle wheel of the *Central America* and fired his final rocket indicating that it was soon going down. Moments later, the ship was engulfed by the waves taking its treasure in gold bars and coins to the ocean depths.

When the ship went down, many men were dragged down by the undertow. Those that survived grabbed pieces of the wooden superstructure including doors from the ship and even a chair on which to float. That evening, about five hours after the sinking, a Norwegian sailing vessel, the bark *Ellen*, discovered the survivors and during the next 8 hours managed to rescue 50 more men from the waters. Eight days and 20 hours later, the final three survivors were picked up more than 400 miles north of the shipwreck after an incredible ordeal of survival on the high seas. In total, 425 people, including the captain, lost their lives.

The Civil War that followed so quickly after the loss of the *SS Central America* overshadowed this tragedy and dimmed it from historical memory. The *Central America* was, however, the most famous shipwreck of its time, comparable to the *Titanic* in this century.

THE COLUMBUS-AMERICA DISCOVERY GROUP

The Columbus-America Discovery Group was formed in 1985 to conduct multidisciplinary research, develop sophisticated deep-ocean technology, and to locate, explore, and recover the remains of the *SS Central America*. Thomas G. Thompson, director and founder of the *Central America* Project, had an interest in shipwrecks and collected information on shipwrecks around the world. Thompson's background as an ocean engineer gave him the special knowledge concerning the latest advances in robotics, computer control technology, image processing, and other high-tech advances that would make a search for a deep ocean shipwreck possible.

In the early 1980s, new technologies were developed for sonar search and for remotely operated recovery vehicles. Newly developed sonar technologies could scan large areas of the ocean bottom with high resolution. Advances in robotics, fiber optics, and computers made it possible to build remotely operated underwater vehicles capable of performing a full range of archaeological recovery tasks. This technology eliminated the need for manned submersibles, which were expensive and dangerous to operate in the deep ocean, and made it economically feasible for a small, independent entrepreneur to search for and recover objects on the deep ocean floor.

In the late 1970s, the *SS Central America* emerged from a selection process that had considered several potential deep water recovery projects. The *Central America* had sunk on the Blake Plateau, some 200 miles east of Charleston and 1.5 miles below the ocean surface, in an area with a flat bottom and little current. Because of the great depth, the ship was safe from damage by storms and hurricanes as well as from casual exploration by SCUBA divers or treasure hunters. In addition, this region had a very slow sedimentation rate and a lack of current that meant there was very little chance that the *Central America* would be covered by any sediment, and as a result, the wreck would provide an attractive target for side-looking sonar. The ship was known to be carrying large quantities of gold, making its location and recovery economically attractive to investors, and there was considerable historical information available about the wreck. Finally, the wreck was located off the coast of the United States so that any resulting legal problems could be handled solely through the US courts under US law.

In the early 1980s Thompson began to assemble a limited partnership of private investors to finance the search for and recovery of the *Central America*. He also began to assemble the team of scientists and technicians that would carry out the project. In 1982, Bob Evans joined Tom Thompson as the second project director, and in 1985 Barry Schatz joined the effort as the third.

FINDING THE WRECK OF THE *SS CENTRAL AMERICA*

The Columbus-America Discovery Group had the following goals:

- Locate the wreck of the *SS Central America* and recover gold and historical artifacts in a responsible manner,

- Develop new technology for deep ocean exploration,
- Add to the historical knowledge of the *Central America* and its times, and
- Increase the scientific understanding of the deep ocean environment and its inhabitants.

The first issue addressed was to review and analyze all available information and produce an estimate of the location of the *Central America*. Gathering all of the information available about the wreck was done primarily by Evans. He obtained information from newspaper accounts, many of which were given by survivors of the wreck, ships' logs, books written by the survivors, and testimony given to the committee that investigated the loss. Evans organized this information into a matrix where a row in the matrix corresponded to a single account of the loss. The columns designated times. An entry at a given row and column gave a summary of what was happening at that time according to the account represented by the row. The matrix made it easy to cross-check the numerous accounts and obtain information about what happened at a specific time.

Exhibit 2 shows a map of the general area of the *Central America* sinking. The line of dashes shows the route of the *Central America* during its last voyage. The line terminates at the position relayed by Captain Herndon to the schooner, *El Dorado*, a little over an hour before the *Central America* sank. Also shown are the estimated positions of the *Marine* when she sighted the *Central America* at noon on the day of the loss, and the *Ellen* at 8:00 a.m. the next morning as she was recovering sur-

Exhibit 2 | **THE AREA WHERE THE *SS CENTRAL AMERICA* SANK**

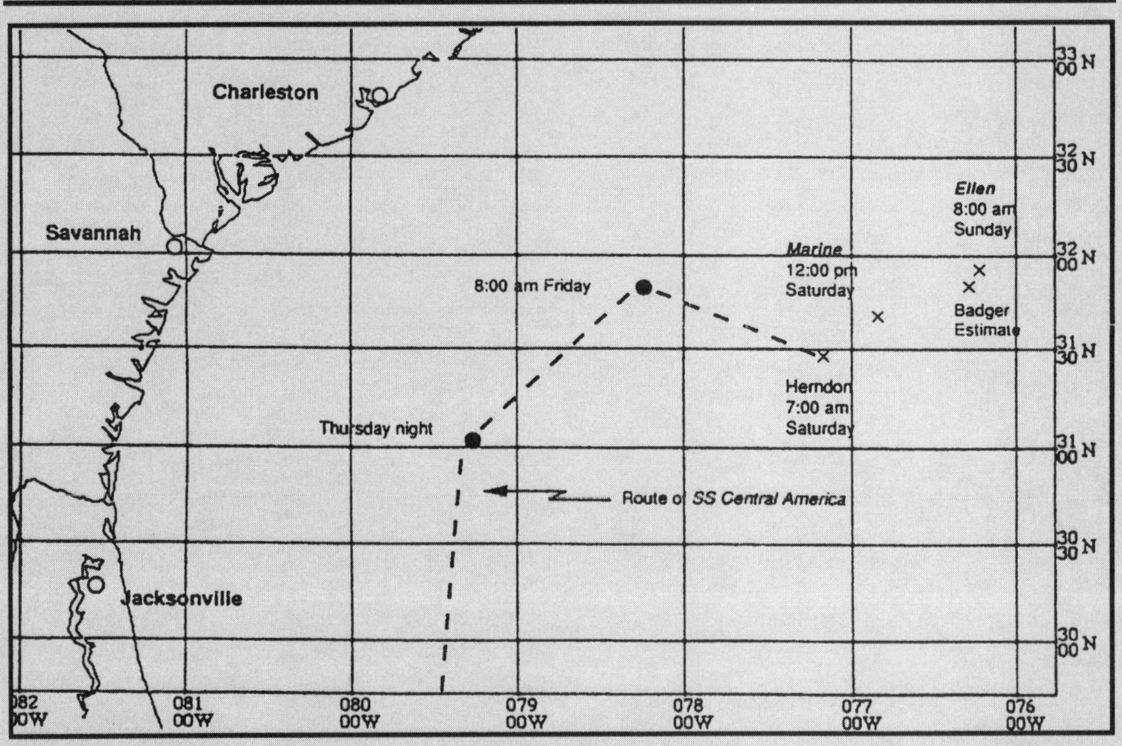

vivors. Near the *Ellen* position is the location of the wreck as estimated by Captain Badger, a passenger on the *Central America* who was rescued by the *Ellen*.

The information appeared to cluster into three self-consistent scenarios, each with different levels of uncertainty. The first scenario based on the position given by Herndon; the second based on the position of the *Marine* when it sighted the *Central America*; and the third based on the celestial fix taken from the *Ellen* at 8:00 a.m. Sunday morning. Each scenario had to be examined more thoroughly to determine the accuracy of its information.

Central America Scenario

The primary piece of information in the *Central America* scenario is the position of the *Central America* passed by Captain Herndon to the *El Dorado*. The position was relayed in the midst of the storm just an hour and a half before the ship sank. This raises the immediate question of when and how this position was taken. The only methods for estimating one's position at sea were to obtain a celestial fix or to dead reckon from the last fix. By studying the accounts of the disaster, Evans determined that there was a clearing in the storm on Saturday morning around 7:00 a.m. at the time of a lunar meridian. Evans also determined that Herndon returned his navigational instruments to the cabin of a passenger on the *Central America* at 8:00 a.m. on Saturday morning. On the basis of this evidence the team surmised that Herndon had taken a celestial fix at 7:00 a.m. on Saturday morning and that the position relayed to the *El Dorado*, 31°21′N, 77°10′W, was this fix.

(Note: Positions are given in terms of degrees and minutes of latitude [North] and longitude [West]. Each degree is divided into 60-minute intervals. In the region of the wreck, each degree of latitude represents about 60 nautical miles [nm], and each degree of longitude about 52 nm.)

How accurate was this fix, and what did it tell about the location of the *Central America* when it sank 13 hours later? The fix was presumably taken using a sextant to determine the altitude of the meridian of the moon measured in degrees from the horizon, with a chronometer used to estimate the Greenwich mean time at which the meridian occurred. Standard navigational tables provide the angular height of the moon's meridian measured from the equator. From these data, latitude and longitude can be computed.

The accuracy of the fix relayed by Captain Herndon was determined by analyzing the errors in the navigational method he used. In particular, the observed path of the moon had a rather broad apex making it difficult to determine the exact point of the meridian when using a sextant, and this adds significant uncertainty to the longitude estimate, with the result that the uncertainty in longitude was estimated to be more than four times greater than the uncertainty in latitude. Characterizing the uncertainties in the estimation of latitude and longitude as normally distributed with mean zero, Barry Belkin of Daniel H. Wagner Associates provided the following estimates of the standard deviations, σ_{lat} and σ_{lon}, of Herndon's fix (expressed in nautical miles):

$$\sigma_{lat} = 0.9 \text{ nm and}$$
$$\sigma_{lon} = 3.9 \text{ nm}$$

Of course the *Central America* did not stay stationary during the time between the celestial fix at 7:00 a.m. and her sinking at 8:00 p.m. that evening. During this time her engines were disabled and no sails hoisted, and she was at the mercy of the winds and currents. In order to account for her movement during this time, the team estimated her drift. There were two components of drift: (a) drift due to the ocean current; (b) drift due to the effects of wind on the ship (leeway). (Exhibit 3)

The ocean current during the storm had to be estimated indirectly. To determine if there was a direction to the current at the time of the loss, the team reviewed the path of the three men who drifted for 8 days on a raft before being picked up by a passing ship. This evidence indicated a generally northeasterly direction to the current.

The team also looked at ocean current data from that region during the past 130 years. The ocean current is the sum of two types of currents: the geostrophic current and the wind-driven current. One can think of the geostrophic current as the current that would be present if there was no wind. To estimate the geostrophic current, the team used ocean current readings that were taken in the month of September in the region from 30°N to 32°N and 76°W to 78°W and spanning the period from the early 1850s to 1974. The region was broken into sixteen 30-minute by 30-minute rectangles. Within each rectangle, the team computed the mean and empirical covariance of the data points lying in the northeast quadrant (because on the days surrounding the sinking the current was in a generally northeasterly direction). This produced bivariate normal distributions with mean vectors having a speed of up to 1.5 nautical miles per hour (kts) in the northeast direction (Appendix 1). The team took these bivariate normal distributions as their best estimate of the distribution of the geostrophic current during the loss of the *Central America*.

Exhibit 3 | **FORCES ACTING ON THE DISABLED *SS CENTRAL AMERICA***

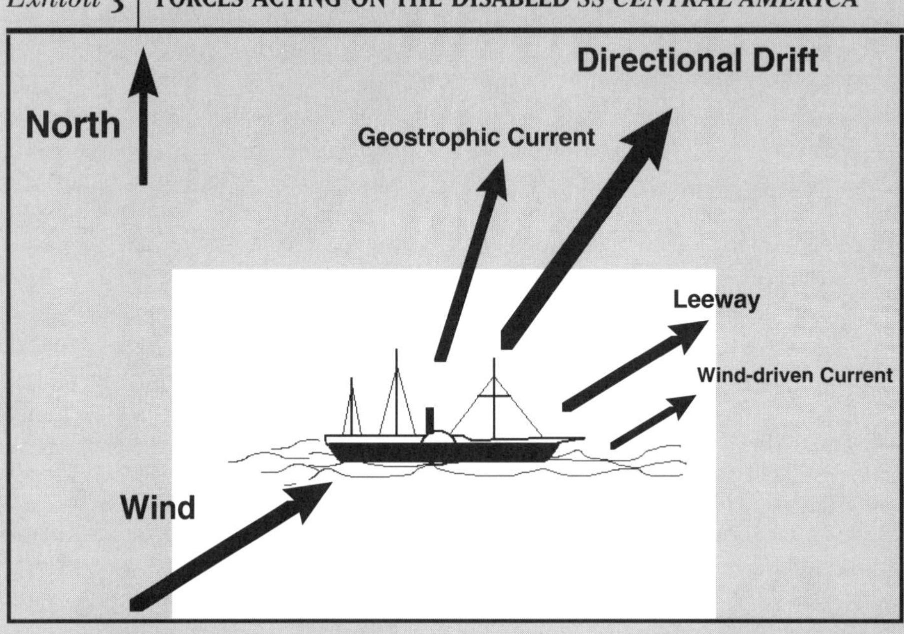

To estimate the wind acting on the ocean surface, Evans returned to the ships' logs and survivors' accounts to find estimates of wind speed and direction during the 2 days preceding the loss of the *Central America* (Appendix 2). To account for the uncertainty in these estimates, the team modeled the winds as having a bivariate normal distribution with mean equal to the value obtained by Evans and a covariance matrix that allowed the wind to vary by as much as 45° from its mean. Roland W. Garwood of the Naval Postgraduate School used his computer model of wind-driven current to estimate the current that would have been produced by the winds as estimated by Evans. Garwood produced estimates for each 6-hour period from 7:00 a.m. on Saturday to 1:00 p.m. on Sunday (Appendix 3). The resulting currents had speeds ranging from 0.2 to 0.4 knots. The uncertainty in these estimates was represented by a bivariate normal distribution with a standard deviation of 0.1 knots in each direction. To obtain the distribution of the total ocean current, the team computed the distribution of the vector sum of the geostrophic and wind-driven current.

The direct action of wind on a ship also contributes to drift (leeway). The leeway factor is the fraction of the wind velocity that is converted to drift as a result of the wind acting on the area of a ship that is above water. Using blueprints of the *Central America*, the leeway factor was estimated to be 3%. Multiplying this by the wind velocity produced the leeway on the *Central America*.

Ellen Scenario

For the *Ellen* Scenario, the project team used the position of the *Ellen* at 8:00 a.m. on Sunday when she was recovering survivors from the *Central America*. The approach was to drift the survivors backward to the time of the sinking of the *Central America* to obtain an estimate of the position of the wreck. At 8:00 a.m. on Sunday, the captain of the *Ellen* took a celestial fix using a meridian of the moon. The recorded position was 31°55′N, 76°13′W. Uncertainty analysis yielded standard deviations of $\sigma_{\text{lat}} = 0.9$ nm and $\sigma_{\text{lon}} = 5.4$ nm. Because people in the water have no leeway, their drift is determined solely by the ocean current. To produce this backward drift, the team set the leeway factor to zero and multiplied the mean vectors for ocean current by minus one, drifting the survivors backward to 8:00 p.m. on Saturday when the *Central America* sank.

Marine Scenario

At 12:45 p.m. on Saturday, the *Marine* sighted the *Central America*. Captain Burt of the *Marine* reckoned his position to be 31°40′N, 76°50′W. The best estimate of the last time that Burt made a celestial fix was at 6:00 a.m. on Friday. For most of the time between this fix and the sighting of the *Central America*, the *Marine* was being driven by the storm under little or no sail. The team estimated the leeway of the *Marine* at 4 percent and applied the wind velocities for that period of time to estimate that the *Marine* traveled 77 nm since the last fix. They also assumed that the error in dead reckoning a position is no more than 25 percent of the distance traveled since the last fix. This resulted in an uncertainty that was circular normal with standard deviation of 9 nm in each direction.

The team also accounted for the distance of the *Marine* from the *Central America* at the time of the sighting. The *Marine* heaved to near the *Central America* at 1:30 p.m., 45 minutes after the sighting. Assuming that the maximum speed of the *Marine* was 8 knots, they calculated that the *Central America* was between 1 and 6 miles from the *Marine* at the time of the sighting.

The *Central America* was sighted off the lee bow of the *Marine*. The *Marine* was reported to be running before the wind that was from the SW at this time. As a consequence, they estimated the *Marine* to be heading NE and the lee direction off the bow to be ENE = 67.5°. They added an uncertainty of ±60° about this direction.

Combining the Three Scenarios

The team looked at each scenario as a whole to determine if there was corroborating evidence that strengthened the credibility of that scenario. As an example, the position estimated by Captain Badger, a passenger on the *Central America*, was very consistent with the *Ellen* scenario. Lieutenant Matthew Maury made an estimate of the location of the wreck based on the information that he had collected in his report to the secretary of the navy. This position also supported the *Ellen* scenario. The celestial fix on which the *Ellen* scenario was based was taken after the storm had passed on a ship that was in no danger of sinking. This position was written in the ship's log. By contrast, Herndon's position, on which the *Central America* scenario was based, was passed verbally to the *El Dorado* in the middle of a storm shortly before the *Central America* sank.

When combining the three scenarios the team assigned a percentage to each scenario. The percentages represented the relative credibility of the scenarios and were required to add to 100. They averaged the three sets of percentages to produce the scenario weights. The results were: *Central America* 23 percent, *Ellen* 72 percent, and *Marine* 5 percent. The *Ellen* received the highest weight or credibility for the reasons discussed previously. The information in the *Marine* scenario was so uncertain that the team gave it a low weight but did not discard it entirely.

With historical information in hand, the Columbus-America Discovery Group set out to develop a probability map of the location of the remains of the *SS Central America*. Once this map had been developed, the team turned to developing an efficient search plan that would produce a high probability of finding the *Central America*.

DEVELOPING A SEARCH PLAN

Fred Newton of Triton Technology was given the task of designing a sonar search that would produce a high probability of finding the *Central America*. The plan had to provide specific directions for performing a search and serve as a basis for estimating the amount of time, effort, and money necessary to assure a high probability of success.

The side scan sonar to be used in the search for the *Central America* was towed behind the search vessel moving at 2 nm per hour and covered a swath of 2,500 meters on either side. Newton estimated the probability of the sonar detecting the wreck as a function of the lateral range of the sonar from the target. Over most of the 2,500 meter range, the signal-to-noise ratio (SNR) produced a detection probability of 0.99. At ranges close to the sensor, increased reverberation from the ocean bottom caused the SNR and the probability of detection to drop. At the outer reaches of the 2,500 meter range, the SNR and the probability of detection also dropped.

Since the ocean bottom was 7,000 to 10,000 feet deep in the search area, the sonar had to be towed from the search ship using a long cable; it was, therefore, desirable to minimize the number of course changes required. Along with the towing cable, a coaxial cable was to be used to relay the sensor responses back to the ship where they would be recorded on an optical disk and displayed on paper.

When developing the search plan, Newton had to take into account the lateral range function for the sensor, the probability of gaps between swaths, and the amount of probability covered by the swath of the sensor. With this in mind he set out to design a plan that would yield a high probability of success in the most efficient way possible.

Where were the remains of the *SS Central America*? How could the wreck be found? How long would a search take? Was success guaranteed?

Assignment

1. Develop a probability map of the area in which the *S.S. Central America* sank.

Also: Research and Development at ICI: Anthroquinone (Chapter 3).
Laying Oil and Gas Pipelines in the North Sea (Chapter 3).
Carpenter Electronics (Chapter 6).
The Stephen B. Roman (Chapter 6).
Ohio Polymer (Chapter 7).

APPENDIX I

Appendix I | **HISTORICAL OCEAN CURRENTS (in kts)**

Latitude	Longitude	Expected Value of Easterly Current	Expected Value of Northerly Current	Variance Easterly Current	Variance Northerly Current	Covariance
3115.0 N	07715.0W	0.104	0.278	0.545	0.511	0.287
3145.0 N	07715.0W	0.878	1.017	0.663	0.803	0.524
3215.0 N	07715.0W	1.513	1.518	0.713	0.627	0.266
3115.0 N	07645.0W	−0.0773	0.00239	0.285	0.416	0.206
3145.0 N	07645.0W	−0.0609	0.0407	0.394	0.529	0.185
3215.0 N	07645.0W	0.380	0.441	0.355	0.393	0.215
3115.0 N	07615.0W	−0.0796	0.0214	0.296	0.577	0.140
3145.0 N	07615.0W	0.0491	0.0350	0.234	0.387	0.0893
3215.0 N	07615.0W	0.206	0.203	0.451	0.431	0.255

APPENDIX 2

Appendix 2 | WIND SYNOPSIS (AS PREPARED BY BOB EVANS)

The individual perspective and nautical experience of each observer were considered when making these estimates of approximate wind speeds and directions. All the raw data were of a subjective nature and while many other variations in the interpretation of this storm are possible, the data represent a reasonable estimate of the conditions experienced on the *SS Central America* during the storm in which she sank.

Day	Time	Wind Direction	Wind Speed
10 Thursday	12:00 pm	NE	35 knots
	1:00 pm	NE	36
	2:00 pm	NE	37
	3:00 pm	NE	38
	4:00 pm	NE	40
	5:00 pm	NE	42
	6:00 pm	NE	44
	7:00 pm	NE	45
	8:00 pm	NE	47
	9:00 pm	NE	49
	10:00 pm	NE	50
	11:00 pm	NE	51
11 Friday	12:00 am	NE	52
	1:00 am	NE	53
	2:00 am	NE	54
	3:00 am	NNE	55
	4:00 am	NNE	56
	5:00 am	NNE	57
	6:00 am	NNE	58
	7:00 am	NNE	60
	8:00 am	NNE	65
	9:00 am	NNE	70
	10:00 am	NNE	75+
	11:00 am	N	75+
11 Friday	12:00 pm	NNW	75+
	1:00 pm	NW	70
	2:00 pm	NW	65
	3:00 pm	NW	64
	4:00 pm	NW	63
	5:00 pm	NW	62
	6:00 pm	NW	61
	7:00 pm	WNW	60
	8:00 pm	WNW	60
	9:00 pm	WNW	60
	10:00 pm	WNW	59
	11:00 pm	WNW	58

(continued)

Appendix 2 | CONTINUED

Day	Time	Wind Direction	Wind Speed
12 Saturday	12:00 am	WNW	56
	1:00 am	WNW	55
	2:00 am	WNW	52
	3:00 am	W	48
	4:00 am	W	45
	5:00 am	W	40
	6:00 am	WSW	35
	7:00 am	WSW	35
	8:00 am	WSW	34
	9:00 am	WSW	33
	10:00 am	WSW	32
	11:00 am	SW	30
12 Saturday	12:00 pm	SW	30
	1:00 pm	SW	30
	2:00 pm	SW	30
	3:00 pm	SW	29
	4:00 pm	SW	28
	5:00 pm	SW	27
	6:00 pm	SW	26
	7:00 pm	SW	25
	8:00 pm	SW	25
	9:00 pm	SW	25
	10:00 pm	SW	25
	11:00 pm	SW	25
13 Sunday	12:00 am	SW	25
	1:00 am	SW	25
	2:00 am	SW	25
	3:00 am	SW	25
	4:00 am	SW	25
	5:00 am	SW	25
	6:00 am	SW	25
	7:00 am	SW	25
	8:00 am	SW	25
	9:00 am	SW	25
	10:00 am	SW	25
	11:00 am	SW	25

APPENDIX 3

Appendix 3 | WIND BLOWN CURRENT ESTIMATES

Date and Time	East (kts)	North (kts)	Variances (kts^2)
12 0700	0.37	0.45	0.10
12 1300	0.69	−0.49	0.10
12 1900	−0.23	−0.65	0.10
13 0100	−0.37	0.23	0.10
13 0700	0.44	0.30	0.10

6

MANAGEMENT SCIENCE/OPERATIONS RESEARCH IN SUPPORT OF MANAGEMENT DECISION MAKERS

CHANGING TECHNOLOGY OF MANAGEMENT

Management must be aware of and respond to technological innovation in products, design, and production methods but also, importantly, the changing technology of management itself. This chapter introduces some new developments in management technologies: technologies aimed at producing a leaner, more effective, and more productive management.

Shop-floor automation is expected to eliminate more than half the jobs in North American manufacturing firms by the year 2000, despite the fact that average output per firm is expected to increase. The pressures from well-designed, high-quality, effectively marketed imports driving this trend also are present in the service sector. The corporate "downsizer" is a highly sought senior manager who can sweep through an organization, eliminating both line workers and management positions. Often, the "downsizer" appears when profits disappear, but increasingly major corporations are proacting by eliminating management positions even in times of relative prosperity.

Eliminating management positions may reduce the amount of management work that has to be done ("the bureaucracy"), and those managers who remain will have fewer subordinates and fewer layers of command. The managers who survive will require superior people skills to obtain the very best from the relatively few humans who remain in the organization, and they will rely heavily on technology to perform the expanded management task required of them. Management science/operations research (MS/OR) is a critical component of new management technologies.

Technological Background

Technologies directed toward improving managerial productivity and effectiveness are evolving from research in many fields, including MS/OR, management information systems (MIS), and artificial intelligence (AI). While these have historically been distinctly different research streams, all three disciplines are today very much concerned with developing improved methods to make use of **data**, **models**, and **knowledge** to improve managerial efficiency and effectiveness.

Developments in MIS, MS/OR, and AI have been greatly influenced and stimulated by the evolution of computers and computing, which has provided increasingly powerful engines to implement new ideas. An outstanding feature of the past 40 years has been the technological development that has continually reduced the cost of computing and data storage. This technological development continues in the **supercomputers** of today, which provide the number "crunching" performance that is invaluable in computationally intensive applications (for example, large-scale optimization, weather forecasting, military logistics, and weaponry).

In 1969, the already high energy level of the computer industry received a quantum boost forward with the invention at Intel Corporation of the microprocessor–a computer on a single wafer of silicon. Initially, **personal computers** (PCs) were not taken very seriously, but all that changed in August 1981, when IBM announced its entry into personal computing with the IBM PC. Each succeeding generation of microprocessors has increased the power and reduced the cost of desktop computing available to the manager.

Telecommunication are a vital piece of hardware technology. We now think in terms of **networks** of computers sharing storage and printing devices and capable of accessing the Internet and, through this, messaging with each other and with other national and international networks. The managerial workstation provides the executive with access to corporate data, external databases, and electronic communications. For the first time, there is the computing power on the executive's desk capable of collecting data from corporate or national data bases, running advanced MS/OR models, and exploiting the knowledge of the modeler or the user. The executive of today must be able to thrive in this data- and computation-intensive environment.

The popular PC **spreadsheets** (Microsoft Excel, Lotus 1-2-3, QuattroPro, and so on) provide data analysis and modeling environments that can be used by management directly. These tools also contain powerful languages that can also be used to develop and deliver **applications softwarc** for use by others (for example, Visual Basic in Excel).

Applications software are programs designed to perform specific computational or data processing tasks. Common applications software includes word processors, spreadsheet programs, and database management programs. There also is a very active market in MS/OR applications software.

Box 6-1

MIDDLE MANAGERS—A THREATENED SPECIES?

"Computers operated by junior clerical staff have diminished the middle managers' role of being responsible for the administration of routine systems." [Management is under pressure from rapidly changing technology and production methods.] "Organizations that are able to seize (technological) opportunities quickly will gain a competitive edge. [In the future] managers will require unprecedented technical skills and the ability to relate these to their businesses." Sir Pat Lowry, President, The Institute of Personnel Management, *The Daily Telegraph,* October 27, 1988.

MS/OR professionals have produced and marketed a vast array of MS/OR applications software. One of the earliest development areas was project management, in which PERT and critical path methods were made available in easy-to-use software packages. In addition to the solvers available in the major spreadsheets, a large variety of stand-alone optimization software is available (for example, see Table 4-3). Simulation software has become an important applications market with a large number of packages that address many different problem areas and include a variety of graphics and animation options (some examples are listed in Table 5-9). Decision analysis models, including multicriteria decisions, data modeling, and inventory control models, are also available as applications software. These packages can be used by MS/OR modelers to develop recommendations for managerial action, and, importantly, to develop decision-aiding systems for use by the managerial user.

The Institute for Operations Research and the Management Sciences [INFORMS] regularly reviews MS/OR applications software and publishes reviews in its magazine *OR/MS Today.* The INFORMS website [www.INFORMS.org] and that of the publisher of *OR/MS Today* [www.Lionheart.com] provide on-line access to these software surveys.

Decision Support Systems

Our understanding of the role of **computer-based information systems** in an organization has evolved over time. The earliest types of systems were **transaction processing systems,** which primarily maintained records and automated routine clerical tasks (for example, payroll systems, invoicing and billing systems, accounting record keeping). As these types of systems were improved, and new systems were developed to provide managerial reports and statistical analyses and to allow data queries, the more general term **management information systems** was applied.

A pivotal idea that has emerged is a type of information systems known as **decision support systems** (DSS). Keen and Scott Morton used the term "decision support" to imply the use of computers to

1. assist managers in their decision processes in semi-structured tasks,
2. support, rather than replace, managerial judgment,
3. improve the effectiveness of decision making rather than its efficiency.

From *Decision Support Systems: An Organizational Perspective*, Addison-Wesley Publishing Company, Reading, Massachusetts, 1978.

This idea caused a considerable controversy. Many attempted to improve on this definition of DSS, and many divergent views appeared. House summarized the situation in 1983:

> ... No generally accepted definition of such systems (DSS) can be realistically stated at this point in time. The majority of current systems which are characterized as DSS do appear to be flexible, do deal principally with unstructured problems, and are at least partially interactive.
>
> From *Decision Support Systems*, Petrocelli, New York, 1983.

MS/OR specialists, who had been developing models to help decision makers address all manner of problem situations, and who, in many cases, had worked closely with managers in reaching decisions for complex, "unstructured" problems were surprised at the fuss the term **DSS** had caused. Naylor expressed a typical view of DSS from MS/OR:

> DSS is a redundant term currently being used to describe a subset of management science that predates the DSS movement.
>
> From *Interfaces*, 1982;12:4.

With the benefit of hindsight, it is clear that management information systems professionals were not the first people to use DSS, but their labeling of "decision support systems" and their discussion of the formalization of DSS have been pivotal for one simple reason: the DSS idea proved to be marketable. Managers had proved reluctant to buy systems designed to tell them what they must do but were willing, perhaps even eager, to buy systems that were advertised as supporting them and helping to improve their effectiveness. MS/OR professionals and software developers were not shy to recognize the marketability of the label "DSS," and a host of products were advertised under this label. The market success of DSS lead to Naylor agonizing in 1982 "... it seems that virtually every computer hardware and software firm in the industry refers to its products as DSS."

Structure in Management Tasks

The degree of "structure" within a management task is central to the DSS concept. The different decision-making levels (**operational**, **tactical**, and **strategic**; see Chapter 3) generally involve differing amounts of structure, although examples of highly structured, semistructured, and unstructured tasks can be found at all levels. Table 6-1 provides examples of different types of activities at the three decision-making levels. In general, however, the degree of structure to a decision decreases as responsibility for the decision moves up through the organization.

Operational decision making tends to be highly structured–deciding, for example, how to blend gasolines within an oil refinery. These decisions are immediate and short term and require little judgment.

Tactical decision making is generally less structured and longer term than operational decision making and often requires considerable managerial judgment. Examples include setting budgets and production levels.

Strategic decision making is generally the least structured and is the responsibility of the most senior managers of the organization. Strategic decision making is often long term and highly judgmental, such as, launching a major new product or buying out a competitor.

How amenable a problem is to MS/OR analysis and solution depends on both the degree of structure to the problem and the decision-making level. MS/OR models can "make" decisions for structured tasks at the operational level where workable solutions can often be derived using modeling techniques and can usually be implemented without great opposition from management because the cost of mistakes is often quite low. There are many such systems in place: for example, inventory control systems that manage inventories of a large number of items, extrapolating usage data to forecast demand, computing reorder quantities for items that are approaching stockouts, and printing orders to suppliers for restocking. Management's role in implementing such a system evolves from one of deriving solutions and implementing them to one of monitoring the system and identifying exceptions and abnormalities.

Table 6-1 | **EXAMPLES OF TASKS AT DIFFERENT DECISION LEVELS**

	Level of Decision Making		
Degree of Structure	**Operational**	**Tactical**	**Strategic**
Structured	Order materials	Derive master schedule	Lease or buy building
Semistructured	Schedule equipment maintenance	Budgeting	Mergers or acquisitions
Unstructured	Hire operators	Hire management	Select a board of directors

Adapted from A. Gorry and Scott Morton, A Framework for Management Information Systems, *Sloan Management Review*, 1971; 13.

At the other end of the scale, many unstructured strategic problems are very difficult to automate much above the provision of raw data. Here, managers feel that they have a unique skill, and furthermore, the cost of poor decisions is very high. Thus, it is difficult to develop a model that might be useful, and even harder to persuade management that such a model could provide useful help with their decision process. Hiring a new vice president of marketing is an example of an unstructured strategic decision.

Between these two extremes, there exists a host of situations where there is sufficient structure to develop some form of useful model but human knowledge and judgment are still required. This is the territory of the DSS. DSS containing appropriate MS/OR models, useful data, and presented in a user-friendly package that a decision maker can use (Figure 6-1) have proved useful in supporting many different decision tasks at all levels of the organization. There appears to be a willingness of management to accept this kind of support if it improves managerial effectiveness–that is, if use of the DSS leads to improved decision making. The challenge facing DSS developers and advocates is to push the area of application of DSS toward less-structured problems at higher levels of the firm.

In 1982, Sprague and Carlson proposed a general structure for a DSS (shown in Figure 6-1) that included both a **database** and a **model base**. Their DSS integrates access to data with the use of appropriate models. Just as the data exist in a formal structure (a database), so the models exist in a similar structure (the model base). The role of the DSS is to select both appropriate data and an appropriate model to maximize the value added to the data in responding to an inquiry from the decision maker. The knowledge needed to solve the problem resides outside the DSS with the decision maker, but this knowledge is brought to bear on the problem by including the decision maker in the problem-solving loop.

Figure **6-1** | **SPRAGUE AND CARLSON VIEW OF A DECISION SUPPORT SYSTEM**

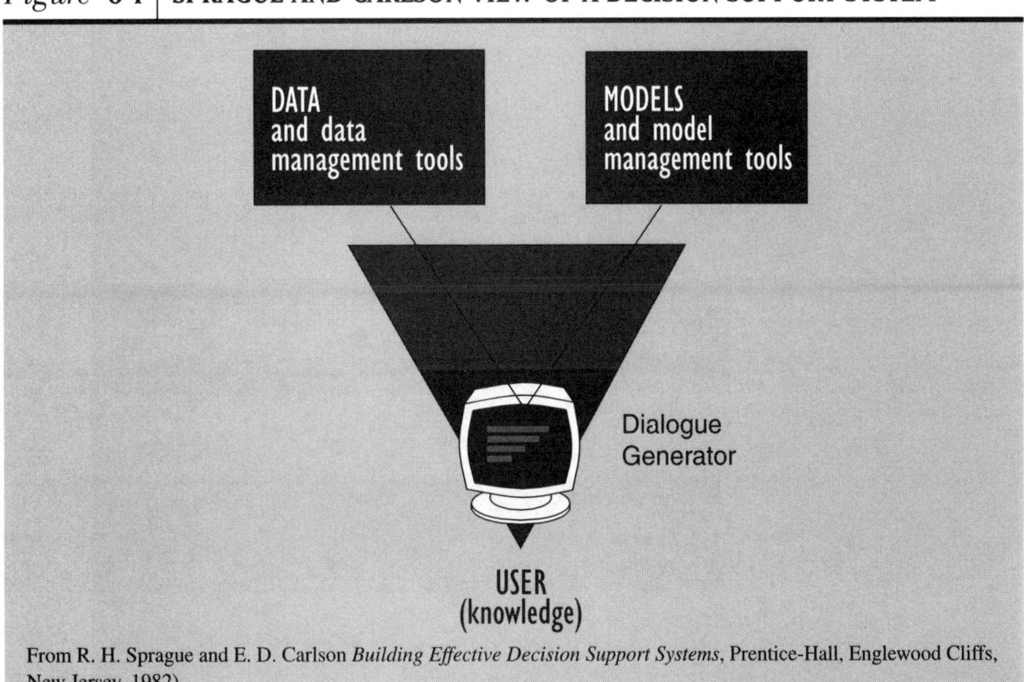

From R. H. Sprague and E. D. Carlson *Building Effective Decision Support Systems*, Prentice-Hall, Englewood Cliffs, New Jersey, 1982)

The **dialogue generator** is an important feature of the DSS of Sprague and Carlson; in MS/OR, this would be called a **user interface**. The role of the user interface in the process of problem resolution in situations in which there is no clear optimal solution ("semistructured" or "unstructured" problems in the language of DSS) is to reduce the problem-solving cycle time.

Problem solving using a DSS proceeds via an iterative series of cycles: the decision maker submits an inquiry to the DSS or model, which responds with some output. The decision maker processes this information, incorporating personal knowledge, and submits a new inquiry. This iterative process continues until a solution is reached that the decision maker judges to be acceptable or the best possible. Figure 6-2 illustrates this process.

Analysis of semistructured or unstructured problems using a DSS requires the user to perform three functions during each iteration of the problem-solving cycle.

- First, formulate an inquiry that can be understood by the system.
- Second, receive and comprehend the response from the system.
- Third, analyze the response and think up an appropriate new inquiry.

The cycle time for each iteration is the sum of the DSS or model processing time, the receiving and comprehending time, and the user's thinking or response time, and the time to formulate and input a new query.

Cycle time = *DSS processing time* + *receiving and comprehending time* + *response time* + *new query formulation time*

The **system processing time** is an important design feature of a DSS. Although occasionally this can be quite long, in general, the more senior the manager, the faster the system must respond. Achieving fast DSS response times often requires clever data and model management, good (and computationally fast) models, considerable programming skill, and, often, a powerful computer.

The **user's thinking or response time** is less controllable but can be reduced through training and experience with the problem situation and use of the DSS.

The objective of the user interface is to minimize the **receiving and comprehending time** and the **new query formulation time**.

Figure **6-2** **PROBLEM SOLVING WITH A DSS**

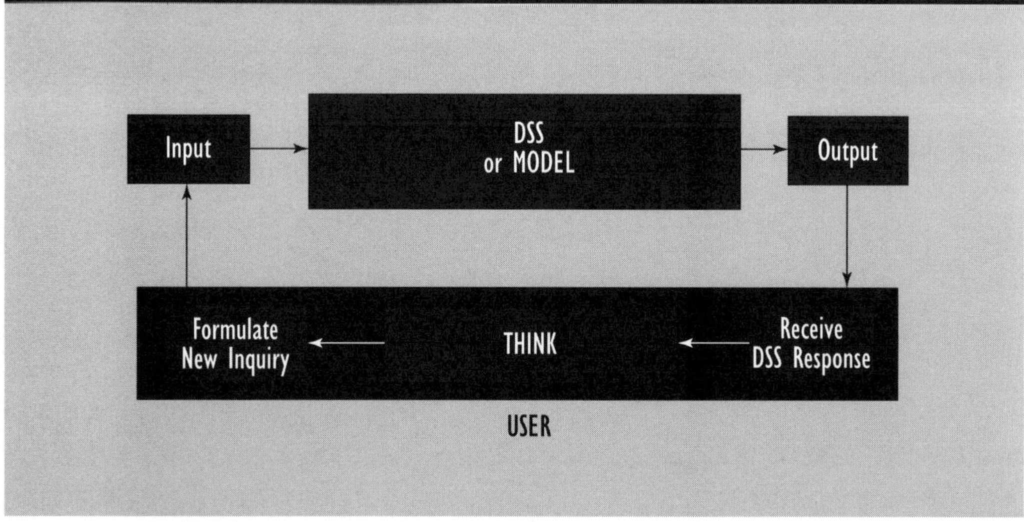

Increasingly, "intelligence" is included in the interface; although this used to mean the use of a human "chauffeur" to work between the executive and the system, increasingly, ideas from **artificial intelligence** are appearing in human/computer interfaces.

Designing interfaces for effective human/computer interaction involves elements of cognitive psychology, ergonomics (human factors engineering), software engineering, and management. On the input side, the classic interaction styles (menus, form fill-in, command languages, and direct manipulation [for example, with a mouse or other cursor pointing device]) each has advantages and disadvantages. On the output side, there is a heavy emphasis on computer-generated graphics (including "animation" or dynamic graphics) and on color coding (in both graphic and tabular data), with windowing used to enable the user to combine elements of different displays on the same screen. It is useful to differentiate between two different forms of computer-generated graphics: **iconic graphics** and **presentation graphics**.

In an **iconic** graphic display, each picture element (or **icon**) maps to an element of the real situation, such as a computerized street map, where the lines map to streets, the intersections to street corners, and so on. A **presentation** graphic display presents a summary of some data—the familiar bar charts, line graphs, and pie charts are presentation graphics. Computer-generated graphics appear to be most easily understood when they have some iconic structure that links them to the real world problem; for example, interactive computer-generated maps have provided the basis for many successful DSS designed to support routing decisions for vehicles or people around geographic areas.

The **WIMP** (Windows, Icons, Mouse, Pull-down menus) interface and the interactive spreadsheet with command menus are two widely admired and copied styles of DSS interface.

Decision Support Systems Application Areas

The use of DSS is widespread today. Some recent examples include:

- French National Railways (SNCF) uses a DSS called RailPlus to help schedulers design the best schedule for their high speed trains (TGVs) and a second DSS called RailCap to help planners allocate passenger-carrying capacity (TGV vehicles) to routes. These DSS are credited with generating incremental revenues of more than $2 million annually with a 3% reduction in train operating costs.

- Taco Bell restaurant managers use a DSS to help them determine the most cost-effective workforce schedules. This DSS provides demand-dependent staffing levels derived from store simulations and workforce schedules derived using integer programming and is estimated to save more than 1 hour of direct labor cost per day for each restaurant. In addition, the DSS reduces the manager's time to derive staff schedules from 4 to 6 hours per week to less than 1 hour per week. The estimated benefit of the DSS by 1996 exceeded $53 million.

- More than 40 of the United States have adopted a DSS called PONTIS to help plan the allocation of funds for the maintenance and rehabilitation of bridges. This system is being used to plan Federal government expenditures of some $2.8 billion annually on the maintenance and repair of an inventory of some 565,000 bridges.

A survey of journals published between 1988 and 1994 found 271 articles describing DSS applications broken down by application area as summarized in Table 6-2.

The findings of H. B. Eom and S. M. Lee from an earlier survey on the types of MS/OR models and tools used in the published DSS applications are summarized in Table 6-3. Optimization and simulation each feature prominently together with statistical analysis. Sig-

Table 6-2 | APPLICATION AREAS FOR 271 PUBLISHED DSSs

Application Area	No. of Published DSSs
Corporate DSS	194 of 271
Major areas (within corporate DSS)	
Production or operations management	79
Information systems	37
Marketing/transportation/logistics	25
Finance	20
Strategic management	12
Human resources management	8
Multifunctional management	6
International business	4
Accounting	3
Noncorporate DSS	77 of 271
Major areas (as proportion of noncorporate DSS)	
Government	28
Education	14
Military	10
Hospital and health care	9
Urban and community planning	7
Miscellaneous	6
Natural resources	3

From S. B. Eom, S. M. Lee, C. Somarajan, and E. Kim, *OR Insight* 1997;10:2.

nificantly, even before 1988, computer-generated graphics were included in almost 25% of the DSS.

DSS have long been widely used in manufacturing and distribution. In one of several surveys, (Plenert, G. *Production and Inventory Management Journal* 1st quarter 1992) found DSS used for sales order processing, forecasting, aggregate production scheduling, finished goods distribution, master production scheduling and material requirements planning, bill of materials planning and routing, capacity requirements planning, and inventory and quality control. The use of DSS, however, has spread beyond the traditional economic sectors into new areas.

An investigation of the use of DSS in the U.S. health care industry (S. Butters and S. B. Eom, *Journal of Systems Management*, 43:6, 1992) found major DSS applications for financial planning, cost accounting, and the analysis of productivity. DSS were also found to be used by management to help understand product line costs, revenues, and profitability and for nurse scheduling and the analysis of nursing costs. Emergency medical services vehicle deployment, blood distribution, and equipment purchasing also were problems that were being tackled by DSS. The authors conclude that in the case of the health care industry:

> The computer-based DSS is an indispensable management tool that enhances management's ability to plan strategically on a more informed basis and department heads' ability to control their operations in a more cost effective way.

R. R. Trippi (*Interfaces*, 1990;20:5) reviewed the use of DSS in real estate investments and concluded that most existing DSS are focused on the choice phase of the decision process and are used for the selection of projects suitable for acquisition, retention, improve-

Table 6-3 **MS/OR MODELS USED IN A SAMPLE OF 203 PUBLISHED DSS APPLICATIONS 1971 THROUGH 1988**

Type of Model	No. of DSSs Found (Sample of 203)
Decision trees	8
Optimization models	
Linear	18
Integer	19
Nonlinear	6
Simulation models	
Stochastic	41
Deterministic	24
Other MS/OR models	
Transportation models	6
Network models	15
Inventory models	8
Goal programming	9
Dynamic programming	4
Queuing models	3
Markov models	6
Game theory	1
Multiple-criteria decision making	11
Forecasting and statistical models	40
Tools used	
Graphics	46
Artificial Intelligence	12

From H. B. Eom and S. M. Lee "A Survey of DSS Applications," *Interfaces* 1990;20:3.

ment, and refinancing from a prespecified list. He found many off-the-shelf software packages available, as well as spreadsheet-based DSS.

S. S. Nagel and M. K. Mills (*Interfaces*, 1991;21:2) reviewed the use of DSS in the legal profession and concluded that the most useful type of DSS for lawyers used a spreadsheet form and multicriteria decision-making theory. The benefits of this type of system included better framing of the alternatives, goals, and relations; overcoming analytical problems; and associating diverse users and uses. DSS software has been used in most legal fields. Nagel and Mills state:

> The strength of legal decision-making software is that it permits one to combine explicit data when available, intuitive experience, and personal values, and confront ethical considerations in an easily grasped format.

ARTIFICIAL INTELLIGENCE AND DECISION SUPPORT SYSTEMS

A DSS is designed to be used by a human who brings knowledge into the problem-solving process. Efforts to incorporate knowledge, in addition to data and models, within DSS began with work in artificial intelligence on knowledge-based systems.

Storing and Processing Knowledge Using Knowledge-Based or Expert Systems

Knowledge-based, or "expert," systems (KBS) are a development from research into artificial intelligence (AI).

Box 6-2

ARTIFICIAL INTELLIGENCE

"Any senior manager in any business of almost any size who is not at least learning about artificial intelligence (AI), and sticking a tentative toe or two into AI's waters, is simply out of step, and dangerously so."

Tom Peters, the author of *In Search of Excellence,* quoted in *The Rise of the Expert Company,* E. Feigenbaum, P. McCorduck, and H. P. Nii, Random House, 1988.

Even if this assertion is only partially true, it is clear that developing a basic understanding of AI and of what it can and cannot do for a company may be time well spent.

Artificial Intelligence

In 1956, the term **artificial intelligence** was coined by John McCarthy to describe a stream of research involving **heuristic search techniques**. Many problem-solving processes that appear to be intelligent involve some type of systematic search of possible solutions. For example, computerized speech recognition involves producing an electronic imprint of a spoken sound and then searching through a library of imprints to try to find a match.

The major AI application areas include:

Robotics (building machines that can perform mechanical tasks previously requiring human skill, such as frame-welding and body-painting on an automobile assembly line)

Machine vision (developing systems that can "see")

Machine learning (developing systems that can "learn")

Natural language processing (developing systems that can interpret commands and sentences delivered in standard spoken languages)

Speech recognition (transcribing speech into type)

Successful developments in any of these areas will likely have a significant impact on our lives, but the area that appears to have the greatest managerial potential is that of **knowledge-based systems.** KBS could possibly lead to radical changes in the way firms are managed.

Knowledge has some apparent similarities with data, suggesting that organizations might develop and store "knowledge bases" within the organization from which they could read and write knowledge. In practice, corporate knowledge is difficult to extract and store, in part because much of it exists in the minds of employees. This raises a number of interesting issues. Who owns knowledge? Who can buy and sell knowledge?

AI has made great progress in developing schemes to represent knowledge and constructing knowledge bases. A **knowledge base** encapsulates the rules, probabilities, facts, and relationships that constitute the knowledge the organization uses for some activity. "**Knowledge engineers**" can "debrief" individuals and store their knowledge in knowledge bases so others may have access. Knowledge formalized within a knowledge base can even be "taught" new things and be updated.

Knowledge-based systems (KBS) emerged from universities in the mid-1960s from efforts to build software that could mimic human expert problem solving. An important early KBS was MYCIN, built in the 1970s to diagnose bacterial infections of the blood. Early versions of MYCIN used some 500 "if-then" rules to store the knowledge, a form of knowledge base that has become common.

The CATS system at General Electric Company (GE) was an early commercial KBS that illustrates some changes in management thinking that this technology has caused. For 40 years, David Smith, GE's best diesel-electric locomotive troubleshooter, had advised locomotive engineers around the United States on the appropriate repairs to make during locomotive servicing. As Smith approached retirement, the traditional approach would have been to assign a young engineer as an apprentice to Smith in an effort to absorb Smith's knowledge before it left GE on his retirement. One problem with this approach was that the apprentice might leave GE, taking away the knowledge. Instead, beginning in 1980, GE decided to try to build a locomotive troubleshooting KBS based on Smith's knowledge. Three years later, GE installed a system called CATS on a PC in every GE locomotive repair shop. CATS enabled a novice engineer to uncover the fault and subsequently led the engineer through the required repair procedures, including parts drawings and specific demonstrations of how the repair should be made.

Stand-alone systems, like CATS, have become common (and profitable), but the major managerial benefits will occur when ideas from KBS begin to be integrated into the major decision support and information systems of the organization.

KBS builders are frequently referred to as "knowledge engineers," a term that reflects their role in capturing the knowledge of an expert within the KBS. In 1983, it was estimated that fewer than 200 people worldwide had the knowledge, skills, and expertise required to design and build an KBS. In 1990, estimates put the number between 2,000 and 2,500. Today, KBS have become an area of explosive growth, with new examples appearing daily.

In 1989, it was thought that some 100 of the Fortune 500 companies had implemented significant KBS, whereas most others were investigating and developing applications. A variety of estimates and forecasts suggest that the KBS market reached $1 billion annually in about 1991.

WHAT IS A KNOWLEDGE-BASED SYSTEM?

A precise scientific definition of KBS has proved controversial, but from a pragmatic perspective, KBS can be thought of as computer programs that attempt to solve a particular problem in the same way that a human expert would. A KBS attempts to replicate the thought process used by the expert, including the use of heuristics or rules of thumb. Often what differentiates experts from novices are the number of blind alleys they explore when solving problems. The expert typically takes much less time, can more quickly rule out paths that will not be fruitful, and is more astute in determining what additional information is required. This ability to sort through the myriad of options both efficiently and effectively sets experts apart. KBS developers attempt to understand how an expert goes about solving a problem and then automate that understanding.

Importantly, there must be one or more "experts" who can help solve a problem before a KBS can be constructed. Sometimes finding "experts" can be enlightening: the employee who has achieved recognition as the one who can solve the problem (for example, forecast interest rates) may turn out to be one who built a reputation on a few lucky guesses.

If there is a human expert who can solve a particular problem reliably, then developing an KBS to mimic this expert's problem-solving process may be a more effective option than attempting to use optimization or simulation or other MS/OR tools. In many cases, building such an KBS has not been very complex; some "expert knowledge" is not particularly mysterious.

Building an KBS requires construction of an "inference engine" and a "user interface" in addition to the knowledge base.

The **inference engine** is the name given to the logic or program that manages the search through the knowledge to come up with expert-like recommendations. A high-quality inference engine searches through the knowledge base efficiently and does not waste time exhaustively searching through irrelevant rules or executing redundant looping. The form of the "inference engine" will change depending on the way the knowledge is represented.

The **user interface** is the part of the KBS through which input is received and output is communicated. Many KBS interfaces are also capable of describing the logic sequence by which results were generated and so "explaining" their reasoning to the user.

KBS are constructed using KBS languages or KBS "shells."

KBS languages provide a means of representing instructions to input, output, or process knowledge. Early KBS were written in languages (such as LISP [for LISt Processing] and PROLOG [for PROgramming LOGic]) specifically designed for the complex data types, such as objects, that constitute the knowledge base. Many recently developed KBS are written in newer, powerful general-purpose languages, such as C++.

A KBS Shell is a prepackaged version of an inference engine and interface that can be readily customized to a particular application. Shells typically contain functionality that is common to a particular class of KBS (for example, those based on the application of "if-then" rules) and greatly reduce the time that must be devoted to development of input, output, and processing algorithms.

Are KBS MS/OR, or are they "information systems"? KBS are a particular form of model. There are many instances where this form of model has proved to be more useful in resolving a decision situation than other forms of MS/OR models. The MS/OR problem solver should be aware that a KBS is often a useful modeling option.

The potential value of KBS has been explained by contrasting KBS with human intelligence. According to the AI literature (adapted from Kaplan, *The AI Magazine*, Summer 1984), KBS have several important advantages over human intelligence:

KBS Can Be Permanent. Human intelligence is perishable; workers can change employment or forget things.

KBS Can Be Easily Duplicated. Transferring knowledge from one person to another often requires a lengthy period of apprenticeship, but once in the computer, knowledge can be easily copied and moved.

KBS Can Be Consistent and Thorough. Human intelligence is often erratic because people do not perform consistently and they forget.

KBS Can Be Documented. Human intelligence is difficult to reproduce because a person may reach a conclusion but at some later date be unable to recreate the reasoning process that led to that conclusion or even recall the assumptions that were part of the decision.

KBS Never Get Sick. They also never take a coffee break or a vacation, and they do not mind working 24 hours a day.

However, human intelligence has some advantages over KBS:

Human intelligence is creative. KBS are rather uninspired.

Human intelligence enables people to benefit by, and use, sensory experience directly. KBS must work with symbolic input.

Human reasoning is able to make use of a very wide context of experience and bring that to bear on individual problems. KBS typically gain their power by having a narrow focus.

These advantages of human intelligence over KBS demonstrate certain limitations of KBS. For example, KBS often have difficulty telling when a question is outside the realm of the system's expertise and are often unable to check a conclusion to see if it is reasonable.

Often-cited benefits to the firm of implementing KBS include:

- Ensuring consistency and accuracy of decision making within the organization
- Reducing costs
- Reaching decisions more quickly
- Freeing experts to work on less routine problems
- Capturing the expertise of a specific expert
- Developing a training mechanism for new experts

From an MS/OR perspective, these advantages and disadvantages apply to almost any kind of model. Optimization or simulation models are **permanent** and **easily duplicated**, can be **consistent and thorough**, can **reduce costs**, can be **documented**, and **never get sick**. There are, however, many applications when KBS logic has proven to provide the benefits of modeling.

Teknowledge, Inc., a company that builds KBS tools, suggested eight common situations that point to use of a KBS.

1. When the knowledge required to perform a particular task effectively is available only at a central location; requests for advice are channeled to a small group of people who are always in demand. For example, a key product design team may be spending an excessive portion of their time on the telephone advising repair personnel.
2. If a written document or flowchart exists that is intended to facilitate the use of a program, procedure, or piece of equipment. Often these are so long and detailed that they become useless in practice; the users may resort to folklore-like methods, relying excessively on procedures that appear to work empirically.
3. When an organization turns away work or loses business to competitors because an overworked human expert is required to make judgments or recommendations, even in routine cases. For example, to reduce unnecessary or expensive work, a locomotive repair center requires a supervisor to approve all diagnoses and recommendations before work is undertaken. Although costs are controlled, the average downtime may increase to a point where it is economical for customers to send broken equipment to other centers for repair.
4. When turnover in equipment or personnel leads to an excessive amount of time spent on training rather than on doing. For example, a company updates its line of test equipment each year, and field engineers must spend several weeks annually attending training sessions.
5. When a large amount of mainly routine data must be scanned by a highly trained expert on a continuing basis. For example, a mutual fund manager may scan many different stock prices continually looking for new investment opportunities.
6. When a variety of information from heterogeneous sources must be monitored and integrated to determine the possibility of an important event. For example, a stock broker may constantly examine information from multiple sources to attempt to foresee changes in market trends.
7. When a critical judgment must be made in a very short time interval to capture a gain or avoid a potential disaster. For example, an investment analyst may want to put a new but complex investment strategy in place quickly to respond to stock price changes, or a machine may need to be shut down quickly when a potential problem is detected.

8. Where an optimal solution to a routing, planning, or configuration task is too expensive or time consuming to determine and, as a consequence, a minimally effective process of guesswork has been substituted. For example, a computer company has to engineer and produce parts lists for its equipment customized for individual customers, including the proper cables, components, and mounting arrangement, to allow the equipment to perform as ordered. Errors and delays in this process become a serious problem as orders increase.

WHAT MAKES EXPERT SYSTEMS DIFFERENT?

The fundamental difference between KBS and conventional computer systems is that KBS deal with knowledge, whereas conventional systems deal with models, information, and data.

> Knowledge is not synonymous with information. Rather, knowledge is information that has been interpreted, categorized, applied and revised.
>
> From E. Feigenbaum and P. McCorduck, *The Fifth Generation: Artificial Intelligence and Japan's Computer Challenge to the World*, Addison-Wesley, Reading, Massachusetts, 1983.

Both knowledge bases and traditional databases are designed to store information, but they differ significantly in the types of information they can store and the types of interrelationships between data they can handle. Databases contain definite facts, such as "Today's sales were $3,000,216" and "The Marketing Department budget is $6,500,000." However, databases cannot deal with complex descriptions or rules that describe causal relationships or uncertain knowledge about the stored facts.

Knowledge bases, like databases, also store definite facts, but knowledge bases can also store cause-and-effect knowledge, rules, and imprecise and probabilistic information such as "Increasing advertising usually increases sales." This is an example of not only a rule but also of an imprecise, uncertain, or "fuzzy," chunk of knowledge. Fuzzy knowledge is knowledge qualified by words such as "usually," "most," "many," "almost," "more frequently," and so on. Unlike databases, knowledge bases, and the inference engines within KBS that manipulate knowledge bases, are designed to handle uncertain information. In the database, sales are a number. In a knowledge base, sales may depend on advertising expenses and competitors' prices.

STORING KNOWLEDGE AND MAKING INFERENCES

Data can be stored in databases. Can knowledge be stored in "knowledge bases"? The answer is a definitive "Yes" and the methods by which this can be achieved are improving all the time. The issue is one of "knowledge representation": How can the knowledge of an expert be recorded in a way that enables a nonexpert to access, work with, and benefit from this knowledge?

To illustrate knowledge representation and inference engines, we will examine three basic methods for storing knowledge: **examples**, **rules**, and **frames**.

Examples are the simplest form of knowledge representation: a set of example cases can link data (or "factors") to an expert conclusion or opinion. As an illustration, we could collect all the commercial loan applications considered by the loan experts at a financial institution during a particular week. For each loan application, we would have the application form (listing the data about the application) and the loan officer's decision. By coding the data from the forms together with the expert's decisions and entering them into the computer, we create a "knowledge base" for the "commercial loan problem."

Could we use this knowledge base to make a decision without the expert? This would require an inference engine that would take a new application for a loan and search our knowledge base to find a previous application that matched the new one. When a match is found, we retrieve the expert's decision from the previous application: we have used expert knowledge without the human expert.

There are several problems with this simple general approach. The first is that there may be no case that matches the new case exactly. This situation is likely if the application form is complex with many data items, or if we only have a small number of example cases. Solving this problem by adding more examples may not be the answer: the computer may grind to a halt! The alternative is not to insist on an exact match but to find an example case that is "close enough." We now have to be concerned about what "close enough" means in terms of the many different factors from the application form. Finding "approximate matches" is a major research area.

The second problem encountered with examples are contradictions: we may have two identically coded application forms that produced different expert opinions. This could be because different experts reviewed the forms or because some factors pertinent to the loan decision do not appear on the application form (for example, the impression gained by the loan officer of the applicant during an interview,) or, perhaps, on "close calls" the expert sometimes goes one way and sometimes the other.

Producing a set of examples that would make a useful knowledge base therefore requires that we perform some "knowledge engineering." The objective in doing this is to produce an "exhaustive" set of examples–one that would provide a match for any new case–and to eliminate contradictions so the nonexpert user does not have to choose from more than one expert opinion. This form of knowledge engineering leads naturally to the second form of knowledge representative: **rules**.

Rules are generalized examples, such as, "Approve a commercial loan to any applicant who can provide personal collateral to the bank which exceeds 150% of the loan amount."

A rule like this summarizes knowledge from a great number of example cases. If we had a set of examples of expert action or opinion, we could use these to try to infer what "rules" the expert was following. Alternatively, we could question an expert directly about the rules being used to guide decision making.

Knowledge engineers work with experts to try to define a set of rules which encapsulate the expert's knowledge and which cover a high percentage of the situations likely to be encountered with minimal contradictions. The existence of a large number of successful rules-based commercial expert systems confirms that this approach is both possible and economically viable.

An important issue in rules-based knowledge is that of rule sequence. As an illustration, suppose we have two rules:

A. Approve a commercial-loan application to any applicant who can provide personal collateral in the amount of 150% of the loan amount or greater.
B. Do not approve a loan to any individual who has never worked full-time.

If we have an applicant who has never worked full-time but who can provide 150% personal collateral, the recommendations that result from applying these rules are contradictory. The inference engine that processes the rules will have to be concerned about the **sequence** in which the rules are applied.

There are two basic alternatives to draw inferences from a rules-base. First, we can apply the rules **procedurally**: that is, we start at the top of the rule "stack" and apply the rules one-by-one until we find a rule that applies to the present case, and then stop. **Procedural rule bases** resemble a series of If ... Then ... Else statements: they are highly structured and conceptually straightforward and can be coded in a standard computer language. However, when they become large, they are difficult to validate and to update; when adding a new rule, it is very important to determine the correct position for the new rule in the rule sequence.

The alternative is to process the rules **simultaneously** (that is, nonprocedurally); we apply all the rules and determine which ones apply to the new case. We then take the conclusions from all the rules that apply and check for contradictions. If there are contradictions, we must do some more inferencing to determine which is the best result for the current case, or we may send the case to a human expert for resolution. Nonprocedural rule bases require special-purpose logic and inference engines but are straightforward to maintain because the rules themselves are often fairly simple. Updating or revising the knowledge base is often straightforward because a new rule can be added to the bottom of the rules' stack without concern about sequence. KBS based on nonprocedural rule processing appear to the user to be more "intelligent" than procedural systems: both the "answers" and the effects of adding new rules are less predictable.

Frames are the third way to represent knowledge that we consider. Frames focus on the conclusions rather than the data. For example, in our commercial loan example, instead of looking first at details of the applicant, we look at the results: first consider the result "Approve" and begin to list the characteristics of applicants which make up the decision "Approve." These characteristics become the frame for the result "Approve." For each possible result, we construct a similar frame. To process a new application, we search the stack of frames, attempting to match the details of the application to a frame. Reaching a conclusion using frames is straightforward if an exact match is required (and can be found), but it becomes much more sophisticated if inexact matches or probabilities are involved. The latter requires the inference engine to identify the frame that the applicant is *most likely* to match or to provide a conclusion based on calculation of the probabilities of the applicant matching all possible frames.

Frame-based knowledge has the advantages of allowing easy updating because new frames can be added without changing the basic structure of the inference engine. Sophisticated inference engines result in these KBS appearing quite "intelligent," and the results obtained can be difficult to replicate intuitively.

In summary, examples, rules, and frames are closely related methods for representing similar knowledge. They differ in the type of inference necessary to draw a conclusion from the knowledge and in their ease of validation, maintenance, and updating.

EXAMPLES OF KBS APPLICATIONS

A discussion of KBS applications is made difficult because so many companies believe (or hope?) that they are working on systems that may provide them with a competitive advantage; consequently, they do not want their competitors to find out what they are doing. With that in mind, here is a sampling of operational KBSs:

Campbell Soup. One of the earliest examples of a commercial KBS was Campbell Soup's COOKER. This system diagnosed malfunctions that occurred in the equipment used to sterilize food in cans. Any downtime was expensive and disruptive to shipping schedules. Campbell plant operators and maintenance people handled the day-to-day operation of the equipment and corrected common malfunctions. To support them, Campbell Soup had experts familiar with the design, installation, and operation of the cookers travel around the canning plants as needed. With the implementation of the system, Campbell Soup accrued several benefits, including freeing the experts from diagnostic activities and allowing them to concentrate on design improvements and new processes. The system was used as a training tool for new maintenance personnel. Problems were diagnosed more quickly, and the expertise of the best expert, who retired in 1987, was preserved (from S. Gardiner, Applied Expert Systems: Small Applications, *Solutions*, Peat Marwick, January 1988).

CP Rail. CP developed a system to predict the failure of locomotive engines by analyzing their lubrication fluid. By assessing the concentration of metals and other contaminants in the fluid, the system determined when the engines would require maintenance. Mark Naylor, director of technology, computers, and communications at CP, said that the system raised the average level of analysis to a competence level approaching that of CP's best expert—who had 37 years of field experience and 6 weeks of vacation a year and obviously was not always available. Naylor believed that the major benefit of the system was the uniform level of judgment delivered (from H. Gellman, Competent or Not, Expert Systems Slow to Find a Place in Industry, *The Globe and Mail*, March 13, 1989).

American Express. American Express developed the Authorizer's Assistant to support the authorization of credit card customers' purchases. It was designed to reduce the time needed to process authorization requests and minimize losses from bad credit decisions. The system enabled American Express to realize a 25% reduction in authorization time and improved consistency considerably. Assistant was been found to be 96.5% accurate compared to 85% for the average human authorizer (from P. Hessinger, Artificial Intelligence: Giving Credit to an Expert System, *ComputerWorld*, November 23, 1987).

Alacritous. Alacritous was a small company that focused on providing managers with tools to support the planning function. Their main product, Alacrity Strategy, was a KBS that interviewed managers about their product/business and caused them to think through a number of the key strategic issues. The system produced a written report that summarized the conventional view of the strategic alternatives facing their firm. This KBS (which was marketed initially as "An MBA in a Box") drew on a library of 3,000 rules about strategy and 2,900 recommendations (from Making Strategy Work, Alacritous Limited).

A survey of knowledge engineers reported in 1993 (T. A. Byrd, *Interfaces*, 23:2) found a very broad range of tasks that KBS were handling. The more "managerial" tasks included:

Advising: Fund raising, product functionality, marketing, purchasing, bond purchases

Diagnostics: Industrial systems, equipment, process

Scheduling: Production, airlines, hospital staff, towboats and barges, job shop, plant floor

Planning: Production, computer networks, disaster recovery, travel, mailing list rental, university/teacher class assignment, work-load estimating, project estimating

Analysis: Commission split, quality parameters, market, audit risk, chemical spill, work benefits, loans

Other: Dispatcher, airline gate assignment, production training, foreign currency exchange rate hedging, direct mail prospecting, product quotes, recommend future market actions, credit approval, incident reporting, prioritizing maintenance requests

Listed as the most important benefits that the respondents thought their organizations had realized (in descending order of importance) were:

- More consistency in decision making
- Improved productivity
- More timely business reporting and decisions and
  Workers free to do more creative work
- Improved competitiveness and market share

INTEGRATING DATA, MODELS, AND KNOWLEDGE THROUGH ADVANCED DECISION SUPPORT SYSTEMS

Data reaches the manager from many different sources. In some cases, the data consist of "hard" facts and figures that may be collected in the organization's database, in another organization's database, or the Internet. Other data may be "softer"–opinions of colleagues or estimates of future activity levels. The manager is constantly viewing, validating, selecting, and transforming data, seeking to establish what useful information the data hold about what is happening in and around the organization.

Viewing data alone is rarely very informative. The manager makes use of a wide variety of **models** in seeking to use data. These models may be informal rules-of-thumb, such as, our cost-of-goods-sold is usually about 40% of sales revenues. Most organizations, however, have a host of formal models, including, for example, financial models that link the various items in the financial statements, production models that calculate how many subassemblies must be made to produce a certain volume of finished units, marketing models that relate how much must be spent on advertising and promotion to yield a certain level of sales, pricing models that determine what prices to charge to maximize revenues, and allocation models that determine the best way to spread the scarce resources of the organization around the various products to be produced.

Managers do not accept data without thought, nor do they accept the output from models without question. Each manager brings a wealth of **knowledge** to the task of managing the firm. Knowledge can be very general, such as a code of ethics, or very specific; the last time we raised our prices, the competition followed suit. The manager gains general knowledge through education and specific knowledge through experience doing various management tasks repeatedly. The experienced manager, that is, one who has seen a wide variety of situations before, is a valuable organizational resource.

The roles of data, models, and knowledge in providing decision making support were originally thought of quite separately. The earliest DSS (and also many of the executive information systems of today) emphasized the **data** aspect of managerial support. These systems were designed to provide the manager with the capability to peruse the database of the organization and to select, summarize, and display interesting or pertinent data. Any modeling or knowledge to be applied to the data had to be done either in the manager's head, or "off-line" after the data had been downloaded from the system.

MS/OR models, on the other hand, havc traditionally attempted to provide optimal, or "best," solutions. This is possible when a problem can be formulated in an unambiguous way and "solved" for the best solution. There are a great number of operational problems that can be effectively treated in this way (for example, resource allocation or transportation). Optimizing tactical problems is more difficult, but it is being done increasingly–for example, systems (like OPT) that derive an optimal master schedule for a manufacturer. The optimization of strategic problems is much talked about and increasingly attempted; a good example is the multicriteria analysis by Keeney and Raiffa of the site for a new Mexico City airport (*Decisions with Multiple Objectives: Preferences and Value Tradeoffs*, John Wiley and Sons, New York, 1976). The modeling approach incorporates the selection and use of pertinent data in the modeling, but the use of knowledge is less formal. Both the decision maker's and the modeler's knowledge go into the solution, but the process by which this knowledge is used varies from situation to situation.

Often, complex MS/OR models are embedded in a **data and model management system**. A model (for example, a large-scale mathematical programming problem) might require the input of more than 50,000 variable values and could well produce as many output values. When such a model is used frequently, it is worthwhile to construct an interactive management system around the model. Such management systems use sophisticated interface design ideas to allow interactive access/review/updating of input data, to prompt execution of the model, and to edit the model's output to produce informative displays. The difference between this kind of system and a DSS is one of philosophy: the management model "solves" a structured problem and outputs the solution for implementation, whereas the DSS is a tool to help the decision maker to explore possible solutions to semistructured or unstructured problems.

An expert decision maker can sometimes rely on **knowledge** alone to reach a decision, such as an art expert appraising a painting. Such experts follow a qualitative, intuitive problem analysis process that is often difficult to model. These kinds of intuitive processes often fail when confronted by a quantity of data or when a model can be constructed to demonstrate the suboptimality of the expert's decisions.

A key to effective managerial decision making is to provide technology that encourages the experienced manager to use personal knowledge and experience in conjunction with data and models to arrive at the best possible decisions.

For this reason, there is currently a great deal of interest in integrating KBS concepts with DSS to produce **Expert DSS** (so called **expert DSS** or **intelligent DSS**). There are a number of ways these ideas can be combined:

The **expert front-end** is a KBS that would sit between the DSS and the end-user and serve the purpose of a human "chauffeur," interpreting user requests into DSS commands and translating DSS output into information that the user could understand. An expert front-end could use its own knowledge to respond to DSS queries without always bothering the user, could provide intelligent advice to the user, could include a capability to recognize the user and to tailor the interface to different users, could add custom explanations of DSS actions, and could act as a tutor.

Expert models, which are KBS included in the model base of the DSS, could be used to broaden the areas of application of the DSS and to add more "intelligent" and judgmental solution capabilities.

Expert data management and **expert model management** would involve using a KBS to interpret user requests and to identify and extract the appropriate data or models to determine the DSS response. These types of systems could add judgment to model or data selection and perhaps provide maintenance and restructuring capabilities.

An expert DSS builder is another interesting idea: a KBS that could play the role of the DSS builder, facilitating construction and/or modification of the DSS.

After an extensive review of published DSS applications between 1988 and 1994, Eom and colleagues (S. B. Eom, S. W. Lee, C. Somarajan and E. Kim, "Decision Support System Applications—a Bibliography 1988–1994," *OR INSIGHT* 1997;10:2) report that:

> Expert DSS (knowledge-based DSS, intelligent DSS) are emerging through combining knowledge base and DSS. Approximately 27% of all DSSs (73 of 271) in the survey have enbedded various AI techniques as a component of the systems ... KB modules are being used to formulate problems and select decision models, analyze and interpret the results....

Of the expert DSS available, the most general is expert forecasting software. These packages (for example, SmartForecasts, Forecast Pro) have colorful, graphic, user-friendly interfaces and include several different forecasting models. The user enters the data to be forecast, and a number of statistics about the series are computed. A KBS scans these statistics and selects a forecasting model, and the system then presents the original series plus the forecasts for review and modification.

In the general DSS of Sprague and Carlson (Figure 6-1), data and models are included in the DSS, but the knowledge to solve the problem resides with the user and with the DSS builder, both of whom are external to the DSS. Attempts to incorporate knowledge into the

DSS (as described previously) attempt to internalize the knowledge of user and/or builder into the system. The logical extension of this idea would be an expert DSS where all the knowledge required to solve the problem was internal to the system. Such a system would be a **decision-making system** and, apart from human review and auditing, would provide the kinds of answers to semistructured and unstructured problems that models are able to provide for structured problems.

DECISION-MAKING SYSTEMS

Developments in MS/OR, MIS, and AI motivated by the need to improve managerial productivity and effectiveness have resulted in the implementation of managerial support systems that can speed up and improve managerial decision making. In some cases, such systems present recommended decisions for a broad class of problems within the manager's jurisdiction; in other cases, decision making can be "automated." Some operational problems, particularly inventory management including reordering, have been automated for at least 10 years, but we are now seeing progress being made in expanding the area of application toward less-structured problems, and higher levels of the organization. Consider, for example, the case of AT&T Capital Corporation:

> AT&T Capital Corporation, the largest publicly held leasing and financing company in the United States, owns and manages over $12 billion in assets. In 1992, AT&T began development of three sets of decision automation systems and the associated decision strategies for front-end credit decisions, life-cycle credit-line management, and delinquent account collections. The majority (73 percent) of the credit-granting decisions in AT&T Capital's small-ticket business are now made automatically, including $685 million in new transactions annually. Productivity gains have enhanced competitiveness by reducing response times and increased profitability by reducing credit and collections operating costs by over $3.1 million annually. Finally, improvements in decision quality have led to business volume gains of $86 million annually, while reducing bad debt losses by $1.1 million annually.
>
> From *Interfaces*, 1997;27:1.

Progress such as this is being achieved through integration of MS/OR, MIS, and AI ideas into systems that incorporate databases, model bases, and knowledge bases and that include intelligent data, model, and knowledge base management systems. A good deal of development is directed toward the design and construction of intelligent, graphic, natural language user interfaces that will enable one or more executives to use these complex systems to perform their day-to-day management tasks. Most of the emphasis to date has been on systems to support specific decision-making tasks, but in some applications, it is only a small step to systems that both support and manage the decision making process.

IBM's Logistics Management System (LMS) shows what is possible today.

> LMS monitors and controls the complex manufacturing activities of an entire plant by picking up data automatically, and its knowledge base permits it to reason thoroughly and make necessary corrections so quickly that no individuals or group of individuals can match its performance.
>
> From S. B. Eom, S. W. Lee, C. Somarajan and E. Kim, Decision Support System Applications—a Bibliography 1988–1994, *OR INSIGHT* 1997;10:2.

The challenge today is to provide these systems for more senior managers. This is not a new concept. As early as the mid-1960s, Stafford Beer (*Designing the System*, John Wiley and Sons, Chichester, UK, 1985) was talking about a **situation room** where senior management of an organization could sit and watch the operation of the enterprise and could investigate and implement decisions to control its direction. Because the information gathering and monitoring and control technologies of the 1960s were not sufficiently advanced to implement this concept, Beer's idea was not taken very seriously at the time, but the concept has persisted; we now see situation rooms in several organizations with fairly rigid management rules (for example, the military, engineering–telecommunications and nuclear power plants, and space exploration). As our technology, algorithms, and knowledge continues to develop, we can expect to see attempts to implement Beer's situation room within firms. Much is now going on that represents movement toward this objective.

MANAGEMENT ISSUES

The management issues surrounding decision technology development and adoption are complex. The manager must decide how to move into these technologies in the first place and then establish a reasonable budget in the face of the expected productivity gain and the costs of implementation.

KBSs are a relatively new technology, and as such, their implementation is risky; many attempts to build KBS have failed. There are, however, many compelling examples that demonstrate how well KBSs have worked in some instances for some companies. DEC built the XCON KBS to configure minicomputers and saved more than $20 million annually by eliminating many problems associated with incorrectly ordered or assembled equipment.

DSS may fail because the task chosen is either too large or too small. If it is too small, the users do not need the system. If too large, the system development task becomes insurmountable. DSS also fail for nontechnical reasons, including a lack of senior management commitment, little user interest, high user anxiety, a lack of identifiable benefits, and systems that work but are not practical on a day-to-day basis.

The manager must develop a strategy to minimize the risk of failure without missing significant opportunities. The major ways to minimize the risk of failure include the following:

- Involve the ultimate users of the system during the entire development process.
- Build awareness and ensure top management commitment from the outset.
- Attempt to solve only problems that have been solved successfully before.
- Use standard technology and approaches wherever possible.
- If in doubt, proceed in small steps.
- Plan the validation of the system at the outset and in detail.
- Think about how the system will be maintained.

While all of these suggestions apply equally to traditional systems development, the nature of expertise makes validation and maintenance of KBS particularly important and extremely difficult. Experts are often unsure, rarely know everything, and are learning all the time. Knowledge engineers do not always extract all the relevant knowledge from the domain experts, with the result that some expert knowledge may be missing from the knowledge base. Tasks and conditions change, and unanticipated situations arise leading to the need for new or different knowledge. Often, as users understand KBS and learn how to make these systems work for them, their demands from the KBS increase.

Advanced decision systems are being developed or investigated in virtually every large corporation, and there are many successful applications where a clear bottom line benefit can be demonstrated. These result from the right blend of caution and optimism and putting the right development team in place. These

> systems offer exciting possibilities for problem solving. Like any computer system, however, their success depends on understanding the problem, gaining management commitment, integrating the system into the workflow, winning user acceptance, measuring and demonstrating the results, and ensuring that the system keeps up with company objectives.
>
> From S. Gardiner, Applied Expert Systems: Small Applications, *Solutions* Peat Marwick, January 1988.

SUMMARY

MS/OR models are playing a key role in the development of new technologies to assist managers and improve the effectiveness and efficiency of their decision making.

Advanced decision support technologies (including DSS and KBS) are one competitive weapon in this age of intense, global corporate competition. Several major international corporations have made well-publicized strategic commitments to the use of DSS at high levels of the firm in the expectation that this will improve their competitive positions.

Important examples of the implementation of KBS include DEC, which had early success with a series of KBS to support minicomputer configuration, and Du Pont, where a corporate commitment to KBS has led to the development of literally hundreds of KBS, reportedly saving the company many millions of dollars. At least one of Du Pont's many systems ("Packaging Advisor"; see reading on Du Pont that follows) appears to have provided the company with a significant competitive advantage sustained over a period of time.

Human managers have many unique skills that no computer system yet devised can duplicate, but managers also spend a great deal of their time doing work where computer support can improve both efficiency and effectiveness. Computer systems designed to support managers facilitate the integration of data, models. and knowledge in management decision making. These types of systems, called DSS in the management information systems literature, are developing into the managerial equivalent of "robots"; many expect that their impact will parallel the impact of shop-floor robots on manufacturing employment. If so, organizations that are able to seize these technological opportunities will gain a competitive edge, and the greatly reduced numbers of managers who remain will become very comfortable using new technologies to enhance their productivity.

The future is clear: DSS, KBS, and hybrid managerial support systems will be used in global business competition. Management must decide whether to try to use these technologies to compete and how to react to the use of such advanced systems when used by the competition.

DSS IN ACTION

System Operations Advisor at United Airlines

Operating a fleet of 525 aircraft and more than 2,000 flights daily with a myriad of international destinations, United Airlines has extensively used the power of DSS. MS/OR has been used not only on the strategic and tactical level; the Systems Operations Advisor allows United to use MS/OR at the operational minute-to-minute level as well.

Operations Control Center. The responsibility of United's Operations Control Center in Chicago is to meet departure-completion and customer-service goals in an efficient manner. The five functional groups in the Operations Control Center are meteorology, flight dispatch, flight crew management, in-flight crew management, and system operations control, which is responsible for decisions on delays, cancellations, and routing aircraft for maintenance.

A particular challenge of system operations is to manage aircraft shortages at airports. An aircraft shortage may result from a delayed incoming flight, a canceled incoming flight, or an aircraft with mechanical problems. The nature of the airline industry forces airlines to run as close to capacity as possible due to the high cost of purchasing and maintaining aircraft, with the result that a delay or cancellation in one part of the network can cause secondary delays or cancellations elsewhere. Spare aircraft do exist but may be some distance from the site of shortage, and it not generally economically feasible to fly in a spare aircraft each time a shortage occurs.

Airline operations problems are handled by aircraft controllers in Operations Control. Real-time flight information is provided to these controllers by a transaction-processing mainframe, but unfortunately, the great amounts of textual information and slow interface make this system impractical to use to manage aircraft shortages, especially multiple simultaneous aircraft shortages. United Airlines MS/OR team developed the System Operations Advisor—a real-time decision support system linked to the transaction-processing mainframe—specifically to manage real-time operations.

System Operations Advisor. The System Operations Advisor is composed of three subsystems: the status monitor (SMIT), the delay and swap advisor (DSA), and the cancellation advisor (CAD), which has not yet been implemented. The SMIT system operates through a graphic user interface and alerts controllers of problems such as delays and cancellations. When a delay occurs, the operations controllers switch to the DSA.

Delay and Swap Advisor. Once in the DSA subsystem, the controller selects subfleets of aircraft in which a swap would be allowed. Within each subfleet, the controller can choose to remove a particular aircraft (for example, for maintenance) or restrict an aircraft to only a swap but not a delay. Once the subfleets are selected and constraints entered, the DSA subsystem constructs a minimum-cost-flow network within 5 seconds and displays the solutions in terms of delay passenger minutes (the product of delay minutes and number of passengers affected) and the number of swaps. Using this information, the controller can choose the best option and reschedule or swap flights as necessary.

Value of the System Operations Advisor DSS. In the 6-month period between October 1993 and March 1994, the System Operations Advisor saved more than 27,000 minutes of potential delay. Assuming a conservative cost of $20 per minute, in this short period the system saved United $540,000 in delay costs and, more significantly, reduced the number of delays charged to aircraft controllers by 50%.

From A. Rakshit, et al., System Operations Advisor: A Real-Time Decision Support System for Managing Airline Operations at United Airlines, *Interfaces,* 1996;26:2.

Du Pont's Audit Portfolio DSS

Internal auditing is performed by organizations seeking to maintain the integrity of internal financial controls. This task grows larger and more important as the firm increases in size. For E.I. Du Pont de Nemours and Company, Inc., there are almost 10,000 possible auditable units, with the result that internal auditing is a large and complex task. Because not all 10,000 units can be audited annually, an audit portfolio must be chosen yearly. Choosing this portfolio is paramount to the integrity of the audit. The units chosen have to include the riskiest units (risk defined as audit management's discomfort with failing to audit a particular unit), and over a period of time, all units should be audited. To further complicate selection, a lack of an accepted definition of audit risk means that different managers view different units as having different levels of risk.

Choosing the audit portfolio manually is time and resource consuming and requires a large staff. Du Pont decided to develop a DSS to aid audit unit selection and to manage the dynamic 10,000-unit audit universe.

DSS Challenges. The design of this DSS was an elaborate process that had to encapsulate many components of the audit unit selection process. These included determining an agreed-on list of risk-contributing attributes, identifying the magnitude of the impact of these attributes, fleshing out managers' decision rules for identifying risk, and determining an optimum selection policy.

Ideally, to determine the riskiness of auditable units, Du Pont would like the opinion of all auditing managers on all 10,000 units. "Conceptually, we could envision a voting process in which each member of our audit management team would rank all auditable units in our company's audit universe into risk strata and assign each a position within each stratum" (from *Interfaces*, 1996; 26:3). Because this approach was not feasible, the DSS would have to manage this challenge.

Developing the DSS. The first two steps were to identify and rate, in terms of importance, the risk-contributing attributes. Based on this scale of attributes, each manager was asked to rate his or her segment of units on this scale. From this data, the decision rules used for determining the riskiness of an audit unit by each manager were captured using a statistical analysis.

At this point, the DSS performed **synthetic voting**. In this process, each individual manager's attribute scores of an audit unit were converted to an audit-unit risk value using that manager's decision rules and attribute importance values. These audit-unit risk values were used to vote units into one of four strata: low, moderate, sensitive, or high risk. In this way, the intensity of a manager's opinion on certain criteria was captured.

The final step was to select an audit selection policy that would pull out units to be audited based on audit risk and four other factors: time since last audit, mandatory requirements, changing emphasis of internal auditing, and resource constraints.

Functioning DSS. The completed DSS selected a portfolio by randomly sampling the audit universe after the inclusion or exclusion of necessary units determined using an optimization that ensured that resource constraints were met so the final portfolio was manageable by staff. For completeness and as an aid to understanding, the DSS is also capable of producing 150 reports and statistical tests of the input data and the resulting portfolio.

This DSS has enabled Du Pont to automate the task of synthesizing the opinions of all auditing managers on all auditable units, which was previously thought to be infeasible. The DSS has also guaranteed that no unit goes unaudited for more than 10 years and keeps a database of the dynamic audit universe. Du Pont has also been able to reduce the staff required for internal auditing.

Wayne G. Moore, Regional Audit Manager, wrote, "The system has facilitated the reorganization and productive management of Du Pont's internal auditing functions."

From E. Lieb and J. Gillease, "Du Pont Uses a Decision Support System to Select Its Audit Portfolio," *Interfaces*, 1996;26:3.

Arachne DSS at NYNEX

NYNEX is the regional Bell operating company for the northeastern United States, serving New York, Massachusetts, and the New England states with the exception of Connecticut. The NYNEX network represents a $30 billion investment with additions averaging $2.5 billion annually.

NYNEX interoffice facilities network planners must plan expenditures of $200,000,000 annually to respond to increasing customer demand and intense competition from other telephone carriers. To address this problem, NYNEX Science and Technology organization developed a DSS they named "Arachne."

Jerry Johnson, General Manager of Network Design for NYNEX, stated, "I could not manage without [Arachne]. The developers use sophisticated techniques to produce a [DSS] that addresses my ... planning problem, allowing me to do a faster and better planning job with far fewer resources."

Arachne and the NYNEX Network. The NYNEX network has two parts. The first, called the "local loop," connects customers to one of 1,229 central office switching nodes. The second part of the network are the interoffice facilities (IOF), which link the central offices. These links may be copper cables, fiberoptic cables, or microwaves links carrying digital or analog signals. The objective of Arachne is to ensure that these IOF links are developed in a cost-effective manner to position NYNEX for the future while achieving the maximum benefit for each dollar invested.

Arachne uses the existing network and 5-year demand forecasts for traffic between each pair of central offices to generate a 5-year plan. This plan identifies where NYNEX requires new capacity, what technologies and equipment should be used to develop this added capacity, and how equipment should be moved to accommodate changing demand patterns. Finally, Arachne schedules construction of the new capacity by quarter and computes the cost of the plan.

IOF Planning Process. IOF capacity planning is a very complex problem. The physical links (copper or fiberoptic cables or microwaves) can carry many layers of traffic depending on what equipment is installed at the ends of the links and how the various signals are multiplexed. The first step in creating a new link is to assess whether there is capacity on the available physical links to carry the new demand. If not, a new physical link must be installed, or the demand must be switched on some alternative routing where capacity does exist. Routing decisions made at one level of the network therefore affect routings at other parts of the network.

The data required to evaluate capacity expansion decisions are considerable. They include thousands of nodes and their existing equipment (switches, and so on), tens of thousands of connections, and forecasted demand between each pair of nodes.

Other important features of the planning process include the development and maintenance of a single detailed and accurate view of the network that is used throughout the corporation and differing planning approaches used in different geographical areas (because they differ in traffic density, demand patterns, local government rules, and so on). At any time, NYNEX had a 5-year plan in place, with various projects in different stages of progress: modification of this plan in response to new demand forecasts had to take into account the fact that NYNEX had varying levels of commitment to the projects in progress.

Arachne works with the existing corporate systems and uses a combination of optimization and rules of thumb to develop expansion options for consideration by NYNEX planners. Decomposing IOF planning into three otimizable subproblems and then combining the optimum solutions using sensible rules enables Arachne to derive very good solutions to the overall network planning problem.

Costs and Benefits of Arachne. Arachne cost about $1.2 million to develop initially with approximately $3.7 million further development costs for a total investment of about $5 million.

Before Arachne, the network planners could not complete their task in the 6-month interval between forecasts, but now this process takes about 4 weeks. Planners now have a 5-month window to review and adjust the plan, challenge the rules that they used, and conduct sensitivity analyses. NYNEX now can plan globally, whereas before Arachne, they only had time to plan locally.

The use of Arachne has improved both routing efficiency and network utilization. Improved routing efficiency means that calls are being linked using shorter routes and this tends to depress network efficiency. The improved network efficiency that has resulted indicates that there is now less "spare" capacity on the network. Direct savings were computed for the initial run of Arachne, because on this occasion, the plan developed using Arachne could be compared directly with the plan developed manually.

Through improved balancing of routing efficiency and network utilization, NYNEX avoided $15.7 million in capital expenditures from the first use of Arachne. Arachne's ability to identify links where demand has decreased to a point where capital equipment could be removed for reinstallation elsewhere saved $17.7 million after the first run of Arachne. In addition, the direct interface between the planners, through Arachne, to the corporate database saved $5.0 million annually.

The direct benefits of the first use of Arachne, therefore, were on the order of $33 million for an investment of $5 million.

Johnson stated, "Scientists from NYNEX Science and Technology ... have produced a tool, called Arachne, which I could not manage without, ... allowing me to do a faster and better planning job with far fewer resources."

From T. Barnea, et al., "Arachne: Planning the Interoffice Facilities Network at NYNEX," *Interfaces*, 1996;26:1.

CoverStory: A KBS to Write Marketing News from Data

Ocean Spray Cranberries, a $1 billion fruit-processing cooperative, has developed an expert system, called CoverStory, to automate the processing of data to track their sales and assess the effectiveness of their marketing programs. Before CoverStory, Ocean Spray had to rely on information from such survey and polling companies as SAMI and A.C. Nielsen and data from retail stores and syndicated warehouses.

Point-of-sale computers now collect data on billions of sales transactions every week. The scanning cash register reading bar codes on packages provides many advantages to retailers, including more accurate price input, faster processing of purchased items, and improved inventory control. In addition, these systems have allowed retailers to accumulate information on both individual purchasing habits and individual product and package sales. This information is valuable to managers involved in retail marketing who are interested in maximizing sales of all products and to management at the manufacturer trying to maximize sales of individual products.

However, a major problem exists: the installation of scanners collecting point-of-sale transactions data increases the amount of data available by a factor of 100 to 1000. The issue is how can all these data be processed in a short period to make it available in a timely fashion for management decision making. Any system developed for processing this information must be highly automatic with little human input and must be able to adapt to handle the inevitable growth in the volume of information collected.

Ocean Spray started using Information Resources Inc.'s (IRI) InfoScan national and local market tracking service, which was based on information from 2,500 different scanner-equipped stores and 70,000 individual households. CoverStory was an expert system designed by IRI to analyze this scanner data, which used marketing models (information on displays, features, distribution, pricing, and so on) to determine the top products or markets with respect to change, resulting in a determination of "winners" and "losers." CoverStory then calculated and ranked the possible causes of these changes and produced easily read reports on its findings (Figure 6-3).

CoverStory provides management with summaries and analysis across a wide variety of situations that are used every day in planning and managing: "It no longer seems possible to consider life without it." KBS technology has enabled a single marketing professional to alert Ocean Spray management to key problems and opportunities for four business units with scores of products in dozens of markets representing sales of hundreds of millions of dollars.

From J. D. Schmitz, G. D. Armstrong, and J. D. C. Little, "CoverStory: Automated News Finding in Marketing," *Interfaces*, 1990;20:6.

Cotton Insect Consultant for Expert Management

Millions of dollars are spent each year on applications of insecticides to control cotton pests. In 1987 in Mississippi, $47 million was spent on cotton insect management, but despite this expenditure, an estimated $50 million in cotton yield was lost due to insect damage. An equally important concern was the threat of serious environmental damage posed by inappropriately or poorly timed insecticide application.

Professors R. O. Bowden, R. G. Lutrell, and W. S. Shin at Mississippi State University (MSU) developed an expert system, called the Cotton Insect Consultant for Expert Management (CIC-EM), to help farmers determine the level and type of treatment required to combat any one of 13 cotton insects.

Creating CIC-EM. CIC-EM began with an interview between Lutrell, whose background in entomology qualified him as an expert, and Bowden, whose role was the "knowledge engineer." Bowden developed a program that linked the possible combinations of the crop state variables (At what stage is the crop?) with each of the 13 insects and asked for a recommendation from Lutrell of "spray," "probably spray," "probably not spray," or "do not spray." More than 5,200 scenarios were created for Luttrell to assess and respond to, and common attributes were identified that would allow the knowledge to be summarized in approximately 750 rules.

In designing CIC-EM, blocks of knowledge about each insect were organized into **frames**. These frames allow new information about an insect or even new insects to be incorporated fairly easily. The ability to update the expert system easily is crucial because recommended actions may change as insects develop resistance to insecticides.

Before wide-scale implementation of the system, 13 other researchers were invited to evaluate the system's performance, and 10 of the 13 recommended the system's use. Interestingly, the more experienced researchers were more supportive of the system. This may suggest a reluctance on the part of the younger participants to endorse a system that they perceived might threaten their careers! The only weaknesses of the system identified during this test were its inability to consider the accuracy of the information it processed and extraneous environmental conditions such as weather.

Use of CIC-EM. CIC-EM users, who are likely to be either farmers or representatives of insecticide producers, begin a session by entering background information, which normally includes the planting date and current calendar date but may be expanded to include location, weather conditions, presence of endangered species, or presence of waterways. Next,

Figure 6-3 | **EXAMPLE OF COVERSTORY FRONT PAGE**

To: **Sizzle Brand Manager**

From: **CoverStory**

Date: **07/05/89**

Subject: **Sizzle Brand Summary for 12 Weeks Ending May 21, 1989**

Sizzle's share of type in Total United States was 8.3 in the C&B Juice/Drink category for the 12 weeks ending 5/21/89. This is an increase of 0.2 points from a year earlier but down 0.3 from last period. This reflects volume sales of 8.2 million gallons. Category volume (currently 99.9 million gallons) declined 1.3% from a year earlier.

Sizzle's share of type is 8.3 – up 0.2 from the same period last year.

Display activity and unsupported price cuts rose over the past year – unsupported price cuts from 38 points to 46. Featuring and price remained at about the same level as a year earlier.

partly due to 11.3 pts rise in % ACV with Display vs 1 year ago.

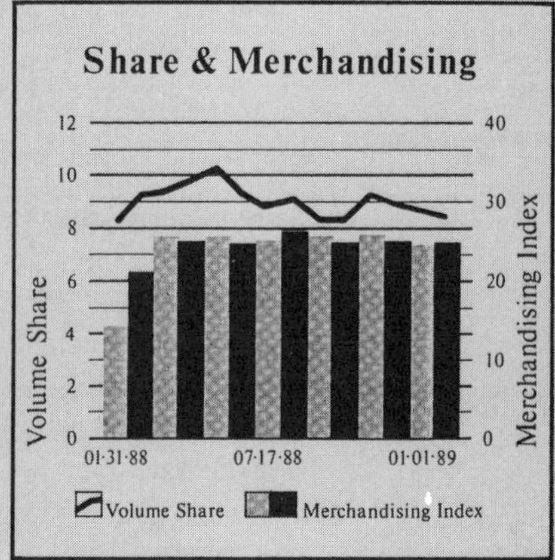

Components of Sizzle Share

Among components of Sizzle, the principal gainer is

Sizzle 64 oz: up 0.5 points from last year to 3.7

and losers:

Sizzle 48 oz - 0.2 to 1.9

Sizzle 32 oz - 0.1 to 0.7

Sizzle 64 oz's share of type increase is

Competitor Summary

Among Sizzle's major competitors, the principal gainers are:

Shakey: up 2.5 points from last year to 32.6

Private Label + 0.5 to 19.9 (but down 0.3 since last period)

and loser

Generic Seltzer - 0.7 to 3.5

Shakey's share of type increase is

Reprinted by permission, J. D. Schmitz, G. D. Armstrong, and J. D. C. Little, "CoverStory—Automated News Finding in Marketing," *Interfaces* 20:6, Copyright 1990, the Institute for Operations Research and the Management Sciences (INFORMS), 901 Elkridge Landing Road, Linthicum, MD 21090 USA.

CIC-EM interacts with the user to determine whether the crop is ahead, on, or behind schedule and, using color graphics to display insect pictures, helps the user to identify the pest in question. Finally, the system analyzes all the information and applies Lutrell's knowledge to suggest action, provide a warning about the dangers of chemical use, and list the necessary application rates. This whole process takes only 3 to 5 minutes.

The strengths of this system lie in its flexibility and user-friendliness, which allow for quick access to an extensive knowledge base. Perhaps more importantly, CIC-EM structures the user's decision-making process, taking some of the guesswork out of a crucial resource allocation issue. CIC-EM's greatest strength may be its ability to minimize environmental impact while simultaneously doing a better job of controlling insects.

Overall Impact. The Mississippi Cooperative Extension Service distributed CIC-EM on a limited basis for the 1991 growing season. Potential savings from implementation could reach $5 million if its recommendations save a single insecticide application per season over the almost 1 million acres of cotton planted in Mississippi alone. This represents a substantial return on a modest development cost.

Speculating about the future, CIC-EM's development could have a major impact on the agricultural industry as a whole. Hard-hit farmers could look to use expert systems as decision-making aids in insecticide applications for other crops, for fertilizer application, or in deciding what seed variety is most appropriate. At a retail level, homeowners might be able to get help to fight common pests in a more ecologically sound manner. Do not be surprised if major chemical producers look to such systems as competitive weapons. A system that recommends only the products of a certain company might be a highly effective sales aid!

From R. O. Bowden, R. G. Luttrell, and W. S. Shin, "Decision Aid for Managing Cotton Insects," *Interfaces*, 1992;22:4.

XCON at Digital Equipment Corporation

Digital Equipment Corporation (DEC) was founded in 1957 by Kenneth H. Olsen to build small, fast computers that were cheap, simple, and fun to design and use. The company started selling circuit modules that later become the building blocks for DEC's first computer, which was called a programmed data processor (PDP-1). These sold for $120,000 at a time when comparable systems were selling for $1,000,000. By the time the PDP-8 was developed, the use of integrated circuits allowed it to be priced at $18,000. This computer was dubbed a minicomputer, and a new generation of computers was born.

The Issue. The underlying technology behind the PDP computers allowed many different combinations of hardware and software to be configured into a working computer. The hallmark of the PDP was the customization of each computer system for each customer. This customization process helped gain customer loyalty, but as new components were introduced, the number of possible computer combinations escalated, and an administrative and manufacturing nightmare resulted.

By 1974-1975, there were 50 types of central processors and 400 core options, each with 10 versions, taking the total possible working combinations into the millions. The complex manufacturing task began with the sales representatives, who took the order and passed it on to the technical editors, who checked it for technical correctness and completeness. This difficult task required many knowledgeable people as well as technical manuals and catalogs. As a result, technical editors had their own solutions and there was no optimal configuration (if it worked ... it was right!): many examples of the "same" system could exist.

A critical manufacturing operation occurred at the final assembly and testing (FAT) plants, where the systems were assembled and tested (and any changes made) and then disassembled to be shipped to the customer. This seemed to be an unnecessary and expensive step, but it was necessary if configuration errors or problems were to be solved away from the customers' premises.

Development of a Solution. A natural step for DEC would be to develop a computer system to configure the PDP computers, and experimentation began in the 1970s using the programming languages of the day (FORTRAN and BASIC). Although these efforts to solve the problem failed, a better understanding resulted. At this point, DEC turned to an academic researcher, John McDermott at Carnegie-Mellon University, who was experimenting with AI. McDermott became interested in the problem and became optimistic about the capability of expert systems to provide a rule-based solution.

The first prototype was called the R1. The Digital staff thought it had potential and should be supported, with the group manager of Systems Manufacturing Administration, David O'Reilly, emerging as the sponsor for the project. McDermott promised that by September 1979 (with the necessary support and funding), R1 would be able to correctly configure 75% of the orders given and be easily modified or extended to configure any orders it configured incorrectly. This program, the first commercial expert system, was delivered a day and a half early. To signify the movement from Carnegie-Mellon to DEC, and the transition from a prototype to a commercial system, R1 was renamed XCON (eXpert CONfigurer).

Implementing XCON. Moving XCON to DEC meant a move from a low-risk experiment staffed by researchers from Carnegie-Mellon to an expensive in-house project staffed by DEC employees. For the system to be useful, it had to be easily modified. Because the program was written in OPS, Digital had to learn this new programming language. Issues in project management, funding, and staffing were all critical. Albert Cavanagh became the first AI Manager at Digital, and much of his time was spent trying to fund AI projects by explaining AI to other departments.

Company initiatives to reduce costs led to a program that specified that each project must pass a strict ROI analysis. Cavanaugh felt he was spending more time justifying his group's existence than doing meaningful work on XCON. Again, O'Reilly emerged as the sponsor and, in an emotional memo to the Operations Committee, asked members to "lay off" XCON.

Despite this rough start, XCON emerged as a success for Digital and provided both cost savings and increased knowledge of the design and use of expert systems.

Results. XCON provided many benefits over manual configuration. Tests showed that XCON could outperform a technical editor in most areas. By December 1979, it was considered superior to human technical editors in areas of consistency, reliability, and transferability to other plants. Furthermore, the program does not forget, obeys every rule, provides a singular configuration authority, and produces more graphic and detailed output.

By 1985, the entire VAX family of systems sold in the United States and Europe were configured by XCON. As Digital's volume increased, no additional technical editors were required. XCON provided about a 98% accuracy rate compared with 65% accuracy for manual configuration. It also increased throughput rate, reduced shipment delays due to configuration errors, and better used the materials on hand. The senior technical editors became available to configure more complex systems. The cost savings were estimated at $15 million per year.

The knowledge gained in this project also led to the use of many other systems, such as XSEL, XSITE, ISA, IMACS, ILRPS, IPMS, and ICSR, in other areas of the organization.

Finally, XCON provided Digital with the reputation of being an expert in the design and use of expert systems.

From J. Martin and S. Oxman, *Building Expert Systems: A Tutorial,* Englewood Cliffs, NJ, Prentice-Hall, 1988, SKUNKWORKS at DEC; "The tale of XCON," Harvard Business School Case 9-687-051, D. Leonard-Barton, "The Case for Integrative Innovation: An ES at Digital," *Sloan Management Review*, Fall 1987.

Expert Systems at Du Pont

The Du Pont Corporation has been an innovator in the use of expert systems. In July 1988, there were about 200 expert systems in routine use throughout Du Pont. By August 1990, the number had increased to more than 600 expert systems, which were estimated to be saving the company more than $75 million annually. By 1991, the annual savings generated were expected to reach $100 million.

Du Pont Corporation. Du Pont is a decentralized organization of 120,000 employees with more than 100 plants worldwide. Du Pont products include fibers, plastics, chemicals, imaging systems, oil, coal, automotive products, electronics, agricultural products, and medical products. Typically, the products sold are several sales away from the end-user. For example, the nylon that Du Pont sells may ultimately end up in the production of carpet that will be sold to a retailer, who in turn sells it to a consumer. Each division is responsible for its own manufacturing, R&D, and information systems. Corporate headquarters provides some centralization and pooling of resources through its Central Research & Development, Engineering, and Information Systems departments.

Competitive pressures have forced Du Pont to take drastic cost-cutting measures. From 1982 to 1987, the workforce at Du Pont was reduced by more than 20% through early retirement incentives. The people who left represented a large portion of Du Pont's expertise and knowledge, and recognition of this, coupled with increased customer demands, prompted Du Pont to put more emphasis on preserving and enhancing its competitive capabilities. One very successful move was to put more decision-making authority into the hands of employees on the plant floor. One of the tools provided to accomplish this task was a network of expert system shells that enabled employees to design their own expert systems.

Ed Mahler, a long-time Du Pont employee, started the Artificial Intelligence (AI) Task Force in 1985 to investigate AI applications for Du Pont. Ed decided not to develop large expert systems that would be used throughout the organization but rather to use expert system shells and assist users in developing their own expert systems. He wanted to provide the education, tools, and support to the divisions so they could build their own expert systems to solve complex problems. Ed believed that the enhancement of decision-making capabilities should be directed at the front-line people who make the decisions, not at those in the head office.

Du Pont's Dispersed Network. This **dispersed approach** to systems development is different from the **specialist approach** used by companies such as Digital Equipment Corporation. The specialist approach involves a centralized development center where specially trained programmers or knowledge engineers use custom tools to create systems (Meador, Mahler, 1990). Du Pont's approach involves putting the decision-making tools into the hands of the decision makers.

Not all organizations are suited for the implementation of this development method. The product and market information required by the individual business unit to operate must be independent from that required by other business units even though administrative information is shared. The products developed must be unique enough to warrant development applications that do not share information with other product developers. The people within each business unit must have the tools and expertise to be able to build their own expert systems. There must be sufficient upper management support to encourage the full education of employees, to ensure widespread acceptance and use of the tools, and to facilitate the necessary cultural change to support the new methods. There are three stages that a company must move through to succeed in a dispersed mode (Meador, Mahler, 1990):

Maverick. A few aggressive pioneers begin to create their own small systems.

Experimentation. The maverick's successes convince a group or manager to address certain problems formally for a trial period.

Culture Change. A group decides to embrace the development of expert systems for a wide variety of applications.

At Du Pont, the manufacturing of its many diverse products requires localized knowledge that differs greatly from one product to another. Even within the 1,700 product lines, great disparity exists because each involves several hundred subtypes of products. Some, such as electronics connectors, have up to 500,000 items in the business unit. With each item being individual, the development expertise required is also individual. Du Pont fosters a high level of independence and technical excellence among its units, which adds to the need to keep decision making at the individual product level.

A philosophy at Du Pont is that bigger is not necessarily better. Problems are broken down into small components, expert system solutions are developed for each component, and then the smaller solutions are later linked to solve large problems.

Table 6-4 shows that expert systems are being used at every step of the product cycle, from customer order input to product shipment (Meador, Mahler, 1990).

Du Pont's hardware systems consist of a variety of mainframes, minicomputers, and PCs. Four large IBM mainframe data centers provide application and database integration for the organization's corporate, department, and business unit levels. The engineering and manufacturing facilities are serviced by Digital VAXs and Hewlett Packard 3000 models. The worldwide offices use a total of 15,000 IBM PCs and 15,000 Apple Macintoshes. There are 30,000 Lotus literate managers and professionals at Du Pont, and more than 1,800 people are now also expert systems literate. The spread of PC-based expert systems use is supported by the existing infrastructure of PCs, whereas the mainframes provide database and communication support. Because the expert system shells used are PC based and user friendly, systems can be developed quickly—from days to months—and relatively cheaply—from a few hundred to a few thousand dollars. Training consists of a basic 2-day course as well as several 1-day specialized courses.

Ed Mahler's vision of letting the decision makers develop their own systems was not something he just decided to implement and then pushed down to the trenches. The feasibility was first tested by a task force that approved 40 different expert system shells to run on the installed workstations and PCs. Senior management agreed to the experiment and provided $3 million in seed money. As the task force saw that successful systems were being generated, a consulting organization within the corporate AI group was chosen to sell the concept, select the standard tools to be used, and establish training programs. Because of the independent nature of the business units, Mahler recognized that change-by-command would not succeed at Du Pont. Therefore, the move toward the use of expert systems was spread by word of mouth using the existing "old boys'" network.

As successes increased in number, so did management support. There was only one hard and fast rule that users had to follow: each system had to have a standard interface for linking into the network and the data files. Otherwise, they could select any of the available tools that would run on their workstations or PCs, and they could develop any system that

Table 6-4 | USES OF EXPERT SYSTEM

Activity	Expert System
Find the customer	Qualification advisor Product advisor (800#?)
Make the right offering	Product selection Pricing advisor
Take the order	Forms advisor Credit risk advisor
Schedule production	Scheduling advisor
Order raw material	Vendor selection PO procedure assistant
Make the product	Machine setup advisor Equipment diagnostics Process diagnostics Control advisors Maintenance advisors Regulatory advisors Procedures advisors
Test the product	Quality assurance Test procedures
Package the product	Labeling advisor
Store and ship product	Warehousing advisor Routing advisor Carrier selection

From C. L. Meador and E. G. Mahler, Choosing an Expert Systems Game Plan, *Datamation,* August 1990.

would help them do their job better. Only 50 of all the systems developed have fallen into disuse; the development time discourages the building of useless systems. The development of duplicate systems is avoided through the use of Du Pont's electronic mail; an employee can put out a call to all 1,800 expert system users to determine whether a similar problem has already been worked out.

Currently, Du Pont has made it through the Maverick and Experimentation stages. The vision that Mahler embraced is on the verge of being fully accepted by several of the business units. In 1990, two of them were developing several hundred systems, and their cultures have already begun to change to adapt to the expert system way of doing business.

Artificial Intelligence Task Force. The AI task force worked on several areas to support the users, including training, advisory expert systems, and technology exploration. The task force used its people to improve custom shells that would help users. They did not work on large-scale projects despite the wishes of Ray Cairns, Vice President of the Information Systems Department, who felt that they should work on larger systems. The AI department recognized that there would be some generic expert systems that could be used to solve similar problems across various business units. For this purpose, competency centers were developed consisting of IS and network professionals to work with business units in the development of systems for such things as real-time process control problems and scheduling systems.

Several concerns face the task force in the future; the greatest are maintaining the task force momentum, monitoring performance, maintaining and tracking the existing systems, supporting end users, and developing better AI tools. As the use of expert systems at Du Pont continues to grow, it will be a challenge to maintain control over what is being developed so people are not continually reinventing the wheel. As the growth of expert system use pushes the culture of the organization into a new realm, there will be unforeseen problems and conflicts that will have to be dealt with.

Ed Mahler. Mahler's vision seems to have become a reality and has brought with it some desirable financial results for the company. One of the reasons that the AI task force has been so successful is that Mahler relied heavily on the existing "old boys'" network at Du Pont to get people to buy into the idea and eventually develop a new network within the AI department.

Mahler has a dynamic personality as well as a personal belief in the expert systems and the people developing them. He uses these characteristics to charge people up, to hold them together, and to be their champion. He believes that his role is to do three things:

1. Help the group develop a vision.
2. Develop a productive work environment.
3. Create a sense of urgency.

His mission is not to build or maintain the systems.

Examples of Expert Systems at Du Pont

Packaging Advisor. This system helps Du Pont customers choose the appropriate materials to be used in the packaging containers manufactured for their specific products. The materials used depend on the type of product, the expected shelf life, and the storage temperature. The customer inputs these variables, and the system advises on the appropriate materials.

Purge Expert. This system automates the purging of impurities from manufactured freon such that maximum impurities are purged with the minimum loss of good product. When done by human operators, the performance levels varied greatly, requiring a batch to be reworked if insufficient impurities were purged, or freon to be wasted if too much material was purged. The system provides consistent performance levels.

Computers and Telecommunication Services Expert System to Diagnose PDP 11/84. This training tool and trouble-shooting guide for repairs of PDP 11/84 computers allowed the number of technicians to be dropped from 10 to four and cut out the need to refer to manuals constantly to interpret manufacturers' codes. One drawback to relying only on the expert system is that the human technicians lose the knowledge of how to diagnose a piece of hardware, which represents the loss of a skill base.

Computers and Telecommunication Services Expert System to Check Hardware Configuration. This system provides a repair technician with the proper configuration for any piece of Ramtek graphics display hardware used in the control rooms at SRW. This information allows proper repair work to be completed before the faulty equipment is reinstalled. Previously, technicians would just reconfigure the repaired part in the same way as before removal from the system; however, often the configuration was faulty, which caused the damage in the first place.

Water Intrusion Expert System. This system was designed to let chemical plant operators at the Sabine Water Works plant in Orange, Texas, know whether more than the optimal percentage of water had been added to the adipic acid. Some water has to be added during the manufacturing process, but at the end all water is distilled out; excess water added increases distillation costs unnecessarily. The system allowed operators to optimize the amount of water added or suggest action in the event that excess water had been added. This system replaces the operator's reliance on Chin Chiao, the plant senior engineer who developed the expert system, to perform the analysis for them.

Transportation Emergency Response System. This system allows people in the field to diagnose, control, and clean up chemical spills occurring in transit.

Maintenance Finish Advisor. This system is used at trade shows to answer customer questions on high-performance paints and to obtain sales leads.

Confidentiality Document Advisor. This system is used to prepare sections of legal documents.

From M. Keil and J. J. Sviokla, Du Pont's Artificial Intelligence Implementation Strategy, Harvard Business School Case 9-189-036, February 1990; J. J. Sviokla, Du Pont's Artificial Intelligence Implementation Strategy: Teaching Note, Harvard Business School Case 5-190-159, May 1990; M. Keil and J. J. Sviokla, Du Pont's AI Task Force: The CTS Expert System, Harvard Business School Case 9-189-067, 1988; M. Keil and J. J. Sviokla, Du Pont's AI Task Force: The Water Intrusion Expert System, Harvard Business School Case 9-189-189, 1989; R. Drawas, A. Metzenbaum, L. Jacobson, and J. Hoffman, AICorp Agrees to Acquire 1st Class Expert Systems, *Business Wire*, Sec. 1, page 1, March 21, 1990; C. L. Meador and E. G. Mahler, Choosing an Expert Systems Game Plan, *Datamation*, August 1990.

EXERCISES

1. Develop a DSS to help a prospective new automobile purchaser or lessor. A new automobile can be purchased outright for a cash amount or purchased for some amount of cash with the balance financed. The amount financed is paid off monthly over some term (usually between 2 and 5 years) with the unpaid balance attracting a monthly interest charge, usually at a fixed rate determined when the loan is signed. Alternatively, the automobile can be leased. Automobile leases are usually for a fixed monthly amount payable at the start of each month and for a fixed term (24 to 48 months). There is often a lump sum payment charged to the lessor, and often the last month's lease payment must be paid up front. Many leases have a "buy-back" provision: the lessor can purchase the automobile at the end of the lease for a fixed amount, which is determined when the lease is signed. Automobile leases often include an extra charge per mile if the automobile is driven more than a predetermined number of miles during the term of the lease. Finally, any cash payments made by the purchaser/lessee must be taken from some investment (such as a saving's account) with a resulting loss of income (usually before tax).
2. Develop a DSS to enable someone to make decisions regarding financial planning for their retirement. An individual of a certain age and annual income has certain expectations about how their income will grow until the date of their retirement (usually age 65 but may be 70 in some cases). The individual can allocate some amount of income to a retirement "fund," which will be invested and can be expected to grow in real terms at some rate. The interest on this fund is usually tax free, as is the annual contribution to this fund up to a certain amount. At retirement, this fund is invested

in an annuity and the payment (interest plus principal) received becomes the retiree's income. This payment may or may not increase with inflation. Annuities expire after a fixed number of years. A retiree may also receive a state or employment-related pension, or both. In planning for retirement, individuals often think in terms of their last year's income: that is: "I would like my annual income when I retire to be at least x% of my final year's salary."

JANICE McCALLUM, R.N., MANAGER NURSING SERVICE

BY GENEVIEVE HAY AND PETER C. BELL

Janice McCallum was manager of nursing services for the fifth floor of the University Hospital. She had been authorized to hire two additional nurses to cover the need for an extra nurse on the night shift, increasing her 12-nurse team to 14 nurses. In addition, one nurse had given notice, and a replacement would have to be hired and trained. These changes meant that she had to develop a new schedule for her nursing staff, a task that she anticipated would take her a few days to complete.

BACKGROUND

Nurse staffing in the hospital was divided by wing and floor number, with a head nurse or a team leader looking after each team. Depending on the number of beds and require care intensity, each floor had up to 50 nurses available for work. Besides the full-time registered nurses, there were part-time registered nurses, nursing assistants, and some nurses who worked at specific times and were not part of the regular schedule. In addition to her other duties, Janice McCallum as manager of nurses was required to develop work schedules for the two teams of nurses who worked on the fifth floor. Developing the work schedules, writing them out, and keeping track of switches, vacations, and absences due to sickness or personal holidays was a time-consuming task.

Janice had two teams to schedule for two 12-hour shifts each day. One team with 12 nurses worked on the Cardiology/Hematology ward. Previously, four nurses were needed on each day shift and two on each night shift, but in the future, the same number would be needed on the day shift, but three were needed on each night shift. The second team was made up of 10 nurses who worked on the General Medicine ward. Three nurses were needed on each day shift and two on each night shift. The number of nurses per shift was determined by the head nurse based on a balance between budget and nursing care considerations.

THE SCHEDULE

The method used to develop a final work schedule was to develop a schedule in the form of master rotation pattern (see Exhibit 1). This pattern had one row for each nurse and one column for each working day. Each row represented a 1-week schedule. The nurses worked through each row, transferring from one row to the next at week end, such that within each team, over the period of either 10 or 12 weeks, each nurse was rotated through the entire master rotation pattern.

The master rotation established a basic work pattern whose columns gave the total shift coverage. (This was calculated by summing in a column, say Tuesday, the number of nurses who were working a particular shift, either day or night.) Construction of a master rotation pattern that met all of the nurses preferences was difficult. Over a 2-week period, the nurses worked an average of 3½ shifts per week. The nurses preferred not to work more than 2 weeks on nights in a row. Between work stretches, nurses preferred 2 days off. This time off was especially important when switching from nights to days. Sometimes the conditions change; nurses wanted 72 hours off when switching from nights to days, or the nurses wanted the stretch of weeks on a particular shift to change (for example, to have 3 weeks of nights rather than 2). When the shift coverage changed, the master rotation pattern had to be revised to accommodate the new requirements or a part-time nurse had to be hired. (This was not preferred because it took time for a nurse to adjust to the specific requirements of the floor.)

Janice used the master rotation pattern to develop a full work schedule, either 10 or 12 weeks long depending on the team. For each week of the work schedule, the master rotation was simply shifted by a week, and this ensured that over the whole period, each nurse went through the entire pattern. It was, therefore, important to make sure that most of the nurses' preferences were met by the master rotation.

The work schedule then had to be modified to suit the

individual preferences regarding vacation time, statutory holidays, and weekends off. The schedule had to be as uniform as possible to ensure the nurses worked the correct average number of shifts a week because each nurse's paycheck was based on the actual number of hours worked in the 2-week period. Nurses liked to receive even paychecks, although this was not entirely possible because night shift work was paid at a higher rate than day shift.

New nurses arriving on the floor worked special schedules during a 4-week training period. They worked 2 weeks on 8-hour shifts on days, Monday to Friday, followed by 1 week of three 12-hour days and two 12-hour nights. After this, they were put onto the regular schedule, taking over for the nurse leaving. During the 4-week training period, the trainee was an extra nurse on duty.

SCHEDULING PROBLEM

Other considerations faced by Janice were how to minimize the use of part-time nurses, how to meet as many nurse preferences as possible, and how to deal with different day to day shift staffing requirements. Many hospitals worked their staff on 8-hour shifts; perhaps the effects of such a change should be investigated?

Janice's immediate problem was how to change the existing 12-nurse pattern to a 14-nurse pattern. As she took out the scheduling forms and looked ahead to writing out, first 14 weeks of a schedule for 14 nurses and then a 10-week schedule for 10 nurses, it occurred to her that a computer should be able to do this task for her. Clearly, the computer could easily print out a schedule from any master rotation pattern, but Janice wondered if the computer could also created the required master rotation?

Assignment

1. How could a simple spreadsheet model help the scheduler; what could a simple model do and what could it not do?
2. Develop a spreadsheet model to assist Janice McCallum (Try to make your model as user-friendly as possible).

Exhibit 1 | **12-WEEK MASTER ROTATION PATTERN USED BY JANICE McCALLUM, R.N., FOR THE 12-NURSE TEAM**

M	T	W	T	F	S	S
D	D			D	D	D
		N	N			
N	N			N	N	N
		D	D			
D	D			D	D	D
		D	D			
N	N			N	N	N
		N	N			
D	D			D	D	D
		D	D			
D	D			D	D	D
		D	D			

CON-TEST: AN EXPERT SYSTEM AT A STEEL WORKS

Jack Davidson, superintendent of casting at the continuous casting (CONCAST) machine at the Parry Sound works of the International Steel Corporation, was being asked to install an expert system to diagnose faults in the slab auto level control system.

INTERNATIONAL STEEL CORPORATION

International Steel Corporation (ISC) was a major international manufacturer of iron, steel, and steel products. As was the case for most major steel corporations, the early 1980s had been a difficult period during which imports from Japan and third-world countries had eroded ISC's market share in its traditional markets, particulárly in North America. As a result, ISC had reported heavy losses for several years and was in the process of "downsizing" both its capacity and workforce.

CONTINUOUS CASTING MACHINE

ISC's integrated steel complex on the banks of the River Ehen had been developed in the late 1970s. The complex used relatively new continuous casting technology to produce a broad range of steel products.

Before the development of continuous casting, the standard basic shapes of semifinished steel were produced by casting the molten steel into ingots. These ingots were then placed in soaking pits to bring them to a uniform temperature before being passed to the primary rolling mills, which rolled them into three products:

Slabs (rectangular product for making plate or sheet)

Blooms (product 150 to 300 millimeters square for making heavy forgings, heavy section, or rails)

Billets (product 50 to 125 millimeters square for conversion into bars, rods, light sections, or tubes)

In the continuous casting process, instead of going through the ingot stage before being reheated and rolled, the molten metal was poured ("teemed") directly into a casting machine to produce the slabs, blooms, or billets. Continuous casting, therefore, eliminated the need for primary and intermediate rolling mills, soaking pits, and the storage and use of a large number of ingot molds. It also increased the yield of usable product from a given weight of steel.

ISC's CONCAST machine had 12 lines: seven producing blooms (about 200 millimeters square) and five producing slabs (about 600 × 400 millimeters).

At the head of each line, the molten steel from the steel-making vessel was teemed from a ladle into a preheated refractory-lined trough called a tundish. From the tundish, the metal flowed into a rectangular water-cooled copper mold that oscillated up and down for set distances at strictly controlled rates during casting. This oscillation overcame the one-time problem of the metal sticking to the walls of the mold. Inside the mold, the liquid metal froze forming a solid skin around a core that remained liquid. The rate of casting was controlled by the withdrawal speed of the slab or bloom, which was accomplished by two sets of rolls that gripped the steel without distorting its shape. The steel was cooled by carefully controlled jets of water while being guided through a secondary cooling chamber—the rate at which the metal was allowed to cool was critical to achieve a perfect product. At the bottom of the casting machine, the product was cut to length and passed to the next stage of manufacture.

FAULT DIAGNOSIS IN THE SLAB AUTO LEVEL CONTROL SYSTEM

Operation of the CONCAST machine was carried out by an automatic control system that controlled a number of key parameters. One of these was the level of the molten metal in the oscillating bath above the mold. If this oscillating liquid level wandered out of range on either level or rate of change of level, then the auto-control system took action. This action ranged from a warning light to a complete line shutdown, depending on the severity of the fault.

Standard operating practice called for the equipment operator to call for a maintenance engineer whenever trouble was indicated. A delay often resulted, since the engineers were often some distance away or were all working on high-priority jobs elsewhere at the plant. Adding to the aggravation of these delays was the fact that after the engineer had arrived and diagnosed the problem, the trouble was often quite minor and could be fixed by the operator.

In response to this situation, the Office of the Chief

Engineer had developed an "expert system" and was proposing that it be installed at the casting machine.

EXPERT SYSTEM

The expert system was a computer program that attempted to duplicate the diagnostic procedures followed by the maintenance engineer. The program was to be accessible to the plant operator, either by using a portable microcomputer or by using a microcomputer with several input/output stations distributed around the casting machine.

When a fault was signaled by the automatic control system, the plant operator started the expert system. The expert system asked the plant operator to input data about the state of the casting machine or to perform certain tests and input the results, in much the same way that the engineer would gather the facts necessary to diagnose the fault.

The output from a sample fault diagnosis run of the expert system is included in Exhibit 1.

The expert system had been developed by engineering using a commercial expert system "shell" that absolved the system developer of the need to program the system. The expert system shell required the system developer to input three system components: a list of the possible faults, the tests needed to diagnose the faults, and a tree structure (input in a tabular form) that presented the sequence in which the tests were performed.

Thirty-one faults that engineering had identified that could be repaired by the plant operators were included in the expert system. Other faults were so serious that engineering would have to be called, or if the diagnostic tests indicated problems with an instrument, the program provided a maintenance contact at the instrument manufacturer.

Fault diagnosis required the expert system designer to lay out a diagnostic tree and a library of questions (or dialog) to enable the user to input the results of each diagnostic test. Several different types of tests could be used, depending on the possible responses (for example, "Yes/No" or "Yes/No/Don't Know" or menu responses, and so on).

An important element of system design was the order in which the tests were carried out. This problem could be thought of in terms of a tree structure with different levels of tests. At the outset, there were several different tests or questions that could be asked independently–these were **level 1 tests**. Each response to a level 1 test could be followed by a **level 2 test** that was only useful if done after a specific response to a level 1 test. Similarly, **level 3 tests** were only used conditional on a certain response to a level 2 test, and so on.

Because only a single test could be done at one time, the system design problem was:

1. To choose the test to be done first from the list of possible level 1 tests
2. To choose the test to be done second from the remaining level 1 tests and from the list of level 2 tests that could be done given the result of the first test
3. To choose the third test from the remaining level 1 tests, the list of level 2 tests that were eligible given the results of the level 1 tests, and from the list of level 3 tests that were eligible if the second test was a level 2 test, and so on

Because a very large number of test sequences were possible, the system designer had had to identify a suitable criterion to use to plan the "best" sequence of tests. Some factors that had influenced the sequencing problem included the costs of the different faults (some permitted operation at reduced capacity whereas others resulted in complete plant shutdown), the costs of the different tests, and the frequency with which the different faults occurred.

After the faults had been identified and the test dialog developed, the expert system shell created the expert system application, so the engineer creating the system did not have to do any computer programming.

Exhibit 1 | EXAMPLE OF FAULT DIAGNOSIS AND RECOVERY USING EXPERT SYSTEM

```
            *********** CON-TEST EXPERT SYSTEM ***********
            ** THIS SYSTEM IS DESIGNED TO ASSIST IN THE **
            ** DIAGNOSIS OF FAULTS ON THE PARRY CONCAST **
            ** AUTO LEVEL CONTROL SYSTEM.               **
            ** THE SYSTEM WAS DESIGNED BY ISC LABS.     **
            **********************************************

Do you have a fault ? Y
Does the fault occur :-
 1. ON LOCAL TEST ?
 2. ON STOPPER TEST ?
 3. ON DETECTOR CALIBRATION ?
 4. ON AUTO SELECT ?
 5. DURING AUTO CASTING ?
 6. CONTROL SYSTEM SETTINGS AND ACTUATOR TESTS ?
 7. EXIT FROM FAULT DIAGNOSIS SYSTEM ?
5
Has the alarm bell on the operators pendant been
intermittently sounding ?
Y
Are there large deviations in level control ?
Y
Does the stopper slowly open and then close rapidly ?
N
Does the stopper position trace on the chart recorder show
large variations in stopper position (greater than + or - 2
divisions on chart recordings) ?
N
Was the slide gear stiff in manual control ?
N
Poor control could be caused by a build up of slag on top of
the tundish steel level, restricting stopper movement.
Investigate and correct if possible. After end of test,
check setting of equipment.
To return to fault menu type Y
To return to system setting data type N
N
Which system setting do you require ?
 1. THE KENT P4000 CONTROLLERS.
 2. THE MOOG ELECTRONICS RACK.
 3. THE SIGNAL CONDITIONING ELECTRONICS RACK.
 4. THE HYDRAULIC ACTUATOR RESPONSES.
 5. LIST OF EQUIPMENT SUPPLIERS.
 6. TO EXIST FROM MENU.
2
THE MOOG ELECTRONICS SETTINGS:
Servo valve drive card:
      GAIN POT SETTING: 9.75 - 9.85
      ZERO POT SETTING: 10.0
Do you want the oscillator/demodulator settings?
Y
      OSCILLATOR/DEMODULATOR ELECTRONICS CARD
      GAIN POT SETTING: 0.65 - 0.75
      ZERO POT SETTING: 1.35 - 2.1
```

Exhibit **I CONTINUED**

```
Do you require the comparator card settings ?
N
DO YOU WISH TO RETURN TO MAIN FAULT FINDING ROUTINE ?
Y
Does the fault occur :-
1. ON LOCAL TEST ?
2. ON STOPPER TEST ?
3. ON DETECTOR CALIBRATION ?
4. ON AUTO SELECT ?
5. DURING AUTO CASTING ?
6. CONTROL SYSTEM SETTINGS AND ACTUATOR TESTS ?
7. EXIT FROM FAULT DIAGNOSIS SYSTEM ?
2
Have you tried the Local Test routine ?
Y
Is the tundish car umbilical cable plugged in correctly and
making good contact ?
(MAKE SURE THAT THE CABLE IS NOT CONNECTED UPSIDE DOWN)
Y
Is the pendant auto/manual switch in the manual position ?
Y
When the pendant stopper button is depressed does the stopper
test light illuminate ?
Y
When the stopper test button is depressed and the stopper
test pot is turned clockwise or anticlockwise does the
actuator move ?
Y
Does the actuator follow the stopper pot movement and hold
it's position without drift ?
(NOTE: THE STOPPER TEST BUTTON ON THE OPERATOR'S PENDANT MUST
BE DEPRESSED THROUGHOUT THIS OPERATION)
N
Are the actuator hydraulic hoses connected correctly ?
(Examine the colour codes for top and bottom)
Y
Does the MOOG oscillator card give 1 volt when the actuator
is retracted and 9 volts when the actuator is fully extended
?
(CHECK THE READING ON THE EDGEWISE METER ON THE KENT P4000
STOPPER CONTROLLER)
N
Are the gain and zero pots on the MOOG OSCILLATOR/DEMODULATOR
board at the main control cabinet set correctly ?
[Approx. settings: GAIN 1.7 Zero 0.7]
N
ADJUST GAIN AND ZERO POTS TO SPECIFIED SETTINGS
```

(continued)

MAKING THE EXPERT SYSTEM "INTELLIGENT"

Another feature that had been discussed was the idea of making the expert system "intelligent."

The system designer had used historical data on the frequency of the possible faults in the design of the test sequence; for example, other things being equal, the most frequently occurring fault was tested for first.

As the system was used, data on the faults identified by the system could be collected at execution time. If the fault frequencies were found to be markedly different from the historical data used to develop the initial system, then the engineering department could be brought back in to redesign the system and reorder the tests. Alternatively, the system could be designed to do this reordering automatically; the system itself could adapt to changing fault frequencies. This could then be considered to be an intelligent expert system.

If it was decided to go ahead with this type of system, the rules to decide when test sequences should be changed would have to be developed.

DECISION TO INSTALL THE EXPERT SYSTEM

Jack Davidson believed that because the expert system had been designed by the same engineers who normally diagnosed and repaired faults at the casting machine, then the logic of the system should be acceptable, but several other issues were a basis for some concern.

Was the expert system efficient, or would it lead to the plant operators spending a lot of time on unnecessary tests?

Were the advantages of the expert system sufficient to overcome the extra costs that it imposed on the plant operators?

If the expert system were installed and used for a period of time, would the system become out of date?

What procedures should be put in place to maintain the system?

Was an "intelligent" system viable?

Assignment

1. Can the design problem be structured as a tree?
2. What decisions does the designer have to make? What criteria should be used to make these decisions?
3. Any decision analysis of the design problem is necessarily complex because of the large number of options. Can you come up with a rule of thumb that would give a "good" but not necessarily the "best" design?
4. Can you suggest an approach to make the system "intelligent"?

A WELL-KNOWN BUSINESS SCHOOL

Wayne Simbirski, Admissions Officer at a well-known business school, had heard that an expert system could "make" decisions that were usually made by human experts.

The school had recently acquired an expert system development tool (or shell) that was advertised as being exceptionally easy to use. A casual meeting with one of the professors responsible for introducing the shell to the school suggested to Wayne that there may be applications for the use of expert systems within the school's admissions process. In particular, the professor mentioned that he had attended conference sessions where speakers had discussed the use of an expert system to select scholarship winners and to select applicants for admission to programs. The latter example was particularly appealing because every year the school had to trim more than a thousand M.B.A. program applicants down to just a few hundred admission offers.

The professor also mentioned that the first stage of expert system design was for the expert to start thinking about the expertise. Wayne saw all the applicant's files and although he had no say in the actual admissions decisions (which were made by the admissions committee of the faculty), his access to the files and the decisions that had been made suggested to him that he should be able to formalize the admissions decision process.

ADMISSION DECISION

Students applying to the well-known business school had to submit several pieces of essential data. This included their score on the Graduate Management Admission Test (or GMAT), the transcript from their first degree program, a record of their work experience, a short essay on why they wanted to attend the well-known business school, and a description of their nonacademic activities and interests.

The first stage of the admission process was to assign

two marks to each student using the scale A (excellent), B (above average), C (average), and D (below average). The first mark was given for the essay, and the second for the degree of excellence displayed in activities unrelated to academic work or normal job responsibilities.

The marks for the essay and nonacademic activities, GMAT, undergraduate record, and work experience were important factors in the admission decision.

GMAT scores typically ranged from 450 to 800, with the higher scores preferred.

Undergraduate record was shown in many different ways on the student's transcripts. Wayne computed each applicant's grade point average (**GPA**) and made a minor adjustment to reflect known differences between universities and programs. **GPA** was measured on a scale from 4 to 1, where 4 indicated an A average in an excellent program at a first-class university.

Not all applicants submitted university transcripts; if none was submitted, Wayne assumed that the applicant had not previously attended university.

Work experience was computed by summing the applicant's months of full-time work experience. A qualitative parameter that was sometimes important was the relevance of the work experience; a month working as a research assistant at a university was not seen as being as relevant as a month working in a bank. To account for this, Wayne computed a "relevant work experience" total for each applicant by summing the number of months of relevant full-time work and half the number of months of less relevant full-time work.

ADMISSION CRITERIA

Admissions decisions were the responsibility of a faculty admissions committee that made one of four decisions:

A. Accept for admission unconditionally.
B. Offer a deferred admission for the next year conditional on the applicant obtaining an additional 12 months of relevant work experience before admission.
C. Send a "weak" rejection letter, encouraging the applicant to reapply at a later date.
D. Send a "strong" rejection letter.

There was an unofficial document that listed the general criteria for admission. These criteria were known to the admissions committee, but it seemed to Wayne that the committee used these as a general guide only and did not adhere to them rigorously. The listed criteria for admission were:

1. Any two from a GMAT score of at least 600, a GPA of at least 3.5, or 5 or more years of relevant work experience, or
2. At least 5 years of relevant work experience, and both a GMAT of at least 500 and a GPA of at least 2.5, or
3. At least 5 years of relevant work experience, a GMAT of at least 500, a mark of A for "excellence" and a mark of A or B on the essay, or
4. At least 3 years of relevant work experience, a GMAT of at least 550, a GPA of at least 3.0, and at least marks of B for both "excellence" and the essay, or
5. At least 1 year of relevant work experience, a grade of A for "excellence," a GPA of at least 3.5 and a GMAT of at least 500

A deferred admission was offered to any applicant who qualified for admission according to the above criteria except for being deficient in work experience. Admission was conditional on the applicant gaining the necessary work experience before entry to the program. Only 1-year deferals were offered; applicants needing more than 1 year of additional work experience were rejected but encouraged to gain the needed experience and then reapply.

Applicants were rejected outright if they had a degree but did not report a GPA of at least 2.5 and a GMAT of at least 500, or, if they had no degree, reported a GMAT below 550, and a mark for "excellence" of C or D.

All others who failed to be accepted were encouraged to reapply at some future time.

EXPERT SYSTEM

Wayne has heard of expert systems with thousands of rules. The admissions decision seemed to him to be fairly straightforward. He wondered whether he could use the expert system shell to build an "M.B.A. Program Admissions Advisor" expert system.

As a first step toward investigating the possibility of such a system, Wayne collected together some examples of the actions of the admissions committee (Exhibit 1).

Assignment

1. What knowledge is used in the admission decision?
2. Can you represent this knowledge as a set of rules?

Exhibit 1 | SOME EXAMPLES OF ADMISSIONS DECISIONS

File No.	GMAT	GPA	Relevant Work Experience (months)	Essay Mark	Activity Mark	Result
1	665	3.80	4	B	D	A
2	604	N.T.	71	C	C	A
3	622	2.75	49	D	C	B
4	465	3.72	62	C	C	A
5	484	3.78	52	C	D	B
6	612	3.03	84	D	D	A
7	712	3.13	54	B	D	B
8	645	2.64	60	B	B	A
9	623	2.89	53	A	A	B
10	576	3.44	65	A	C	A
11	552	3.20	47	C	A	B
12	595	2.87	61	B	B	A
13	587	2.77	44	A	B	B
14	551	N.T.	75	B	A	A
15	555	N.T.	45	B	A	B
16	501	1.66*	71	A	A	A
17	537	1.33*	46	B	A	B
18	696	3.33	52	A	A	A
19	677	3.20	37	B	A	A
20	555	3.10	49	A	A	A
21	571	3.13	39	B	A	A
22	642	3.37	52	B	B	A
23	613	3.19	42	A	B	A
24	577	3.41	52	B	B	A
25	557	3.27	40	B	B	A
26	592	3.60	14	C	A	A
27	580	3.92	3	D	A	B
28	520	3.51	14	C	A	A
29	513	3.81	5	D	A	B
30	509	3.55	26	C	A	A
31	502	3.98	27	A	A	A
32	576	3.92	39	C	A	A
33	520	3.77	43	C	A	A
34	497	2.20*	84	A	A	D
35	523	N.T.	54	A	C	D
36	457	2.64*	60	B	D	D
37	460	3.51	53	A	A	C

(continued)

Exhibit I | **CONTINUED**

File No.	GMAT	GPA	Relevant Work Experience (months)	Essay Mark	Activity Mark	Result
38	490	2.55	66	A	B	C
39	492	3.26	12	C	B	C
40	495	3.67	37	B	A	C
41	472	3.52	38	A	B	C
42	499	3.57	26	C	A	C
43	494	3.62	27	D	B	C
44	478	3.60	14	A	A	C
45	478	3.70	17	D	B	C
46	485	3.71	3	D	A	C
47	477	3.51	6	C	B	C
48	525	3.10	5	A	B	C
49	528	2.13*	13	C	B	C
50	518	3.37	26	B	B	C
51	506	N.T.	39	C	B	C
52	554	3.44	9	B	C	C
53	567	3.37	14	B	B	C
54	593	3.33	29	A	C	C
55	560	2.89	0	A	A	C
56	555	2.45	9	C	D	C
57	490	2.55	14	A	A	C
58	592	2.47	19	B	C	C
59	570	2.72	28	A	A	C
60	552	2.32	26	A	C	C
61	560	2.67	37	B	A	C
62	587	2.42	43	C	C	C
63	604	3.34	9	A	B	C
64	620	3.10	19	D	A	C
65	617	3.22	35	C	A	C
66	640	2.71	8	B	B	C
67	629	2.80	14	A	B	C
68	666	2.73	32	C	B	C
69	600	2.51	47	B	B	C
70	607	2.43	11	C	B	C
71	626	2.48	23	A	C	C
72	647	2.07	24	B	B	C
73	611	2.41	36	C	C	C

N.T. = No transcript submitted.
* = Unofficial transcript.

MUTUAL LIFE ASSURANCE COMPANY: THE KNOWLEDGE ENGINEERING GROUP

BY BETTY VANDENBOSCH, UNDER THE DIRECTION OF PROFESSOR PETER C. BELL; REVISED BY PETER C. BELL.

By June 1990, the first production expert system at Mutual Life Assurance Company of Canada (Mutual) had been in use for almost four months. Brian Cooper, leader of the Knowledge Engineering Group (KEG), which had developed the Group Quotes expert system ("Quality Underwriting-Intelligent Calculations," or QU-IC) wondered what the future should hold for further expert systems development at Mutual.

Thanks to the information sessions arranged by the KEG with help from Bill Yeo, Vice President-Information Systems, senior management seemed to understand the potential for expert systems, and seemed eager to move forward. Mutual was in the last stages of purchasing a mainframe expert system shell that should facilitate the embedding of expert systems logic into traditional applications and enable expert systems to become a part of mainstream data processing.

KEG now consisted of five experienced and capable knowledge engineers but did not yet have a major new application to develop. Should the group focus on finding major new applications? Should they concentrate on bringing expert systems into the mainstream of data processing? Should they make expert systems an available tool for end-user computing? Should they do all of these things? What was the best way to proceed?

MUTUAL GROUP

The Mutual Group was a broad-based group of financial services companies, active in life and health insurance, investments, financial management and counselling, property management, and oil and gas exploration. In 1989, it had assets of $12.5 billion, revenue of $3.3 billion, net income of $125 million, and more than 2,800 employees. The Mutual Life Assurance Company was the lead company of the group, providing life and health insurance, reinsurance, annuities, RRSPs, pensions, mortgages, real estate financing, and corporate lending. According to *Canadian Business*, the Mutual Group was the sixth largest life insurance company in Canada in 1989 (J. Matthews, Pacesetting Service Firms, July 1990, p. 60).

INFORMATION SYSTEMS AT MUTUAL

The Information Systems (IS) Division at Mutual Life had an objective to stay at the forefront of relevant technology and had committed significant resources to research and development, often ahead of many of its competitors. As a result, Mutual often used IS as a way to recruit top-quality people. There was a great deal of movement from IS to the other divisions in the company, so there was good understanding and support of IS throughout the organization.

A staff of more than 300 worked in the IS division at The Mutual Group's head office (Exhibit 1 shows the organizational structure of the division).

Industry cost studies typically showed that Mutual spent a greater proportion of its general and administrative expenses on data processing than its competitors of a similar size and that, overall, general and administrative expenses were lower than those of similar firms. Mutual users were involved in every aspect of the development process. Developers were organized into resource teams by lines of business. Users determined development priorities and were clearly the owners of the systems that were developed. The development process always included joint application design (JAD) sessions among users and developers. End-user computing had been encouraged since the late 1970s.

Employees who had experience in other organizations found that the tool kit that Mutual used for systems development had a much higher degree of integration than was the norm in the industry. In 1985, Mutual began using a tool to automate several aspects of the systems analysis and design process, including helping systems professionals develop systems diagrams and models, validate design data, prototype screens and reports before coding, and create user- and system-related documentation. The IS division found that automating analysis and design allowed production of more thorough and consistent designs, which resulted in better quality systems. (C. Trudel, "CASE Tool Delivers an Assist," *Computing Canada*, May 25, 1989, page 28.)

A successfully piloted document image processing

system illustrated how new technology was typically introduced at Mutual. Bill Yeo and the interested user group agreed that the time had come to experiment so they invested in the system. They shared the cost so the first user would not be burdened with learning costs that would ultimately benefit the entire organization. An article about the system appeared in a computing magazine (*Computing Canada*, July 1989).

EXPERT SYSTEMS AT MUTUAL

David Blackburn, a senior systems engineer at Mutual Life, became interested in expert systems in 1984 and was soon joined by Brian Cooper. Both had come from Support Services and began by doing a lot of reading about the technology. As soon as they were convinced that expert systems might hold promise for Mutual, they surveyed senior managers to find a place to try the new technology. The Mutual Financial Planning subsidiary (MFP) appeared to have a problem that was amenable to an expert systems solution.

MFP consisted of eight offices across the country, each with a few executive financial planners responsible for providing individuals with customized tax and investment advice. The expert system, called FAST (Financial Analysis Support Tool), was designed to support the financial analysis component of the planning process.

Mutual ordered two Xerox LISP machines in August 1985 and purchased an expert system shell called KEE from Intellicorp Inc. The machines arrived in early 1986, and Dave and Brian, together with Kam Lafontaine, an expert planner, started immediately. Dave thought they probably rewrote FAST three times as they experimented with a number of approaches.

Typically, the team would meet and discuss the system and financial planning until they had filled a white board full of notes. Dave and Brian would work on that for a day or two, at which time the team would get back together, review progress, and fill in the gaps that had appeared on the white board as a result of the features that had been implemented. There was always more work on the white board, but they never tried to implement all of the ideas before having Kam come back for another look at the progress they had made. The idea was to keep the iterative process going and never implement so much that they would hesitate to retrace their steps.

While the FAST system was being developed, Xerox announced that it would no longer support the LISP machines Mutual was using. KEG then ordered Sun workstations to replace the Xerox equipment, and they were forced to convert all the software already developed.

The FAST system was ready for implementation in mid-1988 after about 250 days of development time (each day of development time was estimated to cost between $300 and $500). Unfortunately, by that time, the window of opportunity had closed, and FAST was no longer a high priority–executive financial planners had been shifted into a much greater agent support role and could no longer justify the expense of FAST, which was designed for a more sophisticated planning process.

Although the system was in production for only a short time, the participants learned a great deal about how to develop expert systems during the process, an important objective at the outset. While they were converting the system from Xerox to Sun equipment, the group was already looking for another application of expert systems technology.

They found Group Quotes.

QUOTATIONS IN THE GROUP INSURANCE DIVISION

In 1987, the underwriting group in the Group Insurance division realized they had to improve the systems support available for the quotation process. What were once straightforward quotation calculations for group clients, had evolved into complicated, time-consuming, number-crunching procedures. Over the years, the quotation procedures manual had become incredibly complicated and full of special exceptions as a consequence of the increasingly competitive environment Group Insurance faced.

The underwriters were doing a remarkable job using a patchwork of support tools consisting of a mainframe application, APL programs designed by Group actuaries, PC programs, and many many manual calculations. The underwriters were limited in their ability to undertake "what if" analyses because the turnaround required by brokers and the sales force was short, whereas the turnaround provided by the system was long. In addition, it was difficult for underwriters to thoroughly research unusual requests because most of their time was spent on rate calculation.

An expert system was conceived to make the difficult and time-consuming rate calculation aspect of the underwriters' job easier and to produce client quotes more quickly. The objective was to integrate all of the data and procedures required for the entire quotation process.

The first step was to build a prototype to prove that the expert system was a viable solution. A single benefit, the long-term disability benefit was chosen because it was considered to be one of the most difficult to support. The prototype was demonstrated to the senior people in the underwriting group, who were anxious to see the progress that had been made. Bill Yeo also arranged a technology session to showcase QU-IC to the senior executives of the company. KEG believed that the process of demonstrating the system as often as possible was important to maintain a high level of commitment throughout the project.

In March 1989, the *Financial Post* reported that Executive Vice-President David MacIntosh told the annual meeting that the company would spend $250,000 on an expert systems project. The pressure was on to perform. Once the prototype was approved, development of QU-IC took about 1 year with a team of two full-time and three part-time developers working with two experts.

Brian described the development as follows:

> The quotation process was the most complicated thing I hope I ever try to program. It was riddled with exceptions and special cases. It was not exhaustively documented or consistently applied from underwriter to underwriter. There were so many variables and special cases that I doubt we would ever have been able to write specifications for this system. At times it seemed we would never get it right (as we iterated over and over and over), but we did it and the result is better than I think we really expected or hoped it would be.

One of the real challenges was to make the quotation system a "white" rather than a "black" box; just to output a final rate would not have been acceptable. The process had to be transparent, giving the underwriter access to the calculations throughout. In addition, the expertise of senior underwriters had to be built in.

Another difficult aspect of QU-IC's development was the testing and validation phase. About 1 month's worth of historical case studies were tried using the system, and the results were compared with the underwriters' actual recommendations. These cases then formed the basis of a test system to allow ongoing validation as QU-IC inevitably was enhanced.

QU-IC asked underwriters to describe the benefit requested by the prospective group; the type of business of the group;, the age, sex, income, and job titles of all group members; past benefit programs; and the claims history. From this information, QU-IC calculated rates that should be charged for the policy and checked for and noted any unusual situations that should be brought to the underwriter's attention (for example, good or bad claim experience for specific benefits, or an unusual age distribution in the group). The underwriter then used the reports from the analysis to investigate and tune the rate—there were literally hundreds of ways the underwriter could introduce discretionary changes into the pricing procedure.

Nine Sun workstations (each costing about $18,000) were purchased in late 1989 for the Group Quotes system, which went into full operation in February 1990.

By June, the 14 underwriters in the group had processed over 500 quotations using QU-IC. Mutual now owned 22 Sun work stations: 15 for use in Group Quotes and seven for development.

Only 4 months after its implementation, the underwriters believed that developing quotes using QU-IC was both faster and more effective than the old way. Typically, it took about 3 years for an underwriter to become proficient (turnover in the financial services industry averaged about 10% annually, and the average cost of an underwriter, including salary, benefits, office space, and supplies, was about $51,000), but with QU-IC, underwriters with 1 year of experience were doing the same work as 3-year underwriters. In addition, rate calculations that used to take up to 2 or 3 days to complete now took about 1 hour. Underwriters were now able to review more scenarios and undertake more research to produce more informative quotations.

KNOWLEDGE ENGINEERING GROUP

In June 1990, KEG consisted of five people: David Blackburn, Rick Schmidt, and Brian Cooper, with traditional data processing backgrounds, and Janice McGuire and David Sibson, from the Micro-Computer Center.

Brian had a clear idea of the kinds of people that made the best knowledge engineers. He believed that people skills were more important than technical skills, but anyone attracted to KEG would have to have an innate interest in the technology: "After all, technical skills were crucial so that the developers could learn the new technology quickly, and provide early results to the users when they began developing systems." David Sibson and Janice had learned from the more experienced members of the team, acting somewhat like apprentices initially. As Janice said, "I spent a lot of time experimenting and looking at other people's code."

Up to now, KEG had been interested primarily in providing computerized support to people who did extensive analysis and would benefit from a system that adapted to their way of working. KEG had not been interested in propagating the expert's special knowledge to an army of clerks, but rather, in boosting the expert's performance and effectiveness with a highly tailored and powerful analysis support tool.

KEG had developed a standardized approach to investigating and developing expert systems. The group believed that an iterative process employing rapid prototyping with constant feedback was the key to success; the application expert had to be involved throughout.

Typically, the development process began with a study to investigate the merits of employing expert systems technology in a particular situation. This phase involved spending 2 weeks sitting beside a person currently doing the work to understand exactly what was done. With this understanding, the knowledge engineer would work with the managers involved to decide if the application showed promise as an expert system. If it did, a prototype would be built. During the prototype development phase, which lasted from 6 to 8 weeks, the user would be involved about half-time. The prototype either proved or disproved the potential of the concept. If the users and the KEG believed the prototype had merit, they discussed it in detail with the ultimate users of the system using the prototype to demonstrate the potential of the system. After approval of the prototype, the team would begin to build the production system.

KEG had undertaken about 20 studies and developed six prototypes by the middle of 1990. Often, the study phase determined that an expert system was not the most appropriate solution. Sometimes, a prototype would be built for the sole purpose of researching a difficult problem, with the intention of using traditional software development techniques once the problem was understood.

In June, decisions were being made on a group renewal system, which would be an add-on to QU-IC, and a dental claim system. The latter would be an expert systems component of a traditional system designed to lessen the manual intervention required to process dental claims.

CHALLENGES FACING THE KEG

Brian Cooper believed KEG faced a major decision point in determining the its future focus. As he saw it, they had three opportunities: undertake more projects like QU-IC and FAST, integrate expert systems tools and techniques into mainstream data processing, and help users build their own "noncritical" applications. Should they pursue all three avenues or just one or two?

Finding More Projects

To leverage their specialized abilities in building complex analysis systems, KEG wanted to find more applications like QU-IC and FAST. Applications would have to be ill defined (to justify the iterative development style), important or strategic (to justify the exotic development and delivery environment), and manually intense. (It would have to be really hard for someone to do the job, or the system would probably not be cost justified.)

While it might be possible to continue to search out new applications and convince users to allow development, it seemed more effective to try to educate users about the potential of expert systems and try to encourage them to start coming to KEG with their needs.

KEG had already spent a great deal of time building awareness about expert systems, and advertising QU-IC's success throughout the organization but found it a long and slow process to get the organization up to speed. There just was no one beating a path to KEG's door to have work done (as was the case for the rest of IS). In fact, KEG was the only development group in IS that did not face a development backlog of daunting proportions.

Bringing Expert Systems into Mainstream Data Processing

Brian believed the challenge in bringing expert systems into mainstream data processing was one of changing the mind set of the more than 175 developers to convince them to abandon what had worked for them in the past and take the risk of adopting a new methodology. The developers would then have to convince the ultimate decision makers in the user community to use the system. KEG also had to prove the dependability and maintainability of the new technology: Mutual could not afford to have the flaky and the unproven in their traditional DP shop. The company could not operate without reliable systems and had come to depend on IS to provide them with just that.

The second aspect was one of ongoing application support. So far, KEG had undertaken all systems support and data administration for QU-IC because the skills to deal with QU-IC as a regular production system were not yet in Computer Operations. No wonder; QU-IC used a new technology, and workstations that no one else in the company was using. However, as more applications were developed, KEG could no longer go on supporting the operational aspects of implemented systems.

How far and how hard should KEG push? Brian wanted to see some of the useful expert systems tools and techniques adopted in IS. IS management also felt this way and had decided to purchase ADS, a mainframe-based expert systems shell, to enable expert systems logic to be embedded into traditional applications. At the same time, Brian believed that expert systems would remain an important niche in data processing–a niche that could provide a real advantage over competitors but not a way to develop "bread and butter" kinds of applications.

End-User Expert Systems

KEG knew that most organizations experimenting with expert systems were using a different approach from Mutual. Rather than looking for complex analytical tasks, many companies were developing many simple applications or providing simple expert systems technology to end users to develop their own "noncritical" applications. Should KEG do this at Mutual? What would the resource requirements be? Were the skills of the members of KEG "right" for this sort of effort?

QU-IC had proved that expert systems were a viable development technology that could provide Mutual with significant benefits. The challenge now facing KEG was to determine how to proceed to realize the full potential of expert systems technology.

Assignment

1. Compare and contrast DEC's, Du Pont's, and Mutual's approach to expert systems.

Exhibit 1 | **INFORMATION SYSTEMS DIVISION DEPARTMENTS**

Department	Responsibility	Headcount
Computer systems	Mainframe applications development	175
Micro-Computer Centre*	PC-based systems (mostly agent support)	21
Computer operations	Day-to-day running of systems	21
Telecommunications services	Voice and data network	18
Technical services	Operating systems support	20
Support services	Bridge between technical services and developers; data entry	35
Personal computing centre	End user computing and remote user support	32

* KEG reports to the executive responsible for the Micro-Computer Centre.

CARPENTER ELECTRONICS LIMITED

BY PATRICK CHAU AND PETER C. BELL

(THIS CASE DESCRIBES A REAL SITUATION BUT HAS BEEN DISGUISED AT THE REQUEST OF THE COMPANY.)

One afternoon in June 1990, Marcel Seres from the Process Engineering department at Carpenter Electronic's manufacturing plant, began the task of designing the plant that would be used to build the new ZQ8000 multifunction turbo-PC booster board. Marcel, an engineer with extensive training in electronics and systems, had been working at Carpenter for about 1 year. He had been initially assigned to the pilot plant design team and had contributed to the development of a small-scale production line for the ZQ8000 board.

Market research on this new product coupled with the success of the pilot production facility had prompted the Board of Directors to approve the design and development of a full-scale production plant. The board anticipated being on the market with the new products by early 1992, hopefully before any similar products appeared from Carpenter's competitors.

The grapevine, however, had been buzzing; at least four competitors now appeared to have competitive products under development or test.

As Marcel began the task of designing the full-scale production facility he recalled the objectives set by the Vice President, Manufacturing Operations:

> We think the ZQ8000 products are better than anything that the competition may come up with, but we cannot survive if we are not the low-cost producer in this market.

He was keenly aware of the time constraints; a plant design had to be ready for engineering to take over by January 1, 1991.

CARPENTER AND THE ELECTRONICS INDUSTRY

Carpenter Electronics, a North American-based producer of printed circuit boards, had created and exploited a market niche in supplying add-in booster boards that greatly enhanced the power of IBM and IBM-compatible PCs. Carpenter had recently been acquired by Matsushonda, a Japanese electronics giant that was marketing a similar line of products but had not yet had Carpenter's market success.

Add-in printed circuit boards for PCs were the core of Carpenter's business, and Carpenter produced the world's most complete range, employing 1,500 scientific, technical, marketing, and other staff at two modern research and production facilities. In 1989, more than 5 million boards were sold, accounting for revenues of about $250 million, or 80% of total revenues.

A key product for Carpenter had been the ZQ80 turbo booster board for the IBM PC. This board, first marketed in 1985, plugged into most IBM or compatible PCs and boosted their performance to match that of the (then) new line of Intel 80286 microprocessor-based PCs (the "AT" family of PCs).

The ZQ80 had been followed by the ZQ800 board, which made the power of the Intel 80386 microprocessor available to earlier generations of PCs. The new ZQ8000 board would take this development one step further in providing a significant boost in computing performance (almost matching that of the new Intel 80486 microprocessor) but also adding new functionality. By including expanded memory capability and management, network management circuitry, and CD-ROM control hardware, the ZQ8000 would make the full functionality of the new generation of PCs available to owners of 5- and 10-year-old machines, all at quite modest cost.

The ZQ8 line of boards had accounted for about one-fourth of Carpenter's revenues in 1989. The company was hoping that the ZQ8000 line would solidify Carpenter's dominant position in the add-in booster board market.

MANUFACTURING THE ZQ8000 BOARDS

The key to all products in the ZQ8 line were the transducers which Carpenter designed and manufactured. In an effort to maintain and expand its markets, Carpenter followed a strict policy of not marketing transducers separately. The ZQ8000 board required nine transducers of four new designs: two each of type A7 and X4, four of A9, and one BR. Because these transducers were at the leading edge of technology, their manufacture was difficult and complex, and the yields produced were uncertain. This complexity was in sharp contrast to all the other components in the ZQ8000 board, which were common units that were inexpensive and easily obtained.

While precise details of the manufacturing process were a closely guarded company secret, the general process was as follows:

Step 1: Material Preparation. This was a batch step in which a large quantity of transducer material was mixed and annealed, allowed to cool, and then cut and cured. This critical step took 1 week to complete and, occasionally, yielded no useful product. Material preparation had been run in the pilot plant at several different scale-ups from the research scale process. The largest scale that had been "proved" in the pilot plant was a 23-kilogram initial material load (23 kg scale).

Step 2: Separation. The chips of cured material then had to be tested and separated into the different transducer products. The first test was to be performed by an advanced, numerically controlled robot, which was expected to be able to test the complete batch in about 3 hours and isolate raw material for the A7 transducers. A further 2 days of processing was scheduled before material suitable for the X4, A9, and BR transducers could be separated out.

The pilot plant studies suggested that a 23 kg scale of operation initially yielded sufficient material for about 20,000 A7, 12,000 A9, 136,000 X4, and 16,667 BR transducers (Exhibit 1). These initial yields were further and further depleted as processing continued.

Step 3: Parallel Processing. After separation, each type of transducer had to be processed separately. The production process was such that the batches generated by the first stage had to be processed together for the entire process. The processing required varied by transducer type:

A7 cleaning and rectification involved nine steps and could take 7 working days.

X4 processing involved five distinct steps, one of which was an extended oven cure that took 7 weeks.

A9 manufacture involved five steps, with a total processing time of about 44 hours.

BR finishing involved 10 different steps, and included three, required, 24-hour curings.

A flowchart of the processing steps is given in Exhibit 2.

Many of the processing steps were difficult, and the outcomes were uncertain. After each processing step in each of the four parallel production processes, the batch was to be tested. If that particular batch of transducers failed the test, the batch had to be thrown out. While it was known that failures occurred, the only estimates of the probability of a batch failing at any stage were those available from the pilot plant studies. (These probabilities are summarized in Exhibit 3.)

Finally, individual transducers were rejected for various reasons during processing. Chipping, warping, or cracking was common and, when detected by the processing equipment, resulted in rejection of the unit. The result was that the batch sizes became smaller as processing proceeded. Estimates of the rejection rates for each process were available as yield rates for each process obtained from the pilot plant studies.

Step 4: Assembly. The final manufacturing stage involved assembly of the transducers together with other readily available components into the printed circuit boards. This would be accomplished by robots, which were accurate and predictable. At this stage, there would be sufficient value added that it would be worthwhile to repair any boards that failed the final test; therefore, the yield of acceptable boards was 100%.

LABOR AND EQUIPMENT

Two types of labor would be required for the manufacture of transducers. Level I labor was the most skilled and would perform those tasks that required high technology equipment. Although level I workers could perform all of the job steps in the manufacturing process, their collective agreement prevented them from doing tasks that did not require their high level of training. These lower level tasks would be performed by level II labor. Most of the process steps only required human attention for a part of the processing time (Exhibit 6-7 provides the expected labor needs of each manufacturing step).

Many of the steps in the manufacturing process required special equipment, and in most cases, the special equipment could only be used for a single production step. There were, however, two exceptions. Laser etching and laser testing could be performed on the same special-purpose machine, which cost about $1,000,000 and could be used to etch and test both A9 and X4 transducers. The microetching of BR and A7 could also be performed on another piece of special equipment (cost about $550,000).

Because of the importance of the ZQ8000 products to Carpenter, their production facility would be physically separate and would not share labor or equipment with any other manufacturing units.

SCALE OF MANUFACTURING OPERATIONS

Marcel remembered that during the last project meeting, he was told that Carpenter was estimating worldwide demand for ZQ8000 boards at 3,000,000 annually. Because of this high demand, he was asked to consider the pros and cons of building two separate plants (one in Canada and one in the United States) rather than having one large plant. Using the results from the pilot plant and the estimated level of demand, he made some rough calculations on the required production scale of various size plants (Exhibit 4).

The importance of the project to Carpenter meant that Marcel had access to most of Carpenter's people and considerable resources, but it also put him under pressure to perform. He knew he had to come up with the most efficient production system possible, but wondered how he should do this. What process should he follow? What issues had to be decided, and how should these decisions be made? Where should research and development efforts be directed?

Assignment

1. What kind of help is needed by Carpenter's staff?
2. What form of model do you recommend to assist Seres? What would the input to your model be? What output would it produce?
3. How could your model be used to help with Carpenter's other problems?

Exhibit 1 | **INITIAL MATERIAL OUTPUT FROM PILOT BATCH**
23-kilogram scale

Unit	Material Produced per Batch	Required per Board	Maximum No. of Boards per Batch*
A7	20,000	2	10,000
A9	12,000	4	3,000
X4	136,000	2	68,000
BR	16,667	1	16,667

* With no downstream batch failures and 100% downstream yields.

Exhibit 2 | SIMPLIFIED FLOW DIAGRAM OF THE MANUFACTURING PROCESS

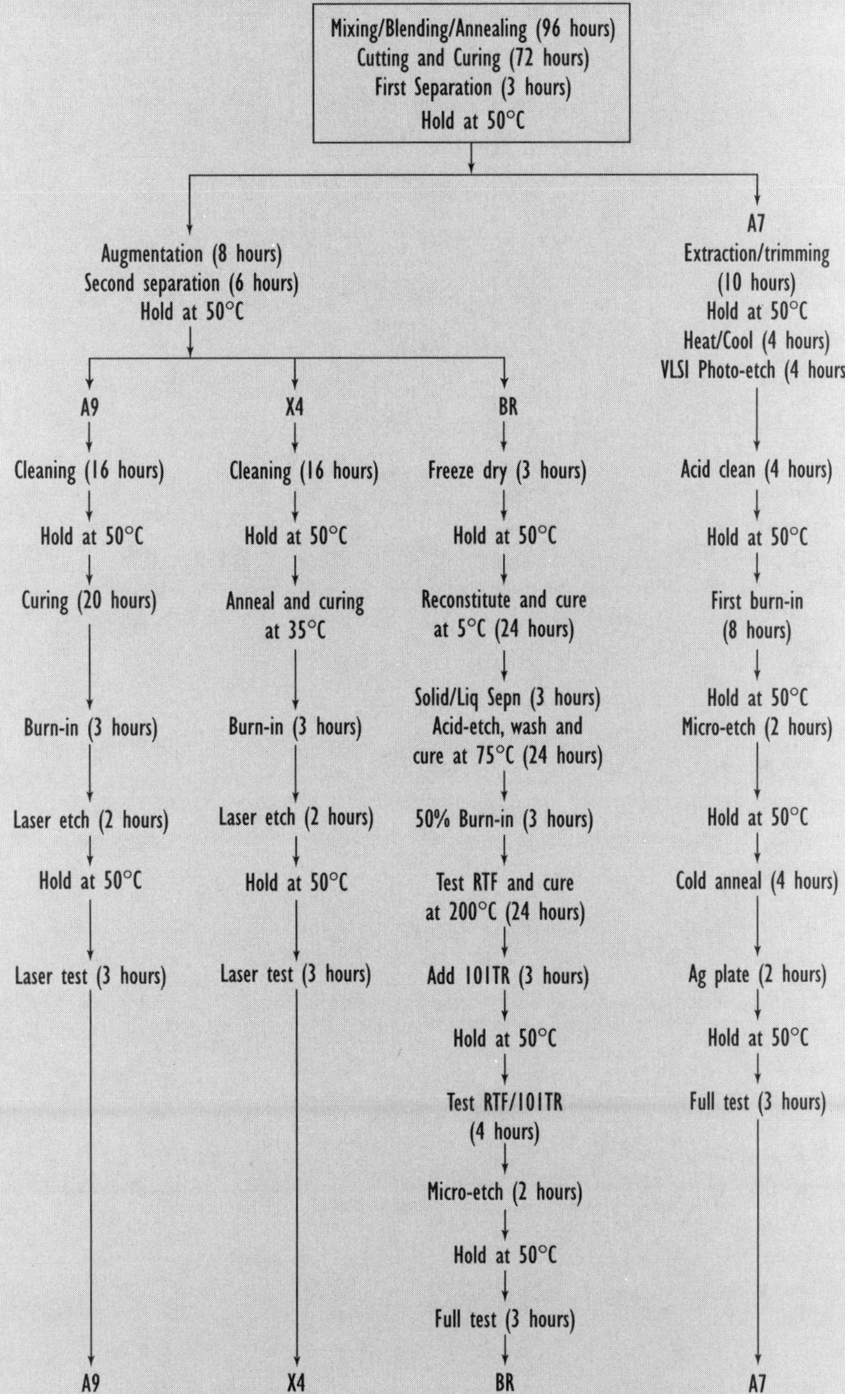

"Hold at 50°C" are inserted to assist scheduling.

Exhibit 3 PROBABILITIES OF FAILURE AND YIELD RATES FOR PROCESS STEPS Estimated from pilot plant studies

	Probability of Failure	Mean Yield (%)	Labor Hours I	Labor Hours II
Material preparation				
Mixing and blending	0.01		12	
Annealing	0.10		18	
First separation	0.07	100	7	9
Second separation		96	3	3
A7 processing				
Extraction	0.02	98		6
Trimming	0.15	98		4
Heat/cool	0.01	85		2
VLSI Photo-etch	0.15	43		3
Acid clean	0.01	85		4
First burn-in	0.05	85		8
Micro-etch	0.01	85		3
Cold anneal	0.02	94		2
Ag plate	0.02	83		2
Full test		97		2
A9 processing				
Cleaning	0.05	92	4	
Curing	0.01	98		2
Burn-in	0.10	95		4
Laser etch	0.15	98		2
Laser test		95		3
X4 processing				
Cleaning	0.05	93	8	
Anneal and curing	0.02	98		2
Burn-in	0.10	95		4
Laser etch	0.15	98		2
Laser test		94		3
BR processing				
Freeze dry	0.06	100	3	
Reconstitute	0.01	100		4
Solid/Liq. Sepn	0.00	92	3	
Acid-etch, wash and hold	0.04	90	6	6
50% burn-in	0.05	90		2
Test RTF		96		4
Add 101TR		100	3	
Test RTF/101TR	0.06	90	4	
Micro-etch	0.01	95		2
Full test		98		3

Exhibit 4 **CALCULATIONS OF REQUIRED BATCH SIZE**
A9 assumed to be bottleneck

	Two Sites		One Site
	Canada	United States	
Estimated demand (000/year)	1,000	2,000	3,000
Demand profile	Assumed constant throughout the year		
Batch process cycle (batches/week)	1	1	1
Plant occupancy (weeks/year)	47	47	47
Batches produced per year	47	47	47
Batch failure rate	15%	15%	15%
Successful batches per year	40	40	40
A9 units required (per batch)	100,000	200,000	300,000
Yield of A9 (units/kg)	12,000/23	12,000/23	12,000/23
Batch size (kg)	200	400	600

HARRISON, YOUNG, PESONEN, AND NEWELL, INC.: DIRECT RESPONSE TV, THE SUPER-TEL CAMPAIGN

It was a beautiful August day. Jacqueline Murdoch sat at her desk in the Bay Street offices of Harrison, Young, Pesonen, and Newell, Inc. (HYPN) and reviewed the spreadsheets on the screen of her personal computer. Today marked the start of week 8 of a 12-week direct response television campaign that HYPN was conducting for Super-Tel, a discount long distance telephone carrier.

Jacqueline had developed the media plan for the Super-Tel campaign and was supervising its execution. Since advertising began, she had been monitoring customer response data coming in from the telemarketing contractor to judge the performance of the advertising plan and with the objective of making adjustments to improve the plan. Within the limits of availability and with sufficient notice, Jacqueline could cancel ads on stations that looked like they would perform poorly or she could try to get the ads moved to better times of the day. She might also be able to buy additional advertising time on stations that had performed well. By studying the incoming data on customer responses, Jacqueline hoped to fine-tune the final weeks of advertising to maximize the number of customer orders received by Super-Tel, while minimizing the costs of obtaining those orders.

HARRISON, YOUNG, PESONEN, AND NEWELL, INC.

HYPN was founded in 1979 by four partners who had worked together at a major branch of a large, full-service advertising agency. These partners noted that 90% of the money spent by organizations on advertising went into the purchasing of media (time on television and radio, or space in magazines, newspapers, and billboards), yet the full-service advertising agencies spent only about 10% of their efforts on managing media purchases. The partners thought that a specialized agency dedicated solely to the planning and purchasing of advertising could offer significant efficiencies and economies compared with a full-service agency.

HYPN initially contracted media planning, purchasing, and management functions to other advertising agencies. Over time, HYPN had shifted their emphasis to working directly for the client organization, who would arrange for a full service or boutique agency to create the ads, and then would have HYPN plan and execute the placement of the ads. HYPN's clients included many major advertisers, including Labatts, Unilever, American Express, Honda, Nike, and Swiss Chalet. By 1988, HYPN had become the largest independent media company in Canada, and by 1994, their billings exceeded $240,000,000. Ten percent of all ads on Canadian television were placed through HYPN.

HYPN's staff of 120 were organized into five basic areas: account management and planning, media buying, research, finance and administration, and response management.

Account Management and Planning services were the liaison with the clients and devised the media plans. Services from the research department were used to determine which media schedule would produce the largest number of viewing impressions by members of the target market at the lowest cost.

Media Buying negotiated the actual purchase of air time or publication space on behalf of **Management and Planning**. At HYPN, media buying was coordinated across customers to increase the overall size of each buy and thus negotiate the best possible rates with the media. Three times annually, HYPN's buying department negotiated major purchases, and with their extensive knowledge of the competitive situation in media, HYPN could ensure that they obtained the best possible rates.

HYPN's **Research Department** was one of the largest in Canada. Through analysis of advertising survey data, the research department supported the work of media planning and advertising placement. In addition, the research department consulted to media companies and the government and had developed innovative research tools of their own. For example, the research department had developed a highly successful method of segmenting target markets clearly and unambiguously according to their habits in the use of media. This allowed advertising to be efficiently targeted to specific market segments.

The **Finance and Administration** department, in addition to serving the needs of HYPN, managed the "Agency of Record" relationships that HYPN had with a number of customers. Some large clients did business with several advertising agencies for their various lines of business. To coordinate the total media buy, the client would appoint one agency as the "Agency of Record," and that agency would arrange the placement of all the advertising created by the other agencies. HYPN has been the agency of record for Sterling Products, Cadbury Beverages, and Neilson Confectionery. In addition, HYPN continued to operate as the media department for several advertising agencies that preferred not to have their own.

The **Response Management** department was where Jacqueline worked. This department specialized in the design and execution of direct marketing campaigns, which some people referred to as "transactional media." Direct marketing campaigns were designed to incite the target audience to respond directly to the advertisement that they had seen, whether this be on television, by direct mail, in print media, or even a telemarketing call. An example would be a mail order ad in a magazine or a television ad with a "1-800" number to call ("Operators are standing by..."). The 1-800 number television ad was a subspecialty in itself and was called "direct response television," or "DRTV." DRTV was Jacqueline's area of expertise.

DIRECT RESPONSE TELEVISION

DRTV advertising had a number of characteristics that distinguished it from more traditional advertising.

The goal of DRTV was to generate responses. These responses could be to receive information about a certain product, to enter a contest (when respondents would be asked if they would mind receiving information about a product in a future mailing), or to order a product directly. Because these came in directly over the telephone, it was possible to measure DRTV advertising effectiveness very quickly and very accurately. Effectiveness could be measured in terms of cost per inquiry or cost per order because not every inquiry (or telephone call) actually translated into a purchase. In addition, because the 800 number shown on the screen could be varied from television station to television station and because most calls occurred shortly after an ad was aired, it was possible to track the productivity of an advertising campaign according to both the stations the ads aired on and the time of day of the ad.

The telephone calls were actually handled by telemarketing call centers who had the facilities to handle large numbers of calls to "800" numbers in short time intervals. Some clients contracted with call centers on their own, whereas in other cases, HYPN would arrange for a center to process calls for a given campaign. The contractor collected information on customers (limited demographic data, postal codes, and so on) together with the times of the calls and the telephone number called and provided this data to HYPN by electronic mail on request (at least weekly, and sometimes daily). HYPN could then analyze this data to monitor progress of the campaign and, where possible, to "fine tune" the placement of future ads.

The direct connection between the placement of an advertisement and the customer response to the ad was unique to DRTV and made it one of the few forms of advertising where performance could be unambiguously established. It was widely believed that a good DRTV campaign could obtain similar results to a traditional campaign costing four times as much. DRTV appeared to work best with general mass market products aimed at people who were comfortable buying by credit card over the telephone.

PLANNING A DRTV CAMPAIGN

In formulating a campaign, the planner first established a budget per unit of product to obtain each sale. This was the allowable margin. The planner then determined the break-even response rate required for the product by dividing the allowable margin per unit into the expected advertising costs. If the break-even response rate looked achievable, the planner next estimated the expected response rate to the ads based on experience with past campaigns for similar products. The expected response was a function of the number of TV spots aired, the attractiveness of the product, the price point, the timing of the ads within the day, the season of the year, the quality of the creative content of the ads, the level of competition, and general economic conditions, with DRTV tending to do well in a poor economy.

The cost per order (CPO), which in mathematical terms was the cost of the media divided by the total orders, was one measure used by the media planner to plan and monitor the campaign. The planner/buyer knew the allowable margin, and if the CPO was less than this, the campaign was on target. If the CPO was greater than the allowable margin, the media had to be adjusted immediately in an attempt to bring the CPO down in line with the allowable margin.

The planner next looked for an allocation of ads to television dayparts and stations for a total cost that would meet the target CPO at the expected response rate. The creation of the ad schedule involved significant judgment concerning the trade-offs between high viewership times at high costs versus lower viewership times at lower costs and involving the choice of different types of ad purchase plans offered by stations. Critical to the success of the plan was the accuracy of the assumptions about the response rate that would be achieved, so it was common to run a small test campaign to test these assumptions before launching the full DRTV campaign.

Television advertising was usually sold in *rotations* in which an ad appeared a specified number of times within certain hours of the day, called a "daypart." Examples of dayparts offered are:

Morning	6:00 AM to 12:00 PM
Afternoon	12:00 PM to 4:00 PM
Access	4:00 PM to 7:00 PM
Prime time	7:00 PM to 11:00 PM
Late night	11:00 PM to 6:00 AM or sign off
Weekends, Saturday and Sunday	6:00 AM to 8:00 PM

In addition to time of day, the time of year was also important. The January-March winter season had the highest TV viewership, with good DRTV response rates, and the second lowest TV advertising rates. The spring and fall seasons had the second highest audiences, with the highest advertising rates (start and end of main TV season) and a DRTV response only about 75% of that of the winter. The summer had the lowest audience, the lowest costs, and the poorest DRTV response at about 50% that of winter. In addition, long weekends tended to have smaller audiences.

DRTV advertising could be purchased under four different contract agreements. In order of decreasing cost/spot, these were:

1. Rate card purchases, which were bought at the station's asking price and were noncancelable and nonpreemptible.
2. Mixed campaigns, which combined some rate card purchases with a per inquiry (PI) element, generally sold on a one-for-one basis.
3. Guaranteed PI purchases, where the station guarantees so many spots, and in return the buyer guarantees a minimum payment in advance, and positioning is negotiated. Under this type of contract, every order or inquiry is worth a certain amount to the station, which is worked off the guarantee with any excess due at the end of the campaign.
4. Straight PI purchases, where the supplier provides a media inventory to the client in return for payment for every call or order generated. Typically, the media planner/buyer would pay 25% of the retail price of the product to the media supplier when payment for the media was on a PI basis (when testing a new product, straight PI was often very desirable).

An ad could be guaranteed to run at a certain time or might be "preemptible": that is, it could be preempted by another ad and bumped to another time or daypart. A preemptible and cancelable ad might, with varying amounts of notice, not be run at all. Typically in Canada

75% of preemptible ads ran, whereas in the United States, only about 25% did. Whether a PI buy was attractive depended on the availability of air time generally. When available air time was tight, PI ads tended to be expensive and run in poor time slots. On other occasions, PI ads could be a very attractive proposition.

Ideally a DRTV campaign should not be budget limited: as long as new orders were being generated within the target CPO, the campaign should continue. In practice, however, a campaign budget was usually set based on estimates of the total market size and absorptive capacity, the fulfillment capability of the sales organization, and historical experience with regard to maximum spending levels and diminishing returns. The advertising allocation criterion was thus usually expressed as the maximum response within the overall budget. A small test campaign was similarly budgeted for one or two "typical" cities with historically low costs per inquiry.

DRTV CAMPAIGN EXECUTION

After completion of a media schedule, and client approval, the DRTV campaign execution began with the contracting of a telemarketing firm to handle the customer calls, assignment of different 800 numbers to ads on different stations, and purchase of initial air time. As the ads ran and the data on call and order distributions was received from the telemarketer, the agency analyzed the campaign's performance, trying to identify which ads, at which times, and on which stations were working best. This information was used to adjust the schedule of future ads, seeking even greater response rates and lower CPOs. While performing this analysis, Jacqueline was mindful that too fast a reaction could be a mistake because viewership and responses were affected by weather conditions and special events. Observations over several weeks were usually more reliable indicators.

SUPER-TEL CAMPAIGN

On this beautiful August afternoon, Jacqueline was analyzing the results of the Super-Tel test campaign. Super-Tel was an alternative long distance telephone service that promised significant discounts off the rates offered by the major carrier, including even higher discounts to the callers' most frequently called numbers. The target market had been identified as women age 18 to 49 years who spent at least $30 per month on long distance telephone charges. In addition, it was thought that members of ethnic communities with relatives abroad would be an important part of the target market.

The DRTV test campaign budget had been set at $720,000. Jacqueline expected to generate 45,000 calls to the telemarketing firm, of which about 40% were expected to convert into purchases of Super-Tel. The target CPO was less than $40. All ads were 60 seconds long, and versions were available in both of Canada's official languages.

The experience from the first 6 weeks of the campaign was that actual purchasers were about 50/50 male/female, with an average spending of $76 per month for long distance calls. The number of calls received was lower than expected, and the conversion rate of calls to orders was also a little lower than expected, with the result that actual CPO was higher than planned CPO. Fortunately, Super-Tel was obtaining customers who spent more than expected, so they were not unhappy with the higher CPO.

Looking over the actual figures to date, Jacqueline wondered whether she could fine-tune this campaign with the objective of improving the response rate, and lowering the CPO. As she worked on the Super-Tel campaign (Exhibits 1 through 5), she realized that she had done this before: Was there, she wondered, a systematic approach to solving this problem that she could use in future campaigns?

Assignment

1. What decisions does Jacqueline have to make?
2. How can MS/OR technology help with these decisions?
3. Develop a DSS to support the management of a direct response campaign (such as the Super-Tel Campaign).

Exhibit 1 **SUPER-TEL DIRECT RESPONSE TELEVISION CAMPAIGN.**
60-SECOND CREATIVE
For the weeks of July 10 to August 21, 1994
Media plan: Budget $458,731 (7 weeks)

Market	Stations	Jul 10	Jul 17	Jul 24	Jul 31	Aug 7	Aug 14	Aug 21	Spend
Toronto	CFTO	$6,509	$6,509	$6,509	$5,990	$5,055	$5,055	$5,055	$40,682
Toronto	CITY	$4,236	$4,236	$4,236	$4,228	$4,228	$4,228	$4,228	$29,619
Toronto	CFMT-L	$2,531	$2,531	$2,531	$2,227	$0	$0	$0	$9,820
Toronto	CFMT-E	$4,005	$4,005	$4,005	$4,005	$4,005	$4,005	$4,005	$28,035
Toronto	CBLT*	$1,256	$1,571	$1,508	$1,382	$1,382	$1,445	$1,382	$9,926
Toronto	WUTV	$2,265	$2,435	$2,435	$2,265	$2,265	$3,286	$3,286	$18,237
Hamilton	CHCH*	$4,228	$4,228	$4,228	$4,712	$4,712	$4,712	$4,712	$31,530
London	CBLN*	$628	$659	$942	$503	$503	$534	$691	$4,460
London	CFPL	$736	$736	$736	$801	$0	$579	$0	$3,587
Windsor	CBET*	$524	$524	$524	$0	$0	$0	$0	$1,571
Kitchener	CKCO	$5,288	$5,288	$5,288	$5,094	$5,094	$5,094	$5,094	$36,243
Barrie	CKVR	$997	$997	$997	$1,696	$2,073	$1,885	$1,382	$10,026
Kingston	CKWS*	$349	$349	$349	$349	$349	$349	$349	$2,441
Ottawa	CJOH	$3,011	$3,011	$3,011	$2,759	$3,249	$3,249	$0	$18,290
Ottawa	CBOT*	$733	$733	$733	$733	$733	$733	$806	$5,204
Pembroke	CHRO	$918	$918	$918	$699	$338	$0	$0	$3,791
Sudbury/SSM	MCTV*	$0	$262	$262	$262	$262	$0	$0	$1,048
Peterborough	CHEX*	$524	$524	$524	$524	$524	$524	$524	$3,665
Montreal	CBMT*	$1,204	$1,204	$1,204	$1,204	$1,204	$1,204	$1,325	$8,549
Montreal	CFCF	$2,020	$2,020	$2,020	$2,821	$2,507	$2,507	$2,507	$16,403
Montreal	WPTZ	$1,673	$1,673	$1,673	$1,744	$1,744	$1,744	$1,744	$11,997
Montreal	WVNY	$0	$0	$0	$0	$0	$0	$1,638	$1,638
Montreal-F	CFJP	$5,118	$5,207	$5,135	$4,414	$3,993	$3,993	$3,939	$31,798
Montreal-F	CFTM	$4,394	$4,394	$4,394	$4,706	$4,353	$4,353	$4,353	$30,947
Quebec City	CFAP	$1,497	$1,750	$1,116	$1,605	$1,605	$1,605	$1,605	$10,782
Quebec City	CFCM	$1,793	$1,793	$1,793	$1,850	$1,919	$1,748	$0	$10,896
Trois Rivieres	CHEM	$1,023	$1,023	$1,023	$1,015	$1,124	$1,124	$0	$6,334
Sherbrooke	CHLT	$1,542	$1,542	$1,542	$1,648	$1,781	$1,664	$1,781	$11,500
Chicoutimi	CJPM	$730	$730	$730	$1,015	$1,104	$993	$0	$5,301
Network	CIII	$5,856	$5,482	$5,856	$5,856	$2,118	$2,118	$2,118	$29,406
Regional Ntwk.	CBC-FR*	$0	$0	$5,228	$6,239	$6,686	$4,677	$6,230	$29,059
Total:		$65,587	$66,334	$71,450	$72,345	$64,908	$63,406	$58,753	$462,783

Exhibit 2 | **SUPER-TEL DIRECT RESPONSE TELEVISION CAMPAIGN: 60-SECOND CREATIVE For the weeks of July 10 to August 21, 1994 Expenditure by station**

Station	Jul 10	Jul 17	Jul 24	Jul 31	Aug 7	Aug 14	Aug 21	Total
GLOBAL	$5,856	$5,482	$5,856	$5,856	$2,118	$2,118	$2,118	$29,404
SRC	$0	$0	$5,228	$6,239	$6,686	$4,677	$6,230	$29,060
CKVR	$997	$997	$997	$1,696	$2,073	$1,885	$1,382	$10,027
CJPM	$730	$730	$730	$1,015	$1,104	$993	$0	$5,302
CHCH*	$4,228	$4,228	$4,228	$4,712	$4,712	$4,712	$4,712	$31,532
CKWS*	$349	$349	$349	$349	$349	$349	$349	$2,443
CKCO	$5,288	$5,288	$5,288	$5,094	$5,094	$5,094	$5,094	$36,240
CBLN*	$628	$659	$942	$503	$503	$534	$691	$4,460
CFPL	$736	$736	$736	$801	$0	$579	$0	$3,588
CFCF	$2,020	$2,020	$2,020	$2,821	$2,507	$2,507	$2,507	$16,402
WPTZ	$1,673	$1,673	$1,673	$1,744	$1,744	$1,744	$1,744	$11,995
CBMT*	$1,204	$1,204	$1,204	$1,204	$1,204	$1,204	$1,325	$8,549
WVNY	$0	$0	$0	$0	$0	$0	$1,638	$1,638
CFJP	$5,118	$5,207	$5,135	$4,414	$3,993	$3,993	$3,939	$31,799
CFTM	$4,394	$4,394	$4,394	$4,706	$4,353	$4,353	$4,353	$30,947
CJOH	$3,011	$3,011	$3,011	$2,759	$3,249	$3,249	$0	$18,290
CBOT*	$733	$733	$733	$733	$733	$733	$806	$5,204
CHRO	$918	$918	$918	$699	$338	$0	$0	$3,791
CHEX*	$524	$524	$524	$524	$524	$524	$524	$3,668
CFCM	$1,793	$1,793	$1,793	$1,850	$1,919	$1,748	$0	$10,896
CFAP	$1,497	$1,750	$1,116	$1,605	$1,605	$1,605	$1,605	$10,783
CHLT	$1,542	$1,542	$1,542	$1,648	$1,781	$1,664	$1,781	$11,500
MCTV*	$0	$262	$262	$262	$262	$0	$0	$1,048
CFTO	$6,509	$6,509	$6,509	$5,990	$5,055	$5,055	$5,055	$40,682
CITY	$4,236	$4,236	$4,236	$4,228	$4,228	$4,228	$4,228	$29,620
CFMT-E	$4,005	$4,005	$4,005	$4,005	$4,005	$4,005	$4,005	$28,035
CFMT-L	$2,531	$2,531	$2,531	$2,227	$0	$0	$0	$9,820
WUTV	$2,265	$2,435	$2,435	$2,265	$2,265	$3,286	$3,286	$18,237
CBLT*	$1,256	$1,571	$1,508	$1,382	$1,382	$1,445	$1,382	$9,926
CHEM	$1,023	$1,023	$1,023	$1,015	$1,124	$1,124	$0	$6,332
CBET*	$524	$524	$524	$0	$0	$0	$0	$1,572
Total	$65,588	$66,334	$71,450	$72,346	$64,910	$63,408	$58,754	$462,790

Exhibit 3 **SUPER-TEL DIRECT RESPONSE TELEVISION CAMPAIGN: 60-SECOND CREATIVE For the weeks of July 10 to August 21, 1994 Calls received by station**

Station	Jul 10	Jul 17	Jul 24	Jul 31	Aug 7	Aug 14	Aug 21	Total
GLOBAL	115	142	148	224	183	148	21	981
SRC	0	0	472	326	574	352	223	1,947
CKVR	50	58	58	32	55	45	21	319
CJPM	12	24	63	18	13	9	5	144
CHCH*	337	316	349	306	210	183	176	1,877
CKWS*	21	20	35	27	13	13	6	135
CKCO	247	223	205	203	201	202	179	1,460
CBLN*	45	26	42	25	25	19	12	194
CFPL	27	24	29	35	3	14	0	132
CFCF	224	365	300	248	103	147	228	1,615
WPTZ	73	79	91	78	117	79	89	606
CBMT*	151	137	181	128	158	104	66	925
WVNY	0	0	0	0	0	0	29	29
CFJP	94	217	188	205	156	159	157	1,176
CFTM	101	233	188	188	153	184	182	1,229
CJOH	95	109	105	67	67	63	12	518
CBOT*	37	31	46	35	35	26	11	221
CHRO	10	30	20	19	7	0	0	86
CHEX*	47	33	54	38	35	19	25	251
CFCM	58	70	72	59	75	37	9	380
CFAP	17	91	51	17	8	3	28	215
CHLT	66	67	91	90	78	88	95	575
MCTV*	6	9	2	3	3	4	0	27
CFTO	346	372	363	263	254	244	204	2,046
CITY	385	377	218	245	228	196	130	1,779
CFMT-E	92	168	113	168	81	126	76	824
CFMT-L	50	112	50	57	14	11	0	294
WUTV	111	202	246	286	213	238	221	1,517
CBLT*	93	157	117	115	160	118	47	807
CHEM	17	34	64	22	32	14	5	188
CBET*	0	0	0	0	0	3	0	3
Total	2,927	3,726	3,961	3,527	3,254	2,848	2,257	22,500

Exhibit 4

SUPER-TEL DIRECT RESPONSE TELEVISION CAMPAIGN: 60-SECOND CREATIVE
For the weeks of July 10 to August 21, 1994
Orders received by station

	Jul 10	Jul 17	Jul 24	Jul 31	Aug 7	Aug 14	Aug 21	Total
GLOBAL	35	45	43	91	79	53	9	355
SRC	0	0	132	107	173	106	78	596
CKVR	21	21	19	11	19	16	6	113
CJPM	3	11	20	5	2	3	2	46
CHCH*	129	99	112	100	67	74	61	642
CKWS*	6	7	14	8	6	3	1	45
CKCO	96	65	74	76	72	68	70	521
CBLN*	17	8	20	7	13	11	1	77
CFPL	9	6	10	15	2	5	0	47
CFCF	79	111	86	78	22	21	45	442
WPTZ	28	26	29	29	46	31	32	221
CBMT*	68	44	66	40	66	30	33	347
WVNY	0	0	0	0	0	0	9	9
CFJP	30	81	71	78	52	54	67	433
CFTM	36	90	70	87	54	78	87	502
CJOH	42	44	27	24	26	21	4	188
CBOT*	9	6	18	15	13	6	5	72
CHRO	4	8	3	4	2	0	0	21
CHEX*	20	12	22	13	8	9	5	89
CFCM	19	19	29	24	22	10	3	126
CFAP	6	28	18	3	4	2	12	73
CHLT	26	21	25	31	29	22	30	184
MCTV*	2	4	1	1	2	1	0	11
CFTO	145	125	112	91	86	85	71	715
CITY	153	150	75	99	95	79	50	701
CFMT-E	39	70	43	60	30	46	30	318
CFMT-L	23	30	25	28	1	3	0	110
WUTV	45	83	86	113	83	102	82	594
CBLT*	44	59	45	41	66	39	21	315
CHEM	5	8	9	12	8	3	1	46
CBET*	0	0	0	0	0	1	0	1
Total	1,139	1,281	1,304	1,291	1,148	982	815	7,960

Exhibit 5 **SUPER-TEL DIRECT RESPONSE TELEVISION CAMPAIGN: 60-SECOND CREATIVE**
For the weeks of July 10 to August 21, 1994
Daypart trending report: Television calls and orders

Daypart			Jul 10	Jul 17	Jul 24	Jul 31	Aug 7	Aug 14	Aug 21	Totals
Morning	0600-1159	Calls	587	878	821	797	690	701	546	5,020
		Orders	204	306	272	299	222	217	193	1,713
Afternoon	1200-1559	Calls	1,160	1,659	1,981	1,707	1,742	1,328	1,029	10,606
		Orders	478	561	679	615	631	494	380	3,838
Access	1600-1859	Calls	366	398	437	309	280	296	240	2,326
		Orders	139	155	139	109	105	93	75	815
Prime	1900-2259	Calls	580	546	523	513	403	375	302	3,242
		Orders	225	196	155	195	150	142	118	1,181
Late	2300-0559	Calls	234	245	199	201	139	148	140	1,306
		Orders	93	63	59	73	40	36	49	413
	Totals:	Calls	2,927	3,726	3,961	3,527	3,254	2,848	2,257	22,500
		Orders	1,139	1,281	1,304	1,291	1,148	982	815	7,960

THE *STEPHEN B. ROMAN*

BY HAMISH TAYLOR AND PETER C. BELL

Dan Wight, controller of the Picton cement plant of Essroc (Canada), was reviewing last year's operations with North American Logistics Manager, François Perrin. The Picton plant had produced some 700,000 tons of cement, most of which had been delivered to Essroc's distribution centers around the Great Lakes by the lake freighter, the *Stephen B. Roman* (Exhibit 1). The *Roman* was owned by the company but operated by a contracted firm, and François noted that the average tonnage carried on the *Roman* during the sailing season, from April to December last year, was a little less than 6,500 tons (the *Roman*'s capacity was 8,500 tons). François saw an opportunity to make better use of the vessel and thereby reduce shipping costs. In particular, under the contractual arrangement for vessel operations, if the vessel was "laid up," Essroc saved about $7,000 per day. A shipping policy of only shipping full loads, and thereby maximizing the number of days the *Roman* was laid up, appeared to be best for the company.

Dan, however, noted that shipping was only one part of a complex manufacturing and distribution process. Shipping only full loads on every trip would maximize the number of days the vessel could be laid up but would affect both manufacturing and the replenishment of inventories of the various products at the distribution centers. The result of implementing such a shipping policy could well be that overall costs would *increase* as a result of increased costs of manufacturing and/or storage. Could manufacturing operations be sustained if the ship was laid up? Dan knew that the vessel dispatcher, Ken Carruthers, had spent long hours trying to derive the best possible manufacturing and distribution schedule, and it was Ken's schedule that had produced the results they were examining.

ESSROC CANADA

Essroc Canada was a wholly owned subsidiary of the Société des Ciments Français, a leading international producer and supplier of cement, ready-mixed concrete, and aggregates for construction markets. Société des Ciments Français was controlled in majority by Ital Ci-

Exhibit 1 | THE *STEPHEN B. ROMAN*

From 1986 Société des Ciments Français Annual Report.

menti and was the third largest cement company in the world, employing approximately 11,000 people in the United States, Italy, Canada, France, Spain, Morocco, and Luxembourg. In North America, Ciments Français operating as the Essroc Cement Group was the fourth largest cement manufacturer, with plants in Pennsylvania, Indiana, Maryland, Quebec, Ohio, and Ontario.

ESSROC'S PICTON PLANT AND THE *STEPHEN B. ROMAN*

The Essroc manufacturing facility in Picton, Ontario (Exhibit 2), with two kilns and approximately 250 employees, was the largest of the North American plants. The plant could produce 1.2 million tons of "clinker" and 900,000 tons of cement annually, and it served major regional distribution centers located in Toronto; Windsor, Ontario; and Oswego and Rochester, New York; as well as the Essroc distribution center in Cleveland, Ohio. The *Stephen B. Roman* delivered cement from Picton to these major distribution centers; smaller distribution centers in Ontario were served by truck and/or rail.

The *Stephen B. Roman* had a complement of 28 and was owned by Essroc but operated through a third-party contractual arrangement. The freighter had a capacity of 8,500 tons of cement in three holds with fixed bulkheads. The forward hold had a capacity of 3,850 tons, the midships hold 1,600 tons, and the aft hold 3,050 tons. The shipping season began on April 1 and ended about December 24.

There were certain restrictions on the *Roman*'s operations. The maximum shipping load into Rochester was only 7,200 tons of cement because of shallow water, although all the other ports had sufficient depth of water for a fully loaded vessel. From August to December, lowered water levels sometimes further restricted the maximum cargo that the *Roman* could carry to Rochester (although the other ports remained unrestricted). Ken (the vessel dispatcher) tried to compensate for this by combining each Rochester trip with an initial delivery to either Oswego or Toronto.

The *Roman* traveled at the same speed and with about the same fuel consumption, whether empty or loaded. Sailing times are given in Exhibit 3.

The variable cost of operating the vessel (wages, fuel, and so on) was approximately $7,000 per day, which could be saved by "laying up" the ship. This saving, combined with the fixed cost of sending the crew home during a lay up (about $12,000), had led to the adoption of a minimum 7-day lay up period: that is, the vessel was only laid up if it could remain so for at least

Exhibit 2 | **THE PICTON PLANT**

From Essroc Canada Brochure.

7 days. The *Roman* was often laid up with a full cargo, so it served as a floating silo at the start of the next operating period. Also, at any time, the *Roman* could be chartered out to another cement company or could haul Essroc cement to a U.S. affiliate in Cleveland if the time and cement were available.

The cost to deliver cement from Picton to Toronto using the Roman was approximately $9 per ton (excluding vessel depreciation or capital charges), compared with $15 per ton by rail and $21 per ton by road. Similar cost differentials applied for the other destinations.

CEMENT PRODUCTION

Cement production is a low technology industry but a critical one in the national economy. Cement production (illustrated in Exhibit 4) began with crushing limestone and then heating the crushed rock with various chemicals in large continuous furnaces (kilns) to produce a chunky intermediate product called clinker, which could be stockpiled. Different types of cement were produced by grinding this clinker in large grinding mills into a powder of varying fineness. At the Picton plant, five different cement types were ground:

- Type I, regular coarse construction cement
- Type II, a low alkali coarse cement satisfying New York State standards
- Type III, a quick-setting fine cement
- Masonry Normal (MasN), a fine grind used in stone masonry and brick laying
- Masonry Special (MasS), another fine grind

Exhibit 3 | ***STEPHEN B. ROMAN*** **SAILING TIMES (ONE WAY)**

From-To	Time (hr)	From-To	Time (hr)
Picton-Toronto	13	Toronto-Rochester	8
Picton-Oswego	7	Toronto-Oswego	12
Picton-Rochester	10	Oswego-Rochester	6
Picton-Windsor	38	Picton-Cleveland	28

Exhibit 4 | CEMENT PRODUCTION PROCESS

How cement is made at our Picton plant

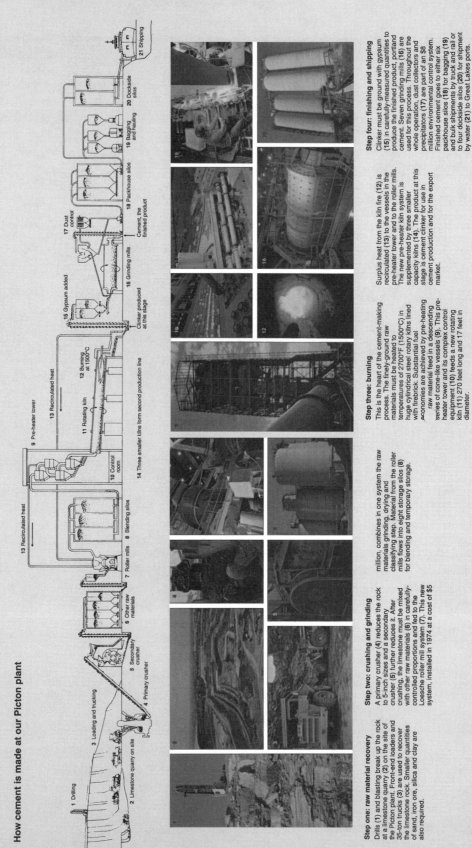

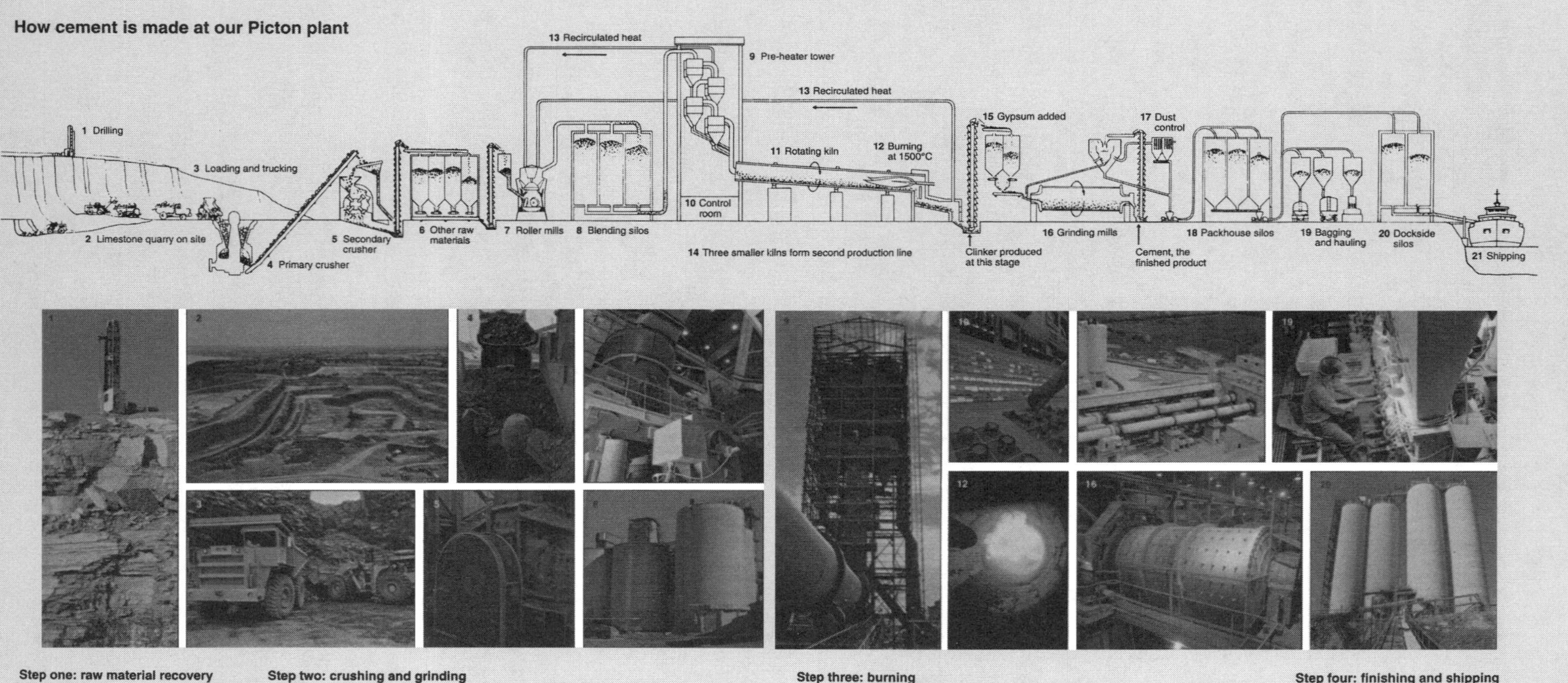

Step one: raw material recovery

Drills (**1**) and blasting break up the rock at a limestone quarry (**2**) on the site of the Picton plant. Front-end loaders and 35-ton trucks (**3**) are used to recover the limestone rock. Smaller quantities of sand, iron ore, silica and clay are also required.

Step two: crushing and grinding

A primary crusher (**4**) reduces the rock to 5-inch sizes and a secondary crusher (**5**) further reduces it. After crushing, the limestone must be mixed with other raw materials (**6**) in carefully-controlled proportions and fed to the Loesche roller mill system (**7**). This new system, installed in 1974 at a cost of $5 million, combines in one system the raw materials grinding, drying and classifying step. Material from the roller mills flows into eight storage silos (**8**) for blending and temporary storage.

Step three: burning

This is the heart of the cement-making process. The finely-ground raw materials must be heated to temperatures of 2700°F (1500°C) in huge cylindrical steel rotary kilns lined with firebrick. Substantial fuel economies are achieved by pre-heating raw material feed in a descending series of cone-like vessels (**9**). This pre-heater tower and its complex control equipment (**10**) feeds a new rotating kiln (**11**) 270 feet long and 17 feet in diameter.

Surplus heat from the kiln fire (**12**) is recirculated (**13**) to the vessels in the pre-heater tower and to the roller mills. The new pre-heater kiln system is supplemented by three smaller capacity kilns (**14**). The product at this stage is cement clinker for use in cement production and for the export market.

Step four: finishing and shipping

Clinker must be ground with gypsum (**15**) in carefully-measured quantities to produce the finished product, portland cement. Seven grinding mills (**16**) are used for this process. Throughout the whole operation, dust collectors and precipitators (**17**) are part of an $8 million environmental control system. Finished cement goes to either six packhouse silos (**18**) for bagging (**19**) and bulk shipments by truck and rail or to four dockside silos (**20**) for shipment by water (**21**) to Great Lakes ports.

From Essroc Canada Brochure.

The market for cement was highly competitive. Customer loyalty was critical because cement from different manufacturers was rarely used on the same construction site, due to differences in setting characteristics and in final color. For Essroc, this had motivated a policy of "zero stockouts" at the various distribution centers. While cement producers were generally aware of substantial projects requiring large amounts of cement, the daily demand was highly weather dependent as construction slowed during wet, cold periods.

PRODUCTION AT PICTON

Production at Picton began with quarrying the limestone and concluded with loading the cement onto the *Roman*. The system was made more manageable, however, by the ability to stockpile the intermediate clinker. Maintenance of a suitable inventory of clinker was relatively straightforward, allowing the production manager to focus attention on scheduling the grinding mills. Once ground, cement had to be stored in weatherproof silos, which were expensive and had limited capacity. Cement types could not be mixed together because of differences in specifications, so scheduling the grinding also effectively involved scheduling the silos. A schematic of the Picton grinding and distribution system is shown in Exhibit 6, including the silo capacities at Picton and at each distribution center.

Mills 5 and 6 were high-volume grinding mills typically restricted to producing cement types I and II. Mill 2 had a lower throughput and was generally used as an overload grinder for cement types I and II. Mill 3 was usually kept on the fine grinds (type III and the two masonry cements), although it could be used to grind any product. Mill 4 was a flexible mill that was used for all types of cement. Production rates for each mill grinding each cement type are shown in Exhibit 5.

Grinding was carried out 24 hours per day. The principal variable cost was electrical power, which varied with the season and time of day. Mills 2, 3, and 4 each used 1,100 KWH per hour of electricity per hour of operation, and Mills 5 and 6 use 2,400 KWH per hour of operation. Hours with peak power costs were Monday to Friday from 7:00 a.m. until 11:00 p.m., while off-peak costs applied to weekends, holidays, and the night period from 11:00 p.m. until 7:00 a.m. next day. The power costs for 1994 are summarized in Exhibit 7.

Products could be rescheduled on the grinding mills with about 20 minutes' notice (given advance notice of the switch). Typically, mill schedules were made for a 2-week period each week, and last-minute amendments, although feasible, were rare.

A complicated series of pipes and pumps transferred cement from the grinding mills to the four dockside silos for onward marine transport, or to the "packhouse" silos that served local needs as well as truck and rail transportation. Contamination by masonry cement was poison to other types of cement because it impaired the ability of the cement to set properly. For this reason, the number 1 dockside silo at Picton was generally reserved for masonry, although after extensive manual cleaning, it could be use for another product if absolutely required (the cleaning crew had to crawl into the silo with long brooms and physically sweep the sides of the silo, an exhausting and dirty job). The other three dockside silos could be used for storing any of cement types I, II, and III before shipping. Once cement had been transferred to a dockside silo, it could only be loaded onto the ship and could not be transferred to the packhouse silos. (The pumping arrangement also made it impractical to transfer cement from the packhouse to the dockside silos). Once cement was loaded into a dockside silo, therefore, that silo could not be used for other cement types until it had been completely emptied.

Dockside silo 1 could load into holds 1 and 2 of the *Roman*, silo 4 into holds 2 and 3, and the other silos into any hold. Cement was loaded at the rate of 800 tons per hour, one hold at a time. Only one cement type could be

Exhibit 5 | **PRODUCTION RATES (tons/hr)**

Cement	Mill 2	Mills 3 and 4	Mills 5 and 6
I	18	22	50
II	16	20	30
III		15	
MasN		16	
MasS		18	

Exhibit 6 | SCHEMATIC OF PICTON GRINDING AND DISTRIBUTION

Grinding Rates (tons/day)

Type	Mill 2	Mills 3&4	Mills 5&6
I	480	480	1080
II	432	432	912
III	0	360	0
MN	0	384	0
MS	0	432	0

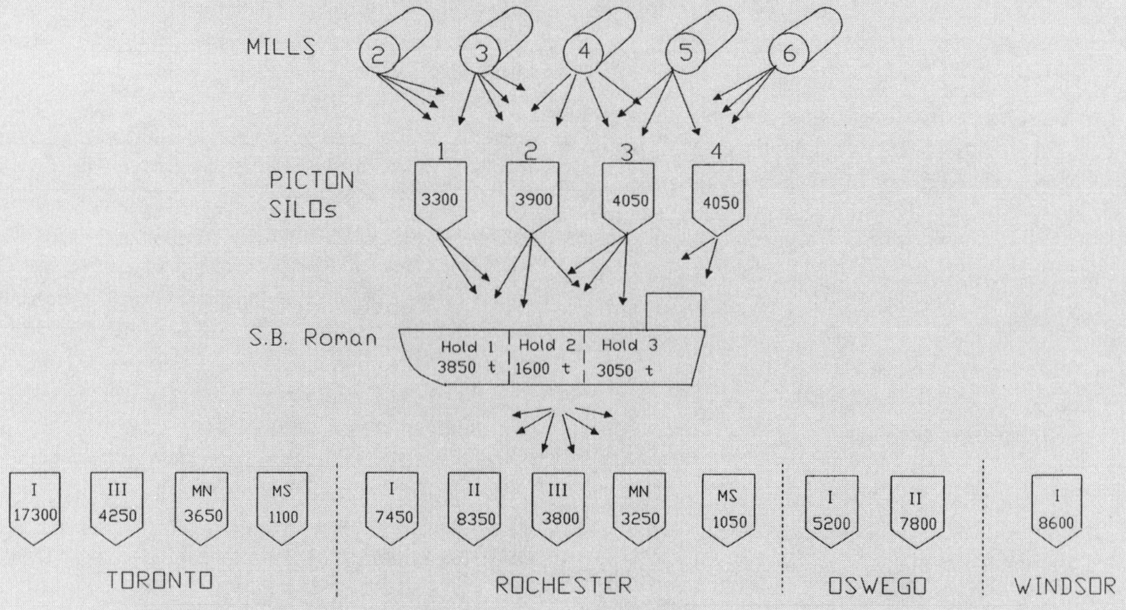

MILLS 2 3 4 5 6

PICTON SILOs: 1 (3300), 2 (3900), 3 (4050), 4 (4050)

S.B. Roman: Hold 1 3850 t | Hold 2 1600 t | Hold 3 3050 t

TORONTO: I 17300, III 4250, MN 3650, MS 1100

ROCHESTER: I 7450, II 8350, III 3800, MN 3250, MS 1050

OSWEGO: I 5200, II 7800

WINDSOR: I 8600

Approximate Demand Rates (tons/day)

Toronto		Rochester		Oswego		Windsor	
I	830	I	269	I	149	I	226
III	154	II	411	II	329		
MN	114	III	126				
MS	23	MN	38				
		MS	29				

loaded into one hold (although a hold's contents could be split between two destinations). Off loading at any destination also occurred one hold at a time, at a rate of 330 tons per hour at Oswego and Windsor, 300 tons per hour at Toronto, and 150 tons per hour at Rochester.

Demand forecasts were important drivers of the entire manufacturing and distribution system. Considerable effort had been spent in trying to improve demand forecasting, but fundamental difficulties remained. Cement demand was driven by construction activity and weather (contractors did not like to pour cement in cool or wet weather), both of which were unpredictable. The

Exhibit 7 | POWER COSTS ($/KWH)

	Winter	Spring	Summer	Fall
On-peak	0.18	0.05	0.10	0.07
Off-peak	0.024	0.025	0.008	0.01

Exhibit 8 | 1995 FORECAST MONTHLY DEMAND

	Toronto				Windsor
Month	**I**	**III**	**MasN**	**MasS**	**I**
January	2,981	833	264	50	2,320
February	4,208	374	640	50	956
March	7,887	825	885	237	1,587
April	11,765	2,173	1,161	232	3,508
May	19,094	3,540	2,461	500	5,205
June	21,076	3,540	3,071	800	5,534
July	19,589	3,540	3,312	800	5,696
August	19,365	3,540	1,312	500	5,780
September	20,751	3,540	1,198	600	5,607
October	21,687	3,540	875	600	5,939
November	16,582	2,520	716	300	3,905
December	9,163	1,810	379	150	2,033
Total	**174,148**	**29,775**	**16,274**	**4,819**	**48,070**

	Rochester				
Month	**I**	**II**	**III**	**MasN**	**MasS**
January	894	836	1,641	135	70
February	1,125	913	1,560	185	171
March	1,883	1,715	2,444	498	301
April	3,183	4,503	2,683	515	315
May	6,022	9,050	2,760	712	565
June	5,252	11,995	2,890	908	763
July	4,419	11,540	2,630	725	599
August	4,024	11,394	3,020	1,200	1,090
September	3,203	10,967	2,760	960	849
October	3,774	11,965	2,760	961	850
November	2,639	8,932	2,095	720	607
December	1,649	4,646	1,585	505	412
Total	**38,067**	**88,456**	**28,828**	**8,024**	**6,592**

	Oswego		Packhouse				
Month	**I**	**II**	**I**	**II**	**III**	**MasN**	**MasS**
January	449	446	820	50	50	46	20
February	817	443	1,395	50	302	25	21
March	1,731	1,148	2,842	50	926	116	118
April	2,611	3,030	4,168	50	594	153	141
May	3,277	7,239	7,387	50	770	285	233
June	3,645	8,294	8,796	50	770	357	320
July	3,018	7,949	8,726	50	770	381	339
August	3,022	8,097	8,117	50	770	169	148
September	2,606	7,525	7,997	50	770	167	148
October	3,012	8,025	7,406	50	770	142	116
November	3,847	4,308	5,941	50	330	105	73
December	2,874	1,874	3,340	50	110	53	40
Total	**30,909**	**58,378**	**66,935**	**600**	**6,932**	**1,999**	**1,717**

method used began with last year's sales for each product, month, and location and used these data to develop a global annual demand estimate for the coming year. This annual estimate was then prorated to products and locations, and then adjustments made for known cement contracts that Essroc Canada had won, or thought that it would win. Forecast demand for next year for each product at each destination, by month, is shown in Exhibit 8. The final step in the forecasting process was to recognize that actual demand was likely to differ from the forecasts, and this had to be taken into account in managing the system. This meant monitoring actual sales against forecasts carefully, maintaining flexibility in production and shipping, and using inventories sensibly to allow unexpectedly high demand to be met.

EXISTING SCHEDULING SYSTEM

Ken Carruthers, the vessel dispatcher, currently used a manual system to plan both the mill production and the *Roman*'s itinerary. A typical example of his worksheet is reproduced in Exhibit 9. As illustrated in the figure, he worked with a 2-week "rolling window," scheduled in 8-hour increments. The first horizontal entry sequence showed the *Roman*'s hold contents and destinations for the trips during the next 2 weeks. Further down the worksheet, grind allocations into each of the four dockside silos was entered, in addition to any grind to be fed to the packhouse silos, including the product, tonnage, and a horizontal line representing the 8-hour time slot that the mill was actually grinding for shipment to that silo. Note in Exhibit 9, for example, the mills were scheduled to grind cement type I into silo one during the off peak times (to minimize power costs) on April 11, 12, and 13.

Ken had several years' experience with this form of scheduling and was able to juggle rates and tonnages mentally to complete the form. Still, a 2-week allocation took him more than a day to complete, and the system was so complicated that he generally could only make a single pass at the allocation; that is, "what-if" analysis was very difficult. Ken observed, "The

Exhibit 9 | **EXAMPLE OF KEN'S WORKSHEET**

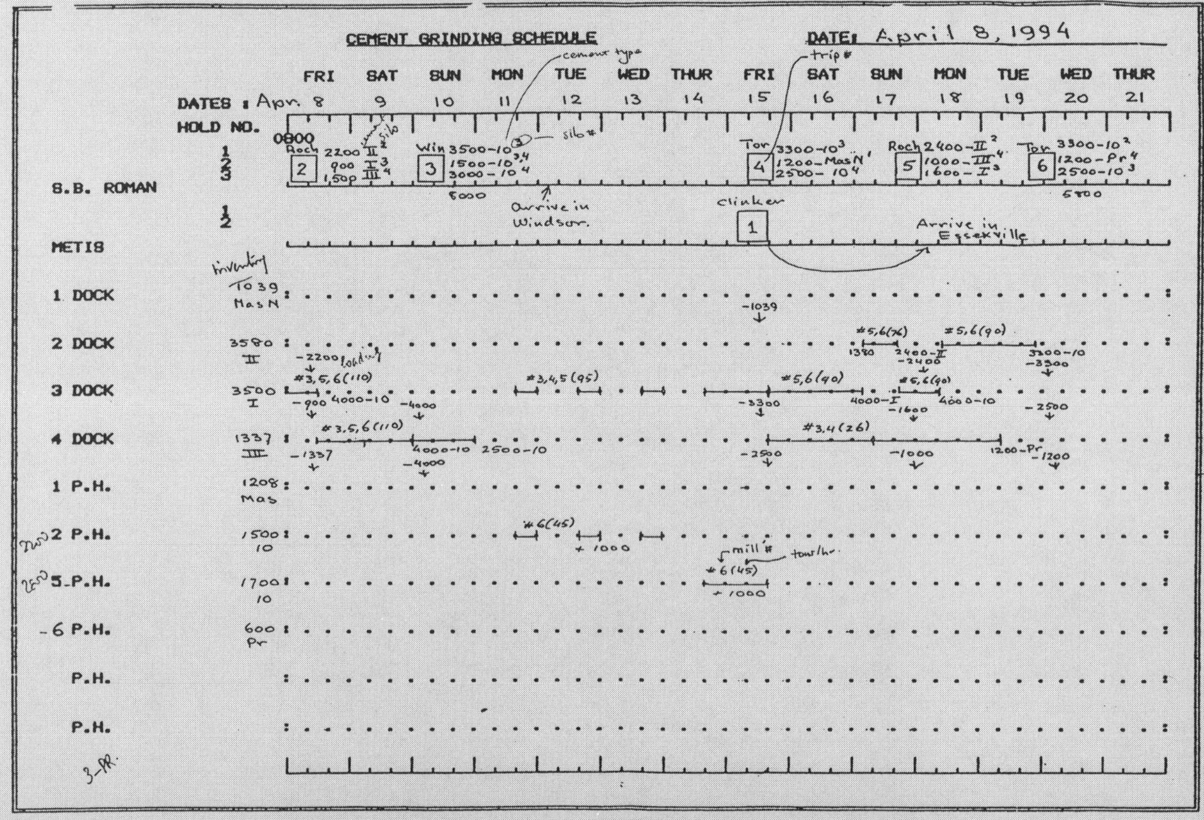

scheduling system is very complicated, and sometimes decisions one makes today can affect operations 6 weeks down the road. However, it must be flexible to meet unforeseen demands, mill take-downs, and vessel operating variations. Also, when I go on vacation, it is difficult for a newcomer to schedule due to the complexity of the system."

THE FUTURE

As they reviewed the data, Dan and François noted that margins in the cement business had been shrinking for some time, and they wondered whether gains could be made from introduction of modern modeling techniques. Could these help Ken with the scheduling problem? In particular, Dan recalled from his undergraduate days the idea of building mathematical programming models of a complex situation as a way to improve decision making.

Assignment

1. What decisions does Ken make?
2. What data does Ken need?
3. What models might help Ken?
4. What knowledge might be helpful?
5. Who has that knowledge?
6. How can a MS/OR specialist help Ken with these decisions?

7

MANAGEMENT SCIENCE/OPERATIONS RESEARCH AS A STRATEGIC WEAPON

The number of corporations that view management science/operations research (MS/OR) as an important component of their corporate strategy is increasing. We examine some of these corporations and the way in which they use MS/OR as a competitive weapon.

CORPORATE STRATEGY, COMPETITIVE STRATEGY, AND DISTINCTIVE COMPETENCIES: A SHORT PRIMER

Michael Porter defined **corporate strategy** as determining what business the corporation should be in and how best to manage the array of business units (From Competitive Advantage to Corporate Strategy, *Harvard Business Review*, May-June, 1990).

A **competitive strategy** is the method of creating competitive advantage at the level of the strategic business units. In assessing its competitive strategy, the firm must determine the products that its customers value that the firm is capable of delivering better than others and that competitors cannot easily replicate. A successful competitive strategy is one that leads to a sustainable competitive advantage.

To execute a successful competitive strategy, the corporation must make use of its **distinctive competencies**. Distinctive competencies are the skills, knowledge, and organizational structures that are internal to the corporation, cross functional boundaries, and are not easily replicated. Distinctive competencies are difficult for competitors to imitate, make a significant contribution to the value the customer attaches to the product, and provide the corporation with the ability to compete in several markets. Distinctive competencies cannot usually be outsourced or purchased.

The example of Federal Express (FedEx) ties together these ideas.

- FedEx's **corporate strategy** is to be a major player in the national and international overnight package business.
- FedEx's **competitive strategy** includes "absolutely, positively" overnight; guaranteed on-time delivery, with friendly staff; and low prices.
- FedEx brings a variety of **distinctive competencies** to this competitive strategy, including its aircraft fleet, hubs and package-handling systems, package-tracking and customer support functions, and logistics support.

Distinctive competencies provide the foundation of a successful competitive and corporate strategy; they enable a corporation to execute strategy more effectively than other companies that might have the same or a similar strategy. The use of information technology (IT) provides a competitive advantage for many globally competitive firms and has become a distinctive competence for these organizations. The potential strategic value of IT was first recognized in 1985:

> Until recently, most managers treated information technology as a support service and delegated it to EDP departments. Now, however, every company must understand the broad effects and implications of the new technology and how it can create substantial and sustainable competitive advantage.... Information technology is changing the way companies operate.
>
> From M.E. Porter and V.E. Millar, How Information Gives You Competitive Advantage, *Harvard Business Review*, 1985; July-August: 149–160.

MS/OR is a key component of IT.

> Today IT must be conceived of broadly to encompass the information that businesses create and use *as well as a wide spectrum of ... technologies that process the information* [emphasis added].
>
> From M.E. Porter and V.E. Millar, How Information Gives You Competitive Advantage, *Harvard Business Review*, 1985; July-August: 149–160.

The strategic importance of information systems is recognized through the existence of senior appointments in IS in many major corporations, including many vice-presidential-level chief information officer (CIO) positions. The average CIO, however, is an information systems professional who has emerged from the data processing department, and most CIOs pay much more attention to hardware and software management and to how data are collected than to how the data are used to achieve a sustainable competitive advantage. Managers of MS/OR activities remain well down the organization structure in most corporations.

There are, however, a growing number of notable exceptions: corporations that manage their MS/OR activities extremely well and in doing so have created a sustainable competitive advantage through investment in MS/OR. In these organizations, senior management recognize their MS/OR as a distinctive competence and consider their MS/OR skills to be a strategically important asset.

We define the term **strategic MS/OR** to be *MS/OR that achieves a sustainable competitive advantage*. Strategic MS/OR is, therefore, a body of work that forms the basis of a distinct competence in MS/OR. Tom Cook is President of Sabre Decision Technologies (SDT) (renamed from American Airlines Decision Technologies [AADT] after a 1994 reorganization that moved the Sabre Reservation Systems Group from American Airlines to AADT). SDT is the MS/OR function for AMR, the parent company of American Airlines. Cook thinks of the objectives of SDT's work in these terms: "The things we are doing are designed to create a competitive advantage"(P. Horner, Eyes on the Prize, *OR/MS Today*, 1991).

As we examine organizations that are world leaders in MS/OR, we will find many examples of "Strategic MS/OR."

MANAGEMENT SCIENCE/OPERATIONS RESEARCH ACTIVITIES AND SUSTAINABLE COMPETITIVE ADVANTAGE

The value of a distinctive competence to a corporation is that it creates a competitive advantage for the firm that is sustainable over a period of time. Competing firms must then react or they will lose market share, and may eventually have to leave the business. Consequently, strategic MS/OR is accompanied by changes in industrial structure, including reorganizations and bankruptcies, and the appearance of new businesses that exploit the particular advantage. Often, these new businesses are spawned from the original innovator.

The existence of strategic MS/OR would be confirmed by finding examples of firms that are achieving a sustainable competitive advantage from their use of MS/OR, but evidence of a sustainable competitive advantage from any source is rarely directly observable. Instead, the existence of strategic MS/OR activities can be inferred from secondary evidence. If MS/OR is a distinctive competence for a firm, then:

- The chief executive officer (CEO) of the firm will know about the firm's MS/OR work and of its importance.
- There will be MS/OR work being done that constitutes the "strategic asset," and this work should be identifiable.
- The MS/OR team will be provided with a certain status and be involved on a regular basis on other major decisions.
- Competitors will know about, and most probably respond to, the firm's successful strategic MS/OR work, perhaps by attempting to copy it.
- There will be evidence that industrial restructuring has occurred, motivated by one firm's successful strategic use of OR.

- New businesses will appear that serve industries where MS/OR has achieved strategic success in the industry.

We review the evidence for each of these items.

CEOs on the Importance of Management Science/Operations Research Activities

Many CEOs of major corporations have spoken out confirming the importance of MS/OR to their organizations.

> MS/OR plays an important part of our ability to manage our diverse businesses.... As we look to the future, MS/OR will continue to be a vital and necessary part of our organization and our goal to remain a world-class company, capable of competing against all comers.
>
> R.E. Howson, Chairman of the Board and Chief Executive Officer, McDermott International, Inc., Plenary Speech to the INFORMS Conference, New Orleans, October 1995.

> OR plays a big role in the five-year ... approximately one billion dollar expansion and modernization program that we launched in 1987. Under the program we have built 22 manufacturing plants—we would not have dared to undertake the expansion at all without MS/OR.... San Miguel's Senior Management appreciates the vital role of MS/OR in attaining our corporate goals, and in implementing the strategies that enable us to achieve adequate growth and satisfactory returns for our various stakeholders.
>
> Francisco Eizmendi Jr., President, San Miguel Corporation, quoted in E. Del Rosario, OR Brews Success for San Miguel, *OR/MS Today*, October 1994.

> Management science is not a project or a set of techniques; it is a process, a way of thinking and managing.
>
> Daniel Elwing, President and CEO of ABB Electric, in D.H. Gensch, N. Aversa, and S.P. Moore, A Choice-Modeling Market Information System that Enabled ABB Electric to Expand its Market Share, *Interfaces*, 1990;20:1.

> Employing OR techniques and modeling skills, the OR department has played a role in the development of long-range plans for the past 17 years and was instrumental in determining the specific growth sequence that allowed FedEx to become the world's largest and most reliable air express carrier. Every major system change ... [was] modeled by OR several years in advance of the actual system change. This enabled the company to grow smoothly.... By modeling various alternatives for future system design, FedEx has, in effect, made its mistakes on paper. Computer modeling works; it allows us to examine many different alternatives and it forces the examination of the entire problem.
>
> Frederick W. Smith, Chairman, CEO, and founder of Federal Express Corporation, in P. Horner, Eyes on the Prize, *OR/MS Today*, August 1991.

These examples suggest that McDermott International, San Miguel Corporation, ABB Electric, and FedEx are candidates for possession of a distinct competence in MS/OR; however, the CEO's knowledge of the value of MS/OR work is a necessary, but not a sufficient, condition for MS/OR to be delivering a sustainable competitive advantage.

Management Science/Operations Research Work that Represents a "Strategic Asset"

There are many examples of MS/OR work that has produced handsome returns. Few can match the example of KeyCorp:

> KeyCorp is a bank holding company in Cleveland with about 1,200 branches and assets of $66.8 billion and equity of $4.7 billion. KeyCorp invested "less than $500,000" in an MS/OR project beginning in 1991 that was expected to reduce expenses by $98 million over 5 years. This represents a payback period for this investment of less than 10 days, or an internal rate of return of about 3,500%!
>
> From S.K. Kotha, M.P. Barnum, and D.A. Brown, KeyCorp Service Excellence Management System, *Interfaces*, 1996;26:1.

While this cost reduction is impressive (although it might be argued that $98 million over 5 years is not a great deal of money for a corporation with $66.8 billion in assets), for this investment to be considered "strategic," it must have created an advantage that was sustainable for some period of time.

Earlier chapters include many examples of MS/OR work that has produced a competitive advantage, particularly a cost advantage, but in many of these examples, it was difficult to sustain this advantage because in many cases the work described was easily replicated. For example, a feed formulator can introduce optimization as a way of reducing the cost of its products, but if this firm prospers, competitors can quickly replicate the work and nullify any advantage. There are, however, some kinds of "strategic problems" that do appear to provide MS/OR groups with the ability to sustain an advantage over a long period of time.

Strategic Management Science/Operations Research Problems. One form of strategic MS/OR problems is the very large, complex, operational problem that is theoretically "optimizable," but for reasons of size and complexity, the optimum solution cannot currently be obtained. Successful MS/OR teams address these problems using a series of heuristics that constrain the problems to a size that can be solved in real time "at the leading edge" of available technique and technology. Once a constrained problem can be optimized, new heuristics are developed that relax the constraints to produce a new problem that with further work, can be optimized to produce an even lower cost solution, at which point the heuristics are changed again and the process repeated.

Strategic MS/OR problems yield increasingly lower cost solutions over a substantial period of time as the solution procedures are refined and developed. The cost advantage is further sustainable if management intervention is required to implement the improved solutions as they are developed.

Sustainability of the competitive advantage, therefore, arises from two sources:

- the MS/OR group has developed skills and knowledge (and perhaps hardware, databases, and code) that a competitor starting work on the same problem cannot easily replicate, and
- management have adapted the firm's structure and operations to take maximum advantage of the low cost solutions that the MS/OR group is producing. These structural changes may involve contracts, labor relations, or facilities design.

The competitor, sensing that a firm is achieving a competitive edge, must first find a way to replicate the MS/OR work. Even if it can do this quickly, it may not be able to implement the results because of structural issues (for example, the union contract might not permit the required changes in working hours or practices, or it may take several years and/or many dollars to renegotiate the contract), or it may find that it obtains much smaller cost savings on implementation than the established firm.

Two problems that have these characteristics are the airline flight crew scheduling problem and the "optimum dynamic pricing" problem.

Airline Flight Crew Scheduling Problem. Crew costs are the second largest cost item for a major airline (after fuel) and amount to more than $1 billion annually ($1.3 billion for

American Airlines [from R. Anbil, E. Gelman, B. Patty, and R. Tanga, Recent Advances in Crew-Pairing Optimization at American Airlines, *Interfaces*, 1991;21:1]). The problem of assigning flight crews to flights is solved as an integer program that selects the low-cost set of crew "tours" that covers all scheduled flights. A critical input for this assignment is a set of feasible crew "tours," in which each tour starts at a crew base, works a feasible set of flights, and returns to the crew base (see Airline Flight Crew Scheduling case at the end of this chapter for a full description of the problem). Developing feasible "tours" to input to the optimization is time consuming but critical: there are a huge number of possible tours. As new tours are developed and tried over a period of time, the cost-effective tours are retained as others are replaced by promising newly developed tours.

A heuristic that makes this problem much more manageable involves limiting the crew tour lengths considered. The problem that has the fewest feasible crew tours is the "1-day" problem, where each crew is constrained to spend every night at its crew base. Over a period of time, good solutions to the 1-day problem can be developed (even if the flight schedule is variable) because the skill and knowledge required to develop new tours can be developed and the database of good 1-day tours can be extended. At some point, however, switching to a "2-day" tour heuristic, where a crew is allowed to spend one night on each tour away from the crew base, becomes possible.

The 2-day problem is much larger that the 1-day problem because there are more flights and many more possible crew tours, but the 2-day problem must have lower cost than the 1-day problem (because any feasible solution to the 1-day problem is a feasible solution to the 2-day problem). It is even possible that a crude solution to the 2-day problem may have lower cost than a near-optimum solution to the 1-day problem. In time, with skill, an OR group can develop near-optimal solutions to the 2-day problem, but now the even larger "3-day" problem looms, again with the promise of cost savings. After the 3-day problem, there awaits the "4-day" problem, and so on. How far can this go? After several years' work, Sabre Decision Technologies (SDT) can now achieve good solutions to the 3-day problem (R. Anbil, E. Gelman, B. Patty, and R. Tanga).

Figure 7-1 illustrates how this continuous improvement process can reduce crew costs over a substantial period of time.

As improved solutions to the n-day problem are developed, management can adapt the organization to take advantage of the promise of lower crew costs. Some fairly straightforward

Figure 7-1 **AIRLINE CREW SCHEDULING PROBLEM COST TRAJECTORY**

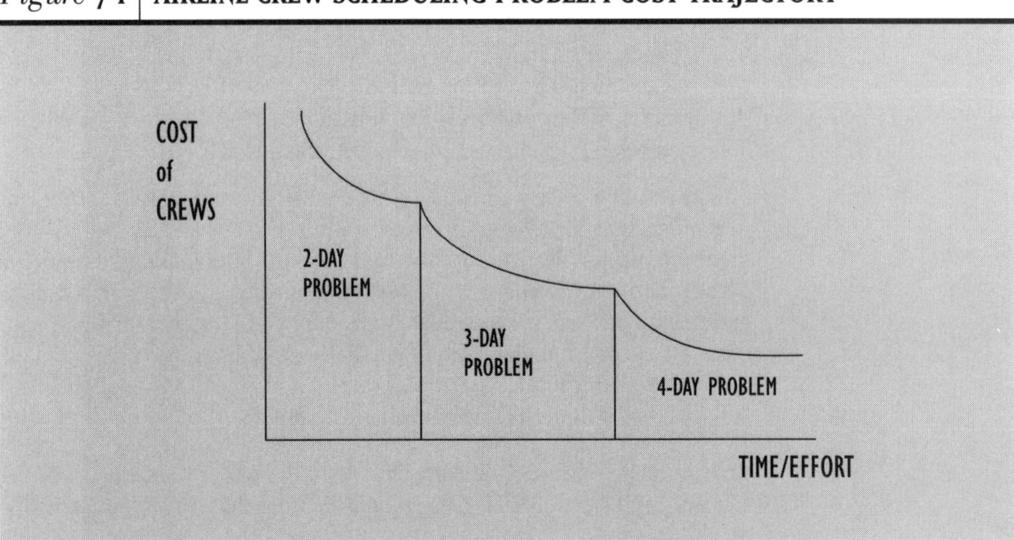

adaptations include changing the numbers of crews available, opening new crew bases, and closing existing ones. Others, such as rescheduling flights to make them less costly to crew, may involve complex tradeoffs and take considerable time to implement. Moving from n-day tours to $(n + 1)$-day tours requires more management intervention, including, perhaps, renegotiated union contracts and possibly even changes in flight regulations, but the airline that can successfully manage these changes will gain greater advantage through lower operating costs. Over time, the operation of the airline becomes "tuned" to the crew assignment algorithms.

Even if a competitor were to "buy" the MS/OR expertise to solve this problem, it would still not be able to achieve the same crew efficiencies immediately because considerable management and structural change would be required to implement the solutions at the same level of effectiveness. It is significant that at the same time SDT was developing advanced algorithms to solve this problem, they were marketing software to their competitors that "solved" the same problem. Clearly, SDT's management did not believe that the software alone was sufficient to counter the cost advantage that American Airlines was obtaining.

Optimum Dynamic Pricing. One of the most important "strategic problems" that has emerged from OR activities is the optimum dynamic pricing problem, known as part of **yield management** at American Airlines (B.C. Smith, J.F. Leimkuhler, and R.M. Darrow, Yield Management at American Airlines, *Interfaces*, 1992;22:1), and also as the **revenue management** (D. Greenfield, OR Overhaul, *OR/MS Today,* April 1996) problem. On January 5, 1996, *Wall Street Journal* columnist Thomas Petzinger Jr. reported "revenue management" to be the number 1 "emerging business strategy." The revenue management or optimum dynamic pricing problem was introduced in Chapter 4, and the general problem can be stated in words:

> Divide the selling horizon for each of our products into periods (hours, days, weeks, or months). Then, for each product and for each period between now and the end of the sales horizon, find product prices for each remaining period that maximize sales revenue while selling out our inventory.

A formal formulation for each product is as follows:

Let p_i be the product price in period i,

q_i be the quantity sold in period i,

$q_i = f_i\,(p_i)$ be the demand curve for period i, and

I be the amount of product to be sold over N pricing periods.

then, for each period, k, $k = 1,2,\ \ldots N$

$$\text{Max } Z = \sum_{i=k}^{N} p_i\, q_i$$

subject to

$$q_i = f_i(p_i) \text{ for } i = k, k+1, \ldots N$$

$$\sum_{i=k}^{N} q_i = I - \sum_{i=1}^{k-1} q_i$$

\+ additional constraints may be added.

Prices obtained by solving this problem are both "optimum" and "dynamic":

Optimum in that the problem is an optimization; the form of the optimization depends on the form of the demand functions. If the demand functions are linear, then the optimization has a quadratic objective.

Dynamic in that with each pricing period, a new set of prices is determined; thus, the price of a product may change within a given solution and also from solution to solution. In general, if sales are strong or demand is high, the optimum price will increase, whereas in periods of weak demand or when sales are lower than expected, prices will decrease.

Figure 7-2 illustrates the iterative nature of optimum dynamic pricing.

Note that this problem reverses traditional business thinking or culture; traditional firms set a product price and allow the market to determine sales volume. In optimum dynamic pricing, the firm determines how much they will sell, and the market (and the firm's skill at revenue maximization) determines what revenue is received for these sales.

The optimum dynamic pricing problem is a strategic OR problem.

The problem is large and complex. A single product problem with daily price changes and a product life of 180 days requires solution of a nonlinear optimization problem with a maximum of 180 variables. An organization with a large number of products (say 10,000) has a significant nonlinear optimization computing load to handle each period.

A firm might introduce dynamic pricing by changing prices weekly. Once weekly prices can be computed and managed, the firm has the opportunity to move to more frequent price changes. In general, the more pricing periods that the sales horizon can be broken into, the higher the revenues that can be obtained; a firm that can manage daily price changes will generally be able to obtain higher revenue that one that can implement only weekly price changes. Similarly, hourly price changes will generally produce higher revenues than daily price changes. However, the more frequent the price changes, the greater are the skill and computation required to compute the optimum prices and bring them into the marketplace.

Solving this problem requires both the algorithmic skill to solve the large nonlinear optimizations and the modeling skill and experience to somehow find and estimate the demand curves (or demand elasticities). The established dynamic pricer will have a significant skills advantage in these two areas.

Each time a price is set, a (p,q) pair is generated that adds to the database available to estimate future demand curves. The established dynamic pricer, therefore, has a significant database of product specific (p,q) pairs that the newcomer cannot replicate.

Figure 7-2 **OPTIMUM DYNAMIC PRICING ITERATIONS**

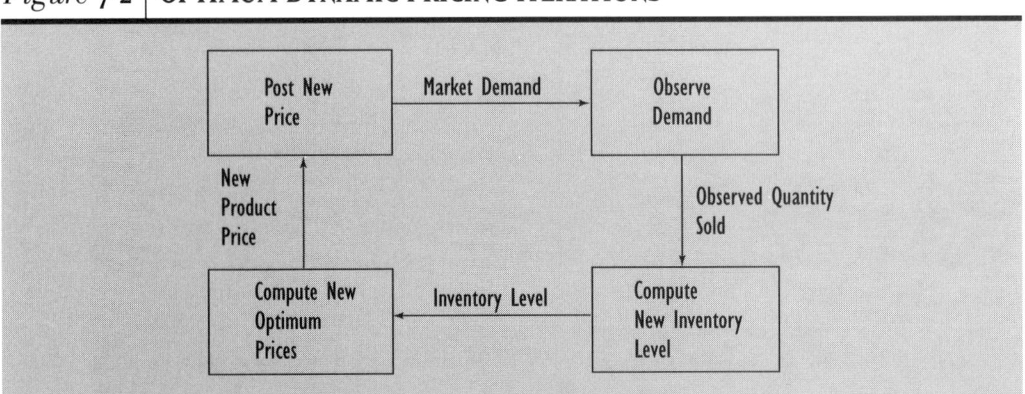

Many exogenous variables (competitor's prices, marketing factors, seasonality, weather, and so on) can be expected to affect demand and be important in demand curve (or elasticity) estimation. Observed values for these exogenous variables may be added to the database and further contribute to the long learning curve for this problem.

The problem has a short run component (Given I units of product to sell over some horizon, how do we set the price each period?) but also an important and difficult-to-solve long-term issue: What is the optimum value for I, the number of units to inject into the market? Determining this optimum quantity involves solving a second optimization that incorporates product acquisition cost data.

Managing optimum dynamic pricing requires that optimum dynamic prices can be computed but also that these prices can be delivered into the marketplace in a timely and effective manner. The firm that has priced products dynamically for some time will have developed the technology and skill to take full advantage of these prices and will be organized in a way that supports the pricing activity. Important among these activities is the development of a marketing approach that promotes the benefits and impact of dynamic prices.

In summary, the firm that has been dynamic pricing for some time will develop skills and knowledge that will provide it with a revenue advantage that a competitor starting dynamic pricing for the first time will be unable to match.

The importance of the optimum dynamic pricing problem has been reinforced by several senior executives, most notably by Robert Crandall, Chairman, President and CEO of American Airlines, who has stated:

> I believe that yield management is the single most important technical development in transportation management since we entered the era of airline deregulation in 1979.... [Dynamic pricing] creates a pricing structure that responds to demand on a flight-by-flight basis. As a result, we can more effectively match our demand to supply.
>
> From B.C. Smith, J.F. Leimkuhler, and R.M. Darrow, Yield Management at American Airlines, *Interfaces*, 1992;22:1.

National Car Rental was essentially bankrupt when it introduced optimal dynamic pricing as part of a new revenue management system. The impact was dramatic:

> [MS/OR] basically saved National Car Rental. And you can go from the CEO of National on down, and they will all say: "just applying these OR models made the life or death difference for this company."
>
> Kevin Geraghty, Aeronomics Inc., in D. Greenfield, OR Overhaul, *OR/MS Today,* April 1996.

Some idea of the management intervention that was required to successfully implement optimum dynamic pricing at National comes from Ernest Johnson, Corporate Vice President, National Car Rental, who stated:

> We got [senior management] to commit to educating the company. In fact, we got them to agree to conduct seminars themselves once the system had been devised. We got them to tour the country and talk to rental agents at all locations, and talk to every reservation agent to explain the differences that they would see in the way pricing and inventory were now going to be handled.... We had to change the culture of the organization.
>
> From D. Greenfield, OR Overhaul, *OR/MS Today,* April 1996.

To replicate a dynamic pricing system like National's, competitors must both develop the algorithms and make the necessary organizational change to allow successful implementation. The time that this will take will provide National with an opportunity to further develop the system and/or the organization in an effort to sustain the competitive advantage that has been created.

A discussion of MS/OR work that represents a strategic asset would be incomplete without recognizing the existence of the MS/OR "industry" in which a large variety of firms sell MS/OR work as their end-product. Important providers of MS/OR include many specialized consultancies (e.g., SDT, Hoskyns, Giro) where the product is "MS/OR work," and this work clearly is a strategic asset for these firms (perhaps their only strategic asset). Another important group of companies are those that sell a product that includes a significant MS/OR component but that is not, of itself, MS/OR. Two rather different examples of this are Innovis Interactive Technologies and AT&T.

Innovis Interactive Technologies. Innovis developed a product called the DesignCenter (M. Lembersky, Enhancing Point-of-Sale Productivity and Satisfaction in Retail Stores, *European Journal of Operational Research*, 1991;54). The DesignCenter was a booth that provided a highly graphic and interactive environment for the design and specification of an outdoor, home-improvement deck. A customer with no training, and using only a single mouse-button, could use the DesignCenter to design their own deck, cost out the design, and finally print a picture of the chosen deck, together with construction instructions and a bill of materials. DesignCenters were made available in late February 1989. By June, more than 100 wood retailers had taken delivery, and by September, well over $150,000,000 worth of decks had been sold.

Although the DesignCenter was not entirely an MS/OR product, its developers were both operational researchers who had worked in the OR group at Weyerhaeuser Company, a major international wood products supplier. The internal logic of the DesignCenter was a combination of rules and algorithms that were closely integrated with a highly user-friendly interactive graphic interface. The system bore many similarities to other forms of visual interactive models that were emerging within MS/OR at this time.

The DesignCenter was a strategic asset for Innovis; it was their only product. The obvious success of the DesignCenter as a vehicle for selling wood and nails suggests that it had the potential to become a strategic asset within the industry, but its history suggests that while the potential was there, it did not quite materialize. Part of the problem appears to be the fact that the DesignCenter sold wood, not specifically Weyerhaeuser wood, and consequently Weyerhaeuser, which had no exclusive retail outlets, could not easily capture the benefits of DesignCenter use and the accompanying competitive advantage. Restructuring of the industry led to the sale of Innovis with the DesignCenter product and the separation of its developers to form their own new company, Lembersky/Chi Inc. A number of DesignCenter clones quickly appeared, including software to design decks that runs on personal computers. The first-mover advantage dissipated quickly, and what looked like a good example of strategic OR now appears to have failed to live up to this expectation.

AT&T. Before deregulation of the North American telephone industry, AT&T made its profits by selling telephones and telephone calls. After deregulation, telephones became low-margin items, and new carriers moved in to cream off profitable sectors of the call business. AT&T faced the problem of developing new revenue producing products, and it found an opportunity in developing and marketing new products that were packages of existing services. One such package product was a **telemarketing system**.

A telemarketing system consists of one or more telemarketing centers, each containing a mass of telephone equipment and many lines to the network, where groups of people answer incoming telephone calls or originate new calls. These telemarketing centers are used to coordinate customer service, perform order processing for catalogue or direct-response television sales, provide field sales staff support or account management, and conduct direct telephone sales and opinion polling. It is estimated that 8 million people will be employed in telemarketing in North America by the year 2000.

The telemarketing product offered by AT&T is rich in MS/OR (T. Spencer III, A.J. Brigandi, D.R. Dargon, and M.J. Sheehan, AT&T's Telemarketing Site Selection System Offers Customer Support, *Interfaces*, 1990;20:1). The key to cost-effectiveness is to select the sites for the call centers and design the communications system to minimize the costs of labor, real estate, and communications, while providing a given level of service. AT&T uses a mixed integer optimization (see reading in Chapter 4) to select minimum cost sites for the centers from the list of politically acceptable sites and assign originating calls to sites to minimize the total cost of the system. In 1988, AT&T used this optimization to help 46 customers who committed $375 million in annual AT&T long distance network services and $31 million in equipment sales from AT&T. Some consulting firms also offer a site selection service, but AT&T competes aggressively because it sees the product as the package, not just the site-selection problem: it is reported that DHL, an express package delivery service, would have had to pay $240,000 to a consultant for advice on site selection for its call centers but AT&T provided the same advice for free in just 10 days (AT&T, The Old Order Changeth, *Focus Employee Annual Report*, 1991).

AT&T has marketed **Cell Center Solutions** for almost a decade and has developed minimum cost systems for hundreds of customers. In doing so, AT&T developed the algorithms and software to solve this complex problem and accumulated a massive database of location data, including available office space, building costs, labor market data, local taxes, and wage rates. The combination of developed skills and experience together with algorithms, software, and databases provides AT&T with a competitive advantage in the "call center" business. Because this advantage appears to have been sustained for a considerable time, this MS/OR work appears to be a "strategic asset" for AT&T.

Management Science/Operations Research Groups that Are Broadly Involved in Corporate Decision Making

In companies where MS/OR has scored a strategic success, the MS/OR group will have gained significant credibility, and as a result, the input of the group will be regularly sought on important decision issues. SDT, FedEx, San Miguel Corporation, and McDermott International provide examples of groups that appear to have gained this expected broad involvement through corporate decision making.

FedEx has had a successful OR group for many years, and this group has historically been involved on major decisions. Joe Hinson, General Manager of Operations Research at FedEx, chairs the corporate strategic planning committee. Hinson reports directly and regularly to CEO Fred Smith, and suggests:

> When you know that you'll be listened to, the weight of your work becomes a little bit heavier and more satisfying. It's nice to know that the answer that you come up with will not be muddled by the time it reaches the top.
>
> From P. Horner, Eyes on the Prize, *OR/MS Today*, August 1991.

A recent article produced by the Harvard Business School MIS History Project (R.O. Mason, J.L. McKenney, W. Carlson, and D.C. Copeland, Absolutely, Positively Operations Research: The Federal Express Story, *Interfaces*, 1996) provides much interesting commentary on OR at FedEx. Although this group has generally documented firms (such as American Hospital Supply, BankAmerica) where information systems provided a strategic advantage (J.L. McKenney, D.C. Copeland, and R.O. Mason, *Waves of Change: Business Evolution Through Information Technology,* Boston, MA, Harvard Business School Press, 1995), they conclude that, "FedEx is an archetype of a company that has succeeded by applying the scientific methods to its operations. Models and analysis have informed many of [FedEx's] crucial, business-shaping decisions. In cases in which OR wasn't used... the company performed poorly."

Five reasons for the success of OR at FedEx are provided:

1. The air cargo industry is a "whole system" business, and not easily managed separately.
2. Fred Smith, the founder and CEO is "devoted to the use of scientific inquiry in his business. OR is a voice to be heard at FedEx."
3. OR has focused on crucial issues and has not been sidetracked in "the esoteric or bogged down in minutia."
4. FedEx OR results and models were considered to be "living things, not imperial edifices cast in concrete.... By means of continual dialogues between the OR team and executive management, they jointly arrived at a shared understanding as to the problems they faced, the pros and cons of the models, and the strengths and weaknesses of what the model results were telling them."
5. "The OR team conducted itself as a learning organization, a center of knowledge and inquiry about the most important dimensions of the business. Captured in their models and databases are literally millions of items ... that characterize all of the most important activities of the business...."

Hinson discusses how deeply his OR group is ingrained in the activities of FedEx.

> An OR department's effectiveness doesn't necessarily have to be measured by the one big home run that saves the company millions of dollars, but rather by giving out lots of good results, providing answers to lots of questions every day and every week of the year, year after year."
>
> From P. Horner, Eyes on the Prize, *OR/MS Today*, August 1991.

San Miguel Corporation's Head of Operational Research, Elise del Rosario, is a corporate Senior Assistant Vice President, and she has established her group as an integral part of corporate strategic decision making. Company President Francisco Eizmendi Jr. suggests the opinion of this group is broadly sought:

> In our strategic planning meetings every year, whenever a division or business unit manager presents a project, we always make sure that Operations Research has gone through the proposal.
>
> From E. Del Rosario, OR Brews Success for San Miguel, *OR/MS Today*, October 1994.

The extent of OR involvement in activities at San Miguel is extraordinary: the OR group tackled 65 projects during 1985-1986, and in 1992, 10 OR projects produced a bottom line impact of $35 million. Furthermore, San Miguel had "OR-type people throughout the organization: Senior vice-presidents, plant managers, production schedulers, economic analysts and so on. Many of these individuals at one time in their career worked in the OR department" (E. Del Rosario).

MS/OR at Babcock and Wilcox (B&W) (now part of McDermott International) achieved a significant success in the late 1960s when B&W's Nuclear Equipment Division was experiencing rapid growth. The resulting scheduling problems were leading to losses of about $15 million annually, prompting *Fortune* magazine to write (in November 1969) that the future of B&W was at stake. A simulation model to aid scheduling, developed by the MS/OR group, was implemented at a cost of about $8 million, and by the time the model was fully operational, the $15 million annual loss had been turned into a $17 million annual profit. As McDermott International CEO Howson states:

> When we acquired B&W, one of the buried treasures we discovered was a well-established, well-respected OR group.... Over the years, our OR staff have used their quantitative, analytical methods to solve many other complicated problems around our company.
>
> From R.E Howson, Chairman of the Board and Chief Executive Officer, McDermott International, Inc., Plenary Speech to the INFORMS Conference, New Orleans, October 1995.

In common with San Miguel Corporation, OR group input is now institutionalized.

> Currently, our OR staff is helping evaluate projects with a total value of over $1 billion. We are convinced that the application of quantitative methods to estimating and contract management increases our company's chances for success. Recently we issued a corporate policy that requires the use of these methods on major proposals and contracts.
>
> From R.E Howson, Chairman of the Board and Chief Executive Officer, McDermott International, Inc., Plenary Speech to the INFORMS Conference, New Orleans, October 1995.

Competitive Reaction to Successful Management Science/ Operations Research

Successful strategic OR provides a competitive advantage over a period of time to the instigator. Competitive corporations would be expected to notice this advantage through declining market shares or profits, and react. This reaction should be noticeable. One extreme reaction would be to declare bankruptcy or sell off the business. The clearest evidence that this has occurred is the case of People Express Airlines (PE). The history of PE, which is well documented in a series of Harvard Business School case studies, is that of a highly successful airline that grew rapidly by paying particular attention to six precepts that closely match some of the common management fads of the day.

These precepts were:

1. Service: commitment to the growth and development of our people;
2. To be the best provider of air transportation;
3. To provide the highest quality of leadership;
4. To serve as a role model for others;
5. Simplicity; and
6. Maximization of profits.

From People Express Airlines: Rise and Decline, Harvard Business School case 9-490-012, 1993.

PE was very "people oriented" and stressed "customer service." Founded in mid-1980, the strategy seemed to work as PE grew to annual revenues of almost $1 billion in 1985. Contemporary writings from the mid-1980s suggested that PE had some problems, but none anticipated that PE would be facing bankruptcy by the end of 1986. The rapid development of the OR group at American Airlines (now Sabre Decision Technologies [SDT]) and its development of optimal dynamic pricing and yield management were not seen as a significant competitive threat at the time. After the fact, it is generally agreed that innovative OR at SDT drove this successful air carrier out of business in just a few short months. Donald Burr, Founder and CEO of PE, "believes that major carriers' use of sophisticated computer programs to immediately match or undercut his prices ultimately killed People Express" (J.A. Bryan, Donald Burr May be Ready to Take to the Skies Again, *Business Week*, January 16, 1989, pp 74–75).

The teaching note, which provides a guide to use of the Harvard Business School PE cases, provides an independent assessment:

> The major carriers met People Express' pricing structure ... and used their reservations systems to achieve optimal pricing and yield management. PE's performance, in essentially all dimensions, immediately declined.... The end was swift.
>
> G. Loveman and M. Beer, People Express Airlines: Rise and Decline, Teaching Note, Harvard Business School case 5-491-080, 1991.

Many other airlines (including Braniff, TWA, Continental, Eastern, Pan American) incurred large losses at this same time leading to bankruptcies and Chapter 11 reorganizations. It is tempting to conclude that OR work at SDT was the driver of these changes; however, these were established airlines that faced new and vigorous competition in this period from new carriers, such as PE, that appeared at the onset of U.S. airline deregulation in December 1981. Established air carriers faced a number of competitive pressures at this time. AMR, the parent company of American Airlines and SDT, reacted to this pressure by investing heavily in MS/OR, and this proved to be a successful strategy. Others that followed different strategies were less successful and did not survive or survived only in greatly trimmed-down form.

Competitive air carriers would be expected to respond to SDT's strategic OR successes by attempting an accelerated OR program. There is some evidence that this was the case as United, Delta, and USAir have all invested significantly in OR. In Spring 1995, USAir was running an advertisement attempting to add 40 professionals to its OR department: "Based upon its past contribution, USAir's OR Department is growing by 40 professionals" (USAir advertisement, *OR/MS Today*, April 1995). The advertisement stated that:

> Our existing OR Department of 37 professionals provides management consulting and decision technology to all divisions of the airline. Grow with us as we find solutions to some of the most complex real-world problems in: ... Transportation Scheduling & Routing, Revenue Management, Operations & Maintenance Planning.

By 1995, AADT had grown to more than 400 professionals, so it is apparent that USAir, with only 37 professionals (expanding to 77), was behind. The problem areas listed are all areas where SDT has published highly profitable MS/OR applications, providing further evidence of "catch up" behavior.

Industrial Restructuring as a Result of Strategic Management Science/Operations Research

The North American airline industry went through major restructuring during the period after deregulation in December 1981. During this time, OR groups have been spawned, and some have flourished. There is broad recognition that OR work is now a critical part of airline operations:

> It is worth emphasizing that a reservations system, with its yield management capacity, is arguably the single most important strategic asset of an airline.
>
> From Beer, People Express Airlines: Rise and Decline, Teaching Note Harvard Business School case 9-490-012, 1991.

Although causality is difficult to establish, there does appear to be strong support for a view that OR has contributed to the observed restructuring, particularly the demise of People Express (discussed earlier) and the growth of American Airlines into the largest air carrier.

OR work at ABB Electric has been credited (Daniel Elwing, President and CEO of ABB Electric, in D.H. Gensch, N. Aversa, and S.P. Moore, A Choice-Modeling Market Information System that Enabled ABB Electric to Expand its Market Share, *Interfaces*, 1990; 20:1) with significant restructuring in the North American market for industrial transformers. ABB entered the electrical transformer market in 1970 and had almost reached a break-even state (with a 6% market share) by 1974. The total market for transformers was about 3,300 units in 1974 but fell to less than 1,000 units in 1975 as a result of events that included the formation of OPEC and the end of the era of cheap energy. Industrial giants Westinghouse, General Electric, and McGraw-Edison and the fledgling ABB were left to fight for a share of a market that remained in the 800 to 1,500 units annually range through 1988. By 1988, ABB had 40% of this shrunken market and Westinghouse and General Electric no longer made industrial transformers.

Between 1974 and 1988, ABB undertook a series of innovative and sophisticated OR projects that transformed the company and its markets. Noteworthy was OR work that after the introduction of the industry's first 5-year product warranty, enabled ABB to develop a manufacturing system to produce extremely high-quality transformers while at the same time becoming the low-cost producer in the industry. In addition, a series of market choice models enabled ABB to develop products that met customers' needs and to target their marketing efforts toward customers who promised the greatest returns.

Although many factors contributed to ABB's success, president Daniel Elwing observed in a statement at the 1988 Board of Directors meeting (by which time ABB sales had grown to exceed $100 million):

> Without the insights from our marketing models, it is unlikely we would have current sales of $25 million; in fact, without the use of these models, it is unlikely we would be here at all.
>
> From Gensch, et al.

Turnarounds. Another form of corporate restructuring is the "turnaround": reviving a failing corporation or revitalized a lethargic one. Citgo invested some $20 to $30 million in MS/OR in 1984-1985 that was instrumental in turning a loss exceeding $50 million annually in 1984 into a pretax profit exceeding $70 million in 1985. John P. Thompson, Chairman of the Board of The Southland Corporation (Citgo's parent company), said,

> We have been very gratified at the success that this approach, with its heavy dependence on [OR] and cooperative effort, has achieved at Citgo. The numerous systems that were developed ... have become an integral part of the Citgo operation, saving many millions of dollars.... we look forward to further [OR] developments, which might provide even greater advantages to Southland in what is becoming an increasingly competitive business climate.
>
> From D. Klingman, N. Phillips, D. Steiger, and W. Young, The Successful Deployment of Management Science throughout Citgo Petroleum Corporation, *Interfaces*, 1987;17.

National Car Rental (D. Greenfield, OR Overhaul, *OR/MS Today,* April 1996) also represents a turnaround largely attributable to OR activities. The National Car Rental case appears particularly compelling: the OR work was a direct order from the CEO, and the company was apparently told that it faced liquidation by its parent company (General Motors) if profits were not significantly increased. "The main thing that we introduced and that is probably unique in most of the car industry, is demand-based pricing. Stop following the competitors around."

Harris Corporation's Semiconductor Division is another good example of an OR-induced turnaround. Harris Semiconductor invested $3.8 million starting in 1992 in an OR project that led to the installation of IMPReSS, a system that used state-of-the-art linear programming to set production, delivery, and inventory levels in 22 manufacturing plants worldwide. (R.C. Leachman, R.F. Benson, C. Liu, and D.J. Raar, IMPReSS: An Automated Production-Planning and Delivery-Quotation System at Harris Corporation–Semiconductor Sector, *Interfaces*, 1996;26:1). In announcing the OR effort on company television, Jon Cornell, Divisional President, emphasized how close to the brink the semiconductor division was: "[The division] will not survive unless we solve our delivery problem. If IMPReSS succeeds, we can succeed. If it fails, we will surely fail." After installation of IMPReSS, Phil Farmer, President and CEO, talked about the dramatic nature of the turnaround: "Our on-time delivery was running about 75%, that was not acceptable. IMPReSS raised our on-time delivery to 95%...." Significantly, "75%" represented the worst performance in the industry, whereas "95%" represented about the best. The financial consequences were that a loss of $100 million annually during 1989-1991 was turned into profits of $20 million in 1993, $30 million in 1994, and $42 million in 1995.

An example of what can be done at modest cost to revitalize a lethargic (or failing?) company is demonstrated by the case of Merit Brass (A.D. Flowers, The Modernization of Merit Brass, *Interfaces*, 1993;23:1). Merit Brass was a traditional firm in the pipe, valve, and fittings industry that recognized that its customer service had slipped and needed improvement. "The company had outgrown its people-intensive systems and needed to implement [MS/OR] methodologies to elevate it to the next level of performance." Merit invested just $78,090 (this included the purchase of two personal computers) plus $19,500 in continuing annual costs in some MS/OR work. The result was an increase in their service level on class A items from 74% to 98% in less than 1 year, while simultaneously reducing inventories to obtain a cost savings of $201,000 annually. Not surprisingly, the "entire top management team at Merit Brass supported these efforts wholeheartedly."

Finally, new corporate startups can catalyze structural change with industries. There are many examples of MS/OR-induced startups in firms selling OR services, but it is more difficult to find examples where MS/OR was clearly instrumental in the formation of a major non-MS/OR corporation. The story of the startup of FedEx, however, provides compelling evidence of the strategic value of MS/OR.

On March 12, 1973, FedEx began its inaugural air-package service serving 11 major cities. After 3 days of operations, service was suspended because of a lack of business; the first day produced just six packages. Founder Fred Smith, however, would not give up. He formed an ad hoc "MS/OR team" to address the problem, and this group worked 18 to 20 hours a day for 15 days straight analyzing the problem. The group concluded that FedEx had opened by serving the wrong cities, and they analyzed 112 cities to determine which were the best candidates for the new air-package service. Using an origin/destination flow model, the MS/OR team developed indicators of each city's market potential that took into account the outbound parcel volume, types of businesses, and availability of air cargo service. A new network of 26 cities was defined that was quite different from the original 11-city network. On April 17, 1973, FedEx began serving its new 26-city network, and the rest, as they say, "is history." FedEx is now the world's largest express transportation company, delivering more than 2 million items to over 200 countries each business day, employing 110,000 people, and operating 500 aircraft and more than 35,000 vehicles (R.O. Mason, J.L. McKenney, W. Carlson, and D.C. Copeland, Absolutely, Positively Operations Research: The Federal Express Story, *Interfaces*, 1996).

New Businesses Serving Management Science/Operations Research-Intensive Industries

There is a rich documentation of the formation of new businesses serving OR-intensive industries. SDT has developed a major external consultancy to the point where it derives about 35% of its revenues from external customers (P. Horner, Eyes on the Prize, *OR/MS Today*, August 1991). Other examples of strong OR consultancies abound, including Hoskyns (B. Scott, Try the Future Now, *OR/MS Today*, June 1996) and perhaps less well known Giro Enterprises.

The road transportation industry has long recognized that appropriate vehicle routing and scheduling can make a significant difference to firm profitability (or public transportation costs). Giro has grown from its formation in 1981 to an employer of some 100 OR professionals in 1994 serving this specialized OR market (J.-M. Rousseau, Marketing OR: From University to Enterprise, presentation to the 1994 National Conference of the Canadian Operational Research Society, Montreal). Specializing in solving mass transit crew-scheduling problems and various types of vehicle-routing problems, Giro has grown from its base in Montreal to the point where it derives 60% of its revenue from outside Canada. HASTUS, its major software product for bus crew scheduling, is used by 80 transit companies in 17 countries. Giro's GeoRoute and GeoBus software provides interactive solutions to routing/scheduling of transit buses, school buses, meter readers, postal services, snow removal, street cleaning, and milk collection, and its fleet management software is used by utilities, government agencies, and business.

Another area of obvious growth supporting OR activities is the growth in the number of companies supplying software to OR practitioners. The number of companies offering optimization packages and simulation software for personal computers has increased dramatically, as has, presumably, the income these companies receive.

Finally, a number of new specialized consultancies have appeared that have "spun-out" from established organizations to concentrate on particular OR innovations. Among these are Insight Logistics, which initially spun-out from British Leyland to concentrate on the development and marketing of visual interactive simulation software, and Aeronomics, which specializes in "revenue management" and includes consultants who formerly worked in the airline industry, including at SDT and Delta Airlines.

CHARACTERISTICS OF FIRMS WITH STRATEGIC OPERATIONS RESEARCH ACTIVITIES

The firms that are the strongest candidates for having a distinct competence in MS/OR activities appear to have several commonalities, particularly in the path that OR has followed as it grew to a position of strategic significance.

First, there has to be a corporate need that initiates the development of an OR capability within the firm. This "need" has often appeared alongside an increasing level of competition with its accompanying uncertainty about the future. Deregulation of previously regulated industries has triggered an expansion of MS/OR, particularly in the North American Airline and banking industries, and more recently within the electric power industry. Actual or impending business failure, or the appearance of new and intense competition, has catalyzed many OR group startups. Regulated or government-owned organizations are poor candidates to have "strategic OR" activities.

Once established, the OR group must capture CEO attention. Those that have done this have successfully taken one, or a combination, of three basic approaches:

- Used MS/OR to address one or more very large and significant problems
- Adopted an MS/OR way of managing throughout critical parts of the organization
- Developed special skills in MS/OR that were marketed to others

Success in one or more of these approaches will have changed the culture of the firm.

This cultural change has required senior management commitment and attention and a host of management changes within the organization. Once implemented, this cultural change is difficult to reverse and provides the MS/OR group with a position of authority within the firm where they are looked to for solutions to existing problems and for help when new problems are recognized.

Eventually, the MS/OR group has become institutionalized in corporate policy, either through the head of the group reporting directly and often to the corporate CEO or through MS/OR appointments to key committees or by written policy that states that the MS/OR group must be involved in certain activities. Consequently, strategic MS/OR groups are functional areas of the business and are as much involved in "operations" as they are in "research."

In the North American air carrier industry, MS/OR is close to becoming a dominant technology; major carriers that do not have a significant investment in MS/OR are finding it very difficult to compete outside niche market areas. Once established as a dominant technology, MS/OR activities and employment in that industry, and in related industries, increase dramatically.

SUMMARY

There are a number of examples of firms that have activities that appear to meet a definition of strategic MS/OR based on the provision of a competitive advantage sustained over a period of time.

Among major corporations, the clearest example of strategic MS/OR activity is that of AMR and SDT over the period from about 1985 to the present. This "MS/OR group" catalyzed massive change in both its parent company and the industry in which it operates (and in other service industries where it has sold its services). Furthermore, this massive change is broadly attributed, both internally and externally, to SDT. When futurist Joseph P. Coates recently opined that "[MS/OR] has wrecked the airline industry" (Bell and Staples, Optimal Dynamic Pricing: The Changing Face of Competition, *Business Quarterly*, 1996;61:1), he was commenting on certain aspects of SDT's impact that he found personally unappealing (such as full aircraft). The success of SDT has been credited with competitor bankruptcies, industrial restructuring, and a competitive advantage of hundreds of millions annually to its parent company, sustained over a significant period of time.

An equally strong candidate for having distinct competence in MS/OR activities is FedEx. Although the FedEx MS/OR group is much smaller than SDT (partly because it does no outside business), MS/OR has been thoroughly ingrained in FedEx activities since start-up in 1973. The FedEx multihub distribution system was designed by the MS/OR group, and its operation and expansion over the years have been managed with the extensive use of MS/OR. MS/OR at FedEx appears to be involved in almost every major decision the corporation takes–and it has been in this position since the very beginnings in 1973.

Other corporations may well have, or have had, strategic MS/OR activities, but the literature on these firms is less extensive. San Miguel Corporation has had an effective OR function since 1971 and has produced significant cost savings year after year to the point where the OR group is involved in decision making throughout the corporation. The very supportive statements of senior management that San Miguel's OR activities are a strategic asset provide strong support, although documentation in the public domain is not very extensive.

ABB Electric during the period of 1974 through about 1988 appears to have achieved a sustained competitive advantage through the use of MS/OR, although this conclusion is based on only a single published work. Documentation of strategic MS/OR at McDermott Corporation is again quite sketchy, although the limited material available supports the importance of MS/OR in the competitive strategy of McDermott. AT&T has a substantial history of successful OR activity, but this is such a huge corporation and there has been so much change in the North American telephone market that the benefits attributable to MS/OR have been dwarfed by other exogenous change. Citgo, Harris Semiconductor, and Merit Brass have all achieved a competitive advantage from their OR work, but the lack of evidence on the sustainability of this advantage prevents the drawing of a strong conclusion.

The MS/OR industry includes many smaller firms (some examples include Giro, Innovis, AutoSimulations, Hosykins, Pristker, and Insight Logistics) that market MS/OR work and where this work represents a strategic asset to these firms; such firms will not survive if their OR work does not provide them with a sustainable competitive advantage. These firms attest to the fact that the MS/OR industry offers a host of exciting entrepreneurial opportunities.

STRATEGIC MS/OR IN ACTION

AMERICAN AIRLINES

In 1982, American Airlines (AA) employed 12 operations researchers. By 1991, after a stream of highly successful projects under the direction of Tom Cook, a former professor of MS/OR, the number of MS/OR specialists employed had grown to more than 300. In 1988, the MS/OR group become a separate division of AMR, the parent company of AA, known as American Airlines Decision Technologies (AADT), with Cook as President. In 1994, the Sabre Information Systems Group was merged with AADT to form Sabre Decision Technologies (SDT).

Management Science/Operations Research Successes at American Airlines

MS/OR tools and systems developed by the Decision Technologies Division have resulted in huge cost savings for AA. Large problems that have been addressed and results published include the following:

Fleet Assignments: Revenue gains of $75 million realized in 1988, as well as a 1.4% increase in operating margins

Flight Crew Scheduling: Annual savings realized in excess of $20 million

Airline Crew Bid Generation System: Productivity improvement of 600%

Performance Analysis and Capacity Planning of Landing Gear Shops: Development of appropriate planning capabilities for future production increases of 100% to 130% per year

Repairable Part Management: One-time savings of $7 million plus recurring annual savings of $1 million

Arrival Slot Allocation System: Reduction in annual air traffic control delays totaling 345,000 minutes for a savings of $5.2 million per year

Yield Management: Revenues from overbooking improvements were $225 million in 1990, revenues from discount-fare controls were $313 million in 1990, productivity savings reached $1 million, and the net quantifiable benefits from yield management improvements were $1.4 billion over 3 years

Systems Improvements

AA has taken a proactive approach to solving potential scheduling, maintenance, and arrival slot problems and is a leader in developing cost-reduction and efficiency methods. MS/OR is fundamental in providing information and solutions to problems that are too large and complicated to be solved manually.

The nature of the airline business, the regulations under which it operates, and the magnitudes of the variables involved (such as the numbers of aircraft, stations, and flights) lend themselves to modeling solutions. The cost savings from these solutions to an organization the size of AA makes a significant resource commitment worthwhile, and models that SDT has developed and used have transformed the airline industry. SDT has become recognized and respected by the highest level of AA management as one of the most profitable and successful parts of the AMR parent organization, thereby giving support and drive to further developments. Although AA is SDT's primary customer, about half of SDT's business comes from external sources.

The models developed for AA are not static but are constantly being improved. Other areas of the operations are being assessed to determine whether modeling applications can improve the processes there as well. AA is committed to low cost operations through the use of MS/OR to address critical and competitively important problems. AMR sees the capabilities of SDT as one of its distinctive competencies.

Fleet Assignments

American Airlines uses mathematical programming to solve its fleet assignment problems. After the marketing group sets the flight schedule, the mathematical program takes the schedule and assigns aircraft types to flights given the following variables:

- 2,300 flights per day covering 150 different cities with over 500 jet aircraft
- Traffic revenue forecasts
- Available resources such as aircraft and gates
- Operating costs
- Maintenance routing for aircraft
- Use of most efficient aircraft types
- Restrictions on certain flights to operate with certain aircraft types
- Limits on the number of aircraft that remain overnight at particular stations
- Limits on the number of arrival and departure slots at a station during the day

The model can run under the assumption that all flights are to be served or under the assumption that certain "wish list" flights may be dropped to fit the available fleet. The objective of the model is to maximize the benefit contributions of the flights less the cost of aircraft used and the cost of stations: that is, to maximize the benefits using the least number of aircraft and the least number of schedule imbalances. By assigning penalties to constraints not met, the cost of different decisions can be estimated. Given the number of variables and constraints, the model matrix becomes quite large, and the complexity of the problem is compounded by the fact that the decision variables (which represent which aircraft is assigned to that flight) must be integers.

The ability to accurately assign the correct size aircraft to a flight has generated gains of 1% in revenue, which translates to $75 million per year. The simplification of the process of assigning aircraft has generated a 1.4% increase in annual operating margins.

Flight Crew Scheduling (TRIP)

SDT uses mixed integer programming to schedule crews onto its flights so as to minimize crew costs by minimizing nonproductive crew time while meeting crew pay guarantees. The derived crew schedule must:

- Meet work rule limitations such as duty periods, rest requirements, and relief on long international flights
- Ensure that each flight segment is covered once and only once with minimum "deadheading" ("deadheading" is flying crew members as passengers to transport them home or to their next flight)
- Ensure that each pairing (flight trip) begins at and returns to the same crew base
- Ensure that minimum/maximum manpower limits for the airline are met and that manpower requirements at a base match availability
- Match crew capabilities to the appropriate fleet of aircraft

The end result is a file containing a set of 1- to 4-day crew trips covering all scheduled flights. The size of these optimization problems (American has 8,300 pilots and 16,200 flight attendants to schedule) requires that they be broken down into smaller subproblems that are solved iteratively until no further improvements can be realized. With further development, the entire fleet will be run as a single problem, allowing the program to achieve the lowest possible cost solutions.

A second system packages the trips into monthly flying assignments called "bidlines" that are then posted for bid by crew members. Those trips not bid on are assigned to reserve crews.

TRIP is constantly being enhanced because a 1% increase in crew use represents savings of $13 million per year. Today, the generator produces 5,000 pairings per second compared with 1986 capabilities of 500 per second.

In 1981, the ratio of *total pay and credit costs* to *total flying hours* was 14.7%; by 1987, it had dropped to 5.2%. Approximately 40% of these savings can be attributed to innovations in the crew pairing optimization program, whereas the remainder is attributable to favorable changes in work rules, improvements in the procedures used in developing the flight crew allocations, and greater availability of computer resources. The optimization-related savings represents a cost reduction of $20 million annually.

Automated Airline Crew Bid Generation System (DEAL and SWAP)

The development of bidlines from the file of crew trips is done in two stages using iterative computer programs. The first stage builds the trip pairings developed by the TRIP program into monthly packages. The DEAL program builds an initial monthly set of bidlines, ignoring the rules of overall flying and credit time for crew members, with the result that these preliminary trip pairings may include flying time that is higher or lower than the legal limits. The SWAP program takes the initial bidlines and performs a series of trip moves and swaps until each bidline falls within the flying time limitations.

The generation systems have improved productivity from the ability to manually produce 10 bidlines per hour to the current ability to produce 60 bidlines per hour.

Performance Analysis and Capacity Planning of a Landing Gear Shop

As the AA fleet continues to expand, the demand for maintenance increases, and this is expected to continue. Each aircraft must receive maintenance on a schedule set by the FAA based on its projected flying hours. An important component of the schedule is maintenance of the landing gear; each aircraft has three or four sets depending on the type. The aircraft is brought to the Maintenance Facility in Tulsa, where the landing gear is disassembled and each part is inspected. A process plan is made up for each part showing the sequence of maintenance work stations to be visited and the estimated processing time at each station. The landing gears are repaired according to this process plan and then reinstalled onto the aircraft.

There are many complications to this process: the aircraft do not always arrive when they are scheduled; there is increased and varying demand for maintenance of different types of landing gear, causing frequent changes to the shop floor component mix; and as the number of aircraft requiring maintenance increases, the capacity of the shop floor becomes inadequate, with a result that aircraft are delayed going back into service.

The QNET model was developed at SDT to evaluate performance of the existing work shop layout and to develop a macrodesign of the landing gear shop. This model views the shop floor as a network of work stations linked by the flow of work pieces and analyzes the work flow as a queuing network. The input into the model is the number of machines at a work station, the failure rate and repair time of each machine, and the expected work load per time period. The model produces output showing the queue length and wait time for each part at each work station and the overall utilization, average queue length, and average wait time for each work station, and it identifies the bottleneck stations by part type and the bottleneck station for the entire system. The model computes the minimum number of machines required at each machining center and attempts to improve the schedule iteratively by decreasing excess inventory while maintaining production feasibility.

Given that there are about 30 work stations and 75 distinct part types arriving from more than 500 aircraft, the optimal solution can provide significant cost savings from efficient use of capacity, reduction in overcapacity and inventory, and minimization of aircraft delays. The model is very effective in planning for long-term capacity growth, which is important when repair requirements growth is projected at 100% to 130% per year. It also provides specific performance criteria against which actual shop performance can be measured.

Repairable Part Management

AA classifies its many aircraft parts as either expendable (parts that are discarded rather than repaired) or rotable (parts of higher value that are repaired and reinstalled into aircraft). There are over 5,000 different rotable parts associated with AA's fleets.

Before each aircraft departure, the aircraft is fully inspected to determine whether each part is functional. If any parts are found to be defective, they are removed, and a working spare part is installed. After the spare part is issued from the station stock, the repair facility or exchange base is notified so the part can be replaced. If the defective part is rotable, it is sent back to the repair facility; otherwise, it is discarded. This process occurs at every base from which flights depart, so an inventory of parts must be kept at each base. However, there is not an equal demand for each possible part at every base. Delays in waiting for parts to arrive essentially count as flight cancellations or delays and can incur high monetary costs as well as loss of goodwill. The option of carrying large inventories at every base becomes cost prohibitive because the average cost of a rotable part is $5,000, with some costing well over $500,000 each.

Two computer systems are used to facilitate the allocation of parts. The Rotable Control System (RCS) tracks the location and status of all rotable parts not currently installed in an aircraft. This system provides data to the Rotables Allocations and Planning System (RAPS). RAPS provides a schedule of least-cost allocation of rotable parts based on the sum of inventory ownership costs and expected shortage costs. It also provides information to inventory managers that facilitate the decision making in the following areas:

- Determining the impact of new fleets on part allocations
- Making surplus and purchase decisions
- Evaluating vendor proposals and terms
- Forecasting future demand
- Anticipating allocation behavior through sensitivity analysis

To provide this information, RAPS establishes a relationship between monthly part removals and monthly flying hours. Both the volume and pattern of the demand for the units in stock determine the level of availability, which is a major influence on the total cost of an allocation.

An extension of RAPS is the Dynamic Redistribution System (DRS), which identifies parts inventories that are reaching a critical shortage volume at a particular station and suggests transfer of parts from stations having excess inventory.

It has been estimated that RPS provided a one-time savings of $7 million and a recurring annual savings of nearly $1 million. In addition, the productivity and analysis capabilities of the materials management analysts have been greatly enhanced. A further use of the models has been to determine the number of maintenance bases required to meet the maintenance demands of AA's fleet. The model has initiated a reduction from 22 to 17 maintenance bases: because the annual inventory carrying costs alone of each base are approximately $215,000, this represents a healthy annual cost savings.

Arrival Slot Allocation System

AA's operating network is based on a hub-and-spoke system comprised of seven main hubs. The flight schedule assigns a scheduled arrival slot for each flight; however, any changes to the schedule cause a second controlled arrival slot to be assigned. These time slots usually span 20 minutes before and after the scheduled or controlled times of arrival. The number of arrivals at a station can be very large; for example, at Chicago O'Hare International Airport, there is capacity for eight arrivals every 5 minutes.

Any changes made to the schedule have a ripple effect on all subsequent arrivals until the slack time between connections can absorb the time losses. The changes also affect passengers, who have to spend extra time at the airport, missing connecting flights, losing baggage, and generating ill will. Therefore, the management and minimization of schedule changes can provide cost savings and reduce complications to the remainder of the schedule while maintaining goodwill with passengers.

Changes are mostly caused by bad weather, when aircraft must change from visual flight rules to instrument flight rules with a corresponding increase in flight separation distances. At O'Hare airport, for example, this drops capacity from eight to five flights every 5 minutes. Other causes of schedule changes are maintenance problems, reallocating crews for flights that have been delayed long enough to overrun existing crew flying hour regulations, and flight cancellations or reschedulings due to weather conditions prohibiting arrival at their original destination.

The process of reallocating arrival slots originates with a message notifying a schedule delay from the air traffic control computer in Washington, DC. The message is forwarded to the dispatcher at the affected station, who then performs calculations to find a satisfactory solution to the arrival slot change problem. The dispatcher returns the new flight information and waits for confirmation. Either the new schedule is confirmed and the dispatcher passes the information to all dispatch desks, or it is rejected and the calculations are reworked to arrive at another solution.

The Automated Arrival Slot Allocation System (ASAS) was developed to provide an integrated system that would do the following:

- Allocate arrival slots efficiently, minimizing delays.
- Calculate delay times and automate the transmission of results with minimal user intervention.
- Give dispatchers more time to perform their everyday activities by turning out results quickly (in a matter of seconds) and allow dispatchers time to simulate several what-if scenarios before committing to a solution.
- Be flexible enough to allow dispatchers to alter the computer generated solution easily and quickly.
- Be highly responsive to any ground delays affecting any airport and accept revisions to ground-delay programs in midanalysis.
- Be flexible enough to accept dispatchers' slot allocations in exceptional cases when the dispatchers have more information than the computer.

The system is composed of four modules:

1. Data integration
2. Heuristic allocation of arrival slots
3. Fine tuning of results to consolidate multiple operating policies
4. Automatic transmission of results for approval

The central module, which includes the MS/OR tools, is the Arrival Slot Allocation Model (ASAM). The model's objective is to minimize a weighted function that measures passenger-minutes of delay where the constraints relate to air traffic control rules. Major delay problems, such as those affecting Chicago O'Hare and Dallas/Fort Worth airports, can be solved in just a few seconds.

ASAS has led to a reduction of average processing time for ground-delay programs from 3 person-hours to 10 person-minutes with an estimated annual savings in flight dispatchers of approximately $455,000. ASAS has also been attributed to direct operating cost savings of $5.2 million during 1989 by reducing air traffic control delays by 345,000 minutes. The many intangible benefits include enhanced passenger goodwill, reduced training for new dispatchers, and more time available to dispatchers to analyze the benefits of different choices.

Yield Management (DINAMO)

AA's innovative yield management systems have revolutionized air travel. These systems take the schedules and fare structure set by the planning departments and determine the product mix to be offered to the customers. Data such as the expected passenger demand, expected volume of cancellations, and other passenger behavior such as reactions to being reaccommodated on another flight are taken into account by the yield management systems.

The development of DINAMO was motivated by three major changes affecting the airline industry and AA; these were:

- Implementation of SABRE reservations systems
- Introduction of Super Saver discount fares
- Airline schedule and price deregulation

AA's response to these changes was a system, called DINAMO (Dynamic Inventory and Maintenance Optimizer), that has three primary areas of analysis:

- Overbooking
- Discount allocations
- Traffic management

Overbooking. On average, half of all flight reservations made are either cancelled or end as a no-show (a passenger who does not cancel but also does not show up for the flight). Airlines have determined that if they limit reservations to the capacity of the flight, flights noted as "sold-out" would, on average, be only 85% filled at take-off because of the probability of no-shows and last-minute cancellations. Overbooking attempts to balance the desire to minimize the risk of lost seat revenues with the risks of oversales (or "bumping"). Oversold passengers must be compensated and reaccommodated onto another flight.

The DINAMO optimization model maximizes the net revenue associated with overbooking decisions and determines the optimal overbooking level as the point at which the marginal revenue gained from allowing an additional reservation is equal to the marginal cost of an additional oversale. A constraint on the maximum number of oversales allowed per flight was added because it was recognized that too many oversold seats (that would have to be reaccommodated) would represent an unacceptable loss of customer goodwill, with a potential negative impact on future seat sales.

Discount Allocation. Airlines offer many different fare types (e.g., business class, full-fare economy, and various discount fares) that make it necessary to allocate the available seats to the different fare classes. DINAMO uses an optimization model to do this. The model weighs the marginal value of a new fare request against the marginal value of all other fares, given the probability of receiving a future request for a higher priced fare if the current request is rejected. Factors taken into consideration include the fact that the marginal value of a fare diminishes with the number of seats that are overbooked and the probability of receiving another fare request diminishes the closer the scheduled flight is to the request day. The popularity of the flight also affects the expected level of future requests.

Traffic Management. About two thirds of all passengers on a flight to a hub airport connect to another flight to continue to their destination. Decisions must be made on how to connect passengers and on the fare types to offer on each connecting flight. With the number of possible connections available, the number of possible desired connections, and the number of fare types, this can branch into an enormous number of options. For example, given a simple airline network with two flights coming into a hub airport DFW from PDX and LAX and two flights connecting out from DFW to LGA and MIA, the number of possible flight routes are:

PDX	DFW	LGA
PDX	DFW	MIA
PDX	DFW	
LAX	DFW	LGA
LAX	DFW	MIA
LAX	DFW	
	DFW	LGA
	DFW	MIA

SDT has developed a series of models to control systemwide reservation availability using models based on a modification within SABRE known as **virtual nesting**.

Virtual Nesting. The many different types of customers, fares, and routes are clustered into similar groups ("buckets"), and certain numbers of seats are then indexed into these buckets. The buckets rank from highest value to lowest (1 to 7). The use of these buckets reduces the number of possibilities included in the models, while the nesting approach ensures that buckets are closed (fully reserved) in sequence from the bottom up. Seats allocated to each bucket are available for that bucket and any above it in ranking (but not below). That is, if bucket 4 is closed, so are buckets 5 through 7; if bucket 3 is open for sale, so are buckets 1 and 2; and if bucket 1 is closed, the flight has been fully overbooked. This ensures that two major objectives are achieved: (1) discount seats are not sold if higher revenue passengers are being turned away, and (2) forecasting excess demand for a bucket results in poor discount allocations for only lower-revenue buckets.

An important problem results from the fact that the value attached to flight segments is more complicated than just the flight revenue. The combined revenue of two separate segments may be higher than the revenue from a direct flight with a stop at the hub, but the direct booking may displace passengers wanting just one leg of the connection. To solve this problem, the model assigns an effective revenue to connecting passengers that is lower than the actual ticket revenue.

Benefits Realized through Yield Management. AA has reduced its spoiled seats (cancellations or no-shows) from the original estimate of 15% per flight to a 1990 average of 3%. The involuntary oversales have been reduced by 62% from 1980 to 1990.

Revenue opportunity is measured as the difference between the minimum revenue expected for a flight (no discount controls) and the maximum revenue expected (perfect discount controls). Performance is measured as the percentage of opportunity revenue actually achieved. The yield management group has estimated that AA achieved 90% of the revenue opportunity resulting from overbooking in 1990, which equates to $225 million. The achieved percentage of revenue opportunity from discount fare controls has jumped from 30% in 1988 to 49% in 1990, representing earned revenue of $313 million for 1990 alone.

Before the implementation of DINAMO, yield management specialists had to review each flight individually, but now only those identified as critical need to be manually reviewed. In 1990, this was only 5% of the flights. The productivity per analyst has increased over 30%, representing an annual savings of $1 million.

Yield management models have allowed AA to offer a greater variety of products for sale while maintaining control over discount seat availability. The net quantifiable benefits to AA has been estimated at $1.4 billion over the 3-year period. Over the 6-year period 1990 through 1995 the total before tax net income of AMR was $187.4 million; far less than the benefits from the DINAMO systems.

Robert Crandall, Chairman, President and CEO of American Airlines, has summed up AA's reaction to these developments:

> I believe that yield management is the single most important technical development in transportation management since we entered the era of airline deregulation in 1979 ... (yield management) creates a pricing structure which responds to demand on a flight-by-flight basis. As a result, we can more effectively match our demand to supply.

From *Interfaces*, 1992;22:1.

From Thirty Years of Airline Operations Research, by Helmut Richter; Applying Integer Linear Programming to the Fleet Assignment Problem, by Jeph Abara; Optimizing Flight Crew Schedules, by Ira Gershkoff; Development of an Automated Airline Crew Bid Generation System, by Russell D. Jones; Performance Analysis and

Capacity Planning of a Landing Gear Shop, by B. Vinod and B.N. Srikar; Repairable Part Management, by Mark J. Tedone, *Interfaces*, 1989; 19:4; American Airlines Arrival Slot Allocation System (ASAS), by Alberto Vasquez-Marquez; Recent Advances in Crew-Pairing Optimization at American Airlines, by Ranga Anbil, Eric Gelman, Bruce Patty, and Rajan Tanga, *Interfaces*, 1991; 21:1; Flight Scheduling and Maintenance Base Planning, Thomas A. Feo, and Jonathan F. Bard, *Management Science*, 1989; 35:12; Yield Management at American Airlines, by Barry C. Smith, John F. Leimkuhler, and Ross M. Darrow, *Interfaces*, 1992; 22:1.

WINNING MANAGEMENT SCIENCE/OPERATIONS RESEARCH AT ABB ELECTRIC

ABB Electric was founded in 1970 with the objective of manufacturing a range of medium power electrical transformers for the North American market. In 1974, just as ABB Electric was approaching a break-even position, the "oil crisis" that followed the formation of OPEC precipitated an industrywide shock that cut industry sales in half. Stalled from further growth, the industry became tremendously competitive almost overnight. ABB was left to compete with established giants such as Westinghouse, McGraw-Edison, and General Electric in the shrinking industry. The only way that ABB could survive was to take customers from the established competitors.

The first market action taken by ABB management was to offer a 5-year warranty on all ABB's products. Because each item cost $300,000 and the industry standard warranty was 1 year, this offer gave ABB instant credibility in the marketplace but required ABB to vastly improve its manufacturing to support the warranty. ABB developed and applied MS/OR models throughout manufacturing to develop the extremely high standard of quality control required. The result was a highly sophisticated concept of manufacturing management that gave ABB the highest quality products in the industry. Remarkably, at the same time, ABB became the low-cost producer.

After success in manufacturing, the use of MS/OR at ABB spread to many other areas, including marketing decision models, design and manufacturing applications, and research and development for new products.

> A strength of ABB Electric is that management science techniques have been applied and developed throughout the entire organization, often integrating various functional areas.

ABB used management science very effectively to support product marketing. Two published applications that have been very successful are modeling customer choice and identifying "switchable" customers.

ABB went to a considerable effort to build a database of transformer purchasers and to try to determine which transformer features were most important to their customers. Multiattribute choice models were developed to predict future customer purchase decisions from a knowledge of past decisions and customer preferences. From these models, ABB was able to predict, with 60% to 70% accuracy, the chosen supplier for each sale of major equipment. ABB could now target its marketing efforts to those sales where it had the best chance of gaining a new customer or holding on to one of its own customers who was likely to switch to a different supplier. ABB also gained a competitive advantage in product design because it knew which product attributes were most important to its customers and could decide on which attributes it could best compete. The models also help ABB to better understand its competition, a necessary success factor in most competitive environments.

In 1974, ABB started developing a customer database by mailing surveys asking customers to rank product attributes. ABB then conducted a statistical analysis to determine which product attributes customers thought were most important. In one market segment, the three most important attributes were found to be warranty, performance ("energy losses"), and appearance, in that order. ABB addressed the warranty issue head-on by offering the best warranty in the industry, but the importance of the appearance of the industrial transformer (more important than price, the availability of spares, or maintenance requirements) proved to a be a surprise. ABB exploited this knowledge through the relatively costless innovation of offering transformers in several different colors.

Using these attributes, ABB conducted an analysis that segmented customers into homogeneous groups, reducing the number of customer segments to 12. ABB then repeated the analysis for each customer segment emerging with a prioritization of attributes for each segment and the market shares of competitive products. These results allowed ABB to develop marketing strategies that focused on those characteristics of the product that each customer segment found to be most important. The models also explained the strength of competition in certain segments; at the end of the first year, ABB had quite accurately predicted market share by supplier, and the models were producing predicted results that were very close to the actual observed results. These results gave the models significant face validity and credibility.

ABB next identified its main competitors in each market segment and how best to compete against them by attribute. In developing specific marketing strategies, the model was used to suggest specific models and product features to emphasize to each segment. In addition, possible new products and modifications emerged. The dissaggregate nature of the models allowed them to be used to predict the decision behavior of both groups of people and individuals, allowing ABB to tailor their contract bids to the criteria of each individual potential customer. Even within the same market segment, ABB's response to similar requests for estimates could be very different depending on who ABB saw as its major competitor for the contract.

Improvements

The initial model proved tremendously successful, and ABB was able to improve the model over time. The concept of the "switchable customers" became important. ABB was able to focus its marketing efforts and eliminate wasted time through identifying the customers who may switch suppliers. ABB identified customers, both its own and competitors, who were unlikely to switch supplier no matter the amount of persuasion used. ABB's strategy was to "essentially... reduce the marketing effort to ABB's and the competitors' brand loyal segments and to expand it to consumers for whom ABB was competitive." The model achieved this differentiation by estimating choice probabilities and determining the statistical significance of the differences in these choice probabilities.

A second improvement to the basic model involved incorporating differing decision process structures. ABB found that not all customers made decisions in the same way: more knowledgeable and experienced buyers tended to consider more attributes and make more trade-offs among the attributes, whereas less knowledgeable customers seldom compared alternatives on more than three attributes.

Results

Daniel Elwing, CEO of ABB Electric, has attributed the company's survival to these models and to MS/OR in general. Elwing created an environment and a management style where MS/OR flourished. Through the use of these models, ABB captured market share steadily, and by 1988 had 40% of the industrial transformer market. ABB was both the lowest cost producer and the highest quality producer in the industry.

ABB President Daniel Elwing observed in a statement at the 1988 board of directors meeting when sales had grown to exceed $100 million that "without the insights from our marketing models, it is unlikely we would have current sales of $25 million; in fact, without the use of these models, it is unlikely we would be here at all."

From D.H. Gensch, N.A. Aversa, and S.P. Moore, A Choice-Modeling Market Information System that Enabled ABB Electric to Expand Its Market Share, *Interfaces*, 1990;20:1.

McDERMOTT INTERNATIONAL

McDermott International, headquartered in New Orleans, has been a major player in the development of the world's offshore oil and gas fields, beginning in the Gulf of Mexico and then around the world. McDermott installed the first platform offshore in the Gulf of Mexico in 1947 in 20 feet of water: today, they are installing production facilities and pipelines in 3,000 feet of water, and expecting to go deeper.

By the 1970s, McDermott was a successful international company with worldwide operations, and in 1978, it acquired Babcock & Wilcox (B&W). B&W was over 100 years old at the time, and it brought a new line of products–equipment for fossil and nuclear power generation, equipment for the U.S. Navy's nuclear fleet, onshore construction, tubular products, and others.

Since the B&W acquisition, McDermott has expanded its capabilities in onshore engineering and construction, including international shipbuilding. McDermott is now an international, multidisciplinary consolidated company with about 25,000 employees and revenues of over $3 billion (nearer to $4 billion if revenues from unconsolidated joint ventures are included).

The common thread that runs through McDermott's five primary lines of business (marine construction, power generation, U.S. government business, engineering, and construction and shipbuilding) is the need to manage the completion of large projects that require engineering of the project, accumulating materials, assembling the materials into a finished product, transporting the product to its installation site, and erecting the product at the site. Often, the materials come from sources all over the world and must arrive at the assembly site on schedule to avoid project delays. Because many of the products made are quite large, account must be taken of limitations on transportation–everything from weather conditions to bridge clearances.

McDermott CEO Howson states:

> Clearly, the ability to model the conditions that can affect such a project is very important to its success. That, of course, is where operations research comes into play in our multidisciplinary, international company. Operations research plays an important part of our ability to manage our diverse businesses.

History of Operations Research at McDermott

MS/OR came to McDermott in 1978 from B&W. Howson states that MS/OR

> brought a new culture to McDermott. B&W's largest customers were U.S. utilities and the U.S. Navy, both of which were conservative by nature. As a result, B&W tended to be analytical and cautious in its approach to business. Operations research, with its ability to create models of processes, was a natural fit. By the time of the acquisition, the application of

> quantitative methods to management of B&W's business had provided a substantial benefit to the company.
>
> B&W first used OR to address management questions about inventory, business plans, research and development projects, and manufacturing. At B&W, as the value of OR was recognized, the OR staff began to tackle more serious problems. One of the most serious problems came in the late 1960s. Demand for the products of B&W's Nuclear Equipment Division, which was then making nuclear power components for both the U.S. Navy and U.S. utilities, was growing rapidly. As is often the case in such situations, the division was having trouble meeting schedules, which was leading to a loss of about $15 million a year.
>
> Several hundred million dollars in contracts were at risk, with the potential of tens of millions of dollars in penalty payments. In November 1969, *Fortune* magazine wrote that the future of B&W was at stake.
>
> Operations Research was called in to look at the situation. The OR staff produced a simulation model for proper sizing and scheduling of the manufacturing operations. It was implemented at a cost of about $8 million for equipment and facilities. By the time it was complete, the $15 million loss had turned into a $17 million profit.

This MS/OR project was leading edge at the time, requiring a great deal of human effort to be expended to deal with limited capacity and a tight deadline. The success of the project proved to be of enormous value to both B&W and the OR department, and when McDermott acquired B&W, they also acquired a well-established, well-respected OR group. McDermott did not have a formal MS/OR function but concluded that MS/OR could make a contribution to the way the corporation was managed. One of the first things the OR staff was asked to do was to improve financial planning and reporting.

McDermott had divisions around the world, with each operating somewhat independently. Each month, the divisions would send to New Orleans a teletype containing operating information, and this information was key-punched and within 2 or 3 weeks, consolidated reports appropriate for management, the board of directors, government agencies, and so on were available. The process was cumbersome, slow, and expensive, often taking an entire month or more to report the results. MS/OR was called and said they could fix it–and they did.

Within a few months, they had an on-line, computerized system for corporate wide financial reporting and planning. Within days of the end of the month, management had the information it needed.

Since that time, OR staff have addressed and solved many other complicated problems. MS/OR provides important support to McDermott's management councils: groups made up of representatives of each of McDermott's operations that address shared technical concerns, common across the company in areas such as engineering, manufacturing, and project management. Some examples of projects include:

- The MS/OR staff has worked with the project management council to develop methods to assess the effect of cost and schedule commitments on risk management.
- The OR staff has worked with division personnel to develop proper risk simulation methods and to teach division personnel how to apply these methods. The OR staff has also evaluated variables such as weather, product performance, and even political risk.

Howson was impressed and took steps to institutionalize these approaches:

> Currently, our OR staff is helping evaluate projects with a total value of over $1 billion. We are convinced that the application of quantitative methods to estimating and contract management increases our company's chances for success. Recently, we issued a corporate policy that requires the use of these methods on major proposals and contracts.

Examples of MS/OR work at McDermott include:

- Simulation models of production operations have been used to properly size and operate manufacturing facilities, to study the installation of subsea pipelines, and to model ocean shipping operations and the transportation and storage of molten sulfur. These models have helped to reduce costs but also helped sell products by showing the customer that McDermott understands technology, has facilities that can meet their needs, and has a plan for completing their work.
- Recently, the OR staff helped the Power Generation Group with their marketing in the important and highly competitive after-market boiler parts repair and replacement business, where maintaining market share is very important to McDermott. The OR group helped to develop a strategy to maintain market share by surveying a large sample of customers to determine what attributes the customer used to select a certain supplier for a particular product or service. The attributes sampled included price, speed of delivery, on-time delivery, quality, warranty, and engineering support. The results enabled the OR group to build a mathematical model to predict how customers will respond to changes in those attributes. The result showed price was an important attribute, but others were also important, and as a result of the work, the managers were able to adjust some of the most influential attributes and create a competitive edge that will not be easily overcome by the competition. An added benefit was that the adjustments could be made at no added cost.
- Most of McDermott's business involves contracts with a longer life than the boiler service business, and accurately determining and then meeting delivery and completion dates for these contracts improve profitability. OR has worked with the manufacturing council on finite capacity scheduling models for several production facilities, with the creation of optimum schedules for personnel and resources that meet contract commitments in a cost-effective manner.
- OR combined with shipbuilding operations helped McDermott win a contract from the U.S. government to develop a revolutionary new simulation-based shipbuilding design program to help U.S. shipyards improve their competitiveness. The goal of simulation-based design is to create three-dimensional models of the ship, the sea, and the shipbuilding process to help shipyards improve schedules and reduce costs. The various models would interact with each other to identify changes in the design that would make operations of the ship more effective or safer or less expensive; make building the ship faster, more predictable, and less risky; and cut the overall cost to the customer of procurement, operation, and disposal. McDermott sees this project as a way to leverage American excellence in computer technology into a competitive advantage for U.S. shipbuilding.
- McDermott made the decision to move away from home-grown software and the programming business and implement an integrated, enterprisewide business system based on commercially available software. OR is helping each operating unit to evaluate its requirements and identify vendors who can meet their needs.
- Earlier in 1995, one of McDermott's joint venture companies signed the largest contract ever for the installation of an offshore pipeline. The contract is worth about $260 million and will result in a lay barge installing some 1,200 miles of pipelines in the North Sea over 4 years. To handle the work, tens of millions of dollars has been invested in upgrading the barge. To ensure the upgrade results in the best possible configuration, the OR staff have been asked to build a computer-animated model of the planned improvement.

CEO Howson sums up OR at McDermott Corporation:

The operations research function at our company probably fits the theme of Managing Interdisciplinary Interfaces about as well as a company could: it is the basis for most of what we do. We must manage interfaces between engineering and construction, between procurement and assembly, between financing and scheduling—the list could go on and on. OR is a key element of managing these interfaces. It provides us an ability to predict, to analyze, and to decide. Without this ability, our chances for success would be lessened considerably.

As we look to the future, OR will continue to be a vital and necessary part of our organization and our goal to remain a world-class company, capable of competing against all comers.

From R.E. Howson, Chairman of the Board and Chief Executive Officer, McDermott International, Inc., address to INFORMS National Conference, New Orleans, October 1995.

CITGO PETROLEUM CORPORATION

In 1983, Southland Corporation, the 7-11 convenience store giant that retailed 2 billion gallons of gasoline annually, took a step to integrate vertically by acquiring Citgo Petroleum Corporation, the oil refining and marketing arm of Occidental Petroleum Corporation. Citgo Petroleum Corporation was one of the nation's largest industrial companies, with 1985 sales in excess of $4 billion, but it had been losing money for several years, culminating in pretax losses of $50 million in 1984.

After the acquisition, Citgo was established as a wholly owned subsidiary with a full debt load, with the intention that Citgo perform independently of Southland. A task force was created to explore all possible areas to improve Citgo's profitability.

The Industry

New legislation in 1982, which sought to make the oil industry more competitive, produced industrywide restructuring between 1983 and 1985. Where formerly integrated oil companies made a profit by extracting crude oil from the ground even though refinery and retail operations might be run at a loss, the new competitive world meant that crude oil could be sold to the highest bidder. Many firms decoupled upstream (refining) and downstream (retailing) operations to reduce cross subsidization. With more sources of crude oil and refined products available, from both off-shore producers and exchange traded products, a narrowing of price-volume relationships occurred, and price elasticity increased (that is, the quantity sold became more sensitive to price changes). In addition to the competitive pressures and the changing characteristic of demand, there was a 20- to 40-fold increase in the cost of financing working capital (a combination of a 10-fold price increase and a 2- to 4-fold increase in interest rates).

Areas Identified for Profit Improvement

The task force identified the following areas for possible savings:

1. Product and crude inventory reductions
2. Accounts receivable and payable
3. Crude oil and feedstock acquisition
4. Variable cost coverage (acquisition, distribution, marketing costs) on products sold
5. Refinery cost reductions

6. Refinery profit maximization
7. Personnel reductions

Over a period of time, a number of systems were designed and implemented to address these issues and harness the possible cost savings.

Refinery Linear Programming System

A linear programming (LP) model was the basis for the central control system in the refinery. Using data on equipment and crude oil availabilities, the LP model optimized production of the various end products of the refinery. Specific uses of the system included:

Crude selection and acquisition economics

Refinery run levels

Product component production levels

Feedstock selection and acquisition economics

Unit turnaround options

Hydrocracker conversion

The task force conducted an audit to determine the quality of the existing LP system and the underlying data. The findings lead to the following action items:

1. Data on costs, unit yields, and crude assays were inaccurate or out of date, with much of the data not maintained independently of the system. To correct this, a physical measurements database was created to provide consistency between planning and operations and allow easy updating.
2. New software was implemented that increased the speed of the system and allowed more end users access through a user-friendly interface.
3. The LP model was changed to better reflect the true operating constraints.
4. An iterative process of validation and calibration was undertaken to further improve the accuracy of the model.

Process Control Equipment Using Nonlinear Optimization Models

Process control equipment that included nonlinear optimization models was installed to measure and optimize energy utilization. The energy audit disclosed major steam losses and a lack of adequate metering. The introduction of the equipment and models has provided improved data for planning and has reduced energy consumption.

New process control equipment was installed on all key units, and procedures to evaluate operator performance and train operators were institutionalized. The automated 24-hour attention to temperature and flow provided for efficient and quality refining, increasing yields and reducing costs. All readings from the equipment were maintained in a database that was used to analyze operator efficiency, unit productivity, and failures. These readings provide data for in-process inventories and for the refinery LP model.

Integrated Maintenance Information System

The maintenance information system performed a number of functions within the refinery, including the following:

Tracking the $12 million parts inventory

Work order generation, approval, and tracking

Development of work plans for personnel

Provision of instructions for delivering materials when a job was ready to be executed

This system has resulted in lower inventory requirements, less equipment downtime, and better utilization of staff.

PC Optimization-Based Scheduling System

The optimization scheduling system schedules the distribution of crude oil from storage tanks to the refinery. The automation of the pipeline and a new tank-gauging system have provided the necessary data for the scheduling system. These measures have resulted in a $20 million reduction in the inventory of crude oil, and processing costs have been reduced through better sequencing of the various inventories.

TRACS

The TRACS system (Tracking, Reporting, and Aggregation of Citgo Segmented Sales) was a database management system combined with an expert system. It was used for marketing planning purposes, providing a comparison between potential selling options and distribution channels. TRACS is able to evaluate sales at all Citgo-owned terminals and all exchange terminals, including all variable costs of supplying sales, such as transportation, handling, and marketing expenses. The TRACS system was used extensively during 1986 for strategic marketing planning.

PASS

PASS (Production Acquisition and Supply System) was a corporatewide, on-line management database with fourth-generation language features. It contained up-to-date operational information on sales and inventory levels, as well as information on various trades and exchanges for all refined products. PASS has been made available to all functions and managers.

Price and volume forecasting was centralized to feed the PASS database, and forecasts were developed using econometric modelling and regression analysis. Because of the massive amount of information provided by the PASS system, the SDM system was created to allow this information to be used to make decisions.

SDM

SDM was an optimization-based Supply, Distribution, and Marketing model that integrated the key economic and physical characteristics of Citgo's supply, distribution, and marketing for an 11-week planning horizon. SDM was used by top management to make decisions on where to sell products, pricing policies, and where to buy or trade products. SDM included a profit maximization model that generated output reports for individual operational managers and used an expert system to generate exception reports, bringing key information to the attention of management. SDM also was used extensively for what-if sessions, allowing management to respond quickly to the dynamics of the commodity market.

Payable Float Optimization System

The payable float optimization system controlled product and crude oil payables using a payment-term maximization program; it also controlled disbursement bank selection. This system has reduced working capital requirements by $8.5 million.

CATS

CATS (Citgo Automated Terminal System) was a transaction processing system at the point of sale that billed customers and provided accurate, up-to-date information on inventory levels for each terminal. This system has reduced the average collection time, with a total reduction of $9 million in working capital requirements.

Total Profit Improvements

Citgo's implementation of MS/OR tools fed by accurate up-to-the-minute data vividly illustrates how the comprehensive and integrated applications of such tools can help companies gain a competitive advantage. Estimates of the cost savings and increased profits were:

1. Reduced working capital requirements by $150 million, leading to interest savings of $18 million per year
2. Improved marketing profits of $2.5 million in 1985
3. Improved refining profits of $50 million in 1985

The total improvement in profits for 1985 was $70 million, with this figure expected to grow as further refinements are made to the many systems as quality data become available. The investment in MS/OR has proved to be attractive with the total cost of all of the systems implemented estimated at $20 to $30 million.

John P. Thompson, Chairman of the Board and Chief Executive Officer of The Southland Corporation, has stated: "We have been very gratified at the success that this approach, with its heavy dependence on management science and cooperative effort, has achieved at Citgo. The numerous systems that were developed for Citgo ... have become an integral part of the Citgo operation, saving many millions of dollars that otherwise would have been lost profits.... We look forward to future management science developments that might provide even greater advantages to Southland in what is becoming an increasingly competitive business climate."

From D. Klingman, N. Phillips, D. Steiger, and W. Young, The Successful Deployment of Management Science throughout Citgo Petroleum Corporation, *Interfaces* 1987;17:1.

TACKLING THE COST OF HEALTH CARE

The costs of providing adequate health care are escalating, in part a result of differences in service levels, lack of measurement and evaluation, and the fact that consumers often do not pay directly for the products. In many cases, these costs are borne by national or regional (state or provincial) governments. All of these issues contributed to the need for a system of product definitions to allow for measurement and evaluation, thus promoting consistency among services from different health service providers. **Diagnosis-related groups** (DRGs) were developed by Professor Bob Feller of Yale University in an effort to begin to control the growing cost of health care in the United States.

A DRG is a classification of a patient according to illness and the bundle of services received during hospitalization for that specific diagnosis. In determining a DRG, a patient is first classified into one of 23 **major diagnostic categories** (MDC). Every illness can be classified into one, and only one, MDC, including diagnoses that involve surgical procedures (Surgical Group) and nonsurgical treatment (Diagnosis Group). Using the *International Classification of Diseases* (ICD) system of coding, each MDC category, Diagnosis Group and Surgical Group, is broken into additional groups based on factors such as:

- Comorbidities/complications
- Age
- Discharge status
- Nonsurgical procedures

This system creates a tree structure with at least four levels:

- MDC
- Operating Room Procedure (Diagnosis Group or Surgical Group)
- ICD classification, and
- Further class differences (as listed above)

When developing this classification system, three characteristics were deemed important: the classifications should be based on information routinely collected by hospitals, the number of MDCs (classes) should be simple enough to be manageable but specific enough to be useful, and within each MDC there should be both a similar pattern of resource intensity, and similar types of patients from a clinical perspective.

Developing Diagnosis-Related Groups

Before the analysis of data to establish DRGs could begin, 2 years were needed to develop the technology required. A panel of physicians was established and asked to explain processes and assist with functional and clinical information. Information from the Uniform Hospital Discharge Data Set (completed for each patient discharged from a hospital in the United States) was analyzed to find similar patterns of care for illnesses and aggregate patients into coherent groups according to the services received. Three obstacles were encountered during this process:

- Not all diseases are equally well understood
- Treatments for the same disease often differ
- Codes that existed at the time were sometimes found to be either too general or too specific (a particular illness sometimes had many different codes, and sometimes none at all)

Impact of Diagnosis-Related Groups

DRGs have met with success when used in conjunction with Medicare's Prospective Payment System (PPS). Patients qualifying for health care paid by the U.S. government under Medicare are classified into one of the DRG codes on discharge, and except for a small number of extreme cases, the hospital is paid a fixed rate based on the classification. The PPS rates are set nationally but are adjusted for local wage rates, even though hospital costs to provide service for each DRG may still differ based on:

- Cost of inputs (labor, materials)
- Number of cases and facility utilization
- Case mix (numbers of each type of different cases)
- Variations in physicians' practices

The combination of the use of PPS rates and DRGs has been successful in making hospitals more accountable for costs. DRGs

> were adopted by Medicare in 1983 to serve as a basis for a prospective payment system for U.S. hospitals. This system has resulted in savings of more than $50 billion in Medicare hospital payments through 1990 and extended the solvency of the Medical Hospital Trust Fund well into the next century. More than 20 countries are currently developing or have adopted DRG-based systems for managing and financing hospital care.
>
> Some of the benefits realized include the following:
>
> - A decrease in the number of admissions
> - A decrease in length of stay
> - A decrease in Medicare Program Costs
> - An increase in profit margins of hospitals

Although the severity of the illnesses of admitted patients has increased, this may simply be due to better coding of illnesses.

From Robert B. Fetter, Diagnosis Related Groups: Understanding Hospital Performance, *Interfaces*, 1991;21:1.

LES ENTERPRISE GIRO, INC.

Jean-Marc Rousseau has visited many of the great cities of the world: Canberra, Melbourne, Singapore, Helsinki, Barcelona, Brussels, Turin, Los Angeles, Stockholm, New York, Boston, Montreal, Edinburgh, Ottawa ... and the list goes on. These cities all use software developed by Rousseau's company, Les enterprises GIRO Inc. (Giro), of Montreal, Canada, as a critical component of the operation of their mass transit systems.

GIRO

The GIRO story began in 1973 when a student of Jean-Marc Rousseau at the University of Montreal investigated the problem of bus driver scheduling at the Montreal Transit System (STUCM) as a master's thesis project. By 1977, university research on this problem had produced a bus crew scheduling technique that was used by the Quebec City Bus System (CTCUQ) to "cost out" various demands from the crew's union during an 8-month strike.

Using this technique, crew schedules with associated costs could be derived quickly in response to union demands for wage increases or changes in working conditions. CTCUQ management could quickly determine the cost to the system of any proposed change rather than wait 3 to 4 weeks for the costs to be derived "the old way." After the end of the strike, a second research contract was signed with CTCUQ that led to derivation of a new bus crew schedule, which produced a demonstrative cost savings to CTCUQ of 1%. In 1979, STCUM undertook a similar test that produced a 3% savings (equivalent to $4 million annually). Although the schedules produced were not perfect, they included fewer problems than those produced by humans.

Between 1979 and 1981, STCUM bus crew schedules were derived by the University of Montreal under a $150,000 research contract. By 1981, however, Jean-Marc was finding conflicts between his role as a university researcher and that of a real-world problem solver. He felt that a real-world problem solver had to take risks and consequently should be rewarded by performance–not a view compatible with that normally ascribed to the university researcher.

In 1981-1982, Giro was formed as a separate company outside the university. Giro was owned by its management and started with a $60,000 contract with STCUM to create a bus schedule for Montreal; 80,000 punched cards were used to input the schedule into the computer! STCUM served as a test site for the new system, which was a batch program with no user interface. STCUM helped develop an interface and significant efforts were made to market the system to other municipalities. These efforts proved to be difficult: every municipality thought that their bus scheduling problem was unique and that only their own employees could derive useable schedules.

The marketing breakthrough came in 1984 through a joint venture with Volvo Transportation Systems. Volvo was selling buses, and a deal was struck with the City of Singapore whereby HASTUS, the GIRO bus scheduling system, was provided as part of a contract for the sale of Volvo buses.

By 1990, HASTUS contained some 1 million lines of computer code. In a major development effort at an estimated cost of 50 person-years, the software was rewritten to a WIMP interactive graphic interface. By 1994, GIRO had 100 employees and $6 to $7 million annual turnover, with 60% of the revenue from outside Canada. GIRO operated in three main areas.

Transit Scheduling. Giro's major product HASTUS is used by more than 80 transit companies in 17 countries.

Routing/Scheduling. This included school buses, meter readers, postal services, snow removal, street cleaning, and milk collection. Giro's software GeoRoute provides interactive map-based solutions that respect one-way street and turn restrictions, pick-up and delivery time, windows, vehicle capacities, and so on.

Fleet Management Software for Utilities (including Bell Canada) Government Agencies and Business. This software schedules maintenance, task orders, budgets, and spare parts inventory and provides vehicle costs and employee timekeeping.

In 1984, Giro began a project with Canada Post Corporation (CPC) as a result of the initiative of a student who had been employed as a CPC driver. CPC faced many routing problems, including deriving the routes for letter carriers and mail box collection. As a result of a number of small contracts over several years and a marketing agreement with CPC (a widely respected showcase for Giro products), Giro postal routing software is being tested in France, Germany, and the United Kingdom.

In 1986, university research on bus routing produced savings of 5% to 15% of the $300 million spent on buses in Montreal. This led to a contract with Montreal Transit, which led to a software product, *GeoBus,* that derives "optimal" bus routes for a metropolitan area.

In 1985, Giro had software for school bus routing that produced routes that were feasible but not "optimal." By 1989, this software had been developed into an interactive graphic package that was in use in 25 school boards in Canada but still did not include optimization.

From J.-M. Rousseau, Marketing O.R.: From University to Enterprise, presentation to the 1994 National Conference of the Canadian Operational Research Society, Montreal.

EXERCISES

EXAMPLES OF OPTIMUM DYNAMIC PRICING

1. Perishable Product Pricing

We have 3,000 units of product to sell over a 5-day period. From historical sales data, we have estimated the following demand curves:

P = price/unit in $
Q = number of units sold

Day 1: P = 10 − 0.01 Q
(valid for prices between $3 and $8)

Day 2: same as day 1

Day 3: P = 15 − 0.01Q
(valid for prices between $6 and $10)

Day 4: P = 20 − 0.01Q
(valid for prices between $6 and $12)

Day 5: same as day 1

Assignment

1. Formulate as a **Solver** problem in Excel. What are the revenue maximizing prices for days 1 through 5? What is the maximum possible revenue?
2. If the price must be the same on each day, what is the revenue maximizing price? What is the revenue? What is the revenue penalty for operating a fixed price policy?
3. Suppose that on day 1 we post the optimal price (from 1 above) but sales are 10% above estimated demand. Re-solve the problem by computing new optimal prices for days 2 through 5 assuming demand is 10% above expected each day except the last day. What is the revenue?
4. Repeat question 3 with an assumption of a fixed single price for the 5 days. What is the revenue? Again, compute the revenue penalty for operating a fixed price policy.
5. Is 3,000 the optimal number of units to order? Would you order more, or fewer?
6. Repeat questions 3 and 4 under an assumption that demand is 10% below expected each day except the last. Assume inventory clearing prices on the last day. What is the revenue penalty from fixed pricing?

2. Hotel Room Pricing

A hotel has 500 rooms. During a typical week in the holiday season, the hotel is busy on Monday, Tuesday, Wednesday, and Thursday nights with primarily business people, but there is generally space available on Friday, Saturday, and Sunday nights. Hotel management provided the demand estimates shown in Table 7-1. Assume linear demand functions over the range of all nonnegative room rates and demands.

Table 7-1 **HOTEL MANAGEMENT PROVIDED THE FOLLOWING DEMAND ESTIMATES**

Room Rate	Days	Estimated Demand (rooms/day)
\$160	Mon, Tue, Wed, Thur	500
	Fri, Sat, Sun	200
\$175	Mon, Tue, Wed, Thur	350
	Fri, Sat, Sun	125

Assignment

1. What is the revenue maximizing room rate if the hotel posts only a single rate good for any day of the week? What weekly occupancy results?
2. What are the revenue maximizing room rates if the hotel posts a "midweek" rate good for the peak demand period (MTWT), and a different "weekend" rate good for Friday, Saturday, or Sunday. What is the new weekly occupancy? What is the revenue increase?

   Another option is for the hotel to offer a discounted weekly rate to attract vacationers who will stay for the full week. Management estimates that demand will be 40 per week at \$900 per week and 160 per week at \$800 per week. Again, assume a linear demand curve.
3. If the hotel posts a weekly rate and a single daily rate (good for any night), what are the revenue maximizing prices? What is the occupancy rate? What is the revenue gain?
4. If the hotel posts three rates (a midweek rate, a weekend rate, and a weekly rate), what are the revenue maximizing prices? What is the occupancy rate? What is the revenue gain?

OHIO POLYMER, INC.

THIS CASE DESCRIBES A REAL SITUATION BUT HAS BEEN DISGUISED.

"Sandy, I cannot negotiate this contract without better information." Norman Vincent, Chief Executive Officer of Ohio Polymer Inc., was visibly upset by the vague answers he was getting from Sandy Carson, Ohio's Vice President, Planning. "We are about to sign a multimillion dollar annual contract, and I'm unconvinced that we know what we're doing. Your people don't seem to have asked the right questions."

Negotiations between Ohio Polymer and ProBut Hydrocarbon Inc. were scheduled to begin next week. ProBut was extending its ethylene gas pipeline and had offered to install a branch pipeline to deliver ethylene to Ohio Polymer. Because Ohio often bought ethylene on the high-priced "spot" market, this looked like a cost-saving opportunity, but before installing the branch line, ProBut wanted a signed supply contract with Ohio Polymer. Sandy Carson had the responsibility to advise CEO Norman Vincent on these negotiations.

Sandy returned to his office and immediately addressed Vincent's basic questions about the contract. How much contract ethylene should Ohio try to obtain? How much should they be prepared to pay?

BACKGROUND

Ohio Polymer Inc. was a large chemical company that operated a major ethylene complex that included nine different plants. Five of these plants produced four finished products: high-pressure polyethylene (HPPE) that was produced in two plants, ethyl benzene, ethylene oxide, and low-pressure polyethylene (LPPE). These four products were produced from the same raw material feedstock–ethylene gas. Ohio Polymer also supplied ethylene by pipeline to a small local manufacturer with a plant nearby. Mean daily consumption of ethylene was approximately 615 tons.

Ohio's complex (Exhibit 1) included three plants where ethylene gas was manufactured at an average rate of 580 tons per day. The production process required a large initial capital investment but resulted in a very low variable cost per ton of ethylene. Each ethylene plant consisted of several furnaces that operated in parallel, served by some connecting headgear. As each furnace operated almost independently, each plant could operate at partial capacity if any of the furnaces broke down. However, if the headgear (which provided ethylene supply to all the furnaces in the given plant) failed, then the whole plant had to be shut down. Data on the frequency of furnace and headgear breakdowns were routinely collected by plant management and was readily available (Exhibit 2).

The ethylene-using plants also operated at discrete levels for the same reasons. Extensive data on the operation of the user plants also were available (Exhibit 3).

Breakdowns of the nine different plants resulted in some days with surplus ethylene and others when there was a shortage. Some balancing of supply and demand was possible, using a system of high pressure storage tanks. If excess ethylene was produced, then it was first liquefied (the liquefier had a capacity of 300 tons per day) and then stored in these tanks that had a maximum capacity of 900 tons. Maintaining pressure over the high pressure tanks was estimated to cost $1 per ton stored for 1 day.

If the amount of ethylene produced was greater than the liquefaction rate or the storage tank was full, then the excess gas had to be flared (burned). Any attempt to voluntarily cut ethylene production resulted in damage to the firebricks that lined the furnaces, accelerating the need for a further shut down to reline the furnace walls. This alternative was not considered feasible.

When ethylene demand exceeded production, ethylene from the storage tanks could be evaporated (the evaporator had a capacity of 400 tons per day) and piped to the user plants. When the storage tanks were empty or the shortage was greater than the maximum evaporation rate, production was maintained by using spot-purchased ethylene. Because of the short lead time involved and the relatively expensive mode of transportation (by truck), spot purchases were relatively expensive (the average price was $200 per ton). Because the average amount of ethylene produced (580 tons per day) was less than the average tonnage required (615 tons per day), there were always several road tankers full of

Exhibit 1 **FLOW DIAGRAM OF ETHYLENE DISTRIBUTION (PLANT CAPACITIES IN TONS/DAY)**

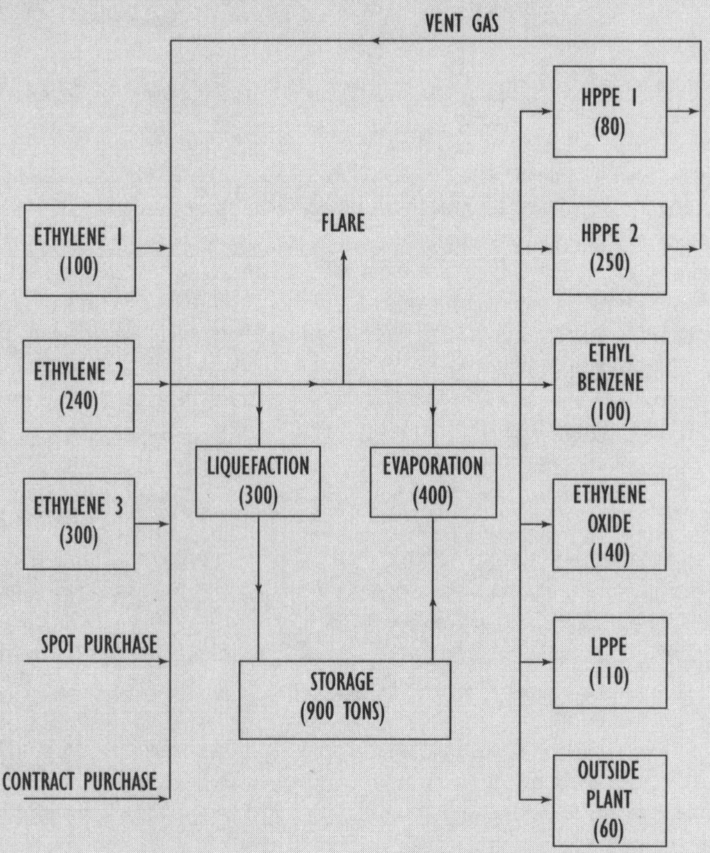

ethylene waiting at the plant to provide spot ethylene as soon as it was needed.

The extensive pipelines within the complex enabled the operating engineers to operate the complex in such a way that the ethylene from any producer plant could be used by any user plant, all plants had access to the storage tanks, and any user plant could use spot-purchased ethylene.

NEW OPPORTUNITY

An alternative source of ethylene had recently become available when ProBut began installation of a nearby main trunk pipeline. ProBut was prepared to install a branch pipeline into the Ohio Polymer complex, but before they would begin construction of this new branch line, ProBut required a contract to supply Ohio Polymer with a fixed daily tonnage of ethylene ("take or pay"). ("Take or pay" contracts were common in industrial gas purchase agreements: in these contracts, the buyer paid a fixed daily price for a maximum quantity of gas but received no credit if less than this maximum amount was actually taken.) Such a contract would reduce Ohio's dependence on expensive spot-market ethylene.

Any contract between Ohio Polymer and ProBut would likely involve several million dollars annually and would be negotiated at the highest level of the firm. For Ohio, this meant that CEO Norman Vincent would conduct the negotiation. As Sandy Carson had discovered, Vincent had become greatly disturbed when he found that the team assigned to this contract was unable to answer some basic questions concerning the value of contract gas to Ohio Polymer.

These were not easy questions to answer. At first instance, it appeared that the pipeline gas would substitute for spot purchases, but the contract would require Ohio to pay for gas on days when it already had excess gas. On some of these days, Ohio would not be able to store the gas and would have to flare it or just not take delivery. Perhaps Ohio should install additional storage tanks and/or increase liquefaction and/or evaporation plant capacity?

How could Sandy provide help to CEO Norman Vincent to enable him to conclude a successful negotiation with ProBut?

Assignment

1. Flowchart a model to address Polymer's problem.
2. What results will your model provide?
3. Use the model of Ohio Polymer's operations to address the following issue:

   You have been asked to sit in on the contract negotiations as a source of technical advice. You are expected to be able to offer price/quantity suggestions but will not have time to run the simulation during the negotiations. Derive one or more "decision aids" from the model output that will enable you to propose responses to contract offers and to explain the rationale behind your reactions to the negotiating team.

Exhibit 2 | ETHYLENE-PRODUCING PLANTS OPERATING DATA

Plant	Capacity (tons/day)	Operating Level %	Operating Level Tons/day	Probability*
Ethylene 1 (2 furnaces)	100	0	0	0.02
		50	50	0.09
		100	100	0.89
Ethylene 2 (4 furnaces)	240	0	0	0.015
		25	60	0.03
		50	120	0.06
		75	180	0.12
		100	240	0.775
Ethylene 3 (5 furnaces)	300	0	0	0.01
		20	60	0.02
		40	120	0.04
		60	180	0.07
		80	240	0.11
		100	300	0.75

Mean production = 580.1 tons/day.

* Probabilities were computed by expressing the time each plant operated at each operating level as a fraction of the total operating time.

Exhibit 3 | **ETHYLENE-USER PLANT OPERATING DATA**

Plant	Capacity (tons/day)	Operating Level %	Operating Level Tons/day	Probability*
HPPE 1	80 (gross)	0	0	0.1
	70.8 (net)	100	70.8	0.9
HPPE 2	250 (gross)	0	0	0.03
	221.25 (net)	25	55.3	0.025
		50	110.6	0.1
		75	165.9	0.4
		100	221.2	0.445
Ethyl benzene	100	0	0	0.05
		50	50	0.05
		100	100	0.9
Ethylene oxide	140	0	0	0.05
		100	140	0.95
LPPE	110	0	0	0.08
		50	55	0.14
		100	110	0.78
Outside plant	60	0	0	0.01
		33.3	20	0.015
		66.7	40	0.17
		100	60	0.805

Note: The HPPE plants vent 11.5% of their ethylene feed back into the system as "vent gas" (see Exhibit 1).

Mean consumption = 615.1 tons/day (net).

* Probabilities were computed by expressing the time each plant operated at each operating level as a fraction of the total operating time.

PROBUT HYDROCARBON, INC.

BY PETER C. BELL AND CHRISTOPH HAEHLING VON LANZENAUER

Robert G. Black, Vice President for Facilities Planning at ProBut Hydrocarbon (ProBut), was pleased. He just had received a letter (Exhibit 1) from Sandy Carson, Vice President for Planning at Ohio Polymer Inc. (Polymer), indicating a strong interest in the proposed branch pipeline. Earlier in the Fall, Bob had proposed to connect Polymer's large ethylene complex to ProBut's main ethylene pipeline, a connection that would involve installing 19 kilometers of high pressure underground pipe. ProBut was prepared to underwrite the investment in the pipeline if a firm supply contract between the two companies could be agreed and signed.

Sandy Carson's letter not only proposed a meeting for a first round of negotiations on January 20/21 but also identified the key agenda items. Apparently, it was Polymer's intention to reach a tentative agreement on the major points of the contract during the proposed meeting and to prepare a *Memorandum of Agreement* as a basis for discussion and, hopefully, approval by Polymer's Senior Management Group.

Bob Black, although elated about the positive response his idea has received from Polymer, was also keenly aware that he and his staff would have to do a significant amount of work in preparing for this negotiating session. In particular, any contract negotiated by Bob would have to be approved by ProBut's Investment Committee, and this committee would require substantive evidence supporting the projected benefits that would flow to ProBut from the proposed branch pipeline. Bob also recalled the unpleasant experience when on another occasion, one of the committee members asked penetrating questions concerning several contingencies that he was not prepared for. Bob was, therefore, determined not to repeat such an experience and knew that he had to do his homework to demonstrate the financial viability of the project and also to ensure that "no money was left on the table."

PIPELINE PROPOSAL

In preparing for the upcoming negotiation, Bob Black felt that adequate information and analyses were essential. While he had reasonable control of the cost and other relevant aspects of the branch pipeline (Exhibit 2), he was not sure how much ethylene Polymer would be prepared to buy on a daily basis.

The pipeline proposal had emerged after a conversation with "Skeets" West, Plant Manager of ProBut's ethylene plant. In this conversation, Skeets had bemoaned the fact that on most days, ProBut produced more ethylene than it could use. On some days, significant quantities of the excess gas could be sold on the spot market, whereas on other days, there was little demand for "spot," and gas often had to be flared because the storage tanks were full. The high variability of the demand for spot gas produced major operating problems for ProBut because plants could not be turned on or off easily (it took several days to start-up a producer plant). Skeets had suggested to Bob that he try to negotiate an agreement with the truckers who purchased spot gas from ProBut whereby these companies would guarantee to take a relatively small but stable amount of ethylene (less than 100 tons per day in total) every day in return for a discount. If such a deal could be agreed, Skeets and his operating engineers could plan daily operations to take into account this demand for ethylene.

After investigating this idea, Bob realized that it was a nonstarter. The purchasers of spot gas were a group of independent truckers who loaded their road tankers with ethylene and then drove to a location where they could resell the gas. Often, after arriving at a site, they had to wait several days until the gas was needed and they could unload. Because the truckers had no place to store ethylene, there was no way they could contract for a fixed daily quantity of gas. This line of inquiry, however, led Bob to approach Polymer.

Bob knew that Polymer was generally short of gas and was by far the largest single buyer (and never a seller) on the spot market. With the completion of the new pipeline, Polymer could now be connected to this line at a reasonable cost. Perhaps Polymer could be persuaded to buy gas directly from ProBut under the kind of guaranteed "take-or-pay" contract that Skeets had in mind? Bob was optimistic that an agreement could be reached, particularly if there was a cost advantage from delivering the ethylene through a pipeline rather than by road tanker. If the volume of gas contracted for delivery through the pipeline was large enough, it seemed that this would be the case.

Bob approached Polymer with an offer to supply a fixed, daily quantity of gas to be delivered through the new branch pipeline. To meet Skeets' requirements, the contract would require Polymer to agree to take a fixed quantity of ethylene every day over a substantial time period. If a long-term contract with Polymer could be agreed on, ProBut would capacitate the branch pipeline to deliver the contracted amount over a 24-hour period to minimize the installation cost. If Polymer wanted to purchase more gas than was provided for by the contract, they would still have to purchase this gas by the truckload on the spot market.

POLYMER'S NEED FOR ETHYLENE

Bob knew that the demand for ethylene at the Polymer complex over the past 2 years had generally exceeded supply and that Polymer met this shortage by buying ethylene on the spot market. The proximity of ProBut's facility to Polymer meant that this spot market gas was usually purchased from ProBut by independent truckers who delivered the ethylene to Polymer. Sandy had included data on Polymer's spot purchases for the last several months with his letter (see Exhibit 3). Bob undertook a preliminary analysis of this data (Exhibit 4) and found a high degree of variability around an average daily purchase of about 35 tons per day: on many days, Polymer appeared to have no need for additional ethylene, whereas on some days, the purchases far exceeded the daily average.

Bob also realized that Polymer had to flare-off gas fairly often, indicating that there was a high degree of variability in Polymer's plant operating levels and that their capacity for storing ethylene when production exceeded needs was limited. It was clear that if ProBut supplied ethylene to Polymer under a contract requiring Polymer to take a fixed daily amount of gas, Polymer would not achieve 100% utilization of this gas; there would be days when some or all of the contract gas would have to be flared-off. Thus, the ethylene to be delivered by the pipeline would have to cost Polymer less than the spot-purchased gas (which was only purchased when absolutely needed).

Bob knew that Polymer was unlikely to sign a contract that would entirely eliminate the need for spot purchases. Given the high transportation cost (about 59% of the current spot price of $200.00 per ton went to pay for trucking), there would be sufficient independent trucking capacity to ensure an uninterrupted supply to Polymer. In fact, the projected savings resulting from fewer spot purchases seemed to be the incentive for Polymer to enter into such a supply contract.

While reviewing these data, Bob wondered what analyses to undertake to prepare for the upcoming negotiations. Bob felt that his analysis would have to demonstrate a return of at least 18% with a high degree of confidence to secure a favorable response to the contract from the Investment Committee.

Assignment

This case is designed to be used in conjunction with Ohio Polymer.

1. As ProBut management, conduct a negotiation with Ohio Polymer's management and arrive at a mutually satisfactory contract for the supply of ethylene gas.

Exhibit 1 | LETTER FROM SANDY CARSON TO BOB BLACK

Mr. Robert Black
Vice President for Facilities Planning
ProBut Hydrocarbon Inc.

Dear Bob:

I enjoyed our telephone conversation last week, and have discussed your proposed branch pipeline initiative with Norman Vincent, our CEO.

We are enthusiastic about your proposal, and we look forward to our scheduled meeting on January 20/21 to work out the details of the ethylene supply agreement. I propose that we address the following issues:

1. How much ethylene can you supply to us daily by pipeline?
2. What will be the price/ton (or price/day) for the contract gas?
3. What will be the term of the contract?
4. Other issues, including time frame for installation, etc.

I am enclosing a list of our daily spot purchases for a 15-month period (from July 7 to the following September 30) to provide you with some background on our needs.

I look forward to our meeting on January 20.

Sincerely,

Sandy Carson
Vice President
Ohio Polymer, Inc.

Exhibit 2 | PROBUT HYDROCARBON INCORPORATED INTERNAL MEMO

DATE: October 7

TO: Bob Black, Vice President, Planning

FROM: Jen Parker, Engineering

RE: Proposed Branch Pipeline

Bob:

Further to your request, I have collected relevant facts and information for the proposed branch pipeline from the main to the Ohio Polymer plant.

1. Pipeline Parameters
   a) Length of line: approx. 19 km (the exact length may be somewhat different following the survey results).
   b) Given the anticipated transmission volume of about 50 tons/day to the Ohio Polymer Plant, a 3 ½" line is proposed.
   c) The volume could be transported without any additional compressor stations. Further, the volume could be increased by up to 50% if such need arises.
   d) The inclusive cost (land, construction, materials, etc.) for the line described under b) would be about $96,000 per km.
   e) Annual operating and maintenance costs are currently $400/km/year.
   f) The life expectancy for the line under normal operating conditions is 40 to 50 years.
2. Environmental Impact Study

   As you know, an Environmental Impact study has to be carried out for this proposal. Following our practice, we should employ an outside consulting firm for this study. Given the assessment we obtained for the main pipeline, I don't anticipate any major problems.
3. Approval by the Regulatory Agency

   Approval for the project has to be obtained from our Regulatory Agency. With a positive Environmental Impact study, no problem with the approval is foreseen, although it may take up to a year to obtain the final approval.
4. Liability Issues

   The proposed pipeline would not trigger an increase in our liability insurance cost. Any risks will be covered by our existing umbrella policy.

If there is any other information that you require, please do not hesitate to contact me again.

Exhibit 3 | SPOT ETHYLENE PURCHASES BY OHIO POLYMER (tons/day)

July 7–31							63	182	0	0	0	0	168	0	229	62
	0	0	0	0	0	0	0	0	100	62	0	28	0	0	81	
August 1–31	0	14	0	109	187	7	72	57	122	0	0	0	0	0	0	0
	47	67	132	67	122	127	22	0	0	0	0	0	0	0	0	
September 1–30	0	0	0	0	0	0	0	0	0	0	0	0	0	0	0	0
	0	0	0	0	0	0	0	0	0	0	0	0	0	0		
October 1–31	0	0	47	0	0	94	42	0	3	67	0	0	0	0	40	0
	0	0	0	0	0	0	0	0	0	0	0	0	0	0	0	
November 1–30	0	0	0	0	0	0	0	0	0	155	62	122	72	7	52	107
	0	119	62	307	0	34	0	118	117	62	62	2	62	0		
December 1–31	0	0	0	0	0	0	0	0	115	42	0	18	0	0	0	0
	18	0	0	0	18	0	0	0	0	0	70	127	62	122	7	
January 1–31	0	29	0	0	0	0	0	0	0	0	0	0	0	0	2	51
	0	3	0	19	0	0	0	36	62	0	299	17	0	18	0	
February 1–28	0	241	0	0	50	0	0	0	138	0	139	1	0	194	0	0
	0	237	41	197	127	0	109	67	0	0	0	0				
March 1–31	0	396	67	7	62	242	0	0	85	41	57	172	62	0	13	11
	0	0	0	0	152	0	0	0	0	0	0	0	0	0	0	
April 1–30	0	0	0	0	0	0	0	0	0	0	0	0	0	0	0	237
	0	98	62	0	179	0	0	0	0	0	50	202	0	0		
May 1–31	0	0	94	0	0	35	0	0	85	0	0	0	0	0	0	0
	129	22	112	0	24	7	0	0	120	242	62	102	122	72	0	
June 1–30	199	112	57	0	0	24	7	62	2	242	187	47	67	67	62	57
	0	0	45	0	0	34	102	7	7	0	0	0	51	0		
July 1–31	0	135	0	14	7	0	0	6	37	67	0	18	7	96	62	67
	0	228	42	127	0	79	122	42	0	99	122	182	42	187	0	
August 1–31	4	7	62	0	0	0	0	0	0	156	0	0	0	12	11	7
	7	187	0	0	0	0	0	0	0	0	0	0	0	0	0	
September 1–30	21	67	0	0	0	0	53	62	67	0	99	7	122	7	7	127
	7	117	122	127	0	0	0	0	44	0	114	0	0	69		

Exhibit **4** | **OHIO POLYMER SPOT PURCHASES**

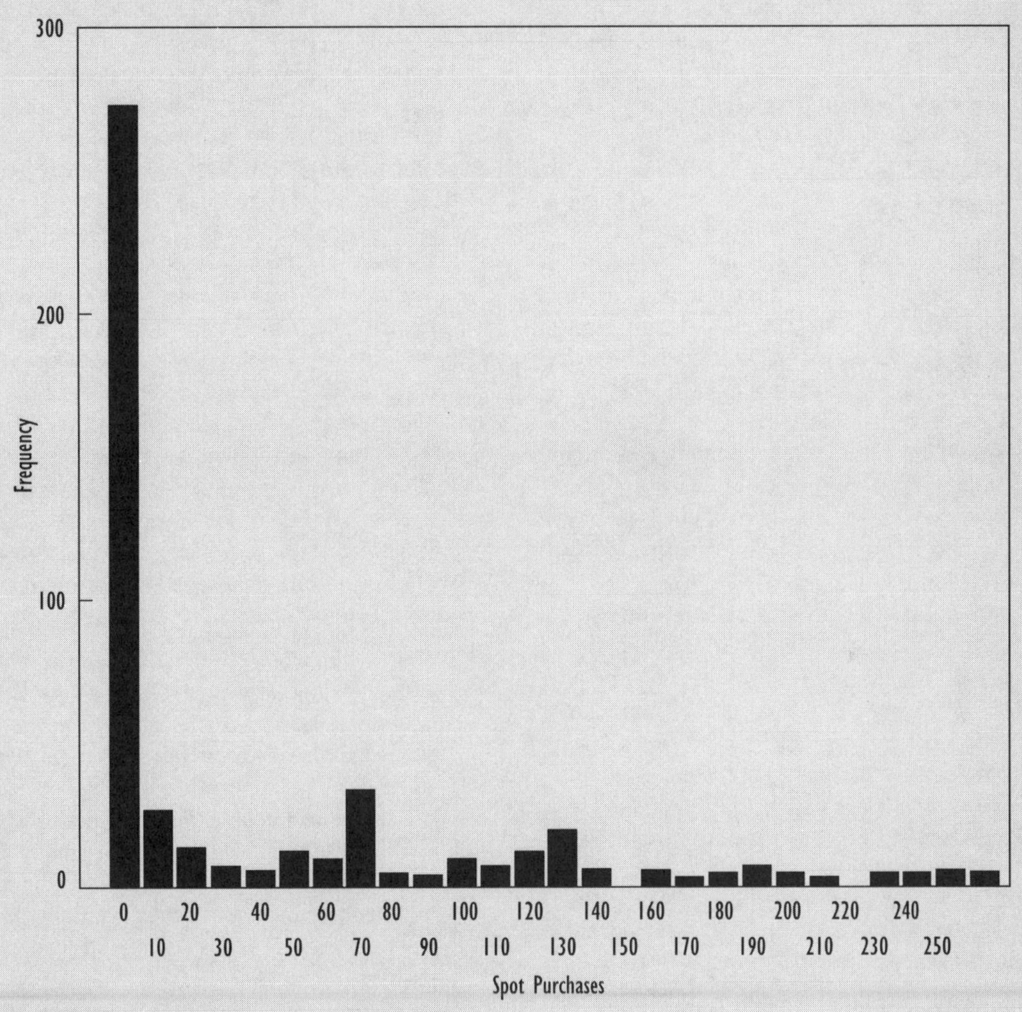

Descriptive Statistics:	Mean	33.11042
	Std. Dev.	60.05096
	Count	451
	Max. Value	396.1
	Min. Value	0

AIRLINE FLIGHT CREW SCHEDULING

Airlines must assign air crews to flights. Air crew costs are the airlines' second highest component of direct operating cost (next to fuel). For a major air carrier, these costs amount to well over a billion dollars annually, and the difference between good crew assignments and bad ones may exceed $100 million annually. The very competitive market in which North American air carriers operate makes crew scheduling a critical activity.

FLIGHT OPERATIONS

Flight schedules are firmed up about 6 weeks in advance. These schedules list the flights to be flown and the specific aircraft that have been assigned to each flight. A typical large air carrier will operate about a dozen different types of aircraft, with each type having different flight crew requirements.

A flight crew consists of a pilot, copilot, and usually a flight engineer plus from one to 14 cabin attendants. Pilots are normally certified to fly only one type of aircraft, and cabin crew are generally trained for service on one type of aircraft.

Flight crews operate from "crew base" cities. For example, American Airlines might hire and maintain 10 "747" crews in Chicago. A crew base city can be anywhere on the air carrier's route network; a major carrier would operate up to a dozen crew base locations. The location of crew bases is an important feature of crew assignment; new crew bases can be opened and existing ones closed. There is little cost associated with maintaining a crew base (other than the cost of the crews, who have to be paid wherever they are based).

In planning flight crew assignments, Federal Aviation Authority (FAA) rules must be followed rigidly along with the terms of employment of the various crew members that are covered by legal contracts negotiated between the carriers and the associations representing the various crew groups. These terms must be rigidly adhered to in the short term, although renegotiations allow some flexibility in the longer term. These contracts provide a number of restrictions on working hours for crew personnel as well as specifying the terms and conditions under which crew are paid. These contracts are very complex and include many conditions that affect the way in which crews can be scheduled for work. The FAA also sets work rules for flight crews; there is little hope of making significant changes in these rules.

Air Crews are normally scheduled to work a 3-day "tour." A crew for a particular aircraft type reports for duty at the crew base airport at a designated time, usually 1 hour before the scheduled take-off. The crew will fly a working day (a minimum of 8.5 paid hours at normal time and longer at overtime rates) not necessarily on the same aircraft but always on the same type of aircraft. At the end of their working day, the crew will "layover" at their destination. The crew contracts mandate that this layover must be at least 9.5 hours. The crew then works a second working day, lays over again, works a third working day, and then must be returned to the crew base city.

Once the crew starts a working day, all members of the crew must be paid whether flying or not until the working day ends (that is, for at least 8.5 hours). Time in the air is paid at a higher rate than time on the ground. The crew members are not paid during layovers (although meals and accommodations must be paid by the carriers; a major airline will pay several million dollars each month for hotel rooms). The crew can be flown as passengers, but when this is done, all crew must be paid as if they were working the flight.

When scheduling crews, there are a number of important issues.

- The carrier would prefer to keep the same crew with the same aircraft as long as possible. This minimizes outbound flight delays because of the nonavailability of crew if an inbound flight is delayed.
- If a crew must change aircraft, there is a difficult issue to resolve. If the on-ground time is too short, there is an increased probability that the outbound flight will be delayed. If the on-ground time is too long, the crew is likely to be paid for nonproductive time.
- Other issues include the location of crew base cities (Can cost be lowered by moving a crew base?) and the terms of the air crew contracts (Does adding or deleting a certain clause lead to higher or lower crew costs?).
- A "typical" day for a major carrier would involve 200 to 600 aircraft flying (with crews!).

SOLVING THE PROBLEM

The crew scheduling problem can be solved as an Integer Programming Problem (IP). This approach can be profitable (American Airlines reports saving of at least $20 million annually by using an approach based on ILP), but it is still very labor intensive.

The basic idea is to use IP to choose the lowest cost crew schedule for a particular class of aircraft/crew from a set of predefined individual crew "tours." A **tour** is a working schedule for a crew that starts at a their crew base city, assigns that crew to a series of flights over a multiday (usually 3 days) period, and returns the crew to their crew base and does not violate any conditions of employment or agency rules. The expected cost for each tour can be computed from a knowledge of pay rates, expected times for the crew in the air and on the ground, layover cities, and hotel and accommodation rates, plus any costs to fly the crew as passengers.

Once a set of potential tours has been devised, the lowest cost subset of these tours that covers the flight schedule can be chosen using IP. The variables are a set of 0-1 integer variables attached to each tour: if the tour is selected to be worked, the variable has value 1; if the tour is not worked, the variable has value zero. A constraint matrix is formed where each column represents a possible crew tour and each row represents a flight. If the possible tour includes that flight, the coefficient is given value 1–otherwise value 0. The cost coefficient for each column (variable) is the cost associated with that tour. A set of constraints is formed by requiring that the sum of the variables in each row be 1 (that is, each flight must have exactly one crew assigned to it).

For an airline with 200 flights per day for one type of aircraft, solving a 3-day crew tour problem would have 600 constraints (representing the 200 × 3 flights) in the ILP matrix. The number of columns is determined by the number of potential, feasible tours that can be generated. Clearly, the cost of the solution can be reduced through the addition of new (and efficient) potential crew tours.

A "tour-generator" program can be developed to create and cost-out feasible crew tours, which can then be input into the ILP to see whether they reduce the cost of the best available solution. In the case of an air carrier of reasonable size, there are so many possible crew tours that it is quite unlikely that the optimal solution can ever be found.

LONG-RUN ISSUES

The cost of providing crews might be reduced by opening new crew base cities or closing old ones, by changing from 3-day crew tours to 4-day crew tours, by allowing flexible-length crew tours, or by changing the crew's conditions of appointment through renegotiation of their union contract. The availability of a crew-scheduling system allows the cost savings from alternatives such as these to be investigated.

Assignment

Assign crews to the example route network in Exhibit 1 under the following assumptions:

Exhibit 1 | **SINGLE FLEET: CREW ASSIGNMENT EXAMPLE**

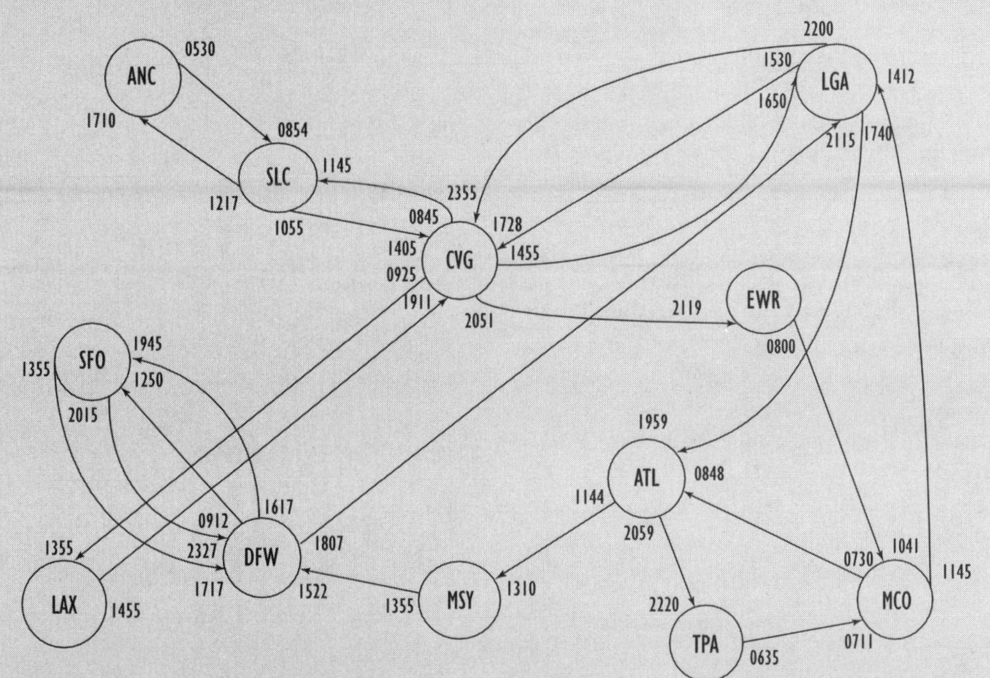

Each crew costs $600 per hour whether flying or not. A crew is paid for 8.5 hours each 24-hour period whether they work or not. A crew can work up to 12 hours per day, but all hours over 8.5 are billed at time and a half. A crew that is flying but not working ("deadheading") is paid as if they were working.

Assume that crews are based at DFW, CVG, and/or ATL.

In model 1, assume that crews must be back at their crew base after each shift (maximum of 12 hours).

In model 2, assume that crews can be away from home for up to 3 days (two nights) and can overnight anywhere at a cost of $1,000 per night.

After solving model 2, address the issue of whether there are lower-cost crew locations than DFW, CVG, and ATL.

BABCOCK AND WILCOX: CONSOLIDATED FORECASTING

The Babcock and Wilcox case is in Chapter 5.

Assignment

Write a report to Jan D'Ailly that addresses the following issues:

> How is B&W using the data (such as that in the exhibit) to derive the financial forecasts and the shop workload estimates?
>
> How could an assessment of "risk" be included in their analysis? Explain carefully what you mean by "risk." What advantage would this provide to B&W?
>
> Evaluate the way the uncertainties associated with contract tendering and winning are handled in the exhibit. Can you suggest an alternative approach that might lead to improved consolidated forecasts? If your approach were adopted, what changes to the method you propose (above) would be required?

INNOVIS INTERACTIVE TECHNOLOGIES

BY PETER C. BELL AND MARK R. LEMBERSKY

The DesignCenter had been brought successfully to market. Dr. Mark Lembersky, President, and Dr. Uli Chi, Vice-President, of Innovis Interactive Technologies now faced the task of planning the next step in the company's development.

THE PRINCIPALS

Dr. Mark R. Lembersky was born in Pittsburgh and trained as an electrical engineer at the Massachusetts Institute of Technology. He received his doctorate in Operations Research from Stanford University and joined the Weyerhaeuser Company after teaching for a few years at Oregon State University. At Weyerhaeuser, Mark managed a broad portfolio of technology development activities before becoming director of systems and finance at the corporate group level. From 1985 to 1987, Mark was Division General Manager, Weyerhaeuser Engineered Products, before becoming the founding President of Innovis Interactive Technologies in 1987.

Dr. Uli H. Chi received degrees in mathematics and computer science at the University of Washington. In 10 years with Weyerhaeuser Company, Uli established and led the Advanced Computing Unit of Weyerhaeuser's Research and Development Division and consulted on the successful and innovative application of computers to industrial problems. Immediately before becoming founding Vice President of Innovis, Uli managed Weyerhaeuser's decision simulators business program.

EMERGENCE OF INNOVIS

The seedling that grew into Innovis was planted in 1977 when Mark Lembersky began applying computers to problems in the logging industry of Washington State. A critical problem was the cutting of rough logs into timber products: the value of a tree could vary as much as 50% depending on how it was cut. Mark and Uli collaborated on the development of a "decision simulator" for training the woods workers who, working at remote locations, had to make thousands of these daily decisions.

This interactive computer program (VISION) displayed a graphic image of a rough log on the screen and offered the user the chance to make log-cutting decisions using a joy-stick control. The screen would then display the economic consequences of the logger's decision and recommend a better alternative. As the loggers worked with the VISION software, their decision-making skills improved dramatically. In the next 10 years, Weyerhaeuser attributed more than $100 million in increased profits to improved log-cutting decision making as a result of use of the VISION software. VISION was granted one of the first U.S. patents issued to a software program.

Donald Rush, Group Vice President for Timberlands, Weyerhaeuser Company, summarized the impact of VISION:

> I'm convinced that improved [log cutting] instructions in our Western operations led to approximately $60 million more profit [by 1985]. VISION has changed the West Coast mentality of doing business. We're doing a better job of matching our logs to the marketplace than ever before.
>
> VISION also showed us there was more variation in Southern raw material values than we'd believed—and that, consequently, there was an opportunity to upgrade the average value of our Southern trees. Implementation in the South led to enhanced profits of over $40 million.
>
> I reviewed these figures carefully and, in fact, reported them to our chief operating officer. They are, if anything, on the conservative side.
>
> I've seen the effect VISION has had on the thinking of even some of our most traditional woods workers. And I've seen the effect this effort has had on the thinking of our top managers—even beyond what I've just described for the South and West.
>
> Top managers were involved in the funding, testing, and implementation of VISION. Our chief executive officer, George Weyerhaeuser, used it. So did our chief operating officer, myself, and many others. We all realized from our interaction that there was more we could do with our timber resources—and we took action. For example, I've seen us commit many million of scarce capital dollars to completely automate log processing facilities so VISION-like procedures can be used online to process tree stems. Also, we've funded and developed other systems based on the same principles for such different areas as facility design and truck-routing.
>
> VISION changed our corporate behaviour in ways that have made us more money, and these changes have persisted. The contributions to the bottom line have not only held up over the years, but have actually increased in importance over time and under adverse industry economic conditions.

Lembersky and Chi received the 1985 Franz Edelman Award for Management Sciences Achievement from the Institute for Management Sciences for the VISION system. This award is presented annually to the winner of an international competition to select the best application of management science in the public or private sectors.

The Lembersky/Chi collaboration at Weyerhaeuser produced other innovative uses of interactive computer-generated graphics. Notable among these was an interactive planning tool that allowed management to see moving pictures of the operation of a proposed facility (such as a sawmill) and to make on-the-spot changes to evaluate capital investment and production alternatives. Managers were able to discover for themselves where and how bottlenecks developed, could change conveyor speeds or machine center throughputs, and could see the results immediately on-screen–all before the plant was built.

THE COMPANY

Innovis Interactive Technologies was founded in 1987 as a Weyerhaeuser subsidiary company with Mark as President and Uli as founding Vice-President.

The Innovis philosophy centered on the concept of "People Controlling Technology." Innovis used the term "Tools for the Imagination" to describe its products, which "were to be designed with a definite look and feel yet be so easy to use that creativity transcended the computer technology: to foster imagination and increase the abilities of people." Innovis would not use threatening or difficult-to-use technology; instead people would enjoy the look and feel of easy-to-use controls and displays, enabling them to think more clearly, analyze accurately, and better evaluate important decisions.

Mark's view was that Innovis would remain small because larger organizations would not be able to match Innovis' success in offering creative and custom-made solutions for clients. Mark and Uli would personally oversee development of each Innovis "tool for the imagination," working with a small, select group of designers, programmers, and hardware experts.

While Innovis itself would remain small, it had access to the resources of the Weyerhaeuser group. Weyerhaeuser engineers and lumber specialists, marketing people, and so on, were all available to Innovis, if needed.

The first Innovis project had been the DesignCenter.

DesignCenter

An Innovis press release described the DesignCenter:

> NEW INNOVIS SYSTEM LETS CONSUMERS DESIGN HOME IMPROVEMENT PROJECTS BY COMPUTER WITHOUT COMPUTER TRAINING
>
> "Do-it-yourselfers" are building their dream home project in their mind and within their budget on a computer design system created by Innovis Interactive Technologies.
>
> The sales aid for the lumber and home improvement industries is premiering in home centers and lumber yards with the introduction of the Weyerhaeuser DesignCenter. Consumers and contractors using the Innovis system design a home deck on a computer screen in minutes and can then view the deck at any angle. People with no computer training are designing with their own imagination what has until recently been the sole preserve of highly trained computer professionals.
>
> "It's pretty amazing stuff," says MIT architecture department member Tim Johnson, about the system's innovative blend of sophisticated computer-based technology and easy-to-use controls. "It brings a lot of expertise down to the level of the laymen," Johnson says.
>
> The ability to create a custom-designed deck project in the retail home center is expected to increase sales for forest product giants like Weyerhaeuser Company, which believes the Innovis DesignCenter will capitalize on an expected 7 percent growth for the home remodeling industry through the early 1990's.
>
> Bill Blankenship, the Weyerhaeuser Northern Region Vice President of Sales and Distribution, sees a unique opportunity for the home repair and remodel market. "We found that as consumers attempted to translate their ideas into shape, confusion and frustration often resulted. The DesignCenter technology simplifies this process and lets consumers visually bring their design ideas to life," Blankenship says.
>
> The computer system designed especially for Weyerhaeuser's corporate goals ironically unleashes human creativity that has been overwhelmed by a technologically dominated society. The University of Maryland's Ben Shneiderman, an expert in human-computer interaction, believes new systems should correct the imbalance.
>
> "Many current systems make the user the victim of the machine," Shneiderman says. "If people have a sense of control, it will empower them to create, innovate, and experience the joy of putting their own ideas to work."
>
> "If you need an instruction manual, we haven't designed it right," says Innovis President Mark Lembersky, who designs the Weyerhaeuser subsidiary's systems with co-founder and Vice President Uli Chi. Allowing consumers to easily chooses shapes, railings and stairs for their deck is part of what Lembersky and Chi are marketing as Tools for the Imagination.
>
> "What we have put together is human-focused; the technology is there as a tool," Lembersky says.
>
> DesignCenter goes beyond showing the finished design by including a printed list of materials and a construction plan for the project. The computer also projects the amount and the cost of materials needed for the job down to the last nail. The salesperson has the option of printing out the plan, materials cost and image of the completed deck design.
>
> "What this type of programming really does is allow you to be creative without the headache of figuring the cost of material," says master carpenter Norm Abram, longtime sidekick to Bob Vila on PBS' *This Old House*. "You can instantly make cost calculations that you can't make sitting at home with your calculator," says Abram, who hosts the new TV program *The New Yankee Workshop*.
>
> Any prospective deck buyers with second thoughts can project two different designs onto the screen and compare the differences in style and cost.
>
> As Innovis' first major customer, Weyerhaeuser has no second thoughts. The company has purchased hundreds of the revolutionary do-it-yourself systems.
>
> "I think the Innovis DesignCenter will be just as exciting and imaginative for the home center industry, as it will be for Weyerhaeuser's retail customers," says Blankenship.
>
> Lembersky plans to build on his DesignCenter success at Innovis by incorporating the latest in high technology with a continuing quest for human-focused systems that complement the power of imagination in solving the needs of individuals, industries and institutions.
>
> We'll look at technology in terms of making it even easier for people to use the technology and do even more for their organization.

The DesignCenter was test marketed at six retail lumber outlets, and the response was overwhelmingly enthusiastic. Lumber sales increased several times as the stores were able to provide deck design assistance, construction plans, and materials in a fraction of the time that this took previously. After the test market, Weyerhaeuser began installation of the DesignCenter nationwide.

The DesignCenter as first marketed consisted of a special purpose microcomputer with a high-quality color graphic display monitor, installed in a booth that prominently displayed the "Weyerhaeuser DesignCenter" motif. There was no keyboard; all input to the system was done using a trackball and by pressing a single key. The microcomputer was equipped with a color printer capable of producing high-quality color renditions of the decks that customers had designed (Exhibit 1). On request (usually controlled by a salesperson), the system would also output a complete parts list for the deck (tied into store inventories to ensure that items listed could be supplied) (Exhibit 2), as well as a set of construction plans for the deck (Exhibit 3).

THE NEXT STEP

The success of the DesignCenter would be a tough act to follow. The number of DesignCenters installed in lumber and/or do-it-yourself stores suggested development of a second module to add to the deck-design module, but there was no obvious market like the deck market.

Many other possibilities existed, including applications outside the lumber business. The next step was a critical one for Innovis: whatever project was selected would clearly absorb most of their energies for some time.

The **DesignCenter** and **Tools for the Imagination** are trademarks of Innovis Interactive Technologies.

Assignment

1. What are Innovis' areas of special competence?
2. What might they do next?

Exhibit I | **DesignCenter RENDITION OF EXAMPLE DECK**

Exhibit 2 | DesignCenter EXAMPLE FOR DECK PARTS LIST

DECK MATERIALS PACKAGE

Component	SKU	Quantity	Lumber
Post	99–999–999	11	8' – 4 x 4 LifeWood
Beam	99–999–999	2	8' – 2 x 10 LifeWood
Beam	99–999–999	12	10' – 2 x 10 LifeWood
Joist	99–999–999	1	8' – 2 x 6 LifeWood
Joist	99–999–999	21	10' – 2 x 6 LifeWood
Joist	99–999–999	1	12' – 2 x 6 LifeWood
Joist	99–999–999	4	16' – 2 x 6 LifeWood
Joist splice	99–999–999	1	8' – 2 x 4 LifeWood
Joist splice	99–999–999	1	16' – 2 x 4 LifeWood
Decking	99–999–999	56	8' – 2 x 6 LifeWood Wey-Dec
Decking	99–999–999	44	16' – 2 x 6 LifeWood Wey-Dec
Blocking–railing	99–999–999	1	8' – 2 x 6 LifeWood
Bridging	99–999–999	1	14' – 2 x 6 LifeWood
Bracing	99–999–999	1	8' – 2 x 6 LifeWood
Bracing	99–999–999	3	8' – 4 x 4 LifeWood
Stair stringer	99–999–999	3	10' – 2 x 12 LifeWood
Stair tread	99–999–999	8	8' – 2 x 6 LifeWood
Railing post	99–999–999	10	8' – 4 x 4 LifeWood
Railing top	99–999–999	14	8' – 2 x 4 LifeWood Dec-Cap
Railing bottom	99–999–999	11	8' – 2 x 4 LifeWood Dec-Cap
Railing baluster	99–999–999	132	LifeWood Colonial Spindle

Component	SKU	Quantity	Other Materials
Foundation pier	99–999–999	11	Precast concrete pier
Foundation concrete	99–999–999	11 bags	60 lbs premix concrete
Beam bolt	99–999–999	50	1/2" x 8" galvanized bolt, washers and nut
Ledger screw	99–999–999	27	1/2" x 7" galvanized lag screw and washer
Brace angle	99–999–999	8	16-Gauge 5" galvanized framing angle
Brace screw	99–999–999	6	1/2" x 7" galvanized lag screw and washer
Stair strap	99–999–999	6	16-Gauge 1" x 18" galvanized tie strap
Railing bolt	99–999–999	38	1/2" x 7" galvanized bolt, washers and nut
Nails	99–999–999	19 lbs	16d galvanized nails
Nails	99–999–999	30 lbs	12d galvanized nails
Nails	99–999–999	2 lbs	10d galvanized nails
Nails	99–999–999	3 lbs	8d galvanized nails
Nails	99–999–999	1 lbs	Galvanized hanger nails

Deck Value: $1747.13, plus tax
Price valid today, 11-15-1989

Exhibit 3 | DesignCenter CONSTRUCTION DETAILS FOR EXAMPLE DECK

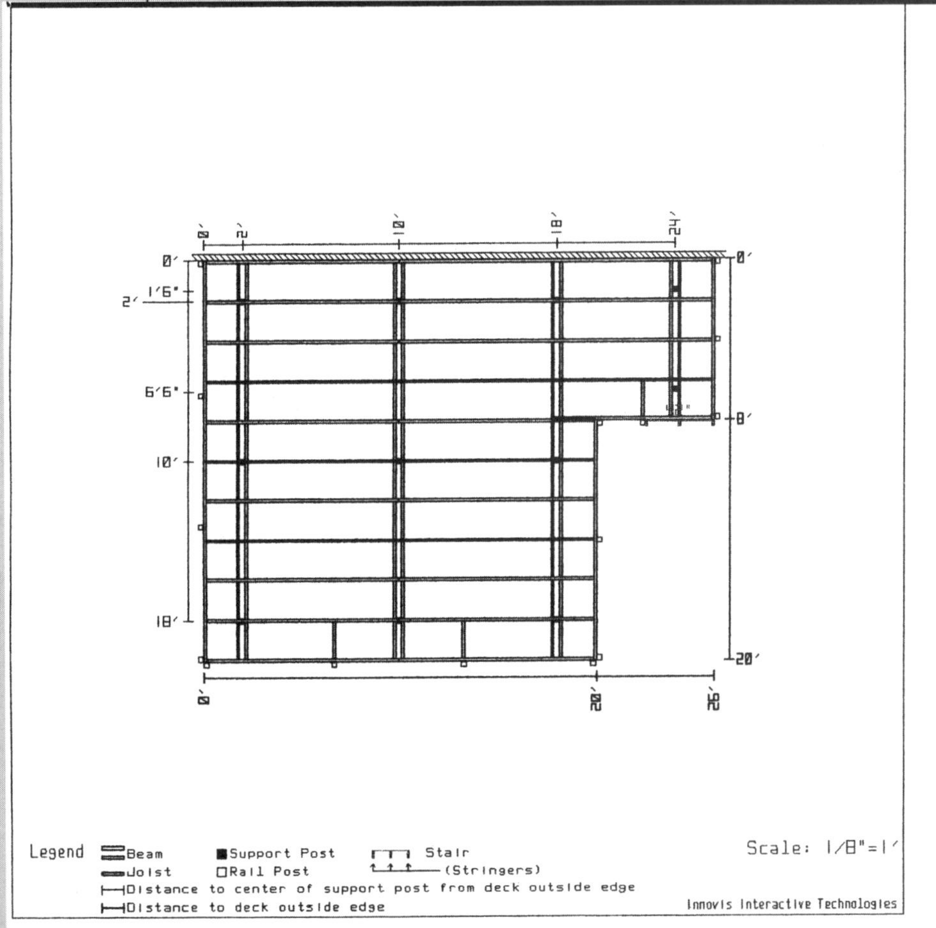

Site description: You selected a 40 PSF live load and a precast pier foundation.

Deck and post height:
You selected a height of 60" from the top of decking to level ground (this means the top of posts will be 53" above level ground).
Your salesperson can provide information for uneven or sloped ground.

Joists:
Set joists on top of beams and 23-13/16" center to center.

Be sure to follow the Deck Construction Detail available from your store salesperson.

WARNING: YOUR DESIGN REQUIRES KNEE BRACES, BEAM SPLICES AND BRIDGING BETWEEN JOISTS. YOUR MATERIALS LIST INCLUDES THE NECESSARY ITEMS. SEE THE DECK CONSTRUCTION DETAIL.

THE SUGGESTED DESIGN IS NOT A FINISHED BUILDING PLAN. THE SUGGESTED DESIGN IS BASED ON 0.40 TREATED GRADE 2 OR BETTER SOUTHERN YELLOW PINE LUMBER. YOU ARE RESPONSIBLE FOR ALL MEASUREMENTS BEING CORRECT, FOR VERIFYING THAT THE SUGGESTED DESIGN OR ANY SUBSTITUTIONS OR MODIFICATIONSMEETS ALL LOCAL BUILDING CODES AND REQUIREMENTS, FOR VERIFYING THAT THE SUGGESTED DESIGN OR ANY SUBSTITUTIONS OR MODIFICATIONS ARE CONSISTENT WITH CONDITIONS AT THE CONSTRUCTION SITE, FOR PROPER CONSTRUCTION AND USE OF MATERIALS, AND FOR THE COMPLETED STRUCTURE. CHECK THE DESIGN WITH YOUR ARCHITECT.

PRO-FORMS, INC.

J.B. Bryson ("JB" to everyone who knew her), General Manager of Pro-Forms, Inc., read the invitation with interest: "You are invited to attend a retirement party for Iris David...." Was Iris that old? Was Iris essential to Pro-Forms' operations? If so, what should Pro-Forms do when Iris retired? Perhaps JB should use this opportunity to conduct a thorough review of their operations.

PRO-FORMS, INC.

Pro-Forms had been in business since 1964 as a printer of business forms—invoices, order books, receipts, brochures, charge card slips, and so on. Pro-Forms specialized in producing paperwork that required multipart, multipaper stock, individually numbered (perhaps also multicolor) printing and collating (Box 7-1).

Pro-Forms produced thousands of different business forms, with the basic types being single part versus multipart and "snap" (separate forms) versus continuous forms (for computer use). Most forms were produced to order, although Pro-Forms had its own line of common generic forms (message pads, memo pads, and so on) that it supplied to a number of office specialty stores.

After more than 20 years of family ownership, Pro-Forms was now a subsidiary of a large multinational and was judged each year based on two numbers: profit and return on net assets (RONA). They had achieved a RONA of about 20% last year, although this had been below the target set for them (25%); as a result they were under some pressure to cut costs, reduce assets, or improve revenues. The current weakness of the dollar and their recent below-target performance meant that capital was always scarce; the parent company preferred to invest in European operations. The catch was that to improve productivity and support other needed change, some investment in equipment was necessary. Any monies that could be recovered by permanently reducing working capital needs could be immediately reinvested in equipment, giving Pro-Forms two possible benefits: management could choose to reinvest the funds or improve their RONA directly through the decrease in net assets.

ORDER PROCESS

Pro-Forms processing of a new customer order usually began with a telephone call to a customer representative. The "rep" entered details of the order into Pro-Forms information system, quoted an approximate price, and generally quoted delivery in about 6 weeks. The customer was responsible for sending in the artwork or design of the form (which was often a copy from a previous order).

Once the copy was in-hand and the customer had passed a credit check, a formal price quotation was prepared. The customer rep specified the production steps involved in producing the job together with time estimates for each step and, working with a pricing manual that contained paper and ink styles and costs, press costs, and other costs, produced the quotation. This quotation took into account the number of forms, the number of parts per form, and the type and size of paper, together with the number of ink colors, the type of collating or binding, and whether numbering was required.

If the order was a repeat order with no artwork changes, the plates used to print the previous order were retrieved from storage and checked to see if reuse was possible. If the plates had been damaged (which was rare) or new artwork or modifications were required, an "artwork charge" was estimated and added to cover the cost of special logos or art design. The formal quotation arrived at was just a guide: it was common for the rep to shave the calculated price to ensure that the

Box 7-1

PRO-FORM PRODUCT

A typical Pro-Form product was an order for 5,000, five-part, 10" by 8½" requisition forms, with the top copy green print on white paper stock, the second part black print on yellow stock, the third part green ink on pink stock, the fourth black ink on green stock, and the bottom part red ink on goldenrod stock, with forms numbered consecutively beginning at number 15,001. All parts except the first on self-carbon paper, with pricing and cost details "blacked out" on parts 3 through 5. Forms to be stacked in 1000s, glued together singly.

quoted price was competitive. The final price quotation was telephoned to the customer. Once the customer had accepted the quotation, processing the order was initiated by moving a production order onto Iris David's workstation.

PRODUCTION OF FORMS AT PRO-FORMS

A business form was processed through four or five production stages: prepress, press, collating, finishing and packing, and possibly binding.

Prepress

Prepress was the name given to the work area where the form was readied for printing. Within the prepress area, there were several different departments, including artwork, composing, masking, photography, and plate making. A new form order required that the artwork be prepared and that an image of the form be transferred to metal plates, from which the images of the form would be printed. Pro-Forms had two technologies available:

Older Photographic Technology. Under this process, the form was laid out on a personal computer wordprocessor and printed onto paper. The paper image was then combined with original artwork and photographed. After development of the photographic negative, acid etching was used to transfer the image onto the metal printing plate.

More Modern "Preup" Computerized Typesetting and Layout Machine. This new technology began at a computer workstation where the form was laid out on the screen. A digital image of the form was then written to a floppy disk. The disk was taken to an etching machine where a laser "burnt" the image directly onto a metal printing plate.

The "Preup" machine and laser etching equipment had cost Pro-Forms more than $250,000 about a year ago, but this process was much faster and more reliable than photoetching. Photoetching, however, had one big advantage in that if a customer submitted some complex artwork (such as a photograph), this could be pasted directly onto the paper image and then photographed. Laser-etching required that all artwork be digitized and the form design be prepared entirely on the workstation.

A metal printing plate was prepared for each image of each color required on each form. In some cases, each part of the form carried the same image; in other cases, the image was different. For example, a credit card charge slip printed in black and red, three parts, with each denoting the purpose of that part ("Customer Copy," "Merchant Copy," and so on), required six printing plates. Small forms were handled by composing multiple copies onto a single plate.

The last step in the prepress process was to print a "proof" of each part of each form from the new plates. These proofs were then sent to the customer for approval. If the customer approved the proofs by signing the approval copy, the form was ready for printing. If the customer found errors that were the fault of Pro-Forms, these had to be corrected while trying to retain the original delivery date promised to the customer. Correcting these errors was given a high priority because the artwork had to be corrected, new plates made, and a second set of proofs run off and sent to the customer for approval. The customer was told that if the corrected proofs were approved within 24 hours, the order would not be delayed.

Sometimes the customer would check the proofs and realize that their original design was in error. In this case, Pro-Forms would consider the corrected proofs as a new order and would quote a new price and reschedule the job into prepress as a new order (and also invoice the customer an artwork charge for the incorrect prepress work).

Plant manager John McCarthy had firm opinions about the role of prepress: "Our operations have really changed over the last year or so: prepress used to be a service department, now they are a production department—we seem to be always waiting for jobs to finish prepress." JB explained, "Our market has really changed: we used to have an average order size of about $10,000—this meant long press runs with a relatively short prepress stage. Our average order size is now about $1,500, but the prepress stage still takes the same amount of time: prepress has become the bottleneck."

"We had hoped to speed up prepress by buying a Preup computerized typesetting and layout machine for about $250,000," John continued, "but we have found that our customers are now demanding the extra options that this machine can provide and the prepress time has not gone down."

Printing

Pro-Forms' five presses were the traditional heart of their printing business. These continuous-feed, three- or four-color, web offset presses cost several hundred thousand dollars each, although similar presses were available on the used equipment market for around $200,000.

Pro-Forms had one 22-inch press, two 17-inch presses, one 14-inch press, and one 13-inch press. The size of the press referred to the web length, which limited the length of the printed form. For example, the 22-inch press could print one image of a 22-inch-long form or two images of an 11-inch-long form or four images of a 5.5-inch-long form on each rotation of the press. Each press also had a maximum page width, but below that maximum it could print almost any width of form, each printing from continuous rolls of paper.

Operation of these presses was a highly skilled job with the quality of the printed forms being heavily dependent on the skill and care of the operator. Each print job required considerable setup to mount the printing plates, fill and adjust ink levels, mount the paper roll, and make the many fine adjustments necessary to produce a top-quality printed form. At the end of the print run, the press had to be stripped down, the plates and paper unloaded, and the ink reservoirs emptied and cleaned. For many jobs, the setup and strip down took longer than the actual printing.

The efficiency of press operation could be improved by selecting the sequence of jobs carefully. In particular, color changes were very time consuming, so it was desirable to group jobs that used the same ink colors. When a color change was necessary, it took much less time to change to a darker color than to a lighter color because the clean up required for a darker color was much less thorough. The presses, therefore, tended to operate in color cycles—starting with the lighter colors, jobs would be sequenced so that the colors became darker and darker until black was reached. The press would then be thoroughly cleaned and a similar cycle repeated. (This description is idealized because many jobs required four colors, in which case minimizing the color changes was a very complex problem.)

Another important consideration was the width of the roll of paper fed into the press. Forms were printed in a wide variety of widths, and it was not economical to stock every size of paper roll for every type and color of paper. Forms could be printed on wider paper and trimmed to size; for example, an 8⅝-inch-wide form could be printed on 9-inch wide stock with ⅜ inch trimmed off. Any such trim was waste.

Some jobs with particular size or color requirements could only be printed on one particular press. In other cases, a job could be printed on several presses, although the combination of presses at Pro-Forms meant that only a single press was generally the best choice for any job; moving the job to a different press would raise printing costs or increase waste paper.

Exhibit 1 | STEPS REQUIRED TO PRINT SAMPLE FORM

Major cleaning of press (remove all previous ink)
Retrieve required red ink from ink inventory and charge press with red ink
Retrieve required black ink from ink inventory and charge press with black ink
Mount red image plate for first part of form
Mount black image plate for first part of form
Collect sufficient paper of first type from paper inventory and mount first paper roll
Run short burst until ink flow is good, carefully check image, if OK then
Run 5,500 copies, mounting additional paper rolls if needed
Stop press
Mount red image plate for second part of form
Mount black image plate for second part of form
Collect sufficient paper of second type from paper inventory and mount first paper roll
Run short burst, carefully check image, if OK then
Run 5,500 copies, mounting additional paper rolls if needed
Stop press
Mount red image plate for third part of form
Mount black image plate for third part of form
Collect sufficient paper of third type from paper inventory and mount first paper roll
Run short burst, carefully check image, if OK then
Run 5,500 copies, mounting additional paper rolls if needed
Stop press
Major cleaning of press
Stop press
Return unused ink to ink inventory
Return unused paper to paper inventory

A modern press was an expensive piece of equipment, and one of the frustrations of Pro-Forms' business was the fact that most of the time the presses were not printing. The reason for this was the need for frequent setups. As an example, Exhibit 1 outlines the printing steps required for an order for 5,000 three-part charge slips printed in black and red with each part on a different paper stock. (Note that 10% extra forms were printed on each order to allow for wastage when new paper rolls were mounted and images had to be aligned.)

Pro-Forms' presses had rated capacities of 10,000 to 20,000 images per hour (depending on the paper size and paper stock), with the result that the press was idle for most of the time that a job was booked at the press. In the example above, if the charge slip was quite small so four images appeared on each plate, each press run would require 1,375 images. The three press runs would require less than 20 minutes of actual printing time interspersed within a set of jobs that typically took considerably longer than 1 hour.

Each press had its own operator, and any operator could work any press. Operating a press was a skilled trade, and all Pro-Forms' operators belonged to a union, with the result that working conditions and practices were strictly controlled and difficult to change. Pro-Forms press operators all worked a single 8-hour shift, 5 days per week, with a ½-hour lunch break. Any additional hours were charged at a minimum of time and a half. Within the work rules, Pro-Forms' press operators had a long history of being very cooperative: for example, whenever possible, they took their lunch break when the press was operating (one operator could look after all three presses if they were all printing).

Sometimes an operator made a major error, for example, by printing the wrong second (or third) image onto a particular first (or other) part. Sorting out these errors was a major problem, often resulting in multiple additional setups and major last-minute schedule changes (and, often, overtime).

Collating

Collating was performed on two collating machines located in the press room at the end of the presses. These collating machines took the rolls of the different parts as they had come off the press, merged them together (adding carbons if required), cut the forms to size (snap forms), crimped or glued the forms together, cut or folded the forms as necessary, and numbered the individual forms if required. The collating machines were very fast (although they could be slow if cutting and/or folding was required), and because these machines combined single parts from several print runs into multipart forms, collating was rarely a bottleneck. In the example above, a printing job that might take 2 or 3 hours produced three rolls of paper that could be combined and cut into 5,000 forms in less than 20 minutes.

Finishing and Packing

Forms were prepared for shipment in many different ways. Continuous forms were "accordion" packed into boxes; snap forms could be glued, crimped, stapled, or bound in multipart pads or singly. Sometimes a cardboard backing was added to the pads and sometimes not. Finally, the finished orders were packaged in paper, boxes, or plastic and shipped to the customer.

These finishing operations were conducted in a finishing area where about 10 people worked many different pieces of equipment. It was rare for a completed job to take more than 24 hours from collating to shipment.

In some instances, Pro-Forms served as a warehouse for the customer, storing the bulk of the order and shipping small lots to the customer on request. This warehousing service was an extra that the customer paid for directly.

Binding

A few jobs required some form of binding that required special purpose binding equipment. The small number of jobs involved meant that there were rarely backlogs at the bindery.

SCHEDULING AT PRO-FORMS

Iris David had been the scheduler at Pro-Forms for about 8 years since Dan Markin retired. Dan had been with Pro-Forms for more than 20 years, beginning as a printer's assistant and ending up as scheduler. Iris had learned how to schedule the plant from Dan.

The plant printed about 6,000 orders for business forms annually, and at any one time there were about 6 weeks' worth of orders in the plant at various stages. The plant worked a two-shift, Monday through Friday, 80-hour week with overtime scheduled only rarely.

When a new order arrived at the plant, it was first made into a work order. This work order included detailed form design, colors, quantities, and prices, but in addition, listed prepress requirements with "standard" prepress times prepared from standard lists by the customer rep. The work order also listed the press that the job was to be printed on and how it was to be collated and shipped.

The work order was then sent to Iris David, who

tentatively scheduled the job on the designated press. Because of the 6-week load of orders in the plant, this generally meant adding the job to the end of the list of jobs waiting for that press, giving the job a tentative printing date about 6 weeks in the future. Iris then sent the work order to prepress, together with the tentative press date. It was then the responsibility of prepress to have the job ready for printing by the press date. The presses were scheduled for 72 hours per week. The 8-hour buffer allowed for breakdowns or unexpectedly long press runs and provided some flexibility for day-to-day scheduling.

About twice a day, Iris consulted her workstation and noted the return of proofs from customers. She wrote the job data (job number, quantity, ink colors, job steps, cost, and price) on a single line onto a 3- by 2-inch white card and inserted the card in her planner. In the planner, these cards were arranged vertically in pockets in a metal folder, and the sequence of jobs could be changed by removing cards from the planner and changing their locations. Each page corresponded to a particular press or collator with the jobs at the bottom of the page being scheduled on the equipment first. As Iris slotted each card into the end of the schedule for the chosen press, she would shuffle jobs around a bit to try to slot the work together by color or by paper type. Because the schedule for each press was on a separate page, it was much easier to resequence jobs on the same press than to switch jobs across presses. Finally, as the press operators would often collect ink or paper for an upcoming job several days before printing started, Iris would not change the schedule in the final week before printing.

There were a number of exceptions to this general scheduling process. While the sales force were aware of the 6-week backlog of orders in the plant and generally promised a 6-week delivery time when selling an order, there were many sales where a shorter delivery schedule was necessary to land the order. In these cases, the rep called Iris directly and tried to negotiate an early press date. Sometimes this was possible, but once the order was received and sent through to prepress, no formal recognition of the "rush" nature of the order (other than the tentative press date) was kept. It was, therefore, up to the rep, often at the prodding of the customer, to expedite the job through the plant.

While the production scheduling system did not take formal account of promised delivery dates, there were a number of informal ways that due date considerations entered into scheduling. First, an attempt was made to keep track of the urgency of each order. Some customers would order forms when they had an ample inventory on hand, and therefore delivery dates for these customers were known not to be critical. Others were known to order when they were almost out of stock, and here the promised delivery date was an important marketing tool in what was a highly competitive business. In some cases, where a form could not be printed in time to meet a customer need, a quantity of standard forms (without customer names or special requirements) was provided gratis to help the customer out until the printed forms could be shipped.

Iris' desk was located in a small office just off the press area, reflecting the long-held view that the presses were the heart of any printing operation. Iris was constantly in contact with the press operators, who were her friends. When she had time, she tried to juggle the schedule to help them out by, for example, grouping together jobs that used the same ink color (about 40% of the jobs used black ink) or jobs that used the same paper stock. In this way, she could improve press productivity through reducing setups.

On Monday of each week, Iris printed "Print Shop Work Tickets" for all scheduled jobs using a printer in her office by keying in the job numbers from her scheduler. As each job "went to press," she handed the Work Ticket to the press operator and removed the job from her scheduling system. When the job was printed, the top copy of the Work Ticket (on which the operator had written the actual press time) was returned to Iris, and the remainder followed the job through collating and finishing. Iris was responsible for entering the actual press time data into the order database. As the orders were printed, she updated her schedule by waiting until all the jobs in the first page of the planner had been scheduled and the cards removed: this empty page was then taken out of the loose leaf stand and moved to the beginning of the schedule.

It was common for the printers to spend time in Iris' office while the presses were actually running. Before, during, or after the usual shop floor banter, the press operators would check through the schedule for their press and would note ink colors or paper types needed for upcoming jobs. The press operators would manage their own ink and paper inventories around their presses: when a job that used, say, green ink had been completed, the operator would check the schedule to see when green ink would be needed again. If it was in the next week or so, the remaining ink would be kept handy rather than returned to inventory. Similarly, if one operator finished with the green ink, and was not scheduled to need it again, he or she would check to see if another press would be using it soon. In this way, the press operators avoided many trips to the ink and paper inventory. One result of this was that the presses were surrounded by tubs of ink and rolls of paper, some (perhaps many?) of which seemed to be very dusty.

PAPER ORDERING

The raw material for production consisted of 120 different types of paper. Each type was stocked in several widths, resulting in approximately 600 different paper stock items. The minimum order size, set by the paper manufacturers, was 1,000 pounds for each paper type and width, with the result that a complete paper inventory would be huge. However, not every every possible print width had to be inventoried because a slitter machine could be used to cut narrower widths from larger size rolls. The 40 3/8-inch width, known as a "mill roll," could be cut down to any set of sizes and was kept in inventory for just that purpose. Each slitting operation, however, usually generated a strip of waste paper that was too narrow to use. For example, if two 20-inch widths were cut from a mill roll, there was a 3/8-inch strip of waste paper that could only be recycled (for which Pro-Forms received no revenue).

Paper types and widths with a high consistent demand were always kept in inventory; sizes that were rarely used were always cut when needed. Stockouts were not tolerated: the demands of the presses were always filled no matter how much waste paper was produced.

Pro-Forms' paper inventory value was about $736,000, accounting for about 40% of net assets. The carrying cost of inventory was estimated at 19% per year, and the cost of trim waste was simply the cost of the waste paper. The cost of placing an order was negligible because deliveries were coming in constantly. Furthermore, Pro-Forms was a large enough buyer that every purchase was discounted by the trade maximum discount, even those orders at minimum quantity. Delivery times varied but rarely exceeded 3 weeks.

Paper ordering was based on a reorder point, standard order quantity system. When the stock of an inventory type and size fell below the reorder point, an order of standard size was placed. Orders were therefore based on the quantities that production was ordering from inventory, but meeting these orders could involve slitting (and the accompanying waste).

One high volume type of paper was 24M white. The pounds of **24M white** output from production, by size, for the past 3 months are summarized in Exhibit 2 (p. 362). Exhibit 3 (p. 363) summarizes the end-of-month inventory for 24M white sizes for the last 3 months, and Exhibit 3 summarizes current reorder points and order quantities for the same stock items.

INTERVIEW WITH JB

JB reacted to Iris' pending retirement by calling in a consultant. After the consultant had spent 2 days working through Pro-Forms' operations, they met for an interview. The consultant asked JB to talk about her perception of the problems and opportunities that Pro-Forms faced. Among the issues discussed were the following:

Low Press Utilization

The folklore of the printing industry was that high press utilizations were needed to produce profits, but Pro-Forms' presses were actually running less than 20% of the time. JB wondered whether they were doing enough to try to maximize press utilization.

Pro-Forms attempted to cope with low press utilizations in a number of ways. First, starting with the customer, Pro-Forms' representatives were instructed to try to sell the customer on a larger order by providing substantial discounts. Doubling the size of an order often added only a few minutes to the total production time (because the production process was almost all setup time), allowing discounts of 60% to 70% to be given for the extra copies. Second, Pro-Forms would speculate on frequent customers: if a customer was observed to order 10,000 of the same form each month, Pro-Forms would print 60,000, ship 10,000, and inventory the balance. In these cases, it was important that when a new order arrived, there was someone who knew and could pick up the fact that this particular product was in stock. There had been one situation (which was much talked about) where Pro-Forms had speculated on a customer who ordered 5,000 forms each week by printing 100,000 forms. Three weeks later on receipt of another order for 5,000 forms, Pro-Forms had printed another 100,000! The mistake was not noticed until the second stack of 95,000 remaining forms had been added to the inventory of 90,000. (Luckily, the customer kept ordering, and the design of the form did not change until the inventory had all been shipped.)

Poor Customer Service

Pro-Forms tried hard to work to a rule of 6 weeks for a new order, 4 weeks for a reorder, but even the 6-week delivery date was optimistic: in busy or vacation periods, 8 weeks was common. There was no standard process in place to expedite an order. If a customer complained, the customer reps could try to persuade Iris to move the order forward, but after a couple of confrontations with her, they generally gave up.

When a valued customer in desperate need of a new supply of forms called, Pro-Forms' reps were told to try a number of options. First, they may have a few forms from the customer's last order in inventory (Pro-Forms would keep "overcount" forms for a year or so before recycling them; the "overcount" was the useable remains of the 10% print overrun). Second, Pro-Forms printed and inventoried generic forms in common types (for example, telephone message pads) and would try to sell a supply of generic forms to the customer to tide them over while a new order was printed. Finally, where appropriate, Pro-Forms offered to produce the same form as the last order without customer proofs in 3 weeks (because no prepress or proof time was necessary). If all this failed, Pro-Forms would quote a high price and expedite the order. When an order was expedited, a customer representative was given the task of "walking" the order through the plant. When this was done, the order could be produced in 24 hours, although this generally meant working a press overtime and frequently left the remainder of the schedule in tatters (and often left Iris quite upset!).

New customers, and most occasional customers, were always told that delivery was 4 or 6 weeks (or longer). If a generic form was not acceptable, and if there were no overrun forms in inventory, the customer went elsewhere.

JB knew that the long production times were costing Pro-Forms some customers but was not sure what to make of this. On the one hand, business was being turned away (which was bad), but on the other hand, their order books were full and Pro-Forms was operating at full capacity. If they turned away fewer potential customers, how would they produce these orders?

Pricing

JB thought that there was an opportunity to improve pricing. There seemed to be a number of problems with the way Pro-Forms developed price quotations for new orders.

First, price calculations were very complex and had to be done before the job was scheduled, yet the cost of producing the job very much depended on the schedule. The new Preup technology was much more expensive than the older Photo-etch, and press time costs for printing varied (by more than a factor of 2) according to the press used. The customer rep performing the price calculations chose a production method for the order and used this as a basis for the price calculation, but the process actually used could be quite different.

Second, it did not make sense that two orders for the exact same form should be quoted different prices because the load on the plant resulted in them being processed differently; hence, the reps were given latitude to "fudge" the price quotations. How could this latitude be controlled so that loss-making orders were not taken?

Finally, JB noted that "we have all the data on actual job times (both prepress and press) for completed jobs in the computer, but we don't do anything with this."

Press Operator Overtime

The press operators were the highest paid employees in the plant and were employed according to strict rules set by their union (and agreed to by Pro-Forms in their collective agreement). Once a job had started on a press, it was left to the operators' discretion to determine whether the job had to be finished before the end of the day or whether there was some point where the job could be suspended overnight without problems. Often a press would be scheduled for a 5-hour job, 1 hour before the end of the second shift, even though the next job on the schedule was a 1-hour job. In many of these situations, the operator would decide to finish the job before leaving, resulting in 4 hours of overtime pay. Iris had been approached about this issue but had argued that had the overtime not been worked, the schedule would have been delayed. JB remained skeptical because she had noted that overtime costs were consistently high in November and December and just before the operators' summer vacations.

"Comfort Zone"

Another frustration that JB mentioned was what she called our "Comfort Zone." She explained this as follows:

"It basically takes us less than 3 days to actually produce a form (less than 1 day in each of prepress, printing, and finishing). If you add to that 48 hours for customer proofs, there is no reason why we cannot deliver any order in 1 week. Why then does it take us 6 weeks to push an order through the plant? It is because this plant is very comfortable with the 6-week backlog. If we worked overtime until we cleared out all the orders in the plant, would we be able to work to and maintain a 1-week delivery? No, because the reps would shave prices and get more orders until we were back to 6-weeks delivery! This plant is comfortable with 6 weeks' worth of orders on the books and no matter what we do, this seems to be where we end up."

INTERVIEW WITH SOME CUSTOMERS

After the interview with JB, the consultant talked to five customers (four large customers and one occasional customer). These customers all held the view that Pro-Forms was a fine company to deal with: the reps were friendly and helpful, the pricing was competitive, and the quality of the work was acceptable.

When queried (carefully) about delivery times, the customers were sympathetic. They all recognized that quality printing took time, that printing a form was a complex process, and that they could not expect overnight service on their orders. They were all adamant that they must see proofs before the job was run off (one large customer had found two errors in their last set of proofs).

In the discussion of delivery times, a consensus emerged that the delivery time itself was not a major problem, but uncertainty in the delivery time was a major problem. One large customer wondered why the reps could not provide firm delivery dates: "Why can't the rep slot the job directly into the schedule and tell us when it will be printed and shipped?" Another suggested that it would be valuable if the reps could sometimes schedule an order for 5-week completion instead of 6: "Surely this would not change the schedule much, and would be a useful service for large, regular customers [such as himself]?"

Another large customer suggested that she was quite good at keeping supplies of the 100 or so different forms she needed in stock, but every now and then something happened, and she realized that she was running out of copies of an important form. Sometimes Pro-Forms could run her off a small order within a few hours to keep her going while they were printing her reorder, but other times they could not. How come she could not rely on them to keep her supplied?

Finally, the smaller customer wondered how long Pro-Forms could continue to be so inflexible and so unaccommodating to its customers. Competition was intensifying everywhere. There were other places that did custom printing, and there was certainly an opportunity for someone with more of a customer orientation to begin printing business forms.

Assignment

1. There are several areas of Pro-Forms' operation where MS/OR appears to have potential. Identify some of these and try to prioritize them: which areas hold the greatest potential?
2. For each area that you identify, address the following issues:

   What decisions are being and have to be made, and who is (or should be) the decision maker?

   What criterion (or criteria) should be used to make the decision(s)?

   Outline one or more models that will help with these decisions. What additional information will you need to build your model(s)?

Exhibit 2 **PRO-FORMS, INC. PAPER USE FOR LAST 3 MONTHS**
24M White (pounds)

Size	Quantity	No. of Uses	Size	Quantity	No. of Uses
4 1/4"			12 1/4	899	2
5 1/2	60	2	13 1/2	730	2
5 3/4	195	2	14	5,150	1
6 1/8	345	6	14 3/8		
6 1/4			14 5/8	4,460	3
6 1/2	100	2	14 7/8	33,000	1
6 5/8			15	3,590	3
7 1/4			15 1/4	3,775	5
7 5/8	1,095	16	15 5/8	2,000	1
8	745	8	16	655	2
8 1/8			17	4,140	5
8 1/2	3,355	27	18 1/4	2,250	5
8 5/8	420	6	18 3/4		
8 3/4			19	3,685	3
9			19 1/4	1,305	2
9 1/8	1,740	20	20	8,020	4
9 1/2	395	6	21 1/4	1,200	1
9 3/4	380	3	21 3/4	625	1
9 7/8	320	1	22	980	1
10	985	8	22 3/4	410	1
10 5/8	1,045	6	23 1/4	3,490	3
11	2,498	14	23 3/4	935	1
11 1/4			24	2,280	1
11 1/2	800	5	24 1/2	3,000	1
11 5/8	3,195	24	25 1/4	2,635	2
12	1,008	7			

Exhibit 3 **PRO-FORMS, INC. MONTH END INVENTORIES**
24M White (pounds)

Size	January	February	March
7 5/8	2,424	2,765	2,871
8	3,972	1,842	681
8 1/2	1,994	2,660	1,356
9 1/8	2,714	1,369	1,628
9 1/2	5,925	5,298	4,933
10	1,590	2,000	5,770
11	1,546	1,710	1,517
11 5/8	2,440	2,009	1,122
12	1,720	1,031	248
13	1,446	1,740	2,236
14	0	365	149
14 7/8	12,917	12,186	5,434
15	6,191	5,591	6,141
15 1/4	564	1,817	5,268
17	2,019	2,604	2,322
19	465	465	465
21 1/4	2,153	2,153	2,153
23 1/4	3,219	3,114	1,846
24	364	593	593
25 1/4	0	100	126
40 3/8	0	3,000	1,699

Exhibit 4 | **PRO-FORMS, INC. REORDER POINTS AND QUANTITIES 24M White (pounds)**

Size	Reorder Point	Reorder Quantity
7 5/8	1,000	1,000
8	2,000	1,000
8 1/2	2,000	1,000
9 1/8	2,000	1,000
9 1/2	1,000	1,000
10	1,000	1,000
11	1,500	1,000
11 5/8	2,000	1,000
12	750	1,000
13	1,000	1,000
14	1,000	1,000
14 7/8	10,000	1,000
15	5,000	1,000
15 1/4	500	1,000
17	2,500	1,000
19	1,000	1,000
21 1/4	2,000	1,000
23 1/4	3,000	1,000
24	1,000	1,000
25 1/4	500	1,000
Mill roll*	2,000	2,400

* 30-Inch-diameter rolls; all others are 40-inch-diameter.

NATIONAL CAR RENTAL

BY DOUG ROTH UNDER THE SUPERVISION OF PROFESSOR PETER BELL. REPRODUCED WITH PERMISSION OF INFORMS. COPYRIGHT © 1998, INFORMS.

In 1992, National Car Rental (National) was losing millions of dollars every month. General Motors (GM), National's parent company, was forced to take a $744 million charge against the ownership of National. Despite cutting costs and reducing staff, the company was still unprofitable, with the result that morale was very low. GM stated that if National did not become profitable, so that it could be sold, it would be liquidated and all 7,500 employees would lose their jobs. GM estimated the cost of liquidation at $2 billion.

Turnaround specialists Jay Alix and Associates were called in, and Larry Ramaekers was assigned to lead the turnaround and act as president. Looking to the airline industry, Ramaekers noted the success of their new **yield management** or **revenue management** technology and decided to go for a revenue-based turnaround as opposed to a cost-cutting turnaround: if revenue management technology could be successfully applied at National, revenues would be increased without a significant increase in costs. Time was short; a working system was needed in only 3 months, and a foundation system for all 172 corporate centers within 1 year.

National conducted extensive meetings with several top consultants in the hope that they could provide the tools to save their sinking company. Finally, National turned to Aeronomics, a consulting company from Atlanta that employed several former airline revenue management specialists. Aeronomics' assignment was straightforward: save the company.

CAR RENTAL INDUSTRY

In the 1980s, the car rental industry was in turmoil. Low profit margins were subsidized by tax credits. When the tax credits disappeared, these low profit margins were eroded even further. North American automobile manufacturers purchased the troubled major rental companies and flooded them with cars through low-cost fleet deals. The car manufacturers placed more emphasis on using their car rental subsidiaries to soak up excess production than to produce profits.

In the early 1990s, economic conditions and improvements in design and production quality increased demand for American-made cars. Consequently, the manufacturers dramatically raised vehicle prices to their car rental subsidiaries. These increased fleet costs, combined with the fact that the car rental industry was slow to apply technology, precipitated the industry into crisis.

National, like all the major car rental companies, depended largely on corporate customers that possessed large numbers of employees who needed rental cars. National attempted to win these customers by offering low "corporate rates." Thus, peak demand for rental cars occurred midweek, forcing all rental companies to regularly turn down price-insensitive customers at this time. In addition, the need to have sufficient cars to meet midweek demand resulted in large numbers of idle cars over the weekends.

To stimulate rentals, the car rental industry allowed price-sensitive leisure customers to book multiple reservations with no prepayment required and often at very low prices due to early booking discounts and/or low weekend rates. Penalties for cancellations or no-shows were rare. Customers arriving as much as 12 hours after the specified time of the reservation were given the reserved car, at the reserved rate. These policies, which were standard for the rental industry, resulted in no-show and cancellation rates that sometimes exceeded 50% of all reservations.

To combat this high no-show rate, companies oversold their fleet in an attempt to avoid having idle cars sitting on their lots. "Walk-ups" were also used by location managers to try to manage car inventories; a walk-up was a customer who called wanting a car the same day. Walk-ups were turned away when necessary to avert an impending oversell situation or encouraged through aggressive pricing when there were excess vehicles in inventory.

PRICING AT NATIONAL CAR RENTAL

National struggled with the same challenges as its competitors, but other factors made it critical for National to change quickly. National's business was predominantly corporate customers, and its strategy focused on these business renters. As a consequence, National neglected leisure customers, who were needed on weekends and low-demand weekdays.

In February 1992, the severity of National's situation prompted National's executives to initiate a pilot revenue management project. Specifically, two problems provided cause for alarm.

First, competitors were raising the rental price on days of peak demand as the required day of rental approached, but National was not doing this. For example, if booked today, the price this Sunday at National was $45 per car, the price for next Sunday was $45, and the price for Sunday a year from now was still $45. High or low demand and the time to the actual rental day did not matter. A complicating factor was that pricing was a shared responsibility. Changing prices was a time-consuming manual process that involved location managers, marketing, regional vice presidents, senior management, and the pricing group, who all shared input, with no single person ultimately responsible for a location's pricing decisions.

Second, National was turning down customers (citing a lack of cars) on the same days that it ended up with excess capacity. Inventories (car rental days) were controlled by field managers without a system to advise them when to increase or restrict availability. No demand forecasts were made at either the local or corporate level.

REVENUE MANAGEMENT PROBLEM

National identified three areas that it thought should be addressed to enhance overall profitability:

Capacity Management. Improving fleet use by not turning away customers on days when surplus cars would be available.

Pricing. More frequent price changes could enhance corporate revenues through sensitivity to consumer price tolerance.

Reservations Control. Accepting bookings based on length of rent (LOR) would enable National to increase leisure and corporate business to positively affect the bottom line.

Capacity Management

The two key features of capacity management were planned upgrades and overbooking.

Planned Upgrades. In the car rental business, the demand for rental cars fell into definite market segments. Business renters typically demanded midsized cars. Low-valued leisure customers preferred economy cars with low rates. More affluent leisure customers often demanded specialty vehicles, such as minivans or four-wheel-drive vehicles.

To accomplish market segmentation, the car rental company could not directly substitute one vehicle type for another; there was a definite upgrade hierarchy that needed to be managed. It was inappropriate to put higher-class customers in economy cars. However, if National restricted economy bookings to only economy cars, it would miss a large revenue opportunity. The difference in the holding costs of the different vehicle classes was small enough to justify having sufficient high-valued inventory to meet the high-demand periods, and few economy customers complained about getting a more luxurious car than the one they booked as long as the rate was the same. Typical fleet planning policy was, therefore, to acquire more large and midsize cars than expected demand required and fewer economy cars.

Planned upgrades could, however, cause a distortion of availability when an economy customer turned up and drove away in a high-valued car, and then the high-valued car was not there when needed for high-valued customers. National, therefore, had to decide in advance the number of economy, midsized, and luxury bookings it would accept for each renting day in its 60-day planning horizon.

Overbooking. High levels of no-shows and cancellations in the industry made overbooking a standard procedure. National regularly accepted more reservations than it had vehicles available in an attempt to avoid having idle cars on the actual day of rental. National realized that idle car inventory cost money: however, running out of vehicles also cost money. National estimated that it incurred a cost of about $130 per customer to rectify a situation where a customer arrived with a reservation when National had no car available. A second issue was the fact that customer satisfaction surveys, which were widely reported in trade magazines and other publications, used "reservation but no car" statistics to compare the service provided by the various rental companies and the results could greatly hurt or enhance a company's reputation.

Finally, a rate cut designed to stimulate demand on a day when National had excess inventory, such as a weekend, could also increase demand on a day when capacity was already strained.

Exhibit 1 | **TYPICAL CAR RENTAL RESERVATION PATTERNS**

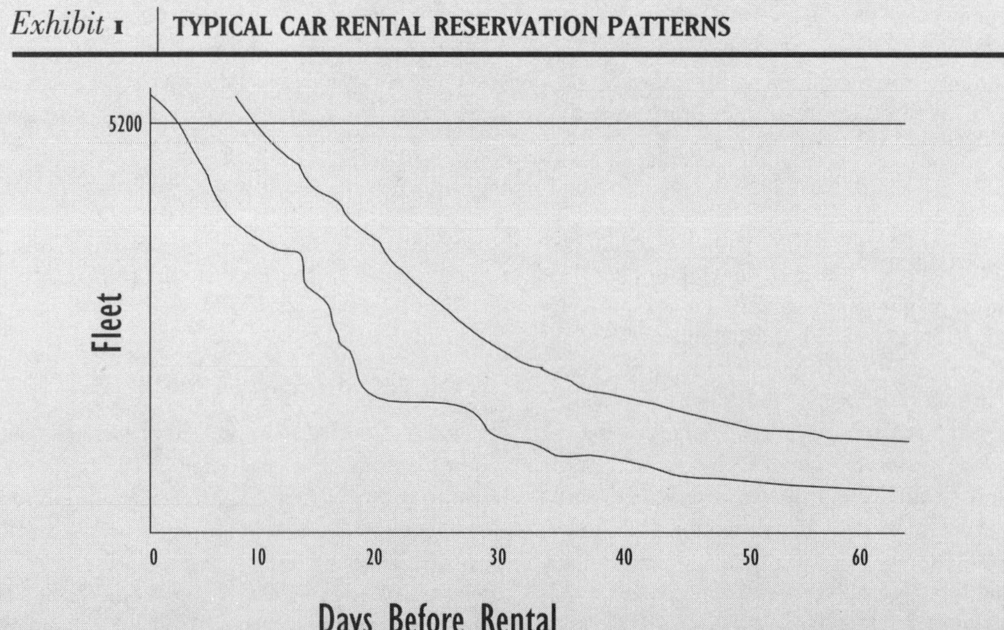

Pricing

The car rental population was made up of two major segments: **corporate** and **leisure**. Corporate customers typically booked close to the date of rental, were inflexible in rental and return date and times, did not shop competitors extensively, and most importantly expected to pay a predetermined fixed rate reimbursed by their company. Leisure customers, on the other hand, booked in advance, were reasonably flexible in time of pick-up, and shopped competitors extensively looking for the best value.

Currently, National used fixed rate pricing. In Exhibit 1, the bottom line represents a typical booking rate curve for one location over the 60 days before a rental day. The horizontal line represents the available fleet of 5,200 cars at that location. By the day of rental, National had reached its target of 5,500 rentals, which, after cancellations, would be expected to provide the target vehicle use. The second booking curve (slightly above the first) represented the case of slightly greater demand, where the increased demand over the 60-day time period before rental day caused National to run out of inventory 5 to 6 days before the actual rental day. Because rentals were accepted on a first-come, first-served basis, this second case would leave no vehicles for corporate customers or price-insensitive walk-ups.

While revenue produced by each car could be increased by simply raising rental rates, the rental car market was extremely competitive, with the result that a price move that made the company more expensive than its competitors could quickly damage utilization levels. In addition, a higher revenue for each car rented was not worth much if most of the fleet was sitting idle on the lot. National recognized the desirability of increasing revenue, but this had to be accomplished while working within these two realities of the car rental industry.

Reservations Control

Capacity management and pricing both provided a degree of reservations control, but both operated at the aggregate level. The actual reservations booking division was required to further refine the booking process and, in particular, to decide which customer's booking requests should be accepted or rejected. Two rental terms were common to the reservations division:

- **Minimum length-of-rent** (LOR) policies placed restrictions on the minimum number of rental days
- **Constrained days**, which were calendar days where the demand for vehicles was expected to be at sell-out capacity

It was thought that by either accepting or rejecting reservations based on LOR and constrained days, car rental companies could increase utilization and, in turn, profitability, while remaining competitively priced.

CHALLENGE

National needed answers, and it needed them fast. National would be able to access historical booking rates, information on various class segments' demand, and the various statistics and costs for cancellations, walk-ups, and so on. However, National was unsure what information was necessary to improve capacity through both overbooking and planned upgrades, along with pricing and reservation systems.

How should National handle overbooking and LOR-based customer acceptance or rejection? How should prices be set, and planned upgrades managed? In short, how could National apply new "revenue management" technology to save the company?

Assignment

1. Suggest a model to accept or reject rentals based on the length of rental.
2. How should "planned upgrades" be handled?
3. Suggest a model to review prices and suggest price changes.
4. How should overbooking levels be set?

INDEX

D

N

O

P

T

U

V